MOS 2010 Study Guide for Microsoft® Word, Excel®, PowerPoint®, and Outlook®

Joan Lambert
Joyce Cox

PUBLISHED BY
Microsoft Press
A Division of Microsoft Corporation
One Microsoft Way
Redmond, Washington 98052-6399

Library of Congress Control Number: 2011922801

ISBN: 978-0-7356-4875-3

Printed and bound in the United States of America.

6 7 8 9 10 11 12 13 14 M 8 7 6 5 4 3

Microsoft Press books are available through booksellers and distributors worldwide. If you reed support related to this book, email Microsoft Press Book Support at mspinput@microsoft.com. Please tell us what you think of this book at http://www.microsoft.com/learning/booksurvey.

Microsoft and the trademarks listed at http://www.microsoft.com/about/legal/en/us/IntellectualProperty /Trademarks/EN-US.aspx are trademarks of the Microsoft group of companies. All other marks are property of their respective owners.

The example companies, organizations, products, domain names, email addresses, logos, people, places, and events depicted herein are fictitious. No association with any real company, organization, product, domain name, email address, logo, person, place, or event is intended or should be inferred.

This book expresses the author's views and opinions. The information contained in this book is provided without any express, statutory, or implied warranties. Neither the authors, Microsoft Corporation, nor its resellers, or distributors will be held liable for any damages caused or alleged to be caused either directly or indirectly by this book.

Acquisitions Editor: Rosemary Caperton
Editorial Production: Online Training Solutions, Inc.
Cover: Jelvetica

[2013-02-01]

Contents

Taking a Microsoft Office Specialist Exam xix

    Microsoft Office Specialist Certification xix

    Selecting a Certification Path xix

    Test-Taking Tips xx

    Certification Benefits. xxi

    For More Information xxii

Using This Book to Study for a Certification Exam. xxiii

    Features and Conventions of This Book. xxiv

Using the Book's Companion Content xxv

    Exam 77-881: Microsoft Word 2010. xxv

    Exam 77-882: Microsoft Excel 2010 xxvii

    Exam 77-883: Microsoft PowerPoint 2010. xxviii

    Exam 77-884: Microsoft Outlook 2010 xxx

Modifying the Display of the Ribbon xxxi

    Dynamic Ribbon Elements. xxxi

    Changing the Width of the Ribbon xxxii

    Adapting Procedure Steps xxxv

Your Companion eBook. xxxvii

Getting Support and Giving Feedback xxxix

    Errata xxxix

    Getting Help with Microsoft Office 2010 xxxix

    We Want to Hear from You xl

        Stay in Touch xl

Exam 77-881 **Microsoft Word 2010**

    Prerequisites. 2

        Selecting Text. 2

        Moving Around in a Document 3

What do you think of this book? We want to hear from you!

Microsoft is interested in hearing your feedback so we can continually improve our books and learning resources for you. To participate in a brief online survey, please visit:

microsoft.com/learning/booksurvey

1   Sharing and Maintaining Documents   5

1.1   Apply Different Views to a Document 6

Switching Views 6

Modifying the Program Window 16

Magnifying Document Content 17

Splitting a Document Window 18

Displaying Multiple Program Windows 20

Practice Tasks 22

1.2   Apply Protection to a Document 22

Marking a Document as Final 22

Restricting Formatting and Editing Changes 24

Restricting Document Access 26

Practice Tasks 27

1.3   Manage Document Versions 28

Practice Tasks 29

1.4   Share Documents 29

Sending Documents 29

Saving Documents in Shared Locations 31

Publishing Documents as Blog Posts 33

Practice Tasks 35

1.5   Save a Document 36

Practice Tasks 41

1.6   Apply a Template to a Document 42

Practice Tasks 44

Objective Review 44

2   Formatting Content   45

2.1   Apply Font and Paragraph Attributes 46

Applying Character Formatting 46

Applying Styles 49

Practice Tasks 52

2.2   Navigate and Search Through a Document 53

Moving Around in a Document 53

Searching for Content and Formatting 54

Practice Tasks 57

2.3   Apply Indentation and Tab Settings to Paragraphs 58

Indenting Paragraphs 58

Setting Tab Stops 59

Practice Tasks 62

2.4   Apply Spacing Settings to Text and Paragraphs 63
        Practice Tasks 64
2.5   Create Tables. 65
        Creating Basic Tables. 65
        Formatting Tables 67
        Inserting Preformatted Tables. 69
        Practice Tasks 70
2.6   Manipulate Tables in a Document. 70
        Modifying Table Data 70
        Modifying Table Structure 72
        Practice Tasks 75
2.7   Apply Bullets to a Document 75
        Practice Tasks 78
      Objective Review 78

3   Applying Page Layout and Reusable Content   79

3.1   Apply and Manipulate Page Setup Settings 80
        Controlling Page Settings. 80
        Setting Page Breaks. 82
        Setting Section Breaks 83
        Flowing Text in Columns. 85
        Practice Tasks 86
3.2   Apply Themes. 87
        Practice Tasks 90
3.3   Construct Content in a Document by Using the Quick Parts Tool. 90
        Practice Tasks 93
3.4   Create and Manipulate Page Backgrounds 94
        Practice Tasks 96
3.5   Create and Modify Headers and Footers. 96
        Practice Tasks 100
      Objective Review 100

4   Including Illustrations and Graphics in a Document   101

4.1   Insert and Format Pictures in a Document 102
        Inserting Pictures. 102
        Formatting Pictures. 103
        Practice Tasks 105

4.2   Insert and Format Shapes, WordArt, and SmartArt. 105
        Inserting and Formatting Shapes 105
        Inserting and Modifying WordArt 108
        Inserting and Modifying SmartArt Diagrams 110
        Practice Tasks 112
4.3   Insert and Format Clip Art 112
        Practice Tasks 114
4.4   Apply and Manipulate Text Boxes. 115
        Practice Tasks 117
        Objective Review. 118

5   Proofreading Documents   119
5.1   Validate Content by Using Spelling and Grammar Checking Options 120
        Practice Tasks 124
5.2   Configure AutoCorrect Settings 125
        Practice Tasks 127
5.3   Insert and Modify Comments in a Document. 127
        Practice Tasks 130
        Objective Review. 130

6   Applying References and Hyperlinks   131
6.1   Apply a Hyperlink. 132
        Inserting Hyperlinks 132
        Inserting Bookmarks. 134
        Practice Tasks 136
6.2   Create Endnotes and Footnotes 136
        Practice Tasks 138
6.3   Create a Table of Contents. 138
        Practice Tasks 142
        Objective Review. 142

7   Performing Mail Merge Operations   143
7.1   Set Up Mail Merge. 144
        Preparing Source Documents 144
        Merging Source Documents 148
        Checking for Errors 156
        Practice Tasks 157

7.2   Execute Mail Merge 158

    Previewing the Results of a Mail Merge Operation 158

    Completing the Mail Merge Operation 159

    Practice Tasks 160

Objective Review 160

Exam 77-882   Microsoft Excel 2010

Prerequisites 162

    Managing Worksheets 162

    Managing Worksheet Content 162

    Managing Excel Tables 163

    Managing Data Entries 163

1   Managing the Worksheet Environment   165

1.1   Navigate Through a Worksheet 166

    Practice Tasks 168

1.2   Print a Worksheet or Workbook 168

    Printing Part or All of a Workbook 168

    Setting Page Breaks 170

    Printing Gridlines and Headings 172

    Printing Page Headers and Footers 174

    Practice Tasks 175

1.3   Personalize the Excel Environment 175

    Managing Program Functionality 175

    Customizing the Ribbon and Quick Access Toolbar .177

    Managing Workbooks 183

    Practice Tasks 185

Objective Review 186

2   Creating Cell Data   187

2.1   Construct Cell Data 188

    Pasting Structured Data 188

    Inserting and Deleting Data 189

    Practice Tasks 192

2.2   Apply Auto Fill 193

    Filling a Data Series 193

    Copying Data 197

    Practice Tasks 198

2.3   Apply and Manipulate Hyperlinks. 198
        Creating Hyperlinks. 198
        Modifying Hyperlinks 201
        Practice Tasks 201
    Objective Review. 202

3   Formatting Cells and Worksheets   203

3.1   Apply and Modify Cell Formats. 204
        Formatting Cell Content. 204
        Formatting Cell Fills and Borders 207
        Setting Row Height and Column Width 208
        Formatting Numbers. 210
        Practice Tasks 214
3.2   Merge or Split Cells 215
        Practice Tasks 216
3.3   Create Row and Column Titles. 216
        Practice Tasks 218
3.4   Hide or Unhide Rows and Columns 218
        Practice Tasks 219
3.5   Manipulate Page Setup Options for Worksheets 220
        Practice Tasks 222
3.6   Create and Apply Cell Styles. 222
        Practice Tasks 224
    Objective Review. 224

4   Managing Worksheets and Workbooks   225

4.1   Create and Format Worksheets. 226
        Practice Tasks 227
4.2   Manipulate Window Views. 228
        Freezing and Splitting Windows 228
        Displaying Multiple Windows 229
        Practice Tasks 230
4.3   Manipulate Workbook Views. 231
        Switching Worksheet Views. 231
        Customizing the Program Window 231
        Customizing Worksheet Appearance. 232
        Changing the Zoom Level 232
        Practice Tasks 233
    Objective Review. 234

5   Applying Formulas and Functions   235

5.1   Create Formulas 236

        Practice Tasks 240

5.2   Enforce Precedence 240

        Practice Tasks 241

5.3   Apply Cell References in Formulas 242

        Practice Tasks 244

5.4   Apply Conditional Logic in Formulas 245

        Creating Conditional Formulas 245

        Nesting Functions 246

        Practice Tasks 247

5.5   Apply Named Ranges in Formulas 247

        Practice Tasks 249

5.6   Apply Cell Ranges in Formulas. 250

        Practice Tasks 251

        Objective Review 251

6   Presenting Data Visually   253

6.1   Create Charts Based on Worksheet Data. 254

        Plotting Charts 254

        Applying Layouts and Styles 257

        Moving and Sizing Charts 258

        Editing Data 259

        Configuring Chart Elements. 260

        Practice Tasks 263

6.2   Apply and Manipulate Illustrations. 264

        Inserting and Formatting Clip Art. 264

        Inserting and Modifying SmartArt Diagrams .265

        Inserting and Formatting Shapes 267

        Capturing Screenshots 269

        Practice Tasks 270

6.3   Create and Modify Images. 271

        Practice Tasks 273

6.4   Apply Sparklines. 273

        Practice Tasks 275

        Objective Review 276

7   Sharing Worksheet Data with Other Users   277

    7.1   Share Spreadsheets 278

        Saving Workbooks in Specific Formats 278

        Sending Workbooks 283

        Practice Tasks 284

    7.2   Manage Comments 285

        Practice Tasks 287

    Objective Review 287

8   Analyzing and Organizing Data   289

    8.1   Filter Data 290

        Practice Tasks 293

    8.2   Sort Data 293

        Practice Tasks 295

    8.3   Apply Conditional Formatting 295

        Practice Tasks 300

    Objective Review 300

Exam 77-883   ## Microsoft PowerPoint 2010

Prerequisites 302

        Understanding PowerPoint Views 302

        Moving Around in a Presentation 303

        Selecting Text 303

1   Managing the PowerPoint Environment   305

    1.1   Adjust Views 306

        Switching Views 306

        Zooming In and Out 307

        Practice Tasks 308

    1.2   Manipulate the PowerPoint Window 308

        Working with Multiple Program Windows 308

        Sizing Panes in Normal View 310

        Practice Tasks 311

    1.3   Configure the Quick Access Toolbar 311

        Practice Tasks 313

    1.4   Configure PowerPoint File Options 314

        Practice Tasks 318

    Objective Review 318

2   Creating a Slide Presentation   319

2.1   Construct and Edit Photo Albums. 320
      Creating Photo Albums. 320
      Editing Photo Albums 322
      Practice Tasks 323
2.2   Apply Slide Size and Orientation Settings 324
      Practice Tasks 325
2.3   Add and Remove Slides 326
      Inserting New Slides 326
      Reusing Slides. 327
      Inserting Outlines 330
      Rearranging Slides. 330
      Deleting Slides 331
      Hiding Slides. 332
      Practice Tasks 332
2.4   Format Slides. 333
      Applying and Modifying Themes 333
      Formatting the Background of Slides. 336
      Inserting Footer Information 338
      Dividing a Presentation into Sections 339
      Customizing Slide Masters. 342
      Practice Tasks 343
2.5   Enter and Format Text. 344
      Entering Text in Text Placeholders 344
      Entering Text in Independent Text Boxes 344
      Editing Text. 345
      Formatting Characters and Paragraphs. 346
      Formatting Bulleted and Numbered Lists 350
      Practice Tasks 354
2.6   Format Text Boxes 354
      Changing the Shape of Text Boxes 354
      Sizing and Positioning Text Boxes. 356
      Aligning Text Boxes 359
      Formatting Text Boxes 360
      Adjusting the Text Layout. 362
      Setting Default Formatting 363
      Practice Tasks 364
Objective Review. 364

3   Working with Graphical and Multimedia Elements   365

3.1   Manipulate Graphical Elements. 366
    Opening the Format Dialog Box. 366
    Applying Styles, Borders, and Effects. 366
    Sizing and Positioning a Graphic. 368
    Changing the Stacking Order 370
    Grouping Graphics. 371
    Aligning Graphics. 371
    Linking Graphics to Other Information 372
    Practice Tasks 374
3.2   Manipulate Images 374
    Cropping Images 374
    Formatting Images 376
    Compressing Pictures 378
    Resetting or Replacing Images 379
    Practice Tasks 379
3.3   Modify WordArt and Shapes. 380
    Working with WordArt. 380
    Working with Shapes 381
    Practice Tasks 383
3.4   Manipulate SmartArt. 384
    Creating Diagrams. 384
    Making Design Changes. 386
    Changing Shapes in Diagrams. 387
    Converting Diagrams to Shapes or Bullet Points 388
    Practice Tasks 388
3.5   Edit Video and Audio Content. 389
    Inserting and Editing Video Content 389
    Inserting and Editing Audio Content 392
    Practice Tasks 395
Objective Review. 396

4   Creating Charts and Tables   397

4.1   Construct and Modify Tables. 398
    Inserting Tables and Editing Table Content. 398
    Changing Table Structure. 399
    Formatting Tables 402
    Inserting and Modifying Excel Worksheets. 404
    Practice Tasks 406

4.2   Insert and Modify Charts 406
    Inserting Charts and Editing Chart Data 406
    Changing the Chart Type and Layout 409
    Practice Tasks 412
4.3   Apply Chart Elements 412
    Practice Tasks 414
4.4   Manipulate Chart Layouts. 414
    Selecting Chart Elements 414
    Sizing and Positioning Elements 415
    Practice Tasks 416
4.5   Manipulate Chart Elements 416
    Practice Tasks 420
  Objective Review. 420

5   Applying Transitions and Animations   421

5.1   Apply Built-In and Custom Animations 422
    Applying Built-In Animations. 422
    Applying Fancier Animations. 423
    Copying Animations 424
    Practice Tasks 424
5.2   Apply Effect and Path Options 425
    Fine-Tuning Animation Effects. 425
    Adjusting Motion Paths 426
    Practice Tasks 427
5.3   Manipulate Animations. 428
    Practice Tasks 432
5.4   Apply and Modify Transitions Between Slides .432
    Practice Tasks 434
  Objective Review. 434

6   Collaborating on Presentations   435

6.1   Manage Comments in Presentations 436
    Practice Tasks 438
6.2   Apply Proofing Tools. 438
    Using AutoCorrect. 438
    Correcting Spelling Mistakes. 440
    Finding and Replacing Text and Fonts. 441
    Using the Thesaurus 442
    Comparing and Combining Presentations 444
    Practice Tasks 445
  Objective Review. 446

7   Preparing Presentations for Delivery   **447**

   7.1   Save Presentations 448

           Practice Tasks 453

   7.2   Share Presentations 453

           Compressing Media. 453

           Packaging for CD Delivery 454

           Creating Videos 455

           Practice Tasks 457

   7.3   Print Presentations 457

           Previewing and Printing 457

           Printing Handouts and Notes 459

           Practice Tasks 461

   7.4   Protect Presentations. 462

           Removing Extraneous Information. 462

           Assigning Passwords 463

           Marking as Final 465

           Attaching Digital Signatures 465

           Practice Tasks 466

     Objective Review. 466

8   Delivering Presentations   **467**

   8.1   Apply Presentation Tools 468

           Practice Tasks 470

   8.2   Set Up Slide Shows. 470

           Adjusting Slide Show Settings 470

           Setting Up Presenter View 472

           Broadcasting Slide Shows. 473

           Creating Custom Slide Shows 474

           Practice Tasks 476

   8.3   Set Presentation Timing 476

           Practice Tasks 478

   8.4   Record Presentations. 478

           Practice Tasks 479

     Objective Review. 480

Exam 77-884 Microsoft Outlook 2010

Prerequisites. 482
    Module-Specific Behavior 482
    Switching Views. 483
    Creating Outlook Items 483
    Addressing Messages 484
    Editing and Formatting Message Content. 484

1   Managing the Outlook Environment   485

  1.1 Apply and Manipulate Outlook Program Options 486
    Managing Mail Module Options. 486
    Managing Calendar Module Options. 496
    Managing Contacts Module Options. 502
    Managing Tasks Module Options 504
    Managing Notes Module and Journal Options .505
    Managing Language Options 506
    Managing Advanced Options 507
    Practice Tasks 512
  1.2 Manipulate Item Tags 512
    Working with Color Categories. 512
    Setting Message Sensitivity and Importance 515
    Setting Message Properties. 516
    Flagging Items for Follow-Up 517
    Changing Read Status. 519
    Practice Tasks 519
  1.3 Arrange the Content Pane 519
    Displaying and Hiding Program Window Panes. 519
    Displaying Module Content. 525
    Displaying List Views. 527
    Modifying List Views. 527
    Working with the Status Bar 528
    Practice Tasks 530
  1.4 Apply Search and Filter Tools. 531
    Using Instant Search 531
    Using Search Folders. 533
    Practice Tasks 534

1.5   Print an Outlook Item 535
     Printing Items 535
     Printing Messages 535
     Printing a Calendar 536
     Printing Contact Records 537
     Practice Tasks 539
   Objective Review 540

2   Creating and Formatting Item Content   541

2.1   Create and Send Email Messages 542
     Formatting Messages 542
     Setting Message Options 542
     Sending Messages 544
     Practice Tasks 545
2.2   Create and Manage Quick Steps 545
     Practice Tasks 549
2.3   Create Item Content 549
     Inserting Visual Elements 549
     Inserting SmartArt Graphics 551
     Inserting Charts 553
     Inserting Screen Images 555
     Modifying Visual Elements 556
     Creating Hyperlinks 557
     Practice Tasks 559
2.4   Format Item Content 560
     Applying Text and Paragraph Formatting 560
     Applying and Managing Styles 562
     Applying and Managing Style Sets 565
     Applying and Managing Themes 566
     Practice Tasks 568
2.5   Attach Content to Email Messages 569
     Practice Tasks 570
   Objective Review 570

3   Managing Email Messages   571

3.1   Clean Up the Mailbox 572
     Managing Mailbox Size 572
     Managing Conversations 574
     Saving Messages and Message Attachments 575
     Practice Tasks 576

3.2   Create and Manage Rules. 576

      Managing Mail by Using Outlook Rules 576

      Creating Automatic Reply Rules 579

      Practice Tasks 580

3.3   Manage Junk Email 581

      Working with Junk Email Messages 581

      Configuring Junk Email Options 582

      Practice Tasks 585

3.4   Manage Automatic Message Content 585

      Creating and Using Automatic Signatures. 585

      Setting a Default Theme, Stationery, and Fonts. 587

      Identifying Response Text 589

      Practice Tasks 589

    Objective Review 590

4   Managing Contacts   591

4.1   Create and Manipulate Contacts. 592

      Creating Contact Records. 592

      Creating Electronic Business Cards. 596

      Practice Tasks 599

4.2   Create and Manipulate Contact Groups 600

      Practice Tasks 602

    Objective Review 602

5   Managing Calendar Objects   603

5.1   Create and Manipulate Appointments and Events. 604

      Scheduling Appointments 604

      Scheduling Events 606

      Setting Recurrence and Privacy Options 608

      Working with Appointments and Events. 609

      Practice Tasks 610

5.2   Create and Manipulate Meeting Requests 611

      Creating Meeting Requests 611

      Scheduling Meetings. 614

      Responding to Meeting Requests. 617

      Rescheduling and Canceling Meetings 619

      Practice Tasks 621

5.3   Manipulate the Calendar Pane 622
      Arranging Calendar Content 622
      Displaying Different Views. 625
      Displaying Multiple Calendars. 625
      Changing Calendar Colors 629
      Practice Tasks 629
Objective Review 630

6   Working with Tasks, Notes, and Journal Entries   631

6.1   Create and Manipulate Tasks 632
      Creating Tasks. 632
      Displaying Views of Tasks. 635
      Managing Tasks 637
      Managing Task Details 638
      Managing Task Assignments 640
      Finalizing Tasks. 642
      Practice Tasks 643
6.2   Create and Manipulate Notes 644
      Creating Notes. 644
      Displaying Views of Notes 644
      Organizing Notes. 645
      Practice Tasks 646
6.3   Create and Manipulate Journal Entries. 646
      Activating the Outlook Journal 646
      Automatically Recording Information .647
      Editing Journal Entries. 648
      Practice Tasks 650
Objective Review 650

Index. 651

About the Authors 691

What do you think of this book? We want to hear from you!

Microsoft is interested in hearing your feedback so we can continually improve our books and learning resources for you. To participate in a brief online survey, please visit:

microsoft.com/learning/booksurvey

Taking a Microsoft Office Specialist Exam

Desktop computing proficiency is increasingly important in today's business world. As a result, when screening, hiring, and training employees, employers can feel reassured by relying on the objectivity and consistency of technology certification to ensure the competence of their workforce. As an employee or job seeker, you can use technology certification to prove that you already have the skills you need to succeed, saving current and future employers the trouble and expense of training you.

Microsoft Office Specialist Certification

Microsoft Office Specialist certification for Microsoft Office 2010 is designed to assist employees in validating their skills with programs in the Office 2010 software suite. The following certification paths are available:

- A Microsoft Office Specialist (MOS) is an individual who has demonstrated proficiency by passing a certification exam in one or more of the Office 2010 programs, including Microsoft Word, Excel, PowerPoint, Outlook, and Access, or in Microsoft SharePoint.

- A Microsoft Office Specialist Expert (MOS Expert) is an individual who has taken his or her knowledge of Office 2010 to the next level and has demonstrated by passing a certification exam that he or she has mastered the more advanced features of Word 2010 or Excel 2010.

Selecting a Certification Path

When deciding which certifications you would like to pursue, you should assess the following:

- The program and program version(s) with which you are familiar
- The length of time you have used the program and how frequently you use it
- Whether you have had formal or informal training in the use of that program
- Whether you use most or all of the available program features
- Whether you are considered a go-to resource by business associates, friends, and family members who have difficulty with the program

Candidates for MOS-level certification are expected to successfully complete a wide range of standard business tasks, such as formatting a document or worksheet and its content; creating and formatting visual content; or working with SharePoint lists, libraries, Web Parts, and dashboards. Successful candidates generally have six or more months of experience with the specific Office program, including either formal, instructor-led training or self-study using MOS-approved books, guides, or interactive computer-based materials.

Candidates for MOS Expert-level certification are expected to successfully complete more complex tasks that involve using the advanced functionality of the program. Successful candidates generally have at least six months, and may have several years, of experience with the programs, including formal, instructor-led training or self-study using MOS-approved materials.

Test-Taking Tips

Every MOS certification exam is developed from a set of exam skill standards (referred to as the objective domain) that are derived from studies of how the Office 2010 programs or SharePoint are used in the workplace. Because these skill standards dictate the scope of each exam, they provide critical information about how to prepare for certification. This book follows the structure of the published exam objectives; see "Using This Book to Study for a Certification Exam" at the beginning of this book for more information.

The MOS certification exams for the Office 2010 programs and SharePoint are performance based and require you to complete business-related tasks in the program for which you are seeking certification. You might be told to adjust program settings or be presented with a file and told to do something specific with it. Your score on the exam reflects how well you perform the requested tasks within the allotted time.

Here is some helpful information about taking the exam:

- Keep track of the time. You have 50 minutes to complete the exam. Your exam time does not officially begin until after you finish reading the instructions provided at the beginning of the exam. During the exam, the amount of time remaining is shown at the bottom of the exam interface. You can't pause the exam after you start it.

- Pace yourself. At the beginning of the exam, you will be told how many questions are included in the exam. Some questions will require that you complete more than one task. During the exam, the number of completed and remaining questions is shown at the bottom of the exam interface.

- Read the exam instructions carefully before beginning. Follow all the instructions provided in each question completely and accurately.

- Enter requested information as it appears in the instructions, but without duplicating the formatting unless you are specifically instructed to do so. For example, the text and values you are asked to enter might appear in the instructions in bold and underlined text, but you should enter the information without applying these formats.

- Close all dialog boxes before proceeding to the next exam question unless you are specifically instructed not to do so.

- Don't close task panes before proceeding to the next exam question unless you are specifically instructed to do so.

- If you are asked to print a document, worksheet, chart, report, or slide, perform the task, but be aware that nothing will actually be printed.

- Don't worry about extra keystrokes or mouse clicks. Your work is scored based on its result, not on the method you use to achieve that result (unless a specific method is indicated in the instructions).

- If a computer problem occurs during the exam (for example, if the exam does not respond or the mouse no longer functions) or if a power outage occurs, contact a testing center administrator immediately. The administrator will restart the computer and return the exam to the point where the interruption occurred, with your score intact.

> **Strategy** This book includes special tips for effectively studying for the Microsoft Office Specialist exams in Strategy paragraphs such as this one.

Certification Benefits

At the conclusion of the exam, you will receive a score report, indicating whether you passed the exam. You can print with the assistance of the testing center administrator. If your score meets or exceeds the passing standard (the minimum required score), you will be contacted by email by the Microsoft Certification Program team. The email message you receive will include your Microsoft Certification ID and links to online resources, including the Microsoft Certified Professional site. On this site, you can download or order a printed certificate, create a virtual business card, order an ID card, view and share your certification transcript, access the Logo Builder, and access other useful and interesting resources, including special offers from Microsoft and affiliated companies.

Using the Logo Builder, you can create a personalized certification logo that includes the MOS logo and the specific programs in which you have achieved certification. If you achieve MOS certification in multiple programs, you can include up to six of them in one logo.

Microsoft Access 2010 Certified
Microsoft Excel 2010 Certified
Microsoft Outlook 2010 Certified
Microsoft PowerPoint 2010 Certified
Microsoft Word 2010 Certified

You can include your personalized logo on business cards and other personal promotional materials. This logo attests to the fact that you are proficient in the applications or cross-application skills necessary to achieve the certification.

For More Information

To learn more about the Microsoft Office Specialist exams and related courseware, visit:

www.microsoft.com/learning/en/us/certification/mos.aspx

Using This Book to Study for a Certification Exam

The Microsoft Office Specialist (MOS) exams for individual Microsoft Office 2010 programs are practical rather than theoretical. You must demonstrate that you can complete certain tasks rather than simply answering questions about program features. The successful MOS certification candidate will have at least six months of experience using all aspects of the application on a regular basis; for example, using Microsoft Outlook at work to send messages, track contact information, schedule appointments and meetings, track and assign tasks, and take notes.

This book has been designed to guide you in studying the types of tasks you are likely to be required to demonstrate in the MOS exams for Microsoft Word 2010, Excel 2010, PowerPoint 2010, and Outlook 2010.

Each part of the book covers one exam. The coverage for each exam is divided into chapters representing broad skill sets, and each chapter is divided into sections addressing groups of related skills. Each section includes review information, generic procedures, and practice tasks you can complete on your own while studying. When necessary, we provide practice files you can use to work through the practice tasks. You can practice the procedures in this book by using the practice files supplied or by using your own files. (If you use your own files, keep in mind that functionality in some Office 2010 programs is limited in files created in or saved for earlier versions of the program. When working in such a file, *Compatibility Mode* appears in the program window title bar.)

As a certification candidate, you probably have a lot of experience with the program you want to become certified in. Many of the procedures we discuss in this book will be familiar to you; others might not be. Read through each study section and ensure that you are familiar with not only the procedures included in the section, but also the concepts and tools discussed in the review information. In some cases, graphics depict the tools you will use to perform procedures related to the skill set. Study the graphics and ensure that you are familiar with all the options available for each tool.

Throughout this book, you will find Strategy tips presenting additional methods of study you can pursue on your own to ensure that you achieve mastery of a skill set and are successful in your certification effort.

Features and Conventions of This Book

If you have worked with previous versions of Word, Excel, PowerPoint, or Outlook, or if you need help remembering how to perform a particular task, the following features of this book will help you locate specific information:

- **Detailed table of contents** Scan a listing of the topics covered in each chapter and locate specific topics.

- **Chapter thumb tabs** Easily locate the beginning of the chapter you want.

- **Detailed index** Look up specific tasks and general concepts in the index, which has been carefully crafted with the reader in mind.

You can save time when you use this book by understanding how special instructions, keys to press, buttons to click, and other conventions are indicated in this book.

Convention	Meaning
1 **2**	Numbered steps guide you through step-by-step procedures.
→	An arrow indicates a procedure that has only one step.
Practice Files	This paragraph at the end of a chapter introduction provides information about the practice files provided as part of the companion media for use in the chapter.
See Also	These paragraphs direct you to more information about a given topic in this book or elsewhere.
Tip	These paragraphs provide a helpful hint or shortcut that makes working through a task easier, or information about other available options.
Strategy	These paragraphs provide additional exam study tips.
Interface elements	In procedures, the names of program elements (such as buttons and commands) are shown in bold characters.
Key combinations	A plus sign (+) between two key names means that you must hold down the first key while you press the second key. For example, "press Ctrl+Home" means "hold down the Ctrl key and press the Home key."
User input	In procedures, anything you should enter appears in bold italic characters.

Using the Book's Companion Content

Before you can complete the exercises in this book, you need to copy the book's practice files to your computer. These practice files, and other information, can be downloaded from here:

http://go.microsoft.com/FWLink/?Linkid=206095

Go to the detail page in your web browser and follow the instructions for downloading the files.

> **Important** The Microsoft Word 2010, Excel 2010, PowerPoint 2010, and Outlook 2010 programs are not available from this website. You should purchase and install those programs before using this book.

The following tables list the practice files for this book.

Exam 77-881: Microsoft Word 2010

Folder/Objective	File
Word\Objective1 1 Sharing and Maintaining Documents	*ExecutiveResume.dotx*
	Finalizing.docx
	Orchestra.docx
	Password.docx
	Saving1.docx
	Saving2.docx
	Saving3.docx
	UrbanResume.dotx
	Versions.docx
	Viewing1.docx
	Viewing2.docx

(continued)

Folder/Objective	File
Word\Objective2 2 Formatting Content	*Characters.docx* *Finding.docx* *Lists.docx* *ModifyTable.docx* *Paragraphs.docx* *RoomPlanner.docx* *SortTable.docx* *Styles.docx* *Table.docx* *Tabs.docx* *TabularList.docx*
Word\Objective3 3 Applying Page Layout and Reusable Content	*Background.docx* *Columns.docx* *CustomTheme.docx* *Header.docx* *Numbers.docx* *Pages.docx* *Parts.docx* *SavedText.docx* *Theme.docx*
Word\Objective4 4 Including Illustrations and Graphics in a Document	*ClipArt.docx* *Logo.png* *Picture.docx* *Shapes.docx* *SmartArt.docx* *TextBoxes.docx* *WordArt.docx*
Word\Objective5 5 Proofreading Documents	*Comments.docx* *Letter.docx*
Word\Objective6 6 Applying References and Hyperlinks	*Contents.docx* *Footnotes.docx* *Hyperlinks.docx* *OtherLogos.docx*
Word\Objective7 7 Performing Mail Merge Operations	*AnniversaryLetter.docx* *CustomerList.xlsx*

Exam 77-882: Microsoft Excel 2010

Folder/Objective	File
Excel\Objective1 1 Managing the Worksheet Environment	*HeaderFooter.xlsx* *PageBreaks.xlsx* *PopulationData.xlsx* *PrintArea.xlsx* *Properties.xlsx*
Excel\Objective2 2 Creating Cell Data	*FillCopies.xlsx* *FillCustom.xlsx* *FillSeries.xlsx* *Hyperlink.xlsx* *InsertingDeleting.xlsx*
Excel\Objective3 3 Formatting Cells and Worksheets	*FormatCells.xlsx* *HeightWidth.xlsx* *Hiding.xlsx* *Hyperlink.xlsx* *Layout.xlsx* *RowColumnFormatting.xlsx*
Excel\Objective4 4 Managing Worksheets and Workbooks	*AirQualityData.xlsx* *PersonalMonthlyBudget.xlsx* *PopulationData.xlsx* *SalesReport.xlsx*
Excel\Objective5 5 Applying Formulas and Functions	*CellRange.xlsx* *ConditionalFormula.xlsx* *MultiplicationTable.xlsx* *Sales.xlsx* *SalesBySeason.xlsx* *SummaryFormula.xlsx*

(continued)

Folder/Objective	File
Excel\Objective6 6 Presenting Data Visually	ChartElements.xlsx ClipArt.xlsx DataSource.xlsx Editing.xlsx Logo2.jpg PersonalMonthlyBudget.xlsx Picture.xlsx Plotting.xlsx Pollution.pptx Shapes.xlsx SizingMoving.xlsx SmartArt.xlsx Sparklines.xlsx VariegatedGrass.jpg
Excel\Objective7 7 Sharing Worksheet Data with Other Users	Comments.xlsx Saving.xlsx
Excel\Objective8 8 Analyzing and Organizing Data	ConditionalFormatting.xlsx Filtering.xlsx Sorting.xlsm

Exam 77-883: Microsoft PowerPoint 2010

Folder/Objective	File
PowerPoint\Objective1 1 Managing the PowerPoint Environment	BuyingTripsA.pptx BuyingTripsB.pptx WaterSaving.pptx

Folder/Objective	File
PowerPoint\Objective2 2 Creating a Slide Presentation	*AnnualGeneralMeeting.pptx* *BuyingTrips.pptx* *Chrysanthemum.jpg* *CommunityService.pptx* *Daisies.jpg* *Frangipani.jpg* *Harmony.pptx* *Hydrangeas.jpg* *Orientation.docx* *Projects.pptx* *Service.pptx* *Tulips.jpg* *WaterLilies.jpg* *WaterSaving.pptx*
PowerPoint\Objective3 3 Working with Graphical and Multimedia Elements	*Bear.wmv* *Bravo.jpg* *InMyBackyard.pptx* *ManagingYourTime.pptx* *PhotoAlbum.pptx* *Pollution.pptx* *ShareholdersMeeting.pptx* *StatusMeeting.pptx*
PowerPoint\Objective4 4 Creating Charts and Tables	*AirQuality.pptx* *Costs.xlsx* *Temperature.pptx* *TimeManagement.pptx* *WaterConsumption.xlsx* *WaterSaving.pptx* *WaterStrategies.pptx*

(continued)

Folder/Objective	File
PowerPoint\Objective5 5 Applying Transitions and Animations	*AnnualMeeting.pptx* *BackyardEcology.pptx* *NaturalBackyard.pptx* *NaturalGardening.pptx* *PersonalJournal.pptx*
PowerPoint\Objective6 6 Collaborating on Presentations	*AnnualMeetingA.pptx* *AnnualMeetingB.pptx* *CommunityService.pptx* *CompanyMeeting.pptx* *WaterUse.pptx*
PowerPoint\Objective7 7 Preparing Presentations for Delivery	*Color.pptx* *Harmony.pptx* *HealthyEcosystems.pptx* *Meeting.pptx* *YinYang.png*
PowerPoint\Objective8 8 Delivering Presentations	*BackyardEcosystems.pptx* *DirectorsMeeting.pptx* *Landscaping.pptx* *Meeting.pptx*

Exam 77-884: Microsoft Outlook 2010

Folder/Objective	File
none 1 Managing the Outlook Environment	none
Outlook\Objective2 2 Creating and Formatting Item Content	*Brochure.docx* *KauaiLighthouse.jpg* *Regulations.docx* *Strategy.pptx*
none 3 Managing Email Messages	none
Outlook\Objective4 4 Managing Contacts	*OTSI-Logo.png*
Outlook\Objective5 5 Managing Calendar Objects	*Agenda.docx*
Outlook\Objective6 6 Working with Tasks, Notes, and Journal Entries	*ServiceProject.docx*

Modifying the Display of the Ribbon

The goal of the Microsoft Office working environment is to make working with Office documents, including Microsoft Word documents, Excel workbooks, PowerPoint presentations, Outlook email messages, and Access database tables, as intuitive as possible. You work with an Office file and its contents by giving commands to the program in which the document is open. All Office 2010 programs organize commands on a horizontal bar called the *ribbon*, which appears across the top of each program window whether or not there is an active document.

Ribbon tabs   Ribbon groups

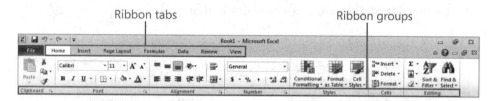

Commands are organized on task-specific tabs of the ribbon, and in feature-specific groups on each tab. Commands generally take the form of buttons and lists. Some appear in galleries. Some groups have related dialog boxes or task panes that contain additional commands.

Throughout this book, we discuss the commands and ribbon elements associated with the program feature being discussed. In this topic, we discuss the general appearance of the ribbon, things that affect its appearance, and ways of locating commands that aren't visible on compact views of the ribbon.

> **Tip** Some older commands no longer appear on the ribbon but are still available in the program. You can make these commands available by adding them to the Quick Access Toolbar.

Dynamic Ribbon Elements

The ribbon is dynamic, meaning that the appearance of commands on the ribbon changes as the width of the ribbon changes. A command might be displayed on the ribbon in the form of a large button, a small button, a small labeled button, or a list entry. As the width of the ribbon decreases, the size, shape, and presence of buttons on the ribbon adapt to the available space.

For example, when sufficient horizontal space is available, the buttons on the Review tab of the Outlook program window are spread out and you're able to see more of the commands available in each group.

If you decrease the width of the ribbon, small button labels disappear and entire groups of buttons are hidden under one button that represents the group. Click the group button to display a list of the commands available in that group.

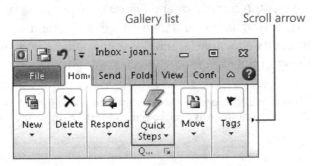

When the window becomes too narrow to display all the groups, a scroll arrow appears at its right end. Click the scroll arrow to display hidden groups.

Changing the Width of the Ribbon

The width of the ribbon is dependent on the horizontal space available to it, which depends on these three factors:

- **The width of the program window** Maximizing the program window provides the most space for ribbon elements. You can resize the program window by clicking the button in its upper-right corner or by dragging the border of a nonmaximized window.

> **Tip** On a computer running Windows 7, you can maximize the program window by dragging its title bar to the top of the screen.

- **Your screen resolution** Screen resolution is the size of your screen display expressed as pixels wide × pixels high. The greater the screen resolution, the greater the amount of information that will fit on one screen. Your screen resolution options are dependent on your monitor. At the time of writing, possible screen resolutions range from 800 × 600 to 2048 × 1152. In the case of the ribbon, the greater the number of pixels wide (the first number), the greater the number of buttons that can be shown on the ribbon, and the larger those buttons can be.

  On a computer running Windows 7, you can change your screen resolution from the Screen Resolution window of Control Panel.

- **The density of your screen display** You might not be aware that you can change the magnification of everything that appears on your screen by changing the screen magnification setting in Windows. Setting your screen magnification to 125 percent makes text and user interface elements larger on screen. This increases the legibility of information, but means that less information fits onto each screen.

On a computer running Windows 7, you can change the screen magnification from the Display window of Control Panel. You can choose one of the standard display magnification options, or create another by setting a custom text size.

> **See Also** For more information about display settings, refer to *Windows 7 Step by Step* (Microsoft Press, 2009), *Windows Vista Step by Step* (Microsoft Press, 2006), or *Windows XP Step by Step* (Microsoft Press, 2002) by Joan Lambert and Joyce Cox.

The screen magnification is directly related to the density of the text elements on screen, which is expressed in dots per inch (dpi) or points per inch (ppi). (The terms are interchangeable, and in fact are both used in the Windows dialog box in which you change the setting.) The greater the dpi, the larger the text and user interface elements appear on screen. By default, Windows displays text and screen elements at 96 dpi. Choosing the Medium - 125% display setting changes the dpi of text and screen elements to 120 dpi. You can choose a custom setting of up to 500 percent magnification, or 480 dpi, in the Custom DPI Setting dialog box.

Tip You can choose a magnification of up to 200 percent from the lists or choose a greater magnification by dragging across the ruler from left to right.

Adapting Procedure Steps

The screen images shown in the procedures in this book were captured at a screen resolution of 1024 × 768, at 100 percent magnification, and with the default text size (96 dpi). If any of your settings are different, the ribbon on your screen might not look the same as the one shown in the book. For example, you might see more or fewer buttons in each of the groups, the buttons you see might be represented by larger or smaller icons than those shown, or the group might be represented by a button that you click to display the group's commands.

When we instruct you to give a command from the ribbon in a procedure, we do it in this format:

* On the **Insert** tab, in the **Illustrations** group, click the **Chart** button.

If the command is in a list, we give the instruction in this format:

* On the **Page Layout** tab, in the **Page Setup** group, display the **Breaks** list, and then click **Page**.

If differences between your display settings and ours cause a button on your screen to look different from the one mentioned in this Study Guide, you can easily adapt the steps to locate the command. First, click the specified tab. Then locate the specified group. If a group has been collapsed into a group list or group button, click the list or button to display the group's commands. Finally, look for a button that features the same icon in a larger or smaller size than that shown in the book. If necessary, point to buttons in the group to display their names in ScreenTips.

If you prefer not to have to adapt the steps, set up your screen to match ours while you read and work through the procedures in the book.

Your Companion eBook

The eBook edition of this book allows you to:

- Search the full text
- Print
- Copy and paste

To download your eBook, please see the instruction page at the back of this book.

Getting Support and Giving Feedback

Errata

We've made every effort to ensure the accuracy of this book and its companion content. If you do find an error, please report it on our Microsoft Press site at oreilly.com:

1. Go to microsoftpress.oreilly.com.
2. In the **Search** box, enter the book's ISBN or title.
3. Select your book from the search results.
4. On your book's catalog page, in the list of links under the cover image, click **View/Submit Errata**.

You'll find additional information and services for your book on its catalog page. If you need additional support, please send an email message to Microsoft Press Book Support at *mspinput@microsoft.com*.

> **Tip** Product support for Microsoft software is not offered through the O'Reilly website or the Microsoft Press Book Support email address.

Getting Help with Microsoft Office 2010

If your question is about Microsoft Word 2010, Excel 2010, PowerPoint 2010, or Outlook 2010, and not about the content of this Microsoft Press book, your first recourse is the Microsoft Office Help system. You can find general or specific Help information in a couple of ways:

- In the program window, you can click the Help button (labeled with a question mark) located in the upper-right corner of the web browser window to display the program-specific Help window.

- In the left pane of the Backstage view, you can click Help to access Microsoft Office Help resources.

If your question is about Word 2010, Excel 2010, PowerPoint 2010, Outlook 2010, or another Microsoft software product and you cannot find the answer in the product's Help system, please search the appropriate product solution center or the Microsoft Knowledge Base at:

support.microsoft.com/

In the United States, Microsoft software product support issues not covered by the Microsoft Knowledge Base are addressed by Microsoft Product Support Services. Location-specific software support options are available from:

support.microsoft.com/gp/selfoverview/

We Want to Hear from You

At Microsoft Press, your satisfaction is our top priority, and your feedback our most valuable asset. Please tell us what you think of this book at:

www.microsoft.com/learning/booksurvey/

The survey is short, and we read *every one* of your comments and ideas. Thanks in advance for your input!

Stay in Touch

Let's keep the conversation going! We're on Twitter: twitter.com/MicrosoftPress.

Microsoft Word 2010

This part of the book covers the skills you need to have for certification as a Microsoft Office Specialist in Microsoft Word 2010. Specifically, you need to be able to complete tasks that demonstrate the following skill sets:

1 Sharing and Maintaining Documents

2 Formatting Content

3 Applying Page Layout and Reusable Content

4 Including Illustrations and Graphics in a Document

5 Proofreading Documents

6 Applying References and Hyperlinks

7 Performing Mail Merge Operations

With these skills, you can create and manage the documents most commonly used in a business environment.

Prerequisites

We assume that you have been working with Word 2010 for at least six months and that you know how to carry out fundamental tasks that are not specifically mentioned in the Microsoft Office Specialist objectives for Word 2010. Before you begin studying for this exam, you might want to make sure you are familiar with the information in this section.

Selecting Text

Before you can edit or format text, you need to select it. You can select any amount of text by dragging through it. You can select specific units of text as follows:

- To select a word, double-click it. The word and the space following it are selected. Punctuation following a word is not selected.
- To select a sentence, click anywhere in the sentence while holding down the Ctrl key. The first character in the sentence through the space following the ending punctuation mark are selected.
- To select a paragraph, triple-click it. The paragraph and paragraph mark are selected.

You can select adjacent words, lines, or paragraphs by positioning the cursor at the beginning of the text you want to select, holding down the Shift key, and then pressing an arrow key or clicking at the end of the text that you want to select.

To select non-adjacent blocks of text, select the first block, hold down the Ctrl key, and then select the next block.

To select a block of text quickly, you can use the selection area—the empty area to the left of the document's text column. When the pointer is in the selection area, it changes from an I-beam to a right-pointing arrow. From the selection area, you can select specific units of text as follows:

- To select a line, click in the selection area to the left of the line.
- To select a paragraph, double-click in the selection area to the left of the paragraph.
- To select an entire document, triple-click anywhere in the selection area.

To deselect text, click anywhere in the document window except the selection area.

Moving Around in a Document

You can view various parts of the active document by using the vertical and horizontal scroll bars. Scrolling the document does not move the cursor—it changes only the part of the document displayed in the window. For example, if you drag the vertical scroll box down to the bottom of the scroll bar, the end of the document comes into view, but the cursor stays in its original location.

Here are some other ways to use the scroll bars:

- Click the up or down scroll arrow on the vertical scroll bar to move the document window up or down one line of text.

- Click above or below the scroll box to move up or down one windowful.

- Click the left or right scroll arrow on the horizontal scroll bar to move the document window to the left or right several characters at a time.

- Click to the left or right of the scroll box to move left or right one windowful.

You can also move around in a document by moving the cursor. You can click to place the cursor at a particular location, or you can press a key or a key combination to move the cursor.

The following table shows the keys and key combinations you can use to move the cursor quickly.

Pressing this key or combination	Moves the cursor
Left Arrow	Left one character at a time
Right Arrow	Right one character at a time
Down Arrow	Down one line at a time
Up Arrow	Up one line at a time
Ctrl+Left Arrow	Left one word at a time
Ctrl+Right Arrow	Right one word at a time
Home	To the beginning of the current line
End	To the end of the current line
Ctrl+Home	To the beginning of the document
Ctrl+End	To the end of the document
Ctrl+Page Up	To the beginning of the previous page
Ctrl+Page Down	To the beginning of the next page
Page Up	Up one screen
Page Down	Down one screen

1 Sharing and Maintaining Documents

The skills tested in this section of the Microsoft Office Specialist exam for Microsoft Word 2010 relate to viewing and managing documents. Specifically, the following objectives are associated with this set of skills:

1.1 Apply Different Views to a Document

1.2 Apply Protection to a Document

1.3 Manage Document Versions

1.4 Share Documents

1.5 Save a Document

1.6 Apply a Template to a Document

Word provides many tools with which to manage the way you work with documents and share documents with other people.

This chapter guides you in studying ways of viewing documents, preventing unwanted changes, working with document versions, sharing documents with other people, saving documents, and changing the appearance of a document by applying a template.

> **Practice Files** Before you can complete the practice tasks in this chapter, you need to copy the book's practice files to your computer. The practice files you'll use to complete the tasks in this chapter are in the Word\Objective1 practice file folder. A complete list of practice files is provided in "Using the Book's Companion Content" at the beginning of this book.

1.1 Apply Different Views to a Document

Switching Views

In Word, you can display a document in a variety of views, each suited to a specific purpose. The standard views include Print Layout view (the default), Full Screen Reading view, Web Layout view, Outline view, and Draft view.

➤ To switch views

→ On the **View** tab, in the **Document Views** group, click the **Print Layout**, **Full Screen Reading**, **Web Layout**, **Outline View**, or **Draft View** button.

→ In the lower-right corner of the program window, on the **View Shortcuts** toolbar, click the **Print Layout**, **Full Screen Reading**, **Web Layout**, **Outline**, or **Draft** button.

> **See Also** For more information about the View Shortcuts toolbar, see the "Magnifying Document Content" topic later in this section.

Working in Print Layout View

Print Layout view displays a document on the screen the way it will look when printed. You can see elements such as margins, page breaks, headers and footers, and watermarks.

➤ To hide or display space between pages in Print Layout view

→ Point to the gap or line between any two pages, and when the pointer changes to two opposing arrows, double-click the mouse button.

→ On the **Display** page of the **Word Options** dialog box, in the **Page display options** section, clear or select the **Show white space between pages in Print Layout view** check box.

➤ To display page thumbnails

1. On the **View** tab, in the **Show** group, select the **Navigation Pane** check box.

2. In the **Navigation Pane**, click the **Browse Pages** tab.

Working in Full Screen Reading View

Full Screen Reading view displays a magnified view of the document content. In this view, the ribbon is replaced by one toolbar at the top of the screen with buttons for saving and printing the document, accessing reference and other tools, translating text, highlighting text, and inserting comments.

Document management tools   Navigation buttons   Full Screen Reading view options

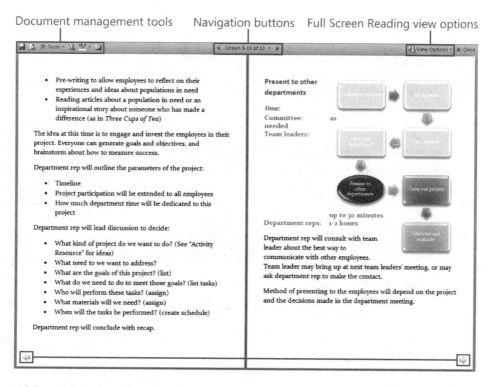

While working in Full Screen Reading view, you can save, preview, and print the document; translate content; and highlight or comment on content, by using the document management tools located at the left end of the title bar. In addition, you can access research tools, highlight and comment on document content, and search for specific text by using the commands on the Tools menu.

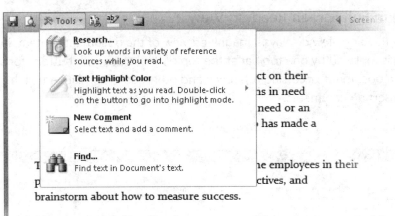

ct on their

...s in need

...need or an

...has made a

T... ...e employees in their
p... ...ctives, and
brainstorm about how to measure success.

Department rep will outline the parameters of the project:

You can navigate from page to page or jump to a specific screen or heading within the document by using the buttons available in the navigation tools area in the center of the title bar.

Jump To A Page Or Section In The Document button

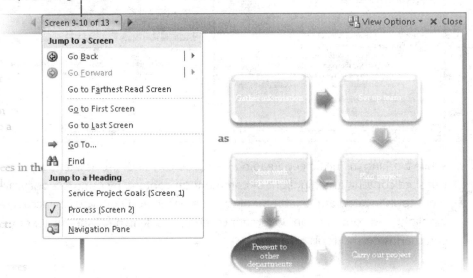

You can control the appearance of the document and the functionality within the document by using commands available from the View Options menu.

➤ **To move from page to page in Full Screen Reading view**

→ Click the **Next Screen** or **Previous Screen** button in the center of the title bar.

→ Click the arrows located on the outer edges at the bottom of the pages.

➤ **To move to a specific location in the document in Full Screen Reading view**

→ Click the **Jump to a page or section in the document** button, and then click the screen or heading you want to move to.

➤ **To change the way content is displayed in Full Screen Reading view**

→ On the **View Options** menu, do any of the following:

  ○ Click **Don't Open Attachments in Full Screen** to prevent email attachments and documents from a Microsoft SharePoint site from opening in Full Screen Reading view.

  ○ Click **Increase Text Size**, **Decrease Text Size**, **Margin Settings**, or **Show Printed Page** to change the amount of text shown on each page.

  ○ Click **Show One Page** or **Show Two Pages** to change the number and width of pages shown in the Full Screen Reading window.

  ○ Click **Allow Typing** to allow or prevent editing, and **Track Changes** to track changes made to the document while editing is allowed.

  ○ Click **Show Comments and Changes** or **Show Original/Final Document** to manage the display of tracked changes and comments.

➤ **To switch from Full Screen Reading view to the previous view**

→ Click the **Close full screen reading view** button.

Working in Web Layout View

Web Layout view displays the document the way it will look when viewed in a web browser. In this view, you can see backgrounds and other effects. You can also see how text wraps to fit the window and how graphics are positioned.

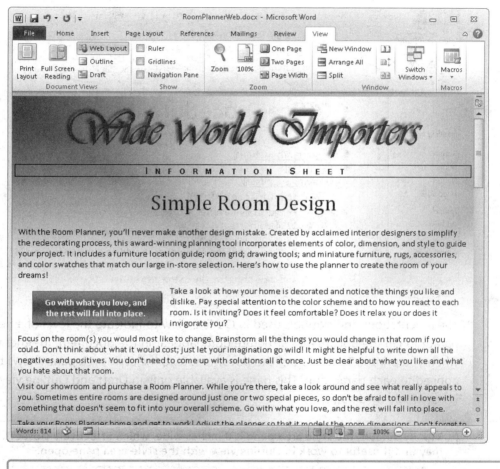

See Also For information about the ribbon, see "Modifying the Display of the Ribbon" at the beginning of this book.

Working in Outline View

Outline view displays the structure of a document as nested levels of headings and body text, and provides tools for viewing and changing its hierarchy.

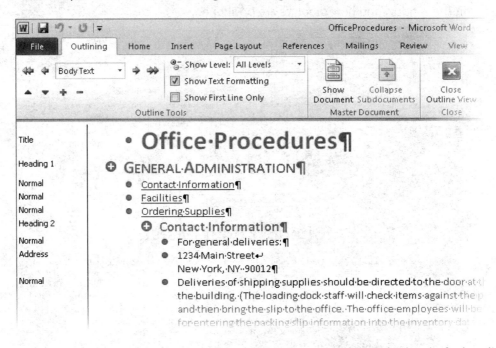

The indentations and symbols used in Outline view to indicate the level of a heading or paragraph in the document's structure don't appear in the document in other views or when you print it. To the left of the document text, the style area pane shows the style applied to each paragraph. This pane is available only in Draft and Outline views, and it is not visible by default.

> **Tip** By default, the style area pane is 0 inches wide, which effectively closes it. You may find it useful to work in Outline view with the style area pane open.

When working in Outline view, you can control the level of content that is displayed, promote or demote the level of headings or body text, and easily move entire sections of text. You can also work with the subdocuments of a master document.

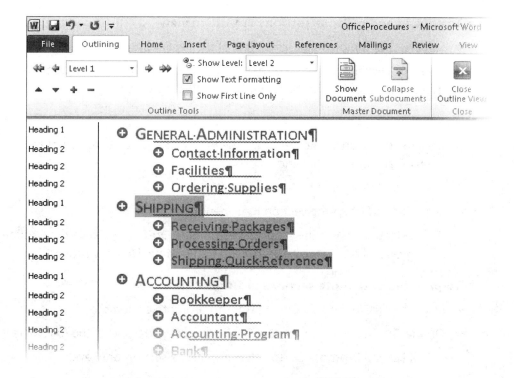

> ➤ **To display or hide styles in the margin in Outline view**

→ On the **Advanced** page of the **Word Options** dialog box, in the **Display** section, do one of the following, and then click **OK**:

- ○ To display styles, enter a positive dimension (for example, *0.5"*) in the **Style area pane width in Draft and Outline views** box.

- ○ To hide styles, enter *0"* in the **Style area pane width in Draft and Outline views** box.

> ➤ **To display only content at a specific level and above in Outline view**

→ On the **Outlining** tab, in the **Outline Tools** group, in the **Show Level** list, click the lowest content level you want to display.

➤ **To expand and collapse sections in Outline view**

→ Double-click the plus sign to the left of the section.

→ Select or click in the section. Then on the **Outlining** tab, in the **Outline Tools** group, click the **Expand** button or the **Collapse** button.

➤ **To reorganize a document in Outline view**

→ Click the plus sign to the left of any heading to select that section of the document. Then do any of the following:

  ○ Drag the section to its new location.

  ○ Cut and paste the section to its new location.

  ○ Select or click in the section. Then on the **Outlining** tab, in the **Outline Tools** group, click the **Move Up** button or the **Move Down** button.

➤ **To promote or demote sections in Outline view**

→ Select or click in the section you want to promote or demote.

→ On the **Outlining** tab, in the **Outline Tools** group, do one of the following:

  ○ Click the **Promote** button to promote the section one level.

  ○ Click the **Demote** button to demote the section one level.

  ○ Click the **Promote to Heading 1** button to promote the section to a first-level heading.

  ○ Click the **Demote to Body Text** button to demote a heading to body text.

➤ **To expand and collapse subdocuments in Outline view**

→ Select or click in the subdocument. Then on the **Outlining** tab, in the **Master Document** group, click the **Expand Subdocuments** button or the **Collapse Subdocuments** button.

➤ **To open a subdocument from Outline view**

→ On the **Outlining** tab, in the **Master Document** group, click the **Show Document** button.

Working in Draft View

Page break indicator

Draft view displays the content of a document with a simplified layout so that you can type and edit quickly. You cannot see layout elements such as headers and footers.

➤ **To display or hide styles in the margin in Draft view**

→ On the **Advanced** page of the **Word Options** dialog box, in the **Display** section, do one of the following, and then click **OK**:

○ To display styles, enter a positive dimension (for example, *0.5"*) in the **Style area pane width in Draft and Outline views** box.

○ To hide styles, enter *0"* in the **Style area pane width in Draft and Outline views** box.

Modifying the Program Window

When you want to focus on the layout of a document, you can display horizontal and vertical rulers and gridlines to help you position and align elements.

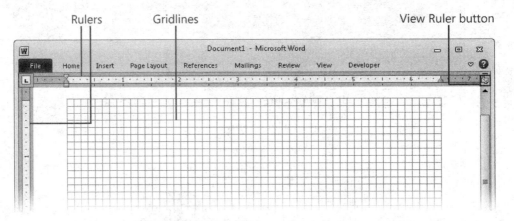

When you are fine-tuning the layout of a document, you might find it helpful to display formatting marks and hidden characters. Formatting marks, such as tabs and paragraph marks, control the layout of your document, and hidden characters provide the structure for behind-the-scenes processes, such as indexing.

➤ **To display or hide rulers**

→ At the top of the vertical scrollbar, click the **View Ruler** button.

→ On the **View** tab, in the **Show** group, select or clear the **Ruler** check box.

➤ **To turn the display of the vertical ruler on or off**

→ On the **Advanced** page of the **Word Options** dialog box, in the **Display** section, select or clear the **Show vertical ruler in Print Layout view** check box.

➤ **To display or hide gridlines**

→ On the **View** tab, in the **Show** group, select or clear the **Gridlines** check box.

➤ **To display or hide formatting marks and hidden characters**

→ On the **Home** tab, in the **Paragraph** group, click the **Show/Hide ¶** button.

Magnifying Document Content

You can adjust the magnification of the document by using the tools available from the ribbon or from the View Shortcuts toolbar located at the right end of the status bar.

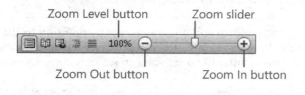

Fixed magnification levels

Page-related magnification levels

View Shortcuts toolbar

The View Shortcuts toolbar includes tools for changing the view and the magnification of the document window.

Zoom Level button   Zoom slider

Zoom Out button   Zoom In button

See Also For information about changing the view, see the "Switching Views" topic earlier in this section.

> ➤ **To zoom in or out in 10 percent increments**

→ On the **View Shortcuts** toolbar, click the **Zoom In** button or the **Zoom Out** button.

> ➤ **To zoom to a specific magnification**

→ On the **View Shortcuts** toolbar, drag the **Zoom** slider.

→ On the **View** tab, in the **Zoom** group, click the **100%**, **One Page**, **Two Pages**, or **Page Width** button.

Or

1. On the **View Shortcuts** toolbar, click the **Zoom level** button.

Or

On the **View** tab, in the **Zoom** group, click the **Zoom** button.

2. In the **Zoom** dialog box, click a fixed magnification level or a page-related magnification level, or in the **Percent** box, enter or select a magnification level. Then click **OK**

> ➤ **To display multiple pages**

→ On the **View** tab, in the **Zoom** group, click the **Two Pages** button.

Or

1. On the **View Shortcuts** toolbar, click the **Zoom level** button.

Or

On the **View** tab, in the **Zoom** group, click the **Zoom** button.

2. In the **Zoom** dialog box, click the **Many pages** button, and select the number of pages across and down that you want to display. Then click **OK**.

> **Tip** You can select up to 2 pages down and 4 pages across by pointing to that configuration on the default Many Pages grid. You can select many more pages by dragging through the grid. The number of pages you can select is dependent on your screen resolution.

Splitting a Document Window

It can be cumbersome to work in a long document that requires you to frequently scroll up and down to view data elsewhere in the document.

In any view other than Full Screen Reading view, you can view multiple parts of a document at one time by splitting the window. You can then independently scroll and work in two views of the document at one time. Each part of the split window has its own ruler; commands on the ribbon apply to the active content in either part of the split window or to the entire document shown in both parts of the split window.

Split bar (active)   Split bar (inactive)

Separate scroll bars

➤ To split the window

→ Drag the split bar from the top of the vertical scroll bar to the location where you want to split the window.

> **Tip** You can change the program window area allocated to each split pane by dragging the split bar up or down.

→ On the **View** tab, in the **Window** group, click the **Split** button. Then click in the location where you want to split the window.

➤ To remove a split

→ Double-click the split bar that divides the pane.

→ Drag the split bar to its original location at the top of the scroll bar.

→ On the **View** tab, in the **Window** group, click the **Remove Split** button.

Displaying Multiple Program Windows

You can open multiple documents in independent windows, and you can open multiple windows that display the same document.

You can display two windows side by side so that you can see the contents of both simultaneously. When you display windows side by side, Word automatically turns on synchronous scrolling, so that scrolling one window also scrolls the other. You can also stack two or more windows on top of each other. When more than two windows are stacked, the ribbon is hidden automatically. When only two windows are stacked, you can manually minimize the ribbon to display only the tab names and occupy less screen space.

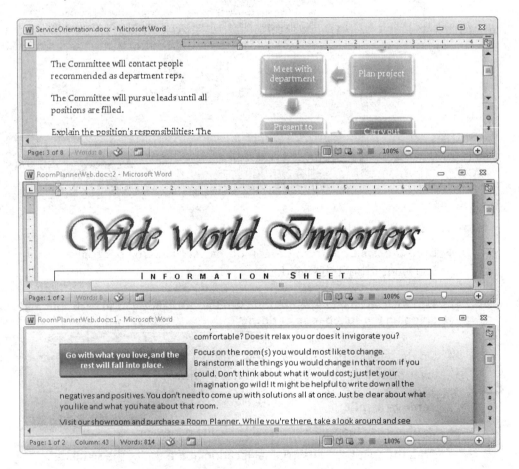

➤ **To open a second instance of a document in a separate window**

→ On the **View** tab, in the **Window** group, click the **New Window** button.

➤ **To stack multiple program windows**

→ In the **Window** group, click the **Arrange All** button.

➤ **To restore stacked program windows**

→ Maximize each program window.

➤ **To display two program windows side by side**

1. In the **Window** group, click the **View Side by Side** button.

2. If more than two documents are open, in the **Compare Side by Side** dialog box, click the document you want to display side by side with the current document.

➤ **To turn synchronous scrolling on or off**

1. Display two program windows by using the **View Side by Side** command.

2. In the **Window** group, click the **Synchronous Scrolling** button.

➤ **To restore side-by-side program windows to their original size**

→ In the **Window** group, click the **View Side by Side** button.

➤ **To switch between multiple program windows**

→ If the window is visible on the screen, click anywhere in the window.

→ Click the Windows Taskbar button representing the window you want to make active.

→ In the **Window** group, click the **Switch Windows** button, and then click the window you want to make active.

Practice Tasks

The practice files for these tasks are located in the Word\Objective1 practice file folder.

- Open the *Viewing1* document, and change the magnification so that you can see two pages side by side. Then zoom to 100%, and jump to the *Shipping* heading. Finally, jump to the top of page 5.

- Open the *Viewing1* and *Viewing2* documents, and switch back and forth between the two open windows. Then arrange the two document windows so that they are stacked one above the other.

- Open the *Viewing2* document, and arrange the screen so that you can see the beginning and end of the document at the same time.

1.2 Apply Protection to a Document

Marking a Document as Final

Before you distribute a document to other people, you can mark it as final to prevent anyone from making changes to it. Marking a document as final has the following results:

- The document is changed to read-only, and some buttons on the ribbon are unavailable.

- A Marked As Final banner appears at the top of the document.

- A Permissions flag on the Info page of the Backstage view indicates that the document has been marked as final.

- A Marked As Final Icon appears on the status bar.

Further changes cannot be made to the document by you or anyone else without first removing the Marked As Final designation.

Unavailable buttons   Read-only indicator   Marked As Final banner

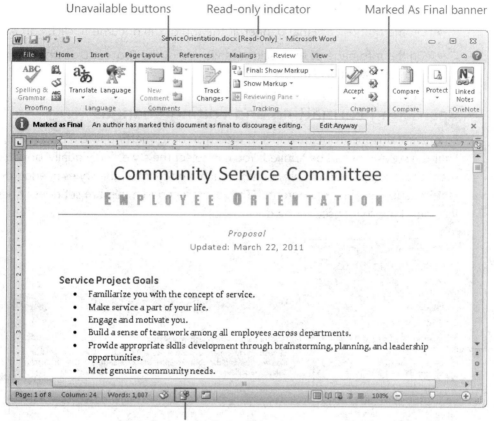

Marked As Final icon

➤ To mark a document as final

1. On the **Info** page of the Backstage view, click the **Protect Document** button, and then click **Mark as Final**.

2. In the **Microsoft Word** dialog box, click **OK** to acknowledge that the file will be marked as final and saved.

3. If a **Microsoft Word** message box informing you that the document has been marked as final appears, click **OK**.

> **Tip** You can select the Don't Show This Message Again check box to prevent the message box from appearing when you mark documents as final in the future.

➤ **To remove the Marked As Final designation**

→ On the **Marked as Final** banner at the top of the document, click **Edit Anyway**.

→ On the **Info** page of the Backstage view, click the **Protect Document** button, and then click **Mark as Final**.

Restricting Formatting and Editing Changes

To prevent anyone from introducing inconsistent formatting into a document, you can limit the styles that can be applied. You can select the styles individually, or you can implement the recommended minimum set, which consists of all the styles needed by Word for features such as tables of contents. (The recommended minimum set doesn't necessarily include all the styles used in the document.)

You can also restrict the ways users can edit a document.

➤ **To restrict formatting changes**

1. On the **Review** tab, in the **Protect** group, click the **Restrict Editing** button.

   Or

   On the **Info** page of the Backstage view, click the **Protect Document** button, and then click **Restrict Editing**.

2. In the **Restrict Formatting and Editing** task pane, in the **Formatting restrictions** section, select the **Limit formatting to a selection of styles** check box, and then click **Settings**.

3. In the **Formatting Restrictions** dialog box, do one of the following, and then click **OK**:

   ○ Clear the check boxes of the styles that you will not allow in the document.

   ○ Click **None**, and then select the check boxes of the styles that you will allow in the document.

4. In the **Start enforcement** section of the **Restrict Formatting and Editing** task pane, click **Yes, Start Enforcing Protection**.

5. In the **Start Enforcing Protection** dialog box, if you want to require a password to use styles other than those you selected, enter a password in the **Enter new password** and **Reenter password to confirm** boxes. Then click **OK**.

➤ **To restrict editing**

1. In the **Restrict Formatting and Editing** pane, in the **Editing restrictions** section, select the **Allow only this type of editing in the document** check box.

2. In the **Allow only...** list, do one of the following:

   ○ To force all changes to be tracked, click **Tracked changes**.

   ○ To disable all changes other than commenting, click **Comments**.

   ○ To disable changes outside of form fields, click **Filling in forms**.

3. In the **Start enforcement** section of the **Restrict Formatting and Editing** task pane, click **Yes, Start Enforcing Protection**.

➤ **To remove formatting and editing restrictions**

1. In the **Restrict Formatting and Editing** pane, click **Stop Protection**.

2. If the **Unprotect Document** dialog box opens, enter the assigned password, and then click **OK**.

Restricting Document Access

If you want only certain people to be able to open and change a document, you can assign a password to protect the document. Word then requires that the password be entered correctly before the document can be opened and changed.

Word offers two levels of password protection:

- **Unencrypted** The document is saved in such a way that only people who know the password can open it, make changes, and save the file. People who don't know the password can open a read-only version. If they make changes and want to save them, they have to save the document with a different name or in a different location, preserving the original.

- **Encrypted** The document is saved in such a way that people who do not know the password cannot open it at all.

➤ **To require a password to open a document**

1. On the **Info** page of the Backstage view, click the **Protect Document** button, and then click **Encrypt with Password**.

2. In the **Encrypt Document** dialog box, in the **Password** box, enter the password you want to assign to the document. Then click **OK**.

   Or

1. In the left pane of the Backstage view, click **Save As**.

2. At the bottom of the **Save As** dialog box, click **Tools**, and then click **General Options**.

3. In the **General Options** dialog box, in the **Password to open** box, enter the password you want to assign to the document. Then click **OK**.

> **Tip** Instead of setting a password, you can select the Read-Only Recommended check box to cause Word to display a message suggesting that the document be opened as read-only.

4. In the **Confirm Password** dialog box, in the **Reenter password to modify** box, enter the password, and then click **OK**.

5. In the **Save As** dialog box, click **Save**. If prompted to do so, click **Yes** to confirm that you want to replace the existing file.

➤ **To require a password to modify a document**

1. In the left pane of the Backstage view, click **Save As**.

2. At the bottom of the **Save As** dialog box, click **Tools**, and then click **General Options**.

3. In the **General Options** dialog box, in the **Password to modify** box, enter the password you want to assign to the document. Then click **OK**.

4. In the **Confirm Password** dialog box, in the **Reenter password to modify** box, enter the password, and then click **OK**.

5. In the **Save As** dialog box, click **Save**. If prompted to do so, click **Yes** to confirm that you want to replace the existing file.

➤ **To remove a password requirement**

1. In the left pane of the Backstage view, click **Save As**.

2. At the bottom of the **Save As** dialog box, click **Tools**, and then click **General Options**.

3. In the **General Options** dialog box, delete the content of the **Password to open** or **Password to modify** box. Then click **OK**.

4. In the **Save As** dialog box, click **Save**. Then click **Yes** to confirm that you want to replace the existing file.

Practice Tasks

The practice files for these tasks are located in the Word\Objective1 practice file folder. Save the results of the tasks in the same folder.

- Open the *Finalizing* document, mark it as final, and save it as *MyFinalizing*. Then close and reopen the document, note the functionality that is unavailable, and remove the Marked As Final designation.

- Open the *Password* document, set the password for the file to *P@ssword*, and save it as *MyPassword*. Then close and reopen the document.

1.3 Manage Document Versions

Like other Office programs, Word automatically saves a temporary copy of an open file every 10 minutes. If you close a file without saving it, you can return to the most recently saved temporary version. You can also display the temporary copies of files that you started but never saved.

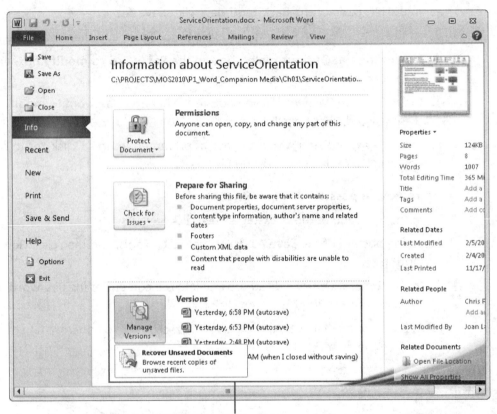

Document versions

> ► **To change the AutoSave frequency**

> → On the **Save** page of the **Word Options** dialog box, in the **Save AutoRecover information every** box, enter a number of minutes from 1 through 120.

> ► **To display a previous (saved) version of the current document**

> → On the **Info** page of the Backstage view, in the **Versions** list, click the version of the file you want to display.

➤ **To replace the current file with a previous version**

1. Display the previous version of the file.

2. On the **Autosaved Version** bar that appears below the ribbon, click **Restore**.

➤ **To display a temporary (unsaved) version of a document**

1. On the **Info** page of the Backstage view, click the **Manage Versions** button, and then click **Recover Unsaved Documents**.

2. In the **Open** dialog box displaying the contents of your UnsavedFiles folder, click the file you want to display, and then click **Open**.

➤ **To delete temporary document versions**

1. On the **Info** page of the Backstage view, click the **Manage Versions** button, and then click **Delete All Unsaved Documents**.

2. In the dialog box prompting you to confirm the deletion, click **Yes**.

Practice Tasks

The practice file for these tasks is located in the Word\Objective1 practice file folder. Save the results of the tasks in the same folder.

- Open the *Versions* document and save it as *MyVersions*. Configure Word to automatically save a draft version of the document every 1 minute.

- In the *MyVersions* document, change the title to *Business Office Procedures*. Then save the document.

- Display and then restore the original version of the *MyVersions* document.

1.4 Share Documents

Sending Documents

Word 2010 provides many simple ways of sharing documents, even without first saving them. From within Word, you can send a document as an email attachment, share a document from a Windows Live SkyDrive site or SharePoint site, or convert a document and send it as a PDF file or an XPS file.

> **Tip** If you have the services of a third-party online fax service provider, you can send a document from within Word as an Internet fax.

➤ To send a document as an email message attachment

1. In the left pane of the **Save & Send** page of the Backstage view, click **Send Using E-mail**.

2. In the right pane of the **Save & Send** page, do one of the following:

   - Click the **Send as Attachment** button to send the document as a .docx file.
   - Click the **Send as PDF** button to send the document as a .pdf file.
   - Click the **Send as XPS** button to send the document as an .xps file.

> **Tip** It is not necessary to provide a file name when sending a document that has not yet been saved.

3. Enter the recipient name and other necessary information in the email message composition window, and then send the message.

➤ To send a link to a shared document

1. Save the document in a shared location.

2. In the left pane of the **Save & Send** page of the Backstage view, click **Send Using E-mail**.

3. In the right pane of the **Save & Send** page, click the **Send a Link** button.

4. Enter the recipient name and other necessary information in the email message composition window, and then send the message.

Saving Documents in Shared Locations

You can share a document with other people by saving it to a Windows Live SkyDrive folder or to a SharePoint site.

> **Tip** A free Windows Live SkyDrive account allows you to store and share up to 25 GB of files, such as photos and Microsoft Office documents, on the Internet. To create a Windows Live SkyDrive folder, visit skydrive.live.com, and sign in with your Windows Live ID.

To develop a document with other users, you need to save it to a SharePoint 2010 site. You then continue to work on it from the site. When another contributor begins making changes to the file stored on the site, Word alerts you to that person's presence. You can display a list of the other people who are actively working on the document and their availability.

As the people working on the document make changes, Word keeps track of them. When you finish working with the document, you save and close it as usual. The next time you open it, you'll see the changes made by anyone else who has worked on the document.

➤ **To save a document to an existing Windows Live SkyDrive folder**

1. In the left pane of the **Save & Send** page of the Backstage view, click **Save to Web**.

2. In the right pane of the **Save & Send** page, in the **Shared Folders** list, click the folder in which you want to save the document. Then click the **Save As** button.

3. In the **Save As** dialog box displaying the selected workspace, enter a file name, select a file format, and then click **Save**.

➤ **To create a Windows Live SkyDrive folder from within Word**

1. In the left pane of the **Save & Send** page of the Backstage view, click **Save to Web**.

2. In the right pane of the **Save & Send** page, click the **New Folder** button.

3. On the Windows Live SkyDrive site, follow the instructions to log in and create a folder.

4. On the **Save & Send** page, click the **Refresh** button.

➤ **To save a document to a SharePoint site**

1. In the left pane of the **Save & Send** page of the Backstage view, click **Save to SharePoint**.

2. In the **Recent Locations** list, click the SharePoint document library in which you want to save the file.

Or

In the **Locations** list, click **Browse for a location**.

> **Tip** You can save a document only to an existing document library; you can't create a document library from within Word.

3. Click the **Save As** button.

4. In the **Windows Security** dialog box, enter your SharePoint site credentials, and then click **OK**.

5. In the **Save As** dialog box, if necessary, browse to the document library in which you want to save the file. Then enter a file name, select a file format, and click **Save**.

Publishing Documents as Blog Posts

You can share the content of a document with other people by publishing it as a blog post. If you have already set up a blog account with a blog service provider, you can register your account with Word the first time you create a blog post. If you haven't yet set up the blog account, you need to register with a service provider before you can publish your first post. Thereafter, Word uses your registered account information when you create or publish a blog post.

You can publish any document as a blog post.

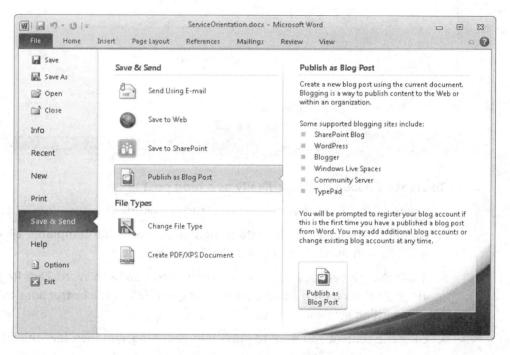

You can also create a blog post by using a template designed specifically for that purpose, publish a draft of the post to your blog space, and then publish the final version.

➤ **To create a document specifically as a blog post**

1. Create a blog account with a provider such as WordPress.

2. On the **New** page of the Backstage view, under **Available Templates**, click **Blog post**. Then in the right pane, click the **Create** button.

3. If you have not already registered your blog account with Word, click **Register Now** in the **Register a Blog Account** dialog box, and follow the instructions to register your existing account.

4. Enter the content you want to publish to your blog, and then save the file.

5. On the **Blog Post** tab, in the **Blog** group, click the **Publish** arrow, and then click **Publish as Draft**.

6. In the **Connect To <Blog Title>** dialog box, enter the space name and password for your blog, and then click **OK**.

7. On the **Blog Post** tab, in the **Blog** group, click the **Home Page** button.

8. Display and review the draft blog post. Make any necessary changes, and then click **Publish**.

➤ **To publish a document as a blog post**

1. In the left pane of the **Save & Send** page of the Backstage view, click **Publish as Blog Post**.

2. In the right pane of the **Save & Send** page of the Backstage view, click the **Publish as Blog Post** button.

3. If you have not already registered your blog account with Word, click **Register Now** in the **Register a Blog Account** dialog box, and follow the instructions to register your existing account.

4. On the **Blog Post** tab, in the **Blog** group, click the **Publish** arrow, and then click **Publish as Draft**.

5. In the **Connect To <Blog Title>** dialog box, enter the space name and password for your blog, and then click **OK**.

6. On the **Blog Post** tab, in the **Blog** group, click the **Home Page** button.

7. Display and review the draft blog post. Make any necessary changes, and then click **Publish**.

Practice Tasks

The practice file for these tasks is located in the Word\Objective1 practice file folder. Save the results of the tasks in the same folder.

> **Tip** You can perform these tasks only if you have a blog account or set up a blog account during the process.

- Create a new document based on the Blog Post document template. Replace the title placeholder with *Walla Walla Music* and paste the first two paragraphs of the *Orchestra* document into the content area. Then save the document as *MyBlogPost*.

- Publish a draft of the *MyBlogPost* document to your blog. Then display the blog post, change the title to *Walla Walla Symphony Orchestra Review*, and publish a final version of the post to your blog.

- Publish the *Orchestra* document directly to your blog.

1.5 Save a Document

The 2007 Microsoft Office system introduced a new set of file formats based on XML, called Microsoft Office Open XML Formats. By default, Word 2010 (and Word 2007) documents are saved in the .docx format, which is a Word-specific Open XML format. The .docx format provides the following benefits:

- File sizes are smaller than with previous file formats.
- It is simpler to recover damaged content because XML files can be opened in a variety of text editors.
- Security is greater because .docx files cannot contain macros, and personal data can easily be identified and removed from files.

Documents saved in the .docx format can be opened by Word 2010 and Word 2007. Users of earlier versions of Word can download a converter that will allow them to open a .docx file in their version of Word.

In addition to the .docx format, Word provides these Open XML formats:

- **.docm** This format is for macro-enabled documents.
- **.dotx** This format is for document templates.
- **dotm** This format is for macro-enabled document templates.

You can save a Word document in many formats, some of which optimize the file for specific uses.

Strategy You should be familiar with the types of file formats in which you can save Word documents and when it is appropriate to use each one.

If you intend to share a Word document specifically with users of Word 2003, 2002, 2000, or 97, you can save it in the .doc file format used by those versions of the program. Word 2010 opens .doc files in Compatibility Mode. Compatibility Mode turns off advanced program features; these features can be re-enabled by saving the file in one of the current file formats.

If you want to save a Word document in a format that can be opened by the widest variety of programs, use one of the following formats:

- **Rich Text Format (.rtf)** This format preserves the document's formatting.

- **Plain Text (.txt)** This format preserves only the document's text.

If you want to ensure that the appearance of the file content is the same no matter what computer or device it is displayed on, or if you want to ensure that other people can't easily modify the file, you can save it in one of the following formats:

- **Portable document format (PDF)** A fixed-layout document format created by Adobe Systems. A PDF file includes the text, fonts, images, and vector graphics that compose the document. The Adobe Reader or Adobe Acrobat software is required to view a PDF document.

- **XML Paper Specification (XPS) document format** A fixed-layout document format created by Microsoft. The XPS document format consists of structured XML markup that defines the layout of a document and the visual appearance of each page, along with rendering rules for distributing, archiving, rendering, processing, and printing the documents.

Each of these formats displays content in a device-independent manner.

When you save a Word document in PDF or XPS format, you can optimize the file size of the document for your intended distribution method. You can also do the following:

- Specify the pages to include in the .pdf or .xps version of the document.
- Include or exclude comments and tracked changes.
- Include or exclude items such as bookmarks and properties.
- Set specific PDF options.

You can save a document as a webpage in any of three formats:

- **Web Page** This format saves the webpage as an .htm file with a folder of supporting files that ensure the page is rendered exactly as you want it.

- **Single File Web Page** This format embeds all the information necessary to render the webpage in one MIME-encapsulated aggregate HTML (.mhtml) file that can be distributed via email.

- **Web Page, Filtered** This format removes any Office-specific tags from the file and significantly reduces the size of the web document and its accompanying folder of supporting files. However, it can also radically change the look of the document. For example, it might change a shaded background to a solid color, making the resulting page difficult to read.

After you save a document as a webpage, it is no longer a Word document. However, you can still open, view, and edit the webpage in Word, just as you would a normal document. (You can also open and edit HTML-format webpages created in other programs.) Making changes can be as basic as replacing text and adjusting alignment, or as advanced as moving and inserting graphics. When you finish modifying the webpage, you can resave it as a webpage, or save it as a regular Word document.

In the Web Options dialog box, which is available from the Tools menu in the Save As dialog box, you can specify which browsers you anticipate will be used to view your webpages. You can also have Word disable any features that are incompatible with the specified browsers.

> **Strategy** View the other pages of the Web Options dialog box to familiarize yourself with the kinds of settings available for webpages.

➤ To save a document in a specific format

1. In the left pane of the Backstage view, click **Save As**.

2. In the **Save As** dialog box, browse to the folder in which you want to save the document. Enter a file name, select a file format, and then click **Save**.

   Or

1. In the left pane of the **Save & Send** page of the Backstage view, click **Change File Type**.

2. In the right pane of the **Save & Send** page, in the **Document File Types** or **Other File Types** list, click the file format in which you want to save the document.

3. Click the **Save As** button.

4. In the **Save As** dialog box, browse to the folder in which you want to save the document. Enter a file name, select a file format, and then click **Save**.

➤ **To save a document as a PDF file or an XPS file**

1. In the left pane of the Backstage view, click **Save As**. In the **Save As** dialog box, browse to the folder in which you want to save the document, and enter a file name. Then in the **Save as type** list, click **PDF (.pdf)**.

Or

In the left pane of the **Save & Send** page of the Backstage view, click **Create PDF/XPS Document**. Then in the right pane, click the **Create PDF/XPS** button. In the **Publish as PDF or XPS** dialog box, browse to the folder in which you want to save the document, and enter a file name.

2. In the **Optimize for** area, click **Standard** to generate a larger, higher-quality file or **Minimum size** to generate a smaller, lower-quality file. Then click **Options**.

3. In the **Options** dialog box, select the document content you want to include in the file, and then click **OK**.

4. In the **Save As** dialog box, click **Save**.

Or

In the **Publish as PDF or XPS** dialog box, click **Publish**.

Practice Tasks

The practice files for these tasks are located in the Word\Objective1 practice file folder. Save the results of the tasks in the same folder.

- Open the *Saving1* document, and save it with the name *MyCompatibility* in a format that users of Word 2003 can work in. Close the *MyCompatibility* document and then open it in Compatibility Mode and note the changes in the document.

- Open the *Saving2* document, and save only page 3 as a PDF file named *MyPDF*, ensuring that the document headings are bookmarked in the *MyPDF* file.

- Open the *Saving3* document, and save it as a single-file webpage named *MyWebpage* that is optimized for display at a screen resolution of 1024×768. Then display the *MyWebpage* file in Windows Internet Explorer.

1.6 Apply a Template to a Document

Every new document you create is based on a document template. A Word 2010 document template is a file with a .dotm or .dotx extension that defines information about style sets and color schemes and can also contain content (words and graphics).

> **See Also** For information about using styles and style sets supplied by a template, see section 2.1, "Apply Font and Paragraph Attributes."

When you create a document from the New page of the Backstage view, you base the document on any of the templates installed in the default template location on your computer, or on other templates that you can download from the Microsoft Office Online site.

> **Tip** By default, templates are stored in the AppData\Roaming\Microsoft\Templates subfolder of your personal folder.

The most common document, a blank document, is based on the Normal document template. Word 2010 also comes with document templates from which you can create a blog post and a variety of faxes, letters, reports, and resumes. From the New page, you can download design templates for dozens of types of documents, including brochures, business cards, calendars, lists, menus, and postcards. Some of these templates were created by Microsoft. Others, known as *community templates*, were created and made available by computer users such as yourself.

After you create a document, you can change the template on which the document is based by applying a different template. Document template options can be easily accessed from the Developer tab, which is not displayed on the ribbon by default.

➤ **To display the Developer tab**

→ On the **Customize Ribbon** page of the **Word Options** dialog box, in the **Customize the Ribbon** pane, under **Main Tabs**, select the **Developer** check box. Then click **OK**.

➤ **To attach a local template to a document**

1. On the **Developer** tab, in the **Templates** group, click **Document Template**.

2. On the **Templates** page of the **Templates and Add-ins** dialog box, in the **Document template** area, click **Attach**.

3. In the **Attach Template** dialog box, navigate to and double-click the template you want to attach.

4. In the **Templates and Add-ins** dialog box, select the **Automatically update document styles** check box, and then click **OK**.

5. On the **Home** tab, in the **Styles** group, click the **Change Styles** button, point to **Style Set**, and then click **Reset to Quick Styles from <template name> Template**.

➤ **To attach a web template to a document**

1. On the **New** page of the Backstage view, in the **Office.com Templates** section, browse to the web template you want to attach.

   Or

   On the **New** page of the Backstage view, in the **Office.com Templates** section header, enter a search term in the **Search Office.com for templates** box, and press Enter. Then locate the web template you want to attach.

2. Select the template and then, in the right pane, click the **Download** button.

3. On the **Developer** tab, in the **Templates** group, click the **Document Template** button.

4. On the **Templates** page of the **Templates and Add-ins** dialog box, in the **Document Template** area, click **Attach**.

5. In the **Attach Template** dialog box, navigate to and double-click the downloaded template.

6. In the **Templates and Add-ins** dialog box, select the **Automatically update document styles** check box, and then click **OK**.

7. On the **Home** tab, in the **Styles** group, click the **Change Styles** button, point to **Style Set**, and then click **Reset to Quick Styles from <template name> Template**.

Practice Tasks

The practice files for these tasks are located in the Word\Objective1 practice file folder. Save the results of the tasks in the same folder.

- Double-click the *ExecutiveResume* document template to open a new document based on the template. In the new document, display the Developer tab on the ribbon. Then save the document as *MyResume*.

- Attach the *UrbanResume* document template to the *MyResume* document and ensure that the document styles are updated to the new template. Then note the differences.

Objective Review

Before finishing this chapter, ensure that you have mastered the following skills:

1.1 Apply Different Views to a Document

1.2 Apply Protection to a Document

1.3 Manage Document Versions

1.4 Share Documents

1.5 Save a Document

1.6 Apply a Template to a Document

2 Formatting Content

The skills tested in this section of the Microsoft Office Specialist exam for Microsoft Word 2010 relate to modifying the appearance and structure of document content, and locating specific content within a document. Specifically, the following objectives are associated with this set of skills:

2.1 Apply Font and Paragraph Attributes
2.2 Navigate and Search Through a Document
2.3 Apply Indentation and Tab Settings to Paragraphs
2.4 Apply Spacing Settings to Text and Paragraphs
2.5 Create Tables
2.6 Manipulate Tables in a Document
2.7 Apply Bullets to a Document

By applying specific styles or formatting to elements of your document, you can organize it and make it easier to read. For example, you can format section headings to indicate the structure of the document or emphasize text by changing its size, applying bold or italic formatting, or underlining it. You can also break down specific points you want to make by setting them up in a bulleted list, or organize data by inserting it in a table.

This chapter guides you in studying ways of formatting document content by applying styles and character formatting; applying indentation and tab settings to paragraphs; and changing the spacing of both paragraphs and text. It also examines ways of navigating through and searching for text; creating and manipulating tables; and creating bulleted lists.

> **Practice Files** Before you can complete the practice tasks in this chapter, you need to copy the book's practice files to your computer. The practice files you'll use to complete the tasks in this chapter are in the Word\Objective2 practice file folder. A complete list of practice files is provided in "Using the Book's Companion Content" at the beginning of this book.

2.1 Apply Font and Paragraph Attributes

Applying Character Formatting

By default, the font used for text in a new Word document is Calibri, but you can change the font at any time. Each font consists of characters, numbers, and/or symbols that share a common design. You can vary the look of the base font by changing the following attributes:

- **Size** Almost every font comes in a range of sizes, measured in points. A point is approximately 1/72 of an inch.

- **Style** The most common styles are regular (or plain), italic, bold, and bold italic.

- **Color** The palette includes the colors of the theme applied to the document and a set of standard colors. You can also specify custom colors.

- **Underline** You can choose from a variety of underline styles as well as change the underline color.

- **Effects** Various enhancements can be applied, such as strikethrough, shadows, or embossing. You can also hide text by applying the Hidden font effect.

- **Case** You can specify small capital letters (small caps), all capital letters, or all lowercase. You can mix the case by specifying that the first word in a selection should have an initial capital letter (sentence case) or all words should have initial capital letters (title case). You can also toggle the case of selected text, changing all uppercase letters to lowercase and lowercase letters to uppercase.

- **Character spacing** You can push characters apart or squeeze them together. This is also called *kerning*.

After you select an appropriate font for a document, you can use these attributes to achieve different effects. Although some attributes might cancel each other out, they are usually cumulative. Collectively, the font and its attributes are called *character formatting*.

You can change the character formatting of a selection by clicking buttons on the Mini Toolbar or in the Font group on the Home tab. You can change several character formats at once from the Font dialog box.

Strategy Word provides so many ways to format text that it would be impossible to detail them all here. Be sure you are familiar with the attributes available from the Font group on the Home tab and from the Font dialog box.

➤ **To apply character formatting to selected text**

→ On the Mini Toolbar, or in the **Font** group on the **Home** tab, click the attribute you want to apply.

> **Tip** You can format a word by clicking anywhere in the word (other than at the beginning or the end) and then clicking the attribute you want to apply.

➤ **To change the font size of selected text**

→ On the Mini Toolbar or in the **Font** group on the **Home** tab, click the **Grow Font** button to increase the font to the next standard size, or click the **Shrink Font** button to decrease the font to the next standard size.

➤ **To change the case of selected text**

→ On the **Home** tab, in the **Font** group, click the **Change Case** button, and then click Sentence case, lowercase, UPPERCASE, Capitalize Each Word, or tOGGLE cASE.

➤ **To apply a special effect to selected text**

→ In the **Font** group, click the **Strikethrough**, **Subscript**, or **Superscript** button.

   Or

1. On the **Home** tab, click the **Font** dialog box launcher.
2. On the **Font** page of the **Font** dialog box, in the **Effects** area, select the check box for the effect you want to apply. Then click **OK**.

➤ **To change the character spacing of selected text**

1. In the **Font** dialog box, display the **Advanced** page.
2. In the **Character Spacing** area, change the **Spacing** setting to **Expanded** or **Condensed**, set the number of points of expansion or contraction, and then click **OK**.

➤ **To highlight selected text**

→ On the Mini Toolbar, in the **Highlight** list, click the color you want.

→ On the **Home** tab, in the **Font** group, in the **Text Highlight Color** list, click the color you want.

> **Tip** If you click the Highlight button without first making a selection, the mouse pointer becomes a highlighter that you can drag across text. Click the Highlight button again or press Esc to turn off the highlighter.

➤ **To clear formatting from selected text**

→ On the **Home** tab, in the **Font** group, click the **Clear Formatting** button.

→ Press Ctrl+Spacebar.

> **Strategy** In addition to character formatting, you can apply various attributes, including alignment, shading, and borders, to entire paragraphs. Be sure you are familiar with these simple types of paragraph formatting.

Applying Styles

Styles are named sets of paragraph and/or character formatting that you can use in place of manual formatting to produce a consistent look throughout a document. There are five types of styles: Character, Paragraph, Linked, Table, and List. The most common types of styles you will use are the following:

- **Paragraph styles** You can use these styles to apply a consistent look to different types of paragraphs, such as headings, body text, captions, quotations, and list paragraphs. Some built-in paragraph styles, such as Heading 1 and Heading 2, are associated with outline levels.

- **Character styles** You can use these styles to change the appearance of selected words.

You can view the available styles in several locations, including the following:

- In the Styles group on the Home tab of the ribbon, the Quick Styles gallery displays the styles designated in the active style set as Quick Styles. Part of the Quick Styles gallery is visible at all times in the Styles group—the number of visible styles depends on the width of your program window and screen resolution. You can scroll the gallery or expand it to display all the current Quick Styles. From the Quick Styles gallery, you can apply and manage all Quick Styles.

- At the right side of the program window, the Styles pane displays all the styles available in the currently active document templates or a subset thereof, such as only those that are currently in use. You can display or hide the Styles pane, and from it you can apply and manage all styles, including those designated as Quick Styles.

> **See Also** For information about templates, see section 1.6, "Apply a Template to a Document."

In the Styles pane, paragraph styles are identified by a paragraph mark, and character styles are identified by the letter *a*. You can point to any style to display a ScreenTip detailing the formatting included in the style.

- At the left side of a document displayed in Draft view or Outline view, the style area pane displays the name of the style attached to each paragraph. The style area pane does not display character styles. You can display or hide the style area pane.

> **See Also** For information about displaying the style area pane, see section 1.1, "Apply Different Views to a Document."

Style area pane   Styles pane

You can tell Word to select all text to which a particular style is applied and then globally switch to a different style. You can also globally clear the formatting of a particular style so that the text reverts to Normal style.

➤ **To display the style area pane in a document**

1. Display the document in Draft view or Outline view.

2. Display the **Advanced** page of the **Word Options** dialog box.

3. In the **Display** area, enter a positive number in the **Style area pane width in Draft and Outline views** box. Then click **OK**.

➤ **To display the Styles pane in the program window**

➔ On the **Home** tab, click the **Styles** dialog box launcher.

➤ **To display visual representations of styles in the Styles pane**

➔ At the bottom of the **Styles** pane, select the **Show Preview** check box.

➤ **To display a specific selection of styles in the Styles pane**

1. At the bottom of the **Styles** pane, click **Options**.

2. In the **Style Pane Options** dialog box, click **Recommended**, **In use**, **In current document**, or **All styles** in the **Select styles to show** list.

3. In the **Select how list is sorted** list, click **Alphabetical**, **As Recommended**, **Font**, **Based on**, or **By type**.

4. Select the check boxes for the types of formatting you want to show as styles, and then click **OK**.

➤ **To apply a character style**

1. Select the text you want to format.

2. In the **Styles** pane, click the character style you want to apply.

➤ **To apply a paragraph style**

1. Select or position the cursor anywhere in the paragraph you want to format.

2. In the **Styles** pane, click the paragraph style you want to apply.

➤ **To apply a Quick Style**

1. Select or position the cursor in the text you want to format.

2. On the **Home** tab, in the **Quick Styles** gallery, click the style you want to apply.

➤ **To clear all instances of a style**

1. On the **Advanced** page of the **Word Options** dialog box, ensure that the **Keep track of formatting** check box is selected in the **Editing options** section.

2. In the **Styles** pane, point to the style you want to clear, click the arrow that appears, and then click **Clear Formatting of Instance(s)**.

➤ **To copy existing formatting to other text**

1. Select the text that has the formatting you want to copy.

2. On the Mini Toolbar or in the **Clipboard** group on the **Home** tab, click the **Format Painter** button once if you want to apply the copied formatting only once, or click it twice if you want to apply the copied formatting multiple times.

3. Click the word or select the text to which you want to apply the copied formatting. If you clicked the **Format Painter** button twice, repeat this step as many times as you want.

4. When you finish, click the **Format Painter** button again, or press the Esc key, to turn off the Format Painter.

Practice Tasks

The practice files for these tasks are located in the Word\Objective2 practice file folder. If you want to save the results of the tasks, save them in the same folder with *My* appended to the file name so that you don't overwrite the original practice file.

- In the *Characters* document, format the *Beautiful Bamboo* heading with the Stencil font. Make it bold and 26 points, apply the Outline effect, and expand the character spacing by 2 points. Then change its color to the light green standard color.

- In the *Characters* document, in the paragraph that begins *Because they are so easy to grow*, format the names *chimonobambusa marmorea, indocalamus tessellatus, pleioblastus chino vaginatus, bambusa glaucophylla*, and *otatea acuminata aztecorum* in small caps. Then change all small caps formatting to italic.

- In the *Styles* document, display the style area pane at the left side of the document in Draft view. Apply the formatting of the *Author Meet and Greet Update* heading to the *Fantasy Author Starts Book Tour* paragraph at the bottom of the document by using the Format Painter.

2.2 Navigate and Search Through a Document

Moving Around in a Document

The Navigation Pane has two pages on which you can display headings and page thumbnails. You can move to specific locations in the document by clicking items on these pages in the Navigation Pane.

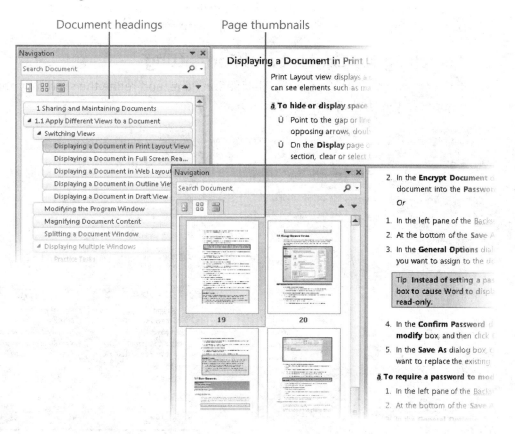

Document headings   Page thumbnails

➤ To display and move to document headings

1. On the **View** tab, in the **Show** group, select the **Navigation Pane** check box.

2. In the **Navigation Pane**, click the **Browse the headings in your document** tab.

3. To move to a specific section of the document, click its heading in the **Navigation Pane**.

> **Tip** The Navigation Pane displays only headings that are formatted with heading paragraph styles. For information about paragraph styles, see section 2.1, "Apply Font and Paragraph Attributes."

➤ **To display and move to pages**

1. In the **Navigation Pane**, click the **Browse the pages in your document** tab.

2. To move to a specific page of the document, click its thumbnail in the **Navigation Pane**.

Tip You can display more or fewer page thumbnails in the Navigation Pane by changing its width. To change the width of the Navigation Pane, drag its right border.

Searching for Content and Formatting

You can search for text from the Navigation Pane, and refine the search by selecting options in the Find Options dialog box.

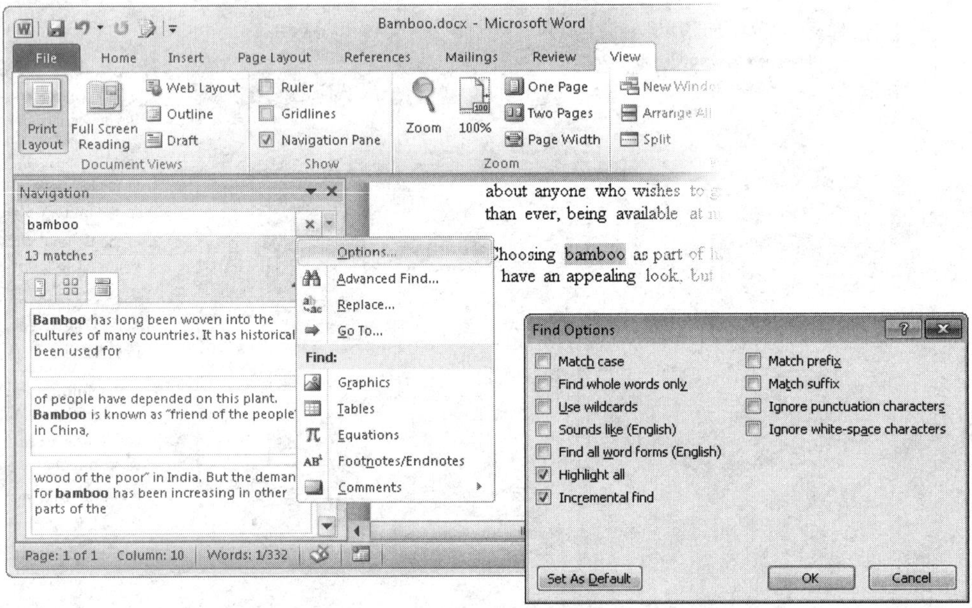

In addition to simple content, you can locate specific formatting, styles, and special characters by using the Find And Replace dialog box.

Paragraph Mark
Tab Character
Any Character
Any Digit
Any Letter
Caret Character
§ Section Character
¶ Paragraph Character
Column Break
Em Dash
En Dash
Endnote Mark
Field
Footnote Mark
Graphic
Manual Line Break
Manual Page Break
Nonbreaking Hyphen
Nonbreaking Space
Optional Hyphen
Section Break
White Space

Find and Replace

Find   Replace

Find what: ban

<< Less   Find In ▾   Find Next   Cancel

Search Options

Search: All

☐ Match case
☐ Find whole wo
☐ Use wildcards
☐ Sounds like (E
☐ Find all word f

☐ Match prefix
☐ Match suffix

☐ Ignore punctuation characters
☐ Ignore white-space characters

Find

Format ▾   Special ▾   No Formatting

Strategy Be familiar with the elements and characters you can locate from the Format and Special menus in the expanded Find And Replace dialog box.

➤ To locate text

1. In the **Search Document** box at the top of the **Navigation Pane**, enter the text you want to locate.

2. In the **Navigation Pane**, click the **Browse the results from your current search** tab.

3. To move to a specific search result, click the entry in the **Navigation Pane**.

4. To refine the search, click the **Find Options and additional search commands** arrow, and then click **Options**.

5. In the **Find Options** dialog box, select the check boxes of additional search parameters, and then click **OK**.

➤ **To locate styles and formatting**

1. On the **Home** tab, in the **Editing** group, click the **Find** arrow, and then click **Advanced Find**.

Or

In the **Navigation Pane**, on the **Browse the results from your current search** page, click the **Find Options and additional search commands** arrow, and then click **Advanced Find**.

2. On the **Find** page of the **Find and Replace** dialog box, click the **Format** button, and then click the type of formatting you want to locate. Refine the formatting identification if necessary, and then click **OK**.

➤ **To locate special characters**

1. On the **Home** tab, in the **Editing** group, click the **Find** arrow, and then click **Advanced Find**.

Or

In the **Navigation Pane**, on the **Browse the results from your current search** page, click the **Find Options and additional search commands** arrow, and then click **Advanced Find**.

2. On the **Find** page of the **Find and Replace** dialog box, click the **Special** button, and then click the character you want to locate.

➤ **To highlight all occurrences of text or formatting**

1. On the **Home** tab, in the **Editing** group, click the **Find** arrow, and then click **Advanced Find**.

2. On the **Find** page of the **Find and Replace** dialog box, specify the text or formatting you want to highlight, click **Reading Highlight**, and then click **Highlight All**.

➤ **To replace text or formatting**

1. On the **Home** tab, in the **Editing** group, click the **Replace** button.

2. On the **Replace** page of the **Find and Replace** dialog box, do the following:

  o Click the **Find what** box, and then specify the text and/or formatting you want to replace.

  o In the **Search Options** area, refine the search specifications as necessary.

  o Click the **Replace with** box, and then specify the replacement text and/or formatting.

3. On the **Replace** page, do one of the following:

- Click **Replace All** to replace all instances of the specified text and/or formatting.

- Click **Find Next** to locate the first instance of the specified text and/or formatting. Then click **Replace** to replace the instance and move to the next, or **Find Next** to move to the next instance without making a change.

➤ **To locate document elements**

➜ In the **Navigation Pane**, on the **Browse the results from your current search** page, click the **Find Options and additional search commands** arrow and then, in the **Find** section, click the element you want to locate.

➜ Below the vertical scroll bar, click the **Select Browse Object** button, and then click the element you want to locate.

Or

1. On the **Home** tab, in the **Editing** group, click the **Find** arrow, and then click **Go To**.

2. On the **Go To** page of the **Find and Replace** dialog box, in the **Go to what** list, click the element you want to locate.

Practice Tasks

The practice file for these tasks is located in the Word\Objective2 practice file folder. If you want to save the results of the tasks, save them in the same folder with *My* appended to the file name so that you don't overwrite the original practice file.

- In the *Finding* document, highlight all instances of *The Taguien Cycle*. Then change all instances of *The Taguien Cycle*, to italic.

- On page 2 of the *Finding* document, change the style of the last four lines of text on the page to Subtitle.

- In the Finding document, replace all instances of nonbreaking spaces with regular spaces.

2.3 Apply Indentation and Tab Settings to Paragraphs

Indenting Paragraphs

In Word, you don't define the width of paragraphs and the length of pages by defining the area occupied by the text; instead, you define the size of the white space—the left, right, top, and bottom margins—around the text.

> **See Also** For information about setting margins, see section 3.1, "Apply and Manipulate Page Setup Settings."

Although the left and right margins are set for a whole document or section, you can vary the position of the paragraphs between the margins. The quickest way to indent a paragraph from the left is to click the Increase Indent button; clicking the Decrease Indent button has the opposite effect. You cannot increase or decrease the indent beyond the margins.

Another way to control the indentation of lines is by dragging markers on the horizontal ruler to indicate where each line of text starts and ends.

- **First Line Indent** Begins a paragraph's first line of text at this marker

- **Hanging Indent** Begins a paragraph's second and subsequent lines of text at this marker at the left end of the ruler

- **Left Indent** Indents the text to this marker

- **Right Indent** Wraps the text when it reaches this marker at the right end of the ruler

Hanging indent marker   First Line indent marker   Right indent marker

Left indent marker

See Also For information about displaying the ruler, see section 1.1, "Apply Different Views to a Document."

Setting a right indent indicates where the lines in a paragraph should end, but sometimes you might want to specify where only one line should end. For example, you might want to break a title after a particular word to make it look balanced on the page. You can end an individual line by inserting a text wrapping break (more commonly known as a *line break*). Word indicates the line break with a bent arrow.

Tip Inserting a line break does not start a new paragraph, so when you apply paragraph formatting to a line of text that ends with a line break, the formatting is applied to the entire paragraph, not just that line.

➤ **To change the indentation of selected paragraphs**

→ On the **Home** tab, in the **Paragraph** group, click the **Increase Indent** or **Decrease Indent** button.

→ On the **Page Layout** tab, in the **Paragraph** group, in the **Indent** area, increase or decrease the **Left** or **Right** settings.

→ On the horizontal ruler, drag the **First Line Indent**, **Left Indent**, or **Right Indent** marker to the location you want.

Tip Left and right margin indents are often used to draw attention to special paragraphs, such as quotations.

➤ **To insert a line break**

1. Position the cursor where you want the break to occur.
2. On the **Page Layout** tab, in the **Page Setup** group, click the **Breaks** button, and then click **Text Wrapping**.

Setting Tab Stops

You can align text in different locations across the page by using tab stops. By default, Word sets left-aligned tab stops every half inch (or every 1.27 centimeters, if Word is set to display measurements in centimeters).

You can set the following types of tabs in any position between the left and right margins:

- **Left Tab** Aligns the left end of the text with the tab stop.

- **Center Tab** Aligns the center of the text with the tab stop.

- **Right Tab** Aligns the right end of the text with the tab stop.

- **Decimal Tab** Aligns the decimal point in the text with the tab stop.

- **Bar Tab** Inserts a vertical bar aligned with the tab stop in the paragraph containing the cursor.

You can set custom tab stops one at a time or set multiple tab stops at the same time in the Tabs dialog box. You also use this dialog box to specify tab leaders—visible marks such as dots or dashes connecting the text before the tab with the text after it.

➤ **To set a custom tab stop**

1. Click the **Tab** button located at the left end of the horizontal ruler until the type of tab stop you want appears.

2. Click the horizontal ruler where you want to set the tab stop.

Or

1. On either the **Home** or **Page Layout** tab, click the **Paragraph** dialog box launcher.

2. At the bottom of the **Paragraph** dialog box, click **Tabs**.

3. In the **Tabs** dialog box, in the **Tab stop position** box, enter a measurement.

4. In the **Alignment** area, click the option you want, click **Set**, and then click **OK**.

➤ **To change the position of an existing custom tab stop**

➜ On the ruler, drag the tab stop to the left or right.

➜ In the **Tabs** dialog box, select the tab in the **Tab stop position** box, enter a new measurement in the **Tab stop position** box, click **Set**, and then click **OK**.

➤ **To set a tab stop with a leader**

1. In the **Tabs** dialog box, set a new tab stop or select an existing one.

2. In the **Leader** area, click the option you want, click **Set**, and then click **OK**.

➤ **To delete a custom tab stop**

➜ Drag the tab stop away from the ruler.

➜ In the **Tabs** dialog box, select the tab, click **Clear**, and then click **OK**.

➤ **To clear all custom tab stops**

➜ In the **Tabs** dialog box, click **Clear All**, and then click **OK**.

Practice Tasks

The practice files for these tasks are located in the Word\Objective2 practice file folder. If you want to save the results of the tasks, save them in the same folder with *My* appended to the file name so that you don't overwrite the original practice file.

- In the *Paragraphs* document, display nonprinting characters and the rulers. Insert a line break to the left of *Update* in the fourth line. Indent the first line of each of the paragraphs following the *Update* heading by a quarter of an inch. Finally, give all the paragraphs below *Esther Valle* left and right indents of half an inch.

- At the end of the *TabularList* document, enter the following, pressing Tab where indicated:

  Self Tab *Other People* Tab *Nature*

  Transformation Tab *Life/death* Tab *Weather*

  Time travel Tab *Telepathy* Tab *Oceans*

  Visible/invisible Tab *Mind control* Tab *Animals*

  Make the first line bold, and indent the entire list. Left-align the second column at the 2-inch mark on the horizontal ruler, and then right-align the third column at the 4-inch mark.

- In the *Tabs* document, for the *Date*, *Time*, *Location*, and *Ticket cost* paragraphs, set a left tab at the 2.5-inch mark and a decimal tab at the 4-inch mark.

2.4 Apply Spacing Settings to Text and Paragraphs

In documents based on the Normal document template, a normal paragraph has internal line spacing of 1.15 lines, and is followed by 10 points of blank space. You can change the look of a paragraph by changing the following:

- **Line spacing** You can adjust the spacing between the lines in a paragraph proportionally or by specifying an exact amount of space.

- **Paragraph spacing** To make it obvious where one paragraph ends and another begins, you can add space above or below, or both.

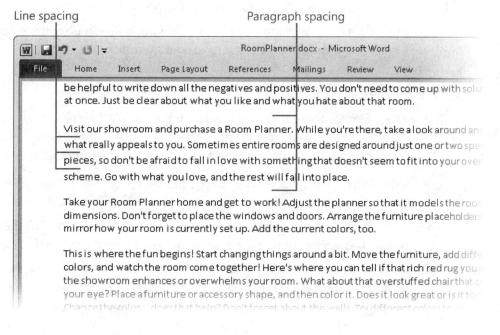

Line spacing   Paragraph spacing

➤ **To change the line spacing of selected paragraphs**

1. On the **Home** tab, in the **Paragraph** group, click the **Line and Paragraph Spacing** button.

2. In the list, select the standard spacing option you want.

    Or

    In the list, click **Line Spacing Options**, change the setting under **Line spacing** on the **Indents and Spacing** page of the **Paragraph** dialog box, and then click **OK**.

➤ **To change the paragraph spacing of selected paragraphs**

→ On the **Page Layout** tab, in the **Paragraph** group, under **Spacing**, change the **Before** or **After** setting.

→ On the **Home** tab, in the **Paragraph** group, click the **Line and Paragraph Spacing** button, and then click **Add Space Before Paragraph**, **Remove Space Before Paragraph**, **Add Space After Paragraph**, or **Remove Space After Paragraph**. (Only two options will be visible, depending on the current Before and After settings of the active paragraph.)

Or

1. On the **Home** tab, click the **Paragraph** dialog box launcher.

2. On the **Indents and Spacing** page of the **Paragraph** dialog box, in the **Spacing** area, change the **Before** or **After** setting, and then click **OK**.

Practice Tasks

The practice files for these tasks are located in the Word\Objective2 practice file folder. If you want to save the results of the tasks, save them in the same folder with *My* appended to the file name so that you don't overwrite the original practice file.

- In the *RoomPlanner* document, change the line spacing of the text in the side-bar on page 2 so that two line spaces appear between the lines of text.

- In the *RoomPlanner* document, change the paragraph spacing of all the text in the main document so that the spacing between each paragraph is 12 points.

- In the *Paragraphs* document, change the spacing after all paragraphs to 12 points, and then remove the spacing after the *Date*, *Time*, *Location*, and *Ticket cost* paragraphs. Change the line spacing of the paragraph that begins *The author of* to 1.5.

2.5 Create Tables

Creating Basic Tables

Numeric data can often be presented more efficiently in a table than in a paragraph of text. Tables make large amounts of data or more complex data easier to read and understand because the data can be structured in rows and columns, frequently with row and column headers.

You can create a table in several ways:

- Select the number of rows and columns you want from a grid to create a table that spans the text column with all the cells of equal size.

- Display the Insert Table dialog box and specify the number of rows and columns, as well as the size of the columns.

- Draw cells the size you want.

- Convert selected text to a table.

> **Tip** You can also insert existing data from a Microsoft Excel worksheet in a Word document, but the intricacies of using the Microsoft Office programs together are not likely to be tested on the Word certification exam.

Most people are accustomed to thinking of a table as a means of displaying data in a quick, easy-to-grasp format. But tables can also serve to organize your pages in creative ways. For example, suppose you want to display two tables side by side. The simplest way to do this is to first create a table with one tall row and two wide columns and no grid-lines. You can then insert one table in the first cell and the other table in the second cell. These nested tables then seem to be arranged side by side.

Payment Schedule	
Interest Rate	3.6%
Years	3
Loan Amount	$155,000.00
Monthly Payment	$4,548.69
Cost of Loan	$163,752.79
3-Year Lease Cost	$180,000.00
Savings	$16,247.21

Payment Schedule	
Interest Rate	5.0%
Years	3
Loan Amount	$155,000.00
Monthly Payment	$4,645.49
Cost of Loan	$167,237.61
3-Year Lease Cost	$180,000.00
Savings	$12,762.39

As with regular tables, you can create a nested table in one of three ways:

- From scratch
- By formatting existing information
- By inserting Excel data

And just like other tables, you can format a nested table either manually or by using one of the ready-made table styles.

> **Tip** You can use tables to organize a mixture of elements such as text, tables, charts, and diagrams.

➤ **To insert a table**

1. On the **Insert** tab, in the **Tables** group, click the **Table** button.
2. In the grid, move the pointer across and down to select the number of columns and rows you want, and then click the lower-right cell in the selection.

   Or

1. On the **Insert** tab, in the **Tables** group, click the **Table** button, and then click **Insert Table**.
2. In the **Insert Table** dialog box, in the **Table size** area, specify the number of columns and rows you want the table to include.

3. In the **AutoFit behavior** area, do one of the following:
   - Click **Fixed column width**, and then specify a standard width for the table columns.
   - Click **AutoFit to contents** to size the table columns to fit their contents. The width of the resulting table may be less than the width of the page.
   - Click **AutoFit to window** to create a table that fits within the page margins and is divided into columns of equal size.
4. In the **Insert Table** dialog box, click **OK**.

➤ **To draw a table**

1. On the **Insert** tab, in the **Tables** group, click the **Table** button, and then click **Draw Table**.
2. Drag the pointer (which has become a pencil) across and down to create a cell.
3. Point to a corner of the cell, and drag to create another cell, or draw column and row boundaries inside the first cell.
4. Press Esc to turn off the table drawing pointer.

> **Tip** You can adjust an existing table by clicking the Draw Table button in the Draw Borders group on the Design tab. You can also change the style, weight, and color of the borders of drawn tables.

➤ **To convert selected text to a table**

1. On the **Insert** tab, in the **Tables** group, click the **Table** button, and then click **Convert Text to Table**.
2. In the **Convert Text to Table** dialog box, adjust the **Table size** and **AutoFit behavior** settings, select the type of text separator, and then click **OK**.

Formatting Tables

To format an existing table, you can apply one of the table styles available on the Table Tools Design contextual tab, which include a variety of borders, shading, text colors, and other attributes to give the table a professional look. The appearance of the built-in styles reflects the table elements selected in the Table Style Options group on the Design contextual tab.

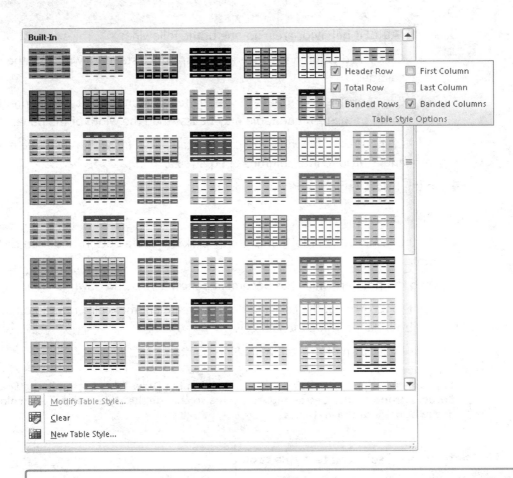

> **Tip** You can click buttons in the Paragraph and Font groups of the Home tab and apply character formatting from the Styles gallery to tables, just as you would to format any text in a Word document.

➤ To apply a built-in table style

1. Click anywhere in the table you want to format.

2. On the Table Tools **Design** contextual tab, in the **Table Styles** gallery, click the built-in style you want to apply.

Inserting Preformatted Tables

Formatting a table to best convey its data is often a process of trial and error. You can get started by creating a Quick Table, a preformatted table with sample data that you can customize.

Double Table

The Greek alphabet

Letter name	Uppercase	Lowercase	Letter name	Uppercase	Lowercase
Alpha	A	α	Nu	N	ν
Beta	B	β	Xi	Ξ	ξ
Gamma	Γ	γ	Omicron	O	o
Delta	Δ	δ	Pi	Π	π
Epsilon	E	ε	Rho	P	ρ
Zeta	Z	ζ	Sigma	Σ	σ
Eta	H	η	Tau	T	τ

Matrix

City or Town	Point A	Point B	Point C	Point D	Point E
Point A	—				
Point B	87	—			
Point C	64	56	—		
Point D	37	32	91	—	
Point E	93	35	54	43	—

Tabular List

ITEM	NEEDED
Books	1
Magazines	3
Notebooks	1
Paper pads	1
Pens	3
Pencils	2
Highlighter	2 colors
Scissors	1 pair

With Subheads 1

Save Selection to Quick Tables Gallery...

Insert Table...
Draw Table
Convert Text to Table...
Excel Spreadsheet
Quick Tables

➤ **To insert a Quick Table**

1. On the **Insert** tab, in the **Tables** group, click the **Table** button, and then point to **Quick Tables**.

2. In the **Quick Tables** gallery, click the preformatted table you want to insert.

Practice Tasks

The practice file for these tasks is located in the Word\Objective2 practice file folder. If you want to save the results of the tasks, save them in the same folder with *My* appended to the file name so that you don't overwrite the original practice file.

- In the *Table* document, convert the tabular list beginning with *Distance* and ending with *$20.00* into a table with two columns and six rows.

- In a new document, create a Matrix Quick Table.

- In a document, draw a table half the width and one-quarter the height of the page. Divide the table into four columns and 6 rows. Then apply the Colorful Shading – Accent 3 table style.

- In a document, insert a table with four columns and five rows. Specify the width of each column as 1.0".

2.6 Manipulate Tables in a Document

Modifying Table Data

After creating a table, you can enter text, numbers, and graphics into its cells. You can edit the information as you would normal text.

You can sort the data within a table by the contents of any table column. If the table includes a header row and/or a total row and multiple data rows, Word sorts only the data rows.

Strategy You should create a table with four or five columns and many rows of data and observe the effect of sorting the table with and without a header row to understand the sorting process.

Sort

Sort by

| Region | ▼ | Type: | Text | ▼ | ◉ Ascending |
| | | Using: | Paragraphs | ▼ | ○ Descending |

Then by

| Customer ID | ▼ | Type: | Number | ▼ | ◉ Ascending |
| | | Using: | Paragraphs | ▼ | ○ Descending |

Then by

| Order Date | ▼ | Type: | Date | ▼ | ○ Ascending |
| | | Using: | Paragraphs | ▼ | ◉ Descending |

My list has
◉ Header row   ○ No header row

Options...   OK   Cancel

You can apply borders and shading to a table manually or select a built-in table style that reflects the current thematic elements of the document. When the edges of table cells are not visually differentiated by borders or other formatting, you can display nonprinting gridlines that define the edges of the table cells.

➤ **To sort content in a table**

   1. Click anywhere in the table.

   2. On the Table Tools **Layout** contextual tab, in the **Data** group, click the **Sort** button.

   3. In the **Sort** dialog box, select the primary column by which you want to sort the content, and up to two additional nested sorting criteria. Then click **OK**.

➤ **To specify a header row for a table**

   1. Click anywhere in the table.

   2. On the Table Tools **Design** contextual tab, in the **Table Style Options** group, select the **Header Row** check box.

> **Tip** When you specify a header row, the built-in table styles change to visually differentiate the header from the rest of the table.

➤ **To display gridlines in a table**

   1. Click anywhere in the table.

   2. On the **Layout** contextual tab, in the **Table** group, click the **View Gridlines** button.

Modifying Table Structure

You can modify a table's structure at any time. To change the structure, you need to know how to select the appropriate parts of the table, as follows:

- **Select a table** Click anywhere in the table. On the Table Tools Layout contextual tab, in the Table group, click the Select button, and then click Select Table.

- **Select a column** Point to the top border of the column. When the pointer changes to a black, down-pointing arrow, click once.

- **Select a row** Point to the left border of the row. When the pointer changes to a white, right-pointing arrow, click once.

- **Select a cell** Triple-click the cell or click its left border.

- **Select multiple cells** Click the first cell, hold down the Shift key, and press the arrow keys to select adjacent cells in a column or row.

The basic methods for modifying table structure are as follows:

- Size the table, columns, or rows.

- Insert or delete rows, columns, or cells.

- Merge or split cells.

> **Tip** You can move a table by pointing to it and then dragging the handle that appears in its upper-left corner. Or click the handle to select the table, and then use the Cut and Paste buttons in the Clipboard group on the Home tab to relocate the table.

From the Table Properties dialog box, you can control many aspects of a table's structure, including the following:

- Specify the preferred width of the entire table, as well as the way it interacts with the surrounding text.

- Specify the height of each row, whether a row is allowed to break across pages, and whether a row of column headers should be repeated at the top of each page.

> **Tip** The Repeat As Header Row... option is available only if the cursor is in the top row of the table. You can also set repeating headers by clicking the Repeat Header Rows button in the Data group on the Layout tab.

- Set the width of each column. Setting the width of a cell also sets the width for its column.

> **Tip** You can also control the widths of selected cells and their columns by changing the Table Column Width setting in the Cell Size group on the Layout tab.

- Set the horizontal and vertical alignment of text within cells.

> **Tip** You can also control the alignment of cell text by clicking buttons in the Alignment group on the Layout tab.

- Control the margins of cells (how close text comes to the cell border) by clicking the Options button on either the Table or Cell page.

> **Tip** You can also control the margins by clicking the Cell Margins button in the Alignment group on the Layout tab.

➤ To display the Table Properties dialog box

1. Click anywhere in the table, or select a row, a column, or the table.
2. On the Table Tools **Layout** contextual tab, in the **Table** group, click the **Properties** button.

➤ To change the size of a selected table

→ Drag the size handle in the lower-right corner of the table.

➤ **To change the width of a selected column**

→ Drag a column's right border to the left or right.

→ Drag the column's **Move Table Column** marker on the horizontal ruler to the left or right.

→ On the **Layout** contextual tab, in the **Cell Size** group, change the **Table Column Width** setting.

➤ **To change the height of a selected row**

→ Drag a row's bottom border up or down.

→ Drag the row's **Adjust Table Row** marker on the vertical ruler up or down.

→ On the **Layout** contextual tab, in the **Cell Size** group, change the **Table Row Height** setting.

➤ **To insert columns or rows**

1. Click anywhere in the column or row adjacent to which you want to add a single column or row, or select the number of columns or rows you want to insert.

2. On the **Layout** contextual tab, in the **Rows & Columns** group, click an **Insert** button.

➤ **To insert cells**

1. Click the cell adjacent to which you want to add a single cell, or select the number of cells you want to insert.

2. On the **Layout** contextual tab, click the **Rows & Columns** dialog box launcher.

3. In the **Insert Cells** dialog box, specify how adjacent cells should be moved to accommodate the new cell or cells, and then click **OK**.

➤ **To delete a table, columns, or rows**

1. Click anywhere in the table, column, or row you want to delete, or select the number of columns or rows you want to delete.

2. On the **Layout** contextual tab, in the **Rows & Columns** group, click the **Delete** button.

3. Click **Delete Columns**, **Delete Rows**, or **Delete Table**.

➤ **To delete cells**

1. Click the cell, or select the number of cells you want to delete.

2. On the **Layout** contextual tab, in the **Rows & Columns** group, click the **Delete** button, and then click **Delete Cells**.

3. In the **Delete Cells** dialog box, specify how adjacent cells should be moved to replace the deleted cell or cells, and then click **OK**.

➤ **To merge or split selected cells**

→ On the **Layout** contextual tab, in the **Merge** group, click the **Merge Cells** button.

→ On the **Layout** contextual tab, in the **Merge** group, click the **Split Cells** button.

➤ **To convert a table to text**

1. Click anywhere in the table.

2. On the **Layout** contextual tab, in the **Data** group, click the **Convert to Text** button.

3. In the **Convert Table to Text** dialog box, do one of the following, and then click **OK**:

- ○ Click **Paragraph marks**, **Tabs**, or **Commas** to separate the content of table cells with one of these standard elements.

- ○ Click **Other**, and then enter any single character in the **Other** box to separate the content of table cells with that character.

Practice Tasks

The practice files for these tasks are located in the Word\Objective2 practice file folder. If you want to save the results of the tasks, save them in the same folder with *My* appended to the file name so that you don't overwrite the original practice file.

- In the *SortTable* document, sort the table in ascending order by State, then by City, and then by Last Name.

- In the *ModifyTable* document, merge the cells in the first row of the Estimate table. Add two rows below the last row. Then adjust the size of the entire table until its right edge aligns with the 4-inch mark on the horizontal ruler.

- In the *ModifyTable* document, expand the height of the header row of the Estimate table to 0.4", and then center align the contents.

- In the *ModifyTable* document, convert the Consultation Fee Schedule table to text, with the column contents separated by tabs.

2.7 Apply Bullets to a Document

You can use lists to clearly present a set of related items in a document. When the order of the items is not important, use a bulleted list.

You can create a single-level or multilevel bulleted list by selecting a bulleted list style and then typing the list, or by typing the list and then applying the style.

After you create a bulleted list, you can modify, format, and customize the list as follows:

- Move items up or down, insert new items, or delete unwanted items.
- Sort list items in ascending or descending order.
- Change the bullet character to a standard symbol or to a picture.
- Change the overall indentation of the entire list or change the relationship of the first "outdented" line to the other lines.
- Change the level of items in a multilevel list.

> **Strategy** The precise formatting of bulleted lists depends on the interplay of settings in their respective galleries as well as paragraph formatting and the location of tab stops. You should create multiple lists, show paragraph marks, and experiment with various settings, observing their effects.

➤ **To create a bulleted list**

1. Enter the list items as separate paragraphs, and then select the paragraphs.

2. On the **Home** tab, in the **Paragraph** group, click the **Bullets** button.

Or

1. Type * (an asterisk) at the beginning of a paragraph, press the Spacebar or the Tab key, type the first item in the list, and then press Enter.

2. Type items and press Enter to add subsequent bulleted items.

3. To end the list, do one of the following:

   ○ Press Enter twice to start the next paragraph at the left margin.

   ○ Press Enter and then Backspace to indent the next paragraph at the same level as the list.

➤ **To change the level of a selected bulleted list**

1. On the **Home** tab, in the **Paragraph** group, click the **Bullets** arrow, and then click **Change List Level**.

2. In the **Change List Level** gallery, click the level you want.

➤ **To change the level of a list item**

→ With the cursor in the item, on the **Home** tab, in the **Paragraph** group, click the **Increase Indent** button to demote the item or the **Decrease Indent** button to promote the item.

➤ **To sort bulleted list items**

1. Select the list items you want to sort.

2. On the **Home** tab, in the **Paragraph** group, click the **Sort** button.

➤ **To change the bullet symbol**

1. Click anywhere in the list you want to format.

2. On the **Home** tab, in the **Paragraph** group, click the **Bullets** arrow and then, in the **Bullets** gallery, click the symbol you want to use.

Or

1. Click anywhere in the list you want to format.

2. On the **Home** tab, in the **Paragraph** group, click the **Bullets** arrow, and then click **Define New Bullet**.

3. In the **Define New Bullet** dialog box, do one of the following, and then click **OK**:

   ○ Click the **Symbol** button. In the **Symbol** dialog box, locate and click the bullet symbol you want to use, and then click **OK**.

   ○ Click the **Picture** button. In the **Picture Bullet** dialog box, locate and click the bullet graphic you want to use, and then click **OK**.

➤ **To turn automatic bulleted list formatting on or off**

1. On the **Proofing** page of the **Word Options** dialog box, in the **AutoCorrect options** section, click the **AutoCorrect Options** button.

2. On the **AutoFormat As You Type** page of the **AutoCorrect Options** dialog box, select or clear the **Automatic bulleted lists** check box, and then click **OK**.

3. In the **Word Options** dialog box, click **OK**.

Practice Tasks

The practice file for these tasks is located in the Word\Objective2 practice file folder. If you want to save the results of the tasks, save them in the same folder with *My* appended to the file name so that you don't overwrite the original practice file.

- In the *Lists* document, convert the paragraphs under each of the bold headings except *The Sequence of Events* to a bulleted list that uses the four-diamond bullet character.

- In the *Lists* document, convert the paragraphs under the heading *The Sequence of Events* to a numbered list with the *A. B. C.* format.

Objective Review

Before finishing this chapter, ensure that you have mastered the following skills:

2.1 Apply Font and Paragraph Attributes

2.2 Navigate and Search Through a Document

2.3 Apply Indentation and Tab Settings to Paragraphs

2.4 Apply Spacing Settings to Text and Paragraphs

2.5 Create Tables

2.6 Manipulate Tables in a Document

2.7 Apply Bullets to a Document

3 Applying Page Layout and Reusable Content

The skills tested in this section of the Microsoft Office Specialist exam for Microsoft Word 2010 relate to creating a document that has a professional, consistent appearance. Specifically, the following objectives are associated with this set of skills:

3.1 Apply and Manipulate Page Setup Settings
3.2 Apply Themes
3.3 Construct Content in a Document by Using the Quick Parts Tool
3.4 Create and Manipulate Page Backgrounds
3.5 Create and Modify Headers and Footers

You can modify the structure of a document in many ways, including changing the page setup, manipulating page breaks, formatting content in columns, and inserting content in text boxes. You can modify the appearance of a document by applying themes, displaying watermarks, formatting the page background, and configuring page headers and footers.

This chapter guides you in studying ways of formatting a document by working with the page setup settings, applying themes, using Quick Parts, adding page backgrounds, and adding headers and footers.

> **Practice Files** Before you can complete the practice tasks in this chapter, you need to copy the book's practice files to your computer. The practice files you'll use to complete the tasks in this chapter are in the Word\Objective3 practice file folder. A complete list of practice files is provided in "Using the Book's Companion Content" at the beginning of this book.

3.1 Apply and Manipulate Page Setup Settings

Controlling Page Settings

Word gives you control of the layout of the pages in a document. You can change the page size, margins, and orientation by clicking the buttons in the Page Setup group on the Page Layout tab. (You can also make the same changes on the Print page of the Backstage view.) All pages of a document have the same margins and are oriented the same way unless you divide the document into sections. Then each section can have independent margin and orientation settings.

> **See Also** For information about changing document layout by using tables, see section 2.5, "Create Tables." For information about changing document layout by using Quick Parts, see section 3.3, "Construct Content in a Document by Using the Quick Parts Tool."

When the automatic hyphenation feature is turned on, Word inserts line breaks and hyphens within words to help achieve a more uniform line length. You can control the way Word hyphenates words, from the Hyphenation dialog box.

Word makes it easier than ever to add sophisticated visual content to your documents. This visual content can consist of pictures created outside of Word, such as a scanned photograph, a clip art image, or an illustration created with a graphics program. Or it can consist of drawing objects that are created within Word, such as a shape, a diagram, WordArt text, or a text box. You can use the buttons on the Insert tab to insert different kinds of visual content.

After you have inserted a visual object, you can format it many ways. The types of formatting you can apply vary with the type of object and, in the case of pictures, with the type of picture.

With automatic hyphenation off

With automatic hyphenation on

...ted visual content to your doc-
...es created outside of Word, such
...illustration created with a graph-
...that are created within Word,
...xt box. You can use the buttons
on the Insert tab to insert different kinds of visual content.

...e inserted a visual object, you can format it many ways. The types
...you can apply vary with the type of object and, in the case of pic-
...type of picture.

Hyphenation

☑ <u>A</u>utomatically hyphenate document
☑ Hyphenate words in <u>C</u>APS

Hyphenation <u>z</u>one: 0.25"
<u>L</u>imit consecutive hyphens to: 2

[<u>M</u>anual...]   [OK]   [Cancel]

When the automatic hyphenation feature is turned off, Word breaks lines between words and after punctuation. You can stop Word from breaking a line between two words that you want to keep together by inserting a nonbreaking space between the words.

➤ **To change the page margins**

1. On the **Page Layout** tab, in the **Page Setup** group, click the **Margins** button.

2. In the **Margins** gallery, click the standard margin set you want.

   Or

   Click **Custom Margins**, specify settings on the **Margins** page of the **Page Setup** dialog box, and then click **OK**.

➤ **To insert a nonbreaking space**

→ Press Ctrl+Shift+Space.

   Or

1. On the **Insert** tab, in the **Symbols** group, click the **Symbol** button, and then click **More Symbols**.

2. On the **Special Characters** page of the **Symbol** dialog box, click **Nonbreaking Space**, and then click **Insert**.

➤ **To automatically break lines and hyphenate words**

→ On the **Page Layout** tab, in the **Page Setup** group, click the **Hyphenation** button, and then click **Automatic**.

➤ **To control hyphenation settings**

1. On the **Page Layout** tab, in the **Page Setup** group, click the **Hyphenation** button, and then click **Hyphenation Options**.

2. In the **Hyphenation** dialog box, specify whether you want Word to automatically hyphenate the document or to hyphenate uppercase words, the maximum distance of a hyphen from the document margin (the hyphenation zone), and how many consecutive lines of a paragraph may be hyphenated. Then click **OK**.

➤ **To turn off automatic hyphenation**

→ On the **Page Layout** tab, in the **Page Setup** group, click the **Hyphenation** button, and then click **None**.

➤ **To selectively hyphenate words in a document**

1. On the **Page Layout** tab, in the **Page Setup** group, click the **Hyphenation** button, and then click **Manual**.

2. For each hyphenation suggested in the **Manual Hyphenation** dialog box, click **Yes** or **No**.

Setting Page Breaks

When you add more content than will fit within the document's top and bottom margins, Word creates a new page by inserting a soft page break (a page break that changes based on the content). If you want to control how pages break, you can insert a manual page break. You can also control whether related paragraphs stay together or can be separated by a page break, and you can specify that a particular paragraph start on a new page.

Tip You can apply these options to individual paragraphs, or you can incorporate them into the styles you define for document elements such as headings.

➤ **To insert a page break**

→ On the **Insert** tab, in the **Pages** group, click the **Page Break** button.

→ On the **Page Layout** tab, in the **Page Setup** group, click the **Insert Page and Section Breaks** button, and then in the list, click **Page**.

→ Press Ctrl+Enter.

➤ **To delete a page break**

1. Display the document in **Draft** view, and then display nonprinting characters.

> **Tip** To display nonprinting characters, click the Show/Hide ¶ button in the Paragraph group on the Home tab.

2. Select the page break, and then press Delete.

➤ **To force a page break before a paragraph**

1. Right-click anywhere in the paragraph, and then click **Paragraph**.

2. On the **Line and Page Breaks** page of the **Paragraph** dialog box, in the **Pagination** area, select the **Page break before** check box. Then click **OK**.

> **Tip** If a page break should always appear before a particular type of paragraph, such as a heading, you can incorporate the Page Break Before setting into the paragraph's style.

➤ **To keep related paragraphs together**

→ On the **Line and Page Breaks** page of the **Paragraph** dialog box, in the **Pagination** area, select the **Keep with next** check box. Then click **OK**.

➤ **To keep all the lines of a paragraph together**

→ On the **Line and Page Breaks** page of the **Paragraph** dialog box, in the **Pagination** area, select the **Keep lines together** check box. Then click **OK**.

➤ **To avoid one line of a paragraph appearing on the page**

→ On the **Line and Page Breaks** page of the **Paragraph** dialog box, in the **Pagination** area, select the **Widow/Orphan control** check box. Then click **OK**.

➤ **To insert a blank page anywhere in a document**

→ On the **Insert** tab, in the **Pages** group, click the **Blank Page** button.

Setting Section Breaks

In addition to controlling pagination with page breaks and paragraph formatting, you can control it with section breaks. A section break identifies a part of the document to which you can apply page settings, such as orientation or margins, that are different from those of the rest of the document.

Simple·Room·Design¶

With·the·Room·Planner,·you'll·never·make·another·design·mistake.·Created·by·acclaimed·interior· designers·to·simplify·the·redecorating·process,·this·award-winning·planning·tool·incorporates·elements· of·color,·dimension,·and·style·to·guide·your·project.·It·includes·a·furniture·location·guide;·room·grid;· drawing·tools;·and·miniature·furniture,·rugs,·accessories,·and·color·swatches·that·match·our·large·in-store·selection.·Here's·how·to·use·the·planner·to·create·the·room·of·your·dreams!¶

¶ ————————Section Break (Continuous)————————

Take·a·look·at·how·your·home· is· decorated· and· notice· the· things·you·like·and·dislike.·Pay· special· attention· to· the· color· scheme· and· to· how· you· react· to· each· room.· Is· it· inviting?· Does·it·feel·comfortable?·Does· it· relax· you· or· does· it· invigorate·you?¶

Focus· on· the· room(s)· you· would· most· like· to· change.· Brainstorm· all· the· things· you· would· change· in· that· room· if· you· could.· Don't· think· about·

to· place· the· windows· and· doors.· Arrange· the· furniture· placeholders· to· mirror· how· your· room· is· currently· set· up.· Add·the·current·colors,·too.¶

This· is· where· the· fun· begins!· Start·changing·things·around·a· bit.· Move· the· furniture,· add· different·colors,·and·watch·the· room· come· together!· Here's· where· you· can· tell· if· that· rich· red· rug· you· saw· in· the· showroom· enhances· or· overwhelms· your· room.· What·

not·quite·sure,·go·back·to·your· planner· for· a· few· more· adjustments.·If·you·are·sure,·go· back· to· the· store· one· more· time· to· see· if· anything· else· catches· your· eye.· Then· make· your·purchases.·You're·almost· there!¶

NOTE:· If· you· decided· to· paint· your·room,·do·that·before·your· new·pieces·are·delivered.·You'll· want· to· start· enjoying· your· new· room· as· soon· as· your· purchases·arrive.·¶

The following types of section breaks are available:

- **Next Page** This break starts the following section on the next page.
- **Continuous** This break creates a new section without affecting page breaks.
- **Even Page** This break starts the following section on the next even-numbered page.
- **Odd Page** This break starts the following section on the next odd-numbered page.

➤ **To insert a section break**

→ On the **Page Layout** tab, in the **Page Setup** group, click the **Insert Page and Section Breaks** button, and in the **Section Breaks** area, click the type of section break you want.

➤ **To specify different page settings for part of a document**

1. Select the part of the document that will have different settings.

2. On the **Page Layout** tab, in the **Page Setup** group, click the **Insert Page and Section Breaks** button, and in the **Section Breaks** area, click the type of section break you want.

3. Click anywhere between the top and bottom section breaks, and change the page settings.

➤ **To specify a different header or footer for a section**

1. Display the document in Print Layout view, and then double-click a header or footer in the section you want to configure.

2. In the active header or footer area, enter the header or footer content you want to display for the current section.

➤ **To delete a section break**

1. Display the document in Draft view, and then display nonprinting characters.

2. Click to the left of the section break, and then press Delete.

Flowing Text in Columns

By default, Word displays text in one column, but you can specify that text be displayed in multiple columns to create layouts like those used in newspapers and magazines. When you format text to flow in columns, the text fills the first column and then moves to the top of the next column. You can insert a column break to force text to move to the next column.

> **Tip** You can align the text in columns the same way you would any text. If you justify the columns for a neater look, you might want to have Word hyphenate the text to ensure that there are no large gaps between words.

You have the choice of one, two, or three equal columns, or two other two-column formats: one with a narrow left column and the other with a narrow right column. No matter how you set up the columns initially, you can change the layout, the widths of the individual columns, and the division between the columns at any time from the Columns dialog box.

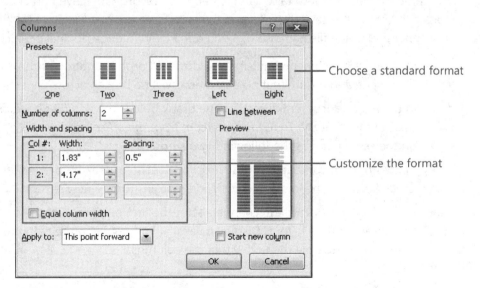

Choose a standard format

Customize the format

➤ **To format an entire document in multiple columns**

→ With the cursor anywhere in the text, on the **Page Layout** tab, in the **Page Setup** group, click the **Columns** button, and then click the number of columns you want.

➤ **To format part of a document in multiple columns**

1. Select the text you want to appear in columns.

2. On the **Page Layout** tab, in the **Page Setup** group, click the **Columns** button, and then click the number of columns you want.

➤ **To change the width of columns**

1. Click anywhere in any column. Then on the **Page Layout** tab, in the **Page Setup** group, click the **Columns** button, and click **More Columns**.

2. In the **Columns** dialog box, do the following, and then click **OK**:

   ○ Clear the **Equal Column Width** check box.

   ○ In the **Width and spacing area**, change the **Width** dimensions or the **Spacing** dimensions.

➤ **To display lines between columns**

➜ In the **Columns** dialog box, select the **Line between** check box.

Practice Tasks

The practice files for these tasks are located in the Word\Objective3 practice file folder. If you want to save the results of the tasks, save them in the same folder with *My* appended to the file name so that you don't overwrite the original practice file.

- In the *Pages* document, implement widow and orphan control for the entire document, and ensure that no paragraphs will be broken across pages.

- In the *Pages* document, insert a page break before the *Facilities* heading, and then ensure that the *To use the intercom from the office* heading will appear on the same page as the following two steps.

- In the *Pages* document, insert a Next Page section break before the *Shipping Quick Reference* heading, and set Wide margins for the new section.

- In the *Columns* document, change all but the first paragraph of the document to a three-column layout. Display a vertical line between the columns, and then hyphenate only the text within the columns.

3.2 Apply Themes

You can enhance the look of an entire document by applying a predefined theme—a combination of colors, fonts, and effects that project a certain feeling or tone. You apply a theme to the entire document from the Themes gallery.

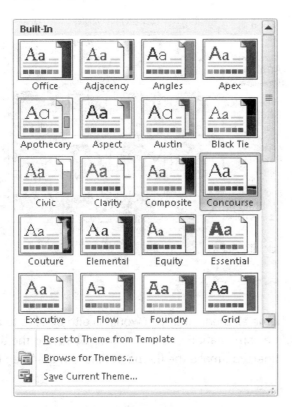

If you like certain aspects of different themes (for example, the colors of one theme and the fonts of another), you can mix and match theme elements.

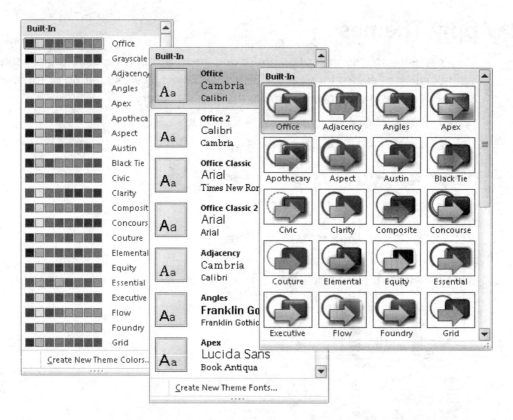

If you create a combination of theme elements that you would like to be able to use with other documents, you can save the combination as a new theme. By saving the theme in the default Document Themes folder, you make the theme available in the Themes gallery.

➤ **To apply a theme**

1. On the **Page Layout** tab, in the **Themes** group, click the **Themes** button.

2. In the **Themes** gallery, click the theme you want.

➤ **To change the theme colors, fonts, or effects**

1. On the **Page Layout** tab, in the **Themes** group, click the **Theme Colors**, **Theme Fonts**, or **Theme Effects** button.

2. In the corresponding gallery, click the color scheme, font set, or combination of effects you want.

➤ **To create a new color scheme**

1. Apply the color scheme that is closest to the one you want.

2. On the **Page Layout** tab, in the **Themes** group, click the **Theme Colors** button, and then click **Create New Theme Colors**.

3. In the **Create New Theme Colors** dialog box, click the box to the right of the presentation element you want to change.

4. In the color palette that appears, do one of the following:

   ○ Click the color you want to apply to the selected element.

   ○ At the bottom of the palette, click **More Colors**. Then, on either the **Standard** page or the **Custom** page of the **Colors** dialog box, click the color you want, and click **OK**.

5. Enter a name for the color scheme in the **Name** box, and then click **Save**.

➤ **To create a new font set**

1. Apply the font set that is closest to the one you want.

2. On the **Page Layout** tab, in the **Themes** group, click the **Theme Fonts** button, and then click **Create New Theme Fonts**.

3. In the **Create New Theme Fonts** dialog box, do the following:

   ○ In the **Heading font** list, click the font you want to use for all heading styles.

   ○ In the **Body font** list, click the font you want to use for all heading styles.

4. Enter a name for the font set in the **Name** box, and then click **Save**.

> **Tip** Custom themes, color schemes, and font sets are saved in the C:\Users\<*username*>\AppData\Roaming\Microsoft\Templates\Document Themes folder. To delete a custom theme, color scheme, or font set, navigate to the folder, right-click the item, and then click Delete.

➤ **To save a modified theme**

1. Adjust the colors, fonts, or effects of the current theme to suit your needs.

2. In the **Themes** gallery, click **Save Current Theme**.

3. In the **Save Current Theme** dialog box, enter a name for the theme in the **File name** box, and then click **Save**.

Practice Tasks

The practice files for these tasks are located in the Word\Objective3 practice file folder. If you want to save the results of the tasks, save them in the same folder with *My* appended to the file name so that you don't overwrite the original practice file.

- Apply the Aspect theme to the *Theme* document.

- In the *CustomTheme* document, change the color theme to Opulent and the font theme to Apex, and then save the combination as a custom theme with the name *MOS Design*.

3.3 Construct Content in a Document by Using the Quick Parts Tool

Longer documents typically include elements such as a cover page and headers and footers to provide identifying and organizing information. To reinforce key concepts and also alleviate the monotony of page after page of plain text, they might also include elements such as sidebars and quotations pulled from the text.

To simplify the creation of professional-looking text elements, Word 2010 comes with ready-made visual representations of text, known as *Quick Parts* or *building blocks*. (The terms *Quick Parts* and *building blocks* seem to be used interchangeably in the Word program and documentation.)

Structural Quick Parts are listed in the Building Blocks Organizer. The Building Blocks Organizer includes Quick Parts for building bibliographies, cover pages, equations, footers, headers, page numbers, tables of contents, tables, text boxes (including sidebars and pull quotes), and watermarks.

Clicking a Quick Part in the left pane of the Building Blocks Organizer displays a preview in the right pane.

The names of some Quick Parts indicate that they belong to a design family, such as Alphabet or Pinstripes. You can sort the list on any column—for example, you might want to sort the list by name to group all the Quick Parts by design family, so that you can preview the entire set before inserting them.

> **Strategy** Spend some time inserting Quick Parts in a test document and saving modified and new Quick Parts in various ways so that you understand the relationship between the Building Blocks Organizer and the Cover Page, Header, Footer, and Text Box galleries.

More information about each Quick Part is available by scrolling the Building Blocks list horizontally. The Behavior column indicates whether Word inserts the building block in the existing text, in its own paragraph, or on its own page. The Description column includes information about the Quick Part, and in some cases, recommendations for its use. For an overview of a particular Quick Part, you can click Edit Properties.

In addition to the Quick Parts that are available from the Building Blocks Organizer, you can insert document properties and fields from the Quick Parts menu. Document properties that are inserted as Quick Parts update automatically when the property changes.

► **To insert any Quick Part**

1. On the **Insert** tab, in the **Text** group, click the **Quick Parts** button, and then click **Building Blocks Organizer**.

2. In the **Building Blocks Organizer**, select the Quick Part you want, and then click **Insert**.

3. In the document, replace any text placeholders in the Quick Part with the information you want to appear in the document.

> **Tip** After you insert a Quick Part, you can resize or reposition it or change its formatting by using commands on the Drawing Tools Format contextual tab.

► **To insert a dynamic document property**

→ On the **Insert** tab, in the **Text** group, click the **Quick Parts** button, point to **Document Property**, and then click the property you want to insert.

➤ **To insert a field**

1. On the **Insert** tab, in the **Text** group, click the **Quick Parts** button, and then click **Field**.

2. In the **Field** dialog box, do the following, and then click **OK**:

   ○ In the **Field names** list, click the field you want to insert.

   ○ In the **Field properties** area, set any properties associated with the field.

➤ **To insert a cover page**

1. Position the insertion point at the beginning of the document.

2. On the **Insert** tab, in the **Pages** group, click the **Cover Page** button.

3. In the **Cover Page** gallery, click the design you want.

4. In the document, replace the text placeholders with the information you want to appear on the cover page.

See Also For information about inserting ready-made headers and footers, see section 3.5, "Create and Modify Headers and Footers."

Practice Tasks

The practice files for these tasks are located in the Word\Objective3 practice file folder. If you want to save the results of the tasks, save them in the same folder with *My* appended to the file name so that you don't overwrite the original practice file.

- In the *Parts* document, insert a Pinstripes cover page. Change the subtitle placeholder to *Information Sheet* and the date placeholder to today's date.

- In the *Parts* document, on page 2, insert a Pinstripes Quote, and use Paste Special to insert an unformatted copy of the last sentence of the fourth para-graph (*Go with what you love...*) in the quote box. Then save the customized pull quote as a Quick Part with the name *Inspiration Quote*.

- In the *SavedText* document, select and save *Wide World Importers* as an AutoText Quick Part named *wwi*. Then in a new paragraph at the end of the document, type *Recommended by* and insert the *wwi* Quick Part.

- In the *SavedText* document, add a footer that includes only the Author, FileName, and SaveDate fields with their default formats and options.

3.4 Create and Manipulate Page Backgrounds

Whether you are creating a document that will be viewed on a printed page, on a computer, or in a web browser, you can make your document stand out by adding a page border, background color, or pattern. You can also add watermarks—faint words or a graphic that appear behind the text but don't interfere with its readability.

> **Tip** You can also add watermarks from the Building Blocks Organizer. For more information, see section 3.3, "Construct Content in a Document by Using the Quick Parts Tool."

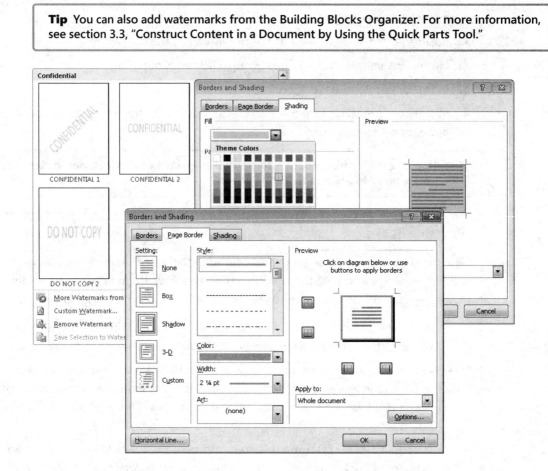

➤ **To add a page border**

1. On the **Page Layout** tab, in the **Page Background** group, click the **Page Borders** button.

2. On the **Page Border** page of the **Borders and Shading** dialog box, under **Setting**, click the type of border you want.

3. To create a line border, make selections in the **Style**, **Color**, and **Width** lists. To create a patterned border, select the pattern you want from the **Art** list.

4. To apply or remove the border from a side of the diagram, in the **Preview** area, click any of the border buttons or any side of the preview diagram.

5. In the **Apply to** list, select the part of the document you want to apply the page border to: the whole document, the current section, or part of the current section.

> **See Also** For information about creating sections, see the "Setting Section Breaks" topic of section 3.1, "Apply and Manipulate Page Setup Settings."

6. To make adjustments to the border margin or position, click **Options**, set the margins, alignment, and positioning, and then click **OK**.

7. In the **Borders and Shading** dialog box, click **OK**.

➤ To add a page background color

1. On the **Page Layout** tab, in the **Page Background** group, click the **Page Color** button.

2. In the **Page Color** palette, click the background color you want.

   Or

1. In the **Page Color** palette, click **More Colors**.

2. On the **Standard** or **Custom** page of the **Colors** dialog box, make a selection, and then click **OK**.

➤ To add a page background pattern

1. In the **Page Color** palette, click **Fill Effects**.

2. In the **Fill Effects** dialog box, click the tab for the type of fill effect you want.

3. Click the options or thumbnails you want, and then click **OK**.

➤ To add a text watermark

1. On the **Page Layout** tab, in the **Page Background** group, click the **Watermark** button.

2. In the **Watermark** gallery, click the thumbnail for one of the predefined text watermarks.

   Or

1. In the **Watermark** gallery, click **Custom Watermark**.

2. In the **Printed Watermark** dialog box, click **Text watermark**.

3. Either select the watermark text you want from the **Text** list, or enter the text in the **Text** box.

4. Format the text by changing the settings in the **Font**, **Size**, and **Color** boxes.

5. Choose a layout, select or clear the **Semitransparent** check box, and then click **OK**.

➤ **To use a picture as a watermark**

1. In the **Watermark** gallery, click **Custom Watermark**.

2. In the **Printed Watermark** dialog box, click **Picture watermark**, and then click **Select Picture**.

3. In the **Insert Picture** dialog box, navigate to the folder where the picture is stored, and double-click the name of the picture.

4. In the **Scale** list, choose how big or small you want the watermark picture to appear in the document.

5. If you want to display a more vibrant picture, clear the **Washout** check box. Then click **OK**.

Practice Tasks

The practice file for these tasks is located in the Word\Objective3 practice file folder. If you want to save the results of the tasks, save them in the same folder with *My* appended to the file name so that you don't overwrite the original practice file.

- In the *Background* document, change the background color to the second lightest green (Olive Green, Accent 3, Lighter 60%).
- Add the Canvas texture to the background of the *Background* document.
- Add the URGENT text watermark to the *Background* document.

3.5 Create and Modify Headers and Footers

You can display information on every page of your document by creating headers and footers—regions at the top and bottom of the pages that can be created and formatted independently. You can have a different header and footer on the first page of a document, different headers and footers on odd and even pages, or different headers and footers for each section. When you create a header or footer, Word applies the header or footer style specified by the document's template, indicates the header and footer areas by displaying dotted borders, and displays a contextual Design tab on the ribbon.

You can enter information in the header and footer areas the same way you enter ordinary text. You can use the commands on the Design tab to enter and format items such as the date and time, move from one header or footer to another, and establish the location and position of the header and footer.

> **Tip** If your document contains section breaks, each successive section inherits the headers and footers of the preceding section unless you break the link between the two sections. You can then create a different header and footer for the current section. For information about sections, see the "Setting Section Breaks" topic of section 3.1, "Apply and Manipulate Page Setup Settings."

If you want to enter page numbers, you can select the style you want from the Page Number gallery. You can format the page numbers in a variety of ways in the Page Number Format dialog box.

	Top of Page	▸	
	Bottom of Page	▸	Two Bars 2
	Page Margins	▸	
	Current Position	▸	
	Format Page Numbers...		
	Remove Page Numbers		

Two Bars 2

1

Vertical Outline 1

Page Number Format

Number format: i, ii, iii, ...

☑ Include chapter number

Chapter starts with style: Heading 1

Use separator: - (hyphen)

Examples: 1-1, 1-A

Page numbering

◉ Continue from previous section

◯ Start at:

OK   Cancel

Vertical Outline 2

With Shapes
Arrow 1

1

More Page Numbers from Office.com ▸

Save Selection as Page Number (Bottom)

➤ **To insert a header or footer**

1. Position the cursor anywhere in the document.

2. On the **Insert** tab, in the **Header & Footer** group, click the **Header** button or the **Footer** button.

3. In the **Header** gallery or the **Footer** gallery, click the design you want.

4. On the Header & Footer Tools **Design** contextual tab, in the **Options** group, do any of the following:

  ○ Select the **Different First Page** check box if you want to use a different header or footer on the first page of the document. You might want to do this if, for example, the first page of the document is a cover page.

  ○ Select the **Different Odd & Even Pages** check box if you want to use different headers or footers for odd pages and for even pages. Select this option if the content of the header or footer is not centered and the document content will be viewed on facing pages.

  ○ Clear the **Show Document Text** check box if you find that you're distracted by the main document text when you're working in the header or footer.

5. In the **Position** group, set the **Header from Top** or **Footer from Bottom** distance.

6. From the **Insert** group, insert the date, time, a picture, a clip art image, or any Quick Parts you want to include in the header or footer.

7. In the header or footer, replace any text placeholders and enter any other information you want to appear.

8. In the **Close** group, click the **Close Header and Footer** button.

➤ **To delete a header or footer**

1. Double-click the header or footer to activate it.

2. Press Ctrl+A to select all the content of the header or footer, and then press Delete.

➤ **To insert the current date and/or time in a header or footer**

1. In the header or footer, position the cursor where you want the date and/or time to appear.

2. On the **Design** contextual tab, in the **Insert** group, click the **Insert Date and Time** button.

3. In the **Date and Time** dialog box, do the following, and then click **OK**:

   ○ Click the format in which you want the date and/or time to appear in the header or footer.

   ○ If you want Word to update the date and/or time in the header each time you save the document, select the **Update automatically** check box.

➤ **To insert a page number in a header or footer**

1. On the **Insert** tab, in the **Header & Footer** group, click the **Insert Page Number** button.

2. In the **Page Number** list, point to a page number position, and then click the page number style you want.

➤ **To change the format of page numbers**

1. In the **Header & Footer** group, click the **Insert Page Number** button, and then click **Format Page Numbers**.

2. In the **Page Number Format** dialog box, in the **Number format** list, click the format you want.

3. Select any other options you want, and then click **OK**.

Practice Tasks

The practice files for these tasks are located in the Word\Objective3 practice file folder. If you want to save the results of the tasks, save them in the same folder with *My* appended to the file name so that you don't overwrite the original practice file.

- In the *Header* document, add a Motion (Even Page) header with the text *The Taguian Cycle*, and specify that the header should not appear on the first page. Then add a Motion (Even Page) footer that displays today's date.

- In the *Numbers* document, add page numbers to the entire document, and format the page numbers as uppercase roman numerals.

Objective Review

Before finishing this chapter, ensure that you have mastered the following skills:

3.1 Apply and Manipulate Page Setup Settings

3.2 Apply Themes

3.3 Construct Content in a Document by using the Quick Parts Tool

3.4 Create and Manipulate Page Backgrounds

3.5 Create and Modify Headers and Footers

4 Including Illustrations and Graphics in a Document

The skills tested in this section of the Microsoft Office Specialist exam for Microsoft Word 2010 relate to inserting and formatting visual elements. Specifically, the following objectives are associated with this set of skills:

4.1 Insert and Format Pictures in a Document
4.2 Insert and Format Shapes, WordArt, and SmartArt
4.3 Insert and Format Clip Art
4.4 Apply and Manipulate Text Boxes

Graphic elements can add flair to a document, provide additional structure, or, more importantly, convey information to the reader.

This chapter guides you in studying ways of inserting and formatting pictures, shapes, and clip art elements; creating decorative text as WordArt objects; illustrating relational concepts with SmartArt diagrams; and presenting information in text boxes.

> **Practice Files** Before you can complete the practice tasks in this chapter, you need to copy the book's practice files to your computer. The practice files you'll use to complete the tasks in this chapter are in the Word\Objective4 practice file folder. A complete list of practice files is provided in "Using the Book's Companion Content" at the beginning of this book.

4.1 Insert and Format Pictures in a Document

Inserting Pictures

You can insert digital photographs or pictures created in almost any program into a Word document. You can also capture and insert images of content displayed on your computer screen directly from Word. By using the built-in screen clipping tool, you can insert screen captures of entire windows or selected areas of on-screen content.

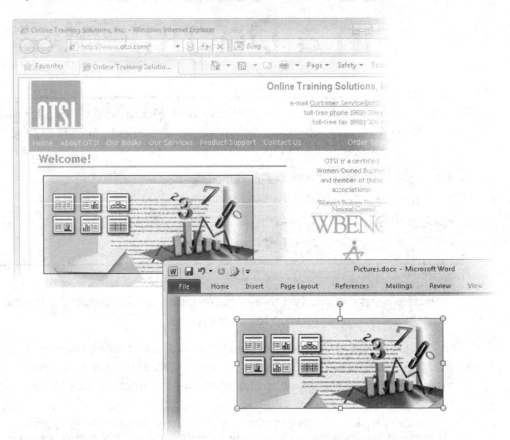

Inserting images in a document can increase the file size of the document dramatically. By default, Word compresses pictures when you save a file. You can turn off automatic compression and compress only the pictures you want. You can also adjust the compression rate to be appropriate for the way the document will be viewed.

➤ **To insert a picture from a file**

1. On the **Insert** tab, in the **Illustrations** group, click the **Insert Picture from File** button.

2. In the **Insert Picture** dialog box, browse to and click the file you want. Then do one of the following:

   ○ Click **Insert** to insert the picture into the document.

   ○ In the **Insert** list, click **Link to File** to insert a picture that will update automatically if the picture file changes.

   ○ In the **Insert** list, click **Insert and Link** to insert a picture that you can manually update if the picture file changes.

➤ **To change the picture compression settings**

1. On the Picture Tools **Format** contextual tab, in the **Adjust** group, click **Compress Pictures**.

2. In the **Compress Pictures** dialog box, set the options and output you want, and then click **OK** twice.

➤ **To capture and insert a screen clipping**

1. Display the content you want to capture.

2. In the Word document, position the cursor where you want to insert the screen clipping.

3. On the **Insert** tab, in the **Illustrations** group, click the **Screenshot** button.

4. In the **Screenshot** gallery, do one of the following:

   ○ Click a window thumbnail to insert a picture of that window into the document at the cursor.

   ○ Click **Screen Clipping**, and then drag across the part of the screen you want to capture.

Formatting Pictures

After you insert an image in a document, you can modify it in many ways. For example, you can crop or resize a picture, change the picture's brightness and contrast, recolor it, apply artistic effects to it, and compress it to reduce the size of the document containing it. You can apply a wide range of preformatted styles to a picture to change its shape and orientation, as well as add borders and picture effects.

> ➤ **To change the size and/or shape of a selected picture**

  → Drag its sizing handles.

  → On the Picture Tools **Format** contextual tab, in the **Size** group, change the **Height** and **Width** settings.

  → On the **Format** contextual tab, click the **Size** dialog box launcher. Then on the **Size** page of the **Layout** dialog box, change the **Height**, **Width**, or **Scale** settings.

> ➤ **To move a picture**

  → Drag the picture vertically to a new location.

  → Select the picture. On the **Format** contextual tab, in the **Arrange** group, display the **Position** gallery, and then click one of the **In Line with Text** or **With Text Wrapping** icons.

> ➤ **To copy a picture to a new location**

  → Hold down the Ctrl key and drag the picture vertically to the second location.

> **Tip** Release the mouse button first, and then the Ctrl key. (If you release Ctrl first, Word moves the image instead of copying it.)

> ➤ **To apply artistic effects to a selected picture**

  → On the **Format** contextual tab, in the **Adjust** group, expand the **Artistic Effects** gallery, and then click the effect you want to apply.

➤ **To apply a style to a selected picture**

→ On the **Format** contextual tab, in the **Picture Styles** group, expand the **Quick Styles** gallery, and then click the style you want to apply.

Or

1. On the **Format** contextual tab, click the **Picture Styles** dialog box launcher.

2. In the **Format Picture** dialog box, on the **Line Color**, **Line Style**, **Shadow**, **Reflection**, **Glow and Soft Edges**, **3-D Format**, and **3-D Rotation** pages, choose the effects you want to apply. Then click **Close**.

Practice Tasks

The practice file for these tasks is located in the Word\Objective4 practice file folder. If you want to save the results of the tasks, save them in the same folder with *My* appended to the file name so that you don't overwrite the original practice file.

- Insert the *Logo* graphic at the beginning of the *Picture* document. Then size the logo so that it is 0.5" high, maintaining the height-to-width ratio.

- Apply the Texturizer effect to the text in the logo, and then place a copy of the logo at the end of the *Picture* document.

- Insert a screen clipping of the Microsoft logo, captured from the home page of the Microsoft website, at the end of the *Picture* document.

4.2 Insert and Format Shapes, WordArt, and SmartArt

Inserting and Formatting Shapes

If you want to add visual interest and impact to a document but you don't need anything as fancy as a picture or a clip art image, you can draw a shape. Shapes can be simple, such as lines, circles, or squares; or more complex, such as stars, hearts, and arrows. You can format shapes by using built-in styles or by applying a fill, outline, and effects. You can add text to shapes, specify the text direction, and format the text, either by using normal formatting techniques or WordArt styles, or by applying a fill, outline, and effects.

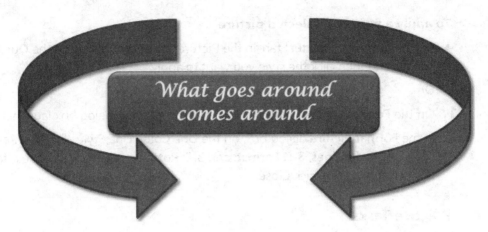

If you build a picture by drawing individual shapes, you can group them so that they act as one object. If you move or size a grouped object, the shapes retain their positions in relation to each other. To break the bond, you ungroup the object.

If your picture consists of more than a few shapes, you might want to draw the shapes on a drawing canvas instead of directly on the page. The drawing canvas keeps the parts of the picture together, helps you position the picture, and provides a frame-like boundary between your picture and the text on the page. You can then draw shapes on the canvas in the usual ways. At any time, you can size and move the drawing canvas and the shapes on it as one unit.

➤ **To open a drawing canvas**

→ On the **Insert** tab, in the **Illustrations** group, click the **Shapes** button, and then click **New Drawing Canvas**.

> **Tip** If you prefer to always use the drawing canvas when creating pictures with shapes, display the Advanced page of the Word Options dialog box. Then under Editing Options, select the Automatically Create Drawing Canvas When Inserting AutoShapes check box, and click OK.

➤ **To draw a standard shape**

1. On the **Insert** tab, in the **Illustrations** group, click the **Shapes** button.
2. In the **Shapes** gallery, click the shape you want, and then do one of the following:
   - ○ Click anywhere on the page to insert a standard-size shape.
   - ○ Drag anywhere on the page to draw a shape the size you want.

➤ **To add text to a selected shape**

→   Click the shape, and then enter the text.

→   Right-click the shape, click **Add Text**, and then enter the text.

> **Tip** For more control over the text within a shape, you can insert the text in a text box. For more information, see section "4.4, "Apply and Manipulate Text Boxes."

➤ **To customize a selected shape**

1.   On the Drawings Tools **Format** contextual tab, in the **Insert Shapes** group, click the **Edit Shape** button, and then click **Edit Points**.

2.   Drag the intersection points that appear on the shape to change its form.

> **Tip** You change the size and location of a shape by using the same techniques as you do with other graphic elements.

➤ **To change a selected shape to another shape**

→   On the **Format** contextual tab, in the **Insert Shapes** group, click the **Edit Shape** button, point to **Change Shape**, and then click the shape you want.

➤ **To format a selected shape**

→   On the **Format** contextual tab, do any of the following:

o   In the **Shape Styles** gallery, click the built-in style you want to apply.

o   In the **Shape Styles** group, in the **Shape Fill**, **Shape Outline**, and **Shape Effects** galleries, click the settings you want.

➤ **To format text attached to a selected shape**

→   On the **Format** contextual tab, do any of the following:

o   In the **WordArt Styles** gallery, click the built-in style you want to apply.

o   In the **WordArt Styles** group, in the **Text Fill**, **Text Outline**, and **Text Effects** galleries, click the settings you want.

o   In the **Text** group, click **Text Direction**, and then click the direction in which you want the text to flow.

➤ **To stack multiple shapes**

→ Drag the shapes so that they overlap.

➤ **To change the stacking order of multiple shapes**

1. Select the shape you want to move up or down in the stack.

2. On the **Format** contextual tab, in the **Arrange** group, do any of the following:

   ○ Click the **Bring Forward** or **Send Backward** button to move the shape up or down one level.

   ○ In the **Bring Forward** list, click **Bring to Front** to move the shape to the top of the stack.

   ○ In the **Bring Forward** list, click **Bring in Front of Text** to move the shape on top of the surrounding text.

   ○ In the **Send Backward** list, click **Send to Back** to move the shape to the bottom of the stack.

   ○ In the **Send Backward** list, click **Send Behind Text** to move the shape behind the surrounding text.

➤ **To group shapes**

1. Select the first shape, hold down the Ctrl key, and then click the additional shapes you want to group.

2. On the **Format** contextual tab, in the **Arrange** group, click the **Group** button, and then click **Group**.

➤ **To ungroup shapes**

1. Select the grouped shapes.

2. On the **Format** contextual tab, in the **Arrange** group, click the **Group** button, and then click **Ungroup**.

Inserting and Modifying WordArt

When you want a text banner that is fancier than one you can create by applying character formatting, you can use WordArt. WordArt text can swirl, grow bigger from one end to the other or in the middle, take on a three-dimensional shape, and change color from one letter to the next. The WordArt object is attached to the paragraph that is active at the time you create the WordArt object, but you can move it independently of the surrounding text.

> **To insert a WordArt object**

1. On the **Insert** tab, in the **Text** group, click the **WordArt** button.

2. In the **WordArt** gallery, click the text style you want.

3. Replace the placeholder text in the WordArt object.

4. Set the size and other attributes of the text as you would with any other text.

> **Tip** You change the size, shape, and location of a WordArt object by using the same techniques as you do with other graphic elements.

> **To create a WordArt object from existing text**

1. Select the text.

2. On the **Insert** tab, in the **Text** group, click the **WordArt** button.

3. In the **WordArt** gallery, click the text style you want.

4. Set the size and other attributes of the text as you would any other text.

> **To format the background of a selected WordArt object**

→ On the Drawing Tools **Format** contextual tab, do any of the following:

  ○ In the **Shape Styles** gallery, click the built-in style you want to apply.

  ○ In the **Shape Styles** group, in the **Shape Fill**, **Shape Outline**, and **Shape Effects** galleries, click the settings you want.

> **To format the text of a selected WordArt object**

→ On the **Format** contextual tab, do any of the following:

  ○ In the **WordArt Styles** gallery, click the built-in style you want to apply.

  ○ In the **WordArt Styles** group, in the **Text Fill**, **Text Outline**, and **Text Effects** galleries, click the settings you want.

  ○ In the **Text** group, click **Text Direction**, and then click the direction in which you want the text to flow.

Inserting and Modifying SmartArt Diagrams

When you need your document to clearly illustrate a concept such as a process, cycle, hierarchy, or relationship, you can create a dynamic, visually appealing diagram by using SmartArt diagrams. After selecting the type of diagram you want and inserting it into the document, you add text either directly in the diagram's shapes or from its text pane. SmartArt diagrams can be only text or text and pictures.

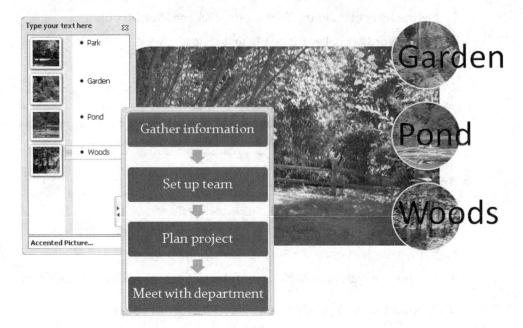

➤ **To insert a diagram**

1. On the **Insert** tab, in the **Illustrations** group, click the **Insert SmartArt Graphic** button.

2. In the left pane of the **Choose a SmartArt Graphic** dialog box, click the type of diagram you want.

3. In the center pane, click the layout you want, and then click **OK**.

> **Tip** You change the size, shape, and location of a SmartArt diagram by using the same techniques as you do with other graphic elements.

➤ **To add text to a diagram shape**

→ With the diagram selected, click the shape, and enter the text.

→ In the text pane, click the bullet for the shape, and enter the text.

> **Tip** If the text pane is not open, click the tab on the left side of the diagram's frame, or click the Text Pane button in the Create Graphic group on the SmartArt Tools Design contextual tab.

➤ **To change the layout of a selected diagram**

→ To switch to a layout in the same diagram category, on the SmartArt Tools **Design** contextual tab, in the **Layouts** gallery, click the layout you want.

→ To switch to a layout in a different diagram category, on the **Design** contextual tab, in the **Layouts** gallery, click **More Layouts** and then, in the **Choose a SmartArt Graphic** dialog box, choose the layout you want.

➤ **To delete a shape from a SmartArt diagram**

→ Click the shape, and then press the Delete key.

➤ **To change the color scheme of a selected diagram**

→ On the **Design** contextual tab, in the **SmartArt Styles** group, click the **Change Colors** button and then click the color scheme you want.

➤ **To apply a style to a selected diagram**

→ On the **Design** contextual tab, in the **SmartArt Styles** gallery, click the style you want to apply.

➤ **To apply a style to a a selected diagram shape**

→ On the SmartArt Tools **Format** contextual tab, in the **Shape Styles** gallery, click the style you want to apply.

Or

1. On the **Format** contextual tab, click the **Shape Styles** dialog box launcher.

2. In the **Format Shape** dialog box, on the **Line Color**, **Line Style**, **Shadow**, **Reflection**, **Glow and Soft Edges**, **3-D Format**, and **3-D Rotation** pages, choose the effects you want to apply. Then click **Close**.

> **Strategy** Many formatting options are available from the Design and Format contextual tabs. Be familiar with the options available on the contextual tabs as well as in the associated dialog boxes.

Practice Tasks

The practice files for these tasks are located in the Word\Objective4 practice file folder. If you want to save the results of the tasks, save them in the same folder with *My* appended to the file name so that you don't overwrite the original practice file.

- At the end of the *Shapes* document, draw a circle 1.5 inches in diameter in the upper-left corner of a new drawing canvas. Then create a copy of the circle in the upper middle of the drawing canvas and another in the upper-right corner. Draw curved lines resembling strings below each circle. Group the shapes, and then move the group to the top of the document.

- At the end of the *SmartArt* document, insert a Vertical Process diagram. In the text pane, enter *The Journey*, *The Battle*, and *The Twist* as bullet points. Then add a new shape containing the words *True Climax*.

- At the beginning of the *WordArt* document, insert *Welcome Esther Valle!* in a Gradient Fill WordArt Style with 44-point text.

- In the *WordArt* document, change the words *Extra! Extra!* into a Fill WordArt style, and change the color of the letters to orange with a red outline. Make the object two inches wider, and then apply the perspective Diagonal Lower Left shadow style.

4.3 Insert and Format Clip Art

Clip art comes in many different styles and formats, including illustrations, photographs, videos, and audio clips. The only thing the clips have in common is that they are free and available without any copyright restrictions. You can search for clip art objects by using keywords, and store the images you might want to use in the Microsoft Clip Organizer. You can also edit the keywords associated with an image and view its properties.

➤ To locate and insert a clip art object

1. On the **Insert** tab, in the **Illustrations** group, click the **Clip Art** button.

2. In the **Clip Art** pane, in the **Search for** box, enter a keyword, and click **Go**.

3. In the results list, click the thumbnail of the image you want.

> **Tip** You change the size, shape, and location of a clip art object by using the same techniques as you do with other graphic elements.

➤ **To temporarily store a clip art image on the Microsoft Office Clipboard**

→ In the **Clip Art** pane, point to the image, click the arrow that appears, and then click **Copy**.

➤ **To store a clip art object in the Clip Organizer**

1. In the **Clip Art** pane, point to the image, click the arrow that appears, and then click **Make Available Offline**.

2. In the **Copy to Collection** dialog box, select or create the folder in which you want to store the clip art object, and then click **OK**.

➤ **To save a clip art object as a file**

1. Insert the clip art object in a document.

2. Right-click the clip art object, and then click **Save as Picture**.

3. In the **File Save** dialog box, browse to the location in which you want to save the file, name the file, select a file type, and then click **Save**.

➤ **To open the Clip Organizer**

→ On the Windows **Start** menu, click **All Programs**, **Microsoft Office**, **Microsoft Office 2010 Tools**, and then **Microsoft Clip Organizer**.

Practice Tasks

The practice file for these tasks is located in the Word\Objective4 practice file folder. If you want to save the results of the tasks, save them in the same folder with *My* appended to the file name so that you don't overwrite the original practice file.

- In the *ClipArt* document, insert a stylized dollar clip art image at the end of the *Greg Guzik* paragraph, and make it 0.25 inch square. Then insert a copy of the image at the beginning of the paragraph.

- Search for other stylized dollar clip art images, and save several of them to the Clip Organizer.

- In the *ClipArt* document, replace the dollar image with a new one from the Clip Organizer. Then resize and reposition it as you like.

4.4 Apply and Manipulate Text Boxes

When you want text that is not part of the main flow to appear on a page, you can create a text box in one of several built-in styles. If none of the predefined text-box building blocks meets your needs, you can draw and format your own text box. You can make your custom text boxes available from the Text Box gallery by saving them as building blocks.

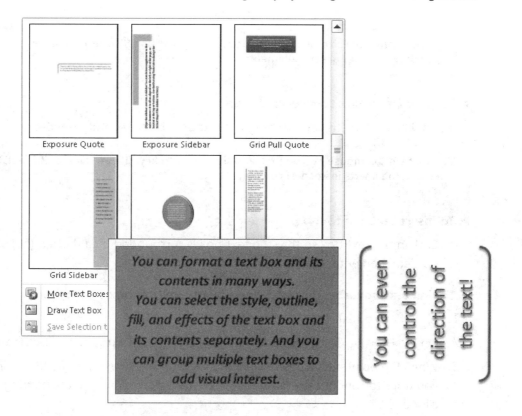

> ➤ **To insert a predefined text box**
>
> → On the **Insert** tab, in the **Text** group, click the **Text Box** button, and then click **Draw Text Box**.
>
> *Or*
>
> **1.** On the **Insert** tab, in the **Text** group, click the **Quick Parts** button, and then click **Building Blocks Organizer**.
>
> **2.** In the **Building Blocks Organizer** dialog box, click any building block that is a member of the **Text Boxes** gallery, and then click **Insert**.

➤ **To insert a custom text box**

→ On the **Insert** tab, in the **Text** group, click the **Text Box** button, and click **Draw Text Box**. Then do one of the following:

  o Click anywhere on the page to insert a dynamic text box that resizes as you enter text.

  o Drag anywhere on the page to draw a text box of a fixed size.

> **Tip** You change the size, shape, and location of a text box by using the same techniques as you do with other graphic elements.

➤ **To copy a text box to a new location**

→ Hold down the Ctrl key and drag the text box to the second location.

> **Tip** Release the mouse button first, and then the Ctrl key. (If you release Ctrl first, Word will move the image instead of copying it.)

➤ **To insert text in a text box**

→ Click in the text box so that the text box is surrounded by a dashed (not solid) border. Then enter text as you would in a document.

➤ **To link text boxes so that text flows from one text box to another**

1. Click the first text box.

2. On the Drawing Tools **Format** contextual tab, in the **Text** group, click **Create Link**.

3. When the pointer changes to a pitcher shape, point to an empty text box in which you want to continue the text, and when the pointer changes to a pouring pitcher, click once.

➤ **To change the direction of text in a selected text box**

→ On the **Format** contextual tab, in the **Text** group, click the **Text Direction** button, and then click the direction you want.

➤ **To format a text box**

1. Click the text box frame so that the text box is surrounded by a solid (not dashed) border.

2. On the **Format** contextual tab, do any of the following:
   ○ In the **Shape Styles** gallery, click the built-in style you want to apply.
   ○ In the **Shape Styles** group, in the **Shape Fill**, **Shape Outline**, and **Shape Effects** galleries, click the settings you want.

➤ **To change the default formatting for text boxes**

→ Select a formatted text box, right-click its border, and then click **Set as Default Text Box**.

➤ **To save a selected text box as a building block**

1. On the **Insert** tab, in the **Text** group, click the **Text Box** button, and then click **Save Selection to Text Box Gallery**.

2. In the **Create New Building Block** dialog box, enter a name and description, select or create a category, and then click **OK**.

Tip When you exit Word after saving a custom building block, you'll be asked whether you want to save changes to the template in which you stored the building block. If you want the building block to be available for future documents, click Save; otherwise, click Don't Save.

Practice Tasks

The practice file for these tasks is located in the Word\Objective4 practice file folder. If you want to save the results of the tasks, save them in the same folder with *My* appended to the file name so that you don't overwrite the original practice file.

- In the *TextBoxes* document, insert a Simple Text Box. Then cut and paste the paragraph of the document into the text box.

- Continuing in the *TextBoxes* document, decrease the size of the text box to 1.5 inches high by 2.5 inches wide, and then draw another text box of the same size below the first one. Link the two text boxes so that the overflow text from the first box is displayed in the second text box.

- Continuing in the *TextBoxes* document, color the first text box Light Blue with a Blue border and the second text box Light Green with a Green border. Then apply an Offset Diagonal Top Right shadow to both boxes.

Objective Review

Before finishing this chapter, ensure that you have mastered the following skills:

4.1 Insert and Format Pictures in a Document

4.2 Insert and Format Shapes, WordArt, and SmartArt

4.3 Insert and Format Clip Art

4.4 Apply and Manipulate Text Boxes

5 Proofreading Documents

The skills tested in this section of the Microsoft Office Specialist exam for Microsoft Word 2010 relate to reviewing and validating document content and working with AutoCorrect settings. Specifically, the following objectives are associated with this set of skills:

5.1 Validate Content by Using Spelling and Grammar Checking Options
5.2 Configure AutoCorrect Settings
5.3 Insert and Modify Comments in a Document

In the days of handwritten and typewritten documents, people might have tolerated a typographical or grammatical error or two because correcting such errors without creating a mess was difficult. Word-processing programs such as Word have built-in spelling and grammar checkers, so now documents that contain these types of errors are likely to reflect badly on their creators. Word provides three tools to help you with the chore of eliminating spelling and grammar errors: visual error indicators, the spelling and grammar checker, and the AutoCorrect feature.

When reviewing the content of a document, it can be useful to insert information in comments, either for your own reference or to initiate discussion with someone else.

This chapter guides you in studying ways of checking the spelling and grammatical accuracy of document content, configuring Word to automatically correct frequently misspelled words, and inserting and viewing comments in documents.

> **Practice Files** Before you can complete the practice tasks in this chapter, you need to copy the book's practice files to your computer. The practice files you'll use to complete the tasks in this chapter are in the Word\Objective5 practice file folder. A complete list of practice files is provided in "Using the Book's Companion Content" at the beginning of this book.

5.1   Validate Content by Using Spelling and Grammar Checking Options

Word automatically indicates suspected spelling and grammar errors by using colored error indicators. Red wavy underlines indicate potential spelling errors and green wavy underlines indicate potential grammar errors. You can correct the indicated error by choosing a replacement word or phrase from the built-in dictionary, or you can instruct Word to ignore this instance or all instances of the underlined word or phrase.

As you know, operating an import business in the global arena requires careful consideration of current economic and environmental conditions, as well as of political issues that could affect our ability to maintain a viable business. When we select our product sorces, we strive to not only to improve the local economy but to to ensure the preservation of fr[...] complex balancing act, but we are commited to maximizing our positive [...] no negative impacts.

sources
sores
scores
forces
source's
Ignore
Ignore All
Add to Dictionary
AutoCorrect ▸
Language ▸
Spelling...
Look Up ▸

An exciting and challenging venture, and we would like to invite you to [...] to discuss any information you might need with Sidney Higa, one of our [...] may contact Sidney through our main number at (925) 555-0167, through[...] sidney@wideworldimporters.com, or by regular mail at our corporate ad[...]

In the meantime, here is a packet of informational material that includes [...] suppliers, a travel manual used by our purchasing agents in the field, and [...] which outlines our commitment to supporting grass-root businesses such [...]

> **Tip** You might also see blue wavy underlines, which indicate words that are correctly spelled but that might be incorrectly used in a particular context.

With the spelling and grammar checker, you can check the spelling or grammar of selected content or an entire document. From the Spelling And Grammar dialog box, you can review and correct any issues that don't match the built-in spelling and grammar rules.

As you know, operating an import business in the global arena requires careful consideration of current economic and environmental conditions, as well as of political issues that could affect our ability to maintain a viable business. When we select our product sorces, we strive to not only to improve the local economy but to to ensure the preservation of fragile ecologies. It is a complex balancing

no negative impacts

An exciting and cha

to discuss any inforr

may contact Sidney

sidney@wideworldi

In the meantime, he

suppliers, a travel n

which outlines our

Spelling and Grammar: English (U.S.)

Repeated Word:

> When we select our product sorces, we strive to not only to improve the local economy but to **to** ensure the preservation of fragile ecologies.

Suggestions:

☑ Check grammar

- Ignore Once
- Ignore All
- Add to Dictionary
- Delete
- Delete All
- AutoCorrect

Options...   Undo   Close

The buttons available in the Spelling And Grammar dialog box vary based on the type of issue being addressed, as follows:

- If the spelling and grammar checker flags a suspected misspelling, it suggests corrections.
- If the tool flags a suspected breach of grammar rules, it tells you which rule you have broken and suggests corrections.

Options on the Proofing page of the Word Options dialog box control the dictionaries used by Word when checking the spelling and grammar of message content, as well as the language in which button labels, tab names, Help content, and ScreenTips are displayed.

➤ To replace an underlined word or phrase with a suggested correction

→ Right-click the underlined word or phrase and then, at the top of the context menu, click the replacement word or phrase.

➤ To remove an error indicator without making changes

→ Right-click the underlined word or phrase, and then click **Ignore**.

➤ **To check spelling and grammar in a document**

1. On the **Review** tab, in the **Proofing** group, click the **Spelling & Grammar** button.

2. In the **Spelling and Grammar** dialog box, for each error that is flagged, do one of the following:

   ○ Click **Ignore Once** to move to the next error without making a change.

   ○ Click **Ignore All** to move to the next error and instruct Word to not flag any further instances of the selected word or phrase as an error.

   ○ Click **Add to Dictionary** to add the selected word or phrase to the dictionary that is currently in use.

   ○ Click a suggested correction in the **Suggestions** box, and then click **Change** to implement the change for the currently selected word or phrase.

   ○ Click a suggested correction in the **Suggestions** box and then click **Change All** to implement the change for all instances of the currently selected word or phrase in the document.

   ○ Click **Delete** to delete the currently selected word or phrase.

   ○ Click **Delete All** to delete all instances of the currently selected word or phrase in the document.

➤ **To hide spelling or grammar errors in a document**

1. In the **Spelling and Grammar** dialog box, click **Options**.

   Or

   In the left pane of the **Word Options** dialog box, click **Proofing**.

2. In the **Exceptions for** section of the **Proofing** page, do any of the following:

   ○ To hide all wavy red underlines, select the **Hide spelling errors in this document only** check box.

   ○ To hide all wavy green underlines, select the **Hide grammar errors in this document only** check box.

➤ **To customize the spelling and grammar-checking settings**

1. In the **Spelling and Grammar** dialog box, click **Options**.

Or

In the left pane of the **Word Options** dialog box, click **Proofing**.

2. In the **When correcting spelling in Microsoft Office programs** section of the **Proofing** page, select the spelling correction options and dictionaries you want to use in all Office programs, including Word.

3. In the **When correcting spelling and grammar in Word** section of the **Proofing** page, select the spelling-checking and grammar-checking options you want to use in Word. (You can select different options in other Office programs.)

Practice Tasks

The practice file for these tasks is located in the Word\Objective5 practice file folder. If you want to save the results of the tasks, save them in the same folder with *My* appended to the file name so that you don't overwrite the original practice file.

- In the first paragraph of the *Letter* document, correct the spelling of the word *sorces* by selecting the correct spelling from the context menu.

- Check the spelling and grammar of the *Letter* document, and do the following from within the Spelling And Grammar dialog box:

  ○ Correct the duplicate instances of the word *to* in the first paragraph.

  ○ Add the company name *Contoso* to the dictionary so that Word doesn't flag future instances of it as a spelling error.

5.2 Configure AutoCorrect Settings

The AutoCorrect feature corrects commonly misspelled words, such as *adn* to *and*, so that you don't have to correct them yourself. AutoCorrect includes a long list of frequently misspelled words and their correct spellings. In addition to correcting spelling errors, the AutoCorrect feature corrects common capitalization issues.

If you frequently misspell a word that AutoCorrect doesn't change, you can add it to the list in the AutoCorrect dialog box. If AutoCorrect frequently changes a word or letter combination that you want it to leave as it is, you can create an exception to the AutoCorrect rules for that specific word or letter combination.

AutoCorrect Exceptions

First Letter | INitial CAps | Other Corrections

Don't correct:

appt
desktopA
joanlamb
mgmt
microsoft

Add

Delete

☑ Automatically add words to list

OK | Cancel

> **Strategy** Be familiar with the different types of AutoCorrect exceptions you can create.

➤ To add a misspelling to the AutoCorrect list

1. Select the misspelled word and then, on the **Proofing** page of the **Word Options** dialog box, click **AutoCorrect Options**.

   Or

   Right-click the misspelled word, point to **AutoCorrect**, and then click **AutoCorrect Options**.

2. On the **AutoCorrect** page of the **AutoCorrect** dialog box, enter the correct spelling in the **With** box. Click **Add**, and then click **OK**.

   Or

1. On the **Proofing** page of the **Word Options** dialog box, click **AutoCorrect Options**.

2. On the **AutoCorrect** page of the **AutoCorrect** dialog box, enter the misspelling in the **Replace** box and the correct spelling in the **With** box. Click **Add**, and then click **OK**.

➤ To modify the default automatic correction options

1. On the **Proofing** page of the **Word Options** dialog box, click **AutoCorrect Options**.

2. On the **AutoCorrect** page of the **AutoCorrect** dialog box, clear the check box of anything you don't want Word to automatically correct. Then click **OK**.

➤ To reverse an automatic correction

→ Click the **Undo** button.

→ Press Ctrl+Z.

➤ **To create an exception to the AutoCorrect settings**

1. On the **Proofing** page of the **Word Options** dialog box, click **AutoCorrect Options**.

2. On the **AutoCorrect** page of the **AutoCorrect** dialog box, click **Exceptions**.

3. In the **AutoCorrect Exceptions** dialog box, enter the text you do not want the AutoCorrect feature to change on the appropriate page, click **Add**, and then click **OK**.

➤ **To remove an AutoCorrect exception**

1. On the **Proofing** page of the **Word Options** dialog box, click **AutoCorrect Options**.

2. On the **AutoCorrect** page of the **AutoCorrect** dialog box, click **Exceptions**.

3. In the **AutoCorrect Exceptions** dialog box, click the exception you want to remove, click **Delete**, and then click **OK**.

Practice Tasks

The practice file for these tasks is located in the Word\Objective5 practice file folder. If you want to save the results of the tasks, save them in the same folder with *My* appended to the file name so that you don't overwrite the original practice file.

- In the *Letter* document, locate the misspelled word *commited*. From the context menu, add the misspelled word to the AutoCorrect list so that Word automatically corrects future instances to *committed*.

- Modify the AutoCorrect options so that Word automatically corrects the misspelled word *avalable* to *available*. Test the AutoCorrect modification by entering the following text at the end of the second paragraph:

  Sidney will not be avalable May 10-14.

5.3 Insert and Modify Comments in a Document

You can insert comments within a document to ask questions, make suggestions, or explain changes. Depending on the document view, comments are shown in balloons, in the Reviewing Pane, or inline.

When shown in balloons, each comment is associated with specific text that is highlighted in the document in the same color as the balloon and is preceded in the balloon by the initials of the person who created the comment and a sequential number.

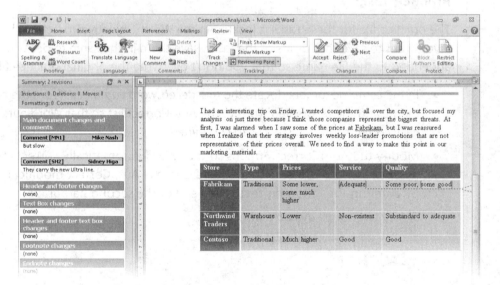

When shown in the Reviewing Pane, each comment header displays the comment number and the name of the person who entered the comment.

You can add information within an existing comment or respond to a comment with a secondary response comment. Response comments are indicated by the letter *R* followed by the response number in the comment header.

> **Strategy** Practice displaying only specific types of review markup.

➤ **To insert a comment about selected text**

1. On the **Review** tab, in the **Comments** group, click the **New Comment** button.

2. In the comment balloon, enter the comment.

➤ **To hide or display comments**

➡ On the **Review** tab, in the **Tracking** group, click the **Show Markup** button, and then click **Comments**.

➤ **To display comments in the margin**

➡ Turn on the display of comments. On the **Review** tab, in the **Tracking** group, click the **Show Markup** button, point to **Balloons**, and then click **Show Revisions in Balloons** or **Show Only Comments and Formatting in Balloons**.

➤ **To display comments in the Reviewing Pane**

➡ Turn on the display of comments. On the **Review** tab, in the **Tracking** group, click the **Reviewing Pane** arrow, and then click **Reviewing Pane Vertical** or **Reviewing Pane Horizontal**.

> **Tip** To change the size of the Reviewing Pane, point to its border and then, when the pointer changes to a double-headed arrow, drag the border.

➤ **To display comments in ScreenTips**

➡ Turn on the display of comments. On the **Review** tab, in the **Tracking** group, click the **Show Markup** button, point to **Balloons**, and then click **Show All Revisions Inline**.

➤ **To display comments from a specific reviewer**

1. On the **Review** tab, in the **Tracking** group, click the **Show Markup** button, and then point to **Reviewers**.

2. Click to place a check mark next to each reviewer whose comments you want to display, and click to clear the check mark next to each reviewer whose comments you want to hide.

➤ **To move between comments**

➡ On the **Review** tab, in the **Comments** group, click the **Previous** button or the **Next** button.

➤ **To edit a comment**

1. Display comments either in the Reviewing Pane or in balloons.

2. Click the comment, and then change the text by using normal editing techniques.

➤ **To respond to a comment**

1. Display comments either in the Reviewing Pane or in balloons.

2. Click the comment. Then on the **Review** tab, in the **Comments** group, click the **New Comment** button.

3. Enter your comment response.

➤ **To delete a comment**

1. Display comments either in the Reviewing Pane or in balloons.

2. Click the comment. Then on the **Review** tab, in the **Comments** group, click the **Delete** button.

   Or

   Right-click the comment, and then click **Delete Comment**.

Practice Tasks

The practice file for these tasks is located in the Word\Objective5 practice file folder. If you want to save the results of the tasks, save them in the same folder with *My* appended to the file name so that you don't overwrite the original practice file.

- Open the *Comments* document, and in the fifth column of the table, add the comment *They carry the new Ultra line* to the words *some good*. Then delete the comment associated with the word *competitors* in the first paragraph.

- In the *Comments* document, add *These are special order* in a new paragraph at the end of the second comment. Then respond to the comment associated with *Adequate* with a new comment balloon containing the text *If I were a real customer, I would have left*.

Objective Review

Before finishing this chapter, ensure that you have mastered the following skills:

5.1 Validate Content by Using Spelling and Grammar Checking Options

5.2 Configure AutoCorrect Settings

5.3 Insert and Modify Comments in a Document

6 Applying References and Hyperlinks

The skills tested in this section of the Microsoft Office Specialist exam for Microsoft Word 2010 relate to creating references and hyperlinks within documents. Specifically, the following objectives are associated with this set of skills:

6.1 Apply a Hyperlink
6.2 Create Endnotes and Footnotes
6.3 Create a Table of Contents

You may want to refer the reader of a document to another location in the document, to another document, or to a webpage for further information. You can do this by inserting a hyperlink in the document to the other location. You can also supply additional information to a reader by including footnotes or endnotes in the document. You can provide a master reference to the document content by including a table of contents that links the reader to the headings within the document.

This chapter guides you in studying ways of inserting hyperlinks, ways of inserting endnotes and footnotes, and methods of creating a table of contents.

> **Practice Files** Before you can complete the practice tasks in this chapter, you need to copy the book's practice files to your computer. The practice files you'll use to complete the tasks in this chapter are in the Word\Objective6 practice file folder. A complete list of practice files is provided in "Using the Book's Companion Content" at the beginning of this book.

6.1 Apply a Hyperlink

Inserting Hyperlinks

Like webpages, Word documents can include hyperlinks that provide a quick way to connect to related information, or to perform tasks such as opening another document, downloading a file, displaying a webpage, or sending an email message. You insert a hyperlink from text or a graphic element to a specific target file or location. You can specify whether the target information should be displayed in the same window or frame as the document or in a new window or frame. You can also specify default settings for all hyperlinks.

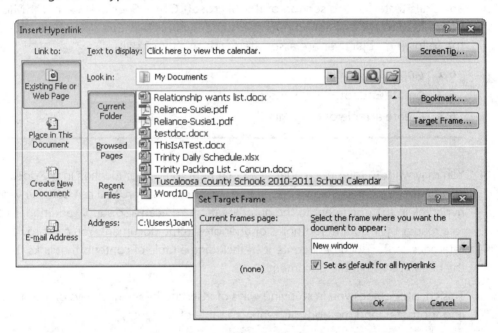

Within the document, hyperlinked text appears underlined and in the color specified for hyperlinks by the document's theme. (Hyperlinked graphics do not have a visual indicator.) You can display the hyperlink target by pointing to the hyperlinked text or graphic. You can jump to the hyperlink target by holding down the Ctrl key and clicking the linked text or graphic. After you click hyperlinked text, it appears in the color specified for followed hyperlinks.

➤ **To insert a hyperlink to a file**

1. Select the text or graphic object to which you want to attach the hyperlink.

> **Tip** You can change the selected text from within the Insert Hyperlink dialog box by changing it in the Text To Display box.

2. On the **Insert** tab, in the **Links** group, click the **Insert Hyperlink** button.

    Or

    Right-click the selection, and then click **Hyperlink**.

3. In the **Insert Hyperlink** dialog box, on the **Link to** bar, click the **Existing File or Web Page** button.

4. In the **Look in** area, browse to the file.

    Or

    In the **Address** box, enter the absolute path to the file.

5. Click **Target Frame**. In the **Set Target Frame** dialog box, specify where the hyperlink target will be displayed, and then click **OK**.

6. In the **Insert Hyperlink** dialog box, click **OK**.

➤ **To insert a hyperlink to a webpage**

1. Select the text or graphic object to which you want to attach the hyperlink, and then open the **Insert Hyperlink** dialog box.

2. On the **Link to** bar, click the **Existing File or Web Page** button.

3. In the **Address** box, enter the URL of the webpage.

4. Click **Target Frame**. In the **Set Target Frame** dialog box, select **New window**, and then click **OK**.

5. In the **Insert Hyperlink** dialog box, click **OK**.

➤ **To insert a hyperlink to a heading or bookmark within the document**

1. Select the text or graphic object to which you want to attach the hyperlink, and then open the **Insert Hyperlink** dialog box.

2. On the **Link to** bar, click the **Place in This Document** button.

3. In the **Select a place in this document** box, click the heading or bookmark.

4. In the **Insert Hyperlink** dialog box, click **OK**.

➤ **To insert a hyperlink that opens an email message form**

1. Select the text or graphic object to which you want to attach the hyperlink, and then open the **Insert Hyperlink** dialog box.

2. On the **Link to** bar, click **E-mail Address**.

3. In the **E-mail address** box, enter the email address to which you want to send the message.

Or

In the **Recently used email addresses** list, click the email address to which you want to send the message.

4. In the **Subject** box, enter the subject of the message.

5. In the **Insert Hyperlink** dialog box, click **OK**.

➤ **To modify a hyperlink**

1. Right-click the hyperlink, and then click **Edit Hyperlink**.

2. In the **Edit Hyperlink** dialog box, make the necessary changes, and then click **OK**.

➤ **To remove a hyperlink**

➜ Right-click the hyperlink, and then click **Remove Hyperlink**.

Inserting Bookmarks

Whether you are creating a document or working in a document created by someone else, you can insert named bookmarks to identify information to which you might want to return later. (Word automatically creates bookmark names for headings down to the fourth level by duplicating the heading and then removing articles, spaces, and punctuation and capitalizing the first letter of each word.) You can move to bookmarked locations within a document either by creating hyperlinks to the bookmarks or by browsing to them.

> **Tip** The automatically created bookmarks appear on the Place In This Document page of the Insert Hyperlink dialog box.

Find and Replace

Find	Replace	Go To

Go to what:

| Page |
| Section |
| Line |
| **Bookmark** |
| Comment |
| Footnote |

Enter bookmark name:

animals

| animals |
| chickens |
| cows |
| fruits |
| horses |
| plants |

Previous   Go To   Close

➤ **To insert a bookmark**

1. Place the cursor at the location in which you want to insert the bookmark.

Or

Select the text or object to which you want to attach the bookmark.

2. On the **Insert** tab, in the **Links** group, click the **Bookmark** button.

3. In the **Bookmark** dialog box, enter a name for the bookmark in the **Bookmark name** box, and then click **Add**.

Tip Bookmark names cannot contain spaces. If you enter a space and then type a character, the Add button becomes inactive. To name bookmarks with multiple words, either run the words together and capitalize each word or replace the spaces with underscores for readability.

➤ **To move to a bookmark**

1. Open the **Bookmark** dialog box, and then click the bookmark you want to move to.

2. Click **Go To**, and then click **Close**.

Or

1. On the **Home** tab, in the **Editing** group, click **Go To** in the **Find** list.

2. On the **Go To** page of the **Find and Replace** dialog box, in the **Go to what** list, click **Bookmark**.

3. In the **Enter bookmark name** list, click the bookmark you want.

4. Click **Go To**, and then click **Close**.

Practice Tasks

The practice files for these tasks are located in the Word\Objective6 practice file folder. If you want to save the results of the tasks, save them in the same folder with *My* appended to the file name so that you don't overwrite the original practice file.

- In the *Hyperlinks* document, create a hyperlink from the logo at the top of the page to the *OtherLogos* document. Then test the hyperlink.

- In the *Hyperlinks* document, create a hyperlink that, when clicked, creates an email message that is addressed to you and has a subject of *MOS Test Message*. Then test the hyperlink.

6.2 Create Endnotes and Footnotes

When you want to provide a reference or comment about a statement in a document—for example, to explain an assumption or cite the source for a different opinion—you can enter the comment as a footnote or as an endnote. Doing so inserts a number or symbol called a *reference mark*, and your associated comment appears with the same number or symbol either as a footnote or as an endnote. Footnotes appear either at the bottom of the page or immediately after the last text on the page. Endnotes appear at the end of the document or document section. In most views, footnotes or endnotes are divided from the main text by a note separator line.

Word applies default styles to the reference marks for footnotes and endnotes. By default, footnote reference marks use arabic numerals (1, 2, 3, and so on), and endnote reference marks use roman numerals (i, ii, iii, and so on). You can change the numbering and reference marks associated with footnotes and endnotes.

```
Footnote and Endnote                    [?] [X]
Location
  ● Footnotes:     Bottom of page          [▼]
  ○ Endnotes:      End of document         [▼]
                              [ Convert... ]

Format
  Number format:   1, 2, 3, ...            [▼]
  Custom mark:     [        ]   [ Symbol... ]
  Start at:        1    [▲▼]
  Numbering:       Continuous              [▼]

Apply changes
  Apply changes to:  Selected text          [▼]

  [   Insert   ]   [   Cancel   ]   [   Apply   ]
```

➤ **To create a footnote or endnote**

1. Place the cursor in the location from which you want to reference the footnote or endnote.

2. On the **References** tab, in the **Footnotes** group, click the **Insert Footnote** button or the **Insert Endnote** button.

3. In the linked area at the bottom of the page or end of the document or section, enter the note text.

➤ **To change the number format of existing footnotes or endnotes**

1. On the **References** tab, click the **Footnotes** dialog box launcher.

2. In the **Footnote and Endnote** dialog box, in the **Location** area, click **Footnotes** or **Endnotes**.

3. In the **Format** area, in the **Number format** list, click the format you want.

4. With **Whole document** shown in the **Apply changes to** box, click **Apply**.

➤ **To change the formatting of footnote or endnote reference marks**

1. In the document text, select the reference mark for any footnote or endnote.

2. On the **Home** tab, in the **Editing** group, click the **Select** button, and then click **Select Text with Similar Formatting**.

3. On the **Home** tab, apply the character formatting you want the reference marks to have.

➤ **To change the location of footnotes or endnotes**

1. On the **References** tab, click the **Footnotes** dialog box launcher.

2. In the **Footnote and Endnote** dialog box, do any of the following, and then click **OK**:

   ○ Click **Footnotes** and then, in the list, click **Bottom of page** or **Below text**.

   ○ Click **Endnotes** and then, in the list, click **End of document** or **End of section**.

➤ **To delete a footnote or endnote**

➜ In the document text, select the reference mark of the footnote or endnote you want to delete, and then press Delete.

Practice Tasks

The practice file for this task is located in the Word\Objective6 practice file folder. If you want to save the results of the tasks, save them in the same folder with *My* appended to the file name so that you don't overwrite the original practice file.

* In the *Footnotes* document, cut the last sentence from the end of the first paragraph to the Microsoft Office Clipboard. Then insert a footnote after the first sentence in the second paragraph, and paste the cut item as the text of the footnote.

6.3 Create a Table of Contents

If you create a long document divided into parts by headings you have designated by applying styles (Heading 1, Heading 2, and so on), you can add a table of contents (TOC) to the beginning of the document to give readers an overview of the document's contents and to help them find specific sections. If the document will be printed, you can indicate with a page number the starting page of each section. If the document will be distributed electronically, you can link each heading and subheading in the table of contents to the section in the document so that readers can jump directly there with a click of the mouse.

Office Procedures

Contents

General Administration *1*

Contact Information 2

Facilities 3

Office 3

Warehouse 3

Phone System 3

Ordering Supplies 5

Business Stationery, Letterheads, Invoices, Packing Slips, Receipts 5

Supplies 5

Shipping *7*

Receiving Packages 8

The Table Of Contents gallery offers three standard table formatting options that use nine levels of built-in TOC styles (TOC 1, TOC 2, and so on). If none of these formats meets your needs, you can choose from several other styles, such as Classic, Fancy, and Simple, in the Table Of Contents dialog box.

Built-In

Automatic Table 1

Contents
Heading 1 ....
    Heading 2 ....
        Heading 3 ....

Automatic Table 2

Table of Contents
Heading 1 ....
    Heading 2 ....
        Heading 3 ....

Manual Table

Table of Contents
Type chapter title (level 1) ....
    Type chapter title (level 2) ....
        Type chapter title (level 3) ....
Type chapter title (level 1) ....

More Table of Contents from Office.com

Insert Table of Contents...

Remove Table of Contents

Save Selection to Table of Contents Gallery...

Table of Contents

Index | Table of Contents | Table of Figures | Table of Authorities

Print Preview

Heading 1 1

Heading 2 3

Heading 3 5

☑ Show page numbers
☑ Right align page numbers
Tab leader: [.......]

Web Preview

Heading 1

Heading 2

Heading 3

☑ Use hyperlinks instead of page numbers

General

Formats: [From template]

Show levels:

From template
Classic
Distinctive
Fancy
Modern
Formal
Simple

Options...   Modify...

OK   Cancel

After you select the style you want, Word identifies the table of contents entries (based on the document heading levels) and creates the table at the cursor as one field. You can edit the text of a table of contents, but it is much easier to have Word update the table for you. You can tell Word to update only the page numbers, or if you have changed, added, or deleted headings, you can have Word update (re-create) the entire table.

> **Tip** You can change the formatting or content within the table, but any individual for-matting changes you make will be lost if you update the table of contents. Therefore it is best to wait until the table of contents is complete before manually formatting any of its content.

> **See Also** For information about applying styles, see section 2.1, "Apply Font and Paragraph Attributes."

➤ To create a standard table of contents

1. Ensure that headings within the document are styled with Heading styles.

2. Position the cursor where you want to insert the table of contents.

3. On the **References** tab, in the **Table of Contents** group, click the **Table of Contents** button.

4. In the **Table of Contents** gallery, click the table of contents style you want.

➤ To create a custom table of contents

1. On the **References** tab, in the **Table of Contents** group, click the **Table of Contents** button, and then click **Insert Table of Contents**.

2. In the **Print Preview** area of the **Table of Contents** dialog box, do any of the following:

   ○ Show or hide the page number of each heading by selecting or clearing the **Show page numbers** check box.

   ○ Display page numbers at the right table margin or immediately following the heading by selecting or clearing the **Right align page numbers** check box.

   ○ Specify the characters that appear between the heading and the page number by clicking the **Tab leader** arrow and then clicking **(none)**, dots (.......), dashes (-----), or underscores (_____).

3. In the **Web Preview** area of the **Table of Contents** dialog box, specify whether page numbers are included in tables of contents created in web documents by selecting or clearing the **Use hyperlinks instead of page numbers** check box.

4. In the **General** area of the **Table of Contents** dialog box, do any of the following:

    ○ In the **Formats** list, select one of the default Word TOC formats.

    ○ In the **Show levels** list, enter or click to select the number of outline levels you want to include in the table of contents.

5. In the **Table of Contents** dialog box, click **OK**.

➤ **To create a table of contents with custom TOC styles**

1. Position the cursor where you want to insert the table of contents.

2. On the **References** tab, in the **Table of Contents** group, click the **Table of Contents** button, and then click **Insert Table of Contents**.

3. In the **Table of Contents** dialog box, click **Modify**.

4. In the **Style** dialog box, select a TOC style you want to modify, and then click **Modify**.

5. In the **Modify Style** dialog box, change the font, paragraph, tabs, border, and other formatting to suit your needs, and then click **OK**.

6. Repeat steps 4 and 5 to make additional style modifications. When you finish, click **OK** in the **Style** dialog box.

7. In the **Table of Contents** dialog box, click **OK**.

➤ **To update a table of contents**

1. Right-click the table of contents, and then click **Update Field**.

2. In the **Update Table of Contents** dialog box, click **Update page numbers only** or **Update entire table**, and then click **OK**.

    Or

1. Position the cursor in the table of contents.

2. On the **References** tab, in the **Table of Contents** group, click the **Update Table** button.

3. In the **Update Table Of Contents** dialog box, click **Update page numbers only** or **Update entire table**, and then click **OK**.

Practice Tasks

The practice file for these tasks is located in the Word\Objective6 practice file folder. If you want to save the results of the tasks, save them in the same folder with *My* appended to the file name so that you don't overwrite the original practice file.

- At the beginning of the *Contents* document, create a table of contents based on heading styles that uses the Classic format and dotted line page-number leaders.

- Insert manual page breaks within the *Contents* document, and then update the entire table of contents to reflect your changes.

Objective Review

Before finishing this chapter, ensure that you have mastered the following skills:

6.1   Apply a Hyperlink

6.2   Create Endnotes and Footnotes

6.3   Create a Table of Contents

7 Performing Mail Merge Operations

The skills tested in this section of the Microsoft Office Specialist exam for Microsoft Word 2010 relate to merging data into documents. Specifically, the following objectives are associated with this set of skills:

7.1 Set Up Mail Merge
7.2 Execute Mail Merge

Many businesses and other organizations communicate with their customers or members by means of letters, newsletters, and promotional pieces that are sent to everyone on a mailing list. The easiest way to generate a set of documents that are identical except for certain information—such as the name and address of the recipient—is to use the mail merge process. You can use the mail merge process to easily produce a set of personalized documents and mailing labels.

This chapter guides you in studying the steps required to create form letters, email messages, envelopes, labels, catalogs, and directories that contain variable information. You study how to set up source documents, set up mail merge documents manually or by using the Mail Merge wizard, check mail merge documents for errors, preview mail merge operations, and produce merged documents in various final delivery formats.

> **Practice Files** Before you can complete the practice tasks in this chapter, you need to copy the book's practice files to your computer. The practice files you'll use to complete the tasks in this chapter are in the Word\Objective7 practice file folder. A complete list of practice files is provided in "Using the Book's Companion Content" at the beginning of this book.

7.1 Set Up Mail Merge

Preparing Source Documents

The mail merge process combines static information stored in one document (the main document) with variable information stored in another document (the data source). The main document contains the static text that will appear in all the merged documents. It also contains placeholders—called *merge fields*—that tell Word where to insert the variable information. The data source contains the variable information. You can prepare either source document first, but because you must insert the correct merge field names into the main document, it can be useful to prepare the data source first.

Preparing a Data Source

A valid data source is a structured document, such as a Word table, Microsoft Excel worksheet, Microsoft Access database table, or Microsoft Outlook contact list, that contains sets of information—called *records*—in a predictable format.

A typical data source file consists of a matrix of rows and columns. Each row contains one record, such as the complete name and address of a customer, and each column contains a particular type of information—called a *field*—such as the first name of all the customers. In the first row of the data source, each field is identified by its column header—called a *field name*.

	A	B	C	D	E	F
1	FirstName	LastName	Address1	City	State	PostalCode
2	Charlie	Keen	991 S. Mississippi Rd.	St. Louis	MO	89203
3	Raman	Sarin	8808 Backbay St.	Boston	MA	88337
4	Jed	Brown	666 Fords Landing	Westover	WV	66954
5	George	Schaller	401 Rodeo Dr.	Auburn	WA	34923
6	Patrick	Sands	4568 Spaulding Ave. N.	Seattle	WA	12345
7	Andreas	Schou	14 S. Elm Dr.	Moscow	ID	02912
8	Bob	Kelly	12 Juanita Ln.	Helena	MT	42665
9	Jim	Kim	78 Miller St.	Seattle	WA	81233
10	Eli	Bowen	27 Christopher St.	Seattle	WA	67645
11	Colleen	Bracy	18 Elm St.	Tulalip	WA	77483

Row 1 (Field names) — Rows 2–11 (Record)

> **Tip** Because field names are also used as the merge fields in the main document, they cannot contain spaces. To make the field names readable with no spaces, capitalize each word, as in *PostalCode*, or replace the spaces with underscores, as in *Last_Name*.

You can select recipients by entering them into a new recipient list, by referencing an existing data source, or by importing an Outlook contact list. When you import an Outlook contact list, all the contacts contained therein are automatically selected as recipients.

➤ To create a recipient list by entering information

1. On the **Mailings** tab, in the **Start Mail Merge** group, click the **Select Recipients** button, and then click **Type New List**.

2. In the **New Address List** dialog box, enter the first recipient's information.

3. For each additional recipient, click **New Entry** (or press Tab) and then enter the recipient's information.

4. When the recipient list is complete, click **OK**.

5. In the **Save Address List** dialog box displaying the contents of your My Data Sources folder, enter a name for the recipient list file, and then click **Save**.

➤ To select recipients from an existing file

1. On the **Mailings** tab, in the **Start Mail Merge** group, click the **Select Recipients** button, and then click **Use Existing List**.

2. In the **Select Data Source** dialog box, browse to and select the file containing the recipient list. Then click **Open**.

> ➤ **To select recipients from an Outlook contact list**

1. Start Outlook and, if necessary, provide the credentials for your email account.

2. In Word, on the **Mailings** tab, in the **Start Mail Merge** group, click the **Select Recipients** button, and then click **Select from Outlook Contacts**.

3. In the **Select Contacts** dialog box, click the contact list you want to reference, and then click **OK**.

4. To use only a subset of the contacts in the contact list, do one of the following in the **Mail Merge Recipients** dialog box:

   - Clear the check box located between *Data Source* and *Last* in the list header to clear all the selection check boxes. Then select only the recipients you want.

   - Clear the selection check boxes of individual recipients.

Preparing a Main Document

You can create a Word document and then use it as the main document for a mail merge process, or you can create a document specifically for the mail merge process. Either way, you insert merge fields into the document in the location in which you want to insert variable information from the data source.

Merge fields

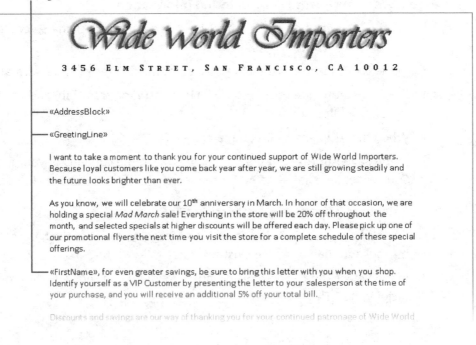

«AddressBlock»

«GreetingLine»

I want to take a moment to thank you for your continued support of Wide World Importers. Because loyal customers like you come back year after year, we are still growing steadily and the future looks brighter than ever.

As you know, we will celebrate our 10th anniversary in March. In honor of that occasion, we are holding a special *Mad March* sale! Everything in the store will be 20% off throughout the month, and selected specials at higher discounts will be offered each day. Please pick up one of our promotional flyers the next time you visit the store for a complete schedule of these special offerings.

«FirstName», for even greater savings, be sure to bring this letter with you when you shop. Identify yourself as a VIP Customer by presenting the letter to your salesperson at the time of your purchase, and you will receive an additional 5% off your total bill.

Discounts and savings are our way of thanking you for your continued patronage of Wide World

You can insert specific named merge fields or you can insert an address block or greeting line (salutation) that you tailor to suit your needs.

> ➤ **To insert a single merge field**
>
> → On the **Mailings** tab, in the **Write & Insert Fields** group, click the **Insert Merge Field** arrow and then, in the list, click the merge field you want to insert.

> ➤ **To insert multiple merge fields**
>
> **1.** On the **Mailings** tab, in the **Write & Insert Fields** group, click the **Insert Merge Field** button.
>
> **2.** In the **Insert Merge Field** dialog box, for each field you want to insert, click the field and then click **Insert**. After you insert the fields you want, click **Close**.

> ➤ **To insert an address block**
>
> **1.** On the **Mailings** tab, in the **Write & Insert Fields** group, click the **Address Block** button.
>
> **2.** In the **Insert Address Block** dialog box, specify the address elements you want to include, and preview the results. Then click **OK**.

> **To insert a greeting line**

1. On the **Mailings** tab, in the **Write & Insert Fields** group, click the **Greeting Line** button.

2. In the **Insert Greeting Line** dialog box, select the format of the salutation you want to use for recipients whose records include the salutation's required elements, and select the generic salutation you want to use for other recipients. Then click **OK**.

Merging Source Documents

You can merge a main document with a data source manually or by using the Mail Merge wizard.

Setting Up a Manual Mail Merge

> **Strategy** Be familiar with the different types of mail merge documents you can create.

The first step in the manual mail merge process is to specify the type of merge documents you want to create: letters, email messages, envelopes, labels, or a directory. You then select or create a data source and identify the records in the data source that you want to include in the mail merge operation. You create your main document and insert merge fields from the data source into it. You preview the results and check for errors, and then you merge the documents.

You perform all of these steps by using the commands available on the Mailings tab of the ribbon.

> **See Also** For information about selecting data sources, creating data sources, and in-serting fields, see the "Preparing Source Documents" topic earlier in this section. For information about previewing and completing mail merge operations, see section 7.2, "Execute Mail Merge."

> **To set up a manual mail merge for letters**

1. Open a new blank document.

2. On the **Mailings** tab, in the **Start Mail Merge** group, click the **Start Mail Merge** button, and then click **Letters**.

3. On the **Mailings** tab, in the **Start Mail Merge** group, click the **Select Recipients** button, and click the type of data source you will use. Then select or create the data source, and refine the recipient list as appropriate.

4. In the document, enter the static text that you want to appear in all letters.

5. Position the insertion point in a location where you want to insert variable information from the data source, and then use the commands in the **Write & Insert Fields** group on the **Mailings** tab to insert the fields you want.

➤ **To set up a manual mail merge for email messages**

1. Open a new blank document.

2. On the **Mailings** tab, in the **Start Mail Merge** group, click the **Start Mail Merge** button, and then click **E-mail Messages**.

3. On the **Mailings** tab, in the **Start Mail Merge** group, click the **Select Recipients** button, and click the type of data source you will use. Then select or create the data source, and refine the recipient list as appropriate.

4. In the Word document, enter the content of the email message and merge fields for any variable information from the data source that you want to include.

➤ **To perform a manual mail merge for an envelope based on an address in a document**

1. In the document, select only the lines of the address. (Do not select any blank lines above or below the address.)

2. On the **Mailings** tab, in the **Create** group, click the **Envelopes** button.

3. In the **Envelopes and Labels** dialog box, do the following if necessary:

- ○ Edit the address in the **Delivery address** box.

- ○ Enter a return address in the **Return address** box.

> **Tip** You can have Word supply the return address. Display the Advanced page of the Word Options dialog box. Toward the bottom of the page, under General, enter the return address in the Mailing Address box, and click OK. The address then appears by default as the return address in the Envelopes And Labels dialog box. If you want to use envelopes with a preprinted return address, you must select the Omit check box to avoid duplication.

- ○ Click **Options**, select the envelope size, the feed method (horizontally or vertically and face up or face down), and the font and font size of both the address and the return address.

4. In the **Envelopes and Labels** dialog box, do one of the following:

   ○ To print the envelope, insert an envelope in the printer according to the selected feed method, and then click **Print**.

   ○ To have Word insert the address in the format required for an envelope on a separate page at the beginning of the current document, click **Add to Document**.

➤ **To set up a manual mail merge for multiple envelopes**

1. Open a new blank document, and display paragraph marks.

2. On the **Mailings** tab, in the **Start Mail Merge** group, click the **Start Mail Merge** button, and then click **Envelopes**.

3. In the **Envelope Options** dialog box, do the following, and then click **OK**:

   ○ On the **Envelope Options** page, choose the envelope size and specify the font and location for the delivery address and the return address.

   ○ On the **Printing Options** page, verify that the selected printer is the one you want to use, specify the way you will insert the envelopes into the printer, and choose the feed location. (For envelopes, this is usually *manual paper feed*.)

4. On the **Mailings** tab, in the **Start Mail Merge** group, click the **Select Recipients** button, and click the type of data source you will use. Then select or create the data source, and refine the recipient list as appropriate.

5. In the document formatted by Word to match your selections, position the cursor at the upper-left paragraph mark and then enter the return address as you want it to appear on all envelopes.

6. Position the insertion point at the centered paragraph mark. On the **Mailings** tab, in the **Write & Insert Fields** group, click the **Address Block** button.

7. In the **Insert Address Block** dialog box, specify the address elements you want to include, and preview the results. Then click **OK**.

➤ **To set up a manual mail merge for labels**

1. Select labels of an appropriate size for your purpose. Note the brand name and product number.

2. Open a new blank document, and display paragraph marks.

3. On the **Mailings** tab, in the **Start Mail Merge** group, click the **Select Recipients** button, and click the type of data source you will use. Then select or create the data source, and refine the recipient list as appropriate.

4. On the **Mailings** tab, in the **Start Mail Merge** group, click the **Start Mail Merge** button, and then click **Labels**.

5. In the **Label Options** dialog box, do the following, and then click **OK**:

   ○ In the **Printer information** area, click the type of printer you intend to use. If you choose **Page printers**, select the printer tray.

   ○ In the **Label information** area, click the label brand in the **Label vendors** list, and then click the product number in the **Product number** list.

   Or

   To set up the mail merge for custom labels, click **New Label**. In the **Label Details** dialog box, enter a name, margin dimensions, page size, and the number of labels across and down each sheet. Then click **OK**.

6. In the document formatted by Word to match your selections, position the cursor in the first cell. On the **Mailings** tab, in the **Write & Insert Fields** group, click the **Address Block** button.

7. In the **Insert Address Block** dialog box, specify the address elements you want to include, and preview the results. Then click **OK**.

➤ **To set up a manual mail merge for a catalog or directory**

1. Open a new blank document, and display paragraph marks.

2. On the **Mailings** tab, in the **Start Mail Merge** group, click the **Start Mail Merge** button, and then click **Directory**.

3. On the **Mailings** tab, in the **Start Mail Merge** group, click the **Select Recipients** button, and click the type of data source you will use. Then select or create the data source, and refine the recipient list as appropriate.

4. In the Word document, enter the merge fields you want to include in the catalog or directory, and then press Enter. Ensure that a blank paragraph mark ends the main document.

Setting Up a Mail Merge by Using the Mail Merge Wizard

The Mail Merge wizard guides you through the process of merging a main document and a data source.

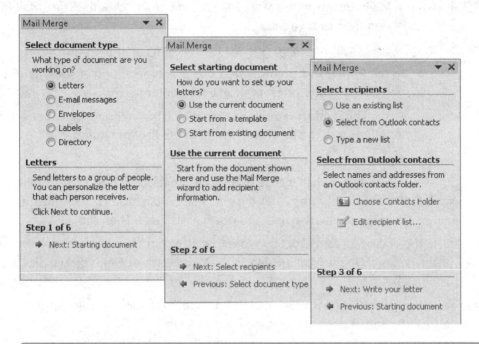

> **See Also** For information about selecting data sources, creating data sources, and inserting fields, see the "Preparing Source Documents" topic earlier in this section. For information about previewing and completing mail merge operations, see section 7.2, "Execute Mail Merge."

➤ **To set up mail merge for letters by using the Mail Merge wizard**

1. Create a document containing the text of the letter.

2. On the **Mailings** tab, in the **Start Mail Merge** group, click the **Start Mail Merge** button, and then click **Step by Step Mail Merge Wizard**.

3. In the **Mail Merge** task pane, with the **Letters** option selected, at the bottom of the pane, click **Next: Starting document**.

4. With the **Use the current document** option selected, click **Next: Select recipients**.

5. With the **Using an existing list** option selected, click **Browse**. Then in the **Select Data Source** dialog box, identify the data source, and click **Open**.

6. If necessary, in the **Select Table** dialog box, click the table you want to use as your data source, and then click **OK**.

7. In the **Mail Merge Recipients** dialog box, sort or filter the records as necessary, and then click **OK**.

8. At the bottom of the **Mail Merge** task pane, click **Next: Write your letter**, and then insert the required merge fields in the main document, either by clicking items in the task pane or by clicking buttons in the **Write & Insert Fields** group on the **Mailings** tab.

> **Tip** Clicking Address Block or Greeting Line opens a dialog box in which you can refine the fields' settings, whereas clicking individual fields from the Insert Merge Field list inserts them with their default settings.

➤ **To set up mail merge for email messages by using the Mail Merge wizard**

1. Create a document containing the text of the email message.

2. On the **Mailings** tab, in the **Start Mail Merge** group, click the **Start Mail Merge** button, and then click **Step by Step Mail Merge Wizard**.

3. In the **Mail Merge** task pane, click **E-mail messages**, and then click **Next: Starting document**.

4. With the **Use the current document** option selected, click **Next: Select recipients**.

5. Click **Select from Outlook contacts**, and then click **Choose Contacts Folder**. If the **Choose Profile** dialog box opens, select the Outlook profile from which you want to choose your recipients, and then click **OK**. Then in the **Select Contacts** dialog box, identify the data source, and click **OK**.

6. In the **Mail Merge Recipients** dialog box, sort or filter the records as necessary, and then click **OK**.

7. In the **Mail Merge** task pane, click **Next: Write your e-mail message**, and insert the necessary merge fields.

8. Preview the merged email messages, and then click **Next: Complete the merge**.

9. Click **Electronic Mail**, and in the **Merge to E-mail** dialog box, do the following:

  ○ Verify that **Email_Address** is selected in the **To** box.

  ○ Enter a message subject in the **Subject line** box.

  ○ Select the message format you want in the **Mail format** box.

10. With the **All** option selected in the **Send records** area, click **OK**.

➤ **To set up mail merge for envelopes by using the Mail Merge wizard**

1. Open a new blank document, and display paragraph marks.

2. On the **Mailings** tab, in the **Start Mail Merge** group, click the **Start Mail Merge** button, and then click **Step by Step Mail Merge Wizard**.

3. On the **Select document type** page of the **Mail Merge** task pane, click **Envelopes**, and then click **Next: Starting document**.

4. With **Change document layout** selected on the **Starting document** page, click **Envelope options**.

5. In the **Envelope Options** dialog box, do the following, and then click **OK**:

   ○ On the **Envelope Options** page, choose the envelope size, and specify the font and location for the delivery address and the return address.

   ○ On the **Printing Options** page, verify that the default printer shown is the one you want to use, specify the way you will insert the envelopes into the printer, and choose the feed location. (For envelopes, this is usually manual feed.)

6. At the bottom of the **Mail Merge** task pane, click **Next: Select recipients**.

7. On the **Select recipients** page, click the type of data source you will use. Then select or create the data source, and refine the recipient list as appropriate.

8. At the bottom of the **Mail Merge** task pane, click **Next: Arrange your envelope**.

9. In the document formatted by Word to match your selections, position the cursor at the upper-left paragraph mark, and then enter the return address as you want it to appear on all envelopes.

10. Position the cursor at the centered paragraph mark. On the **Arrange your envelope** page of the **Mail Merge** task pane, click **Address Block**.

11. In the **Insert Address Block** dialog box, specify the address elements you want to include, and preview the results. Then click **OK**.

➤ **To set up mail merge for labels by using the Mail Merge wizard**

1. Open a new blank document.

2. On the **Mailings** tab, in the **Start Mail Merge** group, click the **Start Mail Merge** button, and then click **Step by Step Mail Merge Wizard**.

3. On the **Select document type** page of the **Mail Merge** task pane, click **Labels**, and then click **Next: Starting document**.

4. With **Change document layout** selected on the **Starting document** page, click **Label options**.

5. In the **Label Options** dialog box, do the following, and then click **OK**:

   ○ In the **Printer information** area, click the type of printer you intend to use. If you choose **Page printers**, select the printer tray.

   ○ In the **Label information** area, click the label brand in the **Label vendors** list, and then click the product number in the **Product number** list.

   Or

   To set up the mail merge for custom labels, click **New Label**. In the **Label Details** dialog box, enter a name, margin dimensions, page size, and the number of labels across and down each sheet. Then click **OK**.

6. At the bottom of the **Mail Merge** task pane, click **Next: Select recipients**.

7. On the **Select recipients** page, click the type of data source you will use. Then select or create the data source, and refine the recipient list as appropriate.

8. At the bottom of the **Mail Merge** task pane, click **Next: Arrange your labels**, and then ensure that you can see the left edge of the main document.

9. With the cursor positioned in the first cell, click **Address block** on the **Arrange your labels** page.

10. In the **Insert Address Block** dialog box, click **OK** to accept the default settings.

11. In the **Mail Merge** task pane, click **Update all labels**.

➤ **To set up mail merge for a catalog or directory by using the Mail Merge wizard**

1. Open a new blank document, and display paragraph marks.

2. On the **Mailings** tab, in the **Start Mail Merge** group, click the **Start Mail Merge** button, and then click **Step by Step Mail Merge Wizard**.

3. In the **Mail Merge** task pane, click **Directory**, and then click **Next: Starting document**.

4. In the **Mail Merge** task pane, with the **Directory** option selected, at the bottom of the pane, click **Next: Starting document**.

5. With the **Use the current document** option selected, click **Next: Select recipients**.

6. In the **Mail Merge** task pane, click the type of data source you will use. Then select or create the data source, and refine the recipient list as appropriate.

7. At the bottom of the **Mail Merge** task pane, click **Next: Arrange your directory**, and insert the necessary merge fields.

Checking for Errors

You can validate that a main document and data source will merge successfully by using the Auto Check feature. When running an automatic check, you can simulate or complete the merge. You can display errors on screen as the merge occurs, or write errors to a separate document.

Checking and Reporting Errors ? x

- ○ Simulate the merge and report errors in a new document.
- ● Complete the merge, pausing to report each error as it occurs.
- ○ Complete the merge without pausing. Report errors in a new document.

[OK] [Canc]

Invalid Merge Field ? x

This merge field is used in the main document, but it does not exist in the data source.

First

You can remove the invalid merge field from the main document.

[Remove Field]

Or, you can replace it with a valid merge field from the data source.

Fields in data source:

FirstName ▼

Sample data:

Charlie

[OK] [Cancel]

➤ **To validate a mail merge operation before merging source documents**

1. Prepare the main document and data source, and set up the mail merge for the type of output you want.

2. On the **Mailings** tab, in the **Preview Results** group, click the **Auto Check for Errors** button.

3. In the **Checking and Reporting Errors** dialog box, click **Simulate the merge and report errors in a new document**. Then click **OK**.

4. For each error that the Auto Check feature reports, in the **Invalid Merge Field** dialog box, click **Remove Field** or choose the matching field from the **Fields in data source** list.

➤ **To validate a mail merge operation while merging source documents**

1. Prepare the main document and data source, and set up the mail merge for the type of output you want.

2. On the **Mailings** tab, in the **Preview Results** group, click the **Auto Check for Errors** button.

3. In the **Checking and Reporting Errors** dialog box, do one of the following, and then click **OK**:

   ○ Click **Complete the merge, pausing to report each error as it occurs**, and then click **OK**.

   ○ Click **Complete the merge without pausing. Report errors in a new document**, and then click **OK**.

4. For each error that the Auto Check feature reports, in the **Invalid Merge Field** dialog box, click **Remove Field** or choose the matching field from the **Fields in data source** list.

Practice Tasks

The practice files for these tasks are located in the Word\Objective7 practice file folder. Save the results of the tasks in the same folder for reuse in section 7.2.

- Set up a form letter using the *AnniversaryLetter* document as the main document and the *CustomerList* workbook as the data source.

- At the top of the main document, insert merge fields for a standard address and an informal greeting line. At the beginning of the third paragraph, insert a merge field for the recipient's first name, type a comma followed by a space, and change *For* to *for*.

- Before merging the source documents, edit the data source from within Word to include the following contact:

  Heidi Steen

  678 Pine Street

  Agriculture, WA 10003

- Before merging the source documents, sort the recipient list in ascending order by postal code.

- Without merging the source documents, save the main document as *AnniversaryFormLetter*. Check the document for errors, and then retain it for use in the section 7.2 practice tasks.

- Create a sheet of labels for all the records in the *CustomerList* workbook other than the two recipients whose addresses are not in the state of Washington (WA). Save the label document as *MyMergedLabels*, and then close it.

7.2 Execute Mail Merge

Previewing the Results of a Mail Merge Operation

After you specify the data source you want to use and enter merge fields in the main document, you can preview the merged documents before performing the actual merge. You can exclude recipients during this preview.

➤ **To preview the results of a mail merge operation**

1. On the **Mailings** tab, in the **Preview Results** group, click the **Preview Results** button.

2. In the **Write & Insert Fields** group, click the **Highlight Merge Fields** button. Verify that the highlighted merge fields are correctly specified and placed.

3. In the **Preview Results** group, click the **Next Record** button or **Previous Record** button to display each merged document that will be generated. Click the **First Record** button or **Last Record** button to display the first or last merged document that will be generated.

4. To preview the mail merge results for a specific record, click the **Find Recipient** button in the **Preview Results** group. In the **Find Entry** dialog box, enter a name or other record detail in the **Find** box, and then click **Find Next**.

   Or

1. Display the **Preview your e-mail messages** page of the **Mail Merge** task pane.

2. In the **Mail Merge** task pane, click the **Next Record** button or **Previous Record** button to display each merged document that will be generated.

3. To preview the mail merge results for a specific record, click **Find a recipient**. In the **Find Entry** dialog box, enter a name or other record detail in the **Find** box, and then click **Find Next**.

➤ To exclude a displayed recipient from a mail merge operation

→ On the **Preview your e-mail messages** page of the **Mail Merge** task pane, under **Make changes**, click **Exclude this recipient**.

Completing the Mail Merge Operation

When you are ready, you can either send the merged documents directly to the printer or you can merge them one after the other into a new document, separated by page breaks. If you merge to a new document, you have another chance to review and, if necessary, edit the merged documents before sending them to the printer.

➤ To execute a manual mail merge operation to a new document

1. On the **Mailings** tab, in the **Finish** group, click the **Finish & Merge** button, and then click **Edit Individual Documents**.

2. In the **Merge to New Document** dialog box, specify the records that you want to include in the merge document, and then click **OK**.

➤ To execute a mail merge operation to a new document from the Mail Merge wizard

1. In the **Mail Merge** task pane, display the **Complete the merge** page.

2. In the **Mail Merge** task pane, click **Edit individual letters**.

> **Tip** The Edit link reflects the type of mail merge document you're working with.

3. In the **Merge to New Document** dialog box, click **All**, and then click **OK**.

➤ To execute a manual mail merge operation to an email message

1. On the **Mailings** tab, in the **Finish** group, click the **Finish & Merge** button, and then click **Send E-mail Messages**.

2. In the **Merge to E-mail** dialog box, do the following, and then click **OK**:

   ○ In the **Message options** area, ensure that the correct field appears in the **To** list, enter the message subject in the **Subject line** box, and choose the message format you want from the **Mail format** list.

   ○ In the **Send records** area, indicate the records to which you want to send the email message.

➤ **To execute a mail merge operation to an email message from the Mail Merge wizard**

1. In the **Mail Merge** task pane, display the **Complete the merge** page.

2. In the **Merge** section of the **Mail Merge** task pane, click **Electronic mail**.

3. In the **Merge to E-mail** dialog box, enter the subject of the email message in the **Subject line** box, and then click **OK**.

➤ **To execute a mail merge operation to a printer from the Mail Merge wizard**

1. In the **Mail Merge** task pane, display the **Complete the merge** page.

2. In the **Mail Merge** task pane, click **Print**.

3. In the **Merge to Printer** dialog box, specify the range of records you want to merge to the printer, and then click **OK**.

4. In the **Print** dialog box, select the printer you want to use, and then click **OK**.

Practice Tasks

The practice files for these tasks are located in the Word\Objective7 practice file folder. You will need to complete the practice tasks in section 7.1 before performing the tasks in this section.

- Preview the results of the mail merge operation that will be executed by merging the *AnniversaryFormLetter* document you created in the tasks for section 7.1 with the *CustomerList* workbook.

- Exclude the recipient *Garth Fort* from the mail merge operation.

- Merge the source files to a new document that contains all the letters. Save the document as *MyMergedLetters*, and close it.

Objective Review

Before finishing this chapter, ensure that you have mastered the following skills:

7.1 Set Up Mail Merge

7.2 Execute Mail Merge

Microsoft Excel 2010

This part of the book covers the skills you need to have for certification as a Microsoft Office Specialist in Microsoft Excel 2010. Specifically, you will need to be able to complete tasks that demonstrate the following skills:

1 Managing the Worksheet Environment

2 Creating Cell Data

3 Formatting Cells and Worksheets

4 Managing Worksheets and Workbooks

5 Applying Formulas and Functions

6 Presenting Data Visually

7 Sharing Worksheet Data with Other Users

8 Analyzing and Organizing Data

With these skills, you can create, populate, format, and manage the types of workbooks most commonly used in a business environment.

Prerequisites

We assume that you have been working with Excel 2010 for at least six months and that you know how to carry out fundamental tasks that are not specifically mentioned in the Microsoft Office Specialist objectives for Exam 77-882, "Microsoft Excel 2010." Before you begin studying for this exam, you might want to make sure you are familiar with the information in this section.

Managing Worksheets

➤ **To insert a new worksheet**

→ Click the **Insert Worksheet** button at the right end of the worksheet tab section.

   Or

1. Right-click the worksheet tab before which you want to insert a new worksheet, and then click **Insert**.

2. On the **General** page of the **Insert** dialog box, click **Worksheet**, and then click **OK**.

➤ **To delete a worksheet**

→ Right-click the worksheet tab, and then click **Delete**.

➤ **To rename a worksheet**

1. Right-click the worksheet tab, and then click **Rename**.

2. Type the new worksheet name, and then press Enter.

Managing Worksheet Content

➤ **To select all the content in a worksheet**

→ At the junction of the row and column headings (above row 1 and to the left of column A), click the **Select All** button.

➤ **To select an individual column or row**

→ Click the column heading (labeled with the column letter) or the row heading (labeled with the row number).

➤ **To size a column or row to fit its contents**

→ Select the column or row, and then double-click its right or bottom edge.

Managing Excel Tables

➤ **To select the data in a table, table column, or table row**

→ Point to the upper-left corner of the table. When the pointer changes to a diagonal arrow, click once to select only the data, or twice to select the data and headers.

→ Point to the top edge of the table column. When the pointer changes to a downward-pointing arrow, click once to select only the data, or twice to select the data and headers.

→ Point to the left edge of the table row. When the pointer changes to a right-pointing arrow, click once to select only the data, or twice to select the data and headers.

Managing Data Entries

You enter text or a number in a cell simply by clicking the cell and typing the entry. A Cancel (X) button and an Enter (check mark) button appear between the Formula Bar and Name box, and the indicator at the left end of the status bar changes from *Ready* to *Enter*, because what you have typed will not be recorded in the cell until you "enter" it.

Excel allows a long text entry to overflow into an adjacent empty cell and truncates the entry only if the adjacent cell also contains an entry. However, unless you tell it otherwise, Excel displays long numbers in their simplest form, as follows:

- If you enter a number with fewer than 12 digits in a standard-width cell (which holds 8.43 characters), Excel adjusts the width of the column to accommodate the entry.

- If you enter a number with 12 or more digits, Excel displays it in scientific notation. For example, if you enter 12345678912345 in a standard-width cell, Excel displays 1.23457E+13 (1.23457 times 10 to the 13th power).

- If you enter a value with many decimal places, Excel might round it. For example, if you enter 123456.789 in a standard-width cell, Excel displays 123456.8.

- If you manually set the width of a column and then enter a currency value that is too large to be displayed in its entirety, Excel displays pound signs (#) instead of the value.

➤ **To complete a data entry**

→ Click the **Enter** button (the check mark) on the **Formula Bar** to complete the entry and stay in the same cell.

→ Press Enter or the Down Arrow key to complete the entry and move to the next cell in the same column.

→ Press the Tab key or the Right Arrow key to complete the entry and move to the next cell in the same row.

→ Press Shift+Enter or the Up Arrow key to complete the entry and move to the previous cell in the same column.

→ Press Shift+Tab or the Left Arrow key to complete the entry and move to the previous cell in the same row.

1 Managing the Worksheet Environment

The skills tested in this section of the Microsoft Office Specialist exam for Microsoft Excel 2010 relate to working with workbooks and with individual worksheets, and configuring Excel program options. Specifically, the following objectives are associated with this set of skills:

- **1.1** Navigate Through a Worksheet
- **1.2** Print a Worksheet or Workbook
- **1.3** Personalize the Excel Environment

Each Excel workbook consists of individual worksheets (three by default, but you can add and remove worksheets at will) which, when printed, are divided into pages. You can personalize many aspects of Excel functionality and of the Excel program window to tailor the Excel working environment so that you can most efficiently create and manipulate data on worksheets. You can also control the page layout of a worksheet so that, when printed, each page displays the information you want.

This chapter guides you in studying methods for moving among cells, pages, and named data ranges in a worksheet; printing all or selected workbook content; setting up content for printing by inserting page breaks, changing page layout options, and adding headers or footers; and personalizing the Excel environment by managing program functionality, customizing the ribbon and Quick Access Toolbar, and managing workbook properties, AutoSaving, and versioning.

> **Practice Files** Before you can complete the practice tasks in this chapter, you need to copy the book's practice files to your computer. The practice files you'll use to complete the tasks in this chapter are in the Excel\Objective1 practice file folder. A complete list of practice files is provided in "Using the Book's Companion Content" at the beginning of this book.

1.1 Navigate Through a Worksheet

You can move around in a worksheet in many ways, including the following:

- Pressing directional keyboard keys and key combinations
- Specifying a named cell or range of cells

> **See Also** For information about naming a cell or range of cells, see section 5.5, "Apply Named Ranges in Formulas."

- Specifying a property of the cell in the Go To Special dialog box

➤ **To move by one cell**

→ Press the Up Arrow key to move one cell up.

→ Press the Down Arrow key to move one cell down.

→ Press the Right Arrow key or the Tab key to move one cell to the right.

→ Press the Left Arrow key or Shift+Tab to move one cell to the left.

➤ **To move by one screen**

→ Press Page Up or Page Down to move up or down.

→ Press Alt+Page Up or Alt+Page Down to move to the left or right.

➤ **To move to the edge of the current data region**

→ Press Ctrl+Up Arrow, Ctrl+Down Arrow, Ctrl+Left Arrow, or Ctrl+Right Arrow.

➤ **To move to the next nonblank cell**

→ Press End, and then press the Up Arrow, Down Arrow, Left Arrow, or Right Arrow key.

➤ **To move to the beginning of the current row**

→ Press Home.

➤ **To move to the beginning of a worksheet**

→ Press Ctrl+Home.

➤ **To move to a specific location**

1. On the **Home** tab, in the **Editing** group, display the **Find & Select** list, and then click **Go To**.

2. In the **Go To** dialog box, enter a cell, cell range, or range name in the **Reference** box, and then click **OK**.

➤ **To move to a location that has a specific property**

1. On the **Home** tab, in the **Editing** group, display the **Find & Select** list, and then click **Go To Special**.

2. In the **Go To Special** dialog box, click the property on which you want to search, and then click **OK**.

➤ **To move to a named cell or range**

→ Enter the name in the **Go To** dialog box, and then click **OK**.

→ Enter the name in the **Name** box, and then press Enter.

➤ **To move to the last populated cell on a worksheet**

→ Press Ctrl+End.

→ In the **Go To Special** dialog box, click **Last cell**, and then click **OK**.

Practice Tasks

The practice file for these tasks is located in the Excel\Objective1 practice file folder. If you want to save the results of the tasks, save them in the same folder with *My* appended to the file name so that you don't overwrite the original practice file.

- Open the *PopulationData* workbook. Using the techniques described in this section, move to cell J6 of the NST03 worksheet.

- Using the techniques described in this section, move to the first worksheet cell that contains a comment.

- Move to the cell range named US_2006.

- Move to the last populated cell in the worksheet.

1.2 Print a Worksheet or Workbook

Printing Part or All of a Workbook

An Excel workbook can contain many separate worksheets of data. You can print part or all of an individual worksheet, a selected worksheet, or all the worksheets that contain content at one time. By default, Excel prints only the currently active worksheet(s).

If you want to print only part of a worksheet, you can do so from the Print page of the Backstage view or, if you will often print the same portion of a worksheet, you can define that portion as the print area.

After defining the print area of a worksheet, you can add selected ranges to it. A contiguous range becomes part of the original print area definition; a range that is noncontiguous or a different shape becomes a separate print area and is printed on a separate page. You can also remove ranges from the print area.

If you don't want to limit printing to the print area, you can permanently clear the print area or temporarily ignore it by selecting an option on the Print page of the Backstage view.

➤ **To print all populated worksheets in a workbook**

→ On the **Print** page of the Backstage view, in the **Settings** area, display the first **Print** list, and then click **Print Entire Workbook**.

➤ **To print a single worksheet**

1. Display the worksheet you want to print.

2. On the **Print** page of the Backstage view, in the **Settings** area, display the first **Print** list, and then click **Print Active Sheets**.

➤ **To print specific worksheets**

1. Display the first worksheet in the workbook that you want to print.

2. Select additional worksheets in one of these ways:

  ○ To select adjacent worksheets, press Shift and then click the tab of the last worksheet in the workbook that you want to print.

  ○ To select nonadjacent worksheets, press Ctrl and then click the tab of each additional worksheet you want to print.

3. On the **Print** page of the Backstage view, in the **Settings** area, display the first **Print** list, and then click **Print Active Sheets**.

Tip When multiple worksheets are selected, [Group] appears in the title bar. Many commands are not available when a group of worksheets is active. To release the group selection, click the tab of any worksheet that is not part of the group.

➤ **To print a portion of a worksheet without defining a print area**

1. In the worksheet, select the range of cells you want to print.

2. On the **Print** page of the Backstage view, in the **Settings** area, display the first **Print** list, and then click **Print Selection**.

➤ **To define a selected range as the print area**

  → On the **Page Layout** tab, in the **Page Setup** group, click the **Print Area** button, and then click **Set Print Area**.

➤ **To add a selected range to the print area**

  → On the **Page Layout** tab, in the **Page Setup** group, click the **Print Area** button, and then click **Add to Print Area**.

Tip The Add To Print Area option will not be displayed if the area of the worksheet designated as the print area is currently selected.

➤ **To remove a range from the print area**

1. On the **Page Layout** tab, click the **Page Setup** dialog box launcher.

2. On the **Sheet** page of the **Page Setup** dialog box, change the range reference in the **Print area** box, and then click **OK**.

➤ **To clear the print area**

→ On the **Page Layout** tab, in the **Page Setup** group, click the **Print Area** button, and then click **Clear Print Area**.

➤ **To ignore the print area**

→ On the **Print** page of the Backstage view, in the **Settings** area, display the first **Print** list, and then click **Ignore Print Area**.

Tip The Ignore Print Area setting remains active (indicated by a check mark) until you turn it off by clicking it again.

See Also For information about scaling worksheets and about changing page margins, orientation, and size, see section 3.5, "Manipulate Page Setup Options for Worksheets."

Setting Page Breaks

When the cell entries in a worksheet will not fit within the margins of one printed page, Excel indicates which cells will print on which page by inserting a soft page break. Page breaks are indicated in Normal view as dashed lines. If you want to control how pages break, you can insert manual page breaks. Before printing a worksheet, you can preview the page breaks and fine-tune their placement.

Geographic Area	Population Estimates		Change, 2006 to 2007		National Ranking of Regions and States			
					Population Estimates		Change, 2006 to 2007	
	########	########	Number	Percent	########	########	Number	Percent
United States	301,621,157	298,754,813	2,866,338	1.0	(X)	(X)	(X)	(X)
Northeast	54,680,626	54,590,172	90,454	0.2	4	4	4	4
Midwest	66,388,735	66,128,483	260,312	0.4	3	3	3	3
South	110,454,786	108,894,582	1,560,204	1.4	1	1	1	1
West	70,096,950	69,141,582	955,368	1.4	2	2	2	2
Alabama	4,627,851	4,590,240	37,611	0.8	23	23	21	27
Alaska	683,478	677,450	6,028	0.9	47	47	41	23
Arizona	6,338,755	6,165,689	173,066	2.8	16	16	6	2
Arkansas	2,834,797	2,809,111	25,686	0.9	32	32	27	22
California	36,553,215	36,249,872	303,343	0.8	1	1	2	25
Colorado	4,861,515	4,766,248	95,267	2.0	22	22	7	8
Connecticut	3,502,309	3,495,753	6,556	0.2	29	29	40	44
Delaware	864,764	852,747	12,017	1.4	45	45	35	14
District of Columbia	588,292	585,459	2,833	0.5	50	50	46	36
Florida	18,251,243	18,051,508	133,735	1.1	4	4	4	19
Georgia	9,544,750	9,342,080	202,670	2.2	9	9	3	5
Hawaii	1,283,388	1,278,635	4,753	0.4	42	42	42	37
Idaho	1,499,402	1,463,878	35,524	2.4	39	39	23	4
Illinois	12,852,548	12,777,042	75,506	0.6	5	5	11	33
Indiana	6,345,289	6,302,646	42,643	0.7	15	15	18	31
Iowa	2,988,046	2,972,566	15,480	0.5	30	30	33	34
Kansas	2,775,997	2,755,817	20,180	0.7	33	33	28	28
Kentucky	4,241,474	4,204,444	37,030	0.9	26	26	22	24
Louisiana	4,293,204	4,243,288	49,916	1.2	25	25	16	16
Maine	1,317,207	1,314,910	2,297	0.2	40	40	47	46
Maryland	5,618,344	5,602,017	16,327	0.3	19	19	31	40
Massachusetts	6,449,755	6,434,389	15,366	0.2	14	13	34	42
Michigan	10,071,822	10,102,322	-30,500	-0.3	8	8	51	50
Minnesota	5,197,621	5,154,586	43,035	0.8	21	21	17	28
Mississippi	2,918,785	2,899,112	19,673	0.7	31	31	30	30
Missouri	5,878,415	5,837,639	40,776	0.7	18	18	19	29
Montana	957,861	946,795	11,066	1.2	44	44	36	17
Nebraska	1,774,571	1,763,755	10,806	0.6	38	38	37	32
Nevada	2,565,382	2,432,427	72,955	2.9	35	35	12	1
New Hampshire	1,315,828	1,311,821	4,007	0.3	41	41	43	39
New Jersey	8,685,920	8,666,075	19,845	0.2	11	11	29	43
New Mexico	1,969,915	1,942,302	27,613	1.4	36	36	26	13
New York	19,297,729	19,281,988	15,741	0.1	3	3	32	47
North Carolina	9,061,032	8,869,442	191,590	2.2	10	10	5	6
North Dakota	639,715	637,460	2,255	0.4	48	48	48	38
Ohio	11,466,917	11,463,513	3,404	-	7	7	44	49
Oklahoma	3,617,316	3,577,536	39,780	1.1	28	28	20	18
Oregon	3,747,455	3,691,084	56,371	1.5	27	27	15	11
Pennsylvania	12,432,792	12,402,817	29,975	0.2	6	6	24	41
Rhode Island	1,057,832	1,061,641	-3,809	-0.4	43	43	50	51
South Carolina	4,407,709	4,330,108	77,601	1.8	24	24	10	10
South Dakota	796,214	788,467	7,747	1.0	46	46	39	20
Tennessee	6,156,719	6,074,913	81,806	1.3	17	17	9	15
Texas	23,904,380	23,407,629	496,751	2.1	2	2	1	7
Utah	2,645,330	2,579,535	65,795	2.6	34	34	14	3
Vermont	621,254	620,778	476	0.1	43	43	49	48
Virginia	7,712,091	7,640,249	71,842	0.9	12	12	13	21
Washington	6,468,424	6,374,910	93,514	1.5	13	14	8	12
West Virginia	1,812,035	1,808,699	3,336	0.2	37	37	45	45

NST03

➤ **To insert a manual page break**

1. Click the cell in column **A** above which you want to insert a horizontal page break.

   Or

   Click the cell in row **1** to the left of which you want to insert a vertical page break.

   Or

   Click a cell anywhere in the worksheet above and to the left of which you want to insert both horizontal and vertical page breaks.

2. On the **Page Layout** tab, in the **Page Setup** group, click the **Breaks** button, and then click **Insert Page Break**.

➤ **To delete a manual page break**

1. Click any cell below or to the right of the page break you want to remove.

2. On the **Page Layout** tab, in the **Page Setup** group, click the **Breaks** button, and then click **Remove Page Break**.

➤ **To delete all manual page breaks**

→ On the **Page Layout** tab, in the **Page Setup** group, click the **Breaks** button, and then click **Reset All Page Breaks**.

➤ **To preview and adjust page breaks**

1. On the **View** toolbar located at the right end of the status bar, click the **Page Break Preview** button and, if a message box appears, click **OK**.

2. To adjust an existing page break, drag it in the direction of either of its arrows.

Printing Gridlines and Headings

When you print a worksheet with the default settings, the gridlines, row headings, and column headings are not printed. If you want to include these elements, you can turn them on for printing.

> **See Also** For information about printing row and column titles, see section 3.3, "Create Row and Column Titles."

Table 3: Estimates of Population Change for the United States, Regions.		
Geographic Area	Population Estimates	Change, 20

Geographic Area	July 1, 2007	July 1, 2006	Number
United States	301,621,157	298,754,819	2,866,338
Northeast	54,680,626	54,590,172	90,454
Midwest	66,388,795		
South	110,454,786		
West	70,096,950		
Alabama	4,627,851		
Alaska	683,478		
Arizona	6,338,755		
Arkansas	2,834,797		
California	36,553,215		
Colorado	4,861,515		
Connecticut	3,502,309		
Delaware	864,764		
District of Columbia	588,292		

— Standard print settings

	A	B	C	D
	Table 3: Estimates of Population Change for the United States, Regi			
2				
3				
4	Geographic Area	Population Estimates		Chang
5		July 1, 2007	July 1, 2006	Number
38	Nebraska	1,774,571	1,763,765	10
39	Nevada	2,565,382	2,492,427	72
40	New Hampshire	1,315,828	1,311,821	4
41	New Jersey	8,685,920	8,666,075	19
42	New Mexico	1,969,915	1,942,302	27
43	New York	19,297,729	19,281,988	15
44	North Carolina	9,061,032	8,869,442	191
45	North Dakota	639,715	637,460	2
46	Ohio	11,466,917	11,463,513	3
47	Oklahoma	3,617,316	3,577,536	39
48	Oregon	3,747,455	3,691,084	56
49	Pennsylvania	12,432,792	12,402,817	29
50	Rhode Island	1,057,832	1,061,641	

Printing gridlines and headings

> **To print gridlines**
→ On the **Page Layout** tab, in the **Sheet Options** group, under **Gridlines**, select the **Print** check box.

> **To print column and row headings**
→ On the **Page Layout** tab, in the **Sheet Options** group, under **Headings**, select the **Print** check box.

Tip Selecting the Print check box in the Sheet Options group selects the corresponding check box on the Sheet page of the Page Setup dialog box. You can set these print options in either place.

Printing Page Headers and Footers

You can display information on every page of a printed worksheet by creating and formatting headers and footers. You can have a different header and footer on the first page or different headers and footers on odd and even pages. When you create a header or footer, Excel opens header and footer areas and displays the Header & Footer Tools Design contextual tab on the ribbon. You can enter information in the header and footer areas in the following ways:

- Select information, such as the company name, the file name, or the worksheet name, from a list.

- Type the information the same way you would enter ordinary text.

- Use commands on the Design contextual tab to enter and format items such as the page number or the date and time.

> ➤ **To insert a header or footer**

1. On the **Insert** tab, in the **Text** group, click the **Header & Footer** button.

2. Click the left, center, or right area of the header, and use a combination of typing and the commands on the Header & Footer Tools **Design** contextual tab to create the header you want.

3. On the **Design** contextual tab, in the **Navigation** group, click the **Go to Footer** button.

4. Repeat step 2 to create the footer.

5. Click away from the footer area to review the header and footer in Page Layout view.

➤ **To change the header or footer**

→ On the **Insert** tab, in the **Text** group, click the **Header & Footer** button, and then make your changes.

Practice Tasks

The practice files for these tasks are located in the Excel\Objective1 practice file folder. If you want to save the results of the tasks, save them in the same folder with *My* appended to the file name so that you don't overwrite the original practice file.

* Configure the SalesByCategory worksheet of the *PrintArea* workbook so that printing with the default settings will print only columns B and C with gridlines.

* On the Orders worksheet of the *PageBreaks* workbook, insert a page break before row 31. Then review the page breaks, and ensure that only columns A through D will appear on the first page.

* In the *HeaderFooter* workbook, create a header that will print on all the pages of the Orders worksheet except the first. On the left, enter today's date; in the center, enter the name of the workbook; and on the right, enter the page number. Return to Normal view, and then change the center section of the header to reflect the name of the worksheet instead of the workbook.

* Configure the print settings of the *HeaderFooter* workbook so that page numbers print at the bottom of each page instead of the top.

1.3 Personalize the Excel Environment

Managing Program Functionality

You can control the settings and appearance of many Excel features from the Excel Options dialog box. The Excel Options dialog box is divided into pages of general Office settings, Excel functionality-specific settings, feature-specific settings (for the ribbon and the Quick Access Toolbar), and security-related settings.

Tip Most of the options you will use to personalize the Excel environment are located on the Formulas and Advanced pages of the Excel Options dialog box. The settings on these pages are all covered in this book. However, the Excel Options dialog box contains other options that are not covered in this book. Be sure to look through the Excel Options dialog box for other options you might be interested in using.

Managing Formula Options

From the Formulas page of the Excel Options dialog box, you can configure settings that pertain to calculations, working with formulas, and automatic error checking.

> **Strategy** Study the settings available on the Formulas page of the Excel Options dialog box and be ready to demonstrate that you can locate and use them.

Managing Advanced Options

From the Advanced page of the Excel Options dialog box, you can configure settings that pertain to editing and moving data, including graphic elements in worksheets; working with program window elements; working with elements of a specific workbook or worksheet; and other, more advanced options.

> **Strategy** Study the settings available on the Advanced page of the Excel Options dialog box and be ready to demonstrate that you can locate and use them.

Customizing the Ribbon and Quick Access Toolbar

In all Microsoft Office 2010 programs, you can create a more efficient working environment by modifying the commands available on the ribbon and the Quick Access Toolbar.

> **See Also** For information about the ribbon, see "Modifying the Display of the Ribbon" at the beginning of this book.

Customizing the Ribbon

You can customize the ribbon to display more or fewer tabs and groups of commands. You can choose from among all the commands available in the program to create custom tabs and groups of commands.

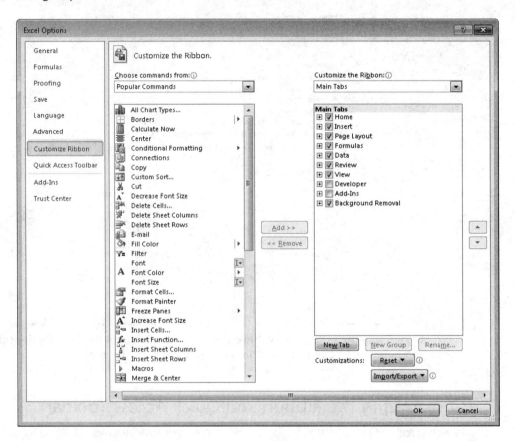

While working in the program window, you can minimize the ribbon to increase the available working space. The minimized ribbon displays only the tab names.

➤ To minimize the ribbon

→ To the right of the ribbon tab names, click the **Minimize the Ribbon** button.

➤ To select a command from the minimized ribbon

→ On the minimized ribbon, click the tab on which the command appears, and then work with the command as usual.

➤ **To expand the ribbon**

→ On the minimized ribbon, to the right of the tab names, click the **Expand the Ribbon** button.

➤ **To hide a ribbon tab**

1. On the **Customize Ribbon** page of the **Excel Options** dialog box, in the **Customize the Ribbon** list, click the category containing the tab you want to hide.

2. In the **Customize the Ribbon** pane, clear the check box of the tab you want to hide.

➤ **To remove a group of commands from a tab**

1. On the **Customize Ribbon** page of the **Excel Options** dialog box, in the **Customize the Ribbon** list, click the category containing the tab you want to modify.

2. In the **Customize the Ribbon** pane, expand the tab you want to modify (click the plus sign to the left of the tab name).

3. Click the group you want to remove from the tab, and then click **Remove**.

➤ **To create a custom group**

1. In the **Customize the Ribbon** pane, click the tab you want to modify.

2. Below the pane, click **New Group**.

3. With the **New Group (Custom)** group selected, click **Rename**.

4. In the **Rename** dialog box, enter a name for the group in the **Display name** box and, optionally, select an icon to represent the group from the **Symbol** gallery. Then click **OK**.

➤ **To add a command to a custom group**

1. In the **Customize the Ribbon** pane, click the group you want to modify.

2. In the **Choose commands from** list, click the group of commands containing the command you want to add.

3. In the **Choose commands** pane, click the command. Then click the **add** button.

> **Tip** You can't add commands to a predefined group.

➤ **To remove a command from a custom group**

1. In the **Customize the Ribbon** pane, locate the group you want to modify.

2. If necessary, expand the tab you want to modify (click the plus sign to the left of the tab name).

3. Click the command you want to remove, and then click **Remove**.

➤ **To move a group on a tab**

1. In the **Customize the Ribbon** pane, click the group you want to move.

2. To the right of the pane, click the **Move Up** button to move the group to the left, or the **Move Down** button to move the group to the right.

➤ **To create a custom tab**

1. In the **Customize the Ribbon** pane, click **New Tab**.

2. In the pane, click **New Tab (Custom)**, and then click **Rename**.

3. In the **Rename** dialog box, enter a name for the tab in the **Display name** box, and then click **OK**.

➤ **To move a tab on the ribbon**

1. In the **Customize the Ribbon** pane, click the tab you want to move.

2. To the right of the pane, click the **Move Up** button to move the tab to the left, or the **Move Down** button to move the tab to the right.

➤ **To reset a tab to its default configuration**

→ On the **Customize Ribbon** page of the **Excel Options** dialog box, in the **Reset list**, click **Reset only selected Ribbon tab**.

➤ **To reset the ribbon to its default configuration**

→ On the **Customize Ribbon** page of the **Excel Options** dialog box, in the **Reset list**, click **Reset all customizations**.

Tip If you upgraded to Office 2010 from a previous version of Office, you might notice that some commands you used in the previous program version are not available from the ribbon. A few old features have been abandoned, but others that people used infrequently have simply not been added to the default ribbon.

If you want to use one of these sidelined features, you can make it a part of your program working environment by adding it to the ribbon. You can find a list of all the commands that do not appear on the ribbon but are still available in a program by displaying the program's Options dialog box and then clicking Commands Not In The Ribbon in the Choose Commands From list.

Customizing the Quick Access Toolbar

In the program window, the Quick Access Toolbar displays the Save button, the Undo button, and the Redo button. To save time, you can place frequently used commands on the Quick Access Toolbar. To save even more time, you can move the Quick Access Toolbar from its default position above the ribbon to below the ribbon, so your mouse has less distance to travel from the content you're working with to the command you want to invoke. If you add all the buttons you use most often to the Quick Access Toolbar, you can hide the ribbon to gain screen space.

From the Quick Access Toolbar page of the Excel Options dialog box, you can modify the Quick Access Toolbar by adding, moving, or removing commands and command group separators. You can modify the Quick Access Toolbar that appears in the program window or create a custom Quick Access Toolbar that appears only in the currently active workbook.

➤ **To add a button to the Quick Access Toolbar for all workbooks**

1. On the **Quick Access Toolbar** page of the **Excel Options** dialog box, in the **Choose commands from** list, click the category containing the command you want to add.

2. In the **Choose commands** pane, locate and double-click the command.

> **Tip** In the Choose Commands pane, items with down-pointing arrows in boxes display tab groups when clicked, and items with left-pointing arrows display a gallery or menu when clicked.

➤ **To create a Quick Access Toolbar that is specific to the active workbook**

→ On the **Quick Access Toolbar** page of the **Excel Options** dialog box, in the **Customize Quick Access Toolbar** list, click **For <name of workbook>**. Then add buttons to the toolbar as usual.

➤ **To change the order of the buttons on the Quick Access Toolbar**

→ In the **Quick Access Toolbar** pane, click the command you want to move, and then click **Move Up** to move it to the left or **Move Down** to move it to the right.

➤ **To separate Quick Access Toolbar buttons into groups**

1. In the **Quick Access Toolbar** pane, click the command before which you want to place a separator.

2. At the top of the **Choose commands** pane, double-click **Separator**.

➤ **To remove a button from the Quick Access Toolbar**

→ In the **Quick Access Toolbar** pane, double-click the command you want to remove.

➤ **To restore the default Quick Access Toolbar**

1. On the **Quick Access Toolbar** page of the **Excel Options** dialog box, in the **Reset** list, click **Reset only Quick Access Toolbar**.

2. In the **Reset Customizations** message box, click **Yes**.

➤ **To display the Quick Access Toolbar below the ribbon**

→ On the **Quick Access Toolbar** page of the **Excel Options** dialog box, select the **Show Quick Access Toolbar below the Ribbon** check box.

→ At the right end of the Quick Access Toolbar, click the **Customize Quick Access Toolbar** button, and then click **Show Below the Ribbon**.

→ Right-click an empty area of the Quick Access Toolbar, and then click **Show Quick Access Toolbar below the Ribbon**.

Managing Workbooks

You can manage not only the content of a workbook, but also certain types of information associated with the file.

Working with Properties

Before distributing a workbook, you might want to attach properties to it so that the file is readily identifiable in the Details view of any browsing dialog box, such as the Open dialog box. You can attach properties to a workbook in the Document Information Panel. Particularly useful are properties called *keywords* in the Document Information Panel, which are identified as *tags* in Windows Explorer and in the Details view of browsing dialog boxes.

You can view the properties of the current workbook on the Info page of the Backstage view. You enter keywords in the Document Information Panel or on the Summary page of the Properties dialog box, separating multiple keywords with semicolons.

Document Properties ▼		Location:	C:\Users\Public\Documents\Properties.xlsx		* Required field	X
Author:	Title:		Subject:		Keywords:	
Category:	Status:					
Comments:						

➤ **To display and edit properties associated with an Excel workbook**

  1. In the right pane of the **Info** page of the Backstage view, click **Properties**, and then click **Show Document Panel**.

  2. In the **Document Information Panel**, click the **Property Views and Options** button, and then click **Document Properties – Server** to display properties associated with a server version of the document (for example, properties used in a document workspace), **Document Properties** to display the common properties stored with the document, or **Advanced Properties** to display the **Properties** dialog box.

  3. Enter any properties you want to associate with the document.

> **Tip** In the Document Information Panel, fields marked with a red asterisk are required; required fields are usually associated with the requirements of a Microsoft SharePoint document library in which the workbook is saved.

➤ **To display all properties associated with an Excel workbook**

→ In the right pane of the **Info** page of the Backstage view, click **Show All Properties**.

→ In the right pane of the **Info** page, click **Properties**, and then click **Advanced Properties** to display the **Properties** dialog box.

➤ **To display properties in a browsing dialog box**

1. Display the dialog box contents in Details view.

2. Right-click any column heading, and then click the property you want to display

> **Tip** Clicking a property that is preceded by a check mark removes it from the display. To add or remove more than one property or a property that is not displayed in the basic list, click More, make selections in the Choose Details dialog box, and then click OK.

Working with Versions

Like other Office programs, Excel automatically saves a temporary copy of an open file every 10 minutes. If you close a file without saving it, you can return to the most recently saved temporary version. You can also display the temporary copies of files that you started but never saved.

➤ **To change the AutoSave frequency**

→ On the **Save** page of the **Excel Options** dialog box, in the **Save AutoRecover information every** box, enter a number of minutes from 1 through 120.

➤ **To display a previous (saved) version of the current workbook**

→ On the **Info** page of the Backstage view, in the **Versions** list, click the version of the file you want to display.

➤ **To replace the current file with a previous version**

1. Display the previous version of the file.

2. On the **Autosaved Version** bar that appears below the ribbon, click **Restore**.

➤ **To display a temporary (unsaved) version of a workbook**

1. On the **Info** page of the Backstage view, click the **Manage Versions** button, and then click **Recover Unsaved Workbooks**.

2. In the **Open** dialog box displaying the contents of your UnsavedFiles folder, click the file you want to display, and then click **Open**.

➤ **To delete temporary workbook versions**

1. On the **Info** page of the Backstage view, click the **Manage Versions** button, and then click **Delete All Unsaved Workbooks**.

2. In the dialog box prompting you to confirm the deletion, click **Yes**.

Practice Tasks

The practice file for these tasks is located in the Excel\Objective1 practice file folder. If you want to save the results of the tasks, save them in the same folder with *My* appended to the file name so that you don't overwrite the original practice file.

*   Attach the keywords *magazine* and *advertising* to the *Properties* workbook.

*   Configure Excel so that it does not provide the AutoComplete information for formulas that you enter. Check the setting by entering *=SUM(* in a worksheet cell and verifying that a tooltip displaying the correct formula structure does not appear.

*   Configure Excel to move to the next cell to the right when you press Enter. Check the setting by entering content in a worksheet cell and then pressing Enter.

*   Display the Developer tab on the ribbon. Then remove the Macros group from the View tab.

*   The Quick Print button is not available, by default, on any ribbon tab. Add this button to the Quick Access Toolbar, make it the leftmost button, and visually separate it from the other buttons.

*   For the current workbook only, create a Quick Access Toolbar that contains buttons for inserting pictures, charts, and tables. Then display the Quick Access Toolbar below the ribbon.

*   Remove your customizations from the Excel Options dialog box, the ribbon, and both Quick Access Toolbars, and display only the standard Quick Access Toolbar above the ribbon.

Objective Review

Before finishing this chapter, ensure that you have mastered the following skills:

1.1   Navigate Through a Worksheet

1.2   Print a Worksheet or Workbook

1.3   Personalize the Excel Environment

2 Creating Cell Data

The skills tested in this section of the Microsoft Office Specialist exam for Microsoft Excel 2010 relate to inserting structured data in worksheet cells. Specifically, the following objectives are associated with this set of skills:

2.1 Construct Cell Data

2.2 Apply Auto Fill

2.3 Apply and Manipulate Hyperlinks

You might populate a worksheet from scratch or paste existing data from another source file. You can perform various operations on data when pasting it into a worksheet, either to maintain the original state of the data or to change it. When creating data from scratch, you can quickly enter a large amount of data that follows a pattern by filling a numeric or alphanumeric data series. You can fill any of the default series that come with Excel or create a custom data series. In addition to numeric and alphanumeric data, Excel supports various types of hyperlinks from cells or embedded objects to locations inside or outside of the workbook.

This chapter guides you in studying ways of pasting data by using the Paste Special feature, filling a data series and copying data by using Auto Fill, and creating and modifying hyperlinks.

> **Practice Files** Before you can complete the practice tasks in this chapter, you need to copy the book's practice files to your computer. The practice files you'll use to complete the tasks in this chapter are in the Excel\Objective2 practice file folder. A complete list of practice files is provided in "Using the Book's Companion Content" at the beginning of this book.

2.1 Construct Cell Data

Pasting Structured Data

The cut, copy, and paste features are used by virtually everyone who uses Excel. However, Excel offers additional advanced techniques for pasting that a great many Excel users are unaware of or rarely use, even though they allow the user to do some very powerful data manipulation.

Using the Paste Special feature, you can perform mathematical operations when you paste data over existing data, you can transpose columns to rows and rows to columns, and you can be selective about what you want to paste from the source cells. You have the option to paste only values, formulas, formatting, data validation, comments, or column widths. You can choose to exclude borders when you paste. You can also link data that you've copied, so that if the source data changes, the copied data will also change.

Click to open the Paste Special dialog box

Strategy In this section, we discuss some of the most common advanced paste techniques. Experiment with all the options in the Paste Special dialog box.

➤ **To transpose rows and columns**

1. Select the row(s) or column(s) you want to transpose.

2. On the **Home** tab, in the **Clipboard** group, click the **Copy** button.

3. Select the cell into which you want to copy the first value of the transposed data.

4. On the **Home** tab, in the **Clipboard** group, in the **Paste** section of the **Paste** list, click the **Transpose** button.

➤ **To paste formula results from one cell range to another**

1. Select and copy the cell range containing the formulas you want to copy the values from.

2. Select the cell into which you want to copy the first value.

3. On the **Home** tab, in the **Clipboard** group, in the **Paste Values** section of the **Paste** list, click the **Values** button.

> **Tip** Point to any button in the Paste gallery to preview how the copied data will be pasted by using that option.

➤ **To add, subtract, multiply, or divide values in two data ranges**

1. Select and copy the first data range—the numbers you want to add to, subtract from, multiply by, or divide by the second data range.

2. Select the first cell of the second data range—the numbers you want to add to, multiply by, or divide by the numbers in the first range, or subtract the first range from.

3. On the **Home** tab, in the **Clipboard** group, in the **Paste** list, click **Paste Special**.

4. In the **Paste Special** dialog box, in the **Operation** area, click **Add**, **Subtract**, **Multiply**, or **Divide**. Then click **OK**.

Inserting and Deleting Data

Inserting and deleting rows and columns is a natural part of worksheet development, and in Excel 2010, it couldn't be easier. You can insert an entire row above the selected cell or an entire column to the left of it. If you want to insert a cell instead of a row or column, you are given the option of making room by moving cells down or to the right.

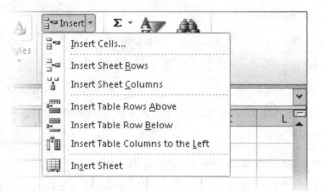

Similarly, you can delete a selected row or column, or you can delete only the selected cells, optionally specifying how the remaining cells should fill the space.

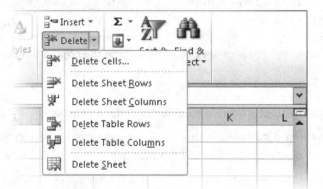

In addition to inserting empty rows, columns, or cells, you can insert cut or copied cell contents directly into an existing table or data range with one command. When you insert a range of cells rather than an entire row or column, Excel requests instructions for making room before inserting a similarly shaped range.

> **Tip** Always select a single cell when inserting cut or copied cells. If you select a range that is a different size and shape from the one you want to insert, Excel displays an error message.

➤ To insert rows or columns

1. Select the number of rows you want to insert, starting with the row above which you want the inserted rows to appear.

Or

Select the number of columns you want to insert, starting with the column to the left of which you want the inserted columns to appear.

2. On the **Home** tab, in the **Cells** group, click the **Insert** button.

➤ To insert cells

1. Select the number of cells you want to insert.

2. On the **Home** tab, in the **Cells** group, click the **Insert** button.

> **Tip** If your selection is one cell or a horizontal range, Excel inserts the new cells above the selection. If your selection is a vertical range, Excel inserts the new cells to the left of the selection.

Or

On the **Home** tab, in the **Cells** group, click the **Insert** arrow, and then click **Insert Cells**. In the **Insert** dialog box, indicate the direction you want to move the existing cells, and then click **OK**.

> **Tip** You can also insert an entire row or column from the Insert dialog box.

➤ To control the formatting of a new insertion

→ Immediately after inserting the rows, columns, or cells that contain formatting or values, click the **Insert Options** button, and then click an option in the list.

➤ To paste copied or cut cells into inserted cells

1. Click a cell at the beginning of the range you want to insert.

2. On the **Home** tab, in the **Cells** group, click the **Insert** arrow, and then click **Insert Cut Cells** or **Insert Copied Cells**.

➤ **To delete selected rows or columns**

→ On the **Home** tab, in the **Cells** group, click the **Delete** button.

➤ **To delete selected cells**

→ On the **Home** tab, in the **Cells** group, click the **Delete** button.

Or

1. On the **Home** tab, in the **Cells** group, click the **Delete** arrow, and then click **Delete Cells**.

2. In the **Delete** dialog box, indicate the direction you want to move the existing cells, and then click **OK**.

> **Tip** You can also delete an entire row or column from the Delete dialog box.

Practice Tasks

The practice file for these tasks is located in the Excel\Objective2 practice file folder. If you want to save the results of the tasks, save them in the same folder with *My* appended to the file name so that you don't overwrite the original practice file.

- In the *InsertingDeleting* workbook, transpose the names in the Magazine column on the Ad Buy Constraints worksheet to the first row of a new worksheet into the new worksheet.

- In the *InsertingDeleting* workbook, practice pasting only the values (with and without borders), formulas, and formatting of cells B4:G9 on the Ad Buy Constraints worksheet.

- On the Ad Buy Constraints worksheet of the *InsertingDeleting* workbook, delete rows to move the column headers to row 1. Delete columns to move the Magazine column to column A. Cut the data from the Mag3 row (B4:F4) and insert it into the Mag2 row (B3:F3). Move the Cost Per Ad data so that it is immediately to the left of the Total Cost cells. Finally, insert two cells in positions B8:B9, shifting any existing data down.

2.2 Apply Auto Fill

Filling a Data Series

You can quickly fill adjacent cells with data that continues a formula or a series of numbers, days, or dates, either manually from the Fill menu, or automatically by dragging the fill handle. When copying or filling data by using the Fill menu commands, you can set specific options for the pattern of the data sequence you want to create.

Click to open the Series dialog box

When creating a series based on one or more selected cells (called *filling a series*), you can select from the following series types:

- **Linear** Excel calculates the series values by adding the value you enter in the Step Value box to each cell in the series.

- **Growth** Excel calculates the series values by multiplying each cell in the series by the step value.

- **Date** Excel calculates the series values by incrementing each cell in the series of dates, designated by the Date Unit you select, by the step value.

- **AutoFill** This option creates a series that produces the same results as dragging the fill handle.

When you use the Auto Fill feature, either from the Fill menu or by dragging the fill handle, the Auto Fill Options button appears in the lower-right corner of the fill range. Clicking the button displays a menu of context-specific fill options.

	A	B	C	D	E
1	1-Aug				
2	2-Aug				
3	3-Aug				
4	4-Aug				
5					

— Fill handle

Auto Fill Options menu:
- ○ Copy Cells
- ◉ Fill Series
- ○ Fill Formatting Only
- ○ Fill Without Formatting
- ○ Fill Days
- ○ Fill Weekdays
- ○ Fill Months
- ○ Fill Years

You can use the Auto Fill feature to create sequences of numbers, days, and dates; to apply formatting from one cell to adjacent cells; or, if you use Excel for more sophisticated purposes, to create sequences of data generated by formulas, or custom sequences based on information you specify.

If you want to fill a series of information that does not match the available series type or unit, you can create a custom fill series consisting of a specific list of data you want your series to conform to. For example, this could be a list of names, regions, or industry-specific reference points.

Custom Lists

Custom Lists tab

Custom lists:
- NEW LIST
- Sun, Mon, Tue, Wed, Thu, Fri, S
- Sunday, Monday, Tuesday, Wed
- Jan, Feb, Mar, Apr, May, Jun, J
- January, February, March, April
- Spring, Summer, Winter, Fall

List entries:
- Spring
- Summer
- Winter
- Fall

[Add] [Delete]

Create a list of entries in the dialog box or import list entries from a worksheet

Press Enter to separate list entries.
Import list from cells: $F$5:$F$8 [Import]

[OK] [Cancel]

➤ **To fill a simple numeric, day, or date series**

1. To create a numeric series in which numbers increment by one, enter the first two numbers of the series in the first two cells of the range you want to fill.

Or

To create a day or date series in which days or dates increment by one, enter the first value of the series in the upper-left corner of the range you want to fill.

Or

To create a series in which numbers, days, or dates increment by more than one, enter as many values as are necessary to establish the series in the first cells of the range you want to fill.

2. Select the cell or cells beginning the series.

3. Drag the fill handle down or to the right to create an increasing series.

Or

Drag the fill handle up or to the left to create a decreasing series.

> **Tip** When using the fill handle, you can drag in only one direction; you can't define a cell range of multiple columns and rows.

➤ **To fill a selective day or date series**

1. Fill the series. Immediately after you release the mouse button, click the **Auto Fill Options** button that appears in the lower-right corner of the cell range.

2. On the **Auto Fill Options** menu, click **Fill Days**, **Fill Weekdays**, **Fill Months**, or **Fill Years**.

➤ **To fill a formatted numeric series**

1. Enter the amount or amounts beginning the series.

2. On the **Home** tab, use the commands in the **Number** group to format the amount or amounts as currency, percentage, fraction, or whatever number format you want.

3. Select the cell or cells beginning the series.

4. Drag the fill handle down or to the right to create an increasing series, or up or to the left to create a decreasing series.

5. Click the **Auto Fill Options** button that appears in the lower-right corner of the cell range. Then on the **Auto Fill Options** menu, click **Fill Series**.

➤ **To set advanced options for a numeric, day, or date series**

1. Enter the number or date beginning the series, and then select the cell range you want to fill.

2. On the **Home** tab, in the **Editing** group, click the **Fill** button, and then in the list, click **Series**.

3. In the **Series** dialog box, select the options you want, and then click **OK**.

➤ **To exclude formatting when filling a series**

1. Fill the series, and then click the **Auto Fill Options** button that appears in the lower-right corner of the cell range.

2. On the **Auto Fill Options** menu, click **Fill Without Formatting**.

➤ **To create a custom fill series**

1. In a series of cells, enter the items you want to use in your custom series, and then select the cells.

2. Display the **Advanced** page of the **Excel Options** dialog box.

3. Scroll to the bottom of the **Advanced** page. In the **General** area, click **Edit Custom Lists**.

4. In the **Custom Lists** dialog box, with the selected cell range shown in the **Import list from cells** box, click **Import**.

5. In the **List entries** list, verify or edit the entries.

6. Click **OK** in each of the open dialog boxes.

➤ **To apply a custom fill series**

→ Select a cell containing any entry from the custom list, and then drag the fill handle to create a series.

> **Tip** Excel fills the series with either lowercase or capitalized entries to match the cell you start with.

Copying Data

You can use the fill functionality to copy text data, numeric data, or cell formatting (such as text color, background color, and alignment) to adjacent cells.

➤ To copy text or currency amounts to adjacent cells

1. In the upper-left cell of the range you want to fill, enter the text or currency amount (formatted as currency) you want to duplicate, and then select the cell.

2. Drag the fill handle up, down, to the left, or to the right to encompass the cell range you want to fill.

➤ To copy numeric data to adjacent cells

1. In the upper-left cell of the range you want to fill, enter the value you want to duplicate, and then select the cell.

2. Drag the fill handle up, down, to the left, or to the right to encompass the cell range you want to fill.

   Or

1. In the upper-left cell of the range you want to fill, enter the value you want to duplicate.

2. Select the entire cell range you want to duplicate the value into.

3. On the **Home** tab, in the **Editing** group, click the **Fill** button, and then in the list, click the first direction in which you want to duplicate the value (**Down** or **Right**).

4. To fill a cell range that includes multiple rows and columns, repeat step 3, selecting the other direction.

> **Tip** You can also fill a cell range up or to the left; if you do so, make sure that the value you want to duplicate is in the lower-right cell of the range you want to fill.

➤ To copy formatting to adjacent cells without changing the cell content

1. Select the cell that has the formatting you want to copy.

2. Drag the fill handle up, down, to the left, or to the right to copy the formatting to the adjacent cells.

3. Click the **Auto Fill Options** button, and then click **Fill Formatting Only**.

Practice Tasks

The practice files for these tasks are located in the Excel\Objective2 practice file folder. If you want to save the results of the tasks, save them in the same folder with *My* appended to the file name so that you don't overwrite the original practice file.

- On the Sheet1 worksheet of the *FillSeries* workbook, fill cells A2:A21 with *Item 1*, *Item 2*, *Item 3*, and so on through *Item 20*. Fill cells B2:B21 with 10, 20, 30, and so on through 200. Then fill cells C2:C21 with *$3.00*, *$2.95*, *$2.90*, and so on through *$2.05*.

- On the Sheet1 worksheet of the *FillSeries* workbook, copy the background and font formatting from cell A1 to cells A2:A21.

- On the Sheet1 worksheet of the *FillCustom* workbook, fill cells B1:K1 with the days *Monday* through *Friday*, repeated twice.

- On the Sheet1 worksheet of the *FillCustom* workbook, create a custom series using the names entered in cells B2:B7. Fill the series in each row to create a rotating duty roster for the two weeks.

- On the Term Schedule worksheet of the *FillCopies* workbook, select cells A2:F14. Using the fill functionality, create a duplicate of the selected term schedule and following empty rows immediately below the original. Ensure that the Period column in the copy of the schedule displays periods 1 through 8.

2.3 Apply and Manipulate Hyperlinks

Creating Hyperlinks

Excel worksheets can include hyperlinks that provide a quick way to connect to related information or to create a prefilled email message. You can create a hyperlink from any cell content to any of the hyperlink locations supported by the Office 2010 programs— to another location on the worksheet, in the workbook, in an external document, or on the web.

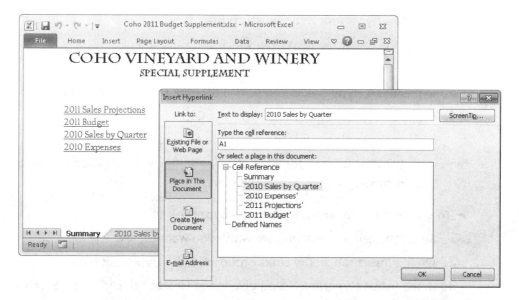

Within the worksheet, an active hyperlink appears underlined and in the color specified for hyperlinks by the applied theme. Pressing Ctrl and clicking the cell takes you to the link's target. After you click the hyperlink, it appears in the theme color specified for followed hyperlinks.

> **Tip** To select a cell containing a hyperlink for formatting, point to the cell and hold down the mouse button until the pointer changes to a plus sign.

➤ To create a hyperlink to a webpage

➜ Enter a URL in the cell, and then press Enter.

Or

1. Select the cell or element from which you want to link.
2. On the **Insert** tab, in the **Links** group, click the **Hyperlink** button.
3. In the **Insert Hyperlink** dialog box, in the **Link to** list, click **Existing File or Web Page**.
4. In the **Address** box, enter the URL of the webpage you want to link to.

Or

Click the **Browse the Web** button. In the web browser window that opens, display the webpage you want to link to. Then minimize or close the browser window.
5. In the **Insert Hyperlink** dialog box, click **OK**.

➤ **To create a hyperlink to an existing file**

1. Select the cell or element from which you want to link.

2. On the **Insert** tab, in the **Links** group, click the **Hyperlink** button.

3. In the **Insert Hyperlink** dialog box, in the **Link to** list, click **Existing File or Web Page**.

4. Do one of the following, and then click **OK**:

    ○ In the **Look in** area, browse to the file you want to link to.

    ○ Click the **Browse for File** button and then, in the **Link to File** dialog box, browse to the file and click **Open**.

➤ **To create an Excel workbook and a hyperlink to it**

1. Select the cell or element from which you want to link.

2. On the **Insert** tab, in the **Links** group, click the **Hyperlink** button.

3. In the **Insert Hyperlink** dialog box, in the **Link to** list, click **Create New Document**.

4. In the **Name of new document** box, enter a name for the workbook.

> **Tip** Do not enter the file extension. The Create New Document hyperlink in an Excel workbook automatically creates an Excel workbook.

5. To create the document in a folder other than your Documents folder, click the **Change** button. Then, in the **Create New Document** dialog box, browse to the folder in which you want to save the file, and click **OK**.

6. In the **When to edit** area, do one of the following:

    ○ Click **Edit the new document later** to create a blank workbook.

    ○ Click **Edit the new document now** to create a workbook and open it in Excel.

7. In the **Insert Hyperlink** dialog box, click **OK**.

➤ **To create a hyperlink to a worksheet or named range within the workbook**

1. Select the cell or element from which you want to link.

2. On the **Insert** tab, in the **Links** group, click the **Hyperlink** button.

3. In the **Insert Hyperlink** dialog box, in the **Link to** list, click **Place in This Document**.

4. In the **Or select a place in this document** box, do one of the following:

    ○ Under **Cell Reference**, click the worksheet you want to link to. Then if you want to link to a specific cell or cell range, enter it in the **Type the cell reference** box.

    ○ Under **Defined Names**, click the named range you want to link to.

5. In the **Insert Hyperlink** dialog box, click **OK**.

➤ **To create a hyperlink that creates a pre-addressed email message**

1. Select the cell or element from which you want to link.

2. On the **Insert** tab, in the **Links** group, click the **Hyperlink** button.

3. In the **Insert Hyperlink** dialog box, in the **Link to** list, click **E-mail Address**.

4. In the **E-mail address** box, enter the message recipient.

5. In the **Subject** box, enter the message subject.

6. In the **Insert Hyperlink** dialog box, click **OK**.

> **Tip** You can specify the text you want to represent the hyperlink in the worksheet cell by entering that text in the Text To Display box.

Modifying Hyperlinks

After creating a hyperlink of any type, you can change the type or target, or remove it without affecting the hyperlinked content.

➤ **To change the target of an existing hyperlink**

1. Right-click the hyperlinked cell or element, and then click **Edit Hyperlink**.

2. In the **Edit Hyperlink** dialog box, change the properties of the hyperlink, and then click **OK**.

➤ **To remove a hyperlink**

→ Right-click the hyperlinked cell or element, and then click **Remove Hyperlink**.

Practice Tasks

The practice file for these tasks is located in the Excel\Objective2 practice file folder. If you want to save the results of the tasks, save them in the same folder with *My* appended to the file name so that you don't overwrite the original practice file.

- On the Employees worksheet of the *Hyperlink* workbook, in cell A12, enter a hyperlink to the website located at www.otsi.com.

- Edit the hyperlink you created in cell A12 so that the cell displays *Please visit our website* instead of the URL.

Objective Review

Before finishing this chapter, ensure that you have mastered the following skills:

2.1 Construct Cell Data

2.2 Apply Auto Fill

2.3 Apply and Manipulate Hyperlinks

3 Formatting Cells and Worksheets

The skills tested in this section of the Microsoft Office Specialist exam for Microsoft Excel 2010 relate to changing the appearance of worksheets and worksheet data. Specifically, the following objectives are associated with this set of skills:

3.1 Apply and Modify Cell Formats

3.2 Merge or Split Cells

3.3 Create Row and Column Titles

3.4 Hide or Unhide Rows and Columns

3.5 Manipulate Page Setup Options for Worksheets

3.6 Create and Apply Cell Styles

Worksheets can contain just a few columns and rows of data or complex calculations involving hundreds of cells. The goal of formatting a worksheet is to structure the data in such a way that no matter what size the worksheet is, key information is readily identifiable. With Excel, you can format the information in an ordinary worksheet on three levels: you can manipulate the worksheet as a whole, work with entire columns or rows, and change individual cells to achieve precisely the results you want. If you define a range of cells as a table, you have additional formatting options available.

This chapter guides you in studying ways of formatting cells and worksheets by using cell formats and styles; merging and splitting cells; and hiding, displaying, and printing row and column titles. You also study page setup options for worksheets.

> **Practice Files** Before you can complete the practice tasks in this chapter, you need to copy the book's practice files to your computer. The practice files you'll use to complete the tasks in this chapter are in the Excel\Objective3 practice file folder. A complete list of practice files is provided in "Using the Book's Companion Content" at the beginning of this book.

3.1 Apply and Modify Cell Formats

Formatting Cell Content

By default, the font used for entries in a new Excel worksheet is Calibri, but you can use the same techniques you would use in any Office 2010 program to change the font and the following font attributes:

- Size
- Style
- Color
- Underline

You can change several attributes at once in the Format Cells dialog box.

> **Tip** By default, row height is dynamic and grows to fit the size of the cell content. If you manually change the height of a row and then change the font size of text in that row, you might have to adjust the row. For more information about adjusting row height, see the "Setting Row Height and Column Width" topic later in this section.

Text formatting can be applied to one cell, an entire row, an entire column, or the entire worksheet.

	A	B	C	D
		Scenario 1 (Best case)	**Scenario 2** (Average case)	**Scenario 3** (Worst case)
1	**Budget Drivers**			
2	Probability of shipping on time	98%	95%	90%
3	Number of building permits released within last 6 months	25,000	30,000	35,000
4	Regional economic growth	3.50%	3.20%	2.00%
5	Competitive strength (products, pricing, promotion, placement)	7	8	9
6	Probability of key supplier performance	99%	95%	90%

You might want to apply the following:

- **Text wrapping** By default, Excel does not wrap text in a cell. Instead, it allows the entry to overflow into the cell to the right if that cell is empty, or hides the part that won't fit if the cell to the right contains its own entry. To make the entire entry visible, you can allow the cell entry to wrap to multiple lines, which increases the height of the row.

> **Tip** Increasing the height of one cell increases the height of the entire row.

- **Alignment** By default, text is left aligned and numbers are right aligned. You can specify a particular horizontal alignment, and you can specify whether multiline entries should start at the top of their cells and go down, be centered, or start at the bottom of their cells and go up.

- **Orientation** By default, entries are horizontal and read from left to right. You can rotate entries for special effect or to allow you to display more information on the screen or a printed page. This capability is particularly useful when you have long column headers above columns of short entries.

> **Tip** You can apply text wrapping, alignment, and orientation formatting to any cell, but bear in mind that some kinds of formatting can detract from the readability of a worksheet if they are applied haphazardly.

> **To format all the characters in a selected cell**

→ On the **Home** tab, click buttons in the **Font** group.

➤ To format some of the characters in a cell

1. In the **Formula Bar** or in the cell, select the text you want to format.

2. On the **Home** tab, click buttons in the **Font** group.

Or

Click buttons on the Mini Toolbar that appears.

➤ To allow the entries in a selected column to wrap

→ On the **Home** tab, in the **Alignment** group, click the **Wrap Text** button.

> **Tip** If all the text in a cell is not visible after you click the Wrap Text button, it might be because the row is set to a specific height.

➤ To align the entries of a selected column

→ On the **Home** tab, in the **Alignment** group, click the **Align Text Left**, **Center**, or **Align Text Right** button to specify horizontal alignment, or click the **Top Align**, **Middle Align**, or **Bottom Align** button to specify vertical alignment.

➤ To change the orientation of a selected row of headers

→ On the **Home** tab, in the **Alignment** group, click the **Orientation** button, and then click the angle you want in the list.

> **Tip** You can change the text alignment, text control, text direction, and text orientation settings on the Alignment page of the Format Cells dialog box.

➤ To apply existing formatting to other cells

1. Select the cell or cells from which you want to copy formatting.

2. On the **Home** tab, in the **Clipboard** group, click the **Format Painter** button to store the formatting of the selected cell for a single use.

Or

In the **Clipboard** group, double-click the **Format Painter** button to store the formatting of the selected cell for multiple uses.

3. Drag the paintbrush-shaped cursor across the cell or cells to which you want to apply the stored formatting.

4. If necessary, click the **Format Painter** button or press Esc to turn off the Format Painter tool.

Formatting Cell Fills and Borders

You can format cells by using borders and shading to make them stand out. You can add predefined borders or custom borders of various styles, colors, and thicknesses to a single cell or to multiple cells. You can apply solid colors, gradients, and patterns to the background of one or more cells as creative ways of delineating structure and drawing attention to key information.

➤ **To change the color of a selected cell**

→ On the **Home** tab, in the **Font** group, click the **Fill Color** button to apply the active color.

→ In the **Font** group, click the **Fill Color** arrow, and then click a theme color or a standard color in the palette.

> **Tip** Clicking More Colors at the bottom of the palette opens the Colors dialog box, where you have a wider range of choices (more than 16 million).

➤ **To add a border to a selected cell**

→ On the **Home** tab, in the **Font** group, click the **Border** button to apply the most recent border.

→ In the **Font** group, on the **Border** menu, click the border you want.

Or

1. In the **Font** group, on the **Border** menu, click **Draw Border**.

2. When the cursor changes to a pencil, drag to draw border lines and boxes.

3. Press Esc to turn off the Draw Border function.

Or

1. In the **Font** group, on the **Border** menu, click **More Borders**.

2. On the **Border** page of the **Format Cells** dialog box, in the **Line** area, click a line style and color.

3. In the **Border** area, click in the preview pane to draw border lines. Click unwanted border lines to remove them.

4. In the **Format Cells** dialog box, click **OK**.

➤ **To remove the border from a selected cell**

→ On the **Home** tab, in the **Font** group, click **No Borders** in the **Border** list.

> **See Also** For information about conditional formatting, see section 8.3, "Apply Conditional Formatting."

Setting Row Height and Column Width

By default, worksheet rows have a standard height of 15 points (1 point equals approximately 1/72 inch) and their height increases and decreases to accommodate the number of lines in their longest entry. You can manually change the height of a row, but it is best to leave it automatic unless you have a good reason to specify a particular height. For example, you might want to specify a narrow row to create a visual break between blocks of data. (You can restore dynamic height adjustment if you need to.)

By default, worksheet columns have a standard width of 8.43 characters. Column width does not always automatically adjust to fit the column contents. You are more likely to want to change column width than row height, usually to accommodate long cell entries. You can have Excel adjust a column to fit its longest entry, or you can adjust it manually. In conjunction with text wrapping, adjusting column widths is a key technique for making as much data as possible visible on the screen or page.

Row headings   Column headings

	A	B	C	D	E	F
1	ID	Project Name	Owner	Days	Start	End
2	1.0	Marketing Research Tactical Plan	R. Ihrig	70	9-Jul	17-Sep
3						
4	1.1	Scope Definition Phase	R. Ihrig	10	9-Jul	19-Jul
5	1.1.1	Define research objectives	R. Ihrig	3	9-Jul	12-Jul
6	1.1.2	Define research requirements	S. Abbas	7	10-Jul	17-Jul
7	1.1.3	Determine in-house resource or hire vendor	R. Ihrig	2	15-Jul	17-Jul
8						
9	1.2	Vendor Selection Phase	R. Ihrig	19	19-Jul	7-Aug
10	1.2.1	Define vendor selection criteria	R. Ihrig	3	19-Jul	22-Jul
11	1.2.2	Develop vendor selection questionnaire	S. Abbas, T. Wang	2	22-Jul	24-Jul
12	1.2.3	Develop Statement of Work	S. Abbas	4	26-Jul	30-Jul
13	1.2.4	Evaluate proposal	R. Ihrig, S. Abbas	4	2-Aug	6-Aug
14	1.2.5	Select vendor	R. Ihrig	1	6-Aug	7-Aug
15						
16	1.3	Research Phase	Y. Li	47	9-Aug	25-Sep
17	1.3.1	Develop market research information needs questionnaire	Y. Li	2	9-Aug	11-Aug
18	1.3.2	Interview marketing group for market research needs	Y. Li	2	11-Aug	13-Aug

> **See Also** For information about text wrapping, see the "Formatting Cell Content" topic earlier in this section.

To adjust rows and columns manually, you can use two methods:

- Drag the border of a row heading or column heading. As you drag, a ScreenTip displays the new dimension of the row or column.

- Adjust the settings in a dialog box.

For the purposes of height and width adjustments, selecting a single cell in a row or column is the same as selecting the entire row or column. You can select multiple rows or columns to change all their heights or widths at the same time.

➤ **To change the height of a selected row**

→ Drag the bottom border of the row heading up or down.

Or

1. On the **Home** tab, in the **Cells** group, display the **Format** list, and then click **Row Height**.

2. In the **Row Height** dialog box, specify the height you want, and then click **OK**.

➤ **To change the width of a selected column**

→ Drag the right border of the column heading to the left or right.

Or

1. On the **Home** tab, in the **Cells** group, display the **Format** list, and then click **Column Width**.

2. In the **Column Width** dialog box, specify the width you want, and then click **OK**.

➤ **To automatically size a row to fit its contents**

→ On the **Home** tab, in the **Cells** group, display the **Format** list, and then click **AutoFit Row Height**.

➤ **To automatically size a column to fit its contents**

→ Double-click the right border of the column heading.

→ On the **Home** tab, in the **Cells** group, display the **Format** list, and then click **AutoFit Column Width**.

> **Tip** You can adjust the width of all the columns in a worksheet at the same time. Click the worksheet selector to select the entire worksheet, and then double-click the border between any two columns. Every column resizes to fit its contents. Empty columns remain unchanged.

Formatting Numbers

> **Strategy** Knowing which number format is appropriate for which type of data is important for efficient worksheet construction. Take the time to explore the formats so that you understand which one to apply when.

By default, all the cells in a new worksheet are assigned the General format. When setting up a worksheet, you assign to cells the format that is most appropriate for the type of information you expect them to contain. The format determines not only how the information looks but also how Excel can work with it.

You can assign the format before or after you type an entry in the cell. You can also just start typing and have Excel intuit the format from what you type. If you choose the format from the list or allow Excel to assign it for you, the format is applied with its default settings. For number and currency formats, you can change those settings in limited ways by clicking buttons on the Home tab. For all formats, you can change them in more precise ways in the Format Cells dialog box.

ABC 123 | **General**
No specific format

12 | **Number**
4590240.00

Currency
$4,590,240.00

Accounting
$4,590,240.00

Short Date
##########

Long Date
##########

Time
##########

% | **Percentage**
459024000.00%

½ | **Fraction**
4590240

10² | **Scientific**
4.59E+06

ABC | **Text**
4590240

More Number Formats...

Format Cells   ? ✕

| Number | Alignment | Font | Border | Fill | Protection |

Category:

General
Number
Currency
Accounting
Date
Time
Percentage
Fraction
Scientific
Text
Special
Custom

Sample
40588

Type:

Up to one digit (1/4)
Up to two digits (21/25)
Up to three digits (312/943)
As halves (1/2)
As quarters (2/4)
As eighths (4/8)
As sixteenths (8/16)

OK   Cancel

If none of the number formats is exactly what you want, you can modify an existing format to define your own. Your format then appears in a list of custom formats so that you can reuse it elsewhere in the workbook.

> **Tip** A custom format is saved in the workbook in which it is created and is not available for other workbooks unless you save the workbook containing the custom format as an Excel template.

> **Strategy** The rules for constructing custom formats are complex. For the exam, you might be asked to modify a format in simple ways, so you should become familiar with the characters used in a format and how to represent and format different types of data.

A number format can include up to four sections that correspond to positive numbers, negative numbers, zero values, and text, separated by semicolons, such as the following:

<POSITIVE>;<NEGATIVE>;<ZERO>;<TEXT>

You don't have to include all the sections in the format, but you must include semi-colons if you leave a section blank. For example, you could configure the following custom formatting:

[Blue]#,##0.00_);[Red](#,##0.00);0.00;"Test "@

This would result in the following display based on the value entered:

Value entered	Value displayed	Description
123 (<positive>)	123.00	Blue text, right aligned, moved one space left
-123 (<negative>)	(123.00)	Red text, right aligned
0 (<zero>)	0.00	Default font color, right aligned
One (<text>)	Test One	Default font color, left aligned

> **See Also** For a full list of characters that are valid in a custom number format, see "Guidelines for Including Text and Adding Spacing" in the Excel Help topic "Create or delete a custom number format."

Format Cells

Number | Alignment | Font | Border | Fill | Protection

Category:

General
Number
Currency
Accounting
Date
Time
Percentage
Fraction
Scientific
Text
Special
Custom

Sample

Type:

[Blue]#,##0.00_);[Red](#,##0.00);0.00;"Test "@

```
h:mm:ss
m/d/yyyy h:mm
mm:ss
mm:ss.0
@
[h]:mm:ss
_($* #,##0_);_($* (#,##0);_($* "-"_);_(@_)
_(* #,##0_);_(* (#,##0);_(* "-"_);_(@_)
_($* #,##0.00_);_($* (#,##0.00);_($* "-"??_);_(@_)
_(* #,##0.00_);_(* (#,##0.00);_(* "-"??_);_(@_)
[Blue]#,##0.00_);[Red](#,##0.00);0.00;"Test "@
```

Delete

Type the number format code, using one of the existing codes as a starting point.

OK | Cancel

➤ **To apply a default data format to a selected cell**

→ On the **Home** tab, in the **Number** group, display the **Number Format** list, and then click a format.

> **Tip** If you want a number to be treated as text, apply the text format.

➤ **To refine a number or currency format**

→ On the **Home** tab, in the **Number** group, click buttons to add a currency symbol, percent sign, or comma; or to increase or decrease the number of decimal places.

Or

1. On the **Home** tab, click the **Number** dialog box launcher.

2. In the **Format Cells** dialog box, with the format selected in the **Category** list, adjust the settings, and then click **OK**.

➤ **To create a custom format**

1. On the **Home** tab, click the **Number** dialog box launcher.

2. In the **Format Cells** dialog box, in the **Category** list, click **Custom**.

3. In the **Type** list, select a format that is close to the one you want, and then in the **Type** box, modify the format to meet your needs.

4. Click **OK** to apply the custom format to the selected cell(s).

➤ **To delete a custom format**

1. On the **Number** page of the **Format Cells** dialog box, in the **Category** list, click **Custom**.

2. In the **Type** list, select the custom format, and click **Delete**. Then click **OK**.

> **Tip** You cannot delete a built-in format from the Type list.

Practice Tasks

The practice files for these tasks are located in the Excel\Objective3 practice file folder. If you want to save the results of the tasks, save them in the same folder with *My* appended to the file name so that you don't overwrite the original practice file.

- On the Expense Statement worksheet of the *FormatCells* workbook, format cell K10 to display its contents in any one of the number formats (Number, Currency, or Accounting) with no decimal places. Then apply the same formatting to cells K11:K23.

- On the Expense Statement worksheet of the *FormatCells* workbook, apply custom number formatting to the TOTAL value in cell K23 that will cause it to be displayed in green if it is a positive number and red if it is a negative number. Do not add formatting for zero or text values. Verify the formatting by entering a value of 3,000 in cell K22.

- On the Expense Statement worksheet of the *FormatCells* workbook, change the font size of the headers in cells A9:K9. In cells A9:K9 and K10:K19, apply a background color that is two shades darker than the current one. Lastly, place a thick box border around the merged cells in row 2.

- On the Expense Statement worksheet of the *RowColumnFormatting* workbook, and set the entire worksheet so that all entries wrap in their cells. Right-align the entries in column A, and bottom-align the headers in row 9. Finally, turn off text wrapping in rows 4, 5, and 9, and turn the headers in row 9 sideways at a 45-degree angle.

- On the Inventory List worksheet of the *HeightWidth* workbook, set the height of row 4 to 6.00, and then drag row 3 to a height of 45.00. Then simultaneously set the width of columns F, G, and H to 10. Finally, reset the width of column B to fit its longest entry.

3.2 Merge or Split Cells

Worksheets that involve data at multiple hierarchical levels often use horizontal and vertical merged cells to clearly delineate relationships. With Excel, you have the following three merge options:

- **Merge & Center** This option merges the cells across the selected rows and columns, and centers the data from the first selected cell in the merged cell.

- **Merge Across** This option creates a separate merged cell for each row in the selection area, and maintains default alignment for the data type of the first cell of each row of the merged cells.

- **Merge Cells** This option merges the cells across the selected rows and columns, and maintains default alignment for the data type of the first cell of the merged cells.

In the case of Merge & Center and Merge Cells, data in selected cells other than the first is deleted. In the case of Merge Across, data in selected cells other than the first cell of each row is deleted.

Merged horizontal cells   Merged vertical cells

	Monday		Tuesday		Wednesday		Thursday		Friday	
	5/30/2010		5/31/2010		6/1/2010		6/2/2010		6/3/2010	
Time In		Total		Total		Total		Total		Total	
Time Out		0.00		0.00		0.00		0.00		0.00	
Meal Break											
Time In		Total		Total		Total		Total		Total	Total Hours Scheduled
Time Out		0.00		0.00		0.00		0.00		0.00	
Total	**0.00**		**0.00**		**0.00**		**0.00**		**0.00**	**0.00**

➤ **To merge selected cells**

→ On the **Home** tab, in the **Alignment** group, click the **Merge & Center** button to center and bottom-align the entry from the first cell.

→ On the **Home** tab, in the **Alignment** group, display the **Merge & Center** list, and then click **Merge Across** to create a separate merged cell on each selected row, maintaining the horizontal alignment of the data type in the first cell of each row.

→ On the **Home** tab, in the **Alignment** group, display the **Merge & Center** list, and then click **Merge Cells** to merge the entire selection, maintaining the horizontal alignment of the data type in the first cell.

➤ **To split a selected merged cell**

→ On the **Home** tab, in the **Alignment** group, click the **Merge & Center** button.

→ On the **Home** tab, in the **Alignment** group, display the **Merge & Center** list, and then click **Unmerge Cells**.

Practice Tasks

The practice file for this task is located in the Excel\Objective3 practice file folder. If you want to save the results of the tasks, save them in the same folder with *My* appended to the file name so that you don't overwrite the original practice file.

- On the Employees worksheet of the *Hyperlink* workbook, merge cells A12:C13 so that the hyperlink is centered across the bottom of the three columns. Then unmerge the cells so that the hyperlink appears in only cell A12.

3.3 Create Row and Column Titles

If a worksheet you will print spans more than one page, you can select an option to print the row and/or column headers, also known as the *titles*, on each page.

See Also For information about printing alphanumeric row and column headings, see section 1.2, "Print a Worksheet or Workbook."

➤ **To print row and column titles on every page**

1. On the **Page Layout** tab, in the **Page Setup** group, click the **Print Titles** button.

2. On the **Sheet** page of the **Page Setup** dialog box, in the **Print titles** area, click in the **Rows to repeat at top** box. Then in the worksheet, select the row(s) containing the column titles you want to print on each page.

3. Click in the **Columns to repeat at left** box. Then in the worksheet, select the column(s) containing the row titles you want to print on each page.

> ## Practice Tasks
>
> The practice file for this task is located in the Excel\Objective3 practice file folder. If you want to save the results of the tasks, save them in the same folder with *My* appended to the file name so that you don't overwrite the original practice file.
>
> - In the *HeightWidth* workbook, configure the Inventory List worksheet to print the row and column headings on each page.

3.4 Hide or Unhide Rows and Columns

If parts of a worksheet contain information you don't want to display, you can hide the rows or columns containing the data. Anyone who notices that column or row headings (column letters or row numbers) are missing can unhide the information unless you protect the workbook. If you don't want to go to the trouble of enforcing protection, you can hide all the column and row headings in the worksheet to make the hidden information harder to detect.

> **See Also** For information about hiding the column and row headings, see "Customizing Worksheet Appearance" in section 4.3, "Manipulate Worksheet Views."

Hidden columns D and E

	A	B	C	F	G	H	
4	Days with AQI data	Days AQI was Good	Days AQI was Moderate	Maximum AQI value	90th percentile AQI value	Median AQI value	Metr
5	365	93	150	237	147	82	River
6	323	98	163	166	122	72	Baker
7	365	168	152	182	106	54	Los A
8	345	182	116	173	114	49	Fresn
9	365	181	123	161	112	51	Visali
10	365	287	65	152	69	35	Tacon
11	365	284	73	155	68	34	Seattl
12	365	187	140	195	101	49	Sacra
13	298	170	117	430	79	48	San D
14	305	243	56	156	63	40	Oran
15	365	303	58	158	66	37	Chico
16	342	289	42	156	59	35	Mode
17	365	301	64	88	59	35	Spok

➤ **To hide selected rows or columns**

→ Right-click the selection, and then click **Hide**.

Or

1. On the **Home** tab, in the **Cells** group, display the **Format** list.

2. In the **Visibility** section of the **Format** list, point to **Hide & Unhide**, and then click **Hide Rows** to hide the selected row(s) or **Hide Columns** to hide the selected column(s).

➤ **To unhide rows or columns**

1. Select the columns or rows on both sides of the hidden column(s) or row(s).

2. Right-click the selection, and then click **Unhide**.

Or

1. Select the rows or columns on both sides of the hidden rows or columns.

2. On the **Home** tab, in the **Cells** group, display the **Format** list.

3. In the **Visibility** section of the **Format** list, point to **Hide & Unhide**, and then click **Unhide Rows** to display the selected row(s) or **Unhide Columns** to display the selected column(s).

➤ **To unhide the first row or column of a worksheet**

1. In the **Name** box to the left of the **Formula Bar**, enter , and then press Enter.

2. On the **Home** tab, in the **Cells** group, display the **Format** list.

3. In the **Visibility** section of the **Format** list, point to **Hide & Unhide**, and then click **Unhide Rows** to display row 1, or **Unhide Columns** to display column A.

> **Tip** To find hidden cells in a worksheet, click the Find & Select button, click Go To Special, select Visible Cells Only, and then click OK. Cells adjacent to hidden cells are identified by a white border.

Practice Tasks

The practice file for this task is located in the Excel\Objective3 practice file folder. If you want to save the results of the tasks, save them in the same folder with *My* appended to the file name so that you don't overwrite the original practice file.

- On the Inventory List worksheet of the *Hiding* workbook, hide the column containing the Inventory ID and the row containing the data's source notes. Then unhide the row, but not the column.

3.5 Manipulate Page Setup Options for Worksheets

You can control the layout of printed worksheets not only by defining a print area and inserting page breaks but also by changing the page margins, the space allocated to the header and footer, the page orientation, and the paper size.

> **See Also** For information about defining a print area and setting page breaks, see section 1.2, "Print a Worksheet or Workbook."

If none of these methods enables you to fit the required amount of information on a printed page, you can avoid having to adjust the font size and the width and height of columns and rows by scaling the worksheet to less than 100 percent. This option achieves the effect you want at print time but does not change the worksheet layout for people who will be viewing it on-screen.

You can scale a worksheet manually or allow Excel to scale it for you by specifying the number of pages you want the printed worksheet to be.

➤ **To change the page margins**

1. On the **Page Layout** tab, in the **Page Setup** group, click the **Margins** button.

2. In the **Margins** list, do one of the following:

   ○ Click the standard margin setting you want.

   ○ Click **Custom Margins**, and then on the **Margins** page of the **Page Setup** dialog box, specify the **Top**, **Bottom**, **Left**, and **Right** margins, and click **OK**.

➤ **To change the height of the header and footer**

1. On the **Page Layout** tab, in the **Page Setup** group, click the **Margins** button, and then click **Custom Margins**.

2. On the **Margins** page of the **Page Setup** dialog box, specify the vertical dimensions of the **Header** and **Footer** areas, and then click **OK**.

➤ **To change the page orientation**

→ On the **Page Layout** tab, in the **Page Setup** group, click the **Orientation** button, and then click **Portrait** or **Landscape**.

➤ **To scale the worksheet when printing**

1. On the **Page Layout** tab, click the **Page Setup** dialog box launcher.

2. On the **Page** page of the **Page Setup** dialog box, in the **Scaling** area, click **Adjust to**. Then change the **% normal size** setting.

   Or

   On the **Page** page of the **Page Setup** dialog box, do one of the following:

   ○ With **Adjust to** selected in the **Scaling** area, adjust the **% normal size** setting.

   ○ In the **Scaling** area, click **Fit to**. Then specify the number of pages horizontally and vertically on which you want to print the worksheet.

3. In the **Page Setup** dialog box, click **OK**.

Practice Tasks

The practice file for these tasks is located in the Excel\Objective3 practice file folder. If you want to save the results of the tasks, save them in the same folder with *My* appended to the file name so that you don't overwrite the original practice file.

- In the *Layout* workbook, display the JanFeb worksheet. Ensure that all the contents will print in a landscape orientation on two pages of letter-size paper.

- In the *Layout* workbook, ensure that all the contents of the JanFeb worksheet will print on two pieces of A5-size paper.

- In the *Layout* workbook, ensure that the contents of the JanFeb worksheet will print at 50 percent of their actual size.

3.6 Create and Apply Cell Styles

You don't have to apply cell formats one at a time. You can quickly apply several formats at once by clicking a style in the Cell Styles gallery. Some of the categories of styles in this gallery are static, whereas others are dynamic and change according to the theme applied to the worksheet.

Good, Bad and Neutral

Normal	Bad	Good	Neutral

Data and Model

Calculation	Check Cell	Explanatory...	Input	Linked Cell	Note
Output	Warning Text				

Titles and Headings

Heading 1	Heading 2	Heading 3	Heading 4	Title	Total

Themed Cell Styles

20% - Accent1	20% - Accent2	20% - Accent3	20% - Accent4	20% - Accent5	20% - Accent6
40% - Accent1	40% - Accent2	40% - Accent3	40% - Accent4	40% - Accent5	40% - Accent6
60% - Accent1	60% - Accent2	60% - Accent3	60% - Accent4	60% - Accent5	60% - Accent6
Accent1	Accent2	Accent3	Accent4	Accent5	Accent6

Number Format

Comma	Comma [0]	Currency	Currency [0]	Percent

New Cell Style...
Merge Styles...

If you need a style that is not already defined, you can manually format a cell and then save the combination of formatting as a cell style that you can easily apply elsewhere.

➤ **To apply a style to a selected cell**

1. On the **Home** tab, in the **Styles** group, click the **Cell Styles** button.

2. In the **Cell Styles** gallery, click the style you want.

➤ **To create a cell style based on a formatted cell**

1. Select a cell that has the combination of formatting you want to save as a style.

2. In the **Cell Styles** gallery, click **New Cell Style**.

3. In the **Style** dialog box, name the style, clear the check boxes of any elements you don't want to include in the style, and then click **OK**.

➤ **To create a cell style from scratch**

1. In the **Cell Styles** gallery, click **New Cell Style**.

2. In the **Style** dialog box, enter a name for the style in the **Style name** box.

3. Click **Format**. In the **Format Cells** dialog box, on the **Number**, **Alignment**, **Font**, **Border**, **Fill**, and **Protection** pages, specify the properties of the custom cell style.

4. Click **OK** in each of the open dialog boxes.

Practice Tasks

The practice file for this task is located in the Excel\Objective3 practice file folder. If you want to save the results of the tasks, save them in the same folder with *My* appended to the file name so that you don't overwrite the original practice file.

- On the Expense Statement worksheet of the *FormatCells* workbook, select cells A9:K9, and apply the 20% - Accent2 cell style. Then change the font style and background color of cells A9:K9, and save the formatting combination as a new cell style.

Objective Review

Before finishing this chapter, ensure that you have mastered the following skills:

3.1   Apply and Modify Cell Formats
3.2   Merge or Split Cells
3.3   Create Row and Column Titles
3.4   Hide or Unhide Rows and Columns
3.5   Manipulate Page Setup Options for Worksheets
3.6   Create and Apply Cell Styles

4 Managing Worksheets and Workbooks

The skills tested in this section of the Microsoft Office Specialist exam for Microsoft Excel 2010 relate to creating, formatting, and displaying worksheets and workbooks. Specifically, the following objectives are associated with this set of skills:

4.1 Create and Format Worksheets
4.2 Manipulate Window Views
4.3 Manipulate Workbook Views

You can easily create, format, and view functional workbooks that contain multiple worksheets.

This chapter guides you in studying how to create and format worksheets, display multiple views of a worksheet or workbook, and display different views of a workbook.

> **Practice Files** Before you can complete the practice tasks in this chapter, you need to copy the book's practice files to your computer. The practice files you'll use to complete the tasks in this chapter are in the Excel\Objective4 practice file folder. A complete list of practice files is provided in "Using the Book's Companion Content" at the beginning of this book.

4.1 Create and Format Worksheets

> **Tip** Basic worksheet-management skills such as creating, deleting, and renaming
> worksheets are covered in the introduction to this part of the book.

Workbooks commonly include multiple worksheets for a single project or purpose. For
example, the first worksheet might display a simple summary of more complex data
presented on other, purpose-specific worksheets. You can move and copy worksheets
within and between workbooks. You can hide worksheets you don't need to use or don't
want other people to see. To work with multiple worksheets at one time—for example,
to apply formatting to several worksheets at once—you can group the worksheets.

When a workbook contains several sheets, it is helpful to change the names on the sheet
tabs to reflect the worksheet contents. You can also assign different colors to the tabs to
categorize them or to make them easily distinguishable.

23	338	322	10	0	0	7-
24	274	236	38	0	0	95
25	274	236	26	12	0	135
26	273	255	17	1	0	102
27	267	253	14	0	0	94
28	315	219	94	2	0	109
29	365	266	92	7	0	146
30	339	298	40	1	0	104

Summary | **All Data** | Washington | Oregon | California

Ready

➤ To copy a worksheet within a workbook or to another workbook

1. Right-click the worksheet tab, and then click **Move or Copy**.

2. In the **Move or Copy** dialog box, if you want to copy the worksheet to another
   workbook, select that workbook in the **To book** list.

3. In the **Before sheet** list, click the worksheet you want to position the copy before.

4. Select the **Create a copy** check box, and then click **OK**.

➤ To reposition a worksheet within a workbook

→ In the **Move or Copy** dialog box, click the worksheet before which you want to
   move the current worksheet, and then click **OK**.

→ Drag the worksheet tab to reposition it.

➤ To hide a worksheet

→ Right-click the worksheet tab, and then click **Hide**.

➤ To display a hidden worksheet

1. Right-click any worksheet tab, and then click **Unhide**.

2. In the **Unhide** dialog box, select the worksheet you want to display, and then click **OK**.

➤ To group worksheets

1. Display the first worksheet you want to include in the group.

2. Select additional worksheets in one of these ways:

- ○ To select adjacent worksheets, press Shift and then click the tab of the last worksheet in the workbook that you want to include in the group.

- ○ To select nonadjacent worksheets, press Ctrl and then click the tab of each additional worksheet that you want to include in the group.

> **Tip** When multiple worksheets are selected, [Group] appears in the title bar. Many commands are not available when a group of worksheets is active. To release the group, click the tab of any worksheet that is not part of the group.

➤ To rename a worksheet

→ Double-click the tab, and then enter the name you want.

→ Right-click the tab, click **Rename**, and then enter the name you want.

➤ To assign a color to a worksheet tab

→ Right-click the tab, click **Tab Color**, and then in the color palette, click the color you want.

Practice Tasks

The practice file for these tasks is located in the Excel\Objective4 practice file folder. If you want to save the results of the tasks, save them in the same folder with *My* appended to the file name so that you don't overwrite the original practice file.

- In the *SalesReport* workbook, and make a copy of the By Product worksheet. Rename the copy *Sales By Product*.

- Group the By Product and Sales By Product worksheets, and then apply the Austin theme to the worksheet group.

- Make the Source Data worksheet the last worksheet in the workbook.

- Hide the By Product-Customer Filtered worksheet.

- Change each of the visible worksheet tabs to a different color.

4.2 Manipulate Window Views

Freezing and Splitting Windows

It can be cumbersome to work in a worksheet that is too long or wide to display legibly in the program window because you have to scroll up and down or back and forth to view data. Similarly, it can be tedious to have to switch back and forth between multiple worksheets in the same workbook if you frequently need to access information in both of them.

You can view multiple parts of a worksheet at one time by freezing rows or columns so that they stay in view while you scroll the rest of the worksheet. You can also split the window and then independently scroll and work in two views of the worksheet at one time.

> **Tip** Another way to bring noncontiguous rows or columns together on one screen is to hide the rows or columns between them. For information about hiding rows and coumns, see section 3.4, "Hide or Unhide Rows and Columns."

➤ To freeze the first row or column of a worksheet

→ On the **View** tab, in the **Window** group, click the **Freeze Panes** button, and then click **Freeze Top Row** or **Freeze First Column**.

➤ **To freeze multiple rows or columns**

1. Select the row below or column to the right of those you want to freeze, by clicking the row heading or column heading.

2. On the **View** tab, in the **Window** group, click the **Freeze Panes** button, and then click **Freeze Panes**.

➤ **To simultaneously freeze columns and rows**

1. Select the cell that is below and to the right of the intersection of the row and column you want to freeze.

2. On the **View** tab, in the **Window** group, click the **Freeze Panes** button, and then click **Freeze Panes**.

> **Tip** You can freeze as many columns and rows as you like depending on what cell is selected when you execute the Freeze Panes command. Selecting a cell in row 1 freezes only columns. Selecting a cell in column A freezes only rows.

➤ **To unfreeze all rows and columns**

→ On the **View** tab, in the **Window** group, click the **Freeze Panes** button, and then click **Unfreeze Panes**.

➤ **To split the window vertically or horizontally**

→ Drag the split bar to the row or column where you want to split the window.

➤ **To remove a split**

→ Double-click the split bar that divides the pane.

→ Drag the split bar to its original location at the top or right end of the scroll bar.

Displaying Multiple Windows

You can open multiple windows that all display the current spreadsheet and then arrange those windows in a variety of ways. You can also open and arrange multiple workbook windows.

➤ **To open a second instance of a workbook in a separate window**

→ On the **View** tab, in the **Window** group, click the **New Window** button.

➤ **To arrange multiple program windows**

1. In the **Window** group, click the **Arrange All** button.

2. In the **Arrange Windows** dialog box, click **Tiled**, **Horizontal**, **Vertical**, or **Cascade**.

3. To include only windows displaying views of the current workbook, select the **Windows of active workbook** check box.

4. In the **Arrange Windows** dialog box, click **OK**.

Practice Tasks

The practice files for these tasks are located in the Excel\Objective4 practice file folder. If you want to save the results of the tasks, save them in the same folder with *My* appended to the file name so that you don't overwrite the original practice file.

- On the Budget worksheet of the *PersonalMonthlyBudget* workbook, freeze rows 1 through 9 so that when you scroll the rest of the workbook, those rows are always visible. Then unfreeze the rows.

- Split the Budget worksheet of the *PersonalMonthlyBudget* workbook so that you can display rows 1 through 9 in one window and scroll the budget data in another window.

- Continuing from the previous task, open the *AirQualityData* and *PopulationData* workbooks. Using the commands in the Window group on the View menu, tile the three windows, and then arrange them so that they overlap.

- Continuing from the previous task, use the New Window command to open a second instance of one of the workbooks. Then arrange only the two windows of the active workbook horizontally.

4.3 Manipulate Workbook Views

Switching Worksheet Views

From the View toolbar at the bottom of the program window, or from the View tab, you can switch among three views of a worksheet:

- **Normal** The worksheet is displayed in the window at 100 percent magnification or at whatever zoom level you select. Page breaks are indicated by black dashed lines.

- **Page Layout** Each worksheet page appears as it will when printed, with space between the individual pages. A ruler appears at the left edge of the window next to the optional row headings. The page header and footer are visible and you can select them for editing.

- **Page Break Preview** The entire worksheet is displayed in the window, with page breaks indicated by bold blue dashed lines and page numbers displayed in the center of each page. You can change the page breaks by dragging the blue lines.

➤ **To display a standard worksheet view**

➜ On the **Zoom** toolbar, click the **Normal**, **Page Layout**, or **Page Break Preview** button.

➜ On the **View** tab, in the **Workbook Views** group, click the **Normal**, **Page Layout**, or **Page Break Preview** button.

Customizing the Program Window

To maximize your work area, you can display the three views in full-screen mode, so that only the title bar is visible. To increase the vertical space of the work area but still have easy access to commands, you can hide the ribbon so that only its tabs are visible, hide the row and column headings, and hide the Formula Bar.

> **See Also** For information about hiding row and column headings, see the next section, "Customizing Worksheet Appearance."

➤ **To hide all program window elements other than the title bar**

➜ On the **View** tab, in the **Workbook Views** group, click the **Full Screen** button.

➤ **To redisplay all program window elements**

➜ Press the Esc key.

➜ Right-click the worksheet, and then click **Close Full Screen**.

➤ **To hide or display the Formula Bar**

→ On the **View** tab, in the **Show** group, select or clear the **Formula Bar** check box.

Customizing Worksheet Appearance

While you are developing a worksheet, you might want to see gridlines and row and column headings to efficiently move among cells. But when you distribute the final worksheet, you can turn off gridlines and headings for a cleaner look.

	A	B	C	D	E	F	G	H
1								
2								
3		Magazine	Cost per Ad	Readers	Number of Ads	Total Cost	Audience	
4		Mag1	$ 30,000.00	100,000	8 $	240,000.00	800,000	
5		Mag2	$ 40,000.00	400,000	8 $	320,000.00	3,200,000	
6		Mag3	$ 27,000.00	350,000	8 $	216,000.00	2,800,000	
7		Mag4	$ 80,000.00	200,000	10 $	800,000.00	2,000,000	
8		Totals				$ 1,576,000.00	8,800,000	
9								
10			Constraints			Total Budget	$ 3,000,000.00	
11						Minimum Audience	10,000,000	
12								
13								
14								
15								
16								

Magazine	Cost per Ad	Readers	Number of Ads	Total Cost	Audience
Mag1	$ 30,000.00	100,000	8 $	240,000.00	800,000
Mag2	$ 40,000.00	400,000	8 $	320,000.00	3,200,000
Mag3	$ 27,000.00	350,000	8 $	216,000.00	2,800,000
Mag4	$ 80,000.00	200,000	10 $	800,000.00	2,000,000
Totals				$ 1,576,000.00	8,800,000

Constraints		
	Total Budget	$ 3,000,000.00
	Minimum Audience	10,000,000
Minimum Ads for Magazines 1 through 3		8
Minimum Ads for Magazine 4		10
Maximum Ads in Any Magazine		20

➤ **To hide or display gridlines**

→ On the **View** tab, in the **Show** group, select or clear the **Gridlines** check box.

➤ **To hide or display row and column headings**

→ On the **View** tab, in the **Show** group, select or clear the **Headings** check box.

Changing the Zoom Level

From the Zoom toolbar at the bottom of the program window, or from the Zoom group on the View tab, you can change the zoom level of a worksheet in any range from 10 percent to 400 percent. You can zoom the entire worksheet or select a range of cells and have Excel determine the zoom level necessary to fit the selection in the program window.

➤ **To change the zoom level in 10 percent increments**

→ On the **Zoom** toolbar, click the **Zoom Out** button (labeled with a minus sign) or the **Zoom In** button (labeled with a plus sign).

➤ **To change the zoom level dynamically**

→ On the **Zoom** toolbar, move the **Zoom** slider to the left to zoom out or to the right to zoom in.

➤ **To set the zoom level to a specific percentage**

1. On the **View** tab, in the **Zoom** group, click the **Zoom** button.

Or

On the **Zoom** toolbar, click the **Zoom level** button.

2. In the **Zoom** dialog box, click a specific magnification level, or click **Custom** and then enter a value from 10 to 400. Then click **OK**.

➤ **To zoom in on selected cells**

1. Select the cell or cell range you want to zoom in on.

2. On the **View** tab, in the **Zoom** group, click **Zoom to Selection**.

Or

1. On the **Zoom** toolbar, click the **Zoom level** button.

2. In the **Zoom** dialog box, click **Fit selection**, and then click **OK**.

Practice Tasks

The practice file for these tasks is located in the Excel\Objective4 practice file folder. If you want to save the results of the tasks, save them in the same folder with *My* appended to the file name so that you don't overwrite the original practice file.

- Open the *PersonalMonthlyBudget* workbook. Display the Budget worksheet in Page Layout view, and then zoom out so you can see the entire first page.

- Select the Projected Monthly Income section of the Budget worksheet, and zoom in to display only the selected cells.

Objective Review

Before finishing this chapter, ensure that you have mastered the following skills:

4.1   Create and Format Worksheets

4.2   Manipulate Window Views

4.3   Manipulate Workbook Views

5 Applying Formulas and Functions

The skills tested in this section of the Microsoft Office Specialist exam for Microsoft Excel 2010 relate to calculating data by using formulas. Specifically, the following objectives are associated with this set of skills:

5.1 Create Formulas
5.2 Enforce Precedence
5.3 Apply Cell References in Formulas
5.4 Apply Conditional Logic in Formulas
5.5 Apply Named Ranges in Formulas
5.6 Apply Cell Ranges in Formulas

Excel has been referred to as the world's most popular database program because you can store vast amounts of data within a single workbook or worksheet. This was not, however, the purpose for which Excel was created. By using the many functions built in to Excel, you can build formulas that perform complex data calculations. Excel 2010 includes many features that simplify the process of creating complex formulas.

This chapter guides you in studying ways of creating basic formulas, controlling the order in which Excel performs calculations within formulas, calculating data based on specific requirements, and referencing data within a formula.

> **Practice Files** Before you can complete the practice tasks in this chapter, you need to copy the book's practice files to your computer. The practice files you'll use to complete the tasks in this chapter are in the Excel\Objective5 practice file folder. A complete list of practice files is provided in "Using the Book's Companion Content" at the beginning of this book.

5.1 Create Formulas

Formulas in Excel can be made up of values that you enter, cell references, names, mathematical operators, and functions. A function can be thought of as a service provided by Excel to do a specific task. That task might be to perform a math operation, to make a decision based on information you give it, or to perform an action on some text.

A function is always indicated by the function name followed by a set of parentheses. For most functions, arguments inside the parentheses either tell the function what to do or indicate the values that the function is to work with. An argument can be a value that you enter, a cell reference, a range reference, a name, or even another function. The number and type of arguments vary depending on which function you're using. It is important to understand the syntax of common functions and be able to correctly enter the function arguments. Fortunately, you don't have to memorize anything; Excel 2010 does an excellent job of walking you through the process of using a function within a formula. You can type a function's syntax yourself if you want, but it's almost always easier to let Excel guide you through the process.

Probably the most common formula used in Excel is one that totals the values in a set of cells. Rather than individually adding the values of all the cells you want to total, you can use the SUM function to perform this task. The following table describes other functions that allow you to summarize information from sets of cells.

Function	Description	Arguments
SUM()	Totals a set of numbers	number1,number2,...,number255
COUNT()	Counts the number of cells that have numbers	value1,value2,...,value255
COUNTA()	Counts the number of cells that are not empty	value1,value2,...,value255
AVERAGE()	Averages a set of numbers	number1,number2,...,number255
MIN()	Finds the minimum value in a set of numbers	number1,number2,...,number255
MAX()	Finds the maximum value in a set of numbers	number1,number2,...,number255

Each of these functions takes up to 255 arguments; each argument can be a range or named reference and can refer to thousands of values.

In the previous table, any argument specified as a number can be a number that is entered directly, a text representation of a number (a number inside of quotation marks), a cell reference, a range reference, or a named reference. Any cells that have text which can't be translated to a number, that are empty, or that have an error are simply ignored by the function.

Also in the table, any argument specified as a value can be any type of value. In the case of the COUNT() function, it will simply ignore any value that it can't interpret as a number. In the case of COUNTA(), it will count every cell that isn't empty.

➤ **To sum values in a cell range**

1. Select the cell immediately below or to the right of the values you want to total.

2. On the **Home** tab, in the **Editing** group, click the **AutoSum** button.

   Or

   On the **Formulas** tab, in the **Function Library** group, click the **AutoSum** button.

3. Verify that the cell range displayed in the formula is correct, and then press Enter.

   Or

1. Select the cell in which you want to place the total.

2. On the **Formulas** tab, in the **Function Library** group, click the **Math & Trig** button, and then in the list, click **SUM**.

3. In the **Function Arguments** box, enter the cell range you want to total, and then click **OK**.

➤ **To count cells containing numeric values**

1. Select the cell immediately below or to the right of the range within which you want to count the cells containing numeric values.

2. On the **Formulas** tab, in the **Function Library** group, click the **AutoSum** arrow, and then in the list, click **Count Numbers**.

3. Verify that the cell range displayed in the formula is correct, and then press Enter.

   Or

1. Select the cell in which you want to place the count.

2. On the **Formulas** tab, in the **Function Library** group, click the **More Functions** button, point to **Statistical**, and then in the list, click **COUNT**.

3. In the **Function Arguments** box, enter the cell range within which you want to count non-empty cells, and then click **OK**.

➤ **To count cells containing any type of value**

1. Select the cell in which you want to place the count.

2. On the **Formulas** tab, in the **Function Library** group, click the **More Functions** button, point to **Statistical**, and then in the list, click **COUNTA**.

3. In the **Function Arguments** box, enter the cell range within which you want to count the cells that contain any type of value, and then click **OK**.

➤ **To average values in a data range**

1. Select the cell immediately below or to the right of the values you want to average.

2. On the **Formulas** tab, in the **Function Library** group, click the **AutoSum** arrow, and then in the list, click **Average**.

3. Verify that the cell range displayed in the formula is correct, and then press Enter.

   Or

1. Select the cell in which you want to place the average.

2. On the **Formulas** tab, in the **Function Library** group, click the **More Functions** button, point to **Statistical**, and then in the list, click **AVERAGE**.

3. In the **Function Arguments** box, enter the cell range that you want to average, and then click **OK**.

➤ **To find the lowest value in a data range**

1. Select the cell immediately below or to the right of the values you want to evaluate.

2. On the **Formulas** tab, in the **Function Library** group, click the **AutoSum** arrow, and then in the list, click **Min**.

3. Verify that the cell range displayed in the formula is correct, and then press Enter.

   Or

1. Select the cell in which you want to place the minimum value.

2. On the **Formulas** tab, in the **Function Library** group, click the **More Functions** button, point to **Statistical**, and then in the list, click **MIN**.

3. In the **Function Arguments** box, enter the cell range you want to evaluate, and then click **OK**.

➤ **To find the highest value in a data range**

1. Select the cell immediately below or to the right of the values you want to evaluate.

2. On the **Formulas** tab, in the **Function Library** group, click the **AutoSum** arrow, and then in the list, click **Max**.

3. Verify that the cell range displayed in the formula is correct, and then press Enter.

   Or

1. Select the cell in which you want to place the maximum value.

2. On the **Formulas** tab, in the **Function Library** group, click the **More Functions** button, point to **Statistical**, and then in the list, click **MAX**.

3. In the **Function Arguments** box, enter the cell range you want to evaluate, and then click **OK**.

Practice Tasks

The practice files for these tasks are located in the Excel\Objective5 practice file folder. If you want to save the results of the tasks, save them in the same folder with *My* appended to the file name so that you don't overwrite the original practice file.

- On the Summary worksheet of the *SummaryFormula* workbook, do the following:
  - In cell B18, create a formula that returns the number of non-empty cells in the Period range. Then in cell B19, create a formula that returns the number of empty cells in the same range.
  - In cell C18, create a formula that returns the average value in the Sales range.
  - In cell D5, create a formula that returns the lowest Sales value for the Fall period.

- On the Sales By Region worksheet of the *Sales* workbook, do the following:
  - Create subtotals of sales amounts first by *Period* and then by *Region*.
  - Find the average sales by *Period* and then by *Region*.
  - Find the maximum and minimum values by *Period* and then by *Region*.

5.2 Enforce Precedence

A formula can involve multiple types of calculations. Unless you specify another order of precedence, Excel evaluates formula content and processes calculations in this order:

1. **Reference operators** The colon (:), space ( ), and comma (,) symbols
2. **Negation** The negative (–) symbol in phrases such as –1
3. **Percentage** The percent (%) symbol
4. **Exponentiation** The raising to a power (^) symbol
5. **Multiplication and division** The multiply (*) and divide (/) symbols
6. **Addition and subtraction** The plus (+) and minus (-) symbols
7. **Concatenation** The and (&) symbol connecting two strings of text
8. **Comparison** The equal (=), less than (<), and greater than (>) symbols and any combination thereof

If multiple calculations within a formula have the same precedence, Excel processes them in order from left to right.

You can change the order in which Excel processes the calculations within a formula by enclosing the calculations you want to perform first in parentheses. Similarly, when you use multiple calculations to represent one value in a formula, you can enclose the calculations in parentheses to instruct Excel to process the calculations as a unit before incorporating the results of the calculation in the formula.

The following table illustrates the effect of changing precedence within a simple formula.

Formula	Result
=1+2-3+4-5+6	5
=(1+2)-(3+4)-(5+6)	−15
=1+(2-3)+4-(5+6)	−7

➤ **To change the order of calculation within a formula**

→ Enclose the calculations you want to perform first within parentheses.

Practice Tasks

There are no practice files for these tasks. Simply open a blank workbook.

- In cell A1 of a worksheet, enter the following formula:

  =5x2+7-12

- Copy the formula from cell A1 to cells A2:A5. Edit each of the copied formulas, placing parentheses around different groupings to view the effect.

5.3 Apply Cell References in Formulas

Formulas in an Excel worksheet most often involve functions performed on the values contained in one or more other cells on the worksheet (or on another worksheet). A reference that you make in a formula to the contents of a worksheet cell is either a relative reference, an absolute reference, or a mixed reference. A relative reference changes in relation to the cell in which the referring formula is originally entered; an absolute reference doesn't change. It is important to understand the difference and to know which to use when creating a formula.

A relative reference to a cell takes the form *A1*. When you copy or fill a formula from the original cell to other cells, a relative reference changes to indicate the cell having the same relationship to the formula cell that A1 did to the original formula cell. For example, copying a formula that refers to cell A1 one row down changes the A1 reference to A2; copying the formula one column to the right changes the A1 reference to B1.

An absolute reference takes the form *$A$1*; the dollar sign indicates an absolute reference to column A and an absolute reference to row 1. When you copy or fill a formula from the original cell to other cells, an absolute reference does not change—regardless of the relationship to the referenced cell, the reference stays the same.

A mixed reference refers absolutely to one part of the reference and relatively to the other. The mixed reference A$1 always refers to row 1, and $A1 always refers to column A.

	A	B	C	D	E
1		Customer	Wingtip Toys		
2		Discount	20%		
3					
4	Quantity	Price Each	Subtotal	Discount	Total
5	100	$ 5.00	$ 500.00	$ 100.00	$ 400.00
6	200	$ 10.00	$ 2,000.00	$ 400.00	$ 1,600.00
7	300	$ 15.00	$ 4,500.00	$ 900.00	$ 3,600.00
8	400	$ 20.00	$ 8,000.00	$1,600.00	$ 6,400.00
9	500	$ 25.00	$ 12,500.00	$2,500.00	$10,000.00
10					

Absolute references   Relative references

	A	B	C	D	E
1			Customer	Wingtip Toys	
2			Discount	0.2	
3					
4		Quantity	Price Each	Subtotal	Discount	Total
5	100	5	=A5*B5	=C5*$C$2	=C5-D5
6	200	10	=A6*B6	=C6*$C$2	=C6-D6
7	300	15	=A7*B7	=C7*$C$2	=C7-D7
8	400	20	=A8*B8	=C8*$C$2	=C8-D8
9	500	25	=A9*B9	=C9*$C$2	=C9-D9
10					

You can reference cells in other worksheets of your workbook. For example, you might prepare a Summary worksheet that displays results based on data tracked on other worksheets. References to cells on other worksheets can be relative, absolute, or mixed.

> **Tip** You can reference a worksheet by whatever name appears on the worksheet tab.

You can reference cells in other workbooks. For example, you might prepare a report that collates data from workbooks submitted by multiple regional managers.

When referencing a workbook located in a folder other than the one your active workbook is in, enter the path to the file along with the file name. If the path includes a non-alphabetical character (such as the backslash in "C:\"), enclose the path in single quotation marks.

➤ To relatively reference the contents of a cell

→ Enter the column letter followed by the row number, like this:

A1

➤ To absolutely reference the contents of a cell

→ Precede the column letter and row number with dollar signs, like this:

$A$1

➤ To absolutely reference a column or row

→ Precede the column letter or row number with a dollar sign.

➤ To reference a cell on a different worksheet in the same workbook

→ Enter the worksheet name and cell reference, separated by an exclamation point, like this:

Data!C2

Or

1. With the cursor positioned where you want to insert the reference, click the tab of the worksheet containing the cell you want to reference.

2. Click the cell or select the cell range you want to reference, and then press Enter to enter the cell reference into the formula and return to the original worksheet.

➤ **To reference a cell in another workbook in the same folder**

→ Enter the workbook name in square brackets followed by the worksheet name and cell reference, separated by an exclamation point, like this:

[Sales.xlsx]Data!C2

→ Enter the path to the workbook, followed the workbook name in square brackets, followed by the worksheet name, enclosing everything in single quotes, Then enter an exclamation point followed by the cell reference, like this:

='C:\PROJECTS\MOS2010\Excel Files\[test.xlsx]Sheet1'!$A$1

Or

1. Open the workbook that contains the cell you want to reference, and then switch to the workbook you want to create the formula in.

2. With the cursor positioned where you want to insert the reference, switch to the second workbook, click the tab of the worksheet containing the cell you want to reference, click the cell or select the range you want to reference, and then press Enter.

Practice Tasks

The practice files for these tasks are located in the Excel\Objective5 practice file folder. If you want to save the results of the tasks, save them in the same folder with *My* appended to the file name so that you don't overwrite the original practice file.

- In the *MultiplicationTable* workbook, on the Practice worksheet, create a formula in cells B2:T20 to complete the multiplication table of the numbers 1 through 20. (Challenge: Create the table in six or fewer steps.) Compare the formulas in your multiplication table with those on the Results worksheet.

- In the *SalesBySeason* workbook, on the Summary worksheet, display the total sales for each period in cells B2:B5 by referencing the corresponding worksheets.

5.4 Apply Conditional Logic in Formulas

Creating Conditional Formulas

You can use a formula to display specific results when certain conditions are met. To do so, you create a formula that uses the conditional logic provided by the IF() function or one of its variations. A basic formula that uses the IF() function performs a logical test and then returns one of two results based on whether the logical test evaluates as TRUE or FALSE.

The correct syntax for the IF() function is as follows:

=IF(logical_test,value_if_true,value_if_false)

> **Tip** The IF() function in Excel is equivalent to an IF...THEN...ELSE function in a computer program.

The logical test and the result can include text strings or calculations. Enclose text strings within the formula in quotation marks. Do not enclose numeric values or calculations in quotation marks.

Excel 2010 includes the additional conditional logic functions shown in the following table.

Function	Description
AVERAGEIF() AVERAGEIFS()	Returns the average of values in a range that meet one or more criteria
COUNTIF() COUNTIFS()	Returns the number of cells in a range that meet one or more criteria
SUMIF() SUMIFS()	Returns the sum of values in a range that meet one or more criteria
IFERROR()	Returns one value if a formula results in an error and another if it doesn't

> **Strategy** Experiment with each of the conditional functions. Follow the prompts given in the tooltip that appears when you begin entering the formula to be sure you provide valid arguments for each function.

Nesting Functions

You can nest additional functions within an IF() function so that Excel evaluates multiple conditions before returning a result. You can use nested functions to do the following:

- Perform a calculation that results in an argument used by the IF() function, like this:

    =IF(SUM(D1:D8)>=80,"Congratulations, you passed!","Sorry, you failed. Please try again.")

- Combine multiple logical tests, like this:

    *=IF(AND(Year=2011,Month="July"),B2*C4,"No")*

You can add logical tests to a conditional formula by using the following functions:

- **AND()** Returns a value of TRUE only if every logical test within it is TRUE.

- **OR()** Returns a value of TRUE if any logical test within it is TRUE.

- **NOT()** Reverses the logical outcome of a logical test, so if the test is TRUE, NOT returns FALSE. For example, NOT(A1=3), returns TRUE as long as the value in cell A1 is not equal to 3. You use this function when you want to check whether a cell is not equal to a certain value.

You place the AND(), OR(), and NOT() functions before the associated arguments.

➤ To use a single conditional logic argument in a formula

→ Enter the function followed by a parenthetical phrase containing the logical test(s), the result if the condition is true, and the result if the condition is false, separated by commas, like this:

=IF(A3<>"",A3+B3,B3+C3)

➤ To use a series of conditional logic arguments in a formula

→ Nest one or more additional functions within the IF() function, like this:

=IF(OR(Month="June",Month="July",Month="August"),"See you next school year!","Enjoy the school year!")

Practice Tasks

The practice file for these tasks is located in the Excel\Objective5 practice file folder. If you want to save the results of the tasks, save them in the same folder with *My* appended to the file name so that you don't overwrite the original practice file.

- On the Expense Statement worksheet of the *ConditionalFormula* workbook, do the following:
  - In cell C25, use the AND() function to determine whether the Entertainment total is less than $200.00 and the Misc. total is less than $100.00.
  - In cell C26, use the OR() function to determine whether the Entertainment total is more than $200.00 or the Misc. total is more than $100.00.
  - In cell C27, use the IF() function to display the text "Expenses are okay" if the function in C25 evaluates to TRUE and "Expenses are too high" if it evaluates to FALSE.
  - In cell C28, use the IF() function to display the text "Expenses are okay" if the function in C26 evaluates to NOT TRUE and "Expenses are too high" if it evaluates to NOT FALSE.
  - Add 60.00 to either the Entertainment column or the Misc. column to check your work.

5.5 Apply Named Ranges in Formulas

To simplify the process of creating formulas that refer to a specific range of data, and to make your formulas easier to create and read, you can refer to a cell or range of cells by a name that you define. For example, you might name a cell containing an interest rate *Interest*, or a range of cells containing nonwork days *Holidays*. In a formula, you can refer to a named range by name. Thus a formula might look like this:

=WORKDAY(StartDate,WorkingDays,Holidays)

A formula that uses named ranges is easier to understand than one that uses standard references, which might look like this:

=WORKDAY(B2,B$3,Data!B2:B16)

Each named range has a scope, which is the context in which the name is recognized. The scope can be the entire workbook or a specific worksheet. The workbook scope allows you to use the same name on multiple worksheets. You can include a comment with each name to provide more information about the range. (The comment is visible only in the Name Manager.)

After defining a named range, you can change the name or the cells included in the named range. You can delete a named range definition from the Name Manager. Note that deleting a cell from a worksheet does not delete any associated named range. Invalid named ranges are indicated in the Name Manager by #REF! in the Value column.

➤ **To define a selected cell or range of cells as a named range**

→ In the **Name** box at the right end of the **Formula Bar**, enter the name, and then press Enter.

Or

1. On the **Formulas** tab, in the **Defined Names** group, click the **Define Name** button.

2. In the **New Name** dialog box, enter the name in the **Name** box.

> **Tip** The New Name dialog box does not indicate whether the selected cell or cells are already part of an existing named range.

3. In the **Scope** list, click **Workbook** to define the named range for the entire workbook, or click a specific worksheet name.

4. In the **Comment** box, enter any notes you want to make for your own reference.

5. Verify that the cell or range of cells in the **Refers to** box is correct, and then click **OK**.

> **Tip** If a cell is part of multiple named ranges, only the first name is shown in the Name box. The Name box displays the name of a multiple-cell named range only when all cells in the range are selected.

➤ **To redefine the cells in a named range**

1. On the **Formulas** tab, in the **Defined Names** group, click the **Name Manager** button.

2. In the **Name Manager** window, click the named range you want to change, and then click **Edit**.

3. In the **Edit Name** dialog box, do one of the following, and then click **OK**.

   ○ In the **Refers to** box, enter the cell range to which you want the name to refer.

   ○ If necessary, click the **Minimize** button at the right end of the **Refers to** box to expose the worksheet area. Then on the worksheet, drag to select the cells that you want to include in the named range.

➤ **To change the name of the cells in a named range**

1. On the **Formulas** tab, in the **Defined Names** group, click the **Name Manager** button.

2. In the **Name Manager** window, click the named range you want to change, and then click **Edit**.

3. In the **Edit Name** dialog box, change the name in the **Name** box, and then click **OK**.

➤ **To delete a named range definition**

1. On the **Formulas** tab, in the **Defined Names** group, click the **Name Manager** button.

2. In the **Name Manager** window, click the named range you want to delete, and click **Delete**. Then click **OK** to confirm the deletion.

Practice Tasks

The practice file for these tasks is located in the Excel\Objective5 practice file folder. If you want to save the results of the tasks, save them in the same folder with *My* appended to the file name so that you don't overwrite the original practice file.

- In the *MultiplicationTable* workbook, on the Results worksheet, define cells A1:T1 as a range named *FirstRow,* and cells A1:A20 as a range named *ColumnA*. Then change the formulas in cells B2:T20 to reference the named ranges.

5.6 Apply Cell Ranges in Formulas

You can refer to the content of a range of adjacent cells. For example, you might use a formula to add the values of a range of cells, or to find the maximum value in all the cells in a row. When referencing a range of cells in a formula, the cell references can be relative, absolute, or mixed.

Select a cell range to enter it in a formula

➤ **To relatively reference the contents of a range of cells**

→ Enter the upper-left cell of the range and the lower-right cell of the range, separated by a colon, like this:

A1:B3

➤ **To enter a relative reference to a range of cells in a formula**

1. Position the cursor where you want to insert the cell range reference.

2. Drag to select the cell range and insert the cell range reference.

➤ **To absolutely reference the contents of a range of cells**

→ Enter the absolute reference of the upper-left cell of the range and the absolute reference of the lower-right cell of the range, separated by a colon, like this:

$A$1:$B$3

Practice Tasks

The practice file for these tasks is located in the Excel\Objective5 practice file folder. If you want to save the results of the tasks, save them in the same folder with *My* appended to the file name so that you don't overwrite the original practice file.

- On the Product Sales worksheet of the *CellRange* workbook, in cells C95, C101, and C104, calculate the sales total for each category by using a relative cell range reference.

- In cell C86 of the Product Sales worksheet, calculate the Cacti sales total by using an absolute cell range reference.

Objective Review

Before finishing this chapter, ensure that you have mastered the following skills:

5.1   Create Formulas
5.2   Enforce Precedence
5.3   Apply Cell References in Formulas
5.4   Apply Conditional Logic in Formulas
5.5   Apply Named Ranges in Formulas
5.6   Apply Cell Ranges in Formulas

6 Presenting Data Visually

The skills tested in this section of the Microsoft Office Specialist exam for Microsoft Excel 2010 relate to adding visual interest to a worksheet. Specifically, the following objectives are associated with this set of skills:

6.1 Create Charts Based on Worksheet Data
6.2 Apply and Manipulate Illustrations
6.3 Create and Modify Images
6.4 Apply Sparklines

You can insert many of the same graphic elements in an Excel workbook that you can insert in other Microsoft Office documents, including clip art, SmartArt diagrams, shapes, screenshots, and pictures. You can also express numeric data by creating charts, and summarize numeric data by using sparklines.

This chapter guides you in studying ways of inserting and modifying charts, graphics images, and sparklines.

> **Practice Files** Before you can complete the practice tasks in this chapter, you need to copy the book's practice files to your computer. The practice files you'll use to complete the tasks in this chapter are in the Excel\Objective6 practice file folder. A complete list of practice files is provided in "Using the Book's Companion Content"at the beginning of this book.

6.1 Create Charts Based on Worksheet Data

Plotting Charts

Charts are an important tool for data analysis and are therefore a common component of certain types of worksheets. You can easily plot selected data as a chart to make it easy to identify trends and relationships that might not be obvious from the data itself.

> **Tip** You must select only the data you want to appear in the chart. If the data is not in a contiguous range of rows or columns, either rearrange the data or hold down the Ctrl key while you select noncontiguous ranges.

Different types of data are best suited for different types of charts. The following table shows the available chart types and the type of data they are particularly useful for plotting.

Chart type	Typically used to show
Column	Variations in value over time or comparisons
Line	Multiple data trends over evenly spaced intervals
Pie	Percentages assigned to different components of a single item (non-negative, non-zero, no more than seven values)
Bar	Variations in value over time or the comparative values of several items at a single point in time
Area	Multiple data series as cumulative layers showing change over time
X Y (Scatter)	Correlations between independent items
Stock	Stock market or similar activity
Surface	Trends in values across two different dimensions in a continuous curve, such as a topographic map
Doughnut	Percentages assigned to different components of more than one item
Bubble	Correlations between three or more independent items
Radar	Percentages assigned to different components of an item, radiating from a center point

To plot selected data as a chart, all you have to do is specify the chart type. If the type of chart you initially selected doesn't adequately depict your data, you can change the type at any time. The 11 chart types each have several two-dimensional and three-dimensional variations, and you can customize each aspect of each variation.

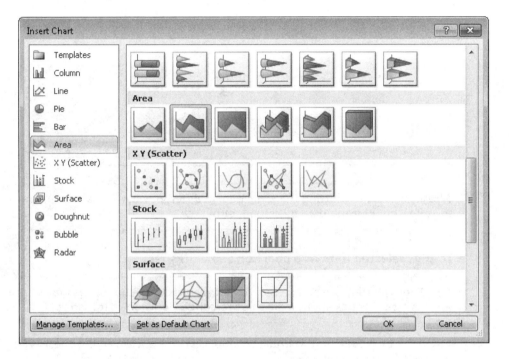

When you plot worksheet data, a row or column of values, which in the charting world are called *data points*, constitutes a set of data called a *data series*. Each data point in a data series is represented graphically in the chart by a data marker and in the chart legend by a unique color or pattern. The data is plotted against an x-axis (or *category axis*) and a y-axis (or *value axis*). Three-dimensional charts also have a z-axis (or *series axis*). Sometimes a chart does not produce the results you expect because the data series are plotted against the wrong axes; that is, Excel is plotting the data by row when it should be plotting by column, or vice versa. You can quickly switch the rows and columns to see whether that produces the desired effect. To see what Excel is doing behind the scenes, you can open the Select Data Source dialog box, which shows you exactly what is plotted where.

```
Select Data Source                                              ?  ✕

Chart data range:  =Sheet1!$A$1:$B$13                              [🔢]

                        [🔢 Switch Row/Column]

Legend Entries (Series)              Horizontal (Category) Axis Labels
[📋 Add]  [📝 Edit]  [✕ Remove] [▲][▼]   [📝 Edit]

Sales                                January                         ▲
                                     February                        ▤
                                     March
                                     April
                                     May                             ▼

[Hidden and Empty Cells]                        [  OK  ]  [ Cancel ]
```

> **Strategy** Practice plotting the same data in different ways. In particular, understand the effects of plotting data by column or by row.

➤ To plot selected data as a chart on the worksheet

> **Tip** Before plotting the data, ensure that it is correctly set up for the type of chart you want to create. For example, a pie chart can display only one data series.

→ On the **Insert** tab, in the **Charts** group, click the button of the chart type you want, and then click a sub-type.

➤ To change the type of a selected chart

1. On the Chart Tools **Design** contextual tab, in the **Type** group, click the **Change Chart Type** button.

2. In the **Change Chart Type** dialog box, click a new type and sub-type, and then click **OK**.

➤ To switch rows and columns in a selected chart

→ On the **Design** contextual tab, in the **Data** group, click the **Switch Row/Column** button.

Or

1. On the **Design** contextual tab, in the **Data** group, click the **Select Data** button.

   Or

   Right-click the chart border or data area, and then click **Select Data**.

2. In the **Select Data Source** dialog box, click **Switch Row/Column**, and then click **OK**.

Applying Layouts and Styles

You can apply predefined combinations of layouts and styles to quickly format a chart. You can also apply a shape style to the chart area to set it off from the rest of the sheet.

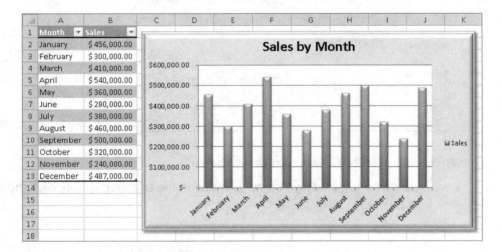

➤ **To change the layout of a selected chart**

→ On the Chart Tools **Design** contextual tab, in the **Chart Layouts** gallery, click the layout you want.

➤ **To apply a style to a selected chart**

→ On the **Design** contextual tab, in the **Chart Styles** gallery, click the style you want.

➤ **To apply a shape style to a selected chart**

→ On the Chart Tools **Format** contextual tab, in the **Shape Styles** gallery, click the style you want.

Moving and Sizing Charts

The charts you create often don't appear where you want them on a worksheet, and they are often too big or too small to adequately show their data. You can move and size a chart by using simple dragging techniques.

If you prefer to display a chart on its own sheet instead of embedding it in the worksheet containing its data, you can easily move it. You can also move it to any other existing worksheet in the workbook.

> **To move a selected chart to a chart sheet**

   1. On the Chart Tools **Design** contextual tab, in the **Location** group, click the **Move Chart** button.

      Or

      Right-click the chart border, and then click **Move Chart**.

   2. In the **Move Chart** dialog box, click **New sheet**, and then if you want, enter a name for the sheet.

   3. Click **OK**.

> **To move a selected chart to a different sheet in the same workbook**

   1. Open the **Move Chart** dialog box, click **Object in**, and then select the worksheet you want from the list.

   2. Click **OK**.

> **To change the size of a selected chart**

   → Point to a handle (set of dots) on the chart's frame, and drag in the direction you want the chart to grow or shrink.

   → Point to a handle in a corner of the chart's frame, hold down the Shift key, and drag in the direction you want the chart to grow or shrink proportionally.

→ On the Chart Tools **Format** contextual tab, in the **Size** group, change the **Shape Height** and **Shape Width** settings.

Or

1. On the **Format** contextual tab, click the **Size** dialog box launcher.

2. In the **Size and Properties** dialog box, change the settings in the **Size and rotate** or **Scale** area, and then click **Close**.

> **Tip** Select the Lock Aspect Ratio check box before changing the settings if you want to size the chart proportionally.

Editing Data

A chart is linked to its worksheet data, so any changes you make to the plotted data are immediately reflected in the chart. If you add or delete values in a data series or add or remove an entire series, you need to increase or decrease the range of the plotted data in the worksheet.

▶ **To edit the data in a chart**

→ In the linked Excel worksheet, change the plotted values.

▶ **To change the range of plotted data in a selected chart**

→ In the linked Excel worksheet, drag the corner handles of the series selectors until they enclose the series you want to plot.

Configuring Chart Elements

To augment the usefulness or the attractiveness of a chart, you can add elements such as a title, axis labels, data labels, a data table, and gridlines. You can adjust each element, as well as the plot area (the area defined by the axes) and the chart area (the entire chart object), in appropriate ways.

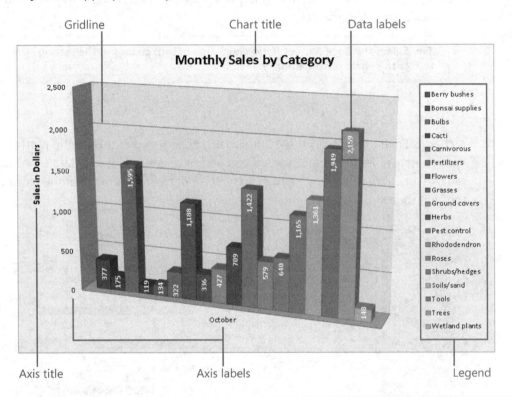

> **Strategy** You can tailor the elements of charts in too many ways for us to cover them in detail here. In addition to choosing options from galleries, you can open a Format dialog box for each type of element. Make sure you are familiar with the chart elements and how to use them to enhance a chart.

➤ To add a chart title

1. On the Chart Tools **Layout** contextual tab, in the **Labels** group, click the **Chart Title** button.

2. In the **Title** gallery, click the option you want.

3. Select the placeholder title, and replace it with the one you want.

➤ **To add or remove axis titles**

1. On the **Layout** contextual tab, in the **Labels** group, click the **Axis Titles** button.

2. In the list, point to **Primary Horizontal Axis Title**, and then click **None** or **Title Below Axis**; or click **More Primary Horizontal Axis Title Options**, make specific selections in the **Format Axis Title** dialog box, and then click **Close**.

   Or

   In the list, point to **Primary Vertical Axis Title**, and then click **None**, **Rotated Title**, **Vertical Title**, or **Horizontal Title**; or click **More Primary Vertical Axis Title Options**, make specific selections in the **Format Axis Title** dialog box, and then click **Close**.

3. Select the placeholder axis title, and enter the text you want to appear as the axis title.

➤ **To add, remove, or move the legend**

1. On the **Layout** contextual tab, in the **Labels** group, click the **Legend** button.

2. In the **Legend** gallery, click the **Show Legend** (**Right**, **Top**, **Left**, or **Bottom**) or **Overlay Legend** (**Right** or **Left**) option you want.

   Or

   Click **More Legend Options**, make specific selections in the **Format Legend** dialog box, and then click **Close**.

➤ **To display data labels**

1. On the **Layout** contextual tab, in the **Labels** group, click the **Data Labels** button.

2. In the **Data Labels** gallery, click **Show** to display the value of each data point on its marker.

   Or

   In the **Data Labels** gallery, click **More Data Label Options**, make specific selections (including the number format and decimal places) in the **Format Legend** dialog box, and then click **Close**.

Tip Data labels can clutter up all but the simplest charts. If you need to show the data for a chart on a separate chart sheet, consider using a data table instead.

➤ **To display the chart data under the axis titles**

1. On the **Layout** contextual tab, in the **Labels** group, click the **Data Table** button.

2. In the **Data Table** gallery, click **Show Data Table** or **Show Data Table with Legend Keys**.

    Or

    Click **More Data Table Options**, make specific selections in the **Format Data Table** dialog box, and then click **Close**.

➤ **To display or hide axes**

1. On the **Layout** contextual tab, in the **Axes** group, click the **Axes** button.

2. In the list, point to **Primary Horizontal Axis** and then click **None, Show Left to Right Axis, Show Axis without labeling**, or **Show Right to Left Axis**; or click **More Primary Horizontal Axis Options**, make specific selections in the **Format Axis** dialog box, and then click **Close**.

    Or

    In the list, point to **Primary Vertical Axis** and then click **None, Show Default Axis, Show Axis in Thousands, Show Axis in Millions, Show Axis in Billions**, or **Show Axis with Log Scale**; or click **More Primary Vertical Axis Options**, make specific selections in the **Format Axis** dialog box, and then click **Close**.

➤ **To display or hide gridlines**

1. On the **Layout** contextual tab, in the **Axes** group, click the **Gridlines** button.

2. In the **Gridlines** list, point to **Primary Horizontal Gridlines** and then click **None, Major Gridlines, Minor Gridlines**, or **Major & Minor Gridlines**; or click **More Primary Horizontal Gridlines Options**, make specific selections in the **Format Major Gridlines** dialog box, and then click **Close**.

    Or

    In the **Gridlines** list, point to **Primary Vertical Gridlines** and then click **None, Major Gridlines, Minor Gridlines**, or **Major & Minor Gridlines**; or click **More Primary Vertical Gridlines Options**, make specific selections in the **Format Major Gridlines** dialog box, and then click **Close**.

➤ **To select a chart element for formatting**

→ On the **Layout** contextual tab, in the **Current Selection** group, click the element you want in the **Chart Elements** list, and then click the **Format Selection** button to open the corresponding **Format** dialog box.

> **Tip** Only those elements that are present in the chart appear in the Chart Elements list.

Practice Tasks

The practice files for these tasks are located in the Excel\Objective6 practice file folder. If you want to save the results of the tasks, save them in the same folder with *My* appended to the file name so that you don't overwrite the original practice file.

- In the *DataSource* workbook, use the data on the Seattle worksheet to plot a simple pie chart.

- In the *Plotting* workbook, on the Sales worksheet, plot the data as a simple 2-D column chart. Then switch the rows and columns.

- In the *Plotting* workbook, on the Sales worksheet, change the chart to a 3-D Clustered Column chart. Then apply Layout 1, Style 34, and the Subtle Effect – Accent 3 shape style.

- In the *SizingMoving* workbook, on the Sales worksheet, increase the size of the chart until it occupies cells A1:L23. Then move it to a new chart sheet named *Sales Chart*.

- In the *Editing* workbook, on the Sales worksheet, change the October sales amount for the Flowers category to *888.25*. Then add the November data series to the chart, and change the way the data is plotted so that you can compare sales for the two months.

- In the *ChartElements* workbook, on the Seattle worksheet, add the title *Air Quality Index Report* to the chart. Then add data labels that show the percentage relationship of each data marker to the whole, with no decimal places.

6.2 Apply and Manipulate Illustrations

Inserting and Formatting Clip Art

You can use royalty-free clip art objects to add visual interest to worksheets.

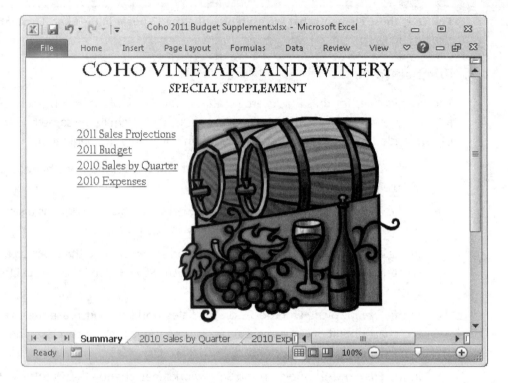

➤ **To locate and insert a clip art object**

  1. On the **Insert** tab, in the **Illustrations** group, click the **Clip Art** button.

  2. In the **Clip Art** pane, enter a keyword in the **Search for** box, and then click **Go**.

  3. In the results list, click the thumbnail of the image you want.

> **Tip** You can change the size, shape, and location of a clip art object by using the same techniques as you do with other graphic elements. For more information see section 6.3, "Create and Modify Images."

➤ **To temporarily store a clip art image on the Microsoft Office Clipboard**

  → In the **Clip Art** pane, point to the image, click the arrow that appears, and then click **Copy**.

➤ **To store a clip art object in the Clip Organizer**

1. In the **Clip Art** pane, point to the image, click the arrow that appears, and then click **Make Available Offline**.

2. In the **Copy to Collection** dialog box, select or create the folder in which you want to store the clip art object, and then click **OK**.

➤ **To open the Clip Organizer**

→ On the Windows **Start** menu, click **All Programs**, **Microsoft Office**, **Microsoft Office 2010 Tools**, and then **Microsoft Clip Organizer**.

Inserting and Modifying SmartArt Diagrams

When you create a worksheet that includes details of a process such as a project schedule, you might want to create an accompanying diagram to illustrate the process visually. You can create professional-looking business diagrams by using the SmartArt graphics feature. By using predefined sets of formatting, you can easily create the type of diagram best suited to the worksheet's information. After selecting the type of diagram you want and inserting it into the document, you add text either directly in the diagram's shapes or from its text pane. SmartArt diagrams can consist of only text, or of text and pictures.

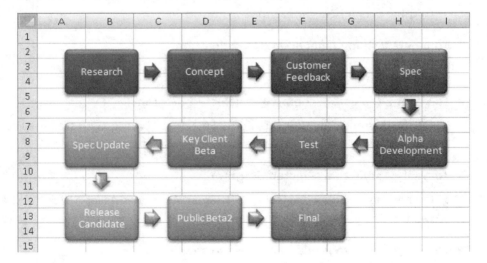

➤ **To insert a diagram**

1. On the **Insert** tab, in the **Illustrations** group, click the **SmartArt** button.

2. In the left pane of the **Choose a SmartArt Graphic** dialog box, click the type of diagram you want.

3. In the center pane, click the layout you want, and then click **OK**.

➤ **To add text to a diagram shape**

→ With the diagram selected, click the shape, and enter the text.

→ In the text pane, click the bullet for the shape, and enter the text.

> **Tip** If the text pane is not open, click the tab on the left side of the diagram's frame, or click the Text Pane button in the Create Graphic group on the SmartArt Tools Design contextual tab.

➤ **To change the layout of a selected diagram**

→ To switch to a layout in the same diagram category, on the SmartArt Tools **Design** contextual tab, in the **Layouts** gallery, click the layout you want.

→ To switch to a layout in a different diagram category, on the **Design** contextual tab, in the **Layouts** gallery, click **More Layouts** and then, in the **Choose a SmartArt Graphic** dialog box, choose the layout you want.

➤ **To delete a shape from a SmartArt diagram**

→ Click the shape's border, and then press the Delete key.

➤ **To change the color scheme of a selected diagram**

→ On the **Design** contextual tab, in the **SmartArt Styles** group, click the **Change Colors** button, and then click the color scheme you want.

➤ **To apply a style to a selected diagram**

→ On the **Design** contextual tab, in the **SmartArt Styles** gallery, click the style you want to apply.

➤ **To apply a style to a selected diagram shape**

→ On the SmartArt Tools **Format** contextual tab, in the **Shape Styles** gallery, click the style you want to apply.

Or

1. On the **Format** contextual tab, click the **Shape Styles** dialog box launcher.

2. In the **Format Shape** dialog box, on the **Line Color**, **Line Style**, **Shadow**, **Reflection**, **Glow and Soft Edges**, **3-D Format**, and **3-D Rotation** pages, choose the effects that you want to apply. Then click **Close**.

> **Strategy** Many formatting options are available from the Design and Format contextual tabs. Be familiar with the options available on these contextual tabs as well as in the associated dialog boxes.

Inserting and Formatting Shapes

To emphasize an important area of a worksheet, you can draw shapes (such as arrows) to which you can add text (such as assumptions or warnings). You can format a shape by changing its style, color, or outline. You can add text to shapes and format the text by using normal formatting techniques or WordArt styles; or by specifying the fill, outline, and effects to be applied to the text. You can format shapes by using built-in styles or by specifying the fill, outline, and effects to be applied to the shape.

	A	B	C	D	E	F	G
1	Region	Sales					
2	NE	$ 460,000.00					
3	NW	$ 500,000.00		Highest sales for any region this year!			
4	SE	$ 200,000.00					
5	SW	$ 400,000.00					
6		$ 1,560,000.00					
7							

If you build a picture by drawing individual shapes, you can group them so that they act as one object. If you move or size a grouped object, the shapes retain their positions in relation to each other. To break the bond, you ungroup the object.

➤ To draw a standard shape

1. On the **Insert** tab, in the **Illustrations** group, click the **Shapes** button.

2. In the **Shapes** gallery, click the shape you want, and then do one of the following:
   ○ Click anywhere on the page to insert a standard-size shape.
   ○ Drag anywhere on the page to draw a shape the size you want.

➤ **To add text to a selected shape**

→ Click the shape and then enter the text.

→ Right-click the shape, click **Edit Text**, and then enter the text.

➤ **To customize a selected shape**

1. On the Drawings Tools **Format** contextual tab, in the **Insert Shapes** group, click the **Edit Shape** button, and then click **Edit Points**.

2. Drag the intersection points that appear on the shape to change its form.

> **Tip** You change the size, shape, and location of a shape by using the same techniques as you do with other graphic elements.

➤ **To change a selected shape to another shape**

→ On the **Format** contextual tab, in the **Insert Shapes** group, click the **Edit Shape** button, point to **Change Shape**, and then click the shape you want.

➤ **To format a selected shape**

→ On the **Format** contextual tab, do any of the following:

○ In the **Shape Styles** gallery, click the built-in style you want to apply.

○ In the **Shape Styles** group, in the **Shape Fill**, **Shape Outline**, and **Shape Effects** galleries, click the settings you want.

➤ **To format text attached to a selected shape**

→ On the **Format** contextual tab, do any of the following:

○ In the **WordArt Styles** gallery, click the built-in style you want to apply.

○ In the **WordArt Styles** group, in the **Text Fill**, **Text Outline**, and **Text Effects** galleries, click the settings you want.

➤ **To change the stacking order of multiple shapes**

1. Select the shape you want to move up or down in the stack.

2. On the **Format** contextual tab, in the **Arrange** group, do any of the following:

○ Click the **Bring Forward** or **Send Backward** button to move the shape up or down one level.

○ In the **Bring Forward** list, click **Bring to Front** to move the shape to the top of the stack.

○ In the **Send Backward** list, click **Send to Back** to move the shape to the bottom of the stack.

> ➤ **To group shapes**

  1. Select the first shape, and then hold down the Ctrl key and select the additional shapes you want to group.

  2. On the **Format** contextual tab, in the **Arrange** group, click the **Group** button, and then click **Group**.

> ➤ **To ungroup shapes**

  1. Select the grouped shapes.

  2. On the **Format** contextual tab, in the **Arrange** group, click the **Group** button, and then click **Ungroup**.

Capturing Screenshots

You can capture and insert images of content displayed on your computer screen directly from Excel. By using the built-in screen clipping tool, you can insert screen captures of entire windows or selected areas of on-screen content.

	A	B	C	D	E	F	G	H	I
4									
5									
6		The screenshot illustrates a sample of the currently available discounts.							
7		Store Name						Cash Back	
8		Auto Zone Coupons & Cash Back						4.0%	
9									
10		eFaucets Coupons & Cash Back						4.0%	
11		Batteries Plus Coupons & Cash Back						6.0%	
12									
13		Botanic Choice Coupons & Cash Back						12.5%	
14		eBatts Coupons & Cash Back						6.0%	
15		Vitamin World Coupons & Cash Back						5.0%	
16									
17		Dr. Leonard's Healthcare Coupons & Cash Back						6.0%	
18		Laptops for Less Coupons & Cash Back						5.0%	
19									
20									

➤ **To capture and insert a screen clipping**

1. Display the content you want to capture.

2. In the Excel worksheet, position the cursor where you want to insert the screen clipping.

3. On the **Insert** tab, in the **Illustrations** group, click the **Screenshot** button.

4. In the **Screenshot** gallery, do one of the following:

- ○ Click a window thumbnail to insert a picture of that window into the document at the cursor.

> **Tip** The Available Windows gallery displays thumbnails of open program windows.

- ○ Click **Screen Clipping**, and then drag across the part of the screen you want to capture.

Practice Tasks

The practice files for these tasks are located in the Excel\Objective6 practice file folder. If you want to save the results of the tasks, save them in the same folder with *My* appended to the file name so that you don't overwrite the original practice file.

- On the My Monthly Budget worksheet of the *PersonalMonthlyBudget* workbook, insert a clip art image that has a budget-related keyword after the Monthly Budget title, and resize it to 0.6 inch high.

- In the *SmartArt* workbook, on the Diagram worksheet, insert a Basic Bending Process diagram. Add the following text to the shapes: *Take order, Create invoice, Fulfill order, Ship order, Order received*. Then apply the Powder style and one of the Colorful color schemes.

- In the *Shapes* workbook, on the Sales By Category worksheet, draw a large, red, left-pointing arrow containing the words *Successful weekend sale* to the right of the Tools Total amount.

- In the *DataSource* workbook, on the Seattle worksheet, insert a screen clipping of slide 5 from the *Pollution* presentation below the data.

6.3 Create and Modify Images

You might want to add images created and saved in other programs or scanned photographs and illustrations to a worksheet such as a catalog of products or a list of employees. If a worksheet will be distributed to people outside your company, you might want to add a logo to the worksheet's header or footer to establish content ownership and reinforce your business identity.

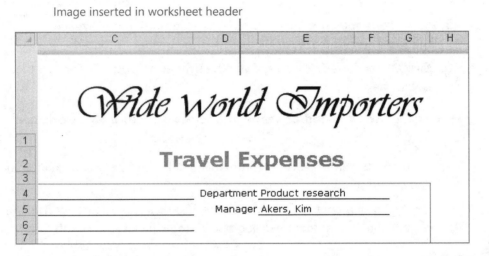

Image inserted in worksheet header

After you insert an image in a document, you can modify it in many ways. For example, you can crop or resize a picture, change its brightness and contrast, recolor it, apply artistic effects to it, and compress it to reduce the size of the document containing it. You can apply a wide range of preformatted styles to a picture to change its shape and orientation, as well as add borders and picture effects.

➤ **To insert a picture on a worksheet**

1. On the **Insert** tab, in the **Illustrations** group, click the **Picture** button.

2. In the **Insert Picture** dialog box, browse to and click the file you want. Then do one of the following:

    ○ Click **Insert** to insert the picture into the worksheet.

    ○ In the **Insert** list, click **Link to File** to insert a picture that will update automatically if the picture file changes.

    ○ In the **Insert** list, click **Insert and Link** to insert a picture that you can manually update if the picture file changes.

➤ **To insert and modify a picture in a worksheet header or footer**

1. On the **Insert** tab, in the **Text** group, click the **Header & Footer** button.

2. Click the left, center, or right section of the header or footer, and then on the Header & Footer Tools **Design** contextual tab, in the **Header & Footer Elements** group, click the **Picture** button.

3. In the **Insert Picture** dialog box, locate and double-click the picture you want.

4. In the **Header & Footer Elements** group, click the **Format Picture** button.

5. In the **Format Picture** dialog box, change settings in the **Size and rotate** area or the **Scale** area to make the picture fit in the header or footer.

6. Click **OK**, and then click away from the header or footer to view the picture in Page Layout view.

➤ **To change the size and/or shape of a selected picture on a worksheet**

→ Drag its sizing handles.

→ On the Picture Tools **Format** contextual tab, in the **Size** group, change the **Height** and **Width** settings.

→ On the **Format** contextual tab, click the **Size** dialog box launcher. Then on the **Size** page of the **Format Picture** dialog box, change the **Height**, **Width**, and **Scale** settings.

➤ **To move a picture on a worksheet**

→ Drag the picture to a new location.

➤ **To copy a picture to a new location on a worksheet**

→ Hold down the Ctrl key, and drag the picture to the second location.

> **Tip** Release the mouse button first, and then the Ctrl key. (If you release Ctrl first, Excel will move the image instead of copying it.)

➤ **To apply artistic effects to a selected picture on a worksheet**

→ On the **Format** contextual tab, in the **Adjust** group, display the **Artistic Effects** gallery, and then click the effect you want to apply.

➤ **To apply a style to a selected picture on a worksheet**

→ On the **Format** contextual tab, in the **Picture Styles** group, display the **Quick Styles** gallery, and then click the style you want to apply.

Or

1. On the **Format** contextual tab, click the **Picture Styles** dialog box launcher.

2. In the **Format Picture** dialog box, on the **Line Color**, **Line Style**, **Shadow**, **Reflection**, **Glow and Soft Edges**, **3-D Format**, and **3-D Rotation** pages, choose the effects that you want to apply. Then click **Close**.

➤ **To replace a selected picture on a worksheet**

1. On the **Format** contextual tab, in the **Adjust** group, click the **Change Picture** button.

2. In the **Insert Picture** dialog box, locate and double-click the replacement picture.

Strategy You can insert and modify other graphics elements such as clip art objects, shapes, business diagrams, and screenshots by using similar techniques. Practice creating or inserting one of each of these elements and then experiment with the various styles and effects that are available.

Practice Tasks

The practice files for these tasks are located in the Excel\Objective6 practice file folder. If you want to save the results of the tasks, save them in the same folder with *My* appended to the file name so that you don't overwrite the original practice file.

- Open the *Picture* workbook, and insert the *Logo2* graphic in the upper-left corner of the Employees worksheet header. Scale the logo so that it does not obscure cell A1 of the worksheet.

- On the Sales worksheet of the *ClipArt* workbook, replace the grass picture with the *VariegatedGrass* picture, and then apply the Paint Strokes artistic effect. Next apply a 5 pt. soft edge to all of the pictures.

6.4 Apply Sparklines

Sparklines are miniature charts that summarize worksheet data in a single cell. Excel 2010 includes three types of sparklines: Line, Column, and Win/Loss. A Line or Column sparkline resembles a chart of the same type. A Win/Loss sparkline indicates whether each data point is positive, zero, or negative.

A sparkline consists of a series of markers. Depending on the sparkline type, you can choose to accentuate the following markers:

- First point
- Last point
- High point
- Low point
- Negative points

You can apply styles and other formatting to sparklines in the same way that you do to other graphic elements.

➤ **To create a sparkline or sparklines**

1. Select the data you want to summarize.

2. On the **Insert** tab, in the **Sparklines** group, click the button of the type of sparkline you want to create.

3. In the **Create Sparklines** dialog box, verify that the data range is correct. In the **Location Range** box, enter or select the cell or cell range in which you want to create the sparkline or sparklines. Then click **OK**.

4. On the Sparkline Tools **Design** contextual tab, in the **Show** group, select the check boxes for the data markers you want to show and clear the check boxes for the data markers you want to hide.

➤ **To change the type of a selected sparkline or sparkline group**

➜ On the **Design** contextual tab, in the **Type** group, click the sparkline type you want.

➤ **To apply a style to a selected sparkline**

➜ On the **Design** contextual tab, do any of the following:

   ○ In the **Style** gallery, click the built-in style you want to apply.

   ○ In the **Style** group, in the **Sparkline Color** gallery, click the color you want.

   ○ In the **Style** group, in the **Marker Color** list, in the **Negative Points**, **Markers**, **High Point**, **Low Point**, **First Point**, and **Last Point** galleries, click the colors you want.

➤ **To delete a sparkline or sparkline group**

➜ Select the sparkline you want to delete. Then on the **Design** contextual tab, in the **Group** group, click the **Clear Selected Sparklines** button.

➜ Select one or more sparklines in the sparkline group you want to delete. Then on the **Design** contextual tab, in the **Group** group, click the **Clear Selected Sparklines** arrow, and click **Clear Selected Sparklines Group**.

Practice Tasks

The practice file for these tasks is located in the Excel\Objective6 practice file folder. If you want to save the results of the tasks, save them in the same folder with *My* appended to the file name so that you don't overwrite the original practice file.

- In the *Sparklines* workbook, on the January worksheet, summarize the data for each day by using a Line sparkline. Apply the Sparkline Style Accent 6, Darker 25% style, and then display all the data markers without placing emphasis on any specific type of data marker.

- In the *Sparklines* workbook, on the February worksheet, summarize the data for each hour by using a Column sparkline. Apply the Sparkline Style Colorful #4 style, and then accentuate the First Point and Last Point data markers.

Objective Review

Before finishing this chapter, ensure that you have mastered the following skills:

6.1   Create Charts Based on Worksheet Data

6.2   Apply and Manipulate Illustrations

6.3   Create and Modify Images

6.4   Apply Sparklines

7 Sharing Worksheet Data with Other Users

The skills tested in this section of the Microsoft Office Specialist exam for Microsoft Excel 2010 relate to saving, sending, and annotating workbooks. Specifically, the following objectives are associated with this set of skills:

7.1 Share Spreadsheets

7.2 Manage Comments

Many of the workbooks you create will contain content intended for reference by other people, or content that you collaborate on with other people.

This chapter guides you in studying ways of saving workbooks in specific file formats for easy access by other people, sending workbooks to other people, and entering comments in workbooks.

> **Practice Files** Before you can complete the practice tasks in this chapter, you need to copy the book's practice files to your computer. The practice files you'll use to complete the tasks in this chapter are in the Excel\Objective7 practice file folder. A complete list of practice files is provided in "Using the Book's Companion Content" at the beginning of this book.

7.1   Share Spreadsheets

Saving Workbooks in Specific Formats

The 2007 Microsoft Office system introduced a new set of file formats based on XML, called Microsoft Office Open XML Formats. By default, Excel 2010 (and Excel 2007) workbooks are saved in the .xlsx format, which is an Excel-specific Open XML format. The .xlsx format provides the following benefits:

- File sizes are smaller than with previous file formats.

- It is simpler to recover damaged content because XML files can be opened in a variety of text editors.

- Security is greater because .xlsx files cannot contain macros, and personal data can easily be identified and removed from files.

Other Excel-specific Open XML formats include .xlsm for macro-enabled workbooks and .xlsb for binary workbooks.

Workbooks saved in the .xlsx format can be opened by Excel 2010 and Excel 2007. Users of earlier versions of Excel can download a converter that will allow them to open an .xlsx file in their version of Excel.

In addition to saving a workbook for use with Excel 2010, you can save it in other formats, including the following:

- **Excel Macro-Enabled Workbook** To be able to store Microsoft Visual Basic for Applications (VBA) macro code or Excel 4.0 macro sheets, use the XML-based .xlsm format.

- **Excel 97-2003** To share an Excel workbook with users of an earlier version of Excel, you can save it in the .xls file format.

- **Single File Web Page or Web Page** You can convert a workbook into HTML so that it can be viewed in a web browser. Saving a workbook in the Single File Web Page format creates one .mht or .mhtml file that contains the content and supporting information, whereas saving a workbook in the Web Page format creates one .htm or .html file that sets up the display structure and a folder that contains separate content and supporting information files.

- **Excel Template** To be able to use a workbook as the starting point for other workbooks, you can save the file as a template.

- **Text (Tab delimited) or CSV (Comma delimited)** If you don't know what program will be used to open the file, you can save it as a delimited text file that can be opened by many programs.

> **Tip** When you save a workbook in one of the text formats, you lose all formatting.

If you intend to share an Excel workbook specifically with users of Excel 2003 or earlier, you can save it in the .xls file format used by those versions of the program. Users of Excel 2010 and Excel 2007 can open an .xls file in Compatibility Mode. Compatibility Mode turns off advanced program features; these features can be re-enabled by saving the file in one of the current file formats.

> **Strategy** Ensure that you are familiar with the types of file formats in which you can save Excel workbooks and when it is appropriate to use each one.

If you want to ensure that the appearance of the file content is the same no matter what computer or device it is displayed on, or if you want to ensure that other people can't easily modify the file, you can save it in one of the following formats:

- **Portable Document Format (PDF)** A fixed-layout document format created by Adobe Systems. A PDF file includes the text, fonts, images, and vector graphics that compose the document. The Adobe Reader or Adobe Acrobat software is required to view a PDF document.

- **XML Paper Specification (XPS) document format** A fixed-layout document format created by Microsoft. The XPS document format consists of structured XML markup that defines the layout of a document and the visual appearance of each page, along with rendering rules for distributing, archiving, rendering, processing, and printing the documents.

Each of these formats displays content in a device-independent manner.

When saving a workbook in one of these formats, you can specify the content that you want to include in the file in the Options dialog box.

You can save a workbook to disk (to your local computer, a network location, or writable media), to a Windows Live SkyDrive, or to a Microsoft SharePoint site.

See Also For information about concurrently saving and sending a workbook, see the "Sending Workbooks" topic later in this section.

Tip A free Windows Live SkyDrive account allows you to store and share up to 25 GB of files, such as photos and Microsoft Office documents, on the Internet. To create a Windows Live SkyDrive folder, visit skydrive.live.com, and sign in with your Windows Live ID.

➤ To save a workbook in a specific format

1. In the left pane of the Backstage view, click **Save As**.

2. In the **Save As** dialog box, browse to the folder in which you want to save the workbook. Enter a file name and select a file format, and then click **Save**.

   Or

1. In the left pane of the **Save & Send** page of the Backstage view, click **Change File Type**.

2. In the right pane of the **Save & Send** page, in the **Workbook File Types** or **Other File Types** list, click the file format in which you want to save the workbook. Then click the **Save As** button.

3. In the **Save As** dialog box, browse to the folder in which you want to save the workbook. Enter a file name, and then click **Save**.

➤ To save a workbook as a PDF or XPS file

1. In the left pane of the Backstage view, click **Save As**. In the **Save As** dialog box, browse to the folder in which you want to save the workbook, and enter a file name. Then in the **Save as type** list, click **PDF (*.pdf)** or **XPS Document (*.xps)**.

   Or

   In the left pane of the **Save & Send** page of the Backstage view, click **Create PDF/XPS Document**. Then in the right pane, click the **Create PDF/XPS** button. In the **Publish as PDF or XPS** dialog box, browse to the folder in which you want to save the workbook, and enter a file name.

2. In the **Optimize for** area, click **Standard** to generate a larger, higher-quality file or **Minimum size** to generate a smaller, lower-quality file. Then click **Options**.

3. In the **Options** dialog box, select the workbook content you want to include in the file, and then click **OK**.

4. In the **Save As** dialog box, click **Save**.

   Or

   In the **Publish as PDF or XPS** dialog box, click **Publish**.

➤ **To save a workbook to an existing Windows Live SkyDrive folder**

1. In the left pane of the **Save & Send** page of the Backstage view, click **Save to Web**.

2. In the right pane of the **Save & Send** page, in the **Shared Folders** list, click the folder in which you want to save the workbook. Then click the **Save As** button.

3. In the **Save As** dialog box displaying the selected workspace, enter a file name and select a file format, and then click **Save**.

➤ **To create a Windows Live SkyDrive folder from within Excel**

1. In the left pane of the **Save & Send** page of the Backstage view, click **Save to Web**.

2. In the right pane of the **Save & Send** page, click the **New Folder** button.

3. On the Windows Live SkyDrive site, follow the instructions to log in and create a folder.

4. On the **Save & Send** page, click the **Refresh** button.

➤ **To save a workbook to a SharePoint site**

1. In the left pane of the **Save & Send** page of the Backstage view, click **Save to SharePoint**.

2. In the right pane of the **Save & Send** page, click **Publish Options**. In the **Publish Options** dialog box, do the following, and then click **OK**:

   ○ On the **Show** page, select the workbook content you want to display when the file is open in a browser window.

   ○ On the **Parameters** page, add any named ranges in the workbook that you want to be editable when the file is open in a browser window.

> **Tip** If the Publish Options button is not available on the Save & Send page, look for it in the Save As dialog box displayed in step 6.

3. In the **Recent Locations** list, click the SharePoint document library in which you want to save the file.

   Or

   In the **Locations** list, click **Browse for a location**.

> **Tip** You can save a workbook only to an existing document library; you can't create a document library from within Excel.

4. Click the **Save As** button.

5. In the **Windows Security** dialog box, enter your SharePoint site credentials, and then click **OK**.

6. In the **Save As** dialog box, if necessary, browse to the document library in which you want to save the file. Then enter a file name and select a file format.

7. If you want to display the file in the browser after saving it, select the **Open with Excel in the browser** check box.

8. In the **Save As** dialog box, click **Save**.

Sending Workbooks

After you save a workbook to disk you can share it with other people by attaching it to an email message created in any program that supports attachments. Excel 2010 provides a simpler way of sharing workbooks, even without first saving them.

From within Excel, you can send a workbook as an email attachment, or convert a workbook and send it as a PDF file or an XPS file.

> **Tip** If you have the services of a third-party online fax service provider, you can send a workbook from within Excel as an Internet fax.

➤ To send a workbook as an email message attachment

1. In the left pane of the **Save & Send** page of the Backstage view, click **Send Using E-mail**.

2. In the right pane of the **Save & Send** page, do one of the following:

   ○ Click the **Send as Attachment** button to send the workbook as an .xlsx file.

   ○ Click the **Send as PDF** button to send the workbook as a .pdf file.

   ○ Click the **Send as XPS** button to send the workbook as an .xps file.

> **Tip** It is not necessary to provide a file name when sending a workbook that has not yet been saved.

3. Enter the recipient name and other necessary information in the email message composition window, and then send the message.

➤ To send a link to a shared workbook

1. Save the workbook in a shared location.

2. In the left pane of the **Save & Send** page of the Backstage view, click **Send Using E-mail**.

3. In the right pane of the **Save & Send** page, click the **Send a Link** button.

4. Enter the recipient name and other necessary information in the email message composition window, and then send the message.

Practice Tasks

The practice file for these tasks is located in the Excel\Objective7 practice file folder. Save the results of the tasks in the same folder.

- Open the *Saving* workbook, and save it with the file name *MOS-Compatible* so that it can be viewed and worked on by a colleague who is using Excel 2003.

- Save the *MOS-Compatible* workbook with the file name *MOS-Template* so that it can be used as the basis for other similar workbooks in the future.

- Save the *MOS-Template* workbook with the file name *MOS-Macro* so that the user will be able to run the attached macro.

- From the Backstage view of the *MOS-Macro* workbook, send the macro-enabled workbook to yourself as an email message attachment.

- From the Backstage view of the *MOS-Macro* workbook, send only the Sales–Revenue worksheet to yourself as a PDF file attached to an email message.

7.2 Manage Comments

In addition to tracking the changes made to a worksheet, you can attach comments to cells without affecting the worksheet functionality. A cell with an attached comment is identified by a red triangle in its upper-right corner. The comment itself appears in a box attached to the red triangle by an arrow. The text of the comment is preceded by the name of the person who added it. By default, comment boxes are hidden.

	A	B	C	D	E	F
11	Alabama	4,627,851	4,590,240	37,611	0.8	23
12	Alaska			6,028	0.9	47
13	Arizona			173,066	2.8	16
14	Arkansas			25,686	0.9	32
15	California			303,343	0.8	1
16	Colorado			95,267	2.0	22
17	Connecticut	3,502,309	3,495,753	6,556	0.2	29
18	Delaware	864,764	852,747	12,017	1.4	45
19	District of Columbia	588,292	585,459	2,833	0.5	50
20	Florida	18,251,243	18,057,508	193,735	1.1	4
21	Georgia	9,544,750	9,342,080	202,670	2.2	9
22	Hawaii	1,283,388	1,278,635	4,753	0.4	42
23	Idaho	1,499,402	1,463,878	35,524	2.4	39

Comment box overlay: **Joan:** AZ was the second fastest-growing state during the survey period

You can work with comments in the following ways:

- Display one comment or all comments.
- Move from comment to comment.
- Edit the content of a displayed comment.
- Resize or move a comment so that it does not obscure important information.

> **To insert a comment about a selected cell**

1. On the **Review** tab, in the **Comments** group, click the **New Comment** button.

   Or

   Right-click the cell, and then click **Insert Comment**.

2. In the comment box, enter the comment.

> **To temporarily display a comment**

→ Point to the cell to which the comment you want to display is attached.

➤ To display or hide one comment

→ Click the cell to which the comment you want to display is attached, and then on the **Review** tab, in the **Comments** group, click the **Show/Hide Comment** button.

→ Right-click the cell to which the comment you want to display is attached, and then click **Show/Hide Comments**.

➤ To display or hide all comments

→ On the **Review** tab, in the **Comments** group, click the **Show All Comments** button.

➤ To move among comments

→ On the **Review** tab, in the **Comments** group, click the **Next** or **Previous** button.

➤ To edit a comment

1. Click the cell to which the comment is attached, and then on the **Review** tab, in the **Comments** group, click the **Edit Comment** button.

   Or

   Right-click the cell to which the comment is attached, and then click **Edit Comment**.

2. Change the text in the comment box by using normal editing techniques.

➤ To resize or move a comment

1. Display the comment, and then click the comment box.

2. Drag its sizing handles to increase or decrease the size of the comment box.

   Or

   Drag its frame to reposition the comment box.

➤ To delete a comment

→ Click the cell to which the comment is attached, and then on the **Review** tab, in the **Comments** group, click the **Delete** button.

→ Right-click the cell to which the comment is attached, and then click **Delete Comment**.

Practice Tasks

The practice file for these tasks is located in the Excel\Objective7 practice file folder. If you want to save the results of the tasks, save them in the same folder with *My* appended to the file name so that you don't overwrite the original practice file.

- Open the *Comments* workbook and display all comments.

- On the Products worksheet of the *Comments* workbook, in cell A59, add the comment *What happened to the common name?* Then delete the comment attached to cell E108.

- On the Products worksheet of the *Comments* workbook, add *These must be special-ordered* to the end of the comment attached to cell A103. Resize the comment box so that all the text of the comment is visible, and move the comment box to an empty area of the worksheet.

- In the *Comments* workbook, hide all comments.

Objective Review

Before finishing this chapter, ensure that you have mastered the following skills:

7.1   Share Spreadsheets
7.2   Manage Comments

8 Analyzing and Organizing Data

The skills tested in this section of the Microsoft Office Specialist exam for Microsoft Excel 2010 relate to identifying and formatting data for analysis. Specifically, the following objectives are associated with this set of skills:

8.1 Filter Data
8.2 Sort Data
8.3 Apply Conditional Formatting

A single Excel workbook can contain over one million rows and 16,000 columns of data. Although it's unlikely that you'll be working with that much data in Excel, you might frequently need to locate specific types of information within a data set or an Excel table. You can filter data to display only the records that meet specific criteria, and sort data to organize it in a logical manner. You can also format the cells within a data range to visually identify data that meets a range of conditions.

This chapter guides you in studying ways of filtering data to locate entries that match specific criteria, sorting data by one or more fields, and formatting data based on a set of conditions.

Practice Files Before you can complete the practice tasks in this chapter, you need to copy the book's practice files to your computer. The practice files you'll use to complete the tasks in this chapter are in the Excel\Objective8 practice file folder. A complete list of practice files is provided in "Using the Book's Companion Content" at the beginning of this book.

8.1 Filter Data

To locate a specific value, you can apply a filter. To filter by multiple criteria, you can apply additional filters to the results of the first one.

Active filter criteria

	A	B	C	D	E	F
1	OrderID ▼	CustomerID ▼	OrderDate ▼	ShippedDate ▼	Freight ▼	ShipName ▼
43	11120	KEMCH	1/29/2011	1/30/2011	2.95	Christian Kemp
44	11121	KEMCH	1/29/2011	1/30/2011	2.95	Christian Kemp
45	11122	KIMTI	1/29/2011	1/30/2011	12.95	Tim Kim
46	11123	KINRU	1/29/2011	1/30/2011	6.95	Russell King
47	11124	SCHJA	1/29/2011	1/30/2011	4.95	Janet Schorr
48	11125	SCHBO	1/29/2011	1/30/2011	12.95	Boris Scholl
49	11126	BRYCH	1/29/2011	1/30/2011	4.25	Chris Bryant
50	11127	BROSC	1/29/2011	1/30/2011	3.25	Scott Brown
63						
64						
65						

Rows that don't meet filter criteria are hidden

In addition to filtering on entire values, you can use ready-made filters to locate values that meet certain criteria. The criteria vary depending on the number format. If the worksheet or table is formatted, you can filter for the cell color, font color, or cell icon.

> **Strategy** Take the time to familiarize yourself with the wide range of ready-made filters and the kinds of criteria you can create with them. Experiment with criteria that include and don't include a specific value.

If none of the ready-made criteria meets your needs, you can create criteria from scratch.

The location of the selection determines which columns in the range are filtered. If you select a populated cell in a data range, filter buttons appear in the column headers for all columns in the range. If you select a row, filter buttons appear in that row, and you can filter only the cells below that row. If you select a column, a filter button appears in the first cell of only that column.

➤ To display rows containing a specific column value

1. Click any cell in the range to be sorted. Then on the **Home** tab, in the **Editing** group, click the **Sort & Filter** button, and click **Filter**.

Or

Click any cell in the range to be sorted. Then on the **Data** tab, in the **Sort & Filter** group, click the **Filter** button.

2. Click the filter arrow for the column by which you want to filter the worksheet, and then click **Select All** to clear all the check boxes.

3. Select the check box(es) of the field value(s) you want to display, and then click **OK**.

➤ To remove a filter

→ On the **Home** tab, in the **Editing** group, click the **Sort & Filter** button, and then click **Clear**.

→ On the **Data** tab, in the **Sort & Filter** group, click the **Clear** button.

> **Tip** If you have finished filtering, you can hide the filtering arrows by displaying the Sort & Filter list from the Editing group on the Home tab and then clicking Filter, or by clicking the active Filter button on the Data tab.

➤ To apply a common filtering criterion

1. Display the filter arrows, and then click the arrow of the column on which you want to filter.

2. Point to **<data type> Filters**, and then click the criterion you want to filter by.

> **Tip** In a column containing date values, you can click All Dates In Period to display all date values in a particular quarter or month.

3. In the **Custom AutoFilter** dialog box, enter the value that completes the criterion. Then if you want, add a second criterion.

4. Click **OK**.

➤ To filter on formatting

1. Display the filter arrows, and then click the arrow of the column on which you want to filter.

2. Point to **Filter by Color**, and then click the formatting you want to filter by.

> **Tip** You can quickly filter a worksheet to display all the rows containing the value or formatting of the active cell. Right-click the cell, point to Filter, and then click the filtering option you want.

➤ To create a custom filter

1. Display the filter arrows, and then click the arrow of the column on which you want to filter.

2. Point to **<data type> Filters**, and then click **Custom Filter**.

3. In the **Custom AutoFilter** dialog box, construct the criterion by which you want to filter, using **And** to specify two criteria or **Or** to specify alternatives.

> **Tip** You can use wildcards when filtering text, but not when filtering numbers.

4. Click **OK**.

> **Tip** Pointing to the filter arrow displays the current filter criteria for the column.

Practice Tasks

The practice file for these tasks is located in the Excel\Objective8 practice file folder. If you want to save the results of the tasks, save them in the same folder with *My* appended to the file name so that you don't overwrite the original practice file.

- Open the *Filtering* workbook. On the OrdersJan worksheet, display only those rows containing WA (Washington state) in the ShipRegion column. Then redisplay all the rows.

- On the OrdersJan worksheet of the *Filtering* workbook, display the orders shipped on January 23, 24, and 25. Then display only the orders that were shipped to states other than Washington (WA) during that time.

- On the OrdersFeb worksheet of the *Filtering* workbook, display only the rows for which the cell in the Freight column has a colored fill. Then display only the rows for which the cell in the Freight column has no fill color. Lastly, redisplay all the rows.

8.2 Sort Data

You can sort the values in one or more columns in a worksheet or table in either ascending or descending order. To sort on multiple columns, you specify in the Sort dialog box the order in which you want them to be sorted.

By default, Excel assumes that the first row in the worksheet contains column headers and does not include it in the sort. It also assumes that you want to sort on the cells' values, but if the worksheet or table is formatted, you can specify that you want to sort on any of the following:

- Cell color
- Font color
- Cell icon

See Also For information about cell icons, see section 8.3, "Apply Conditional Formatting."

You can also specify whether entries starting with uppercase and lowercase letters should be sorted separately and the orientation of the sort (whether you want to sort columns or rows).

> **Tip** You can sort a selected range of data on the content of hidden columns within that range.

➤ To sort a worksheet or table on one column

→ Click any cell in the column. Then on the **Home** tab, in the **Editing** group, click the **Sort & Filter** button, and click the sorting option you want.

> **Tip** The sorting options vary depending on the number format of the data in the column.

→ Click any cell in the column. Then on the **Data** tab, in the **Sort & Filter** group, click the **Sort A to Z** or **Sort Z to A** button.

➤ To sort a worksheet or table on more than one column

1. Click any cell in the range to be sorted. Then on the **Home** tab, in the **Editing** group, click the **Sort & Filter** button, and click **Custom Sort**.

   Or

   Click any cell in the range to be sorted, and then on the **Data** tab, in the **Sort & Filter** group, click the **Sort** button.

2. In the **Sort** dialog box, click the first column you want in the **Sort by** list. Then click the criteria by which you want to sort in the **Sort on** list. Finally, click the order you want in the **Order** list.

> **Tip** The options in the Sort dialog box change if you click Cell Color, Font Color, or Cell Icon in the Sort On list.

3. Click **Add Level**, and repeat step 2 for the second column. Repeat this step for additional columns.

4. Click **OK**.

➤ **To remove a sort level**

1. On the **Home** tab, in the **Editing** group, click the **Sort & Filter** button, and then click **Custom Sort**.

2. In the **Sort** dialog box, click the level you want to remove.

3. Click **Delete Level**, and then click **OK**.

Practice Tasks

The practice file for these tasks is located in the Excel\Objective8 practice file folder. If you want to save the results of the tasks, save them in the same folder with *My* appended to the file name so that you don't overwrite the original practice file.

- In the *Sorting* workbook, sort the data range on the SalesByCategory worksheet by Category only.

- Sort the data range on the SalesByCategory worksheet by Category and then by Sales.

8.3 Apply Conditional Formatting

You can make worksheet data easier to interpret by using conditional formatting to format cells based on their values. If a value meets a particular condition, Excel applies the formatting; if it doesn't, the formatting is not applied.

You set up conditional formatting by specifying the condition, which is called a *rule*. You can select from the following types of rules:

- Highlight cells

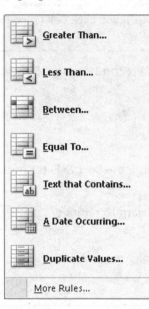

- Top/bottom

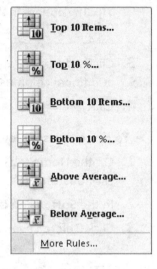

- Data bars

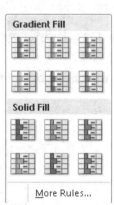

- Color scales

- Icon sets

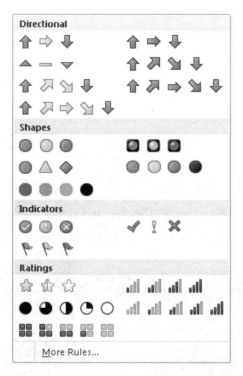

You can also define a rule from scratch in the New Formatting Rule dialog box.

The options available in the Edit The Rule Description area vary depending on the selection in the Select A Rule Type list. You can define multiple conditions for the same range of cells or table.

> **Strategy** Familiarize yourself with all the types of rules and their variations so that you know how to quickly apply any condition that might be requested on the exam.

All the rules you create are listed in the Conditional Formatting Rules Manager, where you can do the following:

- Create and delete rules.
- Edit a selected rule.
- Adjust the order in which Excel processes the selected rule.
- Specify whether Excel should stop processing rules after a cell has met the conditions of the selected rule.

➤ To apply cell fill and font color based on cell value

1. On the **Home** tab, in the **Styles** group, click the **Conditional Formatting** button.

2. In the **Conditional Formatting** list, point to **Highlight Cell Rules** or **Top/Bottom Rules**, and then click the type of condition you want.

3. In the dialog box, complete the condition if necessary for the selected type. Then click one of the available fill, font, or border color options in the list.

> **Tip** You can click Custom Format and then click style, underline, color, and effects on the Font page of the Format Cells dialog box.

4. Click **OK**.

➤ **To display data bars, a color scale, or icons based on cell value**

→ In the **Conditional Formatting** list, point to **Data Bars**, **Color Scales**, or **Icon Sets**, and then click the option you want.

➤ **To create a rule from scratch**

1. In the **Conditional Formatting** list, click **New Rule**.

2. In the **New Formatting Rule** dialog box, in the **Select a Rule Type** list, click the type you want.

3. In the **Edit the Rule Description** area, specify the condition.

4. If the selected conditional formatting rule includes formatting options, click **Format**. Then on the **Font** page of the **Format Cells** dialog box, specify the formatting to apply if the condition is met, and click **OK**.

5. In the **New Formatting Rule** dialog box, click **OK**.

➤ **To modify the conditional format applied to selected cells**

1. In the **Conditional Formatting** list, click **Manage Rules**.

2. In the **Conditional Formatting Rules Manager** dialog box, click the rule you want to change, and then click **Edit Rule**.

3. In the **Edit Formatting Rule** dialog box, make your changes, and then click **OK**.

➤ **To stop testing the cell for subsequent rules if this rule is met**

→ Open the **Conditional Formatting Rules Manager** dialog box, click the rule, select the **Stop If True** check box, and then click **OK**.

➤ **To delete the conditional format applied to selected cells**

→ In the **Conditional Formatting** list, point to **Clear Rules**, and then click **Clear Rules from Selected Cells** or **Clear Rules from Entire Sheet**.

→ Open the **Conditional Formatting Rules Manager** dialog box, click the rule, click **Delete Rule**, and then click **OK**.

Practice Tasks

The practice file for these tasks is located in the Excel\Objective8 practice file folder. If you want to save the results of the tasks, save them in the same folder with *My* appended to the file name so that you don't overwrite the original practice file.

- In the *ConditionalFormatting* workbook, on the Orders worksheet, format the name Seattle in the City column with red text.

- On the Details worksheet of the *ConditionalFormatting* workbook, display the Three Arrows (Colored) icon set for all the values in the Extended Price column. Then show blue data bars for the same values. Finally, in the same column, fill all cells containing values over $100 with bright yellow.

- On the Details worksheet of the *ConditionalFormatting* workbook, configure Excel to first process the rule that makes the cells fill with yellow, and to not process any more rules for cells that meet the first condition.

Objective Review

Before finishing this chapter, ensure that you have mastered the following skills:

8.1   Filter Data

8.2   Sort Data

8.3   Apply Conditional Formatting

Microsoft PowerPoint 2010

This part of the book covers the skills you need to have for certification as a Microsoft Office Specialist in Microsoft PowerPoint 2010. Specifically, you need to be able to complete tasks that demonstrate the following skill sets:

1 Managing the PowerPoint Environment

2 Creating a Slide Presentation

3 Working with Graphical and Multimedia Elements

4 Creating Charts and Tables

5 Applying Transitions and Animations

6 Collaborating on Presentations

7 Preparing Presentations for Delivery

8 Delivering Presentations

With these skills, you can create the types of presentations that are most commonly used in a business environment.

Prerequisites

We assume that you have been working with PowerPoint 2010 for at least six months and that you know how to move around in a presentation, which is not specifically mentioned in the Microsoft Office Specialist objectives for Exam 77-883, "Microsoft PowerPoint 2010." Before you begin studying for this exam, you might want to make sure you are familiar with the information in this section.

Understanding PowerPoint Views

To help you create, organize, and display presentations, PowerPoint provides the following views:

- **Normal** This is the default view. You can work with the content of a specific slide and enter development and delivery notes.

- **Slide Sorter** In this view, the slides of the presentation are displayed as thumbnails so that you can easily reorganize them and apply transitions and timings.

- **Reading View** In this view, each slide fills the screen. You use this view to preview the presentation.

- **Slide Show** In this view, each slide fills the screen. You use this view to deliver the presentation to an audience.

- **Notes Page** In this view, each slide is displayed at the top of a page where you can add speaker notes. You can add speaker notes that consist of only text in the Notes pane in Normal view. However, to create speaker notes that contain elements other than text, such as a graphic or a chart, you must be in Notes Page view.

- **Slide Master, Handout Master, or Notes Master** In these views, the masters that control the default design of the presentation components are displayed. You can make changes to the overall design by working with these masters.

> **See Also** For more information about Normal view, see section 1.2, "Manipulate the PowerPoint Window." For information about applying transitions, see section 5.4, "Apply and Modify Transitions Between Slides." For information about slide timings, see section 8.3, "Set Presentation Timing. For information about delivering a presentation, see Chapter 8, "Delivering Presentations."

Moving Around in a Presentation

When developing a presentation in Normal view, you can move around in several ways.

➤ **To display a specific slide in the Slides pane**

→ On the **Outline** tab or the **Slides** tab of the **Overview** pane, click the slide's icon.

➤ **To move backward or forward one slide at a time**

→ At the bottom of the vertical scroll bar to the right of the **Slide** pane, click the **Previous Slide** or **Next Slide** button.

> **Tip** Clicking the up or down scroll arrow has the same effect.

➤ **To move to a different slide in a presentation**

→ On the vertical scroll bar, drag the scroll box until the adjacent ScreenTip indicates that the slide you want will be displayed if you release the mouse button.

Selecting Text

Before you can edit or format existing text, you have to select it. You can select specific items as follows:

- **A word** Double-click it. The word and the space following it are selected. Punctuation following a word is not selected.

- **A bullet point or subpoint** Click its bullet.

- **Adjacent words, lines, or paragraphs** Drag through them.

- **All the text in a placeholder** In the Slide pane, click inside the placeholder. Then on the Home tab, in the Editing group, click the Select button and click Select All. Alternatively, after clicking the placeholder, press Ctrl+A.

- **All the text on a slide** On the Outline tab, click its slide icon.

- **All the objects on a slide** In the Slide pane, select any placeholder (so that it has a solid border), click the Select button, and then click Select All.

> **Tip** Clicking the Select button, and then clicking Selection Pane displays the Selection And Visibility task pane, where you can specify whether each object on a slide should be displayed or hidden.

Selected text appears highlighted in the location where you made the selection—that is, either in the Slide pane or on the Outline tab of the Overview pane.

1 Managing the PowerPoint Environment

The skills tested in this section of the Microsoft Office Specialist exam for Microsoft PowerPoint 2010 relate to the PowerPoint working environment. Specifically, the following objectives are associated with this set of skills:

1.1 Adjust Views

1.2 Manipulate the PowerPoint Window

1.3 Configure the Quick Access Toolbar

1.4 Configure PowerPoint File Options

The PowerPoint 2010 working environment, also called the *user interface*, makes sophisticated features for creating presentations easily accessible. You can manipulate this environment to make working on a presentation as intuitive as possible.

This chapter guides you in studying methods for controlling the PowerPoint working environment to suit the way you work, including switching to the view most suitable for a particular task, customizing the PowerPoint program window, making frequently used commands available with one click, and modifying program settings.

> **Practice Files** Before you can complete the practice tasks in this chapter, you need to copy the book's practice files to your computer. The practice files you'll use to complete the tasks in this chapter are in the PowerPoint\Objective1 practice file folder. A complete list of practice files is provided in "Using the Book's Companion Content" at the beginning of this book.

1.1 Adjust Views

Switching Views

For efficiency you should know which view to use for a particular task. For example, you could change the order of the first four slides in a presentation in Normal view, but you would probably want to switch to Slide Sorter view to change the order of the first 14 slides.

➤ **To switch to Normal, Slide Sorter, or Reading view**

→ At the right end of the status bar, on the **View Shortcuts** toolbar, click the button of the view you want.

→ On the **View** tab, in the **Presentation Views** group, click the button of the view you want.

➤ **To switch to Slide Show view**

→ At the right end of the status bar, on the **View Shortcuts** toolbar, click the **Slide Show** button.

→ On the **Slide Show** tab, in the **Start Slide Show** group, click the **From Beginning** or **From Current Slide** button.

➤ **To exit Slide Show view**

→ Press the Esc key to return to the previous view.

➤ **To display notes pages**

→ On the **View** tab, in the **Presentation Views** group, click the **Notes Page** button.

➤ **To display the slide master, handout master, or notes master**

→ On the **View** tab, in the **Master Views** group, click the button of the master you want.

Zooming In and Out

You can change the magnification, called the *zoom level*, of the current slide in Normal view or of the slide thumbnails in Slide Sorter view in two ways:

- You can set a specific zoom level by using the Zoom dialog box.

- You can visually adjust the zoom level by using the Zoom slider.

➤ To set a specific zoom level

1. On the **View** tab, in the **Zoom** group, click the **Zoom** button.

   Or

   On the **View Shortcuts** toolbar, click the **Zoom level** button.

2. In the **Zoom** dialog box, click the preset zoom level you want, or type the percentage you want in the **Percent** box. Then click **OK**.

➤ To visually adjust the zoom level

- ➜ At the left or right end of the slider on the status bar, click the **Zoom Out** or **Zoom In** button until the slide is the size you want.

- ➜ On the slider, drag the **Zoom** indicator to the left or right until the slide is the size you want.

➤ **To make the current slide fit the Slide pane**

→ On the **View** tab, in the **Zoom** group, click the **Fit to Window** button.

→ At the right end of the status bar, click the **Fit slide to current window** button.

> **See Also** For more information about the Slide pane, see section 1.2, "Manipulate the PowerPoint Window."

Practice Tasks

The practice file for these tasks is located in your PowerPoint\Objective1 practice file folder. If you want to save the results of the tasks, save them in the same folder with *My* appended to the file name so that you don't overwrite the original practice file.

● In the *WaterSaving* presentation, display the presentation in Slide Sorter view.

● Display the same presentation in Slide Show view, and then return to Slide Sorter view.

● Display the presentation in Normal view, with the active slide zoomed to 50%.

● Expand the size of the active slide to completely fill the space available in the Slide pane.

1.2 Manipulate the PowerPoint Window

Working with Multiple Program Windows

With PowerPoint 2010, each presentation you open is displayed in its own program window. As a result, you can not only switch among open presentations, but you can also view multiple presentations simultaneously. You can arrange windows side by side or in a cascading effect so that you can easily click the one you want.

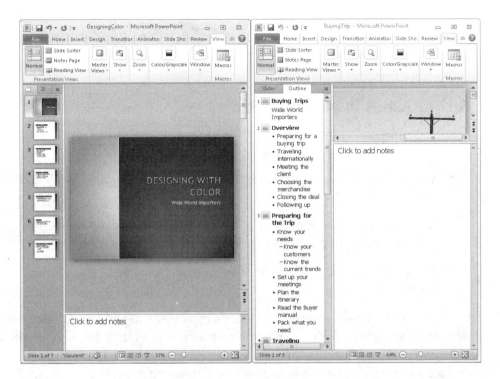

When you want to view two different parts of the same presentation, you can open a second window containing the presentation, arrange the windows side by side, and then scroll the two windows independently.

➤ To switch to a different open presentation

→ On the **View** tab, in the **Window** group, click the **Switch Windows** button, and then click the name of the presentation you want.

➤ To view more than one presentation at the same time

→ On the **View** tab, in the **Window** group, click the **Arrange All** button.

> **Tip** You can also stack overlapping windows by clicking the Cascade button.

➤ **To view different parts of the same presentation**

→ On the **View** tab, in the **Window** group, click the **New Window** button. Then click the **Arrange All** button, and scroll to the parts of the presentations you want to see.

Sizing Panes in Normal View

You carry out most of the development work on a presentation in Normal view, which consists of the following three panes:

- **Overview** This pane appears on the left side of the program window and has two tabs: Slides and Outline.

- **Slide** This pane occupies most of the program window and shows the current slide as it will appear in the presentation.

- **Notes** This pane sits below the Slide pane and provides a place for entering notes about the current slide.

You can adjust the relative sizes of the panes to suit your needs. The adjustments are saved with the presentation that is open at the time and do not affect other presentations.

➤ **To adjust the relative sizes of the Normal view panes**

→ Point to a splitter bar, and when the pointer changes to a double bar with opposing arrows, drag in either direction.

Or

1. On the **View** tab, in the **Window** group, click the **Move Split** button.

2. When a four-headed arrow appears at the junction of the three panes, do either of the following:

   ○ Press the Up Arrow or Down Arrow key to expand or shrink the Notes pane.

   ○ Press the Right Arrow or Left Arrow key to expand or shrink the Overview pane.

3. Press the Esc key to turn off pane splitting.

➤ **To hide a pane or display a hidden pane**

→ Move the splitter bar to shrink the pane as far as it will go.

→ Move the splitter bar back to widen the pane again.

> **Tip** Clicking the Close button in the upper-right corner of the Overview pane closes the pane. Clicking the Normal button in the Presentation Views group of the View tab opens it again.

Practice Tasks

The practice files for these tasks are located in your *PowerPoint\Objective1* practice file folder. If you want to save the results of the tasks, save them in the same folder with *My* appended to the file name so that you don't overwrite the original practice files.

- With the *BuyingTripsA* and *BuyingTripsB* presentations open, display first one and then the other.

- Choose a method to display these two presentations side by side.

- Close *BuyingTripsA*, maximize *BuyingTripsB*, and then in Normal view, hide the Notes pane.

- View slides 2 and 4 of the *BuyingTripsB* presentation side by side.

1.3 Configure the Quick Access Toolbar

By default, the Save, Undo, and Repeat/Redo buttons appear on the Quick Access Toolbar. You can add other frequently used buttons to this toolbar so that they are always available in the upper-left corner of the program window. You add these buttons on the Quick Access Toolbar page of the PowerPoint Options dialog box.

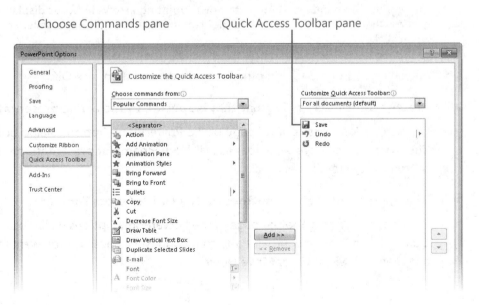

On this page, you can do the following:

- Define a custom Quick Access Toolbar for all presentations or for a specific presentation.
- Add any command from any group of any tab, including contextual tabs.
- Display a separator between buttons.
- Move buttons into the order you want.
- Restore the default Quick Access Toolbar.

If you add many buttons to the Quick Access Toolbar, you can move the Quick Access Toolbar below the ribbon so that they are all visible. If you add all the buttons you use most often to the Quick Access Toolbar, you can hide the ribbon to gain screen space.

> **See Also** For information about the ribbon, see "Modifying the Display of the Ribbon" at the beginning of this book.

➤ To add a button to the Quick Access Toolbar for all presentations

1. On the **Quick Access Toolbar** page of the **PowerPoint Options** dialog box, in the **Choose commands from** list, click the category of commands you want.

2. In the **Choose Commands** pane, click the command you want, and then click **Add**.

> **Tip** In the command list, items with down-pointing arrows in boxes display tab groups when clicked, and items with right-pointing arrows display a gallery or menu when clicked.

3. Repeat steps 1 and 2 to add other commands, and then click **OK**.

➤ To create a Quick Access Toolbar that is specific to the active presentation

→ On the **Quick Access Toolbar** page of the **PowerPoint Options** dialog box, in the **Customize Quick Access Toolbar** list, click **For <name of presentation>**. Then add buttons to the toolbar as usual.

➤ To change the order of the buttons on the Quick Access Toolbar

→ On the **Quick Access Toolbar** page of the **PowerPoint Options** dialog box, in the **Quick Access Toolbar** pane, click the command whose position you want to change, and then click **Move Up** or **Move Down**.

➤ **To group buttons on the Quick Access Toolbar**

➔ On the **Quick Access Toolbar** page of the **PowerPoint Options** dialog box, in the **Choose Commands** pane, double-click **Separator**.

➤ **To remove a button from the Quick Access Toolbar**

➔ On the **Quick Access Toolbar** page of the **PowerPoint Options** dialog box, in the **Quick Access Toolbar** pane, click the command you no longer want, and then click **Remove**.

➤ **To restore the default Quick Access Toolbar**

1. On the **Quick Access Toolbar** page of the **PowerPoint Options** dialog box, click **Reset**, and then click **Reset only Quick Access Toolbar**.

2. In the **Reset Customizations** message box, click **Yes**.

➤ **To display the Quick Access Toolbar below the ribbon**

➔ At the right end of the Quick Access Toolbar, click the **Customize Quick Access Toolbar** button, and then click **Show Below the Ribbon**.

Practice Tasks

You don't need any practice files for these tasks. Simply open a blank presentation.

- You regularly use the ruler, gridlines, and guides when arranging elements on a slide. Add a button to the Quick Access Toolbar for all presentations so that you can display any of these tools without using the ribbon.

- The Quick Print button is not available on any ribbon tab. Add this button to the Quick Access Toolbar, make it the leftmost button, and visually separate it from the other buttons.

- Create a Quick Access Toolbar for the current presentation that contains buttons for inserting pictures, charts, and tables. Then display the Quick Access Toolbar below the ribbon.

- Remove your customizations from both Quick Access Toolbars, and display the toolbar above the ribbon.

1.4 Configure PowerPoint File Options

You can change settings on the pages of the PowerPoint Options dialog box to customize the PowerPoint environment in various ways.

- **General** On this page, you can disable the Mini Toolbar and Live Preview, specify the color scheme and the ScreenTip style, and change the user name and initials.

- **Proofing** This page provides options for adjusting the AutoCorrect settings and for refining the spell-checking and grammar-checking processes.

- **Save** On this page, you can change the default presentation format; the AutoRecover file save rate; the default locations to which PowerPoint saves files; and whether you want fonts to be embedded in the current presentation.

- **Language** On this page, you can change the editing and display languages.

- **Advanced** This page includes options related to editing presentation content; displaying presentations on-screen; printing, saving, and sharing presentations; and a variety of other settings. (You have to scroll the page to see some of these settings.)

- **Customize Ribbon** On this page, you can change the ribbon to suit your needs.

- Quick Access Toolbar On this page, you can customize the Quick Access Toolbar to suit your needs.

> **See Also** For information about changing the Quick Access Toolbar, see section 1.3, "Configure the Quick Access Toolbar."

- **Add-Ins** This page displays all the active and inactive add-ins and enables you to add and remove them.

- **Trust Center** This page provides links to information about privacy and security, and access to security settings.

> **Strategy** Knowing which options are on which page of the PowerPoint Options dialog box makes the customizing process more efficient. To avoid wasting time in the exam, be sure you are familiar with the pages of this dialog box.

➤ **To access the PowerPoint program options**

→ In the left pane of the Backstage view, click **Options**. Then in the left pane of the **PowerPoint Options** dialog box, click the page you want.

Practice Tasks

You don't need any practice files for these tasks. Simply open a blank presentation. Then open the PowerPoint Options dialog box, and make the following changes without clicking OK. When you finish, click Cancel to close the dialog box without implementing your changes.

- Change your user name to *PowerPoint Exam* and your initials to *PE*.
- Turn off the instruction to ignore spelling mistakes in uppercase words.
- Change the AutoRecover interval to 15 minutes.
- Turn off whole-word selection.

Objective Review

Before finishing this chapter, ensure that you have mastered the following skills:

1.1   Adjust Views

1.2   Manipulate the PowerPoint Window

1.3   Configure the Quick Access Toolbar

1.4   Configure PowerPoint File Options

2 Creating a Slide Presentation

The skills tested in this section of the Microsoft Office Specialist exam for Microsoft PowerPoint 2010 relate to working with slides and slide text in a presentation. Specifically, the following objectives are associated with this set of skills:

2.1 Construct and Edit Photo Albums

2.2 Apply Slide Size and Orientation Settings

2.3 Add and Remove Slides

2.4 Format Slides

2.5 Enter and Format Text

2.6 Format Text Boxes

Using templates and reusing slides simplifies the creation of consistent presentations, both for yourself and across your organization. Knowing how to assemble and then manipulate a presentation is important for efficient presentation development. But you also need to know how to work with individual slides and with their text.

This chapter guides you in studying how to create photo albums and then covers ways to create simple text-based presentations. It addresses how to assemble slides from different sources, and how to arrange and format them. It also covers basic techniques for entering, editing, and formatting the text on a slide, including both the text in placeholders provided by the slide layout and the text in independent text boxes that you create as needed.

> **Practice Files** Before you can complete the practice tasks in this chapter, you need to copy the book's practice files to your computer. The practice files you'll use to complete the tasks in this chapter are in the PowerPoint\Objective2 practice file folder. A complete list of practice files is provided in "Using the Book's Companion Content" at the beginning of this book.

2.1 Construct and Edit Photo Albums

Creating Photo Albums

Presentations that consist primarily of photographs are called *photo albums*. You can create a photo album in two ways:

- You can base the presentation on one of the photo album templates that comes with PowerPoint.

> **Tip** To use a slide layout from a photo album template in another type of presentation, first create the photo album and save it. Then reuse the slide with the layout you want in the other presentation. For information about reusing slides, see section 2.3, "Add and Remove Slides."

- You can set up a new blank presentation as a photo album that you design yourself in the Photo Album dialog box, where you can do the following:
  - Add pictures and photographs from files.
  - Insert text boxes.
  - Reorganize the photos.
  - Rotate photos in clockwise and counterclockwise increments of 90 degrees.
  - Adjust contrast and brightness.
  - Add captions below each photo (available only for appropriate picture layouts).
  - Display all photos in black and white.
  - Specify the layout and, for appropriate layouts, how the photos are framed.
  - Apply a theme to the presentation.

> ➤ **To create a photo album from a template**

1. On the **New** page of the Backstage view, click **Sample Templates**.

2. Double-click the photo album template you want, and then save the presentation.

> ➤ **To replace a selected template photograph**

1. On the Picture Tools **Format** contextual tab, in the **Adjust** group, click the **Change Picture** button.

2. In the **Insert Picture** dialog box, locate and double-click the photograph you want.

➤ **To create a custom photo album**

1. Open a new blank presentation, and on the **Insert** tab, in the **Images** group, display the **Photo Album** list, and then click **New Photo Album**.

2. In the **Photo Album** dialog box, click **File/Disk**. Then in the **Insert New Pictures** dialog box, locate and select the pictures you want, and click **Insert**.

3. To include a text box in the layout, click **New Text Box** in the **Photo Album** dialog box.

4. In the **Pictures in album** box, adjust the order of the pictures and text boxes by clicking **Move Down** or **Move Up**.

5. Under the **Preview** box, adjust the angle of rotation, contrast, and brightness of the displayed picture.

6. Under **Picture Options**, specify whether the pictures should have captions and whether they should appear in black and white.

7. In the **Album Layout** area, in the **Picture layout** and **Frame shape** lists, select the options you want.

8. To the right of **Theme**, click **Browse**, and then in the **Choose Theme** dialog box, double-click the theme you want.

9. Click **Create** to set up a presentation that includes a title slide containing the title *Photo Album* and the user name stored in the PowerPoint Options dialog box, as well as slides containing the specified pictures in the specified format.

Editing Photo Albums

After you create any photo album, you can modify a selected photograph by clicking the buttons on the Picture Tools Format contextual tab. For example, you can apply a picture style, border, or effect.

> **See Also** For information about formatting pictures, see section 3.1, "Manipulate Graphical Elements," and section 3.2, "Manipulate Images."

To modify a custom photo album, you can change settings in the Edit Photo Album dialog box, which resembles the Photo Album dialog box in which you created the presentation.

➤ **To edit a custom photo album**

1. On the **Insert** tab, in the **Images** group, display the **Photo Album** list, and then click **Edit Photo Album**.

2. In the **Edit Photo Album** dialog box, make the changes you want, and then click **Update**.

> **Tip** You cannot use the Edit Photo Album dialog box to modify a photo album created from a template. All changes to template-based photo albums must be made on the Picture Tools Format contextual tab.

Practice Tasks

The practice files for these tasks are located in the PowerPoint\Objective2 practice file folder.

- Create a photo album based on the Contemporary Photo Album template. Replace the photograph on the title slide with the *Hydrangeas* practice file, and then save the presentation as *My Contemporary Album*.

- In the *My Contemporary Album* presentation, replace the *Hydrangeas* photograph with the *Tulips* photograph, and surround it with an orange border.

- With a blank presentation open, use the *Chrysanthemum*, *Frangipani*, *Hydrangeas*, and *Tulips* files to create a photo album that displays two photographs on each of two slides, with rounded rectangle frames and no captions. Apply the Black Tie theme, and save the photo album as *My Black Tie Album*.

- Add the *Daisies* and *WaterLilies* photographs to the *My Black Tie Album* presentation, and change the order of the photographs so that *Daisies* and *WaterLilies* appear on slide 2. Display all the photographs in simple black frames, and change the theme to Austin.

2.2 Apply Slide Size and Orientation Settings

By default, slides are sized for an on-screen slide show with a width-to-height ratio of 4:3 (10 inches by 7.5 inches). The slides are oriented horizontally, with slide numbers starting at 1. If you need to print the slides, notes, handouts, or outline of a presentation, you can set the size and orientation to fit the paper.

In the Page Setup dialog box, you can select from the following slide sizes:

- **On-screen Show** For an electronic slide show on screens of various aspects (4:3, 16:9, or 16:10)

- **Letter Paper** For a presentation printed on 8.5-by-11-inch U.S. letter-size paper

- **Ledger Paper** For a presentation printed on 11-by-17-inch legal-size paper

- **A3 Paper, A4 Paper, B4 (ISO) Paper, B5 (ISO) Paper** For a presentation printed on paper of various international sizes

- **35mm Slides** For 35mm slides to be used in a carousel with a projector

- **Overhead** For transparencies for an overhead projector

- **Banner** For a banner for a webpage

- **Custom** For slides that are a nonstandard size

➤ **To set the size of slides**

1. On the **Design** tab, in the **Page Setup** group, click the **Page Setup** button.

2. In the **Page Setup** dialog box, do either of the following, and then click **OK**:

○ In the **Slides sized for** list, select the size you want.

○ In the **Width** and **Height** boxes, enter the sizes you want.

➤ **To change the orientation of slides, notes, handouts, or the outline**

→ On the **Design** tab, in the **Page Setup** group, click the **Slide Orientation** button, and then click **Portrait** or **Landscape**.

→ In the **Page Setup** dialog box, click **Portrait** or **Landscape**.

Tip Slide size and orientation can also be controlled from the Slide Master tab in Slide Master view.

Practice Tasks

The practice file for these tasks is located in the PowerPoint\Objective2 practice file folder. If you want to save the results of the tasks, save them in the same folder with *My* appended to the file name so that you don't overwrite the original practice file.

● In the *Harmony* presentation, size the slides so that you can print them on 8.5-by-11-inch paper.

● Make any changes necessary to print the *Harmony* presentation's speaker notes horizontally on letter paper.

2.3 Add and Remove Slides

Inserting New Slides

When you insert a slide into a presentation, PowerPoint inserts it with the default layout immediately after the current slide. If you want to add a slide with a different layout, you select the layout you want from the New Slide gallery. The available layouts and their design depend on the template used to create the presentation.

After you have inserted a slide, you can change its layout at any time.

If you want to insert a slide that is similar to an existing slide, you can duplicate the existing slide and then change it, instead of having to create the slide from scratch.

➤ **To insert a new slide after the current slide**

→ On the **Home** tab, in the **Slides** group, click the **New Slide** button to insert a slide with the default layout.

→ On the **Home** tab, in the **Slides** group, click the **New Slide** arrow, and then click the layout you want.

➤ **To change the layout of an existing slide**

→ On the **Home** tab, in the **Slides** group, click the **Layout** button, and then click the layout you want.

➤ **To duplicate a slide**

→ On the **Home** tab, in the **Slides** group, click the **New Slide** arrow, and then click **Duplicate Selected Slides**.

→ In the **Overview** pane, on the **Slides** tab, right-click the slide, and then click **Duplicate Slide**.

Reusing Slides

If you save a presentation on your hard disk or in a shared location on your network and then you want to reuse one or more of its slides in a different presentation, you can tell PowerPoint to reuse the existing slides. If you are using PowerPoint Professional Plus and connecting to a Microsoft SharePoint site on which slide libraries are enabled, you can store slides in a slide library so that they are available for use in any presentation by anyone who can access the library. Either way, you insert the slides you want to use from the Reuse Slides task pane.

> **To reuse slides from a saved presentation**

1. Click the slide after which you want to insert reused slides.

2. On the **Home** tab, in the **Slides** group, click the **New Slide** arrow, and then click **Reuse Slides**.

3. In the **Reuse Slides** task pane, click **Browse**, and then click **Browse File**.

4. In the **Browse** dialog box, locate and double-click the presentation containing the slides you want to reuse.

5. In the **Reuse Slides** task pane, click each slide you want to reuse, and then close the task pane.

> **Tip** By default, reused slides take on the formatting of the presentation into which they are inserted. To retain the slides' source formatting, select the Keep Source Formatting check box before inserting the first slide.

➤ **To store slides in a slide library**

1. On the **Save & Send** page of the Backstage view, click **Publish Slides**.

2. In the right pane, click the **Publish Slides** button.

3. In the **Publish Slides** dialog box, select the check box for the slide you want to store in the library.

4. If the URL of your SharePoint slide library does not appear in the **Publish To** box, click the box, and enter the URL.

5. Click **Publish** to store the slide in the slide library.

➤ **To reuse slides from a slide library**

1. Click the slide after which you want to insert a reused slide.

2. On the **Home** tab, in the **Slides** group, click the **New Slide** arrow, and then click **Reuse Slides**.

3. In the **Reuse Slides** task pane, in the **Insert slide from** box, enter the URL of your SharePoint slide library, and then click the **Go** arrow.

   Or

   Click **Browse**, click **Browse Slide Library**, and then in the **Select a Slide Library** dialog box, navigate to the URL of the library and click **Select**.

4. In the **Reuse Slides** task pane, click each slide you want to reuse, and then close the task pane.

Inserting Outlines

If you save an outline containing styled headings as a Microsoft Word document (.doc or .docx) or a Rich Text Format (RTF) file (.rtf), you can open the outline in PowerPoint as a new presentation. You can also insert an outline in an existing presentation. In either case, paragraphs styled as Heading 1 become slide titles, and paragraphs styled as Heading 2 become bullet points.

➤ **To create a presentation based on a Word outline**

1. In the Backstage view, click **Open**.
2. In the **Open** dialog box, click **All PowerPoint Presentations**, and then click **All Files**.
3. Navigate to the outline file, and then double-click it.

➤ **To insert slides from an outline into an existing presentation**

1. Click the slide after which you want to insert slides from the outline.
2. On the **Home** tab, in the **Slides** group, click the **New Slide** arrow, and then click **Slides from Outline**.
3. In the **Insert Outline** dialog box, locate and double-click the outline file.

Rearranging Slides

You can rearrange a presentation's slides at any time so that they effectively communicate your message. You can rearrange a presentation in three ways:

- In Slide Sorter view, you can drag slide thumbnails into the correct order.
- In Normal view, you can drag slides up and down on either the Slides or Outline tab of the Overview pane.
- You can also cut and paste slides in the Overview pane.

> **Tip** On the Outline tab of the Overview pane, you can hide bullet points under slide titles to make it easier to rearrange slides. Double-click the icon of the slide whose bullet points you want to hide. Double-click again to redisplay the bullet points. To expand or collapse the entire outline at once, right-click the title of any slide, point to Expand or Collapse, and then click Expand All or Collapse All.

➤ **To reorganize slides in Slide Sorter view**

1. In Slide Sorter view, on the **View** toolbar, click the **Zoom In** or **Zoom Out** button to adjust the size of the thumbnails as necessary to see the slides you want to move.
2. Drag the slide thumbnails to their new positions.

> **Tip** If you arrange open presentation windows side by side, you can drag slides from one presentation to another. For information about arranging multiple program windows, see section 1.2, "Manipulate the PowerPoint Window."

➤ **To move a slide in Normal view**

→ In the **Overview** pane, on the **Slides** tab, click the slide's thumbnail, and then drag it up or down.

Or

1. On the **Slides** tab, click the slide's thumbnail, and then cut it.
2. Click the thumbnail of the slide after which you want the cut slide to appear, and then paste the slide.

Or

→ In the **Overview** pane, on the **Outline** tab, click the icon of the slide, and then drag it up or down.

Or

1. On the **Outline** tab, click the slide's icon, and then cut the selection. If necessary, click **Yes** to confirm the command.
2. Click the icon of the slide after which you want the cut slide to appear, and then paste the slide.

Deleting Slides

You can easily delete slides you no longer need.

➤ **To delete the current slide**

→ On the **Home** tab, in the **Clipboard** group, click the **Cut** button.

> **Tip** If you might change your mind about the deletion later, use this method so that you can paste the slides back into the presentation from the Microsoft Office Clipboard.

→ In the **Overview** pane, on the **Slides** tab, right-click the slide thumbnail, and then click **Delete Slide**.

→ In the **Overview** pane, on the **Outline** tab, right-click the slide title, and then click **Delete Slide**.

➤ **To delete multiple slides**

1. In the **Overview** pane, on the **Slides** tab, select the slides you want to delete, and then do one of the following:

- ○ Cut the slides.

- ○ Right-click anywhere in the selection, and then click **Delete Slide**.

> **Tip** To select non-contiguous slides, hold down the Ctrl key while you click each slide.

Hiding Slides

If you decide not to include a slide when you deliver a presentation but you don't want to delete the slide entirely, you can hide the slide. Then PowerPoint will skip over that slide during delivery.

➤ **To hide a selected slide**

→ On the **Slide Show** tab, in the **Set Up** group, click the **Hide Slide** button.

→ Right-click the selected slide, and then click **Hide Slide**.

➤ **To display a hidden slide during presentation delivery**

→ Right-click anywhere on the screen, point to **Go to Slide**, and then click the hidden slide, which is identified by the parentheses around its slide number.

Practice Tasks

The practice files for these tasks are located in the PowerPoint\Objective2 practice file folder. If you want to save the results of the tasks, save them in the same folder with *My* appended to the file name so that you don't overwrite the original practice files.

- In the *Service* presentation, add a new slide with the default layout after the title slide. Then add a slide with the Two Content layout.

- Insert the first slide in the *Projects* presentation as slide 4 in the *Service* presentation.

- After slide 4 in the *Service* presentation, create more new slides by inserting the outline stored in the *Orientation* document.

- Reorder the slides in the *Service* presentation so that slide 6 appears before slide 4. Then delete slides 2, 3, and 6, and hide slide 3.

2.4 Format Slides

> **See Also** For information about changing the layout of a slide, see the "Inserting New Slides" topic in section 2.3, "Add and Remove Slides."

Applying and Modifying Themes

The primary formatting of a presentation is dictated by a theme—a combination of colors, fonts, formatting, graphics, and other elements that gives the presentation a coherent look. Even a presentation developed from scratch has a theme, albeit one that consists of only a white background and a basic set of font styles and sizes. You can change the theme applied to a presentation at any time by selecting one from the Themes gallery.

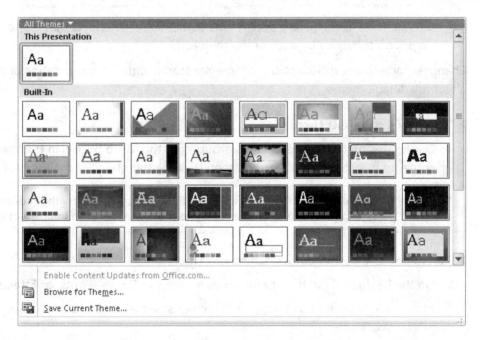

If you like some components of the theme but not others, you can change the following:

- **Colors** Every presentation, even a blank one, has an associated set of 12 complementary colors: four Text/Background colors for dark or light text on a dark or light background; Accent 1 through Accent 6 for the colors of objects other than text; Hyperlink to draw attention to hyperlinks; and Followed Hyperlink to indicate visited hyperlinks. Ten of these colors appear with light to dark gradients in the various color palettes. (The two background colors are not represented in these palettes.)

> **Tip** If none of the color schemes is exactly what you are looking for, you can create your own by clicking Create New Theme Colors at the bottom of the Colors gallery and assembling colors in the Create New Theme Colors dialog box.

- **Fonts** Every presentation, even a blank one, has an associated set of two fonts. The Fonts gallery lists the combination of fonts that is used by each of the themes, in alphabetical order by theme. The top font in each combination is used for titles, and the bottom font is used for other slide text.

> **Tip** You can create a custom font combination by clicking Create New Theme Fonts at the bottom of the Fonts gallery and then specifying the font combination you want in the Create New Theme Fonts dialog box.

- **Effects** The Effects gallery displays the combination of effects that is applied to shapes on the slides by each of the themes.

Changes made to a component of a theme are stored with the presentation and do not affect the default theme.

➤ To apply a different theme

→ On the **Design** tab, in the **Themes** group, click the **More** button in the lower-right corner of the **Themes** gallery, and then click the thumbnail of the theme you want.

> **Tip** If the thumbnail of the theme you want is visible, you can click it without displaying the entire gallery. You can also scroll the gallery to show one row of thumbnails at a time.

➤ To change the theme colors, fonts, or effects

1. On the **Design** tab, in the **Themes** group, click the **Colors**, **Fonts**, or **Effects** button.
2. In the corresponding gallery, click the color scheme, font set, or combination of effects you want.

➤ To save a modified theme

1. Adjust the colors, fonts, or effects of the current theme to suit your needs.
2. In the **Themes** gallery, below the thumbnails, click **Save Current Theme**.
3. In the **Save Current Theme** dialog box, name the theme, and then click **Save**.

➤ **To create a new color scheme**

1. Apply the color scheme that is closest to the one you want.

2. On the **Design** tab, in the **Themes** group, click the **Colors** button, and then at the bottom of the gallery, click **Create New Theme Colors**.

3. In the **Create New Theme Colors** dialog box, click the box to the right of the presentation element you want to change.

4. In the color palette that appears, do one of the following:

   ○ Click the color you want to apply to the selected element.

   ○ At the bottom of the palette, click **More Colors**. Then on either the **Standard** page or the **Custom** page of the **Colors** dialog box, click the color you want, and click **OK**.

5. In the **Name** box at the bottom of the **Create New Theme Colors** dialog box, assign a name to the new color scheme, and then click **Save**.

➤ **To create a new font set**

1. Apply the font set that is closest to the one you want.

2. On the **Design** tab, in the **Themes** group, click the **Fonts** button, and then at the bottom of the gallery, click **Create New Theme Fonts**.

3. In the **Create New Theme Fonts** dialog box, in the **Heading font** list, click the font you want.

4. Repeat step 3 to change the **Body font** setting.

5. In the **Name** box at the bottom of the dialog box, assign a name to the new font set, and then click **Save**.

Tip Custom themes, color schemes, and font sets are saved in the C:\Users\<*username*>\AppData\Roaming\Microsoft\Templates\Document Themes folder. To delete a custom theme, color scheme, or font set, navigate to the folder, right-click the item, and then click Delete.

Formatting the Background of Slides

You can customize the background of all the slides in a presentation by applying a background style from a gallery of predefined solid colors and gradients that reflect the color scheme applied to the presentation.

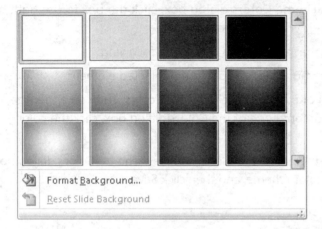

If none of these styles meets your needs, you can use the Format Background dialog box to specify that the background should be filled with the following:

- **Solid color** This simple effect can be customized with varying degrees of transparency.

- **Gradient color** In these visual effects, a solid color gradually changes from light to dark or dark to light. PowerPoint offers several gradient patterns, each with several variations. You can also choose a preset arrangement of colors from professionally designed backgrounds in which the different colors gradually merge.

- **Texture** PowerPoint comes with several preset textures that you can easily apply to the background of slides.

- **Picture** You can also add a picture to the background as a single object or as a tiled image that fills the entire slide.

- **Pattern** You can choose from 48 patterns and specify the foreground and background colors.

When you apply a background by using the Background Styles gallery, all the slides take on the new background. When you apply a background by using the Format Background dialog box, you can control whether the background should be applied to only the current slide or all slides.

> **To apply a predefined background style to all the slides**

→ On the **Design** tab, in the **Background** group, click the **Background Styles** button, and then in the gallery, click the style you want.

> **To fill the current slide's background with a color, gradient, or pattern**

1. On the **Design** tab, click the **Background** dialog box launcher.

2. On the **Fill** page of the **Format Background** dialog box, click the **Fill** option you want.

3. Fine-tune the effect as necessary, and then click **Close**.

➤ **To fill the current slide's background with a texture**

1. On the **Fill** page of the **Format Background** dialog box, click **Picture or texture fill**, and then do one of the following:

   ○ Select an option in the **Texture** list.

   ○ Click **File**, and then in the **Insert Picture** dialog box, locate and double-click the texture file you want.

2. Fine-tune the texture as necessary, and then click **Close**.

➤ **To fill the current slide's background with a picture**

1. On the **Fill** page of the **Format Background** dialog box, click **Picture or texture fill**, and then click **File**.

2. In the **Insert Picture** dialog box, locate and double-click the file you want.

3. Fine-tune the picture as necessary.

> **Tip** You can adjust the brightness, contrast, and color of the picture on the Picture Corrections and Picture Color pages of the Format Background dialog box.

4. Click **Close**.

➤ **To apply a custom background to all the slides**

→ Specify the background as usual, click **Apply to All**, and then click **Close**.

Inserting Footer Information

If you want the same identifying information to appear at the bottom of every slide, you can insert it in a footer. You can specify the following:

- Date and time, in updating or fixed formats
- Slide number
- Custom text

You can omit the footer from the title slide, and apply your settings to the current slide or to all slides.

➤ **To add a footer**

1. On the **Insert** tab, in the **Text** group, click the **Header & Footer** button.

2. In the **Header and Footer** dialog box, in the **Include on slide** area, select the options you want and refine them as necessary.

3. Click **Apply** to add the footer to the current slide, or click **Apply to All** to add it to all slides.

> **Tip** If you want to omit the footer from the title slide, select the Don't Show On Title Slide check box before clicking Apply To All.

Dividing a Presentation into Sections

Dividing a presentation into sections can be a great tool during content development because you can hide all the sections except the one you are currently working on. In a long presentation, sections can make it easier to organize content because you can rearrange entire sections of slides as a unit. You can also use sections to make it easier for audiences to understand the organization of your presentation because you can apply different themes to different sections.

Sections appear as bars across the Slides tab of the Overview pane in Normal view and across the workspace in Slide Sorter view. They do not appear in other views, and they do not create slides or otherwise interrupt the flow of the presentation. When you no longer need the sections in a presentation, you can either leave them where they are or you can delete them at any time.

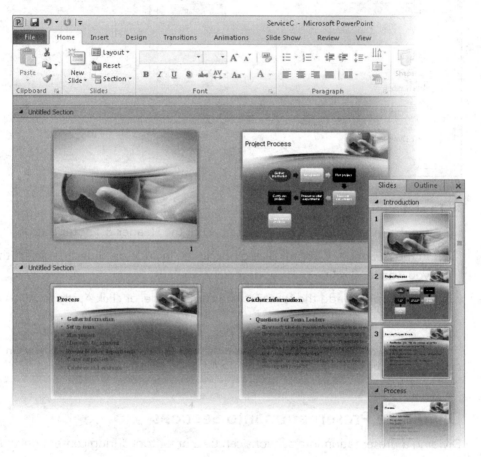

➤ To add a section before the selected slide

→ On the **Home** tab, in the **Slides** group, click the **Section** button, and then click **Add Section**.

➤ **To name a section**

1. Do one of the following:

   ○ Click the section bar, and on the **Home** tab, in the **Slides** group, click **Section**, and then click **Rename Section**.

   ○ Right-click the section bar, and then click **Rename Section**.

2. In the **Rename Section** dialog box, enter the name, and then click **Rename**.

➤ **To hide the slides in a section under the section bar**

→ To the left of the section name, click the black arrowhead.

→ Click the white arrowhead to display the slides again.

➤ **To hide all the slides under their section bars**

→ Click any section bar, and on the **Home** tab, in the **Slides** group, click **Section**, and then click **Collapse All**.

→ Right-click any section bar, and then click **Collapse All**.

→ Click **Expand All** to display the slides again.

➤ **To change the order of sections**

→ Drag the section bars to reorganize the presentation.

→ Right-click a section bar, and then click **Move Section Up** or **Move Section Down**.

> **Tip** Reorganizing sections is easier if all the slides are hidden.

➤ **To apply a different theme to the slides in a section**

→ Click the section bar to select it and its slides, and then apply the theme you want.

➤ **To remove a section**

→ Click the section bar, and then on the **Home** tab, in the **Slides** group, click the **Section** button, and click **Remove Section**.

→ Right-click the section bar, and then click **Remove Section**.

> **Tip** You can also click Remove Section & Slides or Remove All Sections.

Customizing Slide Masters

> **Strategy** There is no objective in the PowerPoint certification exam that relates specifically to a presentation's masters. However, when you want to change the formatting of all the slides in a presentation, or of all the slides of a particular layout, often the fastest method is to make the change to the slide master. So it is worth taking a little time to become familiar with masters and the types of formatting they control.

When you create a new presentation, its slides assume the formatting of the presentation's slide master, which by default contains placeholders for a title, bullet points, the date, the slide number, and footer information. The placeholders control the position of the corresponding elements on the slide. Text placeholders also control the formatting of their text.

On an individual slide, you can make changes to the design elements provided by the master, but you can change the basic design only on the master. When you change a design element on the master, all the slides reflect the change.

To make changes to a presentation's master, you switch to Slide Master view, which adds a Slide Master tab to the ribbon and hides the tabs that aren't needed. In this view, the slide master thumbnail is displayed at the top of the Overview pane, followed by thumbnails of its associated layouts.

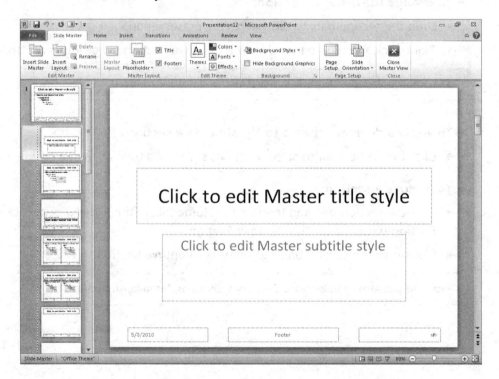

By displaying the slide master and clicking buttons on the Slide Master tab, you can make the following formatting adjustments, which are applied to all the layouts:

- Apply a theme; or change the colors, fonts, or effects associated with the current theme.
- Control the background color, texture, and graphics.
- Specify which placeholders should appear on the slides.

You can also add custom elements that you want to appear on all slides, including graphics such as logos and repeating text such as slogans.

➤ **To switch to Slide Master view**

→ On the **View** tab, in the **Master Views** group, click the **Slide Master** button.

➤ **To close Slide Master view**

→ On the **Slide Master** tab, in the **Close** group, click the **Close Master View** button.

→ On the **View** toolbar at the right end of the status bar, click any view button.

> **Tip** While working in Slide Master view, you can format text placeholders, insert graphic objects, and add animations and transitions by using the same techniques you would use to perform those tasks with slides. For information, see the other chapters in this part of the book.

Practice Tasks

The practice files for these tasks are located in the PowerPoint\Objective2 practice file folder. If you want to save the results of the tasks, save them in the same folder with *My* appended to the file name so that you don't overwrite the original practice files.

- In a blank presentation, ensure that the Apex theme will be automatically applied to any slides you create. Then change the color scheme that will be used for all slides to Verve.
- In a different blank presentation, ensure that the background of any slides you create will be formatted as Style 8. Then change the background that will be used for all slides to the Denim texture.
- In the *CommunityService* presentation, display an automatically updating date in the September 28, 2011 format on all slides except the title slide.
- In the *WaterSaving* presentation, add sections before slide 1, slide 4, slide 6, and slide 12. Assign the name *Introduction* to the first section, and change the theme of that section only to Trek. Then swap the third and fourth sections.

2.5 Enter and Format Text

Entering Text in Text Placeholders

> **Strategy** PowerPoint responds differently to the way you enter text depending on where you are typing. Become familiar with the different ways of creating new slides, new bullet points, and new subpoints so that you can enter text efficiently during the exam.

When you add a new slide to a presentation, the layout you select indicates the type and position of the objects on the slide with placeholders. You can enter text directly into a text placeholder on a slide in the Slide pane, or you can enter it on the Outline tab of the Overview pane. As you type, the text appears both on the slide and on the Outline tab.

➤ **To create a new line of text with the same style and at the same level as the current one**

→ Press Enter.

➤ **To demote the current line of text to the next lower level**

→ Click to the left of the current line, and then press Tab.

→ On the **Home** tab, in the **Paragraph** group, click the **Increase List Level** button.

➤ **To promote the current line of text to the next higher level**

→ Click to the left of the current line, and then press Shift+Tab.

→ On the **Home** tab, in the **Paragraph** group, click the **Decrease List Level** button.

Entering Text in Independent Text Boxes

When you want to add text that is not appropriate for a placeholder, such as annotations or source citations, you can create two types of independent text boxes:

- **Fixed height** The box grows horizontally to fit what you type, even expanding beyond the border of the slide if necessary.

- **Fixed width** The box grows vertically to fit what you type. When the text reaches the right boundary of the box, the height of the box expands by one line so that the text can wrap.

When you click in a text box, a cursor appears, and the box is surrounded by a dashed border. You can then edit the text. Clicking the dashed border changes it to a solid border, indicating that the box itself is selected. You can then manipulate the text box as a unit—for example, you can move or copy it as a whole.

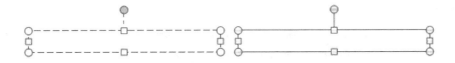

> **See Also** For information about manipulating text boxes, see section 2.6, "Format Text Boxes."

➤ **To insert a fixed-height text box**

1. On the **Insert** tab, in the **Text** group, click the **Text Box** button.

2. Click the slide where you want the upper-left corner of the text box to appear, and then enter the text.

➤ **To insert a fixed-width text box**

1. On the **Insert** tab, in the **Text** group, click the **Text Box** button.

2. Drag to create a text box where you want it to appear, and then enter the text.

Editing Text

After you enter text, you can change it at any time. To replace a selection, you enter the new text. To delete the selection, you press either the Delete key or the Backspace key. If you want to move or copy the selected text, you have three options:

- **Drag-and-drop editing** Use this feature when you need to move or copy text within the same slide or to a slide that is visible on the Outline tab of the Overview pane without scrolling.

- **Cut, Copy, and Paste buttons** Use these commands when you need to move or copy text between two locations that you cannot see at the same time. You can specify how the cut or copied item should look or the format it should have when pasted.

- **Keyboard shortcuts** The main keyboard shortcuts for editing tasks are outlined in the following table.

Task	Keyboard shortcut
Cut	Ctrl+X
Copy	Ctrl+C
Paste	Ctrl+V

If you decide you don't want to keep a change, you can reverse it, and if you undo an action in error, you can reverse that change, too.

➤ **To use drag and drop**

→ Select the text, point to the selection, hold down the mouse button, drag the text to its new location, and release the mouse button.

→ To copy the selection, hold down the Ctrl key while you drag.

➤ **To move or copy a selection**

1. On the **Home** tab, in the **Clipboard** group, click the **Cut** or **Copy** button.

2. Reposition the cursor, and do one of the following:

   ○ Click the **Paste** button to insert the selection in its new location.

   ○ Click the **Paste** arrow, and then in the **Paste Options** list, click the option you want.

   ○ Click the **Paste** arrow, and then click **Paste Special**. In the **Paste Special** dialog box, click the format you want for the pasted object, and then click **OK**.

➤ **To undo an editing action**

→ On the Quick Access Toolbar, click the **Undo** button.

➤ **To undo multiple actions at the same time**

→ On the Quick Access Toolbar, click the **Undo** arrow, and then click the earliest action you want to undo.

➤ **To redo an editing action you have undone**

→ On the Quick Access Toolbar, click the **Redo** button.

> **Tip** You can also undo and redo most formatting actions.

Formatting Characters and Paragraphs

The default formatting of text in placeholders reflects the design of the underlying slide master. However, you can use standard character and paragraph formatting techniques to override the following aspects of the design:

● **Font and size** You can pick a different font or size for any selection.

> **See Also** For information about sizing text boxes to fit their text and about the Autofit feature, see section 2.6, "Format Text Boxes."

● **Color** Picking a color from the applied color scheme creates a pleasing design impact. You can also add colors that are not part of the color scheme, including colors from the standard palette or from the almost infinite spectrum of colors available in the Colors dialog box.

- **Style and effects** You can apply simple styles such as bold and italic, or you can choose more dramatic effects such as shadows, colored underlining, or small caps.

- **Case** You can make selected text all lowercase or all uppercase; ensure that the text is capitalized as a sentence or that each word has an initial capital letter; or switch (toggle) the capitalization of each letter.

- **Character spacing** You can make the space between characters looser or tighter.

- **Fancy text effects** You can apply fancy effects, such as shadows, reflections, and bevels, or rotate or mold text into a shape.

> **See Also** For information about applying fancy text effects to selected characters, see section 3.3 "Modify WordArt and Shapes."

- **Alignment** You can align the text horizontally to the left, right, or center; or you can justify it to span the text box. You can align the text vertically at the top of the text box, in the middle, or at the bottom.

- **Indentation** You can indent the text from the left side of the text box.

- **Line and paragraph spacing** You can adjust the spacing within and between paragraphs.

- **Direction** You can arrange the text in a placeholder so that it is vertical (to the left or right) or stacked.

After you have formatted one text selection to suit your needs, you can quickly apply the same combination of formatting to another selection by using the Format Painter. You can also clear all manual formatting from a selection, so that it reverts to the formatting specified by the design.

➤ **To change the font of selected text**

➜ Either on the Mini Toolbar or in the **Font** group of the **Home** tab, click the font you want in the **Font** list.

➤ **To increase or decrease the size of selected text**

➜ Either on the Mini Toolbar or in the **Font** group of the **Home** tab, click the **Increase Font Size** or **Decrease Font Size** button.

➤ **To precisely size selected text**

→ Either on the Mini Toolbar or in the **Font** group of the **Home** tab, click the size you want on the **Font Size** list.

➤ **To change color of selected text**

→ Either on the Mini Toolbar or in the **Font** group of the **Home** tab, click the color you want in the **Font Color** palette.

Or

1. In the **Font Color** palette, click **More Colors**.

2. On either the **Standard** or **Custom** page of the **Colors** dialog box, specify the color you want, and then click **OK**.

➤ **To change the style or effect of selected text**

→ Either on the Mini Toolbar or in the **Font** group of the **Home** tab, click the button for the style you want.

Or

1. On the **Home** tab, click the **Font** dialog box launcher.

2. In the **Font** dialog box, specify the style or effect you want, and then click **OK**.

➤ **To change the case of selected text**

→ On the **Home** tab, in the **Font** group, click the **Change Case** button, and then click the option you want.

➤ **To change the character spacing of selected text**

→ On the **Home** tab, in the **Font** group, click the **Character Spacing** button, and then click the option you want.

Or

1. On the **Home** tab, in the **Font** group, click the **Character Spacing** button, and then click **More Spacing**.

2. On the **Character Spacing** page of the **Font** dialog box, in the **Spacing** list, click **Expanded** or **Condensed**.

3. Change the **By** setting to the precise amount of space you want between characters, and then click **OK**.

➤ **To change the alignment of selected text**

→ Either on the Mini Toolbar or in the **Paragraph** group of the **Home** tab, click the **Left**, **Center**, or **Right** button.

> **Tip** To justify text, click the Justify button in the Paragraph group.

→ On the **Home** tab, in the **Paragraph** group, click the **Align Text** button, and then click the vertical alignment you want.

➤ **To change the indentation of selected text**

→ Either on the Mini Toolbar or in the **Paragraph** group of the **Home** tab, click the **Increase List Level** or **Decrease List Level** button.

> **Tip** You can click these buttons to increase and decrease the left indent of regular text paragraphs as well as lists.

Or

1. On the **Home** tab, click the **Paragraph** dialog box launcher.
2. In the **Paragraph** dialog box, in the **Indentation** area, change the **Before text** setting, and then click **OK**.

➤ **To change the spacing of selected text**

→ On the **Home** tab, in the **Paragraph** group, click the **Line Spacing** button, and then click the spacing you want.

> **Tip** Clicking Line Spacing Options opens the Paragraph dialog box.

Or

1. On the **Home** tab, click the **Paragraph** dialog box launcher.
2. In the **Paragraph** dialog box, in the **Spacing** area, change the **Before** or **After** settings, or the **Line Spacing** option, and then click **OK**.

➤ **To change the direction of text in a placeholder**

→ Click anywhere in the placeholder, and on the **Home** tab, in the **Paragraph** group, click the **Text Direction** button, and then click the direction you want.

➤ **To copy the formatting of selected text**

→ Either on the Mini Toolbar or in the **Clipboard** group of the **Home** tab, click the **Format Painter** button, and then select the text to which you want to apply the formatting.

➤ **To copy the formatting of selected text multiple times**

1. Either on the Mini Toolbar or in the **Clipboard** group of the **Home** tab, double-click the **Format Painter** button, and then select the text to which you want to apply the formatting.

2. Click the **Format Painter** button to deactivate it.

➤ **To clear all manual formatting from selected text**

→ On the **Home** tab, in the **Font** group, click the **Clear All Formatting** button.

→ Press Ctrl+Spacebar.

Formatting Bulleted and Numbered Lists

Bulleted lists form the foundation of most presentations. You can enter up to five levels of bullets on any slide with a content placeholder. By default, the bullet points you enter are all first-level, but you can easily demote bullet points to subpoints and promote subpoints to bullet points, both on the slide in the Slide pane and on the Outline tab of the Overview pane. (On the Outline tab, you can also change slide titles to bullet points and vice versa.)

If you have entered regular text paragraphs in a placeholder or an independent text box, you can convert the text to a bulleted list or a numbered list. (Numbers are appropriate for items that must appear in a specific order.) You can also convert a bulleted list or numbered list to regular text paragraphs.

The basic look of the bullet points and subpoints is determined by the formatting prescribed on the slide master. However, you can customize a bulleted list by using basic formatting techniques. You can also change the size, color, and symbol of the bullets on the Bulleted page of the Bullets And Numbering dialog box.

For a numbered list, you can change the number scheme, and the size and color of the numbers on the Numbered page of the Bullets And Numbering dialog box.

For both types of lists, you can specify the indenting of each level. If you want to adjust the indenting of multiple levels, it is best to start with the lowest level and work your way up, using equal increments. Otherwise it is easy to create a list that looks uneven and unprofessional.

> **See Also** For information about formatting bullet points as SmartArt diagrams, see section 3.4 "Manipulate SmartArt."

➤ **To demote a bullet point to a subpoint**

→ With the cursor in the bullet point, on the **Home** tab, in the **Paragraph** group, click the **Increase List Level** button.

→ Click to the left of the text of the bullet point, and then press the Tab key.

> **Tip** On the Outline tab of the Overview pane, you can also use these techniques to change a slide title to a bullet point or a numbered item to a lower level.

➤ **To promote a subpoint to a bullet point**

→ With the cursor in the subpoint, on the **Home** tab, in the **Paragraph** group, click the **Decrease List Level** button.

→ Click to the left of the text of the bullet point, hold down Shift, and then press the Tab key.

> **Tip** On the Outline tab of the Overview pane, you can also use these techniques to change a bullet point to a slide title or a numbered item to a higher level.

➤ **To convert selected text to a bulleted list**

→ On the **Home** tab, in the **Paragraph** group, click the **Bullets** button.

➤ **To change the bullets in a selected bulleted list**

1. On the **Home** tab, in the **Paragraph** group, click the **Bullets** arrow.

2. In the **Bullets** gallery, select the bullet style you want.

   Or

1. In the **Bullets** gallery, click **Bullets and Numbering**.

2. On the **Bulleted** page of the **Bullets and Numbering** dialog box, change the size and color of the existing bullet.

3. To change the bullet symbol, click **Customize**, and in the **Symbol** dialog box, choose a font and symbol. Then click **OK**.

4. To use a picture as a bullet, click **Picture**, and in the **Picture Bullet** dialog box, locate and double-click the picture file you want.

5. In the **Bullets and Numbering** dialog box, click **OK**.

➤ **To convert selected text to a numbered list**

→ On the **Home** tab, in the **Paragraph** group, click the **Numbering** button.

➤ **To change the numbers in a selected numbered list**

1. On the **Home** tab, in the **Paragraph** group, click the **Numbering** arrow.

2. In the **Numbering** gallery, select the number scheme you want.

   Or

1. In the **Numbering** gallery, click **Bullets and Numbering**.

2. On the **Numbered** page of the **Bullets and Numbering** dialog box, change the size and color of the numbers, and then click **OK**.

➤ **To adjust the hanging indent of a list**

→ Drag the **First Line Indent** and **Hanging Indent** markers to the left or right on the ruler.

Tip To display the ruler, select the Ruler check box in the Show group on the View tab.

Practice Tasks

The practice file for these exercises is located in the PowerPoint\Objective2 practice file folder. If you want to save the results of the tasks, save them in the same folder with *My* appended to the file name so that you don't overwrite the original practice file.

- In the *BuyingTrips* presentation, on slide 6, create an independent text box containing the text *Be sure to check the manual for important information about the minimum requirements*, arranged on multiple lines.

- On slide 2, in the first bullet point, delete the word *buying*. On slide 5, in the third bullet point, replace *good* with *lasting*. Then move the first bullet point on slide 4 to the top of the bullet list on slide 5. Finally, on slide 3, move the first bullet point and its subpoints so that they follow *Plan the itinerary*.

- On slide 2, make the slide title bold, purple, and small caps. Adjust the character spacing so that it is very loose. Then apply the same formatting to the titles of all the other slides.

- On slide 6, change the bullets to dark red dollar signs. Then on slide 3, increase the hanging indent of the subpoints to a half inch. On slide 8, change the subpoint list to a numbered list, and set the numbering scheme to use purple capital letters.

2.6 Format Text Boxes

> **Tip** If you want to format a placeholder on an individual slide, you can use the same techniques as those you use with text boxes. If you want to make changes to the same placeholder on every slide, it is more efficient to make the adjustments on the presentation's master slide.

Changing the Shape of Text Boxes

Text boxes are shapes that can be manipulated just like any other shape. By default, a new text box is a rectangle, but you can change it to any of the shapes available in the Shapes gallery.

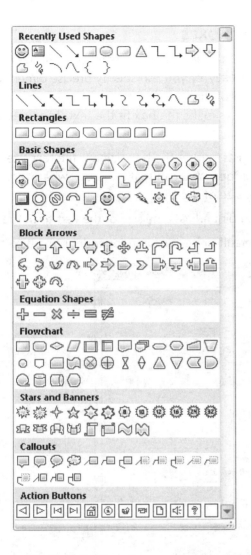

> **➤ To change the shape of a selected text box**

   1. On the Drawing Tools **Format** contextual tab, in the **Insert Shapes** group, click the **Edit Shape** button, and then click **Change Shape**.

   2. In the **Shapes** gallery, click the shape you want.

> **Tip** Changing the shape of a text box has a noticeable effect only if the text box has an outline.

Sizing and Positioning Text Boxes

By default, PowerPoint adjusts the size of an independent text box to fit the text within it. You can drag to change its size manually, or you can specify precise dimensions, but unless you change the Autofit behavior of the box on the Text Box page of the Format Shape dialog box, PowerPoint will always make the box fit the text. The three Autofit options are as follows:

- **Do not Autofit** PowerPoint adjusts neither the box size nor the text size. Any text that does not fit in the box is hidden. You can make the box whatever size you want and manually change the size of the text.

- **Shrink text on overflow** PowerPoint adjusts the size of the text to fit the box.

- **Resize shape to fit text** The default behavior for independent text boxes.

> **Tip** By default, PowerPoint does not adjust the size of content placeholders. If you enter more text than will fit, it adjusts the size of the text and displays the AutoFit Options button so that you can override the default behavior if you want.

Having adjusted the Autofit behavior, you can size a text box visually or by changing the size or scale on the Size page of the Format Shape dialog box.

To move a text box, you can position it manually or by setting precise distances from the upper-left corner or center of the slide on the Position page of the Format Shape dialog box.

➤ **To open the Format Shape dialog box for a selected text box**

→ Ensure that the border is solid, right-click anywhere inside the box, and click **Format Shape**.

→ On the Drawing Tools **Format** contextual tab, click the **Size** dialog box launcher.

➤ **To set the Autofit behavior of a selected text box**

1. Display the **Text Box** page of the **Format Shape** dialog box.

2. In the **Autofit** area, click the option you want, and then click **Close**.

➤ **To size a selected text box**

→ Drag a square text box handle to change the height or width only.

→ If the **Lock aspect ratio** check box is selected on the **Size** page of the **Format Shape** dialog box, drag a round text box handle diagonally to change the size of the box while maintaining the aspect ratio.

→ On the **Format** contextual tab, in the **Size** group, adjust the **Shape Height** or **Shape Width** settings to change the height or width.

→ Display the **Size** page of the **Format Shape** dialog box, do one of the following, and then click **Close**:

  ○ In the **Size and rotate** area, change the **Height** or **Width** setting.

  ○ In the **Scale** area, change the **Height** or **Width** setting.

> **Tip** Select the Lock Aspect Ratio check box if you want the relationship between the height and width to remain constant no matter what the size of the box.

➤ **To move a selected text box**

→ Point to the border of the box, and drag it to the position you want.

Or

1. Display the **Position** page of the **Format Shape** dialog box.

2. If you want to measure from the center of the slide instead of the upper-left corner, click **Center** in the appropriate **From** list.

3. Adjust the **Horizontal** or **Vertical** setting, and then click **Close**.

Aligning Text Boxes

If you create more than one text box on a slide, you can control how the boxes are aligned relative to the slide and to each other in the following ways:

- **Horizontal alignment** The options are Left, Center, and Right.
- **Vertical alignment** The options are Top, Middle, and Bottom.
- **Distribution** The options are Horizontally and Vertically. PowerPoint adjusts the space between the boxes so that they are evenly distributed between the first and last selected boxes.
- **Gridlines and drawing guides** You can display gridlines and set horizontal and vertical guides to assist in aligning text boxes manually.

➤ **To align a selected text box horizontally or vertically**

→ On the Drawing Tools **Format** contextual tab, in the **Arrange** group, click the **Align** button, and then click the horizontal or vertical alignment you want.

➤ **To make the spaces between text boxes even**

→ On the **Format** contextual tab, in the **Arrange** group, click the **Align** button, and then click **Distribute Horizontally** or **Distribute Vertically**.

➤ **To display gridlines**

→ On the **Format** contextual tab, in the **Arrange** group, click the **Align** button, and then click **View Gridlines**.

→ To adjust the size of the grid, on the **Format** contextual tab, in the **Arrange** group, click the **Align** button, and then click **Grid Settings**. Then in the **Grid and Guides** dialog box, adjust the **Spacing** setting in the **Grid settings** area, and click **OK**.

➤ **To display drawing guides**

1. On the **Format** contextual tab, in the **Arrange** group, click the **Align** button, and then click **Grid Settings**.

2. In the **Grid and Guides** dialog box, in the **Guide settings** area, select the **Display drawing guides on screen** check box, and then click **OK**.

3. To adjust the position of the horizontal drawing guide, drag it up or down. To adjust the position of the vertical drawing guide, drag it to the left or right.

> **Tip** If your text boxes overlap, you can click the Bring Forward and Send Backward button in the Arrange group on the Format tab to control the stacking order of shapes, including text boxes.

Formatting Text Boxes

By default, text boxes appear with transparent backgrounds, no border, and no special effects. You can format text boxes in the following ways:

- **Styles** Apply a ready-made combination of fill, outline, and shape effects, such as shadows or bevels.

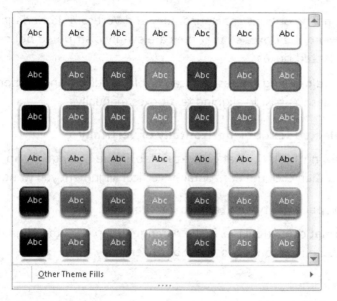

- **Fills** Format the background of the box with a solid color in various shades, a picture, a color gradient, or a texture.

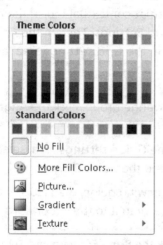

- **Outlines** If you want a text box to have a border when it's not selected, assign an outline color, weight, and style.

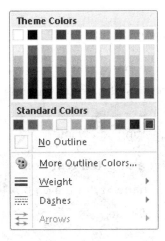

- **Effects** Apply a preset combination of effects, or choose from among seven categories of effects.

You can refine the formatting of the box on the first eight pages of the Format Shape dialog box.

> **Strategy** You should explore the pages of the Format Shape dialog box to understand the many ways you can control text box formatting.

> ➤ **To apply a ready-made style to a selected text box**

1. On the Drawing Tools **Format** contextual tab, in the **Shape Styles** group, click the **More** button.

2. In the **Shape Styles** gallery, click the style you want.

> ➤ **To change the fill, outline, or effect of a selected text box**

1. On the **Format** contextual tab, in the **Shape Styles** group, click the **Shape Fill**, **Shape Outline**, or **Shape Effects** button.

2. In the gallery that appears, click the formatting you want.

> ➤ **To open the Format Shape dialog box for a selected text box**

→ On the **Format** contextual tab, click the **Shape Styles** dialog box launcher.

→ Right-click the box, and then click **Format Shape**.

Adjusting the Text Layout

You can set the following layout options on the Text Box page of the Format Shape dialog box (shown earlier in this section):

- **Alignment** You can specify the horizontal and vertical alignment of text within the text box.

- **Direction** You can specify the direction of text within the text box. Clicking Stacked in this list keeps the individual characters horizontal but makes them run from top to bottom instead of from left to right.

- **Wrapping and margins** You can set whether text should wrap within the text box and the wrapping distance from the four sides of the box.

- **Columns** You can set the number of columns and the spacing between them.

> ➤ **To set the horizontal alignment of text**

1. Select the text box for editing. (It should have a dashed border.)

2. On the **Home** tab, in the **Paragraph** group, click the alignment button you want.

> ➤ **To set the vertical alignment of text in a selected text box**

→ On the **Text Box** page of the **Format Shape** dialog box, in the **Text layout** area, display the **Vertical alignment** list, click the alignment option you want, and then click **Close**.

➤ **To set the direction of text in a selected text box**

→ To rotate the entire text box, on the Drawing Tools **Format** contextual tab, in the **Arrange** group, click the **Rotate** button, and then click the option you want.

→ Drag the green rotating handle attached to the upper-middle handle of the text box to the direction you want.

→ On the **Text Box** page of the **Format Shape** dialog box, in the **Text layout** area, display the **Text Direction** list, click the rotation option you want, and then click **Close**.

➤ **To allow text to wrap in a selected text box**

→ On the **Text Box** page of the **Format Shape** dialog box, in the **Internal margin** area, select the **Wrap text in shape** check box, and then click **Close**.

➤ **To set margins in a selected text box**

→ On the **Text Box** page of the **Format Shape** dialog box, in the **Internal margin** area, adjust **Left**, **Right**, **Top**, and **Bottom** settings, and then click **Close**.

➤ **To flow text in columns in a selected text box**

1. On the **Text Box** page of the **Format Shape** dialog box, click **Columns**.

2. In the **Columns** dialog box, adjust the **Number** and **Spacing** settings, click **OK**, and then click **Close**.

Setting Default Formatting

When you create a text box, PowerPoint applies default settings for the text formatting (for example, font, size, style, and color) and text box formatting (for example, fill color, outline formatting, and special effects). To save formatting steps, you can change the default settings for the presentation you are working on by formatting one text box the way you want it and then specifying the current settings as the default for all new text boxes in the current presentation.

➤ **To make the formatting of a selected text box the default**

→ Right-click the box away from its text, and then click **Set as Default Text Box**.

> **Tip** Clicking the outline of a text box is the most reliable way of getting the Set As Default Text Box option to appear on the shortcut menu.

Practice Tasks

The practice file for this exercise is located in the PowerPoint\Objective2 practice file folder. If you want to save the results of the tasks, save them in the same folder with *My* appended to the file name so that you don't overwrite the original practice file.

* In the *AnnualGeneralMeeting* presentation, on slide 2, use a command to tell PowerPoint to adjust the size of the text in the text box to fit the size of the box. Then make the text box 5 inches tall by 4 inches wide, and position it exactly 2 inches from the top and 3 inches from the left edge of the slide.

* On slide 2, rotate the text in the text box 90 degrees to the left so that it reads from bottom to top. Then arrange the text in two columns with 0.2-inch space between them.

* On slide 3, align the three text boxes so that they are all centered horizontally on the slide and are vertically the same distance apart.

* On slide 3, apply the Intense Effect – Blue, Accent 1 style to the top and bottom text boxes. Change the outline of the center box to 3 pt Blue, Accent 1, and then apply an Offset Right shadow to it.

* On slide 3, make the formatting of the bottom text box the default for all future text boxes created in this presentation.

Objective Review

Before finishing this chapter, ensure that you have mastered the following skills:

2.1 Construct and Edit Photo Albums

2.2 Apply Slide Size and Orientation Settings

2.3 Add and Remove Slides

2.4 Format Slides

2.5 Enter and Format Text

2.6 Format Text Boxes

3 Working with Graphical and Multimedia Elements

The skills tested in this section of the Microsoft Office Specialist exam for Microsoft PowerPoint 2010 relate to the graphics, sounds, and videos you can add to slides. Specifically, the following objectives are associated with this set of skills:

3.1 Manipulate Graphical Elements
3.2 Manipulate Images
3.3 Modify WordArt and Shapes
3.4 Manipulate SmartArt
3.5 Edit Video and Audio Content

These days, presentations are usually delivered electronically and often include more graphics than words. They might also include audio content such as music, and video content such as advertisements or interviews. To meet the demand for more dynamic, visual content, PowerPoint provides many powerful tools for working with graphics and multimedia. Some of these tools work with any type of graphical element, and others are specifically geared to a particular type.

This chapter guides you in studying the common techniques for formatting any graphical element, as well as specific techniques for formatting images, WordArt text, shapes, SmartArt diagrams, videos, and sounds.

> **Practice Files** Before you can complete the practice tasks in this chapter, you need to copy the book's practice files to your computer. The practice files you'll use to complete the tasks in this chapter are in the PowerPoint\Objective3 practice file folder. A complete list of practice files is provided in "Using the Book's Companion Content" at the beginning of this book.

3.1 Manipulate Graphical Elements

> **Tip** This section discusses the techniques you can use to work with all types of graphic elements. For techniques that are specific to a particular type of graphic element, see the subsequent sections in this chapter.

Opening the Format Dialog Box

All graphical and multimedia elements have a Format dialog box that is specific to that type of element. Although PowerPoint provides ready-made styles and effects that you can apply to an element with a few clicks, it is often quicker to use this multipage dialog box to apply custom sets of formatting.

➤ **To open the Format dialog box for a graphic element**

→ Right-click the element, and then click **Format <element type>**.

Applying Styles, Borders, and Effects

After you insert a picture, clip art image, SmartArt graphic, or shape, you can quickly change the way it looks by applying a style. Styles are one-click combinations of borders and effects that are appropriate to each type of graphic element.

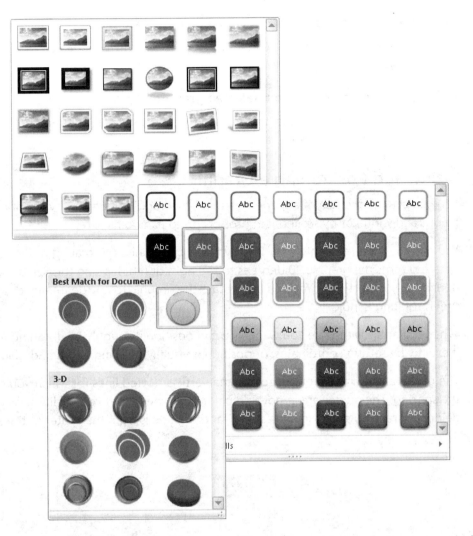

In addition to applying ready-made styles, you can also apply borders and effects to create your own combinations.

➤ To apply a style to a selected graphic element

→ On the **Format** contextual tab for the graphic element type, in the **Styles** gallery, click the thumbnail of the style you want.

> **Tip** For a SmartArt graphic, you can apply a Shape style to a selected graphic shape from the SmartArt Tools Format contextual tab, or you can apply a SmartArt style to the graphic as a whole from the SmartArt Tools Design contextual tab.

➤ **To apply a custom border to a selected graphic element**

→ On the **Format** contextual tab, in the **Border** palette, click the color, weight, and style you want.

➤ **To apply custom effects to a selected graphic element**

→ On the **Format** contextual tab, in the **Effects** palette, click a type of effect, and then click the effect you want.

Sizing and Positioning a Graphic

You can change the size of a graphic element by dragging handles, by specifying the height and width, or by scaling it in proportion to its original size.

You can change the orientation of many types of graphics by rotating or flipping them. Rotating turns the graphic 90 degrees to the right or left; flipping turns it 180 degrees horizontally or vertically. You can also rotate the graphic to any degree by dragging its green rotating handle.

When a graphic is the size you want, you can position it roughly by dragging it, position it exactly by setting coordinates, or position it visually by using a grid and guides.

The grid is a fixed matrix of horizontal and vertical dotted lines for which you can specify the spacing. The guides are a movable pair of horizontal and vertical lines. As you drag a guide, a ScreenTip shows in inches how far the guide is from the center of the slide.

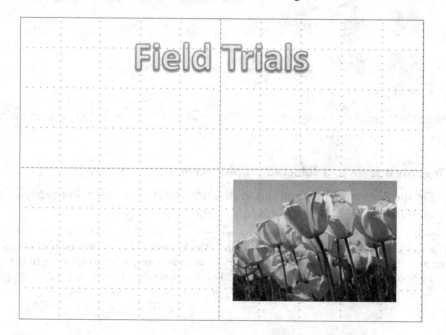

> **Tip** When the Snap Objects To Grid check box is selected in the Grid And Guides dialog box, guides and graphics snap to the grid whether or not it is visible.

➤ To change the size of a selected graphic element

→ Drag a sizing handle until the image is the shape and size you want.

→ On the **Format** contextual tab for the graphic element type, in the **Size** group, change the **Shape Height** or **Shape Width** setting.

Or

1. On the **Format** contextual tab, click the **Size** dialog box launcher.
2. On the **Size** page of the **Format** dialog box, in the **Size and rotate** area, change the **Height** or **Width** setting. Then click **Close**.

> **Tip** You cannot change the height and the width of an image disproportionately unless the Lock Aspect Ratio check box is cleared.

➤ To change the scale of a selected graphic element

→ On the **Size** page of the **Format** dialog box, in the **Scale** area, change the **Height** or **Width** setting. Then click **Close**.

➤ To rotate a selected graphic element

→ Drag the green rotating handle until the image sits at the angle you want.

→ On the **Size** page of the **Format** dialog box, in the **Size and rotate** area, change the **Rotation** setting. Then click **Close**.

Or

1. On the **Format** contextual tab, in the **Arrange** group, click the **Rotate** button.
2. In the **Rotate** gallery, click the option you want.

➤ To position a selected graphic element

→ Drag the image to the position you want.

→ On the **Position** page of the **Format** dialog box, change the **Horizontal** or **Vertical** setting and the adjacent measurement. Then click **Close**.

➤ To display gridlines and guides to assist in positioning graphic elements

→ On the **View** tab, in the **Show** group, select the **Gridlines** or **Guides** check box.

Or

1. Right-click a blank area of the slide, and then click **Grid and Guides**.

2. In the **Grid and Guides** dialog box, select the options you want, and then click **OK**.

> **Tip** To quickly arrange a set of selected graphics that includes pictures, you can apply a SmartArt picture layout to them. Clicking Picture Layout in the Picture Styles group on the Picture Tools Format contextual tab displays a gallery of SmartArt picture diagrams. When you click a layout, PowerPoint moves the graphics into that arrangement, and you can then manipulate the graphics as you would the shapes in any diagram. For information about SmartArt, see section 3.4, "Manipulate SmartArt."

Changing the Stacking Order

When graphics overlap each other, they are *stacked*. The stacking order is determined by the order in which you inserted the graphics, but you can change it by moving graphics in the stack.

> **Tip** If you can't select a graphic because it is covered by others in the stack, click the Selection Pane button in the Arrange group on the Format contextual tab to display the Selection And Visibility task pane, and then select the graphic you want from the Shapes On This Slide list.

➤ **To bring a selected graphic forward in the stack**

→ On the **Format** contextual tab for the graphic element type, in the **Arrange** group, click the **Bring Forward** button to move the graphic forward one step at a time.

→ On the **Format** contextual tab, in the **Arrange** group, display the **Bring Forward** list, and then click **Bring to Front** to move the graphic to the top of the stack.

➤ **To send a selected graphic backward in the stack**

→ On the **Format** contextual tab, in the **Arrange** group, click the **Send Backward** button to move the graphic backward one step at a time.

→ On the **Format** contextual tab, in the **Arrange** group, display the **Send Backward** list, and then click **Send to Back** to move the graphic to the bottom of the stack.

Grouping Graphics

When you have multiple graphic elements on a slide, you can group them so that you can format, copy, and move them as a unit. You can change the attributes of an individual element—for example, its color, size, or location—without ungrouping the graphics.

> **Tip** If you click the buttons in the Images or Illustrations group on the Insert tab to add graphic elements to a slide that does not include a content placeholder, you can group them. However, if the slide does include a content placeholder, you cannot group the graphics no matter which method you use to insert them.

➤ **To group or ungroup selected graphic elements**

→ On the **Format** contextual tab for the graphic element type, in the **Arrange** group, click the **Group** button, and then in the list, click **Group** or **Ungroup**.

➤ **To regroup graphic elements**

1. Select one of the formerly grouped elements.
2. On the **Format** contextual tab, in the **Arrange** group, click the **Group** button, and then in the list, click **Regroup**.

Aligning Graphics

> **Strategy** The alignment options can produce unexpected results when multiple images are selected, depending on whether Align To Slide or Align Selected Objects is turned on. Practice selecting the same images in different orders and then using various commands in the Align list to become familiar with the results.

After inserting pictures, clip art images, shapes, or diagrams in approximate locations, you can align them precisely in several ways. For example, you can:

- Align graphics vertically by their left or right edges or centerline, or horizontally by the top or bottom edges or centerline.
- Distribute graphics evenly within their current space, either horizontally or vertically.
- Align graphics relative to the slide that contains them or to other selected objects.
- Align graphics relative to a position on the slide.
- Align graphics against adjustable horizontal and vertical guides.

➤ **To align selected graphic elements**

→ On the **Format** contextual tab, in the **Arrange** group, click the type of alignment you want in the **Align** list.

> **Tip** By default, a single selected graphic is aligned to the slide and multiple selected graphics are aligned to the first graphic selected.

Linking Graphics to Other Information

You can attach a hyperlink to a graphic element to provide access to supporting details. Clicking the hyperlinked element then takes you directly to the linked details, which might be on a hidden slide, in another presentation, in a file on your computer or your organization's network, or on a website. To let people know the type of information that will be displayed when the link is clicked, you can specify text that should appear in a ScreenTip when they point to the linked element.

> **Tip** You can also use a hyperlink to open an email message window so that people viewing the presentation electronically can easily contact you or your organization.

Editing the graphic does not disrupt the hyperlink; however, deleting the graphic also deletes the hyperlink.

> **Tip** You can attach a hyperlink to any selected object on a slide, such as text, a chart element, or a table.

➤ **To link the selected graphic to a different slide**

   1. On the **Insert** tab, in the **Links** group, click the **Hyperlink** button.

   2. In the **Insert Hyperlink** dialog box, under **Link to**, click **Place in This Document**.

   3. In the **Select a place in this document** list, click the slide you want, and then click **OK**.

> **Tip** To test the hyperlink, you must be in Slide Show view or Reading view.

➤ **To link the selected graphic to a different presentation or a file**

   1. In the **Insert Hyperlink** dialog box, under **Link to**, click **Existing File or Web Page**.

   2. Do one of the following, and then click **OK**:

   ○ With **Current Folder** selected, locate and click the file you want.

   ○ Click **Recent Files**, and then in the list, click the file you want.

➤ **To link the selected graphic to a webpage**

   1. In the **Insert Hyperlink** dialog box, under **Link to**, click **Existing File or Web Page**.

   2. Do one of the following, and then click **OK**:

   ○ In the **Address** box, enter the URL of the webpage.

   ○ Click **Browsed Pages**, and then in the list, click the URL you want.

➤ **To link the selected graphic to an email message form**

   1. In the **Insert Hyperlink** dialog box, under **Link to**, click **E-mail Address**.

   2. In the **E-mail address** box, enter the recipient's address, and in the **Subject** box, enter a message subject (optional).

   3. In the **Insert Hyperlink** dialog box, click **OK**.

➤ **To create a ScreenTip for a linked graphic**

   1. In the upper-right corner of the **Insert Hyperlink** dialog box, click **ScreenTip**.

   2. In the **Set Hyperlink ScreenTip** dialog box, in the **ScreenTip** text box, enter the text you want to appear, and then click **OK**.

Practice Tasks

The practice file for these tasks is located in the PowerPoint\Objective3 practice file folder. If you want to save the results of the tasks, save them in the same folder with *My* appended to the file name so that you don't overwrite the original practice file.

- In the *Pollution* presentation, on slide 4, apply the Bevel Rectangle style and a gold border to the picture. Then make the picture 6 inches high by 6 inches wide, and position it so that its upper-left corner sits at the 3-inch mark on both the vertical and horizontal rulers.

- On slide 4, make the slide title sit on top of the picture. Then bottom-align the arrow with the picture, and right-align the arrow with the slide.

- On slide 4, attach a hyperlink to the picture so that clicking it displays the hidden slide 5.

- On slide 5, link the graphic to the Air Pollution webpage of the Environmental Protection Agency's website (www.epa.gov). Create a ScreenTip that displays the words *Click here to find out what makes air unhealthy* when someone points to the graphic.

3.2 Manipulate Images

Cropping Images

For pictures and clip art images, you can focus attention on a particular part of an image by cropping away the parts you don't need. In addition to being able to crop free-hand, you can use one of several ready-made aspect-ratio settings that take the guesswork out of cropping, including the following:

- Square (1:1)
- Portrait ((2:3, 3:4, 3:5, and 4:5)
- Landscape ((3:2, 4:3, 5:3, 5:4, 16:9, and 16:10)

When you select an aspect ratio, PowerPoint centers a cropping frame of that ratio over the picture. You can then move the picture under the cropping frame so that it encompasses the part of the picture you want.

You can also crop a picture to fill a picture area, to fit a picture area, or to fit any of the shapes in the Shape gallery.

> **To crop a selected image by hand**

1. On the Picture Tools **Format** contextual tab, in the **Size** group, click the **Crop** button.

2. Move the cropping pointer over one of the cropping handles surrounding the image, and drag to crop away the parts of the image you don't want.

3. Click the **Crop** button to turn off the cropping pointer.

> **To crop a selected image to a specific aspect ratio**

1. On the **Format** contextual tab, in the **Size** group, display the **Crop** list, click **Aspect Ratio**, and then click the aspect you want.

2. Move the picture under the cropping frame until the frame encompasses the part of the image you want.

3. Click the **Crop** button to turn off the cropping frame.

> **To crop a selected image to fill or fit the current shape**

→ On the **Format** contextual tab, in the **Size** group, display the **Crop** list, and click **Fill** or **Fit**.

> **To crop a selected image to fit a different shape**

→ On the **Format** contextual tab, in the **Size** group, display the **Crop** list, click **Crop to Shape**, and then in the **Shape** gallery, click the shape you want.

Formatting Images

After you insert a picture or clip art image into your presentation, you can modify it in the following ways:

- Remove the background.
- Make it sharper or softer and adjust the brightness and contrast.

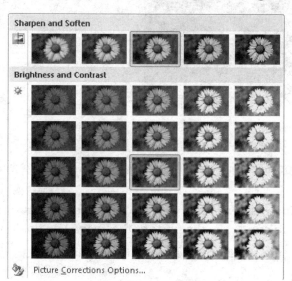

- Tint the image with various shades of a color, or make parts of an image transparent.

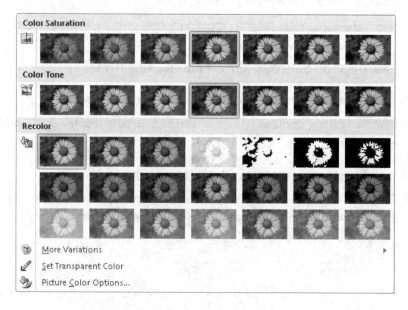

- Apply artistic effects that render the image in other styles, such as a watercolor, etching, or photocopy.

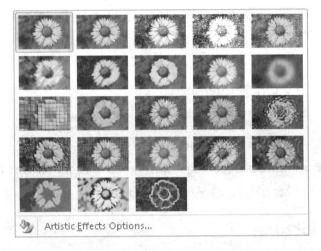

➤ **To remove the background of a selected image**

1. On the Picture Tools **Format** contextual tab, in the **Adjust** group, click the **Remove Background** button.

2. If necessary, adjust the size of the rectangle outside of which the background will be removed.

3. On the **Background Removal** contextual tab, in the **Refine** group, click the **Mark Areas to Keep**, **Mark Areas to Remove**, or **Delete Mark** button, and then click any areas of the picture within the rectangle that you want to adjust, until the picture shows only the areas you want to keep.

4. In the **Close** group, do one of the following:

- ○ Click **Discard All Changes** to restore the background.
- ○ Click **Keep Changes** to remove the designated background areas from the picture.

> **Tip** After removing the background from an image, you might want to crop it to reduce the size of the picture area.

➤ **To modify the sharpness, softness, brightness, or contrast of a selected image**

1. On the **Format** contextual tab, in the **Adjust** group, click the **Corrections** button.

2. In the **Corrections** gallery, in the **Sharpen and Soften** or **Brightness and Contrast** areas, click the option you want.

> **To change the color of a selected image**

1. On the **Format** contextual tab, in the **Adjust** group, click the **Color** button.

2. In the **Color** gallery, in the **Color Saturation**, **Color Tone**, or **Recolor** areas, click the option you want.

> **To make areas of a selected image transparent**

1. In the **Color** gallery, click **Set Transparent Color**.

2. In the image, click the area you want to be transparent.

> **To apply artistic effects to a selected image**

1. On the **Format** contextual tab, in the **Adjust** group, click the **Artistic Effects** button.

2. In the **Artistic Effects** gallery, click the desired effect.

Compressing Pictures

Picture-intensive presentation files can be quite large. You might want to compress the pictures to make the presentation file smaller and more portable.

> **To compress a selected picture**

1. On the Picture Tools **Format** contextual tab, in the **Adjust** group, click the **Compress Pictures** button.

2. In the **Compress Pictures** dialog box, do one of the following, and then click **OK**:

   ○ Select the **Apply only to this picture** check box to compress only the active picture, or clear it to compress all pictures in the presentation.

   ○ Select the **Delete cropped areas of pictures** check box to delete the pixels you crop away, or clear the check box to only hide them.

   ○ Click the resolution (in pixels per inch, or ppi) best suited to your target output.

Resetting or Replacing Images

If you don't like the changes you have made to an image, you can easily restore the original image. If you decide to try a different image, you can simply replace it.

➤ **To discard changes to a selected image**

→ To discard changes other than sizing, on the Picture Tools **Format** contextual tab, in the **Adjust** group, click the **Reset Picture** button.

→ To discard all changes, including sizing, display the **Reset Picture** list, and then click **Reset Picture & Size**.

➤ **To replace a selected image**

1. On the **Format** contextual tab, in the **Adjust** group, click the **Change Picture** button.

2. In the **Insert Picture** dialog box, locate and double-click the replacement picture.

Practice Tasks

The practice file for these tasks is located in the PowerPoint\Objective3 practice file folder. If you want to save the results of the tasks, save them in the same folder with *My* appended to the file name so that you don't overwrite the original practice file.

- In the *PhotoAlbum* presentation, on slide 2, crop both pictures to a portrait aspect ratio of 2:3, with the flowers centered. Then size and position them so that they take up most of the slide.

- On slide 2, increase the contrast of both pictures by 20 percent.

- On slide 3, crop both images to a square aspect ratio, with the flowers centered. Then size and position them so that they are evenly distributed on the slide.

- On slide 3, remove the background of both pictures. Then make the flower on the left look like a line drawing and the flower on the right look like a smooth pastel sketch.

3.3 Modify WordArt and Shapes

Working with WordArt

If you want to add a fancy title to a slide and you can't achieve the effect you want with regular text formatting, you can use WordArt to create stylized text in various shapes. WordArt text can be stretched horizontally, vertically, or diagonally to shape it in fantastic ways. You can also apply additional formatting to achieve unique effects.

➤ **To create WordArt text**

   1. On the **Insert** tab, in the **Text** group, click the **WordArt** button.

   2. In the **WordArt** gallery, click the style you want.

   3. In the text box, enter your text.

➤ **To apply a different style to selected WordArt text**

   → On the Drawing Tools **Format** contextual tab, in the **WordArt Styles** group, display the **WordArt Styles** gallery, and then click the style you want to apply.

Tip You can apply a WordArt style to any text.

➤ **To add special effects to selected WordArt text**

1. On the **Format** contextual tab, in the **WordArt Styles** group, click the **Text Effects** button.

2. In the **Text Effects** gallery, click an effect category, and then choose the one you want.

➤ **To change the shape of selected WordArt text**

1. On the **Format** contextual tab, in the **WordArt Styles** group, click the **Text Effects** button, and then click **Transform**.

2. In the **Transform** gallery, click the shape you want.

3. Size and position the WordArt object the same way you would size and position any other text box.

4. To exaggerate the shape, drag the purple diamond handle to achieve the effect you want.

> **Tip** You can use text effects to format and change the shape of any text.

➤ **To remove WordArt styling from selected text**

→ On the **Format** contextual tab, in the **WordArt Styles** group, display the **WordArt Styles** gallery, and then click **Clear WordArt**.

Working with Shapes

To emphasize key points in a presentation, you can draw shapes, including stars, banners, boxes, lines, circles, and squares. You can also combine shapes to create simple illustrations.

> **Tip** You can create a copy of a selected shape by dragging it while holding down the Ctrl key.

After drawing a shape, you can format it by using the same techniques you would use to format a text box. The quickest way to apply an eye-catching combination of formatting is to use a style. If you format a shape and then want all subsequent shapes you draw in the same presentation to have the same formatting, you can set the formatting combination as the default.

> **See Also** For information about formatting text boxes, see section 2.6, "Format Text Boxes." For information about using styles, see section 3.1, "Manipulate Graphical Elements."

You can add text to a shape and then format it the same way you would format any text, including by applying a WordArt style to it.

If you want to show a relationship between two shapes, you can connect them with a line by joining special handles called *connection points*. Moving a connected shape also moves the line, maintaining the relationship between the connected shapes.

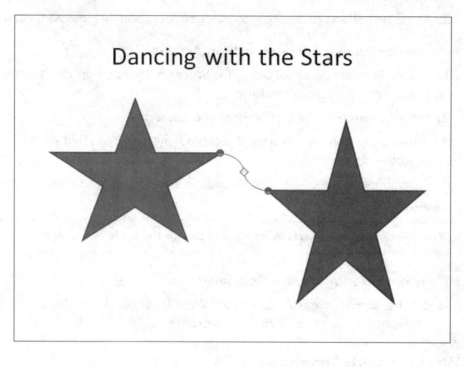

> ➤ **To draw a shape**

1. On the **Insert** tab, in the **Illustrations** group, click the **Shapes** button.

2. In the **Shapes** gallery, click the shape you want.

3. Move the crosshair pointer to the position on the slide where you want the upper-left corner of the shape to be, and drag down and to the right to draw a shape the size you want.

> **Tip** To draw a circle or a square, click the Oval or a Rectangle shape, and hold down the Shift key while you drag.

> ➤ **To change to a different shape**

1. With the shape selected, on the Drawing Tools **Format** contextual tab, in the **Insert Shapes** group, click the **Edit Shape** button.

2. Click **Change Shape**, and then in the **Shapes** gallery, click the shape you want.

> **Tip** If a shape has a yellow diamond handle, you can drag this handle to alter the appearance of the shape without changing its size or angle of rotation.

➤ To make the formatting of the selected shape the default for future shapes

→ Right-click the shape, and click **Set as Default Shape**.

➤ To add text to a selected shape

1. On the **Format** contextual tab, in the **Insert Shapes** group, click the **Text Box** button.

2. Click the shape, and then enter the text.

➤ To connect two shapes

1. In the **Shapes** gallery, under **Lines**, click one of the connector shapes.

2. Point to the first shape, point to a connection point, drag to the second shape, and when its connection points appear, release the mouse button over one of the points.

> **Tip** Connection points are red. If a blue handle appears instead of a red one, the shapes are not connected. Click the Undo button on the Quick Access Toolbar to remove the connection line, and then redraw it.

Practice Tasks

The practice file for these tasks is located in the PowerPoint\Objective3 practice file folder. If you want to save the results of the tasks, save them in the same folder with *My* appended to the file name so that you don't overwrite the original practice file.

- In the *ManagingYourTime* presentation, on slide 1, convert the title into a WordArt object by applying the Gradient Fill – Dark Red, Accent 6, Inner Shadow style.

- On slide 1, mold the WordArt title into an upside-down triangle, with a full reflection offset by 8 points.

- On slide 2, add the word *Time* to the arrow on the left and the word *Money* to the arrow on the right. Format the words with the same WordArt style as the presentation title.

- On slide 2, use an Elbow Connector to connect the left arrow's bottom point with the right arrow's bottom point. Then increase the height of the right arrow to 4 inches.

3.4 Manipulate SmartArt

Creating Diagrams

> **Strategy** Get to know the kinds of diagrams you can create so that you can quickly pinpoint a specific type in the Choose A SmartArt Graphic dialog box. In particular, know the locations of all the diagrams whose names are preceded by .

When you want to illustrate a process or the relationship between hierarchical elements, you can create a dynamic, visually appealing diagram by using SmartArt graphics. By using predefined sets of formatting, you can almost effortlessly put together the type and style of diagram that best conveys your information, such as the following:

- **List** Shows groups of multilevel sequential or nonsequential information.

- **Process** Visually describes the ordered set of steps required to complete a task or workflow.

- **Cycle** Represents a circular sequence of steps, tasks, or events; or the relationship of a set of steps, tasks, or events to a central, core element.

- **Hierarchy** Illustrates the structure of an organization or entity.

- **Relationship** Shows convergent, divergent, overlapping, merging, or containing elements.

- **Matrix** Shows items or concepts as they relate to the whole.

- **Pyramid** Shows proportional, interconnected, or hierarchical relationships in a triangle.

- **Picture** Creates a layout in which you can insert graphics, optionally with captions.

You can easily convert an ordinary bulleted list to a SmartArt diagram that retains the relationship of the bullet levels. Or you can create the diagram and then add text, either directly to its shapes or as a bulleted list in the text pane that opens to the left of the diagram. In this text pane, you can add shapes, delete shapes, and rearrange them by dragging them.

➤ **To create a SmartArt diagram from a bulleted list**

→ Right-click any item in the list, point to **Convert to SmartArt**, and then in the gallery, click the diagram you want.

➤ **To create an empty SmartArt diagram**

1. On a slide that contains a content placeholder, click the **Insert SmartArt Graphic** button.

   Or

   On the **Insert** tab, in the **Illustrations** group, click the **SmartArt** button.

2. In the left pane of the **Choose a SmartArt Graphic** dialog box, click the category you want.

3. In the center pane, click the desired layout.

4. Click **OK**.

➤ **To add text to a SmartArt diagram**

→ Click a shape, and then enter the text.

   Or

1. Open the **Text** pane by doing one of the following:

   ○ Click the button on the left side of the diagram's frame.

   ○ On the SmartArt Tools **Design** contextual tab, in the **Create Graphic** group, click the **Text Pane** button.

2. Replace the bullet point placeholders with your own text.

➤ **To add a shape**

→ In the **Text** pane, at the right end of the bullet after which you want to add the shape, press Enter, and enter the text for the new shape.

→ Click the shape after which you want to add the shape, and then on the **Design** contextual tab, in the **Create Graphic** group, click the **Add Shape** button.

> **Tip** To add a shape before the selected shape, display the Add Shape list, and then click Add Shape Before.

➤ **To promote a subordinate point to a shape or demote a shape to a subordinate point**

➜ Click the subordinate point or shape, and then on the **Design** contextual tab, in the **Create Graphic** group, click the **Promote** or **Demote** button.

> **Tip** Some SmartArt diagrams are not formatted to accept subordinate points within shapes. In hierarchical diagrams, adding a subordinate point in the Task pane adds a subordinate shape, not a bullet point.

➤ **To move an existing shape**

➜ Click the shape, and then on the **Design** contextual tab, in the **Create Graphic** group, click the **Move Up** or **Move Down** button.

➤ **To delete a selected shape**

➜ Press the Delete key.

Making Design Changes

You can customize a diagram as a whole by making changes such as the following:

- Switch to a different layout of the same type or a different type.

> **Tip** If the text in the original diagram doesn't fit in the new layout, the text is not shown. However, it is retained so that you don't have to retype it if you switch again.

- Switch the direction of the layout.
- Add shading and three-dimensional effects to all the shapes in a diagram.
- Select a different combination of colors that coordinates with the presentation's color scheme.
- Apply fancy formatting to the text in all the shapes.

> **See Also** For information about changing the style and adding shading and effects, see section 3.1, "Manipulate Graphical Elements." For information about formatting the text in shapes, see section 3.3 Modify WordArt and Shapes."

➤ **To change the layout of a selected diagram**

→ On the SmartArt Tools **Design** contextual tab, in the **Layouts** gallery, click the layout you want.

> **Tip** To switch to a different layout category, click More Layouts at the bottom of the gallery, and then in the Choose A SmartArt Graphic dialog box, click the desired category and layout.

➤ **To switch the direction of a selected diagram**

→ On the **Design** contextual tab, in the **Create Graphic** group, click the **Right to Left** button.

➤ **To change the color of shapes**

1. On the **Design** contextual tab, in the **SmartArt Styles** group, click the **Change Colors** button.

2. In the **Colors** gallery, click the color scheme you want.

Changing Shapes in Diagrams

In addition to formatting a SmartArt diagram as a whole, you can select an individual shape in a diagram and change it in various ways, including increasing or decreasing its size, altering its form, and changing its color, outline, and effect. In general, you can format the shape and the text within it by using the same formatting techniques you would use for text boxes.

> **See Also** For information about formatting text boxes and their text, see section 2.6, "Format Text Boxes."

➤ **To change a selected shape**

1. On the SmartArt Tools **Format** contextual tab, in the **Shapes** group, click the **Change Shape** button.

2. In the **Shape** gallery, click the shape you want.

➤ **To make a selected shape larger or smaller**

→ On the **Format** contextual tab, in the **Shapes** group, click the **Larger** or **Smaller** button.

→ On the **Format** contextual tab, in the **Size** group, change the **Height** or **Width** setting.

> **Tip** After customizing a diagram, you can revert to the original format by clicking the Reset Graphic button in the Reset group on the SmartArt Tools Design contextual tab.

Converting Diagrams to Shapes or Bullet Points

Just as you can convert a bulleted list to a SmartArt diagram, you can convert a diagram to a bulleted list. You can also convert it to a set of independent shapes.

➤ **To convert a selected SmartArt diagram to a bulleted list**

→ On the SmartArt Tools **Design** contextual tab, in the **Reset** group, click the **Convert** button, and then click **Convert to Text**.

➤ **To convert a selected SmartArt diagram to a set of independent shapes**

1. On the **Design** contextual tab, in the **Reset** group, click the **Convert** button, and then click **Convert to Shapes**.

2. On the Drawing Tools **Format** contextual tab, in the **Arrange** group, click the **Group** button, and then click **Ungroup**.

Practice Tasks

The practice file for these tasks is located in the PowerPoint\Objective3 practice file folder. If you want to save the results of the tasks, save them in the same folder with *My* appended to the file name so that you don't overwrite the original practice file.

- In the *StatusMeeting* presentation, on slide 3, insert an Organization Chart diagram. Then enter *Florian Stiller* as the boss, *Tali Roth* as Florian's assistant, and *Ryan Danner*, *Nate Sun*, and *Erin Hagens* as Florian's subordinates.

- On slide 3, delete the shape for Florian Stiller's assistant from the organization chart. Then assign Florian another subordinate named *Lukas Keller*.

- On slide 4, convert the bulleted list to a Continuous Block Process diagram. Then change the layout to Basic Venn.

- On slide 4, change the style of the diagram to 3-D Polished, and change the colors to Colorful – Accent Colors. Then format the text as Fill – White, Drop Shadow. Finally, change the color of the Administration & HR shape to Dark Red.

3.5 Edit Video and Audio Content

Inserting and Editing Video Content

Sometimes the best way to ensure that your audience understands your message is to show a video. You can insert the following types of videos in slides:

- **Video files** You can insert a digital video that has been saved as a file.

- **Videos from websites** If a video on a public website is in a format supported by Windows Media Player and the owner of the video has made it available to the public, you can insert a link to the video into a slide. Provided the video remains available in its original location, and provided you have an active Internet connection, you will be able to access and play the video from the slide.

- **Clip art videos** Clip art videos are animated graphics, rather than real videos. When you insert a clip art video, it appears as a picture on the slide, and PowerPoint adds a Format contextual tab to the ribbon so that you can adjust the way the picture looks. The clip moves only when you display the slide in Reading view or Slide Show view, and you cannot adjust its action.

After you add a video object, its first frame appears on the slide. When the video object is selected, a play bar appears below it with controls for playing the video.

You can change the way the video object appears on the slide as follows:

- Drag the object to locate it anywhere on the slide.
- Drag its sizing handles to make it larger or smaller.
- Change its appearance by adding styles, frames, and effects.

You can also customize the video so that it plays when and how you want.

➤ To insert a video file

1. If a slide's layout includes a content placeholder, click the **Insert Movie Clip** button.
2. In the **Insert Video** dialog box, locate and double-click the video file you want.

   Or

1. On the **Insert** tab, in the **Media** group, click the **Video** button.
2. In the **Insert Video** dialog box, locate and double-click the video file you want.

➤ To insert a video from a website

1. Display the video you want to use, right-click it, and then click **Copy embed html**.

> **Tip** If you don't see this command, you cannot insert this video into the slide, either because it is the wrong format or because the owner has not made it available for public use.

2. Display the slide into which you want to insert the video.
3. On the **Insert** tab, in the **Media** group, display the **Video** list, and then click **Video from Web Site**.
4. In the **Insert Video from Web Site** dialog box, click in the text box, and then press Ctrl+V (the keyboard shortcut for the Paste command).
5. Click **OK**.

➤ To insert a clip art video

1. On the **Insert** tab, in the **Media** group, display the **Video** list, and then click **Clip Art Video**.
2. In the **Clip Art** task pane, search for and click the video clip you want.
3. Click the arrow that appears to the right of the clip, and then click **Insert**.

➤ **To play the video in Normal view**

➜ Click the video object, and then do either of the following:

  ○ On the object's play bar, click the **Play/Pause** button.

  ○ On the Video Tools **Format** or **Playback** contextual tab, in the **Preview** group, click the **Play** button.

➤ **To change the appearance of a selected video object**

➜ Use the commands on the Video Tools **Format** contextual tab to format the video object just as you would a picture.

> **See Also** For information about using styles and sizing or positioning video objects, see section 3.1, "Manipulate Graphical Elements." For information about formatting pictures, see section 3.2, Manipulate Images."

➤ **To change the settings for a selected video object**

➜ On the Video Tools **Playback** contextual tab, in the **Video Options** group, do any of the following:

  ○ Click the **Volume** button to adjust the volume to low, medium, or high, or to mute the sound.

  ○ Specify whether the video plays automatically when the slide appears or only if you click it.

  ○ Select the **Play Full Screen** check box to expand the video to fill the screen.

  ○ Select the **Hide While Not Playing** check box to make the video object invisible while it is not active. For example, if a video plays automatically when its slide is displayed, you can choose this option to hide the video object when it has finished playing.

  ○ Select the **Loop until Stopped** check box to have the video play continuously until you stop it.

  ○ Select the **Rewind after Playing** check box to ensure that the video starts from the beginning each time it is played.

➤ **To edit a selected video object**

→ On the Video Tools **Playback** contextual tab, in the **Editing** group, do any of the following:

  ○ Click the **Trim Video** button to edit the video so that only part of it plays.

> **Tip** You can find out the total playing time of a video by displaying the Trim Video dialog box.

  ○ Specify **Fade In** and **Fade Out** settings to have the video gradually appear and disappear.

Inserting and Editing Audio Content

You can insert the following types of sounds:

- **Audio files** You can insert an audio file such as a speech or an interview.

- **Audio clips** The audio clips that ship with PowerPoint, which include applause and a phone ring, are available from the Clip Art task pane. You can also download hundreds of sounds from Office Online.

- **Recorded sounds** You can record a sound or narration and attach it to a slide, all from within PowerPoint.

After you add an audio object, it appears on the slide represented by an icon. When the audio object is selected, a play bar appears below its icon with controls for playing the sound.

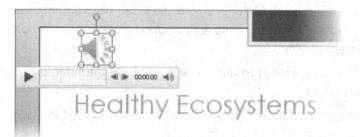

You can change the icon as follows:

- Drag the object to locate it anywhere on the slide.
- Drag its sizing handles to make it larger or smaller.
- Change its appearance by applying styles, borders, and effects.
- Replace the default icon with a picture.

You can also customize the sound so that it plays when and how you want.

➤ **To insert an audio file**

1. On the **Insert** tab, in the **Media** group, click the **Audio** button.

2. In the **Insert Audio** dialog box, locate and double-click the audio file you want.

➤ **To insert an audio clip**

1. On the **Insert** tab, in the **Media** group, display the **Audio** list, and then click **Clip Art Audio**.

2. In the **Clip Art** task pane, search for and click the sound you want.

3. Click the arrow that appears to the right of the sound, and then click **Insert**.

➤ **To attach a sound or narration to a selected slide**

> **Tip** You must have a sound card, microphone, and speakers installed to record and test sounds. Test the microphone before beginning the recording.

1. On the **Insert** tab, in the **Media** group, display the **Audio** list, and then click **Record Audio**.

2. In the **Record Sound** dialog box, click the **Record** button, record the sound or your comments, and then click the **Stop** button.

3. Name the sound or narration, and then click **OK**.

> **See Also** For information about recording an entire presentation, see section 8.4, "Record Presentations."

➤ **To play the sound in Normal view**

> **Tip** You must have a sound card and speakers installed to play sounds.

→ Click the audio icon, and then do either of the following:

  ○ On the icon's play bar, click the **Play/Pause** button.

  ○ On the Audio Tools **Playback** contextual tab, in the **Preview** group, click the **Play** button.

➤ **To change the appearance of a selected audio icon**

→ Use the commands on the Audio Tools **Format** contextual tab to format the audio object just as you would a picture.

> **See Also** For information about using styles and sizing or positioning audio objects, see section 3.1, "Manipulate Graphical Elements." For information about formatting pictures, see section 3.2, Manipulate Images."

➤ **To change the settings for a selected audio object**

→ On the Audio Tools **Playback** contextual tab, in the **Audio Options** group, do any of the following:

  ○ Click the **Volume** button to adjust the volume to low, medium, or high, or to mute the sound.

  ○ Specify whether the sound plays when the slide appears (**Automatically**), only if you click its icon (**On Click**), or throughout the presentation (**Across Slides**).

  ○ Select the **Hide During Show** check box to make an audio object that plays automatically invisible while the presentation is displayed in Reading view or Slide Show view.

  ○ Select the **Loop until Stopped** check box to have the sound play continuously until you stop it.

  ○ Select the **Rewind after Playing** check box to ensure that the sound starts from the beginning each time it is played.

➤ **To edit the sound for a selected audio object**

→ On the **Playback** contextual tab, in the **Editing** group, do any of the following:

  ○ Click the **Trim Audio** button to edit the sound so that only part of it plays.

  ○ Specify **Fade In** and **Fade Out** settings to have the sound gradually increase and decrease in volume.

Practice Tasks

The practice files for these tasks are located in the PowerPoint\Objective3 practice file folder. If you want to save the results of the tasks, save them in the same folder with *My* appended to the file name so that you don't overwrite the original practice files.

- In the *InMyBackyard* presentation, on slide 1, insert the *Bear* video file from your practice file folder. In Normal view, play the video.

- On slide 1, increase the video's brightness and contrast by 20 percent. Then apply the Bevel Rectangle style. Finally, make the video start playing automatically when the presentation is launched and make it play as long as the slide is on the screen.

- In the *ShareholdersMeeting* presentation, on slide 4, insert any audio clip of audience applause (for example, Cheers In Hall).

- On slide 4, use the *Bravo* image in your practice file folder to represent the audio object. Make the image about 2 inches tall, and move it to the lower-right corner of the slide. Then set the sound to play continuously after the icon is clicked.

Objective Review

Before finishing this chapter, ensure that you have mastered the following skills:

3.1   Manipulate Graphical Elements

3.2   Manipulate Images

3.3   Modify WordArt and Shapes

3.4   Manipulate SmartArt

3.5   Edit Video and Audio Content

4 Creating Charts and Tables

The skills tested in this section of the Microsoft Office Specialist exam for Microsoft PowerPoint 2010 relate to the creation of charts and tables. Specifically, the following objectives are associated with this set of skills:

4.1 Construct and Modify Tables

4.2 Insert and Modify Charts

4.3 Apply Chart Elements

4.4 Manipulate Chart Layouts

4.5 Manipulate Chart Elements

It is hard to convey numeric data effectively in a presentation. If you have a small set of data and examining the numbers is important, you can use a formatted table to show clear correlations. If you have a large set of data, or if relationships or trends are more important than actual numbers, you can use a chart to visually represent the data.

This chapter guides you in studying the PowerPoint tools available to help you create tables and charts. You first learn how to create tables, edit their data, modify their structure, and format them appropriately. You'll also see how to incorporate information already available in a Microsoft Excel worksheet in a slide. Then you'll take a look at ways to create charts; change their data, type, and layout; and work with their elements to achieve exactly the effect you want.

> **Practice Files** Before you can complete the practice tasks in this chapter, you need to copy the book's practice files to your computer. The practice files you'll use to complete the tasks in this chapter are in the PowerPoint\Objective4 practice file folder. A complete list of practice files is provided in "Using the Book's Companion Content" at the beginning of this book.

4.1 Construct and Modify Tables

Inserting Tables and Editing Table Content

When you want to present a lot of data in an organized and easy-to-read format, a table is often your best choice. You can create a table in one of the following ways:

- Have PowerPoint insert a table with the number of columns and rows you specify.
- Draw the table by dragging cells the size and shape you need.
- If the table already exists in a Microsoft Access database or a Word document, or on an Excel worksheet, you can copy and paste that table into a slide, rather than re-creating it.

> **See Also** For information about inserting an Excel worksheet, see the "Inserting and Modifying Excel Worksheets" topic later in this section.

To enter information in a table, you simply click a cell and then type. You can also move the insertion point from cell to cell by pressing the Tab key.

	Winter	Spring	Summer	Fall
Minimum	18	41	73	43
Average	29	57	89	54
Maximum	40	72	105	65

When a table is active on a slide, the Table Tools Design and Table Tools Layout contextual tabs are available on the ribbon.

➤ To insert a table

1. In a content placeholder, click the **Insert Table** button.
2. In the **Insert Table** dialog box, specify the number of columns and rows, and then click **OK**.
3. Enter or copy and paste the information into the table structure.

   Or

1. On the **Insert** tab, in the **Tables** group, click the **Table** button.
2. In the grid, point to the upper-left cell, move the pointer across and down to select the number of columns and rows you want, and click the lower-right cell in the selection.
3. Enter or copy and paste the information into the table structure.

➤ **To draw a table**

1. On the **Insert** tab, in the **Tables** group, click the **Table** arrow, and then click **Draw Table**.

2. Position the pencil cursor, and drag down and to the right to create a cell the size you want.

3. On the Table Tools **Design** contextual tab, in the **Draw Borders** group, click the **Draw Table** button, and draw the next cell.

4. Repeat step 3 to draw as many cells as you need.

5. Enter the information into the table structure.

➤ **To edit table content**

→ Use normal editing techniques to change the data within a cell.

➤ **To delete a table**

→ On the Table Tools **Layout** contextual tab, in the **Rows & Columns** group, click the **Delete** button, and then click **Delete Table**.

Changing Table Structure

After you insert a table, you can change its structure in the following ways:

- Add columns or rows.
- Delete columns or rows.
- Combine (merge) selected cells into one cell that spans two or more columns or rows.
- Split a single cell into two or more cells.
- Size columns or rows.
- Size the table.

	Seasonal Temperatures			
	Winter	Spring	Summer	Fall
Minimum	18	41	73	43
Average	29	57	89	54
Maximum	40	72	105	65

➤ To add a row

→ With the cursor in the last cell of the last row, press the Tab key to insert a new row at the bottom of the table.

→ On the Table Tools **Layout** contextual tab, in the **Rows & Columns** group, click the **Insert Above** or **Insert Below** button to insert a row above or below the row containing the cursor.

→ On the Table Tools **Design** contextual tab, in the **Draw Borders** group, click the **Draw Table** button, and draw the row.

➤ To add a column

→ On the **Layout** contextual tab, in the **Rows & Columns** group, click the **Insert Left** or **Insert Right** button to insert a column to the left or right of the column containing the cursor.

→ On the **Design** contextual tab, in the **Draw Borders** group, click the **Draw Table** button, and draw the column.

➤ To delete a row or column

→ On the **Layout** contextual tab, in the **Rows & Columns** group, click the **Delete** button, and then click **Delete Columns** or **Delete Rows** to delete the row or column containing the cursor.

➤ To select table elements

→ To select a cell, point just inside its left border, and when the cursor changes to a black arrow pointing up and to the right, click.

→ To select a column, point above its top border, and when the cursor changes to a black downward-pointing arrow, click.

Or

Click a cell in the column, and on the **Layout** contextual tab, in the **Table** group, click the **Select** button, and then click **Select Column**.

→ To select a row, point outside the table to the left of the row, and when the cursor changes to a black right-pointing arrow, click.

Or

Click a cell in the row, and on the **Layout** contextual tab, in the **Table** group, click the **Select** button, and then click **Select Row**.

➡ To select multiple cells, columns, or rows, select the first element, and then hold down the Shift key as you select subsequent elements.

Or

Drag through adjacent cells, columns, or rows.

➡ To select an entire table, click any cell, and on the **Layout** contextual tab, in the **Table** group, click the **Select** button, and then click **Select Table**.

➤ **To merge two or more selected cells in a row or column**

➡ Select the cells, and then on the **Layout** contextual tab, in the **Merge** group, click the **Merge Cells** button.

Or

1. On the **Design** contextual tab, in the **Draw Borders** group, click the **Eraser** button, and then click the borders between the cells you want to merge.

2. Click the **Eraser** button again to turn it off.

➤ **To split a cell into two or more cells**

1. Click the cell, and on the **Layout** contextual tab, in the **Merge** group, click the **Split Cells** button.

2. In the **Split Cells** dialog box, specify the number of columns and rows you want the cell to be split into, and then click **OK**.

Or

1. On the **Design** contextual tab, in the **Draw Borders** group, click the **Draw Table** button, and then draw borders within the cell for the columns and rows you want.

2. Click the **Draw Table** button again to turn it off.

➤ **To change the size of a selected element**

➡ To change the width of a column, point to the right border of one of its cells, and when the opposing arrows appear, drag the border to the left or right.

Or

On the **Layout** contextual tab, in the **Cell Size** group, adjust the **Table Column Width** setting.

➡ To size a column to fit its entries, point to the right border of one of its cells, and when the opposing arrows appear, double-click.

→ To change the height of a row, point to the bottom border of one of its cells, and when the opposing arrows appear, drag the border up or down.

Or

On the **Layout** contextual tab, in the **Cell Size** group, adjust the **Table Row Height** setting.

→ To evenly distribute the widths of selected columns or the heights of selected rows, on the **Layout** contextual tab, in the **Cell Size** group, click the **Distribute Columns** or **Distribute Rows** button.

→ To change the size of a selected table, point to any handle (the sets of dots) around its frame, and drag in the direction you want the table to grow or shrink.

Or

On the **Layout** contextual tab, in the **Table Size** group, adjust the **Height** or **Width** setting.

Formatting Tables

You can format the text in a table in the same ways you would format regular text. You also have easy access to these options:

- Align text horizontally and/or vertically within a cell.
- Set the text direction.
- Set the cell margins.
- Apply Quick Styles, fills, outlines, and text effects.

In addition to formatting the text in a table, you can format the table itself in the following ways:

- Apply a ready-made table style.
- Customize the style by setting various options.
- Add shading, borders, and effects such as shadows and reflections to individual cells.

Seasonal Temperatures				
	Winter	Spring	Summer	Fall
Minimum	18	41	73	43
Average	29	57	89	54
Maximum	40	72	105	65

➤ **To align text**

→ On the Table Tools **Layout** contextual tab, in the **Alignment** group, click one of the **Align** buttons.

➤ **To set text direction**

→ On the **Layout** contextual tab, in the **Alignment** group, click the **Text Direction** button, and then click one of the rotation options.

➤ **To set cell margins**

→ On the **Layout** contextual tab, in the **Alignment** group, click the **Cell Margins** button, and then click one of the preset options.

→ In the **Cell Margins** list, click **Custom Margins**, and then in the **Cell Text Layout** dialog box, set specific margins.

➤ **To apply Quick Styles and other fancy formatting**

→ On the Table Tools **Design** contextual tab, in the **WordArt Styles** group, click the **Quick Styles** button, and then click the style you want.

→ On the **Design** contextual tab, in the **WordArt Styles** group, click the **Text Fill**, **Text Outline**, or **Text Effects** button, and then click the options you want in the corresponding galleries.

➤ **To apply a table style**

→ On the **Design** contextual tab, in the **Table Styles** gallery, click the style you want.

➤ **To create a custom table style**

→ On the **Design** contextual tab, in the **Table Style Options** group, select or clear the six check boxes to format the table cells to suit your data.

➤ **To format selected cells**

→ On the **Design** contextual tab, in the **Table Styles** group, click the **Shading**, **Border**, or **Effects** button, and then click the options you want.

Inserting and Modifying Excel Worksheets

If you want to use data from an Excel worksheet in a PowerPoint table, you can do any of the following:

- Copy and paste the data as a table.

- Embed the worksheet in a slide as an object.

- Link the slide to the worksheet so that the slide reflects any changes you make to the worksheet data.

Equipment Replacement

Payment Schedule	
Interest Rate	6.0%
Years	10
Loan Amount	$1,550,000
Monthly Payment	$17,208
Cost of Loan	$619,494
10-Year Lease Cost	$1,800,000
Savings	$1,180,506

➤ **To copy and paste Excel data**

1. In the Excel worksheet, select and copy the data you want for the PowerPoint table.

2. Switch to PowerPoint, display the slide, and paste the data.

3. To change the default paste option (which is Use Destination Styles), click the **Paste Options** button, and click the option you want.

➤ **To update copied and pasted Excel data**

➜ Use normal editing techniques to change the data in a cell.

➤ **To embed a worksheet**

1. Copy and paste the Excel data in the usual way.
2. Click the **Paste Options** button, and then click **Embed**.

   Or

1. On the **Insert** tab, in the **Text** group, click the **Insert Object** button.
2. In the **Insert Object** dialog box, click **Create from file**, and then click **Browse**.
3. In the **Browse** dialog box, locate and double-click the workbook. Then click **OK**.

➤ **To eliminate extraneous columns and rows**

1. Double-click the worksheet object.
2. When the worksheet opens in an Excel window within PowerPoint, size the frame around the worksheet so that it is just big enough to contain the active part of the worksheet.
3. Click outside the frame to return to PowerPoint.

➤ **To resize the worksheet**

→ Point any handle (sets of dots) around the worksheet object, and drag to enlarge or shrink it.

➤ **To modify an embedded worksheet**

1. Double-click the worksheet object.
2. Use Excel techniques to edit and format the embedded object.

➤ **To link to a worksheet**

→ Follow the instructions for embedding a worksheet, but in the **Insert Object** dialog box, select the **Link** check box before clicking **OK**.

➤ **To update a linked worksheet**

→ Double-click the table on the slide to open the linked worksheet in Excel, make the changes, and save them.
→ If you update the linked worksheet in Excel and want to synchronize the table on the slide, right-click the table on the slide, and click **Update Link**.

Practice Tasks

The practice files for these tasks are located in the PowerPoint\Objective4 practice file folder. If you want to save the results of the tasks, save them in the same folder with *My* appended to the file name so that you don't overwrite the original practice files.

- In the *TimeManagement* presentation, on slide 2, insert a table with three columns and four rows. In the cells of the top row, enter *Task*, *Minutes/Day*, and *Hours Saved/Week*. Then starting with the second cell, enter the following in the cells of the left column: *Paper documents*, *Email*, and *Calendar*.

- On slide 2, insert a row at the top of the table, and merge its cells. In the merged cell, enter and center the title *Effect of Focused Activity*.

- In the table on slide 2, turn off Banded Rows formatting, and turn on First Column formatting. Then apply the Medium Style 2 - Accent 2 style to the table, and apply a border around the entire table.

- On slide 3, embed the *Costs* worksheet. Then enlarge the worksheet object so that it fills the available space on the slide.

4.2 Insert and Modify Charts

Inserting Charts and Editing Chart Data

You can easily add a chart to a slide to make it easy to see trends that might not be obvious from looking at numbers. When you create a chart in PowerPoint, you specify the chart type and then use a linked Excel worksheet to enter the information you want to plot. As you replace the sample data in the worksheet with your own data, you immediately see the results in the chart in the adjacent PowerPoint window.

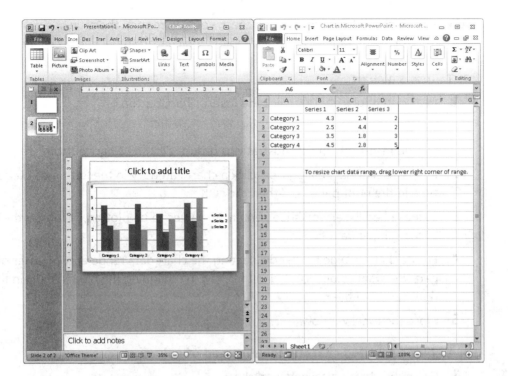

You can enter the data into the linked worksheet by typing it directly, or you can copy and paste it from an existing Excel worksheet, Access table, or Word table. You then identify the chart data range in the linked worksheet to ensure that only the data you want appears in the chart, and close the worksheet to plot the data.

By default, a chart is plotted based on the series of data points in the columns of the attached worksheet, and these series are identified in the legend. You can plot the chart based on the series in the rows instead.

When a chart is active on a slide, the Chart Tools Design, Chart Tools Layout, and Chart Tools Format tabs are available on the ribbon.

After you've plotted your data in the chart, you can reopen the attached worksheet and edit the data at any time. PowerPoint replots the chart to reflect your changes.

➤ **To insert a chart**

1. In a content placeholder, click the **Insert Chart** button.

   Or

   On the **Insert** tab, in the **Illustrations** group, click the **Chart** button.

2. In the **Insert Chart** dialog box, click a chart category in the left pane, click a chart type in the right pane, and then click **OK**.

3. In the linked Excel worksheet, enter the values to be plotted, following the pattern of the sample data.

4. Ensure that the blue border delineating the chart data range encompasses only the data you want to be included in the chart, by dragging the blue triangle in the lower-right corner of the range.

5. Close the Excel window.

➤ **To plot a selected chart by rows instead of columns**

1. Open the chart's attached worksheet.

2. On the Table Tools **Design** contextual tab, in the **Data** group, click the **Switch Row/Column** button.

> **Tip** The worksheet must be open for this button to be active.

➤ **To open the attached worksheet so that you can edit the chart data**

→ Right-click the chart, and then click **Edit Data**.

→ Click the chart, and then on the **Design** contextual tab, in the **Data** group, click the **Edit Data** button.

> **Tip** The chart must be active (surrounded by a frame) when you make changes to the data in the worksheet; otherwise, the chart won't automatically update.

➤ **To select worksheet data for editing**

→ To select a cell, click it.

→ To select a column, click the letter header at the top of the column.

→ To select a row, click the number header at the left end of the row.

→ To select multiple cells, columns, or rows, select the first element, and then hold down the Shift key as you select subsequent elements.

Or

Drag through adjacent cells, columns, or rows.

→ To select an entire worksheet, click the gray cell in the upper-left corner, at the intersection of the letter and row headers.

Changing the Chart Type and Layout

If you decide that the type of chart you initially selected doesn't adequately depict your data, you can change the type at any time. There are 11 chart types, each with two-dimensional and three-dimensional variations.

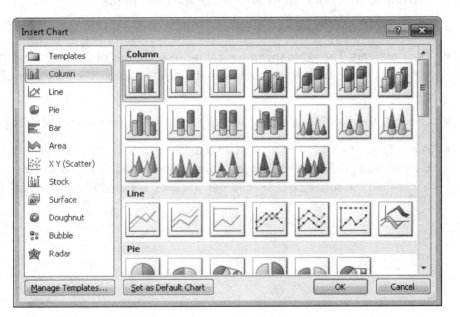

Each chart type has corresponding chart layouts that you can use to refine the look of the chart.

These layouts are preset combinations of the available chart elements, which include the following:

- **Chart area** This is the entire area within the chart frame.

- **Plot area** This is the rectangle between the horizontal and vertical axes.

- **Data markers** These are the graphical representations of the values, or data points, you enter in the Excel worksheet. Sometimes the data markers are identified with data labels.

- **Legend** This provides a key for identifying the data series (a set of data points).

- **Axes** The data is plotted against an x-axis—also called the *category axis*—and a y-axis—also called the *value axis*. (Three-dimensional charts also have a z-axis—also called the *series axis*.) Sometimes the axes are identified with axis labels.

- **Tick-mark labels** These identify the categories, values, or series along each axis.

- **Gridlines** These help to visually quantify the data points.

- **Data table** This table provides details of the plotted data points in table format.

- **Titles** The chart might have a title and subtitle.

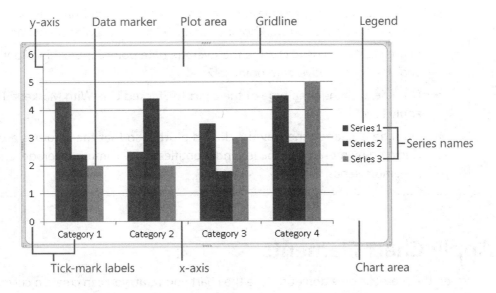

➤ To change the type of a selected chart

1. On the Chart Tools **Design** contextual tab, in the **Type** group, click the **Change Chart Type** button.

2. In the **Change Chart Type** dialog box, select a new type of chart, and then click **OK**.

➤ To apply a preset layout to a selected chart

→ On the **Design** contextual tab, in the **Chart Layouts** gallery, click the layout you want.

Practice Tasks

The practice files for these tasks are located in the PowerPoint\Objective4 practice file folder. If you want to save the results of the tasks, save them in the same folder with *My* appended to the file name so that you don't overwrite the original practice files.

- In the *WaterSaving* presentation, on slide 2, use the data from cells A3:C9 of the *WaterConsumption* workbook to create a Clustered Cylinder column chart.

- In the chart on slide 2, change the Average data point for Brushing Teeth to 4 and the Conservative data point to 2.

- On slide 2, change the type of the chart to Stacked Line With Markers. Then apply Layout 3.

- On slide 3, change the way the data is plotted so that the columns are clustered by month and the legend identifies the Minimum, Average, and Maximum series.

4.3 Apply Chart Elements

When the preset layouts don't produce the chart you want, you can create a custom layout by mixing and matching different chart elements to get exactly the effect you want.

➤ **To add or remove a chart title**

→ On the Chart Tools **Layout** contextual tab, in the **Labels** group, click the **Chart Title** button, and then click the option you want.

➤ **To add or remove an axis**

→ On the **Layout** contextual tab, in the **Axes** group, click the **Axes** button, click **Primary Horizontal Axis** or **Primary Vertical Axis**, and then click the option you want.

➤ **To add or remove an axis label**

→ On the **Layout** contextual tab, in the **Labels** group, click the **Axis Titles** button, click **Primary Horizontal Axis Title** or **Primary Vertical Axis Title**, and then click the option you want.

➤ **To add or remove a legend**

→ On the **Layout** contextual tab, in the **Labels** group, click the **Legend** button, and then click the option you want.

➤ **To add or remove data labels**

→ On the **Layout** contextual tab, in the **Labels** group, click the **Data Labels** button, and then click the option you want.

➤ **To add or remove a data table**

→ On the **Layout** contextual tab, in the **Labels** group, click the **Data Table** button, and then click the option you want.

➤ **To show or hide gridlines**

→ On the **Layout** contextual tab, in the **Axes** group, click the **Gridlines** button, click **Primary Horizontal Gridlines** or **Primary Vertical Gridlines**, and then click the option you want.

➤ **To add or remove a chart wall or chart floor (3D charts)**

→ On the **Layout** contextual tab, in the **Background** group, click the **Chart Wall** or **Chart Floor** button, and then click the option you want.

➤ **To add or remove trendlines, bars, and other analysis tools (line charts)**

→ On the **Layout** contextual tab, in the **Analysis** group, click the button for the type of tool you want, and then click the option you want.

> **Tip** You can also use standard techniques to add pictures, shapes, and independent text boxes to charts.

Practice Tasks

The practice file for these tasks is located in the PowerPoint\Objective4 practice file folder. If you want to save the results of the tasks, save them in the same folder with *My* appended to the file name so that you don't overwrite the original practice file.

- In the *WaterStrategies* presentation, on slide 2, remove the title.
- On slide 3, add a legend at the bottom of the chart. Then add a data table with legend keys at the bottom of the chart, and remove the existing legend.
- On slide 3, add a default vertical axis to the chart, and then add *Temperature* as a rotated axis label.
- On slide 3, display gridlines that allow you to more accurately gauge the value of the chart's data markers.

4.4 Manipulate Chart Layouts

See Also For information about adding and deleting elements, see section 4.3, "Apply Chart Elements." For information about formatting elements, see section 4.5, "Manipulate Chart Elements."

Selecting Chart Elements

You can adjust a chart layout by adding, deleting, moving, and sizing chart elements. To perform any of those tasks, you first have to select the element.

➤ **To select a chart element**

→ If the element is easy to identify, simply click it.

→ If you have trouble clicking some of the smaller chart elements, on the Chart Tools **Format** contextual tab, in the **Current Selection** group, display the **Chart Elements** list, and then click the element you want.

> **Tip** If you want to activate the chart (that is, select the chart area), be sure to click a blank area inside the chart frame. Clicking any of the chart's elements will activate that element, not the chart as a whole.

Sizing and Positioning Elements

If you want more control over the layout of a chart, you can do the following:

- Control the overall size of the chart.
- Adjust the size of chart elements.
- Arrange chart elements precisely.

➤ **To change the size of a selected chart**

→ Point to any handle (the sets of dots around the chart frame), and when the hollow double-headed arrow appears, drag in the direction you want the chart to grow or shrink.

➤ **To change the size of a selected chart element**

→ Point to any handle, and when the hollow double-headed arrow appears, drag in the direction you want the element to grow or shrink.

> **Tip** If an element cannot be sized, the hollow double-headed arrow does not appear.

➤ **To change the position of a selected chart element**

→ Point to the border around the element, away from any handles, and when the four-headed arrow appears, drag to the desired position.

> **Tip** Some elements cannot be moved, even if the four-headed arrow appears.

➤ **To rotate a chart layout**

1. On the Chart Tools **Layout** contextual tab, in the **Background** group, click the **3D Rotation** button.

2. In the **Format Chart Area** dialog box, in the **Rotation** area of the **3-D Rotation** page, set the angle of rotation for each axis, and then click **Close**.

Practice Tasks

The practice file for these tasks is located in the PowerPoint\Objective4 practice file folder. If you want to save the results of the tasks, save them in the same folder with *My* appended to the file name so that you don't overwrite the original practice file.

- In the *Temperature* presentation, on slide 2, make the chart exactly 4.5 inches by 7.5 inches.

- In the chart on slide 2, shrink the size of the plot area by about a half inch. Then stretch the legend so that it spans the plot area.

- On slide 2 on, move the chart title to the left until it aligns with the left end of the gridlines.

4.5 Manipulate Chart Elements

Strategy Each chart element has too many formatting options for us to cover them in detail here. Make sure you are familiar with the elements and how to format them to convey different types of data in different ways.

See Also For information about sizing and positioning chart elements, see section 4.4, "Manipulate Chart Layouts."

You can modify and format a chart to get the effect you want. If you don't want to spend a lot of time on individual chart elements, you can apply styles (predefined combinations of formatting) to the chart area (the entire chart) to create sophisticated charts with a minimum of effort. These styles include the following:

- **Chart Styles** Combinations of data marker, wall, and floor fill colors, as well as background color and bevel effects

- **Shape Styles** Combinations of shape fills, shape outlines, and shape effects

- **WordArt Styles** Combinations of text fills, text outlines, and text effects

You can also apply Shape Style and WordArt Style components individually, both to the chart area and to a selected chart element.

In addition to using styles and style components, you can fine-tune the formatting of a selected chart element in its Format dialog box.

This dialog box is specific to each type of element and includes options such as the following:

- **Chart area** You can specify the background fill, the border color and style, effects such as shadows and edges, the 3-D format and rotation, and the size and position. You can also attach text to be displayed when someone points to the chart.

- **Plot area** You can specify the background fill, the border color and style, effects such as shadows and edges, and the 3-D format and rotation.

- **Data markers** You can specify the background fill, the border color and style, effects such as shadows and edges, and the 3-D format. You can also precisely determine the gap between data points.

- **Legend** You can specify the background fill, the border color and style, and effects such as shadows and edges. You can also specify the legend's position and whether it can overlap the chart.

- **Axes** You can specify the background fill, the line color and style, effects such as shadows and edges, and the 3-D format and rotation. For the category axis, you can also specify the scale, add or remove tick marks, adjust the label position, and determine the starting and maximum values. You can set the number format (such as currency or percentage), and set the axis label alignment.

- **Gridlines** You can set the line color and style, as well as effects such as shadows and edges.

> **Tip** To open the Format Major Gridlines dialog box, right-click any gridline, and then click Format Gridlines.

- **Data table** You can specify the background fill, the border color and style, effects such as shadows and edges, and the 3-D format. You can also set table borders.

> **Tip** To open the Format Data Table dialog box, right-click the selected data table, and then click Format Data Table.

- **Titles** You can specify the background fill, the border color and style, effects such as shadows and edges, and the 3-D format. You can also set the title's alignment, direction, and angle of rotation.

➤ **To apply a Chart Style to a selected chart**

→ On the Chart Tools **Design** contextual tab, in the **Chart Styles** gallery, click the style you want.

➤ **To apply a Shape Style to the chart area or to a chart object**

→ On the Chart Tools **Format** contextual tab, in the **Shape Styles** gallery, click the style you want.

➤ **To apply Shape Style components to the chart area or to a chart object**

→ On the **Format** contextual tab, in the **Shape Styles** group, click the **Shape Fill**, **Shape Outline**, or **Shape Effects** button, and then click the option you want.

➤ **To apply a WordArt Style to the text in a selected chart**

→ On the **Format** contextual tab, in the **WordArt Styles** gallery, click the style you want.

➤ **To apply WordArt Style components to the chart area or to a chart object**

→ On the **Format** contextual tab, in the **WordArt Styles** group, click the **Text Fill**, **Text Outline**, or **Text Effects** button, and then click the option you want.

➤ **To open the Format dialog box for a chart element**

→ If the element is easy to identify, simply double-click it.

→ Right-click the element, and then click **Format <Element>**.

Or

1. If you have trouble double-clicking some of the smaller chart elements, on the **Format** contextual tab, in the **Current Selection** group, display the **Chart Elements** list, and click the element you want.

2. In the **Current Selection** group, click the **Format Selection** button.

> **Tip** Because charts convey at-a-glance summary information, you might want to attach a hyperlink to a chart element to provide access to supporting details. Clicking the hyperlinked element then takes you directly to the linked details, which might be on a hidden slide, in another presentation, in a file on your computer or your organization's network, or on a website. For information about creating hyperlinks, see section 3.1, "Manipulate Graphical Elements."

Practice Tasks

The practice file for these tasks is located in the PowerPoint\Objective4 practice file folder. If you want to save the results of the exercises, save them in the same folder with *My* appended to the file name so that you don't overwrite the original practice file.

- In the *AirQuality* presentation, on slide 3, apply Style 7 to the entire chart. Then with the entire chart still selected, apply the Moderate Effect – Tan, Accent 2 shape style.

- On slide 3, apply the Fill – White, Outline – Accent 1 WordArt style to the chart tile.

- On slide 3, explode the data points in the pie chart by 20 percent, and then set the angle of the first slice at 200.

- On slide 3, move the chart's legend to the right, and then fill its background with the Gray-50%, Accent 6, Darker 25% color.

Objective Review

Before finishing this chapter, ensure that you have mastered the following skills:

4.1   Construct and Modify Tables

4.2   Insert and Modify Charts

4.3   Apply Chart Elements

4.4   Manipulate Chart Layouts

4.5   Manipulate Chart Elements

5 Applying Transitions and Animations

The skills tested in this section of the Microsoft Office Specialist exam for Microsoft PowerPoint 2010 relate to creating movement, both between slides and for slide components. Specifically, the following objectives are associated with this set of skills:

5.1 Apply Built-In and Custom Animations

5.2 Apply Effect and Path Options

5.3 Manipulate Animations

5.4 Apply and Modify Transitions Between Slides

The judicious use of dynamic effects can grab and keep the attention of an audience. By adding transitions between slides, you can visually mark the end of one topic and the beginning of another, and by animating objects on a slide, you can add emphasis, focus, and entertainment.

This chapter guides you in studying the techniques for quickly animating objects, including how to customize animations to suit your needs. It also covers how to add and control dynamic slide transitions.

> **Practice Files** Before you can complete the practice tasks in this chapter, you need to copy the book's practice files to your computer. The practice files you'll use to complete the tasks in this chapter are in the PowerPoint\Objective5 practice file folder. A complete list of practice files is provided in "Using the Book's Companion Content" at the beginning of this book.

5.1 Apply Built-In and Custom Animations

Applying Built-In Animations

If you are delivering a presentation from your computer, you can keep your audience focused and reinforce your message by applying built-in animations to the text and graphics on your slides. You can apply the following types of ready-made effects from the Animation gallery:

- **Entrance** Animate the way the element appears on the slide.

- **Emphasis** Increase or decrease the importance of the element by changing its color, style; or brightness; by making it grow or shrink; or by making it spin.

- **Exit** Animate the way the element leaves the slide.

- **Motion Paths** Move the element around on the slide in various ways, such as diagonally to the upper-right corner or in a circular motion.

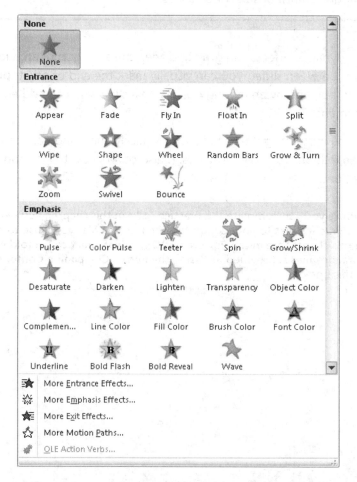

Each animation you add is identified on the slide by an adjacent numbered box that indicates the order in which the animations will occur.

➤ **To apply a built-in animation to a selected object**

→ On the **Animations** tab, in the **Animation** group, click the **More** button, and then in the gallery, click the animation you want.

➤ **To preview the animation for a selected object**

→ On the **Animations** tab, in the **Preview** group, click the **Preview** button.

➤ **To remove an animation from a selected object**

→ In the **Animation** gallery, click **None**.

Applying Fancier Animations

If none of the predefined effects in the Animation gallery meets your needs, you can display additional, professionally designed animations in four categories: Basic, Subtle, Moderate, and Exciting.

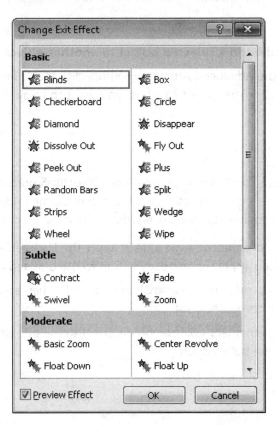

Having applied one animation, you can apply another of a different type. (Applying another of the same type replaces the existing animation.) On the slide, each animation is identified by its own box, with the boxes stacked to the left of the animated object.

➤ **To apply a fancier animation to a selected element**

1. On the **Animations** tab, in the **Advanced Animation** group, click the **More** button to the right of the **Animation** gallery, and then at the bottom of the gallery, click the animation category you want.

2. In the **Change <Animation> Effect** dialog box, click the animation you want.

➤ **To apply an additional animation to a selected animated object**

→ On the **Animations** tab, in the **Advanced Animation** group, click the **Add Animation** button, and then click the additional animation you want to apply.

Copying Animations

If you combine animation effects and want to apply the same combination to another object, you can copy the set with the Animation Painter, which functions the same way as the Format Painter.

➤ **To copy the animations applied to a selected object to another object**

→ On the **Animations** tab, in the **Advanced Animation** group, click the **Animation Painter** button, and then click the object to which you want to copy the animations.

Practice Tasks

The practice file for these tasks is located in the PowerPoint\Objective5 practice file folder. If you want to save the results of the tasks, save them in the same folder with *My* appended to the file name so that you don't overwrite the original practice file.

- In the *NaturalGardening* presentation, on slide 2, apply the Fly In entrance animation to the title. Then apply the same animation to the bulleted list.

- On slide 3, apply the Arc Up motion path animation to the title. Then apply the Flip entrance animation to the bulleted list.

- On slide 2, add the Complementary Color emphasis effect to the title and the Pulse emphasis effect to the bulleted list.

- Copy the animations from slide 2 to slide 3.

5.2 Apply Effect and Path Options

Fine-Tuning Animation Effects

After you apply an animation effect, you can fine-tune its action by using the commands on the Animations tab to do the following:

- Specify the direction, shape, or sequence of the animation. (The options vary depending on the type of animation).

- Specify what action will trigger the animation. For example, you can specify that clicking a different object on the slide will animate the selected object.
- Specify whether you will start an animation by clicking the mouse button or whether PowerPoint should start it with or after the previous one.
- Control how long each animation lasts.
- Delay the start of an animation effect.
- Change the order of the animation effects on a slide.

➤ **To change a selected animation's effect options**

1. On the **Animations** tab, in the **Animation** group, click the **Effect Options** button, and then click the option you want.

2. Click the **Effect Options** button again to apply additional options.

➤ **To change when a selected animation starts**

→ On the **Animations** tab, in the **Timing** group, display the **Start** list, and click **On Click**, **With Previous**, or **After Previous**.

→ When the Start setting is On Click, click the **Trigger** button in the **Advanced Animation** group, click **On Click of**, and then click the object you want to start the animation

➤ **To change the duration of an animation**

→ On the **Animations** tab, in the **Timing** group, increase or decrease the **Duration** option to the setting you want.

➤ **To delay the start of an animation**

→ On the **Animations** tab, in the **Timing** group, increase or decrease the **Delay** option to the setting you want.

> **Tip** You can also change the start, duration, delay, and trigger on the Timing page of the effect options dialog box for the animation, discussed in section 5.3, "Manipulate Animations."

➤ **To change the animation order**

→ On the **Animations** tab, in the **Timing** group, click the up or down arrow under Reorder Animation.

> **Tip** You can also change the order of animations in the Animation pane, discussed in section 5.3, "Manipulate Animations."

Adjusting Motion Paths

If you apply a motion path animation to an object, PowerPoint displays a schematic of the path so that you can adjust its starting and ending points. You can also rotate the path. PowerPoint also displays a schematic for other animations with horizontal or vertical movement, such as the Wave emphasis animation.

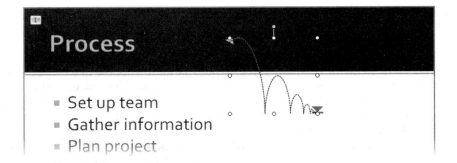

> ➤ **To adjust the height or length of the motion path of a selected animation**

> ➔ Click the path schematic, and drag the handles around the frame.

> ➤ **To rotate the motion path of a selected animation**

> ➔ Click the path schematic, and drag the green rotating handle attached to the frame.

Practice Tasks

The practice file for these tasks is located in the PowerPoint\Objective5 practice file folder. If you want to save the results of the tasks, save them in the same folder with *My* appended to the file name so that you don't overwrite the original practice file.

- In the *BackyardEcology* presentation, on slide 1, change the animation shape of the title to a diamond, and change the animation direction to outward.

- On slide 1, make the subtitle animation start automatically after the title animation, with a delay of 2 seconds.

- On slide 2, set the duration of the bulleted list animations to 2 seconds. Then make the title animation occur before the bulleted list animations.

- On slide 4, adjust the end points of the motion paths of the three pictures so that after each picture appears, its lower-left corner sits on the diagonal bar. (This takes trial and error; when you finish, the first end point will be at the 1 1/8 mark on the vertical ruler, the middle end point will be at the 0 mark, and the right end point will be at the -1 3/8 mark.)

5.3 Manipulate Animations

> **Strategy** You can build sophisticated animation effects involving sequences of multiple settings. Be sure you know where to find various settings and how to change the animation order. And remember that when you have created a set of animations that you like, you can use the Animation Painter to copy the set to another object. For information about the Animation Painter, see the "Copying Animations" topic in section 5.1, "Apply Built-in and Custom Animations."

You can make additional animation adjustments by displaying the Animation pane. This pane shows all the animations applied to the active slide.

If multiple animations are applied to an object, clicking the chevrons in the Animation pane hides and displays them, making it easy to focus on specific objects.

Clicking the arrow that appears when you click an animation in the Animation pane displays a list of actions.

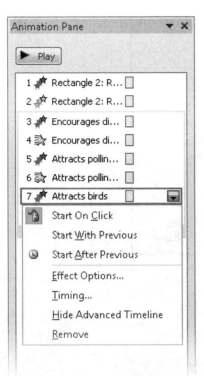

Clicking Effect Options in the list opens a dialog box that is specific to that type of animation. Depending on the type, the refinements you might be able to make include the following:

- Change the animation direction.
- Specify whether the animation should be accompanied by a sound.
- Dim or hide the object after the animation, or make it change to a specific color.
- If the animation is applied to text, animate all the text at once, word by word, or letter by letter.
- Change the Start, Delay, and Duration settings, repeat the animation, and specify what will trigger its action.
- If a slide has more than one level of bullet points, animate different levels separately.
- If an object has embedded text, animate the object and the text together (the default) or separately, or animate one but not the other.
- Specify whether a sequenced animation progresses forward or backward.

Fade   [?] [×]

Effect | Timing | Text Animation

Enhancements

Sound: [No Sound] ▼ 🔊

After animation: Don't Dim ▼

Animate text: All at once ▼

[   ] ⬍ % delay between letters

Fade   [?] [×]

Effect | Timing | Text Animation

Start: On Click ▼

Delay: 0 ⬍ seconds

Duration: 0.5 seconds (Very Fast) ▼

Repeat: (none) ▼

☐ Rewind when done playing

[Triggers ⬍]

⦿ Animate as part of click sequence

○ Start effect on click of: [   ] ▼

○ Start effect on play of: [   ] ▼

Cancel

Fade   [?] [×]

Effect | Timing | Text Animation

Group text: By 1st Level Paragraphs ▼

☐ Automatically after 0 ⬍ seconds

☐ Animate attached shape

☐ In reverse order

OK   Cancel

➤ **To display the Animation pane**

→ On the **Animations** tab, in the **Advanced Animation** group, click the **Animation Pane** button.

➤ **To change the order of the animations on a slide**

➜ In the **Animation** pane, click the animation you want to reorder, and then at the bottom of the pane, click the **Re-Order Up** or **Re-Order Down** arrow.

➤ **To open the effect options dialog box for an animation**

➜ In the **Animation** pane, click the animation, click the arrow that appears, and then click **Effect Options**.

➤ **To change the direction of a text animation**

➜ On the **Effect** page of the effect options dialog box for the animation, in the **Settings** area, display the **Direction** list, and then click the direction you want.

➤ **To add sound to an animation**

➜ On the **Effect** page of the effect options dialog box for the animation, in the **Enhancements** area, display the **Sound** list, and then click the sound you want.

➤ **To dim or hide text, or change its color, after animation**

➜ On the **Effect** page of the effect options dialog box for the animation, in the **Enhancements** area, display the **After animation** list, and then click the effect you want.

➤ **To animate text by word or letter**

➜ On the **Effect** page of the effect options dialog box for the animation, in the **Enhancements** area, display the **Animate text** list, and then click **All at once**, **By word**, or **By letter**.

➤ **To change the start, delay, or duration, or to repeat an animation**

➜ On the **Timing** page of the effect options dialog box for the animation, change the settings to the ones you want.

➤ **To determine the grouping of multiple paragraphs of animated text**

1. On the **Text Animation** page of the effect options dialog box for the animation, display the **Group text** list, and click the option you want.

2. If you want, do any of the following:

   ○ Select the **Automatically after** check box, and set a time in the adjacent box.

   ○ Select the **In reverse order** check box.

Practice Tasks

The practice file for these tasks is located in the PowerPoint\Objective5 practice file folder. If you want to save the results of the tasks, save them in the same folder with *My* appended to the file name so that you don't overwrite the original practice file.

- In the *NaturalBackyard* presentation, on slide 1, attach the Chime sound to the title animation.

- On slide 2, change the animation sequence so that both of the animations attached to the slide title occur before the animations attached to the bulleted list.

- On slide 2, make the color of each bullet point change to green after it appears on the screen.

- On slide 4, set the slide title to animate word by word, with a 50 percent delay between words and a duration of Very Slow.

5.4 Apply and Modify Transitions Between Slides

Transitions control the way successive slides move into view. They include such effects as sliding in, dissolving in from the outer edges or the center, and opening like a vertical blind.

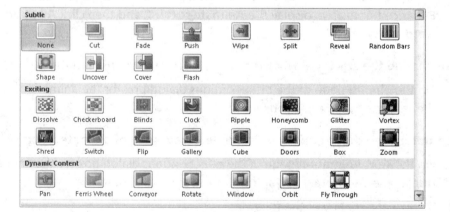

Each slide can have only one transition. You can set transitions in Normal view or Slide Sorter view, and you can set them for one slide, for a group of slides, or for an entire presentation.

Depending on the type of transition, you might be able to refine its effect. In addition, you can specify the following:

- An associated sound
- The transition speed
- When the transition occurs

➤ **To add transitions between slides**

→ On the **Transitions** tab, in the **Transition to This Slide** group, display the **Transitions** gallery, and then click the transition you want.

➤ **To refine the effect of the transition of a selected slide**

→ On the **Transitions** tab, in the **Transition to This Slide** group, click the **Effect Options** button, and then click the effect you want.

➤ **To incorporate a sound into the transition of a selected slide**

→ On the **Transitions** tab, in the **Timing** group, display the **Sound** list, and then click the sound you want.

> **Tip** To associate a sound file of your own with a slide transition, click Other Sound at the bottom of the Sound list. Then in the Add Audio dialog box, find and select the sound file you want to use, and click Open.

➤ **To change the speed of the transition of a selected slide**

→ On the **Transitions** tab, in the **Timing** group, enter the speed you want in the **Duration** box.

➤ **To automate the transition of the selected slide**

1. On the **Transitions** tab, in the **Timing** group, clear the **On Mouse Click** check box.

2. Select the **After** check box, and then enter a time in the adjacent box.

> **See Also** For more information about slide timings, see section 8.2, "Set Up Slide Shows."

➤ **To apply the transition of the selected slide to all the slides**

→ On the **Transitions** tab, in the **Timing** group, click the **Apply To All** button.

➤ **To remove transitions between slides**

1. On the **Transitions** tab, in the **Transition to This Slide** group, display the **Transitions** gallery, and click **None**.

2. In the **Timing** group, click the **Apply To All** button.

Practice Tasks

The practice files for these tasks are located in the PowerPoint\Objective5 practice file folder. If you want to save the results of the tasks, save them in the same folder with *My* appended to the file name so that you don't overwrite the original practice files.

- In the *PersonalJournal* presentation, apply the Cover transition to all the slides in the presentation, and then set the transition speed to 3 seconds.

- In the *PersonalJournal* presentation, make the transition rotate from the bottom.

- In the *PersonalJournal* presentation, add the Wind sound to the transition.

- In the *AnnualMeeting* presentation, remove the transition effects from all the slides.

Objective Review

Before finishing this chapter, ensure that you have mastered the following skills:

5.1   Apply Built-in and Custom Animations

5.2   Apply Effect and Path Options

5.3   Manipulate Animations

5.4   Apply and Modify Transitions Between Slides

6 Collaborating on Presentations

The skills tested in this section of the Microsoft Office Specialist exam for Microsoft PowerPoint 2010 relate to tools for proofing and reviewing presentations. Specifically, the following objectives are associated with this set of skills:

6.1 Manage Comments in Presentations
6.2 Apply Proofing Tools

PowerPoint has tools that you and your colleagues can use to collectively develop presentations. Whether you are reviewing a presentation at the content level or proofing it to ensure that there are no embarrassing mistakes, these tools will help you complete the task efficiently.

This chapter guides you in studying how to insert and review comments. It also covers proofing tasks such as checking spelling and choosing the best word, and describes the process for merging changes made to two different versions of the same presentation.

> **Practice Files** Before you can complete the practice tasks in this chapter, you need to copy the book's practice files to your computer. The practice files you'll use to complete the tasks in this chapter are in the PowerPoint\Objective6 practice file folder. A complete list of practice files is provided in "Using the Book's Companion Content" at the beginning of this book.

6.1 Manage Comments in Presentations

If you are asked to review a presentation, you can give feedback about a slide, without disrupting its text and layout, by inserting a comment in a comment box. If you add a comment without first selecting an object on the slide, the comment is attached to the upper-left corner of the slide. If you select an object before adding the comment, the comment is attached to the upper-right corner of the object.

> **Tip** Your comments are identified by the user name and initials specified on the General page of the PowerPoint Options dialog box.

After you enter your comment, clicking away from the comment box hides the comment but leaves a small comment icon with your initials and a number. Pointing to the icon displays the comment temporarily, and clicking the icon displays the comment until you click somewhere else.

You can turn the display of comments on and off and move quickly back and forth among them. You can respond to a displayed comment by inserting a new one or by activating the comment box for editing so that you can make additions or changes. You can delete comments individually, delete all the comments on the current slide, or delete all the comments in the entire presentation.

> **See Also** For information about annotating slides with an electronic pen or highlighter while displaying a presentation in Slide Show view, see section 8.1, "Apply Presentation Tools."

➤ **To insert a comment**

1. Click the slide or object on the slide to which you want to attach a comment.

2. On the **Review** tab, in the **Comments** group, click the **New Comment** button.

3. In the comment box, enter the comment, and then click away from the comment box to close it.

➤ **To show and hide comments**

→ On the **Review** tab, in the **Comments** group, click the **Show Markup** button.

➤ **To move among comments**

→ On the **Review** tab, in the **Comments** group, click the **Previous** or **Next** button.

➤ **To edit a comment**

→ Quickly activate the comment for editing by double-clicking its icon, and then make your changes or additions in the comment box.

→ Right-click the comment icon, click **Edit Comment**, and then make your changes or additions.

Or

1. Click the comment icon, and then on the **Review** tab, in the **Comments** group, click the **Edit Comment** button.

2. In the comment box, make your changes.

➤ **To delete a specific comment**

→ Right-click the comment icon, and then click **Delete Comment**.

→ Click the comment icon, and then on the **Review** tab, in the **Comments** group, click the **Delete** button.

Tip When you delete a comment, subsequent comments are not renumbered.

➤ **To delete all the comments on the current slide**

→ On the **Review** tab, in the **Comments** group, display the **Delete** list, and then click **Delete All Markup on the Current Slide**.

➤ **To delete all the comments in the presentation**

1. On the **Review** tab, in the **Comments** group, display the **Delete** list, and then click **Delete All Markup in this Presentation**.

2. To confirm the deletion, click **Yes**.

Practice Tasks

The practice files for these tasks are located in the PowerPoint\Objective6 practice file folder. If you want to save the results of the tasks, save them in the same folder with *My* appended to the file name so that you don't overwrite the original practice files.

- In the *WaterUse* presentation, on slide 2, attach the comment *Change date to reflect that of workshop* to the slide. Then on slide 9, attach the comment *Newer data available?* to the citation.

- On the last slide, attach the comment *Native plant graphics would add interest* to the content placeholder. Click away from the comment to close the box, and then edit the comment to read *Colorful native plant graphics would add interest*.

- In the *CompanyMeeting* presentation, delete the comments attached to the title slide. Review the remaining comments in the presentation, and then using only one command, delete them all.

6.2 Apply Proofing Tools

Using AutoCorrect

The AutoCorrect feature detects and automatically corrects many common capitalization and spelling errors, such as *teh* instead of *the* or *WHen* instead of *When*. You can customize AutoCorrect to recognize misspellings you routinely type.

► **To add an entry and its replacement to the AutoCorrect list**

1. On the **Proofing** page of the **PowerPoint Options** dialog box, in the **AutoCorrect options** area, click **AutoCorrect Options**.

2. On the **AutoCorrect** page of the **AutoCorrect** dialog box, in the **Replace** box above the list, enter the misspelling.

3. In the **With** box, enter the correction.

4. Click **Add**, and then click **OK**.

> **Tip** You can also use AutoCorrect entries to automate the typing of frequently used text, such as replacing an abbreviation for the full name of your company.

Correcting Spelling Mistakes

Most misspellings are the result of finger-positioning errors or memory lapses. You can ensure that the words in your presentations are spelled correctly in the following ways:

- By default, PowerPoint checks the spelling of anything you type against its built-in dictionary. To draw attention to words that are not in its dictionary and that might be misspelled, PowerPoint underlines them with a red wavy underline. If you want, you can correct these errors as you make them.

> **Tip** To turn off this on-going spell-checking, on the Proofing page of the PowerPoint Options dialog box, clear the Check Spelling As You Type check box.

- You can ignore the red wavy underlines and instead handle all the potential misspellings in the presentation at one time by clicking options in the Spelling dialog box.

- You can add correctly spelled words that are flagged as misspellings to the supplemental dictionary (called *CUSTOM.DIC*) so that PowerPoint will not flag them in the future.

➤ To correct a word with a red wavy underline

→ Right-click the word, and click the suggested replacement you want.

➤ To check the spelling of the entire presentation at one time

1. With slide 1 active, on the **Review** tab, in the **Proofing** group, click the **Spelling** button.

2. In the **Spelling** dialog box, do one of the following:

- To ignore the flagged word, click **Ignore** or **Ignore All**.

- To change the flagged word, click a suggested correction, or enter the correction in the **Change to** box. Then click either **Change** or **Change All**.

- To delete a duplicated word, click **Delete**.

- To add a spelling to the supplemental dictionary, click **Add**.

- To add a spelling to the AutoCorrect list, click **AutoCorrect**.

3. When a message tells you that the spelling check is complete, click **OK**.

Finding and Replacing Text and Fonts

You can find and change specific words in the following ways:

- Locate each occurrence of a word, part of a word, or a phrase. You can specify whether you want to match the exact capitalization (known as the *case*) or whole words.

- Locate each occurrence of a word, part of a word, or a phrase and replace it with something else. You can replace only a single occurrence or all occurrences. Again, you can specify whether to match capitalization and whole words.

You can also replace a specific font throughout a presentation.

➤ **To find the next instance of specific text**

1. On the **Home** tab, in the **Editing** group, click the **Find** button.

2. In the **Find what** box of the **Find** dialog box, enter the text, and then select the appropriate check boxes.

3. Click **Find Next** until you find the occurrence you want, and then click **Close**.

> **Tip** If you see a message saying that PowerPoint has finished searching the presentation, click OK and then click Close.

➤ **To replace text**

1. On the **Home** tab, in the **Editing** group, click the **Replace** button.

2. In the **Find what** box of the **Replace** dialog box, enter the text you want to replace, and in the **Replace with** box, enter the replacement text. Then select the appropriate check boxes.

3. Click **Find Next**, and then do one of the following:

   ○ To replace the matched instance of the text, click **Replace**.

   ○ To replace all instances, click **Replace All**.

4. Repeat step 3 as necessary, and then click **Close**.

➤ **To replace a font**

1. On the **Home** tab, in the **Editing** group, click the **Replace** arrow, and then click **Replace Fonts**.

2. In the **Replace Font** dialog box, click the font you want to change in the **Replace** list, and click the replacement font in the **With** list.

3. Click **Replace**, and then click **Close**.

Using the Thesaurus

To make sure you're using words that best convey your message, you can use the Thesaurus feature to look up synonyms.

➤ **To find a synonym for a word**

→ Right-click the word, click **Synonyms**, and then click the one you want.

Or

1. Click the word, and then on the **Review** tab, in the **Proofing** group, click the **Thesaurus** button.

2. In the **Research** task pane, point to the synonym you want, click the arrow that appears, and then click **Insert**.

> **Tip** If none of the displayed synonyms suits your purpose, click a word that is close to the meaning you want to display synonyms for that word.

Comparing and Combining Presentations

> **Strategy** Viewing, accepting, and rejecting revisions in PowerPoint is not as intuitive as it is in Microsoft Word. Take some time to practice making changes to a presentation and comparing it with the original version to become familiar with ways of working with this feature.

You can compare two versions of the same presentation by merging changes made in one version into the other. The differences are recorded in the combined presentation as revisions. You can view the suggested changes and then accept or reject them.

➤ **To combine two versions of the same presentation**

1. With one version open, on the **Review** tab, in the **Compare** group, click the **Compare** button.

2. In the **Choose File to Merge with Current Presentation** dialog box, locate and double click the version you want to combine.

➤ **To compare the two versions**

1. In the **Revisions** task pane (which opens automatically after you combine two versions), display the **Slides** tab.

2. On the **Slides** tab of the **Overview** pane, click any slide to see the same slide in the other version.

➤ **To accept or reject revisions**

1. Click a paper and pencil icon to display a box detailing the changes.

2. In the box, do the following:

- ○ To accept all changes to an object, select the **All changes to** check box.
- ○ Select and clear the check box of an individual change to see how the slide looks with and without that change implemented.
- ○ Leave the check box selected to accept the change.

> **Tip** To accept all changes on a slide without displaying the detail box, on the Review tab, in the Compare group, click the Accept arrow, and then click Accept All Changes To The Current Slide. If you change your mind, in the Compare group, click the Reject arrow, and then click Reject All Changes To The Current Slide.

3. On the **Review** tab, in the **Compare** group, click the **Next** button to move to the next slide with changes.

4. Work through the presentation, resolving all the differences.

5. When you see a message that there are no more changes, click **Continue**, and if you want, review your decisions.

6. When you are satisfied with the combined version of the presentation, on the **Review** tab, in the **Compare** group, click the **End Review** button to discard unaccepted changes and all markup.

Practice Tasks

The practice files for these tasks are located in the PowerPoint\Objective6 practice file folder. If you want to save the results of the tasks, save them in the same folder with *My* appended to the file name so that you don't overwrite the original practice files.

- In the *CommunityService* presentation, on slide 2, correct the spelling of *infermation*. Then check the spelling of the entire presentation, correcting any mistakes you find. Add the term *CSCom* to the CUSTOM.DIC dictionary, and add the correct spelling of *employes* to the AutoCorrect substitution table.

- In the *CommunityService* presentation, replace any instances of the word *department* with the word *unit*, matching the capitalization. Then replace any instances of the Times New Roman font with the Calibri font.

- On slide 1, use the Thesaurus to replace the word *Executing* with the synonym *Completing*.

- Compare the *AnnualMeetingA* and *AnnualMeetingB* presentations, and merge the differences between them into *AnnualMeetingB*. Then review the marked differences, accept those on slide 1, and reject all other changes.

Objective Review

Before finishing this chapter, ensure that you have mastered the following skills:

6.1 Manage Comments in Presentations

6.2 Apply Proofing Tools

7 Preparing Presentations for Delivery

The skills tested in this section of the Microsoft Office Specialist exam for Microsoft PowerPoint 2010 relate to tasks you might need to perform after content development but before presentation delivery. Specifically, the following objectives are associated with this set of skills:

7.1 Save Presentations

7.2 Share Presentations

7.3 Print Presentations

7.4 Protect Presentations

When all the content development work is over and you are ready to show a presentation to the world, you need to consider the best way to prepare the presentation for its intended audience. Does the presentation need to be saved in a different format? Do you need to take steps to ensure that the file is clean and can be viewed only by the people you want to view it? Do you need to safeguard it from additional changes?

This chapter guides you in studying the various formats in which you can save a presentation, adjusting the file size to the viewing medium, preparing handouts and speaker notes, removing personal and confidential information, assigning passwords, and marking a presentation as final.

> **Practice Files** Before you can complete the practice tasks in this chapter, you need to copy the book's practice files to your computer. The practice files you'll use to complete the tasks in this chapter are in the PowerPoint\Objective7 practice file folder. A complete list of practice files is provided in "Using the Book's Companion Content" at the beginning of this book.

7.1 Save Presentations

By default, PowerPoint 2010 presentations are saved in PPTX format, which is based on XML. Depending on how you intend to distribute a presentation, you can also save it in a variety of other formats.

You can display descriptions of some of the available file formats by displaying the Save & Send page of the Backstage view and clicking Change File Type.

The available formats include the following:

- **PowerPoint 97-2003 Presentation** If you want to share a PowerPoint presentation with users of an earlier version of PowerPoint, you can save it in the PPT file format. Before saving a presentation in this format, you can use the Compatibility Checker to check whether the presentation includes features that are not supported in previous versions of PowerPoint. You can then decide how to handle any reported issues.

- **PowerPoint Show** When PowerPoint 2010 or Microsoft PowerPoint Viewer is installed on the computer, double-clicking a presentation file saved in the PPSX format opens the presentation in Slide Show view instead of Normal view. Pressing Esc closes the presentation.

- **GIF, JPEG, PNG, TIFF, or other graphic format** You can save slides as images that can be inserted in documents or displayed on webpages. You can save only the current slide or every slide in the presentation as an image.

- **Picture presentation** Each slide is saved as a picture. You might want to save a presentation in this format to decrease its size.

- **Outline** When you want to use the text from a presentation in another program, you can save the presentation file as an outline in RTF format.

- **OpenDocument presentation** Selecting this format saves the presentation in such a way that it can be opened in other presentation programs. Some information is lost, and some formatting and functionality is not preserved.

- **PDF or XPS** Selecting either of these formats saves the presentation as an electronic representation of the printed presentation. These files require a PDF or XPS viewer and can no longer be opened, viewed, or edited in PowerPoint.

➤ **To save a presentation for use in an earlier PowerPoint version**

1. On the **Save & Send** page of the Backstage view, click **Change File Type**, and then double-click **PowerPoint 97-2003 Presentation**.

   Or

   In the Backstage view, click **Save As**. Then in the **Save As** dialog box, in the **Save as type** list, click **PowerPoint 97-2003 Presentation**.

2. In the **Save As** dialog box, specify the file name and storage location, and then click **Save**.

➤ **To check for features unsupported in earlier PowerPoint versions**

1. On the **Info** page of the Backstage view, click **Check for Issues**, and then click **Check Compatibility**.

2. Make a note of any issues reported in the **Compatibility Checker** dialog box, and then click **OK**.

➤ **To save a presentation that can be displayed only in Slide Show view**

1. On the **Save & Send** page of the Backstage view, click **Change File Type**, and then double-click **PowerPoint Show**.

Or

In the Backstage view, click **Save As**. Then in the **Save As** dialog box, in the **Save as type** list, click **PowerPoint Show**.

2. In the **Save As** dialog box, specify the file name and storage location, and then click **Save**.

➤ **To save slides as images**

1. In the left pane of the Backstage view, click **Save As**. Then in the **Save As** dialog box, in the **Save as type** list, click the image format you want.

> **Tip** PNG and JPEG are also available on the Save & Send page.

2. In the **Save As** dialog box, specify the file name and storage location, and then click **Save**.

3. In the message box, click **Every Slide**, and then click **OK** to acknowledge the creation of a folder to hold the images.

Or

In the message box, click **Current Slide Only**.

➤ **To save a picture presentation**

1. On the **Save & Send** page of the Backstage view, click **Change File Type**, and then double-click **PowerPoint Picture Presentation**.

Or

In the Backstage view, click **Save As**. Then in the **Save As** dialog box, in the **Save as type** list, click **PowerPoint Picture Presentation**.

2. In the **Save As** dialog box, specify the file name and storage location, and then click **Save**.

3. In the message box, click **OK** to acknowledge that a copy of the presentation has been saved.

➤ **To save a presentation as an outline**

1. In the left pane of the Backstage view, click **Save As**.

2. In the **File name** box of the **Save As** dialog box, specify the name of the file.

3. In the **Save as type** list, click **Outline/RTF**.

4. Navigate to the folder in which you want to store the outline, and click **Save**.

➤ **To save an OpenDocument presentation**

1. On the **Save & Send** page of the Backstage view, click **Change File Type**, and then double-click **OpenDocument Presentation**.

   Or

   In the left pane of the Backstage view, click **Save As**. Then in the **Save As** dialog box, in the **Save as type** list, click **OpenDocument Presentation**.

2. In the **Save As** dialog box, specify the file name and storage location, and then click **Save**.

3. In the message box warning that some features might no longer be available, click **Yes**.

➤ **To save a presentation in PDF or XPS format**

1. On the **Save & Send** page of the Backstage view, click **Create PDF/XPS Document**, and then click the **Create PDF/XPS** button.

2. In the **Publish as PDF or XPS** dialog box, specify the file name and storage location.

3. If you want to create an XPS document, in the **Save as type** list, click **XPS Document**.

4. In the **Publish as PDF or XPS** dialog box, click **Publish**.

   Or

1. In the left pane of the Backstage view, click **Save As**.

2. In the **Save As** dialog box, specify the file name and storage location.

3. In the **Save as type** list, click **PDF** or **XPS Document**.

4. Click the file size that corresponds to your intended use of the presentation file.

5. Click **Options**, change any of the default settings in the **Options** dialog box, and then click **OK** to close the dialog box.

6. In the **Save As** dialog box, click **Save**.

Practice Tasks

The practice file for these tasks is located in the PowerPoint\Objective7 practice file folder. Save the results of the tasks in the same folder.

- Check the *Color* presentation for compatibility with PowerPoint 2003, and then save it as *My Color 2003* in a format that allows the presentation to be opened and edited in that program.

- Save *My Color 2003* as a presentation that can be opened and viewed only in Slide Show view. Name it *My Color Slide Show*.

- Save *My Color Slide Show* in a format that can be opened as an outline in Microsoft Word. Name the file *My Color Outline*.

- Save the *Color* presentation as *My Color PDF* in a PDF format that is suitable for publishing online. Frame the slides, and exclude all non-printing information.

7.2 Share Presentations

> **See Also** For information about creating handouts for shared presentations, see the "Printing Handouts and Notes" topic of section 7.3, "Print Presentations."

Compressing Media

Before you share a media-intensive presentation with other people, you might want to compress the media to make the presentation file smaller and more portable.

> **To compress media**

1. On the **Info** page of the Backstage view, click **Compress Media**, and then click the quality you want.

> **Tip** The Compress Media button appears on the Info page only if the presentation contains audio or video clips.

2. When compression is complete, click **Close** to close the **Compress Media** progress box.

> **Tip** You can reverse a previous compression by clicking Compress Media and then clicking Undo.

> **See Also** For information about compressing pictures, see the "Compressing Pictures" topic of section 3.2, "Manipulate Images."

Packaging for CD Delivery

If you'll deliver your presentation from a computer other than the one on which you developed it, you need to ensure that the fonts, linked objects, and any other necessary items are available during delivery. You can use the Package For CD feature to save all presentation components to a CD (not a DVD) or other type of removable media. You can include more than one presentation, and you can specify the order in which the presentations should run. As part of the packaging process, you can assign a password and remove extraneous information from the packaged file.

After PowerPoint assembles the files, it creates a folder of supporting files and adds an autorun file. When you insert the presentation CD into your CD/DVD drive, the AutoPlay dialog box opens so that you can run the presentation.

> **Tip** To run a packaged presentation from a CD on a computer that does not have PowerPoint 2010 installed, you need the Microsoft PowerPoint Viewer. The PowerPoint Viewer cannot run presentations saved in the new PowerPoint 2010 format from a CD; it must already be installed on the computer.

➤ **To package the open presentation for delivery on a different computer**

1. On the **Save & Send** page of the Backstage view, click **Package Presentation for CD**, and then click **Package for CD**.

2. In the **Name the CD** box of the **Package for CD** dialog box, enter a name for the package. Then click **Options**.

3. In the **Options** dialog box, do any of the following, and then click **OK**:

   ○ Set passwords to open or modify the presentation.

   ○ Select the **Inspect presentations for inappropriate or private information** check box.

4. In the **Package for CD** dialog box, do one of the following:

   ○ Insert a blank CD in your CD/DVD burner, and if the **AutoPlay** dialog box opens, close it. Then click **Copy to CD**.

   ○ Click **Copy to Folder**. Then in the **Copy to Folder** dialog box, specify the folder in which you want to store the package, clear the **Open Folder When Complete** check box, and click **OK**.

5. Click **Yes** to verify that you want to include linked content.

6. If you indicated in step 3 that you want to inspect the presentation, follow the steps in the Document Inspector, and then click **Close**.

> **See Also** For information about the Document Inspector, see section 7.4, "Protect Presentations."

7. When a message tells you that the packaging operation was successful, click **No** to indicate that you don't want to copy the same package again, and then click **Close**.

8. Test the folder or CD by running the packaged presentation.

Creating Videos

The simplest way to ensure that people can view a presentation whether or not they have PowerPoint installed on their computers is to turn it into a video. While creating the video, you can select the output size and, if the presentation has no slide timings or narration, you can create them. (If a presentation does not have slide timings, by default each slide in the video will display for five seconds.)

➤ **To save the open presentation as a video**

1. On the **Save & Send** page of the Backstage view, click **Create a Video**.

2. In the **Create a Video** pane, click the intended output (**Computer & HD Displays**, **Internet & DVD**, or **Portable Devices**) in the first list.

3. In the second list, do one of the following:

   ○ Click **Don't Use Recorded Timings and Narrations**.

   ○ Click **Use Recorded Timings and Narrations**.

   ○ Click **Record Timings and Narrations**, and then in the **Record Slide Show** dialog box, specify what you want to record, and click **Start Recording**.

   > **See Also** For information about recording slide timings, see section 8.2, "Set Up Slide Shows."

   ○ Click **Preview Timings and Narrations**, and then press Esc or click the mouse button to return to the Backstage view after you have previewed the slides.

4. When you are ready, click **Create Video**.

5. In the **Save As** dialog box, specify the location and name of the file, and click **Save**.

Practice Tasks

The practice file for these tasks is located in the PowerPoint\Objective7 practice file folder.

- Save the *HealthyEcosystems* presentation in the same folder with the name *MyHealthyEcosystems*, and then shrink the file size as much as possible so that you can share the presentation as an email attachment.

- Save the *MyHealthyEcosystems* presentation in a folder named *Delivery* in such a way that it can be transported to a different computer for delivery.

- Save the *MyHealthyEcosystems* presentation as a video that can be played on any computer.

7.3   Print Presentations

Previewing and Printing

If you want to deliver a presentation by using transparencies on an overhead projector, you need to print your presentation on special sheets of acetate. Even if you plan to deliver your presentation electronically, you might want to print your presentation to proof it for typographical errors and stylistic inconsistencies.

Assuming that you have already set the slide size and orientation of your presentation, you can preview it to see how the slides will look when printed. If you will be printing a color presentation on a monochrome (usually black ink) printer, it's a good idea to preview in pure black and white or grayscale (shades of gray) to verify that the text is legible against the background.

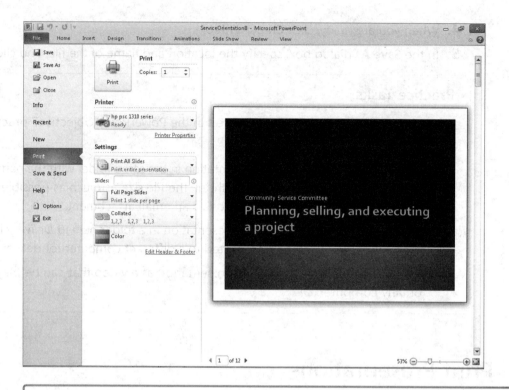

> **Tip** In Normal view, you can see how your slides will look when printed on a mono-
> chrome printer by clicking either the Grayscale or the Black And White button in the
> Color/Grayscale group on the View tab.

When you are ready to print, you can quickly print one copy of each slide on the default
printer with the default settings. You can adjust any of the following settings:

- **Specify the printer to use** You can specify the printer you want to use and set its
  properties (such as paper source and image compression).

- **Specify which slides to print** You can print all the slides, the selected slides,
  or the current slide. You can print only specific slides by clicking the Slides box
  and entering slide numbers and ranges separated by commas (no spaces). For
  example, enter 1,5,10-12 to print slides 1, 5, 10, 11, and 12.

- **Print hidden slides** You can include slides in the printed version that will be hidden
  in the electronic presentation.

- **Specify what to print** You can print slides (one per page), notes pages (one half-
  size slide per page with space for notes), an outline, or handouts. When printing
  handouts, you can specify the number of slides that print on each page (1, 2, 3, 4,
  6, or 9) and the order in which the slides appear on the page.

- **Put a frame around slides** You can print a frame around the slides on the printed page.

- **Scale slides to fit the paper** If you haven't set the size of the slides to match the size of the paper in the printer, PowerPoint can automatically reduce or increase the size of the slides to fit the paper when you print them.

- **Print in high quality** For final output, you can specify that the slides be printed in the printer's highest quality.

- **Print comments and ink markup** You can print electronic or handwritten notes attached to the presentation so that you can review them along with the slides.

- **Print and collate multiple copies** If you want to print multiple copies of a presentation, you can specify whether complete copies should be printed one at a time.

- **Specify the color range** You can print your presentation in color (color on a color printer and grayscale on a monochrome printer), grayscale (on a color or monochrome printer), or pure black and white (no gray on either a color or monochrome printer).

➤ **To preview a presentation**

→ On the **Print** page of the Backstage view, in the right pane, click the **Next Page** or **Previous Page** button to move among the slides.

→ In the right pane of the **Print** page, click the **Zoom In** or **Zoom Out** button or drag the **Zoom** slider to zoom in or out. Click the **Zoom to Page** button to fit the slide to the pane.

➤ **To print one copy of all the slides with the default settings**

→ On the **Print** page of the Backstage view, at the top of the center pane, click **Print**.

➤ **To change the settings for slides, or to print handouts, notes, or an outline**

1. On the **Print** page of the Backstage view, in the center pane, under **Settings**, display the second list, and then click the presentation component you want to print.

2. Change other settings as necessary, and then at the top of the center pane, click **Print**.

Printing Handouts and Notes

You don't need to do anything special to print simple audience handouts that show pictures of a presentation's slides with room for taking handwritten notes. If you want handouts that include text as well as the pictures, you can send the presentation to a Word document in one of five layouts so that you can customize the content in Word.

If you use speaker notes when delivering a presentation to an audience, you can enter text in the Notes pane in Normal view. If you want speaker notes that include pictures or other supporting materials as well as text, you can develop the speaker notes in Notes Page view.

> **Tip** If you use two monitors and Presenter view to deliver the presentation, you don't need to print speaker notes. You can see the notes on one monitor while the audience sees the presentation in Slide Show view through the other monitor. For information about Presenter view, see section 8.2, "Set Up Slide Shows."

The design of handouts and notes is controlled by their masters. You can customize them by using the same techniques you use to customize slide masters.

➤ To create handouts in Word

1. On the **Save & Send** page of the Backstage view, under **File Types** in the middle pane, click **Create Handouts**.

2. In the right pane of the **Save & Send** page, click **Create Handouts**.

3. In the **Send To Microsoft Word** dialog box, click the notes format you want.

> **Tip** If you select Outline Only, the text of the presentation appears in the document as a bulleted list.

4. Under **Add slides to Microsoft Word Document**, click **Paste** or **Paste Link**, and then click **OK**.

5. In Word, add the desired text or other content, and then save the document.

➤ **To display Notes Page view**

→ On the **View** tab, in the **Presentation Views** group, click the **Notes Page** button.

➤ **To customize the handout or notes master**

1. On the **View** tab, in the **Master Views** group, click the **Handout Master** button or the **Notes Master** button.

2. On the **Handout Master** tab or the **Notes Master** tab, make the changes you want by clicking buttons in the **Page Setup**, **Placeholders**, **Edit Theme**, and **Background** groups.

3. On the preview page, customize the text in the **Header**, **Footer**, **Date**, and **Page Number** placeholders. For notes, also make any necessary adjustments to the **Notes** placeholder in the bottom half of the page.

4. Click the **Close Master View** button to return to the previous view.

Practice Tasks

The practice files for these tasks are located in the PowerPoint\Objective7 practice file folder. If you want to save the results of the tasks, save them in the same folder with *My* appended to the file name so that you don't overwrite the original practice file.

- In the *Harmony* presentation, print slides 1, 2, 3, and 5 in grayscale with frames.

- Send the *Harmony* presentation to a Word document, and name that document *MyHandouts*.

- On slide 1 of the *Harmony* presentation, add the note *Establish level of prior knowledge*. Then on slide 3, add the *YinYang* graphic file to the note.

- From the *Harmony* presentation, print one set of handouts with three slides per page in color. Then print a set of speaker notes in grayscale.

7.4 Protect Presentations

Removing Extraneous Information

Presentations are often delivered electronically, as attachments to email messages or as files that can be downloaded from a website. Before distributing a presentation, you will want to remove the identifying and tracking properties attached by PowerPoint while the presentation was being developed. These properties include information such as the author's name, the title, and when the file was created and updated. You might also have attached other properties, such as keywords. To ensure that all properties are removed, you can use the Document Inspector feature, which can also flag and remove items such as comments, notes, and other extraneous content.

➤ **To remove information before distributing a presentation**

1. On the **Info** page of the Backstage view, click **Check for Issues**, and then click **Inspect Document**.

2. In the **Document Inspector** dialog box, clear the check boxes for types of information you don't want to locate, and then click **Inspect**.

3. When the Document Inspector reports its findings, click **Remove All** for any type of information you want to remove.

4. Click **Close** to close the **Document Inspector** dialog box.

Assigning Passwords

The simplest way to control access to a presentation is to assign a password to it. You can assign two types of passwords:

- **Password to open** Assigning this type of password encrypts the presentation so that only people with the password can open and view it.

- **Password to modify** Assigning this type of password does not encrypt the presentation, so anyone can open and view it. However, to make changes or save a copy with a different name, they must supply the password.

Tip You can also assign a password to open a presentation from the Info page of the Backstage view.

To open a presentation to which a password to open has been assigned, you must enter the exact password, including capitalization, numbers, spaces, and symbols. To open a presentation to which a password to modify has been assigned, you can either enter the exact password to open and modify it or open a version that you can view but not modify.

➤ **To set a password for a presentation**

1. In the left pane of the Backstage view, click **Save As**.

2. At the bottom of the **Save As** dialog box, in the **Tools** list, click **General Options**.

3. In the **General Options** dialog box, in the **Password to open** or **Password to modify** box, enter the password you want, and then click **OK**.

4. In the **Confirm Password** dialog box, in the **Reenter password to open** or **Reenter password to modify** box, retype the password you previously entered, and then click **OK**.

> **Tip** In the General Options dialog box, you can enter both passwords. In that case, you will be asked to confirm each in turn.

5. In the **Save As** dialog box, click **Save**.

   Or

1. On the **Info** page of the Backstage view, click **Protect Presentation**, and then click **Encrypt with Password**.

2. In the **Encrypt Document** dialog box, enter the password, and then click **OK**.

3. In the **Confirm Password** dialog box, retype the password you previously entered, and then click **OK**.

➤ **To change the password of an open presentation**

1. In the **General Options** dialog box, change the entry in the **Password to open** or **Password to modify** box, and then click **OK**.

2. In the **Confirm Password** dialog box, in the **Reenter password to open** or **Reenter password to modify** box, retype the new password, and then click **OK**.

3. In the **Save As** dialog box, click **Save**.

   Or

1. On the **Info** page of the Backstage view, click **Protect Presentation**, and then click **Encrypt with Password**.

2. In the **Encrypt Document** dialog box, change the password, and then click **OK**.

3. In the **Confirm Password** dialog box, retype the password you previously entered, and then click **OK**.

➤ **To delete the password of an open presentation**

→ Follow the instructions for changing a password, deleting the existing entry.

Marking as Final

Before distributing a presentation, you should mark it as final. This feature saves the file, deactivates most PowerPoint tools, and displays an information bar at the top of the screen to indicate that no further changes should be made to the presentation. However, you can easily override the final status and make changes to the presentation.

➤ **To mark a presentation as final**

1. On the **Info** page of the Backstage view, click **Protect Presentation**, and then click **Mark as Final**.
2. In the message box, click **OK**, and then click **OK** in the confirmation box.

➤ **To turn off the final status**

→ In the information bar above the document, click **Edit Anyway**.

Attaching Digital Signatures

When you create a presentation that will be distributed to other people via email or the web, you might want to attach a digital signature to it to authenticate its origin. Attaching a digital signature should be the last task you perform on a presentation, because changing the presentation after signing it invalidates the signature.

➤ **To attach a digital signature to a presentation**

1. On the **Info** page of the Backstage view, click **Protect Presentation**, and then click **Add a Digital Signature**.
2. If a message box opens, click **OK**.
3. In the **Sign** dialog box, enter a purpose if desired, and then click **Sign**.
4. In the **Signature Confirmation** message box, click **OK**.

➤ **To view the digital signature attached to a presentation**

1. On the **Info** page of the Backstage view, click **View Signatures**.
2. In the **Signatures** task pane, click the signature, click the arrow that appears to the right, and then click **Signature Details**.
3. In the **Signature Details** dialog box, click **View**.
4. In the **Certificate** dialog box, examine the information on the **General** and **Details** pages, and then click **OK**.
5. In the **Signature Details** dialog box, click **Close**.

➤ **To remove the digital signature**

1. In the **Signatures** task pane, click the signature, click the arrow, and then click **Remove Signature**.

2. In the message box, click **Yes** to permanently remove the signature.

Practice Tasks

The practice file for these tasks is located in the PowerPoint\Objective7 practice file folder. If you want to save the results of the tasks, save them in the same folder with *My* appended to the file name so that you don't overwrite the original practice file.

- In the *Meeting* presentation, remove all identifying and tracking information and comments from the file.

- Assign the password *P@ssword* to the *Meeting* presentation so that the file can be opened but not changed. Then save the presentation with the name *MyPassword*, and close it.

- Open a read-only version of the password-protected *MyPassword* presentation, try to make a change, and then close it. Then open a version you can edit, delete the word *key* in the first two bullets on the last slide, and save the presentation.

- Mark the *Meeting* presentation as final.

Objective Review

Before finishing this chapter, ensure that you have mastered the following skills:

7.1 Save Presentations

7.2 Share Presentations

7.3 Print Presentations

7.4 Protect Presentations

8 Delivering Presentations

The skills tested in this section of the Microsoft Office Specialist exam for Microsoft PowerPoint 2010 relate to preparing a presentation for delivery. Specifically, the following objectives are associated with this set of skills:

8.1 Apply Presentation Tools

8.2 Set Up Slide Shows

8.3 Set Presentation Timing

8.4 Record Presentations

On the surface, delivering a presentation is a simple matter of displaying it in Slide Show view and clicking through the slides. However, PowerPoint provides several options when it comes to delivering a presentation, and it is a good idea to be aware of the possibilities so that you can ensure that the delivery goes as smoothly as possible.

This chapter guides you in studying the tools available for adding value to a presentation, as well as those you can use to deliver the presentation in various ways.

> **Practice Files** Before you can complete the practice tasks in this chapter, you need to copy the book's practice files to your computer. The practice files you'll use to complete the tasks in this chapter are in the PowerPoint\Objective8 practice file folder. A complete list of practice files is provided in "Using the Book's Companion Content" at the beginning of this book.

8.1 Apply Presentation Tools

During a presentation, you can reinforce your message by drawing on slides with an electronic "pen" or changing the background behind text with a highlighter.

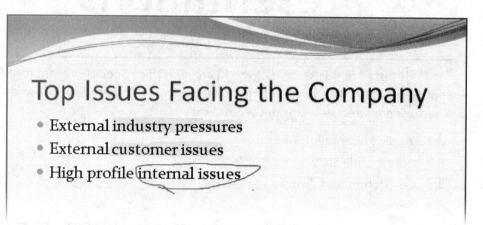

The pen color is determined by a setting in the Set Up Show dialog box, but you can easily change the pen color during the presentation.

➤ **To use a pen or highlighter**

1. In Slide Show view, move the cursor over the slide to display the navigation toolbar. Then click the **Pen** button, and click either **Pen** or **Highlighter**.

    Or

    Right-click anywhere on the screen, click **Pointer Options**, and then click either **Pen** or **Highlighter**.

    > **Tip** Right-clicking the screen displays a shortcut menu only if the Show Menu On Right Mouse Click check box is selected on the Advanced page of the PowerPoint Options dialog box.

2. Use the tool to annotate the slide.

3. Turn off the pen or highlighter by clicking the **Pen** button and then clicking **Arrow**.

    Or

    Right-click the screen, click **Pointer Options**, and then click **Arrow**.

> **Tip** When the pen or highlighter tool is active in Slide Show view, clicking the mouse button does not advance the slide show to the next slide. You need to switch back to the regular pointer to use the mouse to advance the slide.

➤ **To change the pen color before the presentation**

1. On the **Slide Show** tab, in the **Set Up** group, click the **Set Up Slide Show** button.

2. In the **Set Up Show** dialog box, change the **Pen color** setting to the desired color, and then click **OK**.

➤ **To change the pen color during the presentation**

→ Display the navigation toolbar, click the **Pen** button, click **Ink Color**, and then in the palette, click the color you want.

→ Right-click the screen, click **Pointer Options**, click **Ink Color**, and then in the palette, click the color you want.

➤ **To erase an annotation**

→ Display the navigation toolbar, click the **Pen** button, click **Eraser**, and then click the annotation you want to remove.

→ Right-click the screen, click **Pointer Options**, click **Eraser**, and then click the annotation you want to remove.

➤ **To remove all annotations on a slide**

→ On the navigation toolbar, click the **Pen** button, and then click **Erase All Ink on Slide**.

→ Right-click the screen, click **Pointer Options**, and then click **Erase All Ink on Slide**.

➤ **To discard or retain annotations when you close the presentation**

1. Press Esc to stop the presentation.

2. When a message asks whether you want to keep your ink annotations, click **Keep** or **Discard**.

> **Tip** If you click Keep in the message box, you cannot erase the annotations later. You must close the presentation without saving to remove the annotations.

Practice Tasks

The practice file for these tasks is located in the PowerPoint\Objective8 practice file folder. If you want to save the results of the tasks, save them in the same folder with *My* appended to the file name so that you don't overwrite the original practice file.

- In the *Meeting* presentation, change the default pen color to bright blue (the fifth theme color). Then switch to Slide Show view, and on slide 6, underline the word *customer*.

- On slide 6, use a red pen to draw circles around the two instances of *External* and the word *internal*.

- On slide 6, erase the line under the word *customer*. Then highlight the word instead.

- End the *Meeting* presentation, keeping all the ink annotations.

8.2 Set Up Slide Shows

Adjusting Slide Show Settings

The final preparations for delivering a presentation depend on the delivery method. In the Set Up Show dialog box, you can specify the following:

- How the presentation will be delivered
- Whether all slides will be shown, or just a slide subset
- Whether an automatic slide show will loop continuously, be shown without narration, and be shown without animation
- Whether slide timings will be used
- Whether your hardware setup includes multiple monitors, and if so whether you want to use Presenter view
- What pen color and laser pointer color should be used

➤ To set up a presentation for delivery

1. On the **Slide Show** tab, in the **Set Up** group, click the **Set Up Slide Show** button.

2. In the **Set Up Show** dialog box, select the options you want, and then click **OK**.

➤ To specify that narrations should be played during presentation delivery

→ On the **Slide Show** tab, in the **Set Up** group, select or clear the **Play Narrations** check box.

→ In the **Set Up Show** dialog box, in the **Show options** area, select or clear the **Show without narration** check box.

➤ To specify that slide timings should be used during presentation delivery

→ On the **Slide Show** tab, in the **Set Up** group, select or clear the **Use Timings** check box.

→ In the **Set Up Show** dialog box, in the **Advance slides** area, click **Use timings, if present**.

➤ To specify that media controls should be shown during presentation delivery

→ On the **Slide Show** tab, in the **Set Up** group, select or clear the **Show Media Controls** check box.

Setting Up Presenter View

If your computer can support two monitors, or if you will be presenting a slide show from your computer through a projector, you can control the presentation on one monitor while the audience sees the slides in Slide Show view on the delivery monitor or the projector screen.

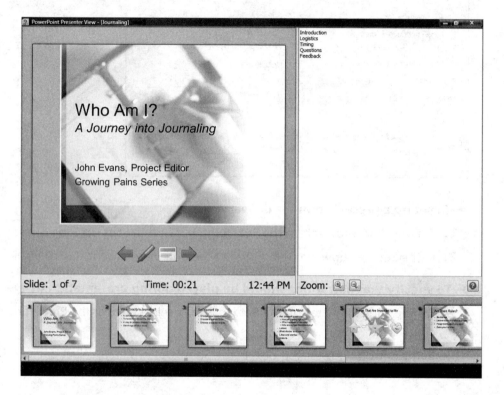

➤ **To deliver a presentation on one monitor and use Presenter view on another**

1. Open the **Set Up Show** dialog box.

2. In the **Multiple monitors** area, in the **Display slide show on** list, click the name of the monitor you want to use to show the slides to your audience.

3. Select the **Show Presenter View** check box, and then click **OK**.

4. With the title slide of the presentation active, switch to Slide Show view.

5. On the control monitor, use the Presenter view tools to control the presentation.

   Or

1. On the **Slide Show** tab, in the **Monitors** group, click the **Show On** arrow.

2. In the list, click the name of the monitor you want to use to show the slides to your audience.

3. In the **Monitors** group, select the **Use Presenter View** check box.

4. With the title slide of the presentation active, switch to Slide Show view.

5. On the control monitor, use the Presenter view tools to control the presentation.

Broadcasting Slide Shows

When the audience for a presentation is scattered in various locations, you can use a broadcast service to make the presentation available over the Internet. The audience can see the presentation in their web browsers and interact via a conference call.

➤ **To broadcast a presentation**

1. On the **Save & Send** page of the Backstage view, click **Broadcast Slide Show** in the center pane, and then click **Broadcast Slide Show** in the right pane.

   Or

   On the **Slide Show** tab, in the **Start Slide Show** group, click the **Broadcast Slide Show** button.

2. In the **Broadcast Slide Show** dialog box, click **Start Broadcast** to connect to the service listed in the Broadcast Service area.

> **Tip** You can click Change Broadcast Service to add a different service.

3. When a link to the website from which the presentation will be broadcast appears, do one of the following:

   - Click **Copy Link** so that you can paste the location of the presentation when notifying your audience about its date and time.

   - Click **Send in Email**, and when your email program opens a message window containing the link, enter the email addresses of the reviewers, and click **Send**.

4. At the appointed time, in the **Broadcast Slide Show** dialog box, click **Start Slide Show**, and click through the slides.

5. When you reach the last slide, click again to return to Normal view.

6. In the **Broadcast View** banner at the top of the workspace, click **End Broadcast**, and then in the message box, confirm that you want to end the broadcast.

Creating Custom Slide Shows

If you need to deliver variations of the same presentation to different audiences, you should first prepare one presentation containing all the slides you are likely to need for all the audiences. Then you can select the slides that are appropriate for a particular audience and group them as a custom slide show.

When you need to deliver the presentation for that audience, you open the main presentation and show the subset of slides by choosing the custom slide show from a list.

➤ To create a custom slide show

1. On the **Slide Show** tab, in the **Start Slide Show** group, click the **Custom Slide Show** button, and then click **Custom Shows**.

2. In the **Custom Shows** dialog box, click **New**.

> **Tip** To change an existing custom show, click Edit in the Custom Shows dialog box.

3. In the **Slide show name** box of the **Define Custom Show** dialog box, enter a name for the custom show.

4. In the **Slides in presentation** list, click the slides you want, click **Add**, and then click **OK**.

5. In the **Custom Shows** dialog box, click **Close**.

   Or

   Click **Show** to switch to Slide Show view with the first slide of the new custom show displayed.

➤ **To deliver a custom show**

→ On the **Slide Show** tab, in the **Start Slide Show** group, click the **Custom Slide Show** button, and then click the custom show you want.

Or

1. In Slide Show view, move the mouse to display the navigation toolbar.

2. On the navigation toolbar, click the **Navigation** button, click **Custom Show**, and then click the show you want.

Practice Tasks

The practice file for these tasks is located in the PowerPoint\Objective8 practice file folder. If you want to save the results of the tasks, save them in the same folder with *My* appended to the file name so that you don't overwrite the original practice file.

- Set up the *DirectorsMeeting* presentation, and to loop continuously without narration or animation.

- Set up the *DirectorsMeeting* presentation so that it starts on slide 2 and advances from one slide to the next only when you click the Next or Previous button on the navigation toolbar.

- In the *DirectorsMeeting* presentation, create a custom show named *Managers* that includes slides 1, 3, 4, 5, 7, and 10. Then edit the custom show to add slide 11.

8.3 Set Presentation Timing

When delivering a presentation, you can move from slide to slide in the following ways:

- **Manually** You control when you move by clicking the mouse button, pressing keys, or clicking commands.

- **Automatically** PowerPoint displays each slide for a predefined length of time and then displays the next slide.

For automatic slide shows, the length of time a slide appears on the screen is controlled by its slide timing. You can apply timings to a single slide, to a group of slides, or to an entire presentation, either by allocating the same amount of time to each slide or by rehearsing the presentation while PowerPoint automatically tracks and sets the timings for you.

Recording	▼ ✕
➡ ‖	0:00:01 ↺ 0:00:01

➤ **To apply the same timing to all slides**

1. On the **Transitions** tab, under **Advance Slide** in the **Timing** group, clear the **On Mouse Click** check box, and select the **After** check box. Then specify the timing in the adjacent box.

2. In the **Timing** group, click the **Apply To All** button.

> **Tip** When you click Apply To All, all the transition effects applied to the current slide are transferred to the other slides. If you have applied different transitions to different slides, those individually specified transitions are overwritten. So it's a good idea to apply all the effects that you want the slides to have in common first. Then you can select individual slides and customize their effects.

➤ **To apply the same timing to a group of slides**

1. Switch to Slide Sorter view, and select the slides.

2. On the **Transitions** tab, under **Advance Slide** in the **Timing** group, select the **After** check box. Then specify the timing in the adjacent box.

➤ **To rehearse a presentation**

1. With slide 1 displayed, on the **Slide Show** tab, in the **Set Up** group, click the **Rehearse Timings** button.

2. Rehearse the presentation.

> **Tip** To repeat the rehearsal for a particular slide, on the Recording toolbar, click the Repeat button to reset the time for that slide to 0:00:00. To start the entire rehearsal over again, click the Recording toolbar's Close button, and when a message asks whether you want to keep the existing timings, click No.

3. At the end of the slide show, click **Yes** to apply the recorded slide timings to the slides.

Practice Tasks

The practice file for these tasks is located in the PowerPoint\Objective8 practice file folder. If you want to save the results of the tasks, save them in the same folder with *My* appended to the file name so that you don't overwrite the original practice file.

- In the *Landscaping* presentation, set a timing of 01:00 for slides 1, 2, and 3.
- Use the quickest method to apply the timing of the first three slides of the *Landscaping* presentation to all the slides.
- Rehearse the delivery of the first three slides of the *Landscaping* presentation, and then apply the rehearsed timings to the slides.

8.4 Record Presentations

You might want to record a presentation while practicing its delivery so that you can correct any flaws before you have to perform before a live audience. You might also want to record a presentation so that people can view it on their computers. When you record a presentation, you can specify the following:

- Whether to record from the first slide or from the current slide
- Whether to include slide and animation timings
- Whether to include narrations and laser pointer movements

Timings recorded with the presentation can be used to move automatically from one slide to the next. Narrations are embedded in each slide as audio objects that can be clicked to play the narration.

➤ **To record a presentation**

1. Assuming that your computer has a sound card, microphone, and speakers and that you have tested the microphone before beginning the recording, open the presentation you want to record, and do one of the following:
   - On the **Slide Show** tab, in the **Set Up** group, click the **Record Slide Show** button.
   - Display the slide from which you want to start the recording, display the **Record Slide Show** list, and then click **Start Recording from Current Slide**.

2. In the **Record Slide Show** dialog box, select or clear the **Slide and animation timings** and **Narrations and laser pointer** check boxes.

3. Click **Start Recording**.

4. Discuss the slides, just as if you were delivering the presentation to a live audience.

> **Tip** You can pause the recording by clicking the Pause button on the Recording toolbar, and you can repeat the recording for the current slide by clicking the Repeat button. You can stop recording by pressing the Esc key.

5. When you have finished delivering the presentation, right-click the screen, and then click **End Show**.

6. Test the recording by switching to Reading view and, if appropriate, clicking the audio icon on each slide.

➤ To repeat the recording for a slide

→ Delete the slide's sound icon, and then record that slide again.

> **Tip** If you are archiving a presentation and want to add comments to a selected slide, on the Insert tab, in the Media group, display the Audio list, and then click Record Audio. After recording your comments, name the sound file for that slide, and click OK. The narration is then attached to a sound icon on the slide.

Practice Tasks

The practice file for these tasks is located in the PowerPoint\Objective8 practice file folder. If you want to save the results of the tasks, save them in the same folder with *My* appended to the file name so that you don't overwrite the original practice file.

- In the *BackyardEcosystems* presentation, record slide timings and narrations for only slide 4.

- Record slide timings and narrations for slides 2 and 3. Then repeat the recording for slide 3.

- Record new slide timings and narrations for the entire *BackyardEcosystems* presentation, starting with slide 1.

Objective Review

Before finishing this chapter, ensure that you have mastered the following skills:

8.1   Apply Presentation Tools

8.2   Set Up Slide Shows

8.3   Set Presentation Timing

8.4   Record Presentations

Exam 77-884

Microsoft
Outlook 2010

This part of the book covers the skills you need to have for certification as a Microsoft Office Specialist in Microsoft Outlook 2010. Specifically, you need to be able to complete tasks that demonstrate the following skill sets:

1 Managing the Outlook Environment

2 Creating and Formatting Item Content

3 Managing Email Messages

4 Managing Contacts

5 Managing Calendar Objects

6 Working with Tasks, Notes, and Journal Entries

With these skills, you can communicate with colleagues and perform the scheduling and tracking tasks that are important to working efficiently in a business environment.

Prerequisites

We assume that you have been working with Outlook 2010 for at least six months and that you know how to carry out fundamental tasks that are not specifically mentioned in the Microsoft Office Specialist objectives for Exam 77-884, "Microsoft Outlook 2010." Before you begin studying for this exam, you might want to make sure you are familiar with the information in this section.

Module-Specific Behavior

Mail

Each time you start Outlook and connect to your email server, any new messages received since the last time you connected appear in your Inbox. Depending on your settings, Outlook downloads either the entire message to your computer or only the message header. The headers, which are listed in the content pane to the right of the Navigation Pane, provide basic information about the message, such as:

- The item type (such as message, meeting request, or task assignment)
- Who sent it
- When you received it
- The subject
- If you forwarded or replied to it
- If it contains attachments
- If it has been digitally signed or encrypted
- If it has been marked as being of high or low importance

Messages you haven't yet read are indicated by closed envelope icons and bold headers. You can view the text of a message in several ways:

- You can open a message in its own window by double-clicking its header in the message list.
- You can read a message without opening it by clicking its header in the message list to display the message in the Reading Pane.

Calendar

When you display the Calendar module, the Navigation Pane changes to display a list of the calendars you can display. When the To-Do Bar is minimized or off, the Navigation Pane also displays the Date Navigator.

Contacts, Tasks, Notes, and Journal

When you display these modules, the Navigation Pane changes to display the various contact, task, or note lists you can display. To the right of the content pane in the Contacts module, you can click alphabetic buttons to quickly jump to contact names starting with a specific letter.

Switching Views

You can use commands on the View tab of the ribbon to display different views of module content. If none of the standard views meets your needs, you can click the View Settings button in the Current View group on the View tab to define a custom view of the information in the current module.

Creating Outlook Items

You can create any type of Outlook item from any module. You can also create folders to contain mail messages, calendar information, contact records, and so on. You must specify the type of items the folder will contain when you create it.

➤ **To create an item specific to the current module**

→ On the **Home** tab, in the **New** group, click the **New <Item>** button.

> **Tip** The New <Item> button is labeled to match the current module. For example, in the Mail module, the New group contains the New E-mail button and the New Items button.

➤ **To create any item from any module**

→ On the **Home** tab, in the **New** group, click the **New Items** button, and then click the type of item you want to create.

➤ **To create a folder**

1. On the **Folder** tab, in the **New** group, click the **New Folder** button.
2. In the **Create New Folder** dialog box, enter a name for the folder in the **Name** box, and then in the **Folder contains** list, click **Calendar Items**, **Contact Items**, **InfoPath Form Items**, **Journal Items**, **Mail and Post Items**, **Note Items**, or **Task Items**.
3. In the **Select where to place the folder** list, click the location in which you want to create the folder.
4. In the **Create New Folder** dialog box, click **OK**.

Addressing Messages

Addressing an email message is as simple as typing the intended recipient's email address into the To box. If you want to send a message to more than one person, separate the addresses with semicolons.

As you type in the To, Cc, or Bcc box, Outlook might display matching addresses in a list below the box. Select a name or email address from the list and then press Tab or Enter to insert the entire name or address in the box.

If your email account is part of an Exchange Server network, you can send messages to another person on the same network by typing only his or her email alias (for example, *joan*)—the at symbol (@) and domain name aren't required.

If a message recipient's address is in your address book, you can type the person's name and Outlook will look for the corresponding email address. (You can either wait for Outlook to validate the name or press Ctrl+K to immediately validate the names and addresses you type.) By default, Outlook searches your Global Address List and main address book, but you can instruct the program to search other address books as well. If no address book contains an entry for the name you typed, when you send the message, Outlook prompts you to select an address book entry or create a new contact.

➤ **To have Outlook search additional address books**

1. On the **Home** tab, in the **Find** group, click **Address Book**.
2. In the **Address Book** window, on the **Tools** menu, click **Options**.
3. In the **Addressing** dialog box, click **Custom**, and then click **Add**.
4. In the **Add Address List** dialog box, click the address list you want to add, click **Add**, and then click **Close**.
5. In the **Addressing** dialog box, click **OK**, and then close the **Address Book** window.

Editing and Formatting Message Content

The certification exam is likely to focus on using Outlook 2010 to manage and organize information. Nevertheless, you should be familiar with the Office 2010 techniques for editing and formatting text; applying themes and page backgrounds; and inserting lists, tables, charts, and graphics. All of these functions work in the same way as they do in Microsoft Word 2010, which is the default Outlook 2010 mail editor.

1 Managing the Outlook Environment

The skills tested in this section of the Microsoft Office Specialist exam for Microsoft Outlook 2010 relate to the Outlook working environment. Specifically, the following objectives are associated with this set of skills:

1.1 Apply and Manipulate Outlook Program Options

1.2 Manipulate Item Tags

1.3 Arrange the Content Pane

1.4 Apply Search and Filter Tools

1.5 Print an Outlook Item

With Outlook 2010, it's easy to configure program settings and the working environment to fit your needs. In addition, Outlook includes sophisticated features for managing, locating, and printing Outlook items such as messages, contact details, and calendar information.

This chapter guides you in studying the program settings available in the Outlook Options dialog box, setting and viewing Outlook item properties, displaying Outlook items in the content pane, working with reminders, displaying information about contacts in the People Pane, locating Outlook items by using Search Folders and the search functionality, and printing Outlook items and attachments.

> **Practice Files** You don't need any practice files to complete the practice tasks in this chapter. For more information about practice file requirements, see "Using the Book's Companion Content" at the beginning of this book.

1.1 Apply and Manipulate Outlook Program Options

You can control the settings and appearance of many Outlook features from the Outlook Options dialog box. The Outlook Options dialog box is divided into pages of general Office settings, Outlook module-specific settings, feature-specific settings (for the ribbon and for the Quick Access Toolbar), and security-related settings.

> **Tip** The Microsoft Office Specialist exam for Outlook 2010 includes objectives related to Outlook-specific settings for the Mail, Calendar, Contacts, Tasks, and Notes modules. The exam also includes objectives for the Outlook Journal, Language options, and Advanced options. These objectives are all covered in this book. However, the Outlook Options dialog box contains other options that are not included on the exam and are not covered in this book. Be sure to look through the Outlook Options dialog box for other options you might be interested in using.

Managing Mail Module Options

Most of the settings you might want to change to modify the way Outlook works are available on the Mail page of the Outlook Options dialog box. These include settings for composing original messages, replies, and forwards; controlling the behavior of Outlook panes and desktop alerts; cleaning up conversations; saving, sending, and tracking messages; and default message format options. Because this is where you'll make most of your changes, we'll take a close look at each of these options.

Compose Messages

The Compose Messages section of the Mail page includes options for changing the behavior of Outlook while you're creating a new message.

Outlook can send and receive email messages in three message formats:

- **Hypertext Markup Language (HTML)** Supports paragraph styles (including numbered and bulleted lists), character styles (such as fonts, sizes, colors, and weight), and backgrounds (such as colors and pictures). Most (but not all) email programs—those that don't display HTML messages as plain text—support the HTML format.

- **Rich Text Format (RTF)** Supports more paragraph formatting options than HTML, including borders and shading, but is compatible with only Outlook and Microsoft Exchange Server. Outlook converts RTF messages to HTML when sending them outside of your Exchange network.

- **Plain Text** Does not support the formatting features available in HTML and RTF messages, but is supported by all email programs.

If many of the people you communicate with most often don't use Outlook as their primary email software program, you might want to change your default message format to one that is compatible with the email programs they use.

➤ **To specify how Outlook will correct and format message content**

1. In the **Compose messages** section of the **Mail** page of the **Outlook Options** dialog box, click the **Editor Options** button.

2. In the **AutoCorrect options** section of the **Proofing** page of the **Editor Options** dialog box, click the **AutoCorrect Options** button.

3. On the **AutoCorrect**, **Math AutoCorrect**, **AutoFormat**, **AutoFormat As You Type**, and **Actions** pages of the **AutoCorrect** dialog box, set the automatic correction and formatting options you want, and then click **OK**.

➤ **To set the default message format**

→ In the **Compose messages** section of the **Mail** page, in the **Compose messages in this format** list, click **HTML**, **Rich Text**, or **Plain Text**.

> **Tip** You can set the format for an individual message by clicking the format you want in the Format group on the Format Text tab of the message composition window.

➤ **To customize the spelling and grammar-checking settings**

1. In the **Compose messages** section of the **Mail** page, click the **Spelling and Autocorrect** button.

2. In the **When correcting spelling in Microsoft Office programs** section of the **Proofing** page of the **Editor Options** dialog box, select the spelling correction options and dictionaries you want to use in all Office programs, including Outlook.

3. In the **When correcting spelling in Outlook** section of the **Proofing** page, select the spelling-checking and grammar-checking options you want, and then click **OK**.

➤ **To customize the way Outlook works with text**

1. In the **Compose messages** section of the **Mail** page, click the **Editor Options** button.

2. On the **Advanced** page of the **Editor Options** dialog box, do any of the following, and then click **OK**:

   ○ In the **Editing options** section, turn on or off advanced editing features, such as how Outlook selects and moves text, whether to track formatting changes, and whether Overtype mode is available.

   ○ In the **Cut, copy, and paste** section, specify whether Outlook will apply source or destination formatting to text copied within a message, between messages, and from other programs, and set options for smart cut and paste (whether to automatically add and remove spaces as needed) and the Paste Options button (whether it appears after a paste operation).

   ○ In the **Display** section, set whether measurements are shown in inches, centimeters, millimeters, points, or picas; whether pixels are shown for HTML features; whether ScreenTips display keyboard shortcuts; and whether character positioning is optimized for layout rather than readability.

> **See Also** For information about signatures, themes, stationery, default fonts, and response identifiers, see section 3.4, "Manage Automatic Message Content."

Outlook Panes

When you open a received message, Outlook changes its status and icon from unread to read. Outlook can also mark messages as read based on actions in the Reading Pane and content pane.

Outlook panes	
Customize how items are marked as read when using the Reading Pane.	Reading Pane...

➤ **To specify how Outlook determines the read status of messages**

1. In the **Outlook panes** section of the **Mail** page, click the **Reading Pane** button.

2. In the **Reading Pane** dialog box, do any of the following, and then click **OK**:

- Select the **Mark items as read when viewed in the Reading Pane** check box, and then enter the number of seconds after which Outlook should mark the item as read.

- Select the **Mark item as read when selection changes** check box.

- Select the **Single key reading using space bar** check box.

> **Tip** You can also control the Reading Pane options from the Outlook Panes section of the Advanced page of the Outlook Options dialog box.

Message Arrival

Outlook can notify you of incoming messages in several ways. If you choose to display a desktop alert, you can control the location, transparency, and duration of the desktop alert.

➤ **To control the way Outlook notifies you of an incoming message**

→ In the **Message arrival** section of the **Mail** page, select or clear the **Play a sound**, **Briefly change the mouse pointer**, **Show an envelope icon in the taskbar**, and **Display a Desktop Alert** check boxes.

➤ **To control desktop alert properties**

1. In the **Message arrival** section of the **Mail** page, click the **Desktop Alert Settings** button.

2. In the **Desktop Alert Settings** dialog box, do the following, and then click **OK**.

- Drag the **Duration** slider to set the length of time (from 3 to 30 seconds) the desktop alert is open.

- Drag the **Transparency** slider to set the transparency (from 0% to 80%) of the desktop alert.

Conversation Clean Up

The Conversation Clean Up feature is new in Outlook 2010. Using the Clean Up command that is available in the Delete group on the Home tab of the Mail module, you can simultaneously move, delete, or ignore all or selected types of messages in an email conversation thread.

```
Conversation Clean Up

   Cleaned-up items will go to this folder: [                    ]  [ Browse... ]
   Messages moved by Clean Up will go to their account's Deleted Items.
   [ ] When cleaning sub-folders, recreate the folder hierarchy in the destination folder
   [ ] Don't move unread messages
   [✓] Don't move categorized messages
   [✓] Don't move flagged messages
   [✓] Don't move digitally-signed messages
   [✓] When a reply modifies a message, don't move the original
```

➤ **To control the functionality of the Clean Up command**

→ In the **Conversation Clean Up** section of the **Mail** page, do the following:

○ If you want to retain (rather than delete) cleaned-up items, specify the location in which you want Outlook to store them. To preserve the location of cleaned-up items, select the **When cleaning sub-folders, recreate the folder hierarchy in the destination folder** check box.

○ To exclude unread, categorized, flagged, or digitally signed messages from the clean-up process, select the **Don't move** check box corresponding to the item type.

○ To exclude original messages from the clean-up process, select the **When a reply modifies a message, don't move the original** check box.

Replies and Forwards

When you open a message and then respond to it, Outlook leaves the original message window open.

When you respond to a message, Outlook inserts the original message below a blank area. You can enter your response in the blank area, or you can respond inline, within the body of the original message. If you respond inline, you can insert identifying text, such as *[your name]* prior to your responses so that the recipient can easily locate them.

You can choose whether and how to include original message text in a response.

Replies and forwards

- ☐ Close original message window when replying or forwarding
- ☐ Preface comments with: Joan Lambert

When replying to a message: [Include original message text ▼]

	Do not include original message
	Attach original message
	Include original message text
	Include and indent original message text
	Prefix each line of the original message

When forwarding a message:

Preface each line in a plain-t

➤ **To close open message windows when you respond to messages**

→ In the **Replies and forwards** section of the **Mail** page, select the **Close original message window when replying or forwarding** check box.

➤ **To insert an identifier before inline responses**

→ In the **Replies and forwards** section of the **Mail** page, select the **Preface comments with** check box. Then in the corresponding text box, enter the text with which you want to preface your response.

> **Tip** You can also control inline response identifiers from the Personal Stationery page of the Signatures And Stationery dialog box.

➤ **To specify the text included in response messages**

→ In the **Replies and forwards** section of the **Mail** page, in the **When replying to a message** and **When forwarding a message** lists, click the original message option you want.

Save Messages

By default, Outlook saves the first draft of a message three minutes after you begin composing the message, and resaves the message every three minutes thereafter. The default location for saved message drafts is the Drafts folder, which is a top-level mailbox folder that appears in the Navigation Pane at the same level as your Inbox. You can alternatively save message drafts in your Inbox, in the Sent Messages folder, or in the Outbox.

When you send a message, Outlook saves a copy of the sent message in the Sent Items folder.

➤ **To specify how and when Outlook saves message drafts**

1. In the **Save messages** section of the **Mail** page, in the **Automatically save items...** box, enter a number of minutes from 1 to 99.

2. In the **Save to this folder** list, click **Drafts**, **Inbox**, **Sent Mail**, or **Outbox**.

➤ **To change how Outlook saves sent messages**

➜ In the **Save messages** section of the **Mail** page, do any of the following:

   ○ To save message responses with the original message rather than in the Sent Items folder, select the **When replying to a message that is not in the Inbox...** check box.

   ○ To delete a message when you forward it, clear the **Save forwarded messages** check box.

   ○ To not save messages that you send, clear the **Save copies of messages in the Sent Items folder** check box.

Send Messages

The Send Messages section of the Mail page includes options for setting message properties and sending messages.

Send messages

Default Importance level: Normal

Default Sensitivity level: Normal

☐ Mark messages as expired after this many days: 0

☐ Commas can be used to separate multiple message recipients

☑ Automatic name checking

☑ Delete meeting requests and notifications from Inbox after responding

☑ CTRL + ENTER sends a message

☑ Use Auto-Complete List to suggest names when typing in the To, Cc, and Bcc lines   Empty Auto-Complete List

By default, when entering multiple email addresses in the To, Cc, and Bcc boxes of a message, you must separate them by using semicolons. If you prefer to separate multiple entries by using commas, you can configure Outlook to allow this option.

When you accept or decline a meeting request or propose a new time for a meeting, the meeting request is deleted from your Inbox. If the meeting was added to your calendar, you can redisplay the request by opening the calendar item. If it wasn't, you have no record of the meeting details. You can configure Outlook to keep the meeting requests.

Outlook builds a list of email addresses and uses that list to suggest full entries as you enter text in the To, Cc, and Bcc boxes. You can delete individual entries from the Auto-Complete list or clear it entirely.

➤ **To allow the use of commas to separate message recipients**

→ In the **Send messages** section of the **Mail** page, select the **Commas can be used to separate multiple message recipients** check box.

➤ **To retain meeting requests after you respond to them**

→ In the **Send messages** section of the **Mail** page, clear the **Delete meeting requests and notifications...** check box.

➤ **To clear the Auto-Complete list**

→ In the **Send messages** section of the **Mail** page, click the **Empty Auto-Complete List** button. Then in the confirmation dialog box, click **Yes**.

➤ **To remove an individual entry from the Auto-Complete list**

→ With the list displayed, press the Down Arrow key to move to the entry you want to remove. Then press the Delete key.

MailTips

MailTips are server-generated messages that appear in the header of a message composition window to notify you of various conditions that apply to that message. MailTips are available only for Exchange Server 2010 accounts that support this feature.

MailTips Options   ? ✕

Settings

A̲pply to this account: 📧 Joanna@litwareinc.com   ▼

S̲elect MailTips to be displayed:

🛡️ Sending Restrictions MailTips
    ☑ Restricted recipient
    ☑ Moderated contact group

📧 Undeliverable Message MailTips
    ☑ Recipient address not valid
    ☑ Message too large for recipient
    ☑ Message too large to send
    ☑ Recipient mailbox is full

ⓘ Informational MailTips
    ☑ Large number of recipients or contact group
    ☑ Recipient is using automatic replies
    ☑ External recipient
    ☑ External recipient in contact group
    ☑ Additional information
    ☑ Mailbox quota about to be exceeded

MailTips bar display options

  ◉ Display automatically when M̲ailTips apply.
  ◯ D̲isplay at all times.
  ◯ N̲ever display MailTips.

☐ E̲xpand the MailTips bar automatically when multiple MailTips apply to a message.

                                                   OK   Cancel

---

➤ To set MailTip preferences for an individual account

1. In the **MailTips** section of the **Mail** page, click the **MailTips Options** button.

2. In the **MailTips Options** dialog box, in the **Apply to this account** list, click the Exchange account to which you want to apply these settings.

3. Select the check boxes for the types of MailTips you want Outlook to display.

4. In the **MailTips bar display options** section, click the display option you want.

5. In the **MailTips Options** dialog box, click **OK**.

Tracking

The Tracking section of the Mail page includes options for requesting notifications when a message you send is delivered to a recipient and when a message is marked by the recipient as read; and options for processing notification requests attached to messages that you receive. This section also includes options for processing responses you receive to meeting requests and voting requests you send.

Tracking

Delivery and read receipts help provide confirmation that messages were successfully received. Not all e-mail servers and applications support sending receipts.

For all messages sent, request:

☐ Delivery receipt confirming the message was delivered to the recipient's e-mail server

☐ Read receipt confirming the recipient viewed the message

For any message received that includes a read receipt request:

◯ Always send a read receipt

◉ Never send a read receipt

◯ Ask each time whether to send a read receipt

☑ Automatically process meeting requests and responses to meeting requests and polls

☑ Automatically update original sent item with receipt information

☐ Update tracking information, and then delete responses that don't contain comments

☐ After updating tracking information, move receipt to: | Deleted Items | | Browse... |

Delivery receipts can be a useful tool when you send an important message and need to know whether it's reached its intended recipient. (However, not all types of email accounts support all types of receipts.) You can request receipts for an individual message by selecting the check boxes in the Tracking group on the Options tab of the message window. Implementing receipts for all outgoing messages is rarely a good idea and is beyond the scope of the Microsoft Office Specialist exam.

When you receive a message that has an attached read receipt request, Outlook prompts you to confirm that you want to send a read receipt. You can make this choice for each individual message or elect to accept or refuse all read receipt requests.

> **Tip** Be cautious when approving read receipt requests, because some mass-mailing companies use these to determine whether an email address is active.

➤ **To automatically accept or refuse all read receipt requests**

→ In the **Tracking** section of the **Mail** page, click **Always send a read receipt** or **Never send a read receipt**.

Other Mail Module Options

In the Message Format section of the Mail page, you can specify how Outlook displays your message content on the screen and the format in which Outlook sends messages outside of your organization. These options are beyond the scope of the Microsoft Office Specialist exam.

The Other section of the Mail page includes options for displaying the Paste Options button, allowing the use of Microsoft InfoPath forms, shading message headers, and expanding conversations when navigating through the Inbox by using the keyboard. You can also specify what occurs when you move or delete an open item. Options include opening the previous or next item in the folder, or returning to the folder without opening another item. These options are beyond the scope of the Microsoft Office Specialist exam.

Managing Calendar Module Options

Options on the Calendar page control settings for displaying and managing Outlook calendars, and for scheduling appointments and resources.

Work Time

By default, Outlook defines the work week as Monday through Friday from 8:00 A.M. to 5:00 P.M. If you work a different schedule, you can change your work week so that other people can make appointments with you only during the times that you plan to be available. Your work week is colored differently in your calendar and by default is the only time displayed to other people on your network who look at your calendar.

Outlook also allows you to specify the first week of the year; this pertains to the week numbers that you can choose to display in the calendar and in the Date Navigator.

➤ **To define your work week**

1. In the **Work time** area of the **Calendar** page of the **Outlook Options** dialog box, set the start time and end time of the work day you want to define.

2. In the **Work week** area, select the check boxes of the days you want to include in your work week.

3. In the **First day of week** list, click the day you want to appear first (on the left) in the Work Week view of your calendar.

4. In the **First week of year** list, click **Starts on Jan 1**, **First 4-day week**, or **First full week**.

> **Tip** Outlook doesn't allow you to define a workday that crosses midnight or to define different start and end times for different days.

Calendar Options

When you create any calendar item using the default settings, Outlook automatically sets a reminder to appear 15 minutes prior to the beginning of the appointment, meeting, or event.

By default, Outlook allows meeting request recipients to propose new meeting times. When you propose a new meeting time, Outlook marks the original meeting time on your calendar as Tentative.

You can easily add the local holidays for more than 80 countries to your Outlook calendar.

➤ **To modify the default reminder settings**

→ To prevent reminders from automatically appearing for new appointments, meetings, and events, clear the **Default reminders** check box.

→ To change the default reminder time, in the **Default reminders** list, click a standard time period from 0 minutes to 2 weeks.

→ To hide the reminder icon on calendar items that have reminders, clear the **Show bell icon on the calendar for appointments and meetings with reminders** check box.

➤ **To modify the meeting time proposal options**

→ To remove the Propose New Time option from meeting requests, clear the **Allow attendees to propose new times for meetings** check box.

→ To automatically accept or decline a meeting request when proposing a new time, click **Accept** or **Decline** in the **Use this response when proposing a new meeting time** list.

➤ **To add the national holidays of a country to your default calendar**

1. In the **Calendar options** section of the **Calendar** page, click the **Add Holidays** button.

2. In the **Add Holidays to Calendar** dialog box, select the check box of the country whose holidays you want to add to your calendar, and then click **OK**.

3. After Outlook adds the selected country's holidays to your calendar, click **OK** in the confirmation message box.

➤ **To control the time period for which your calendar information is available to other Outlook users**

1. In the **Calendar options** section of the **Calendar** page, click the **Free/Busy Options** button.

2. On the **Permissions** page of the **Calendar Properties** dialog box, in the **Permission Level** list, click **Free/Busy time**.

3. In the **Read** area, click the **Other Free/Busy** button.

4. In the **Free/Busy Options** dialog box, in the **Publish** box, enter a number from 0 to 99, and enter a number from 0 to 99 in the **Update free/busy information on the server** box.

5. Click **OK** in the **Free/Busy Options** dialog box and in the **Calendar Properties** dialog box.

➤ **To control the calendar information displayed to specific Outlook users**

  1. In the **Calendar options** section of the **Calendar** page, click the **Free/Busy Options** button.

  2. On the **Permissions** page of the **Calendar Properties** dialog box, select or add a user and then in the **Permission Level** list, click **Free/Busy time**.

  3. In the **Read** area, click **None**; **Free/Busy time**; **Free/Busy time, subject, location**; or **Full Details**.

  4. In the **Calendar Properties** dialog box, click **OK**.

Display Options

Outlook calendars can use any of 15 color schemes. When you create a new calendar, Outlook assigns the next unused color to that calendar. You can change the color of an individual calendar from the Calendar module or specify the default color for new calendars. You can also configure the way Outlook displays information in Schedule view.

> **See Also** For information about Schedule view, see section 5.3, "Manipulate the Calendar Pane."

Specific weeks are referred to in some countries by number to simplify the communication of dates. (For example, you can say you'll be out of the office "Week 24" rather than "June 7-11.") Week 1 is the calendar week in which January 1 falls, Week 2 is the following week, and so on through to the end of the year. Because of the way the weeks are numbered, a year can end in Week 52 or (more commonly) in Week 53.

➤ **To specify the default color of all new calendar colors**

1. In the **Display options** section of the **Calendar** page, in the **Default calendar color** palette, click one of the 15 color boxes.

2. Select the **Use this color on all calendars** check box.

➤ **To display week numbers in the Date Navigator and in the Month view of the calendar**

→ In the **Display options** section of the **Calendar** page, select the **Show week numbers...** check box.

➤ **To modify the Schedule view options**

→ To display all-day events for which the time is indicated as Free, select the **When in Schedule View, show free appointments** check box.

→ To control when Outlook automatically displays or hides Schedule view, select or enter a number from 1 to 30 in the **Automatically switch from vertical layout to schedule view...** box, and select or enter a number from 1 to 29 in the **Automatically switch from schedule view to vertical layout...** box.

→ To prevent Outlook from automatically displaying or hiding Schedule view, clear the **Automatically switch from vertical layout to schedule view...** and **Automatically switch from schedule view to vertical layout...** check boxes.

Time Zones

If you frequently travel or work with colleagues or clients outside of your usual time zone, you might want to change the time zone on your computer so that information such as the receipt time of email messages, appointment times, and the time on the clock in the Windows Taskbar notification area reflects your current location. If you have appointments in both time zones, you can display both time zones on the left side of the Calendar pane, and swap between zones when you travel. That way, you can be sure to correctly enter appointments at the time they will occur in their respective time zones.

➤ **To change time zones**

1. In the **Time zones** area of the **Calendar** page, in the **Time zone** list, click the time zone you want to display.

2. In the corresponding **Label** box, enter a description of up to 32 characters.

➤ **To display multiple time zones**

1. In the **Time zones** area of the **Calendar** page, select the **Show a second time zone** check box.

2. In the corresponding **Time zone** list, click the second time zone you want to display.

3. In the corresponding **Label** box, enter a description of up to 32 characters.

➤ **To switch your calendar between the primary and secondary time zones**

→ In the **Time zones** area of the **Calendar** page, click the **Swap Time Zones** button.

Scheduling Options

By default, the Scheduling Assistant page of a meeting window displays available calendar details for meeting invitees in the scheduling grid and when you point to a scheduled time block.

If you are designated as the manager of a meeting resource such as a conference room or an audio/visual unit, you must by default manually accept or decline resource requests.

➤ **To hide calendar details for meeting invitees**

→ In the **Scheduling assistant** area of the **Calendar** page, clear the **Show calendar details in ScreenTip** and/or **Show calendar details in the scheduling grid** check boxes.

➤ **To automatically process resource requests**

1. In the **Resource scheduling** area of the **Calendar** page, click **Resource Scheduling**.

2. In the **Resource Scheduling** dialog box, select the **Automatically accept meeting requests and remove canceled meetings**, **Automatically decline meeting requests that conflict with an existing appointment or meeting**, and/or **Automatically decline recurring meeting requests** check boxes. Then click **OK**.

Managing Contacts Module Options

Options on the Contacts page control settings for creating and displaying contact records.

The order in which contact records appear in the Contacts module is determined by the File As order and, when contact records are sorted by name, by the content of the Full Name field.

In Business Card view and Card view, Outlook displays a Roman (123, abc) alphanumeric index at the right side of the content pane that you can use to quickly move to contact records beginning with a specific number or letter. If your address book contains entries in other alphabets, you can display a second index.

When displaying a message received from a contact for whom a picture is saved in an address book, Outlook displays the message sender's picture at the right end of the message header. When you are connected to a network that has presence information enabled, Outlook displays an icon representing the message sender's presence (online, busy, away, or offline) next to the message sender's name.

Outlook 2010 includes a Suggested Contacts address book for each account you connect to. When you send a message to a person for whom you do not have a contact record, Outlook creates a contact record for that person in the Suggested Contacts address book corresponding to the account from which you send the message. You can display and search the contents of your Suggested Contacts address books and move contact records from a Suggested Contacts address book to another address book.

➤ **To specify the structure of names in the Full Name field**

→ In the **Names and filing** section of the **Contacts** page of the **Outlook Options** dialog box, in the **Default "Full Name" order** list, click **First (Middle) Last**, **Last First**, or **First Last1 Last2**.

➤ **To specify the order in which contact records appear in the Contacts module**

→ In the **Names and filing** section of the **Contacts** page, in the **Default "File As" order** list, click **Last, First**; **First Last**; **Company**; **Last, First (Company)**; or **Company (Last, First)**.

➤ **To display a second alphanumeric index in the Contacts module**

1. In the **Contacts index** section of the **Contacts** page, select the **Show an additional index** check box.

2. In the **Additional contact index** list, click **Arabic**, **Cyrillic**, **Greek**, **Thai**, or **Vietnamese**.

➤ **To specify the contact information displayed in the Reading Pane and message windows**

→ In the **Online status and photographs** section of the **Contacts** page, select or clear the **Display online status next to name** and **Show user photographs when available** check boxes.

➤ **To prevent Outlook from creating contact records for people you correspond with**

→ In the **Suggested contacts** section of the **Contacts** page, clear the **Automatically create Outlook contacts for recipients that do not belong to an Outlook Address Book** check box.

Managing Tasks Module Options

Options on the Tasks page control settings for creating and managing tasks.

➤ **To automatically set task reminders**

1. In the **Task options** section of the **Tasks** page of the **Outlook Options** dialog box, select the **Set reminders on tasks with due dates** check box.

2. In the **Default reminder time** list, click the time at which you want reminders to appear.

➤ **To change assigned task options**

→ In the **Task options** section of the **Tasks** page, select or clear the **Keep my task list updated with copies of tasks I assign to other people** check box.

→ In the **Task options** section of the **Tasks** page, select or clear the **Send status report when I complete an assigned task** check box.

➤ **To change the color in which tasks appear in task lists**

→ In the **Task options** section of the **Tasks** page, choose the colors you want in the **Overdue task color** and **Completed task color** palettes.

➤ **To change the default task due date**

1. In the **Task options** section of the **Tasks** page, click the **Quick Click** button.

2. In the **Set Quick Click** dialog box, click **Today**, **Tomorrow**, **This Week**, **Next Week**, or **No Date**. Then click **OK**.

Managing Notes Module and Journal Options

Options on the Notes And Journal page control settings for creating notes and for recording activities in the Outlook Journal.

To set the icon color for new notes

➜ In the **Notes options** section of the **Notes and Journal** page of the **Outlook Options** dialog box, in the **Default color** palette, click the color you want.

To set the size of new note windows

➜ In the **Notes options** section of the **Notes and Journal** page, in the **Default size** list, click **Small**, **Medium**, or **Large**.

To set the default font of note text

1. In the **Notes options** section of the **Notes and Journal** page, click the **Font** button.

2. In the **Font** dialog box, change the font settings, and then click **OK**.

To hide the modification date and time in the footer of all note windows

➜ In the **Notes options** section of the **Notes and Journal** page, clear the **Show date and time that the Note was last modified** check box.

To automatically record Outlook items for one or more contacts

1. In the **Journal options** section of the **Notes and Journal** page, click the **Journal Options** button.

2. In the **Journal Options** dialog box, select the check box for each type of Outlook item and file you want to record.

3. Select the check box for each contact for whom you want to record Outlook items and files. Then click **OK**.

Managing Language Options

Options on the Language page control the dictionaries used by Outlook when checking the spelling and grammar of message content, as well as the language in which button labels, tab names, Help content, and ScreenTips are displayed.

ScreenTips are available by default in English, French, and Spanish. To use proofing tools or to display ScreenTips, button labels, tab names, and Help content in a language other than the standard language of your installed Windows operating system, you must install a language pack. Language packs are available for download from the Microsoft Download Center at microsoft.com/downloads/ and are also supplied through Windows Update.

➤ To change the ScreenTip display language to a standard option

→ In the **Choose ScreenTip Language** section of the **Language** page of the **Outlook Options** dialog box, in the **Set your ScreenTip language** list, click **French** or **Spanish**.

Managing Advanced Options

Options on the Advanced page control settings for customizing a wide variety of standard Outlook actions and responses.

Outlook Panes

In the Outlook Panes section of the Advanced page, you can change the content in the Navigation Pane and in the To-Do Bar, and the way Outlook determines when to mark a message as read.

➤ To hide or display buttons in the Navigation Pane

1. In the **Outlook panes** section of the **Advanced** page of the **Outlook Options** dialog box, click the **Navigation Pane** button.

2. In the **Navigation Pane Options** dialog box, select the check boxes of the buttons you want to display, clear the check boxes of the buttons you want to hide, and then click **OK**.

➤ **To change the order of buttons in the Navigation Pane**

1. In the **Outlook panes** section of the **Advanced** page, click the **Navigation Pane** button.

2. In the **Navigation Pane Options** dialog box, for each button you want to move, click its name and then click **Move Up** or **Move Down**.

3. In the **Navigation Pane Options** dialog box, click **OK**.

➤ **To change the font of folder names in the Navigation Pane**

1. In the **Outlook panes** section of the **Advanced** page, click the **Navigation Pane** button.

2. In the **Navigation Pane Options** dialog box, click the **Font** button.

3. In the **Font** dialog box, in the **Font**, **Font style**, and **Size** lists, click the font settings you want, and then click **OK**.

4. In the **Navigation Pane Options** dialog box, click **OK**.

> **See Also** For information about controlling the Reading Pane options, see the "Outlook Panes" subtopic of the "Mail Module Options" topic, earlier in this section.

➤ **To change the content displayed in the To-Do Bar**

1. In the **Outlook panes** section of the **Advanced** page, click the **To-Do Bar** button.

2. In the **To-Do Bar Options** dialog box, do any of the following, and then click **OK**:

   ○ Select the **Show Date Navigator** check box and enter a number from 1 to 9 in the **Number of month rows** box, or clear the **Show Date Navigator** check box.

   ○ Select the **Show Appointments** check box and then select or clear the **Show All Day Events** and **Show Details of Private Items** check boxes, or clear the **Show Appointments** check box.

   ○ Select or clear the **Show Task List** check box.

Outlook Start And Exit

By default, when you first start Outlook, it opens the Mail module and displays your primary Inbox in the content pane. You can specify any folder of any module as the starting location. You can also control whether Outlook empties the Deleted Items folder when you exit the program.

➤ **To change the startup folder**

1. In the **Outlook start and exit** section of the **Advanced** page, click the **Browse** button.

2. In the **Select Folder** dialog box, click the folder you want to start in, and then click **OK**.

➤ **To retain deleted items when exiting**

→ In the **Outlook start and exit** section of the **Advanced** page, clear the **Empty Deleted Items folders when exiting Outlook** check box.

AutoArchive

You can specify a schedule on which Outlook should archive or delete old and expired items.

➤ **To automatically archive Outlook items**

1. In the **AutoArchive** section of the **Advanced** page, click the **AutoArchive Settings** button.

2. In the **AutoArchive** dialog box, select the **Run AutoArchive every** check box, and then select or enter a number from 1 to 60 in the **days** box.

3. In the **AutoArchive** dialog box, do any of the following, and then click **OK**:

   ○ Select or clear the **Prompt before AutoArchive runs** check box.

   ○ Specify the actions you want Outlook to perform with old and expired items, and the folder to which Outlook should move old items.

Reminders

You can control whether the Reminders window opens automatically when a reminder is supposed to appear, and what sound is played when the Reminders window opens.

➤ To prevent the Reminders window from automatically opening

→ In the **Reminders** section of the **Advanced** page, clear the **Show reminders** check box.

➤ To set the sound that plays when the Reminders window opens

1. In the **Reminders** section of the **Advanced** page, select the **Play reminder sound** check box, and then click the **Browse** button.

2. In the **Reminder Sound File** dialog box, browse to the .wav file you want to use, and then click **Open**.

Export

You can export Outlook items and RSS feeds for independent reference or for use in another information management system. You can import electronic business cards and calendars, mail account settings, messages and contact records, and RSS feeds from other file formats for use within Outlook.

➤ To export content from Outlook or import content into Outlook

1. In the **Export** section of the **Advanced** page, click the **Export** button.

2. In the **Import and Export** wizard, select the export or import operation you want to perform, and then click **Next**.

3. Follow the wizard's prompts, and on the final page of the wizard, click **Finish**.

> **Tip** You can also import content into Outlook or export content from Outlook by clicking the Import button on the Open page of the Backstage view.

RSS Feeds

You can control the way that Outlook displays updated RSS feed items, and whether the RSS feeds in your Outlook installation are available to Windows, to Windows Internet Explorer, and to other programs.

➤ To mark updated RSS Feed items as unread

→ In the RSS Feeds section of the **Advanced** page, select the **Any RSS Feed item that is updated appears as new** check box.

➤ To make RSS feeds from Outlook available to Windows and Internet Explorer

→ In the RSS Feeds section of the **Advanced** page, select the **Synchronize RSS Feeds to the Common Feed List (CFL) in Windows** check box.

Send and Receive

By default, if you have an active network connection, Outlook transmits outgoing messages as soon as you send them. You can access the send and receive settings from the Outlook Options dialog box in the same way that you do from the Send/Receive tab of the ribbon.

Other

You can specify a default color category so that clicking in the category box of an item header assigns that category to the item.

➤ To set the default color category

1. In the **Other** section of the **Advanced** page, click the **Quick Click** button.

2. In the **Set Quick Click** dialog box, expand the list and click the category you want to assign. Then click **OK**.

> **Tip** You can assign only a preexisting color category as the default. You cannot create a category from within the Set Quick Click dialog box.

> **Tip** The Advanced page also includes options for developers, dial-up connections, and international communications. None of these options are expected to be within the scope of this exam.

Practice Tasks

There are no practice files for these tasks.

- Configure Outlook to automatically check the spelling of every outgoing message. Test the configuration by sending a message.

- Configure Outlook to automatically close the received email message window when you respond to a message. Test the configuration by responding to a message.

- Add the time zone for a colleague who works in Sydney, Australia to your calendar. Display your calendar and confirm that it shows two time zones.

- Add the Australian national holidays to your calendar. Display your calendar and confirm that December 26 is labeled as Boxing Day.

- Configure Outlook to file contact records in order by first name. Test the configuration by displaying the Contacts module.

- Set the default reminder time for new tasks to 7:30 A.M. Test the setting by creating a task.

- Configure Outlook to automatically empty the Deleted Items folder when you exit the program. Test the configuration by deleting one or more Outlook items and then closing Outlook.

1.2 Manipulate Item Tags

Working with Color Categories

To help you more easily locate Outlook items associated with a specific subject, project, person, or other condition, you can create a category specific to that condition and assign the category to any related items. You can assign a category to any type of Outlook item— a message, an appointment, a contact record, a note, and so on. For example, you might assign contact records for customers to a Customers category.

Assigning messages, appointments, contacts, and tasks to color categories can help you more easily locate information. If you frequently use a particular category, you can assign it as your Quick Click category. You can also assign keyboard shortcuts to up to 11 color categories.

Color categories combine named categories with color bars to provide an immediate visual cue when you view messages in your Inbox, appointments on your calendar, and so on. Depending on the view of the Outlook items, the category may be indicated by a simple colored block or a large colored bar.

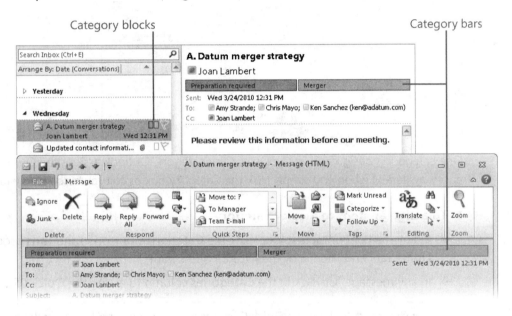

Outlook 2010 comes with six preconfigured color categories that are associated only with the color names. You can rename the six starting categories and create categories. Each category has a name and color, and can also have a shortcut key.

You can rename a default color category and change its color to create categories. If the 25 available categories aren't sufficient, you can assign the same color to multiple categories. You can also create new categories from scratch.

One category is designated as the Quick Click category. Outlook assigns the Quick Click category by default when you simply click the Category box or column associated with an item.

➤ To assign an item to a color category

→ In any mail or contacts folder, click the **Categorize** button in the **Tags** group on the **Home** tab, and then click the category you want.

→ In any message list, click in the **Categories** column to assign the Quick Click category.

> **Tip** You must first set the Quick Click category, as described in the following instructions.

→ In any calendar, click the **Categorize** button in the **Tags** group on the contextual tab (Appointment, Meeting, and so on) that appears for the selected item, and then click the category you want.

→ In any folder, right-click an item or a selection of items, point to **Categorize**, and then click the category you want.

➤ To assign an item to multiple color categories

1. Select the item, display the **Categorize** list, and then click **All Categories**.

2. In the **Color Categories** dialog box, select the check boxes of the categories you want, and then click **OK**.

➤ **To assign a keyboard shortcut to a color category**

1. In the **Categorize** list, click **All Categories**.
2. In the **Color Categories** dialog box, click the category.
3. In the **Shortcut Key** list, click the key combination you want.
4. In the **Color Categories** dialog box, click **OK**.

➤ **To create a custom color category**

1. In the **Categorize** list, click **All Categories**.
2. In the **Color Categories** dialog box, click **New**.
3. In the **Name** box of the **Add New Category** dialog box, type a name for the category.
4. Click the **Color** arrow, and click the color you want to associate with the category.
5. Click the **Shortcut Key** arrow, and click the keyboard shortcut you want.
6. Click **OK** twice.

➤ **To rename a color category**

1. In the **Categorize** list, click **All Categories**.
2. In the **Color Categories** dialog box, click the name of a color category (not its check box), and then click **Rename**.
3. With the category name selected for editing, type the name you want, and then press Enter.
4. Click **OK**.

➤ **To set or change the Quick Click color category**

1. In the **Categorize** list, click **Set Quick Click**.
2. In the **Set Quick Click** dialog box, select the category you want Outlook to use, and then click **OK**.

Setting Message Sensitivity and Importance

When sending a message, you can indicate that a message should be kept private by setting its sensitivity to Confidential, Personal, or Private.

When you receive a message with a sensitivity setting, no indicator appears in the message list. However, in the message window and the Reading Pane, a banner appears in the message header to indicate a sensitivity other than Normal.

You can indicate the priority of a message you are sending by designating it as High Importance or Low Importance.

When you receive a message with a priority setting, a banner appears in the message header in the message window and the Reading Pane to indicate a priority other than Normal. If the Importance field is included in the view, an importance icon appears in the message list.

➤ **To set the sensitivity of a message**

1. On the **Message** tab of the message window, click the **Tags** dialog box launcher.

2. In the **Properties** dialog box, click the option you want in the **Sensitivity** list, and then click **Close**.

> **Tip** You can set the default sensitivity and priority of all new messages in the Send Messages section of the Mail page of the Outlook Options dialog box.

➤ **To designate a message as high or low priority**

→ On the **Message** tab of the message window, in the **Tags** group, click the **High Importance** or **Low Importance** button.

Or

1. On the **Message** tab of the message window, click the **Tags** dialog box launcher.

2. In the **Properties** dialog box, click the option you want in the **Importance** list, and then click **Close**.

➤ **To remove the priority setting from a message you are forwarding**

1. On the **Message** tab of the received message window, in the **Respond** group, click the **Forward** button.

2. On the **Message** tab of the forwarded message composition window, in the **Tags** group, click the active **High Importance** or **Low Importance** button to turn it off.

Setting Message Properties

You can view and set properties for a received message or an outgoing message from the message's Properties dialog box. For received and outgoing messages, you can do the following:

- Set the message Importance and Sensitivity.
- Encrypt the message and its attachments.

- Add a digital signature to the message.
- Cause the message to expire so that it appears crossed out in the message list.
- Associate the message with a contact record.
- Assign the message to a category.

For outgoing messages only, you can do the following:

- Add voting buttons to the message.
- Request a notification when the message is delivered to and read by the recipient.
- Specify an alternative email address for message responses.
- Delay the delivery of a message.

For received messages only, you can display the Internet headers (information about the servers that handled the message en route).

➤ **To open the Properties dialog box**

→ On the **Info** page of the Backstage view of the message window, click the **Properties** button.

Flagging Items for Follow-Up

You can assign a reminder flag for your own reference, to remind you to follow up on a message, contact record, or task. The flags available for messages and tasks are Call, Do Not Forward, Follow Up, For Your Information, Forward, No Response Necessary, Read, Reply, Reply To All, and Review. The flags available for contact records are Follow Up, Call, Arrange Meeting, Send E-mail, and Send Letter. The default flag for any item is Follow Up. Assigning a flag to an email message or contact record adds it to your task list.

If you add a reminder to a flagged item, Outlook displays the Reminders window at the specified time. From the Reminders window, you can dismiss the flag or postpone the reminder to a later time.

> **See Also** For more information about working with tasks created from email messages, contact records, or notes, see section 6.1, "Create and Manipulate Tasks." For information about the Reminders window, see section 1.3, "Arrange the Content Pane."

You can assign a flag to an outgoing message. If you assign a standard flag, it appears only to you. If you specifically flag the message for recipients, Outlook reminds you and/or the recipient to follow up on the message with a specific action.

➤ To flag an item for your follow-up

→ Select the item. On the **Home** tab, in the **Tags** group, click the **Follow Up** button, and then click the flag corresponding to the follow-up time you want to specify.

→ In the content pane, right-click the item, point to **Follow Up**, and then click the flag corresponding to the follow-up time you want to specify.

➤ To set a custom flag

1. Select the item. On the **Home** tab, in the **Tags** group, click the **Follow Up** button, and then click **Custom**.

2. In the **Custom** dialog box, in the **Flag to** list, click the flag you want to appear in the item header.

3. Set the start date and due date to control where the item appears on your task list. Then click **OK**.

➤ To add a reminder to a flagged item

→ In the **Custom** dialog box, select the **Reminder** check box, and then specify the date and time at which you want the reminder to appear.

Or

1. On the **Home** tab, in the **Tags** group, click the **Follow Up** button, and then click **Add Reminder**.

2. With the **Reminder** check box selected in the **Custom** dialog box, specify the reminder date and time. Then click **OK**.

➤ To flag an outgoing message for your follow-up

→ On the **Message** tab of the message composition window, in the **Tags** group, click the **Follow Up** button, and then click the flag corresponding to the follow-up time you want to specify.

➤ To flag an outgoing message for the recipient's follow-up

1. On the **Message** tab, in the **Tags** group, click the **Follow Up** button, and then click **Custom**.

2. In the **Custom** dialog box, select the **Flag for Recipients** check box.

3. Specify the **Flag to** action and the reminder date and time, and then click **OK**.

Changing Read Status

You can set the status of an email message or group of messages to Read or Unread.

➤ **To set the Read status**

1. Select the message or messages for which you want to change the status.

2. Right-click the selection, and then click **Mark as Read** or **Mark as Unread**.

Practice Tasks

There are no practice files for these tasks.

- In your Inbox, assign two messages to the blue category and two to the green category.

- Create a new color category named *Management*. Use the orange color, and assign a shortcut key of Ctrl+F2. Then assign one blue message and one green message to the Management category.

- Assign two contacts to the Management category. Then filter your mailbox to display all items assigned to the Management category.

- Send a message to yourself with the subject *MOS Sensitivity* and flag it as personal.

- After you receive the *MOS Sensitivity* message, set it to expire in five minutes.

- After the *MOS Sensitivity* message expires, mark it as unread.

- Send a message to yourself with the subject *MOS Secret* and flag it as both high priority and confidential.

- After you receive the *MOS Secret* message, forward it to yourself with a normal priority setting.

1.3 Arrange the Content Pane

Displaying and Hiding Program Window Panes

The Outlook program window includes four primary areas in which you work with Outlook items (email messages, contact records, calendar entries, tasks, and notes).

Navigation Pane   Content pane   Reading Pane   To-Do Bar

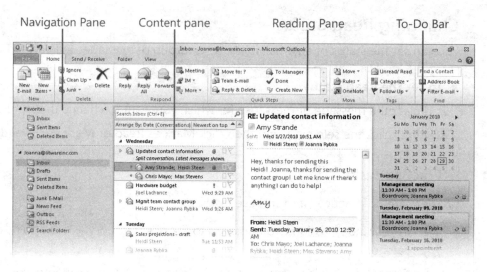

You might find that the default arrangement of these areas is ideal for the way you work. But if you're viewing the program window on a low-resolution screen, don't need all the available tools, or would like more space for the main work area, you can easily change the appearance and layout of the workspace of each of the program window elements. When you start Outlook, the Navigation Pane, To-Do Bar, and Calendar will appear the same way they did when you last exited the program.

> **See Also** For information about displaying and hiding the ribbon in the program window or an item window, see "Modifying the Display of the Ribbon" at the beginning of this book.

Managing the Navigation Pane

The Navigation Pane on the left side of the Outlook window changes depending on which Outlook module you are working in: Mail, Calendar, Contacts, Tasks, or Notes. It also changes when you display the entire contents of your email account folder structure in the Folder List, any shortcuts you have saved in the Shortcuts list, or the Outlook Journals associated with Exchange Server accounts you have configured Outlook to connect to.

Like many aspects of the Outlook window, you can customize the Navigation Pane to suit the way you work. The customization options are located in the Layout group on the View tab of the ribbon.

➤ To display or close the Navigation Pane

→ On the **View** tab, in the **Layout** group, click the **Navigation Pane** button, and then click **Normal** to display the pane or **Off** to hide it.

➤ **To minimize or expand the Navigation Pane**

→ On the **View** tab, in the **Layout** group, click the **Navigation Pane** button, and then click **Minimized**.

→ At the top of the **Navigation Pane**, click the **Minimize the Navigation Pane** button or the **Expand the Navigation Pane** button.

→ Click the **Folders** button on the minimized **Navigation Pane** to temporarily expand it.

➤ **To change the width of the Navigation Pane or To-Do Bar**

→ Drag the divider between the **Navigation Pane** or **To-Do Bar** and the content pane to the right or left.

➤ **To change the space allocated to the navigation buttons**

→ Drag the move handle at the top of the navigation button area up or down.

→ At the bottom of the **Navigation Pane**, click the **Configure buttons** button, and then click **Show More Buttons** or **Show Fewer Buttons**.

➤ **To display or hide navigation buttons**

→ At the bottom of the **Navigation Pane**, click the **Configure buttons** button, point to **Add or Remove Buttons**, and then click the button you want to display or hide.

Or

1. At the bottom of the **Navigation Pane**, click the **Configure buttons** button, and then click **Navigation Pane Options**.

2. In the **Navigation Pane Options** dialog box, select the check boxes of navigation buttons you want to display, and clear the check boxes of navigation buttons you want to hide. Then click **OK**.

➤ **To change the order of navigation buttons**

1. At the bottom of the **Navigation Pane**, click the **Configure buttons** button, and then click **Navigation Pane Options**.

2. In the **Navigation Pane Options** dialog box, click the navigation button you want to move, and click the **Move Up** button or the **Move Down** button. Then click **OK**.

Managing the Reading Pane

The Reading Pane, which displays a preview of the selected Outlook item and commands for working with it, is open by default in the Mail module. You can display the Reading Pane on the right side or at the bottom of the program window in any module, or you can turn it off entirely.

The People Pane at the bottom of the Reading Pane or message window displays extensive information about your previous communications with each message participant.

In its collapsed state, the People Pane displays small thumbnails representing each message participant. If a person's contact record includes a photograph, the photo appears in the People Pane. If no photograph is available, a silhouette of one person represents an individual message participant. A silhouette of three people represents a distribution group.

Resizing bar   Distribution group

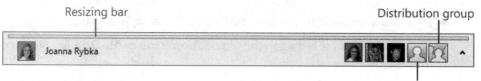

Contact without associated picture

The People Pane can occupy only a certain percentage of the message window, so the amount you can manually adjust the height of the People Pane is dependent on the height of the message window.

In its expanded state, the People Pane displays either large thumbnails or a tabbed breakdown of communications for each message participant.

Toggle button

Scroll to view additional message participants

From the detail view of the People Pane, you can locate items and information associated with the selected contact. The All Items tab of the detailed view displays all your recent communications with the person. If you're looking for a specific item, such as a meeting request or a document attached to a message, you can filter the item list by clicking any of the tabs to the left of the list.

Joanna Rybka   VP of Product Development, Litware, Inc.

All Items	FW: Chris Mayo	8 hours ago
	Chris Mayo (38 KB)	
Activities	FW: Chris Mayo	8 hours ago
Mail	Chris Mayo (38 KB)	
Attachments	A. Datum merger strategy	9 hours ago
Meetings	Merger information	1:26 PM 2/10/2010
Add	Merger information	12:05 PM 2/9/2010
Status Updates	This week's meeting	10:13 PM 1/30/2010

When working with an Exchange account, you can display the People Pane in detail view only if the Cached Exchange Mode feature is enabled. If the Toggle button isn't visible in the expanded People Pane when you're viewing an Exchange account message, the likely problem is that Cached Exchange Mode is not enabled.

> **To display or close the Reading Pane**

→ On the **View** tab, in the **Layout** group, click the **Reading Pane** button, and then click **Right, Bottom,** or **Off.**

> **To expand or contract the People Pane**

→ Click the **Expand/Collapse** button located at the right end of the **People Pane** header.

→ Drag the resizing bar that appears at the top of the **People Pane.**

> **To switch between simple view and detail view**

→ Click the **Toggle** button located near the right end of the expanded **People Pane** header.

> **To set up a connection from Outlook to an online social network**

→ Click the **Add** button located below the contact picture in the **People Pane.**

> **To enable Cached Exchange Mode**

1. On the **Info** page of the Backstage view, in the **Account Settings** list, click **Account Settings.**

2. On the **E-mail** page of the **Account Settings** dialog box, click your Exchange account, and then click **Change.**

3. On the **Server Settings** page of the **Change Account** wizard, select the **Use Cached Exchange Mode** check box, and then click **Next.**

4. On the final page of the **Change Account** wizard, click **Finish.**

Managing the To-Do Bar

The To-Do Bar, which displays the Date Navigator, upcoming appointments, and your task list, is open by default on the right side of the program window in the Mail, Contacts, Tasks, and Notes modules. You can display or close the To-Do Bar, or minimize it to a vertical bar displaying only your next appointment and the number of incomplete tasks you have due today. You can temporarily expand the To-Do Bar by clicking it.

> **Tip** For users who are running Microsoft Office Communicator, the To-Do Bar includes a Quick Contacts section that displays a list of recent correspondents.

By default, the Date Navigator displays a six-week date range. Dates with scheduled appointments are bold.

➤ **To display or close the To-Do Bar**

→ On the **View** tab, in the **Layout** group, click the **To-Do Bar** button, and then click **Normal** to display the pane or **Off** to hide it.

➤ **To minimize or expand the To-Do Bar**

→ On the **View** tab, in the **Layout** group, click the **To-Do Bar** button, and then click **Minimized**.

→ At the top of the **To-Do Bar**, click the **Minimize the To-Do Bar** button or the **Expand the To-Do Bar** button.

➤ **To change the date range displayed in the Date Navigator**

→ Click the left arrow to display the previous month or the right arrow to display the next month.

→ Click the month heading, and then drag to select the month you want to display.

➤ **To select dates for display in the content pane**

→ In the **Date Navigator**, click the specific date to display that date.

→ In the **Date Navigator**, click in the margin to the left of a week to display that week in Week view.

Displaying Module Content

You switch between Outlook program modules by clicking the corresponding button at the bottom of the pane. Additional buttons provide access to the Folder List, to your saved shortcuts, and (if you add its button to the Navigation Pane) to the Outlook Journal. Depending on the space allocated to the buttons, they may be pane-width or iconic.

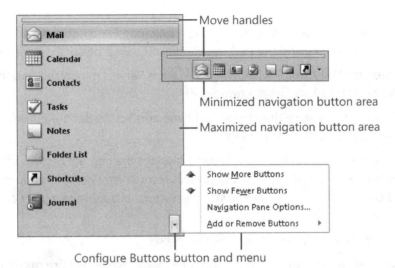

You can minimize the Navigation Pane to a vertical bar on the left side of the window. In the Mail module, information about unread messages in your Inbox appears on the bar. Also in the Mail module, you can display the contents of a folder by clicking that folder on the bar. In any module, you can temporarily expand the Navigation Pane for that module by clicking the Folders button on the bar.

Each Outlook module displays its content in the content pane in multiple views that are appropriate to the module content.

- In the Mail module, the content pane displays the messages in your Inbox or other selected mail folder as well as the Reading Pane, which displays the content of the selected message.

  There are two standard Mail module views:

  o **Normal** In this view, the Navigation Pane and To-Do Bar are maximized.

  o **Reading** In this view, the Navigation Pane, To-Do Bar, and ribbon are minimized.

- In the Calendar module, the content pane displays your calendar for a period of time that you select. The default time period is one day; however, you might find it more useful to have an overview of a longer period of time such as a week or a month.

  There are four standard Calendar module views:

  - **Normal** In this view, the Navigation Pane is maximized, the To-Do Bar is turned off, and the Daily Task List is displayed below the calendar.

  - **Calendar And Tasks** In this view, the Navigation Pane is minimized, the To-Do Bar is turned off, and the Daily Task List is displayed below the calendar.

  - **Calendar Only** In this view, the Navigation Pane is minimized and the To-Do Bar and Daily Task List are turned off.

  - **Classic** In this view, the Navigation Pane and To-Do Bar are maximized and the Daily Task List is turned off.

- In the Contacts module, the content pane displays the contact records saved in the selected address book. By default, the contact records are displayed as business cards, but you can choose among several standard views, including text-only cards and various lists.

  There are three standard Contacts module views:

  - **Normal** In this view, the Navigation Pane and To-Do Bar are maximized.

  - **Cards Only** In this view, the Navigation Pane and To-Do Bar are minimized.

  - **No To-Do Bar** In this view, the Navigation Pane is maximized and the To-Do Bar is turned off.

- In the Tasks module, the content pane displays one of two lists:

  - **To-Do List** This list of tasks is displayed by default and is organized by default in groups by due date. When the To-Do List is displayed, by default the Reading Pane is also displayed.

  - **Tasks List** This list of tasks is displayed in multiple columns with each task preceded by a check box so that you can indicate when the task is complete. When a Tasks List is displayed, by default the Reading Pane is hidden.

  There are two standard Tasks module views:

  - **Normal** In this view, the Navigation Pane and To-Do Bar are maximized.

  - **Reading** In this view, the Navigation Pane, To-Do Bar, and ribbon are minimized.

➤ **To switch between module content views**

→ On the status bar, to the left of the **Zoom** controls, click the view button you want.

Displaying List Views

List views display information in columns, with each column displaying the content of a specific field. You can sort content in a list view by clicking a field column header.

➤ **To display Mail module content in a list view**

→ On the **View** tab, in the **Current View** group, in the **Change View** gallery, click the **Single** button.

➤ **To display Calendar or Contacts module content in a list view**

→ In the **Change View** gallery, click the **List** button.

➤ **To display Tasks module content in a list view**

→ In the **Change View** gallery, click the **Detailed** or **Simple List** button.

➤ **To display Notes module content in a list view**

→ In the **Change View** gallery, click the **Notes List** button.

Modifying List Views

You can add fields to any list view, and remove fields from any list view. After you modify a list view to meet your needs, you can save it as a custom view.

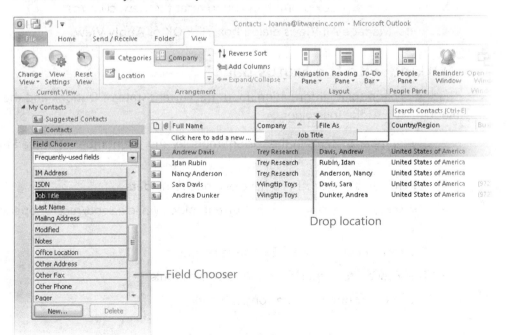

➤ **To add fields to a list view**

1. Right-click any column header, and then click **Field Chooser**.

2. Drag the field you want from the **Field Chooser** window to the column header area and release the mouse button when the red arrows indicate the correct insertion location.

➤ **To remove fields from a list view**

→ Drag the column header of the field you want to remove away from the column header area.

➤ **To save a modified list view**

1. On the **View** tab, in the **Current View** group, display the **Change View** gallery, and then click **Save Current View As a New View**.

2. In the **Copy View** dialog box, enter a descriptive name in the **Name of new view** box.

3. In the **Can be used on** area, click the scope in which you want the view to be available.

4. In the **Copy View** dialog box, click **OK**.

➤ **To reset a folder to the default view**

1. In the **Change View** gallery, click **Manage Views**.

2. In the **Manage All Views** dialog box, click **Reset**.

3. In the message box prompting you to reset the view, click **Yes**.

4. In the **Manage All Views** dialog box, click **OK** or **Apply View**.

Working with the Status Bar

The status bar displays information about the current state of Outlook and the active module, such as the following:

- The number of items in the current module, and the number of unread messages when in the Mail module

- A Reminders button, if you have overdue reminders

- The send/receive status for the current folder, while a send/receive operation is occurring

- The connection status for Exchange accounts

- The view buttons specific to the current module

- The Zoom controls for the content pane

You can modify the content that appears on the status bar.

Customize Status Bar

	Quota Information	Off
✓	Filter	
✓	Items in View	745
✓	Header Items in View	
✓	Unread Items in View	1
✓	Reminders	1
✓	View Shortcuts	
✓	Zoom	100%
✓	Zoom Slider	

Reminders that you set for tasks, appointments, flagged messages, and other Outlook items appear in the Reminders window. From the Reminders window, you can open the item, dismiss the reminder, or reset the reminder to appear at a later time.

> **Tip** Dismissing the reminder for a task marks the task as complete.

➤ To modify the status bar content

1. Right-click an inactive area of the status bar.
2. On the **Customize Status Bar** menu, click a status bar element to display or hide it.

➤ To display overdue reminders

→ On the status bar, click the **Reminders** button.

➤ To dismiss a reminder

→ In the **Reminders** window, click the item, and then click **Dismiss**.

➤ To reschedule a reminder

1. In the **Reminders** window, click the item.
2. In the **Click Snooze to be reminded again in** list, click the time you'd like the new reminder to appear.
3. In the **Reminders** dialog box, click **Snooze**.

   Or

1. In the **Reminders** window, double-click the item.

2. In the item window, change the reminder time. Then close the item window and save your changes.

> **See Also** For information about setting default reminder options, see the "Managing Advanced Options" topic of section 1.1, "Apply and Manipulate Outlook Program Options."

➤ **To display the status of a send/receive operation**

→ On the status bar, click the **Send/Receive** progress bar.

➤ **To connect to an Exchange account**

→ On the status bar, click the **Disconnected** button.

> **See Also** For information about changing the module view, see the "Displaying Module Content" topic earlier in this section.

Practice Tasks

There are no practice files for these tasks.

- Display the Mail module in the default Normal view. Then switch to Reading view to maximize the message viewing space.

- Display the current week in the Calendar module in Calendar And Tasks view. Enter a task on the current day, and then drag the task to the calendar to allocate time to it.

- Display the Contacts module in List view. Add the First Name and Last Name fields to the view, immediately to the right of the Full Name field. Then remove the Full Name field from the view.

- Reset the Contacts module List view to its default settings, and then return the Mail module and Calendar module to their standard views.

1.4 Apply Search and Filter Tools

Using Instant Search

The Instant Search feature of Outlook 2010 makes it easy to find a specific Outlook item based on any text within the item or any attribute, such as the category assigned to it. With this very powerful search engine, you can find any message containing a specified search term, whether the term appears in the message header, in the message itself, or in a message attachment.

Although you can use Instant Search to locate calendar items, contact records, and tasks, you will most often use it to locate messages in your Inbox and other mail folders. You can search a specific mail folder or search all mail folders. As you type the search term, Outlook filters out all messages that don't match, displays only those items containing the characters you enter, and highlights the search term in the displayed messages, making it easy to find exactly what you're looking for. In the lower-left corner of the program window, the status bar displays the number of messages included in the search results.

Unless you specify otherwise, the search results include only the contents of the displayed folder, not any of its subfolders or any other folders. However, you can choose to search all mail folders or all Outlook items. If you search more than one folder, Outlook displays the search results grouped by the folder in which they appear.

You can open, delete, and process a message from the Search Results pane as you would from any other folder. However, if you change a message so that it no longer fits the search criteria, the message is removed from the Search Results pane.

➤ **To search a specific folder**

1. Display the folder contents in the content pane.

2. In the **Search** box at the top of the content pane, enter the search term.

3. On the **Search** contextual tab, in the **Refine** group, click buttons to specify additional search criteria.

➤ **To change the scope of the search operation**

→ On the **Search** contextual tab, in the **Scope** group, click the **All Items** button for the type of item contained in the current folder (for example, **All Mail Items** or **All Calendar Items**) to search all items of that type.

→ On the **Search** contextual tab, in the **Scope** group, click the **All Subfolders** button to include subfolders of the current folder in the search.

→ On the **Search** contextual tab, in the **Scope** group, click the **All Outlook Items** button to include items of all types (including messages, appointments, contact records, and so on) in the search.

> **Tip** The All Items and All Outlook Items searches include all accounts configured in your Outlook installation.

➤ **To return to the original content view**

→ On the **Search** contextual tab, in the **Close** group, click the **Close Search** button.

→ Click any folder in the **Navigation Pane**.

➤ **To quickly return to previous search results**

1. Click in the **Search** box at the top of the content pane to display the **Search** contextual tab.

2. On the **Search** contextual tab, in the **Options** group, click the **Recent Searches** button, and then click the search you want to repeat.

Using Search Folders

A Search Folder is a virtual folder that contains pointers to all the messages in your mailbox that match a specific set of search criteria, regardless of which folders the messages are actually stored in. Outlook 2010 doesn't by default include standard Search Folders. If you want quick access to messages that fit a specific set of criteria, you can create a custom Search Folder.

After you create a Search Folder, Outlook automatically keeps Search Folder contents up to date, and you can access it from the Search Folders node of the Mail module in the Navigation Pane. The names of folders containing unread items are bold, followed by the number of unread items in parentheses. The names of folders containing items flagged for follow up are bold, followed by the number of flagged items in square brackets. The names of folders whose contents are not up to date are italic.

Each unique message in your mailbox is stored in only one folder, but it might appear in several Search Folders. Changing or deleting a message in a Search Folder changes or deletes the message in the folder where it is stored.

➤ To create a Search Folder

1. Display any mail folder.

2. On the **Folder** tab, in the **New** group, click **New Search Folder**.

3. In the **New Search Folder** dialog box, select the type of Search Folder you want to create, and then click **OK**.

> **Tip** You can choose from the standard options presented or click Create A Custom Search Folder to specify other search options.

➤ To change the content that appears in an existing Search Folder

1. Right-click the Search Folder, and then click **Customize This Search Folder**.

2. In the **Customize** dialog box, click **Criteria**.

3. In the **Search Folder Criteria** dialog box, change the criteria that identify the Search Folder contents.

4. Click **OK** in each of the open dialog boxes.

Practice Tasks

There are no practice files for these tasks.

- Use the Instant Search feature to locate a specific message in your Inbox.

- Without changing the search term, expand the search to include all Outlook items.

- Search all Outlook items for anything related to a specific person, such as your manager.

- Search all Outlook items for anything you have assigned to a specific category, such as the Management category. Then search for all items that have attachments.

- Create a Search Folder containing all the messages in your Inbox (not your mailbox) from a specific person, such as your manager.

1.5 Print an Outlook Item

Printing Items

In Outlook 2010, you can print any item from the content pane or from the item window.

➤ **To print an individual item**

→ In the content pane, right-click the item, and then click **Quick Print**.

→ In the program window, on the **Print** page of the Backstage view, specify the print options and settings you want, and then click the **Print** button.

➤ **To print multiple items**

1. In the content pane, select the items you want to print.

2. In the program window, on the **Print** page of the Backstage view, specify the print options and settings you want, and then click **Print**.

Printing Messages

You can print a list of the email messages in your Inbox or print one or more individual email messages. Outlook prints the message as shown on-screen, including font and paragraph formats. You can add information such as page headers and footers.

➤ **To print a list view of all messages in a folder**

→ In the program window, on the **Print** page of the Backstage view, click **Table Style** in the **Settings** section, and then click the **Print** button.

➤ **To print an email message and its attachments**

1. On the **Print** page of the Backstage view, click the **Print Options** button.

2. In the **Print** dialog box, select the **Print attached files** check box. Then click **Print**.

➤ **To print a message attachment**

1. In the **Reading Pane** or message window, select the attachment(s) you want to print.

2. On the **Attachments** contextual tab, in the **Actions** group, click the **Quick Print** button.

Printing a Calendar

When printing a calendar, the amount of detail that appears depends on the period you print and the print style you choose.

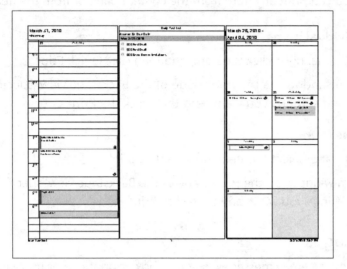

Outlook offers several built-in print styles for calendars, and you can create others if you want. The available print styles vary based on what view you're in when you choose the Print command. The default print styles include:

- **Daily Style** Prints the selected date range with one day per page. Printed elements include the date, day, TaskPad, reference calendar for the current month, and an area for notes.

- **Weekly Agenda Style** Prints the selected date range with one calendar week per page, including reference calendars for the selected and following month.

- **Weekly Calendar Style** Prints the selected date range with one calendar week per page. Each page includes date range and time increments, reference calendars for the selected and following month, and TaskPad.

- **Monthly Style** Prints a page for each month in the selected date range. Each page includes the selected month with a few days showing from the previous and subsequent months, along with reference calendars for the selected and following month.

- **Tri-fold Style** Prints a page for each day in the selected date range. Each page includes the daily schedule, weekly schedule, and TaskPad.

- **Calendar Details Style** Lists your appointments for the selected date range, as well as the accompanying appointment details.

You can select the date or range of dates to be printed and modify the page setup options to fit your needs.

➤ **To print a calendar**

1. In the Calendar module, on the **Print** page of the Backstage view, click **Print Options**.

2. In the **Print** dialog box, do the following:

   ○ In the **Print style** section, select the print style you want.

   ○ In the **Print range** section, specify the date range you want to print.

   ○ To exclude private appointments from the printed calendar, select the **Hide details of private appointments** check box.

3. In the **Print** dialog box, click the **Preview** button.

4. On the **Print** page of the Backstage view, click the **Print** button.

Printing Contact Records

You can print an address book or individual contact records, either on paper or to an electronic file (such as a PDF file or an XPS file), from any address book view.

he item to be printed and

Anderson, Nancy

Full Name: Nancy Anderson
Job Title: Research Associate
Company: Trey Research
E-mail: nancy@treyresearch.net

Davis, Andrew

Full Name: Andrew Davis
Job Title: Account Manager
Company: Trey Research
E-mail: andrew@treyresearch.net

Davis, Sara

Full Name: Sara Davis
Job Title: Assembly Plant Manager
Company: Wingtip Toys
4567 Main Street
Dallas, TX 98052
111 Magnolia Lane
Flower Mound, TX 98053
Bus: (972) 555-0101
E-mail: sara@wingtiptoys.com
E-mail 2: sara@thephone-company.com
Web Page: www.wingtiptoys.com

Dunker, Andrea

Full Name: Andrea Dunker
Job Title: Sales Associate
Company: Wingtip Toys
4567 Main Street
Dallas, TX 98052

1   of 1

Depending on the view, Outlook offers a variety of print styles, such as the following:

- **Card** Contact information displayed alphabetically in two columns. Letter graphics appear at the top of each page and the beginning of each letter group.

- **Small Booklet** Contact information displayed alphabetically in one column. Formatted to print eight numbered pages per sheet. Letter graphics appear at the top of each page and the beginning of each letter group, and a contact index at the side of each page indicates the position of that page's entries in the alphabet. Print double-sided if possible.

- **Medium Booklet** Contact information displayed alphabetically in one column. Formatted to print four numbered pages per sheet. Letter graphics appear at the top of each page and the beginning of each letter group, and a contact index at the side of each page indicates the position of that page's entries in the alphabet. Print double-sided if possible.

- **Memo** Contact information displayed under a memo-like header containing your name. Formatted to print one contact record per sheet.

- **Phone Directory** Contact names and telephone numbers displayed in two columns. Letter graphics appear at the top of each page and the beginning of each letter group.

- **Table** Contact information displayed in a table that matches the on-screen layout.

Table style is available only from the Phone and List views of the Contacts module. All other styles are available from the Business Card and Card views. You can customize the layout of most of the default print styles, and save the modified print styles.

➤ **To print contact records**

1. In the Contacts module, on the **Print** page of the Backstage view, select the contact record printing style you want in the **Settings** list, and then click **Print Options**.

2. In the **Print** dialog box, specify the contact records you want to print, and then click **Print**.

   Or

1. In the Contacts module, select the contact records you want to print.

2. On the **Print** page of the Backstage view, select the contact record printing style you want in the **Settings** list, and then click the **Print** button.

Practice Tasks

There are no practice files for these tasks.

- In your Inbox, select two email messages that have attachments. In one operation, print both messages and their attachments.

- Print your calendar for the next three days so that the daily schedule for each day appears on its own page with space for a task list.

- Select four contact records and print a list of only the names and phone numbers from those contact records.

Objective Review

Before finishing this chapter, ensure that you have mastered the following skills:

1.1 Apply and Manipulate Outlook Program Options

1.2 Manipulate Item Tags

1.3 Arrange the Content Pane

1.4 Apply Search and Filter Toolss

1.5 Print an Outlook Item

2 Creating and Formatting Item Content

The skills tested in this section of the Microsoft Office Specialist exam for Microsoft Outlook 2010 relate to creating, managing, and formatting Outlook items. Specifically, the following objectives are associated with this set of skills:

2.1 Create and Send Email Messages
2.2 Create and Manage Quick Steps
2.3 Create Item Content
2.4 Format Item Content
2.5 Attach Content to Email Messages

Outlook is designed to act as a complete information-management system. It provides many simple yet useful features you can use to work with email messages, contacts, appointments, tasks, notes, and other items. Although the tasks specific to each type of item vary, you use similar techniques to create, manage, and format the content of all Outlook items.

This chapter guides you in studying ways to manage outgoing and incoming messages, including creating and working with Quick Steps. It also guides you in creating and formatting content in email messages, contact records, and other Outlook items, and attaching files or Outlook items to email messages.

> **Practice Files** Before you can complete the practice tasks in this chapter, you need to copy the book's practice files to your computer. The practice files you'll use to complete the tasks in this chapter are in the Outlook\Objective2 practice file folder. A complete list of practice files is provided in "Using the Book's Companion Content" at the beginning of this book.

2.1 Create and Send Email Messages

Formatting Messages

When sending a message to a recipient who uses an email program other than Outlook, you might find it necessary to send the message in plain text or Rich Text Format rather than in the default HTML format.

➤ **To specify the format of an individual message**

→ On the **Format Text** tab, in the **Format** group, click the **HTML**, **Plain Text**, or **Rich Text** button.

> **See Also** For information about setting the default message format, see section 1.1, "Apply and Manipulate Outlook Program Options." For information about formatting message content by using a theme, see section 2.4, "Format Item Content."

Setting Message Options

You can format the appearance of individual messages and set the voting, tracking, and delivery options of an individual message without affecting the default settings.

Message settings and delivery options

> **See Also** For information about setting default message options, see section 1.1, "Apply and Manipulate Outlook Program Options."

➤ **To create an email poll**

1. On the **Options** tab, click the **More Options** dialog box launcher.

2. In the **Voting and Tracking options** area of the **Properties** dialog box, select the **Use voting buttons** check box.

3. In the **Use voting buttons** list, do one of the following, and then click **Close**:

   ○ Click the combination of voting buttons you want in the list.

   ○ Enter the voting button labels you want, separated by semicolons.

➤ **To request a message receipt**

1. On the **Options** tab, click the **More Options** dialog box launcher.

2. In the **Voting and Tracking options** area of the **Properties** dialog box, do any of the following, and then click **Close**:

   ○ Select the **Request a delivery receipt** check box to request notification when the message is delivered to the recipient's mailbox.

   ○ Select the **Request a read receipt** check box to request notification when the message is marked as read.

➤ **To direct responses to an alternative email address**

1. On the **Options** tab, in the **More Options** group, click the **Direct Replies To** button.

   Or

   On the **Options** tab, click the **More Options** dialog box launcher.

2. In the **Delivery options** area of the **Properties** dialog box, enter the email address to which you want responses to be delivered in the **Have replies sent to** box. Then click **Close**.

➤ **To schedule the delivery of a message**

1. On the **Options** tab, in the **More Options** group, click the **Delay Delivery** button.

   Or

   On the **Options** tab, click the **More Options** dialog box launcher.

2. In the **Delivery options** area of the **Properties** dialog box, click the date and time at which you want Outlook to send the message in the **Do not deliver before** lists. Then click **Close**.

➤ **To set an expiration for a message**

1. On the **Options** tab, click the **More Options** dialog box launcher.

2. In the **Delivery options** area of the **Properties** dialog box, select the **Expires after** check box, and then click the date and time at which you want the message to expire. Then click **Close**.

> **See Also** For information about setting reminders on outgoing messages, see section 1.2, "Manipulate Item Tags."

Sending Messages

In addition to the To and Cc fields, which are displayed by default in the message composition window, you can display the From field and the Bcc field. When you display or hide these optional message header fields in an individual message, Outlook retains the setting for all message composition windows.

You can send a message from any account for which you have permission. Valid sending accounts include those that are configured on your computer and other accounts for which you have been delegated permission.

➤ **To display or hide message header fields**

→ On the **Options** tab, in the **Show Fields** group, click the **Bcc** button.

➤ **To specify the sending account**

→ If multiple accounts are configured in Outlook, click the **From** button in the message header, and then click the account from which you want to send the message.

→ If only one account is configured in Outlook, click the **From** button in the message header and then click **Other E-mail Address**. In the **Send From Other E-mail Address** dialog box, enter the account from which you want to send the message in the **From** box.

➤ **To save a sent message in a folder other than the default**

1. On the **Options** tab, in the **More Options** group, click the **Save Sent Item To** button and then click **Other Folder**.

2. In the **Select Folder** dialog box, click the folder to which you want to save the sent message, and then click **OK**.

> **See Also** For information about setting the default location for sent messages, see section 1.1, "Apply and Manipulate Outlook Program Options."

Practice Tasks

There are no practice files for these tasks.

- Send a plain text message to yourself with the subject *MCAS Delivery* that is scheduled to be delivered after noon tomorrow and to expire at midnight tomorrow. Request a receipt when the message is read, and stipulate that the sent message should be saved in your Drafts folder.

- Send a message to yourself with the subject *MCAS Vote* that has *I Will*, *I Might*, and *I Will Not* voting buttons. Respond to the poll when you receive it.

2.2 Create and Manage Quick Steps

With the Quick Steps feature, you can perform multiple processes on one or more email messages with only one click.

In a new installation of Outlook, the Quick Steps gallery includes five standard Quick Steps: Move To, Team E-mail, Reply & Delete, To Manager, and Done. For each of the built-in Quick Steps, you can change its name; edit, add, and remove actions; and specify tooltip text that appears when you point to the Quick Step in the Quick Steps gallery.

You can create Quick Steps that include any combination of up to 12 actions. You can base a new Quick Step on a standard set of actions or an existing Quick Step, or create it from scratch. You can assign shortcut keys (Ctrl+Shift+1 through Ctrl+Shift+9) to up to nine Quick Steps.

> **Tip** The Quick Steps feature is available only in the Mail module. If you connect to multiple accounts, the Quick Steps in each Mail module are specific to that account.

➤ To set up and use an existing Quick Step

1. On the **Home** tab, in the **Quick Steps** gallery, click the Quick Step you want to perform.

2. In the **First Time Setup** dialog box, provide the information required for the selected command, and then click **Save**.

   Or

In the **First Time Setup** dialog box, provide the information required for the selected command, click **Options**, and then follow the instructions for changing the properties of an existing Quick Step.

➤ **To perform an existing Quick Step**

1. Select a message or group of messages.

2. On the **Home** tab, in the **Quick Steps** gallery, click the Quick Step you want to perform.

   Or

   Right-click the selected message(s), point to **Quick Steps**, and then click the Quick Step you want to perform.

➤ **To view the properties of an existing Quick Step**

1. On the **Home** tab, click the **Quick Steps** dialog box launcher.

2. In the **Manage Quick Steps** dialog box, in the **Quick step** list, click the Quick Step you want to view.

➤ **To change the properties of an existing Quick Step**

1. In the **Quick Steps** gallery, right-click the Quick Step you want to modify, and then click **Edit <Quick Step name>**.

   Or

   On the **Home** tab, click the **Quick Steps** dialog box launcher. In the **Manage Quick Steps** dialog box, click the Quick Step you want to modify, and then click **Edit**.

2. In the **Edit Quick Step** dialog box, do any of the following, and then click **Save**:

   - To rename the Quick Step, replace the text in the **Name** box.

   - To replace an action, in the **Actions** list, click the existing action and then click the replacement action. Supply any secondary information necessary for the replacement action.

   - To add an action, click the **Add Action** button. Click **Choose an Action**, and then click the action you want to add. Supply any secondary information necessary for the new action.

   - To assign a shortcut key combination to the Quick Step, in the **Shortcut key** list, click the key combination you want.

   - To change the message that appears when you point to the Quick Step, edit the text in the **Tooltip text** box.

➤ **To create a Quick Step**

1. In the **Quick Steps** gallery, click **Create New** to begin creating a custom Quick Step.

   Or

   Expand the **Quick Steps** gallery, click **New Quick Step**, and then click the basic action set you want the Quick Step to perform, or click **Custom**.

   Or

   Click the **Quick Steps** dialog box launcher. In the **Manage Quick Steps** dialog box, do one of the following:

   ○ Click **New**. Then click the basic action set you want the Quick Step to perform, or click **Custom**.

   ○ In the **Quick step** list, click an existing Quick Step on which you want to base the new Quick Step, and then click **Duplicate**.

2. In the **First Time Setup** or **Edit Quick Step** dialog box, provide the necessary information, and then click **Finish**.

➤ **To reset a built-in Quick Step**

1. On the **Home** tab, click the **Quick Steps** dialog box launcher.

2. In the **Manage Quick Steps** dialog box, in the **Quick step** list, click the Quick Step you want to reset.

3. Click **Reset to Defaults**, and then click **Yes** in the Microsoft Outlook dialog box that opens.

➤ **To delete a Quick Step**

→ In the **Quick Steps** gallery, right-click the Quick Step, and then click **Delete**.

→ Click the **Quick Steps** dialog box launcher. In the **Manage Quick Steps** dialog box, click the Quick Step you want to modify, and then click **Delete**.

Practice Tasks

There are no practice files for these tasks.

- Set up the built-in *Team E-mail* Quick Step to send a message with the subject *MOS Certification Information* to you and two other people. Specify that the message body should be prefilled with the text *New information about MOS Certification*.

- Create a Quick Step named *Categorize MOS* that will do the following:
  - Assign the message to a category named *MOS Study Guide*. (Create the category during the process of creating the Quick Step.)
  - Create a task containing the text of the message.

- Use the *Team E-mail* Quick Step to create a message. Replace the built-in message body content with the text *I'm testing the Outlook 2010 Quick Step feature; please reply to this message*. Then send the message.

- After you receive the two responses to the *MOS Certification Information* message, run the *Categorize MOS* Quick Step on the two messages simultaneously.

- Reset the properties of the *Team E-mail* Quick Step, and delete the *Categorize MOS* Quick Step.

2.3 Create Item Content

Inserting Visual Elements

Using Outlook 2010, you can communicate visual information in the following ways:

- Share photographs with other people by attaching them to or embedding them in messages.

- Explain complicated processes and other business information by creating SmartArt graphics within messages or by embedding SmartArt graphics that you create in other Office 2010 programs.

- Communicate statistical information by creating a chart within a message.

- Decorate message content by inserting clip art images and shapes.

- Share information from websites, documents, and other visual presentations by capturing pictures of things on your screen, using the Screenshot and Screen Clipping tools, and then inserting those screen clippings in your message.

You can insert visual elements into the content pane of an email message, calendar item, or task; or into the Notes pane of a contact record. (You can't insert an image into a note.)

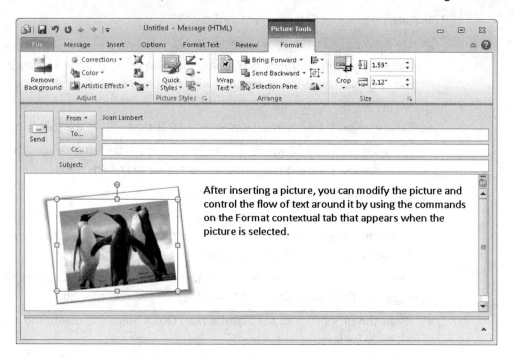

After inserting a picture, you can modify the picture and control the flow of text around it by using the commands on the Format contextual tab that appears when the picture is selected.

➤ **To insert a picture from a file**

1. Position the cursor in the content pane or **Notes** pane where you want the picture to appear.

2. On the **Insert** tab, in the **Illustrations** group, click the **Picture** button.

3. In the **Insert Picture** dialog box, browse to the folder containing the picture you want to insert.

4. Click the picture to select it, and then click **Insert**.

Tip To insert multiple pictures at one time, select the first picture you want to insert. Then either press Shift and click the last picture in a consecutive series, or press Ctrl and click each individual picture.

➤ To locate and insert a clip art image

1. Position the cursor in the content pane or **Notes** pane where you want the image to appear.

2. On the **Insert** tab, in the **Illustrations** group, click the **Clip Art** button.

3. In the **Search** box at the top of the **Clip Art** task pane, enter one or more keywords describing the image you want to locate.

4. In the **Results should be** list, clear the check boxes of any media file types you don't want to search for. Then click **Go**.

5. Scroll through the search results until you locate the image you want to insert.

> **Tip** If you don't find an image that fits your needs, click the Find More At Office.com link to display the Images And More page of the Microsoft Office website. From that page, you can browse categories of images and download images you like to your local clip art collection.

6. Point to any image to display a ScreenTip with information about the file, click the vertical bar that appears on the right side of the image to display a menu of commands, and then click **Insert** on the menu to insert the image.

➤ To insert a shape

→ On the **Insert** tab, in the **Illustrations** group, click the **Shapes** button.

→ In the **Shapes** gallery, click the shape you want to insert.

→ In the content pane or **Notes** pane, drag to draw the shape at the size you want.

Inserting SmartArt Graphics

You can create a SmartArt graphic directly in an email message, contact record, or calendar item. When sending a message, Outlook converts any SmartArt graphics within the message to static graphics.

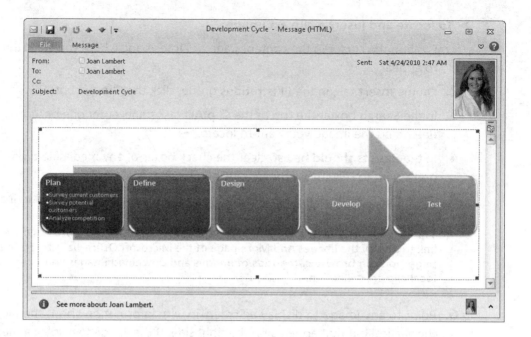

➤ **To create a SmartArt graphic**

1. Position the cursor in the pane where you want the picture to appear.

2. On the **Insert** tab, in the **Illustrations** group, click the **SmartArt** button.

3. In the **Choose a SmartArt Graphic** dialog box, locate the type of graphic you want to create. Click the corresponding icon, and then click **OK**.

➤ **To populate a SmartArt graphic from scratch**

1. Follow the steps to create a SmartArt graphic.

2. In the **Text** pane, for each graphic element you want to label, click the **[Text]** placeholder to the right of the bullet and then enter the label text.

   Or

   In the diagram, click the **[Text]** placeholder in each graphic element you want to label, and then enter the label text.

➤ **To modify the elements included in a SmartArt graphic**

→ In the **Text** pane, do any of the following:

   ○ To insert an element, position the cursor at the end of the preceding element's label text, and then press Enter.

   ○ To demote an element, click the label text, and then press Tab.

   ○ To promote an element, click the label text, and then press Shift+Tab.

   ○ To remove an element, select the label text, and then press Delete.

→ In the SmartArt graphic, do any of the following:

   ○ To insert an element at the same hierarchical level, first click an adjacent element to select it. On the SmartArt Tools **Design** contextual tab, in the **Create Graphic** group, click the **Add Shape** arrow and then click **Add Shape After** or **Add Shape Before**.

   ○ To insert a lower-level element, first click the frame of the existing element. On the **Design** contextual tab, in the **Create Graphic** group, click the **Add Shape** arrow and then click **Add Shape Below**.

   ○ To insert a higher-level element, first click the frame of the existing element. On the **Design** contextual tab, in the **Create Graphic** group, click the **Add Shape** arrow and then click **Add Shape Above**.

   ○ To demote or promote the selected element, on the **Design** contextual tab, in the **Create Graphic** group, click the **Demote** button or the **Promote** button.

   ○ To remove the selected element, press Delete.

> **Tip** You can display or hide the Text pane for any SmartArt graphic by clicking the diagram and then clicking the Text Pane button in the Create Graphic group on the Design contextual tab, or by clicking the Text Pane tab (the opposing arrowheads) on the left side of the diagram's frame.

Inserting Charts

You can create a chart directly in an email message, contact record, or calendar item. Charts you create in an Outlook message look exactly like those you would create in a Microsoft Excel workbook—because they are based on an Excel data source that is created from within Outlook.

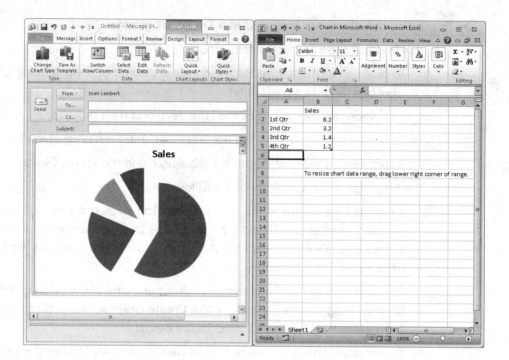

➤ **To create a chart**

1. Position the cursor in the pane where you want the picture to appear.

2. On the **Insert** tab, in the **Illustrations** group, click the **Chart** button.

3. In the **Insert Chart** dialog box, locate the type of chart you want to create. Click the chart icon, and then click **OK**.

4. In the Excel program window that opens, update the mock data with your own. When you finish, close the Excel window.

> **Tip** It's not necessary to save or name the worksheet that contains the data plotted by the chart.

➤ **To modify a chart**

1. Click the chart to activate it, and then display the Excel data sheet by doing one of the following:

   ○ On the Chart Tools **Design** contextual tab, in the **Data** group, click the **Edit Data** button.

   ○ Right-click the chart, and then click **Edit Data**.

2. Update the data, and then close the Excel window.

Inserting Screen Images

You can use the Screenshot and Screen Clipping tools to easily capture images of either an entire window that's open on your screen or a specific area of the screen that you select.

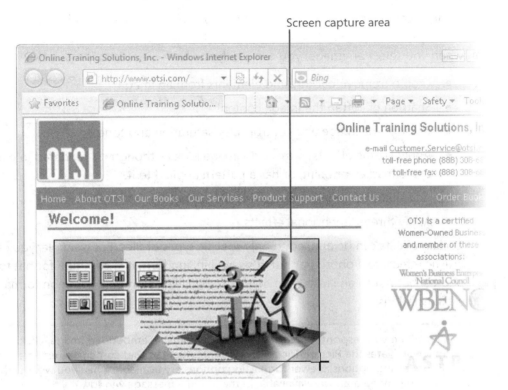

Screen capture area

➤ **To capture and insert a screen image**

1. Ensure that the window you want to capture is not minimized or, if you plan to capture only a portion of a window, that it's visible on the screen.

2. In the Outlook item window, position the cursor in the content pane or **Notes** pane where you want the image to appear.

3. On the **Insert** tab, in the **Illustrations** group, click the **Screenshot** button. In the **Available Windows** gallery displaying the currently open (non-minimized) windows, do one of the following:

   o   To insert an image of an entire open window into the Outlook item, click its icon.

   o   To capture an image of a portion of the content that's visible on your screen, click **Screen Clipping**. Position the Screen Clipping tool in the upper-left corner of the area you want to capture, and then drag to define the capture area.

Modifying Visual Elements

After inserting a visual element, you can modify it by using the commands on the contextual tab that appears when the visual element is selected.

Using functionality that is new in Office 2010, you can modify and enhance images directly in the item window. From the new Picture Tools contextual tab that appears when you select an image, you can do things like:

- Crop or remove background elements from an image.
- Sharpen or soften the image content.
- Colorize the image and control color saturation and tone.
- Apply artistic effects to make an image look as though it's rendered in pencil, chalk, marker, or paint, or has a pattern applied to it.
- Add shadows, reflections, and glowing or soft edges.
- Apply three-dimensional effects.

Certain effects can be applied to only specific types of files. For example, you can apply artistic effects to a photograph that's saved in .jpg format (a common format for digital photos) but not to an illustration that's saved in .wmf format (a common format for clip art illustrations).

> **Tip** When you respond to a message that contains an embedded image, clicking the image activates the Picture Tools Format contextual tab that contains a restricted range of formatting options. (Fewer formatting options are available when you work with the modified image than were available in the original message window.)

> **Strategy** You use the same commands to format visual elements in Outlook that you do in other Office 2010 programs. Each type of visual element that you create in an Outlook message has an associated contextual tab containing formatting commands. As you practice creating visual elements in this section, experiment with the commands that are available on the contextual tabs.

Creating Hyperlinks

Outlook automatically converts URLs that you enter in a message content pane into hyperlinks that the recipient can click to display the webpage. You can manually create a hyperlink from any text or graphic to a heading or bookmark within the message or to an external file or webpage. You can also create a hyperlink that the recipient can click to create a new email message that already has the To and Subject fields populated.

➤ **To create a hyperlink to an existing file**

1. Select the text or graphic from which you want to link.

2. On the **Insert** tab, in the **Links** group, click the **Hyperlink** button.

3. In the **Insert Hyperlink** dialog box, in the **Link to** list, click **Existing File or Web Page**.

4. In the **Look in** area, browse to the file you want to link to.

   Or

   Click the **Browse for File** button and then, in the **Link to File** dialog box, browse to the file and click **Open**.

5. In the **Insert Hyperlink** dialog box, click **OK**.

➤ **To create a Word document and a hyperlink to it**

1. Select the text or graphic from which you want to link.

2. On the **Insert** tab, in the **Links** group, click the **Hyperlink** button.

3. In the **Insert Hyperlink** dialog box, in the **Link to** list, click **Create New Document**.

4. In the **Name of new document** box, enter a name for the document.

5. To create the document in a folder other than your Documents folder, click the **Change** button, browse to the folder in which you want to save the file, and then click **OK**.

6. In the **When to edit** area of the **Insert Hyperlink** dialog box, do one of the following, and then click **OK**:

   ○ Click **Edit the new document later** to create a blank document.

   ○ Click **Edit the new document now** to create a document and open it in Word.

➤ To create a hyperlink to a webpage

1. Select the text or graphic from which you want to link.

2. On the **Insert** tab, in the **Links** group, click the **Hyperlink** button.

3. In the **Insert Hyperlink** dialog box, in the **Link to** list, click **Existing File or Web Page**.

4. In the **Address** box, enter the URL of the webpage you want to link to.

   Or

   Click the **Browse the Web** button. In the web browser window that opens, display the webpage you want to link to. Then minimize or close the browser window.

5. In the **Insert Hyperlink** dialog box, click **OK**.

➤ To create a hyperlink to a heading or bookmark within the message

1. Select the text or graphic from which you want to link.

2. On the **Insert** tab, in the **Links** group, click the **Hyperlink** button.

3. In the **Insert Hyperlink** dialog box, in the **Link to** list, click **Place in This Document**.

4. In the **Select a place in this document** box, click the heading or bookmark you want to link to. Then click **OK**.

➤ To create a hyperlink that creates a pre-addressed email message

1. Select the text or graphic from which you want to link.

2. On the **Insert** tab, in the **Links** group, click the **Hyperlink** button.

3. In the **Insert Hyperlink** dialog box, in the **Link to** list, click **E-mail Address**.

4. In the **E-mail address** box, enter the message recipient.

5. In the **Subject** box, enter the message subject. Then click **OK**.

➤ To change the target of an existing hyperlink

1. Right-click the hyperlinked text or graphic, and then click **Edit Hyperlink**.

2. In the **Edit Hyperlink** dialog box, change the properties of the hyperlink, and then click **OK**.

➤ **To remove a hyperlink**

➔ Right-click the hyperlinked text or graphic, and then click **Remove Hyperlink**.

Practice Tasks

The practice file for these tasks is located in the Outlook\Objective2 practice file folder.

- Create an email message with the subject *MOS Image*. In the message body, insert the *KauaiLighthouse* picture. Resize the picture so it is 4 inches wide, and apply the Bevel Rectangle frame style.

- Create an email message with the subject *MOS Business Graphic*. In the message body, create a SmartArt graphic depicting a life cycle that includes the following stages:

    ○ Plant

    ○ Tend

    ○ Harvest

    ○ Eat

    Use the Block Cycle layout, the Colorful color scheme, and the Cartoon style.

- Create an email message with the subject *MOS Links*. In the message body, enter the following text:

    You can find more information about Microsoft Office 2010 here. Please let me know if you have any questions.

    Insert the following hyperlinks in the message text:

    ○ A link from the words *Microsoft Office* that displays the Office website at office.microsoft.com in a new window.

    ○ A link from the words *let me know* that creates an email message addressed to you with the subject *Office help request*.

2.4 Format Item Content

Applying Text and Paragraph Formatting

You can manually format text in the content pane to differentiate it from your default font. The local formatting options available in Outlook 2010 are the same as those available in Microsoft Word 2010, PowerPoint 2010, and other Microsoft Office 2010 programs, and you might already be familiar with them from working with those programs. Here's a quick review of the types of formatting changes you can make.

- **Font, size, and color** More than 220 fonts in a range of sizes and in a virtually unlimited selection of colors.

- **Font style** Regular, bold, italic, or bold italic.

- **Underline style and color** Plain, multiple, dotted, dashed, wavy, and many combinations thereof, in all colors.

- **Effects** Strikethrough, superscript, subscript, shadow, outline, emboss, engrave, small caps, all caps, or hidden.

- **Character spacing** Scale, spacing, position, and kerning.

- **Paragraph attributes** Alignment, indentation, and spacing.

- **Character and paragraph styles** Titles, headings, and purpose-specific font formatting (for example, for quotes and book titles).

➤ **To apply local formatting to selected text**

→ On the **Message** tab of the message composition window, in the **Basic Text** group, click or select the formatting you want to apply.

→ On the **Message** tab, click the **Basic Text** dialog box launcher. On the **Font** and **Advanced** pages of the **Font** dialog box, click or select the formatting you want to apply, and then click **OK**.

→ On the **Format Text** tab of the message composition window, in the **Font** and **Paragraph** groups, click or select the formatting you want to apply.

→ On the **Format Text** tab, click the **Font** dialog box launcher. In the **Font** dialog box, click or select the formatting you want to apply, and then click **OK**.

→ On the **Format Text** tab, click the **Paragraph** dialog box launcher. On the **Indents and Spacing** and **Line and Page Breaks** pages of the **Paragraph** dialog box, click or select the formatting you want to apply, and then click **OK**.

→ Select the text and then, on the Mini Toolbar, click or select the formatting you want to apply.

> **To apply existing formatting to other text**

1. In the message composition window, position the cursor in the formatted text or paragraph.

2. On the **Message** tab or **Format Text** tab, in the **Clipboard** group, click the **Format Painter** button to store the character and paragraph formatting of the selected text or active paragraph for a single use.

    Or

    In the **Clipboard** group, double-click the **Format Painter** button to store the formatting of the selected text or active paragraph for multiple uses.

3. Drag the paintbrush-shaped cursor across the text to which you want to apply the stored formatting.

4. If necessary, click the **Format Painter** button or press the Esc key to turn off the Format Painter tool.

Tip When working with certain content elements such as tables and graphics, one or more contextual tabs containing formatting commands specific to that element appear on the ribbon. You must select the element to access its formatting commands.

Applying and Managing Styles

A style is a combination of character formatting and paragraph formatting that you can apply to selected text or the active paragraph with one click. You can apply the same styles to the content of an Outlook email message that you can to the content of a Word document. If the existing styles don't exactly meet your needs, you can modify existing styles and create styles from scratch.

Quick Styles gallery

Styles pane

AaBbCcDc	AaBbCcDc	**AaBbC**	AaBbCc	**AaB**	*AaBbCc.*
¶ Normal	¶ No Spaci...	Heading 1	Heading 2	Title	Subtitle
AaBbCcDc	***AaBbCcDc***	**AaBbCcDc**	*AaBbCcDc*	***AaBbCcDc***	AABBCCDC
Emphasis	Intense E...	Strong	Quote	Intense Q...	Subtle Ref...
AABBCCDC	AaBbCcDc				
Book Title	¶ List Para...				

- Save Selection as a New Quick Style...
- Clear Formatting
- Apply Styles...

Styles   ▼ ✕

Clear All	
Balloon Text	¶a
Bibliography	¶
Block Text	¶
Body Text	¶a
Body Text 2	¶a
Body Text 3	¶a
Body Text First Indent	¶a
Body Text First Indent 2	¶a
Body Text Indent	¶a
Body Text Indent 2	¶a
Body Text Indent 3	¶a
Book Title	a
Caption	¶
Closing	¶a
Comment Reference	a
Comment Subject	¶a
Comment Text	¶a
Date	¶a

☐ Show Preview
☐ Disable Linked Styles

Options...

➤ **To display the Styles pane**

→ On the **Format Text** tab, click the **Styles** dialog box launcher.

➤ **To preview the effect of a style on selected text**

→ On the **Format Text** tab, in the **Quick Styles** gallery, point to the style you want to preview.

➤ **To apply a style to selected text**

→ On the **Format Text** tab, in the **Quick Styles** gallery, click the style you want to apply.

→ In the **Styles** pane, click the style you want to apply.

➤ **To modify the formatting of an existing style**

1. In the **Styles** pane, point to the style, click the arrow that appears, and then click **Modify**.

2. In the **Modify Style** dialog box, click the **Format** button, and then click the type of formatting you want to modify.

3. In the dialog box that opens, make the changes you want, and then click **OK**.

4. In the **Modify Style** dialog box, do the following, and then click **OK**:

   ○ Select or clear the **Add to Quick Style list** check box.

   ○ If you want to save the modified style as part of the current document template, click **New documents based on this template**.

➤ **To create a style from scratch**

1. Apply the character and paragraph formatting that you want to include in the new style to text or to a paragraph, and then select the formatted content.

2. In the **Styles** pane, click the **New Style** button.

3. In the **Create New Style from Formatting** dialog box, do the following, and then click **OK**:

   ○ In the **Name** box, enter a name for the style.

   ○ In the **Style type** list, click **Paragraph**, **Character**, **Linked**, **Table**, or **List**.

   > **Tip** The following settings apply to Paragraph and Linked styles and may not be available for other style types.

   ○ In the **Style based on** list, click an existing style if you would like the new style to default to the existing style settings for any element you don't specifically define. Otherwise, click **Normal**.

   ○ In the **Style for following paragraph** list, click the style you want to be applied to a new paragraph when you press Enter at the end of a paragraph that has the new style applied.

   ○ In the **Formatting** section, click or select basic formatting options.

   Or

   In the **Formatting** list, click the type of formatting you want to define, define the formatting you want in the dialog box that opens, and then click **OK**.

   ○ Select or clear the **Add to Quick Style list** check box.

   ○ If you want to save the new style as part of the current document template, click **New documents based on this template**.

➤ **To include or exclude a style in the Quick Styles gallery**

   → In the **Styles** pane, point to the style, click the arrow that appears, and then click **Add to Quick Style Gallery** or **Remove from Quick Style Gallery**.

> **Tip** When pasting content into a message, the Paste Options button appears. From the Paste Options menu, you can choose whether to retain the original formatting of the content, apply the formatting into which you're pasting the content, merge formatting styles, or keep the text only.

Applying and Managing Style Sets

A style set changes the colors, fonts, and paragraph formatting of individual styles. You can change the appearance of all the styles in a message by selecting any of the 14 default style sets (or by creating your own). Selecting a style set changes the appearance of all the text in the current document, as well as the appearance of the icons in the Quick Styles gallery.

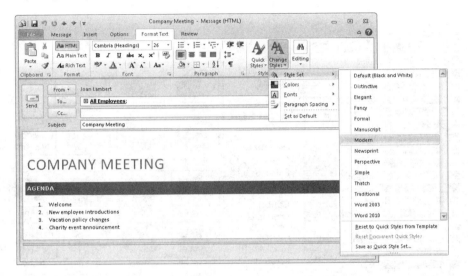

➤ **To preview or select a style set**

→ On the **Format Text** tab of the message composition window, in the **Styles** group, click the **Change Styles** button, click **Style Set**, and then point to or click a specific style set.

➤ **To create a style set**

1. Create the styles you want to include in the style set.

2. On the **Format Text** tab of the message composition window, in the **Styles** group, click the **Change Styles** button, point to **Style Set**, and then click **Save as Quick Style Set**.

3. In the **Save Quick Style Set** dialog box, enter a name for the style set in the **File name** box, and then click **Save**.

Applying and Managing Themes

A theme applies a preselected combination of colors, fonts, and effects to all the message content. The default theme for all Outlook email messages, Word documents, PowerPoint presentations, Excel workbooks, and other Office 2010 documents is the Office theme. You can modify the colors, fonts, and effects of a built-in theme and save customized themes for future use.

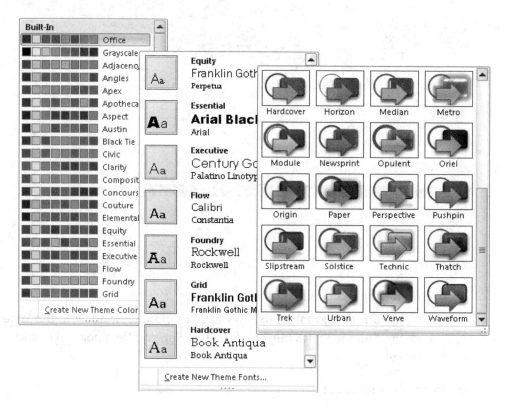

> ➤ **To preview or apply an existing theme**

   1. On the **Options** tab of a message composition window, in the **Themes** group, click the **Themes** button.

   2. In the **Themes** gallery, point to or click a specific theme.

> ➤ **To modify an existing theme**

   1. On the **Options** tab of a message composition window, in the **Themes** group, click the **Colors** button.

   2. In the **Colors** list, click the existing color combination you want to use.

   Or

   In the **Colors** list, click **Create New Theme Colors**. In the **Create New Theme Colors** dialog box, select the colors you want, enter a name for the color scheme in the **Name** box, and then click **Save**.

   3. In the **Fonts** list, click the existing font combination you want to use.

   Or

   In the **Fonts** list, click **Create New Theme Fonts**. In the **Create New Theme Fonts** dialog box, select the heading font and body font you want, enter a name for the font scheme in the **Name** box, and then click **Save**.

   4. In the **Effects** gallery, click the effect scheme you want to use.

> ➤ **To create a custom theme**

   1. Modify any existing theme.

   2. On the **Options** tab of the message composition window, in the **Themes** group, click the **Themes** button and then, in the **Themes** gallery, click **Save Current Theme**.

   3. In the **Save Current Theme** dialog box, enter a name for the theme in the **File name** box, and then click **Save**.

Practice Tasks

The practice file for these tasks is located in the Outlook\Objective2 practice file folder.

- Create a message with the subject *MOS Formatting*. Open the *Regulations* document, and select the content from the beginning of the document to the end of section 2.2. Paste the copied content into the *MOS Formatting* message as unformatted text.

- In the *MOS Formatting* message, format the pasted content as follows:
  - Apply the Title style to the first paragraph.
  - Apply the Subtitle style to the second paragraph.
  - Format the four paragraphs representing categories of rules as a bulleted list.
  - Apply the Heading 1 style to the Definitions and General Rules paragraphs.

- In the *MOS Formatting* message, format the Definitions and General Rules sections as follows:
  - Remove the numbers, periods, and leading spaces from the beginning of the headings and the paragraphs that follow them.
  - Format the paragraphs that follow the headings as numbered lists.

- In the *MOS Formatting* message, display the Styles pane. Modify the Heading 1 style so that it is preceded by an incrementing number followed by a period. Ensure that this places the number 1 at the beginning of the Definitions heading and the number 2 at the beginning of the General Rules heading.

- In the *MOS Formatting* message, define a new number format for the numbered lists so that the paragraphs following the Definitions heading are numbered as 1.1 and 1.2, and the paragraphs following the General Rules heading are numbered as 2.1 and 2.2. Verify that the formatting of the message content now resembles the original document content, and then close the *Regulations* document.

- In the *MOS Formatting* message, change the style set to Thatch. Then change the color scheme associated with the Office theme to Opulent.

2.5 Attach Content to Email Messages

A convenient way to distribute a file (such as a Word document, Excel workbook, PowerPoint presentation, or picture) is by attaching the file to an email message. Message recipients can preview or open the file from the Reading Pane, open it from the message window, forward it to other people, or save it to their computers.

You can also attach Outlook items, such as other messages, calendar items, contact records, notes, and tasks, to outgoing messages. Recipients can save attached items in their own Outlook installations.

➤ **To attach one or more files to a message**

→ Drag the file(s) you want to attach from Windows Explorer into the message area of the message window.

Or

1. On the **Message** tab or **Insert** tab of the message window, in the **Include** group, click the **Attach File** button.

2. In the **Insert File** dialog box, locate and click the first file you want to attach. To attach multiple files, press the Ctrl key and click the additional files.

3. In the **Insert File** dialog box, click **Insert**.

➤ **To attach an Outlook item to a message**

1. On the **Message** tab of the message window, in the **Include** group, click the **Attach Item** button, and then click **Outlook Item**.

2. In the **Insert Item** dialog box, locate and click the item you want to attach.

3. With **Attachment** selected in the **Insert as** area, click **OK**.

Practice Tasks

The practice files for these tasks are located in the Outlook\Objective2 practice file folder.

* Create a message with the subject *MOS Files*. Attach the *Brochure* document to the message. Use a different technique to attach the *Strategy* presentation to the message. Then send the *MOS Files* message to yourself.

* When the *MOS Files* message arrives, preview the attached Strategy presentation in the Reading Pane. Then open the attached *Brochure* document in Word.

* Create a message with the subject *MOS Items*. Attach any contact record and any calendar item to the message. Then send the *MOS Items* message to yourself.

* When the *MOS Items* message arrives, save the attached contact record to your Contacts module and merge it with the original version.

Objective Review

Before finishing this chapter, ensure that you have mastered the following skills:

2.1   Create and Send Email Messages

2.2   Create and Manage Quick Steps

2.3   Create Item Content

2.4   Format Item Content

2.5   Attach Content to Email Messages

3 Managing Email Messages

The skills tested in this section of the Microsoft Office Specialist exam for Microsoft Outlook 2010 relate to managing the messages in your Inbox and other mail folders. Specifically, the following objectives are associated with this set of skills:

3.1 Clean Up the Mailbox
3.2 Create and Manage Rules
3.3 Manage Junk Email
3.4 Manage Automatic Message Content

Even if you use Outlook only for sending and receiving email messages, you can rapidly build up a mass of messages that make it difficult to locate information. Fortunately, Outlook provides features you can use to help save and organize the messages you need and discard those you don't. It also helps you personalize messages and responses.

This chapter guides you in studying ways to manage message conversations and how to save messages and message attachments. You will also learn how to create, modify, and delete Outlook rules; how to manage junk mail; how to manage automatic message content such as signatures, themes, stationery, and fonts; and how to identify response text.

> **Practice Files** You don't need any practice files to complete the practice tasks in this chapter. For more information about practice file requirements, see "Using the Book's Companion Content" at the beginning of this book.

3.1 Clean Up the Mailbox

Managing Mailbox Size

You can manage the size of your mailbox by emptying the deleted items folder and archiving older items. You can use the Mailbox Cleanup tools to locate large folders, large items, and older items, and to manage the archiving and item deletion processes.

> ➤ **To view the size of your mailbox and individual folders within it**

1. On the **Info** page of the Backstage view, click the **Cleanup Tools** button, and then click **Mailbox Cleanup**.
2. In the **Mailbox Cleanup** dialog box, click the **View Mailbox Size** button.

> ➤ **To locate old Outlook items**

→ In the **Mailbox Cleanup** dialog box, click **Find items older than**, click or type to enter a number from 0 to 999 in the **days** box, and then click **Find**.

> ➤ **To locate large Outlook items**

→ In the **Mailbox Cleanup** dialog box, click **Find items larger than**, click or type to enter a number from 0 to 9,999 in the **kilobytes** box, and then click **Find**.

➤ **To archive items in accordance with the default settings**

→ In the **Mailbox Cleanup** dialog box, click the **AutoArchive** button.

Or

1. On the **Info** page of the Backstage view, click the **Cleanup Tools** button, and then click **Archive**.

2. In the **Archive** dialog box, click **Archive all folders according to their AutoArchive settings**, and then click **OK**.

➤ **To perform a custom archival process**

1. On the **Info** page of the Backstage view, click the **Cleanup Tools** button, and then click **Archive**.

2. In the **Archive** dialog box, click **Archive this folder and all subfolders**. Then in the folder structure, click the folder whose contents you want to archive.

3. In the **Archive items older than** box, enter the date before which you want to archive items.

4. In the **Archive** dialog box, click **OK**.

➤ **To stop an active archival process**

1. Display the program window (not the Backstage view).

2. On the status bar, to the right of the **Archiving** progress bar, click the **Cancel archiving** button.

➤ **To view the size of the Deleted Items folder of your default mailbox**

→ In the **Mailbox Cleanup** dialog box, click the **View Deleted Items Size** button.

➤ **To empty the Deleted Items folder of your default mailbox**

1. On the **Info** page of the Backstage view, click the **Cleanup Tools** button, and then click **Empty Deleted Items Folder**.

Or

In the **Mailbox Cleanup** dialog box, click the **Empty** button.

2. In the message box that appears, click **Yes** to confirm that you want to permanently delete the items.

➤ **To empty the Deleted Items folder of any mailbox**

1. Display the **Folder List** in the **Navigation Pane** and expand the mailbox to display its **Deleted Items** folder.

2. Right-click the **Deleted Items** folder, and then click **Empty Folder**.

3. In the message box that appears, click **Yes** to confirm that you want to permanently delete the items.

Managing Conversations

Using the Conversation view and conversation management tools that are new in Outlook 2010, you can view and manage related messages as a group. By default, Outlook displays the contents of your Inbox in Conversation view. When you expand a conversation in your Inbox, all messages in the conversation, regardless of the folder in which they reside, are shown as part of the conversation. You can turn Conversation view on or off at any time and manage the content included within a conversation and the appearance of the content.

➤ **To turn Conversation view on or off**

→ On the **View** tab, in the **Conversations** group, select or clear the **Show as Conversations** check box.

➤ **To manage Conversation view**

→ On the **View** tab, in the **Conversations** group, in the **Conversation Settings** list, click **Show Messages from Other Folders**, **Show Senders Above the Subject**, **Always Expand Conversations**, or **Use Classic Indented View**.

➤ **To delete redundant messages in a conversation**

1. Click a message or a conversation header, or select multiple messages or conversations.

2. On the **Home** tab, in the **Delete** group, click the **Clean Up** button.

3. In the **Clean Up** list, do one of the following:

   ○ To delete all redundant messages from the selected conversations, click **Clean Up Conversation** and then, in the **Clean Up Conversation** dialog box, click **Clean Up**.

   ○ To delete all redundant messages from the current folder but not its subfolders, click **Clean Up Folder** and then, in the **Clean Up Folder** dialog box, click **Clean Up Folder**.

   ○ To delete all redundant messages from the current folder and its subfolders, click **Clean Up Folder & Subfolders** and then, in the **Clean Up Folder** dialog box, click **Clean Up Folder**.

➤ To delete all current and future messages in conversation

1. Click a message or a conversation header, or select multiple messages or conversations.

2. On the **Home** tab, in the **Delete** group, click the **Ignore** button.

3. In the Ignore Conversation dialog box, click **Ignore Conversation**.

> **Tip** Be cautious when using the Ignore Conversation command. Outlook identifies "conversations" based on message subjects. If you receive unrelated messages in the future that have the same message subject as a conversation that you've chosen to ignore, the messages will be deleted.

Saving Messages and Message Attachments

You can save files that you receive as message attachments to your local hard drive so that you can work with them and save changes that you make to them.

To retain messages outside of Outlook, you can save messages as a variety of file types, including text files, Outlook templates, Outlook message files, and HTML files. Choose the file type based on your intended use or distribution.

➤ To save files attached to a selected message

1. In the **Reading Pane** or message window, right-click the attachment and then do one of the following:

   ○ To save the individual file, click **Save As**.

   ○ To save multiple files attached to the message, click **Save All Attachments**. In the **Save All Attachments** dialog box, select the files you want to save, and then click **OK**.

2. In the **Save Attachment** or **Save All Attachments** dialog box, browse to the folder in which you want to save the attachment, and then click **Save**.

   Or

1. In the left pane of the Backstage view, click **Save Attachments**.

2. In the **Save All Attachments** dialog box, select the files you want to save, and then click **OK**.

3. In the **Save Attachment** or **Save All Attachments** dialog box, browse to the folder in which you want to save the attachment, and then click **Save**.

➤ **To save a selected message as a file**

1. In the left pane of the Backstage view, click **Save As**.

2. In the **Save As** dialog box, browse to the folder in which you want to save the message.

3. In the **Save as type** list, click the format in which you want to save the message.

4. In the **Save As** dialog box, click **Save**.

> **Tip** You might find it necessary to save messages externally in order to reduce the size of your mailbox. For information about viewing the size of a mailbox and its subfolders, see the topic "Managing Mailbox Size" earlier in this section.

Practice Tasks

There are no practice files for these tasks.

- Display the contents of your Inbox in Conversation view. Identify a conversation with multiple threads, and delete the redundant messages in the conversation by using the Clean Up command.

- Select a message that has an attached file. Save the file to your Documents folder.

- Select a message that you want to reuse. Save the message as an Outlook template in the default Templates folder.

3.2 Create and Manage Rules

Managing Mail by Using Outlook Rules

You can have Outlook evaluate your incoming or outgoing email messages and make decisions about what to do with them based on instructions you set up, called *rules*. You can create rules based on different message criteria such as senders, recipients, words, attachments, and categories. By using rules, you can have Outlook move, copy, delete, forward, redirect, reply to, or otherwise process messages based on the specified criteria. You can run a rule manually or automatically.

You can set up client rules that are applied to messages stored on your computer for any type of email account. You can set up server rules that are applied to messages as they are received or processed for Microsoft Exchange Server accounts. You can base a rule on one of the 11 templates provided by Outlook, start from a blank rule, or copy and modify an existing rule.

Rules Wizard

Start from a template or from a blank rule
Step 1: Select a template

Stay Organized
Move messages from someone to a folder
Move messages with specific words in the subject to a folder
Move messages sent to a public group to a folder
Flag messages from someone for follow-up
Move Microsoft InfoPath forms of a specific type to a folder
Move RSS items from a specific RSS Feed to a folder
Stay Up to Date
Display mail from someone in the New Item Alert Window
Play a sound when I get messages from someone
Send an alert to my mobile device when I get messages from someone
Start from a blank rule
Apply rule on messages I receive
Apply rule on messages I send

Step 2: Edit the rule description (click an underlined value)

Apply this rule after the message arrives
from people or public group
move it to the specified folder
and stop processing more rules

Example: Move mail from my manager to my High Importance folder

Cancel   < Back   Next >   Finish

➤ To create a rule from scratch

1. On the **Info** page of the Backstage view, click the **Manage Rules & Alerts** button.

2. On the **E-mail Rules** page of the **Rules and Alerts** dialog box, click **New Rule**.

3. In the **Rules Wizard**, do one of the following, and then click **Next**:

   ○ In the **Stay Organized** or **Stay Up to Date** section of the **Select a template** list, click the template on which you want to build the new rule.

   ○ In the **Start from a blank rule** section of the **Select a template** list, click the type of message you want the rule to process.

4. In the **Select condition(s)** list, select the check box for each of the conditions that will identify messages to be processed by the rule. In the **Edit the rule description** area, click each underlined word or phrase, and replace it with a criterion that identifies the target messages. Then click **Next**.

5. In the **Select action(s)** list, select the check box for each of the actions you want Outlook to perform. Specify the criteria for the underlined words or phrases. Then click **Next**.

6. In the **Select exception(s)** list, select the check box for any condition that will identify messages to exclude from the rule action. Specify the criteria for the underlined words or phrases. Then click **Next**.

7. Specify a name for the new rule, do any of the following, and then click **Finish**:

- ○ Select the **Run this rule now...** check box.

- ○ Select the **Turn on this rule** check box.

➤ **To modify an existing rule**

1. Display the **Rules and Alerts** dialog box. On the **E-mail Rules** page, in the **Rule** list, click the rule (not its check box) you want to modify. Click **Change Rule**, and then click **Edit Rule Settings**.

2. In the **Rules** wizard, modify the rule as necessary.

➤ **To create a new rule based on an existing rule**

1. Display the **Rules and Alerts** dialog box. On the **E-mail Rules** page, in the **Rule** list, click the rule (not its check box) you want to use as the basis for the new rule. Then click **Copy**.

2. In the **Copy rule to** dialog box, if the **Folder** list includes multiple accounts or sets of accounts, click the account(s) to which you want the rule to apply. Then click **OK**.

3. On the **E-mail Rules** page, with the copy selected, click **Change Rule**, and then click **Edit Rule Settings**.

4. In the **Rules** wizard, modify the rule as necessary, and specify a unique name for the rule on the final page of the wizard.

➤ **To apply a rule to a specific account or set of accounts**

1. In the **Rules and Alerts** dialog box, click the rule (not its check box) for which you want to specify an account or set of accounts.

2. In the **Apply changes to this folder** list, click the account or set of accounts to which you want to apply the rule.

> **Tip** The Apply Changes To This Folder list is present only when Outlook is configured to connect to multiple Exchange accounts.

➤ **To run a rule on existing messages**

1. Display the **Rules and Alerts** dialog box. On the **E-mail Rules** page, click **Run Rules Now**.

2. In the **Run Rules Now** dialog box, select the check box of each rule you want to run, select the folder(s) and type of messages on which you want to run the rule(s), and then click **Run Now**.

➤ **To delete a rule**

1. Display the **Rules and Alerts** dialog box. On the **E-mail Rules** page, in the **Rule** list, click the rule (not its check box) you want to delete, and then click **Delete**.

2. In the **Microsoft Outlook** dialog box that appears, click **Yes**.

Creating Automatic Reply Rules

Separately from the Outlook rules that you run manually or automatically, you can set up rules that run only when the Automatic Replies feature is active. The Automatic Reply rules are built on a different set of criteria than standard Outlook rules; you can choose from a limited number of conditions, and you can't specify exceptions.

➤ **To create a rule that runs only when you are out of the office**

1. On the **Info** page of the Backstage view, click the **Automatic Replies** button.

2. In the **Automatic Replies** dialog box, click **Rules**.

3. In the **Automatic Reply Rules** dialog box, click **Add Rule**.

4. In the **When a message arrives...** area of the **Edit Rule** dialog box, specify the conditions that define messages to be processed by the rule.

5. To specify additional conditions such as message size, receipt date, importance, and sensitivity, click **Advanced** and, in the **Advanced** dialog box, specify the conditions and then click **OK**.

6. In the **Perform these actions** area, specify the actions to be performed by the rule.

7. In the **Edit Rule** dialog box, click **OK**.

➤ **To specify rules to run while Automatic Replies are turned on**

1. On the **Info** page of the Backstage view, click the **Automatic Replies** button.

2. In the **Automatic Replies** dialog box, click **Rules**.

3. In the **Automatic Reply Rules** dialog box, select the check box for each rule you want to run, and clear the check box for each rule you don't want to run during the current Out of Office period. Then click **OK**.

Practice Tasks

There are no practice files for these tasks.

- Create a subfolder of your Inbox named *High*, and then flag a few messages in your Inbox for follow up today. Create a rule that moves all the messages flagged for follow up to the *High* folder, and run the rule on your Inbox.

- Create a rule that assigns all incoming messages from your manager to the Red category, or to another category of your choosing. Run the rule on your Inbox.

- Create a distribution list that includes only your own email address, and then create a rule that forwards all messages from a specific colleague or friend to the distribution list. Run the rule on your Inbox.

- Delete the three rules you just created. Then move messages back into your Inbox and delete any flags and category assignments you don't want to keep.

3.3 Manage Junk Email

Working with Junk Email Messages

When you open a message from the Junk E-mail folder, Outlook converts the message content to plain text and disables any active links or content within the message. The information bar in the message header provides specific information about the message's status. When you point to the information bar in a suspected junk email message, it turns orange; in a suspected phishing message, it turns pink. Any remote graphics (graphics that are displayed from Internet locations rather than embedded in the message—sometimes called *web beacons*) that were present in the message are converted to URLs so you can easily see where the graphics originated.

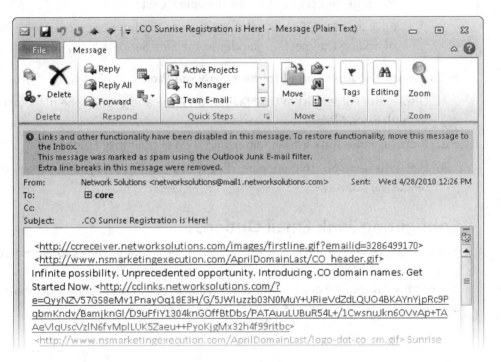

➤ **To process a junk email message**

1. In the **Junk E-mail** folder, select the message you want to process.

2. On the **Home** tab, in the **Delete** group, click the **Junk** button.

3. In the **Junk** list, do one of the following:

    o   Click **Block Sender** to add the message sender to the Blocked Senders list.

    o   Click **Never Block Sender** to add the message sender to the Safe Senders list.

    o   Click **Never Block Sender's Domain** to add the message sender's domain to the Safe Senders list.

    o   Click **Never Block this Group or Mailing List** to add the group to which the message was sent to the Safe Recipients list.

    o   Click **Not Junk** to move the message to the Inbox. You then have the option of adding the message sender to the Safe Senders list.

➤ **To empty the Junk E-mail folder of any mailbox**

1. Display the **Folder List** in the **Navigation Pane** and expand the mailbox to display its **Junk E-mail** folder.

2. Right-click the **Junk E-mail** folder, and then click **Empty Folder**.

3. In the message box that appears, click **Yes** to confirm that you want to permanently delete the items.

Configuring Junk Email Options

In the Junk E-mail Options dialog box, you set specific junk email processing options for each account to which Outlook is configured to connect. The Junk E-mail Options dialog box has five pages. The account for which you're configuring options is shown in the title bar of the Junk E-mail Options dialog box.

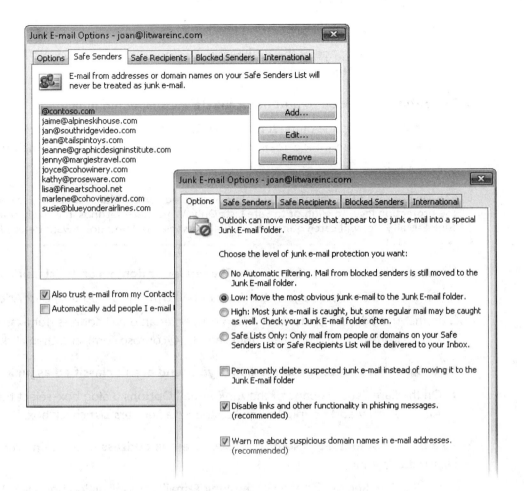

► **To open the Junk E-mail Options dialog box**

→ On the **Home** tab, in the **Delete** group, in the **Junk** list, click **Junk E-mail Options**.

➤ **To choose a junk email protection level**

→ On the **Options** page of the **Junk E-mail Options** dialog box, click **No Automatic Filtering**, **Low**, **High**, or **Safe Lists Only**.

➤ **To configure Outlook to automatically delete suspected junk email**

→ On the **Options** page of the **Junk E-mail Options** dialog box, select the **Permanently delete suspected junk e-mail instead of moving it to the Junk E-mail folder** check box.

> **Tip** Do not select the Permanently Delete Suspected Junk E-Mail... check box if you set the protection level to High or to Safe Lists Only. With these settings, it is likely that the Junk E-Mail Filter will catch quite a few valid messages that you don't want deleted.

➤ **To ensure that messages from a specific sender or domain aren't classified as junk**

1. On the **Safe Senders** page of the **Junk E-mail Options** dialog box, click **Add**.

2. In the **Add address or domain** dialog box, enter an email address (for example, tom@contoso.com) or domain (for example, @contoso.com), and then click **OK**.

➤ **To ensure that responses to messages you send aren't classified as junk**

→ On the **Safe Senders** page of the **Junk E-mail Options** dialog box, select the **Automatically add people I e-mail to the Safe Senders List** check box.

➤ **To ensure that messages sent to a specific email address or domain aren't classified as junk**

1. On the **Safe Recipients** page of the **Junk E-mail Options** dialog box, click **Add**.

2. In the **Add address or domain** dialog box, enter an email address or domain, and then click **OK**.

> **Tip** Add distribution lists or mailing lists of which you are a member to your Safe Recipients List to ensure that messages sent to you through the distribution list or mailing list will never be treated as junk email.

➤ **To ensure that messages from a specific sender or domain are always classified as junk**

1. On the **Blocked Senders** page of the **Junk E-mail Options** dialog box, click **Add**.

2. In the **Add address or domain** dialog box, enter an email address or domain, and then click **OK**.

➤ **To block all messages from a location-specific top-level domain**

1. On the **International** page of the **Junk E-mail Options** dialog box, click the **Blocked Top-Level Domain List** button.

2. In the **Blocked Top-Level Domain List** dialog box, select the check box for each country or region you want to block, and then click **OK**.

➤ **To block all messages with language-specific encoding**

1. On the **International** page of the **Junk E-mail Options** dialog box, click the **Blocked Encodings List** button.

2. In the **Blocked Encodings List** dialog box, select the check box for each language you want to block, and then click **OK**.

Practice Tasks

There are no practice files for these tasks.

- In your Inbox, use a message from someone you trust to add that person's email address to your Safe Senders list.

- Locate a junk email message in your Inbox, Junk E-mail folder, or other folder. Add the message sender to your Blocked Senders list.

- If your Junk E-mail folder contains no messages you want to keep, empty it.

3.4 Manage Automatic Message Content

Creating and Using Automatic Signatures

When you send an email message to someone, you will most likely "sign" the message by typing your name at the end of the message text. You can automatically insert your signature text in outgoing messages by creating an email signature and assigning it to your email account. Your email signature can include additional information that you want to consistently provide to message recipients. If you have more than one email account set up in Outlook, you can instruct Outlook to insert a different signature in messages sent from each account.

➤ To create and assign automatic signatures

1. Display the **Outlook Options** dialog box.

2. In the **Compose messages** section of the **Mail** page, click the **Signatures** button.

3. On the **E-mail Signature** page of the **Signatures and Stationery** dialog box, click the **New** button.

4. In the **Type a name for this signature** box of the **New Signature** dialog box, enter a name that identifies the content or purpose of the signature. Then click **OK**.

5. In the **Edit signature** box, enter the signature text.

> **Tip** If you want to include your electronic business card as part of your signature, click the Business Card button. Then in the Insert Business Card dialog box, locate and click your name, and click OK.

6. Format the signature text by selecting the text and then using the formatting commands at the top of the **Edit signature** area.

> **Tip** Your signature will appear in email messages exactly as it does here.

7. In the **Choose default signature** area, select the email account to which you want to assign the signature. Then in the **New messages** list, click the signature name.

8. If you want to include the signature in message responses, in the **Replies/forwards** list, click the signature name.

9. Make any other changes you want, and then click **OK** in the **Signatures and Stationery** dialog box and in the **Outlook Options** dialog box.

➤ **To manually insert an existing email signature in a message**

1. Position the cursor where you want to insert the email signature.

2. On the **Insert** tab, in the **Include** group, click the **Signature** button.

3. In the **Signature** list, click the name of the email signature you want to insert.

➤ **To remove an email signature from a message**

→ Select and delete the signature content as you would any other text.

Setting a Default Theme, Stationery, and Fonts

The fonts, styles, colors, and backgrounds of content you create in Outlook are governed by a theme. The default theme is named Office. New messages use the 11-point version of the body font and font color specified by the theme (for the Office theme, this is 11-point black Calibri), and responses use the same font, but in blue.

You can change the appearance of message content by changing the theme of the individual message, by applying styles to paragraphs, or by applying local character and paragraph formatting. In addition to formatting messages on a case by case basis, you can change the default look of all new messages by choosing a different theme. If you're happy with the basic theme but want to change the default appearance of text, you can separately specify the font, size, style, and color of the text of new messages, responses and forwarded messages, and messages sent in Plain Text format.

➤ **To format messages with preselected fonts, styles, colors, and backgrounds**

1. In the **Compose messages** section of the **Mail** page of the **Outlook Options** dialog box, click the **Stationery and Fonts** button.

2. On the **Personal Stationery** page of the **Signatures and Stationery** dialog box, in the **Theme or stationery for new HTML e-mail message** area, click the **Theme** button.

3. In the **Theme or Stationery** dialog box, click the theme you want to use. Select or clear the **Vivid Colors**, **Active Graphics**, and **Background Image** check boxes to specify the theme elements you want to include. Then click **OK**.

4. In the **Theme or stationery for new HTML e-mail message** area of the **Signatures and Stationery** dialog box, click the **Font** arrow, do one of the following, and then click **OK**:

   ○ Click **Use theme's font** to use the theme font for new messages and responses.

   ○ Click **Use my font when replying and forwarding messages** to use the theme font for new messages and a custom font for responses.

   ○ Click **Always use my font** to use a custom font for all messages and to use only the styles, colors, and backgrounds of the selected theme.

5. In the **Outlook Options** dialog box, click **OK**.

➤ **To reset to the default theme**

1. In the **Compose messages** section of the **Mail** page of the **Outlook Options** dialog box, click the **Stationery and Fonts** button.

2. On the **Personal Stationery** page of the **Signatures and Stationery** dialog box, in the **Theme or stationery for new HTML e-mail message** area, click the **Theme** button.

3. In the **Theme or Stationery** dialog box, click **(No Theme)**. Then click **OK** three times to close the **Theme or Stationery**, **Signatures and Stationery**, and **Outlook Options** dialog boxes.

➤ **To set the font for specific message types**

1. In the **Compose messages** section of the **Mail** page of the **Outlook Options** dialog box, click the **Stationery and Fonts** button.

2. On the **Personal Stationery** page of the **Signatures and Stationery** dialog box, click the **Font** button corresponding to the type of message for which you want to format the font.

3. In the **Font** dialog box, select the font, style, size, effects, and advanced formatting of the font you want to use. Then click **OK**.

4. In the **Signatures and Stationery** dialog box, click **OK**. Then click **OK** in the **Outlook Options** dialog box.

Identifying Response Text

When you respond to a message, Outlook inserts the original message below a blank area. You can enter your response in the blank area, or you can respond inline, within the body of the original message. If you respond inline, you can insert identifying text, such as *[your name]* prior to your responses so that the recipient can easily locate them.

➤ **To insert an identifier before inline responses**

1. In the **Compose messages** section of the **Mail** page of the **Outlook Options** dialog box, click the **Stationery and Fonts** button.

2. On the **Personal Stationery** page of the **Signatures and Stationery** dialog box, in the **Replying or forwarding messages** area, select the **Mark my comments with** check box.

3. In the **Mark my comments with** text box, enter the text with which you want to identify your responses. Then click **OK**.

4. In the **Outlook Options** dialog box, click **OK**.

> **Tip** You can also control inline response identifiers from the Replies And Forwards section of the Mail page of the Outlook Options dialog box.

Practice Tasks

There are no practice files for these tasks.

- Create an automatic signature and assign it to appear in original messages only for your default email account.

- Set the default theme for outgoing messages to any theme that you like other than Office. Create a message and ensure that it uses the theme. Then reset to the default theme.

- Configure Outlook to insert your initials between asterisks before comments that you insert in message responses.

Objective Review

Before finishing this chapter, ensure that you have mastered the following skills:

3.1 Clean Up the Mailbox

3.2 Create and Manage Rules

3.3 Manage Junk Mail

3.4 Manage Automatic Message Content

4 Managing Contacts

The skills tested in this section of the Microsoft Office Specialist exam for Microsoft Outlook 2010 relate to creating and working with contact records and contact groups. Specifically, the following objectives are associated with this set of skills:

4.1 Create and Manipulate Contacts

4.2 Create and Manipulate Contact Groups

Having immediate access to current, accurate contact information for the people you need to interact with—by email, telephone, mail, or otherwise—is important for timely and effective communication. You can easily build and maintain a detailed contact list, or address book, in Outlook 2010. From your address book, you can look up information, generate messages, and share contact information with people. You can create contact records for individuals or companies, and you can create contact groups to simplify communication with multiple contacts.

This chapter guides you in studying ways of creating, modifying, and sharing contact records; modifying electronic business cards; and creating, managing, and using contact groups.

> **Practice Files** Before you can complete the practice tasks in this chapter, you need to copy the book's practice files to your computer. The practice file you'll use to complete the tasks in this chapter is in the Outlook\Objective4 practice file folder. A complete list of practice files is provided in "Using the Book's Companion Content" at the beginning of this book.

4.1 Create and Manipulate Contacts

Creating Contact Records

You save contact information for people and companies by creating a contact record in an address book.

You can store the following types of contact information in a contact record:

- Name, company name, and job title
- Business, home, and alternate addresses
- Business, home, mobile, pager, and other telephone numbers
- Business, home, and alternate fax numbers
- Webpage address (URL), instant messaging (IM) address, and up to three email addresses
- Photo or other identifying image
- General notes, which can include text and illustrations such as photos, clip art images, SmartArt diagrams, charts, and shapes

You can also store personal and organization-specific details for each contact, such as the following:

- Professional information, including department, office location, profession, manager's name, and assistant's name
- Personal information, including nickname, spouse or partner's name, birthday, anniversary, and the title (such as Miss, Mrs., or Ms.) and suffix (such as Jr. or Sr.) for use in correspondence

In addition to creating contact records from scratch, you can quickly clone information from an existing record to create contact records for several people who work for the same company. You can also create new contact records from email messages. If someone sends you a contact record or an electronic business card, you can easily turn it into a contact record in your own Outlook address book.

> **See Also** For information about creating and sending electronic business cards, see "Creating Electronic Business Cards" later in this section.

You can add to or change the information stored in a contact record at any time.

By default, Outlook files contacts by last name (Last, First order). You can change the default File As setting for new contacts to any of the following:

- First Last
- Company
- Last, First (Company)
- Company (Last, First)

Contact records are useful for more than just storing information; you can also initiate a number of actions that are specific to a selected contact. Commands for initiating communication are available in the Communicate group on the Contact tab of an open contact record window.

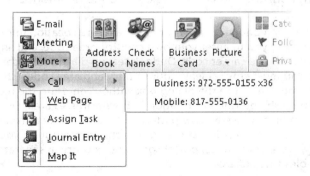

> **Tip** If your organization has a unified messaging system, other options (such as Reply With IM) might appear on the More menu.

Here are some of the actions you can perform from within a contact record by using the commands in the Communicate group on the Contact tab:

- You can create an email message addressed to the contact by clicking the E-mail button.
- You can create a meeting request that includes the contact by clicking the Meeting button.
- If you have Microsoft Office Communicator configured, you can initiate a chat session with the contact by clicking Reply With IM.
- If you have Internet telephone capabilities, you can place a call to the contact by clicking the telephone number you would like Outlook to dial in the Call list.
- You can display the contact's website by clicking Web Page.
- You can create a task assigned to the contact by clicking Assign Task.
- You can create a journal entry assigned to the contact by clicking Journal Entry.
- You can display a map of the contact's address by clicking Map It, or by clicking the Map It button in the Addresses area.

➤ **To create a contact record**

1. In the Contacts module, click the **New Contact** button in the **New** group on the **Home** tab.

   Or

   In any Outlook module, click the **New Items** button in the **New** group on the **Home** tab, and then click **Contact**.

2. In the contact record window, enter the new contact information. To enter multiple phone numbers or addresses, click the arrow at the right end of the field label, click an appropriate description, and then enter the corresponding information.

> **Tip** The first time you enter a phone number for a contact, the Location Information dialog box opens, prompting you to enter your own country, area code, and any necessary dialing information such as a carrier code. Outlook sets up dialing rules based on the information you enter. You must enter at least your country and area code in the dialog box and then click OK; you can't close the dialog box without entering the requested information. When you finish entering information in the Addresses area, Outlook verifies that the address conforms to a standard pattern. If Outlook detects irregularities in the address you enter, the Check Address dialog box opens, prompting you to enter the street address, city, state or province, postal code, and country in separate fields from which it reassembles the address.

3. On the **Contact** tab, in the **Show** group, click the **Details** button, and then enter additional information.

4. In the **Actions** group, click the **Save & Close** button.

➤ **To create a contact record with the same company information**

1. In the **Contacts** pane, double-click the contact record on which you want to base a new contact record for a contact from the same company.

2. On the **Contact** tab, in the **Actions** group, click the **Save & New** arrow, and then click **Contact from the Same Company**.

3. In the contact record window, enter the contact information.

4. Save and close the contact record.

➤ **To create a contact record based on another contact record**

1. In the **Contacts** pane, click the contact record on which you want to base a new contact record.

2. Press Ctrl+C and then Ctrl+V.

3. In the **Duplicate Contact Detected** dialog box, click **Add new contact**, and then click **Add**.

4. In the **Contacts** pane, double-click the duplicate contact record and then, in the contact record window, edit the contact information as required.

5. Save and close the contact record.

➤ **To create a contact record from a message header**

1. In the message window or **Reading Pane**, right-click the name or email address in the **From** field, and then click **Add to Outlook Contacts**.

2. In the contact record window, edit the contact information as required.

3. Save and close the contact record.

➤ **To send a contact record**

→ In the contact record window, in the **Actions** group, click the **Forward** button and then click **As a Business Card**, **In Internet Format**, or **As an Outlook Contact**.

➤ **To create a contact record from an attached or embedded electronic business card**

1. In the message window or **Reading Pane**, right-click the business card, and then click **Add to Outlook Contacts** or **Open**.

2. Save and close the contact record.

➤ **To create a contact record from an attached contact record**

1. In the message window or **Reading Pane**, double-click the contact record to open it in a contact record window.

2. Save and close the contact record.

➤ **To change the default filing order of contact records**

1. On the **Contacts** page of the **Outlook Options** dialog box, in the **Names and filing** area, click the **Default "File As" order** arrow, and then click the filing order you want.

2. In the **Outlook Options** dialog box, click **OK**.

> **Tip** You can change the File As order for an individual contact by selecting the order you want in the File As list in the contact record.

➤ **To change the default mailing address**

1. In the contact record window, click the **Addresses** arrow, and then click the type of address you want to designate as the default.

2. In the **Addresses** area, select the **This is the mailing address** check box.

3. Save and close the contact record.

➤ **To attach a document, message, or other information to a contact record**

1. In the contact record window, on the **Insert** tab, in the **Include** group, click the **Attach File** button or the **Outlook Item** button.

2. In the **Insert File** or **Insert Item** dialog box, locate and then double-click the file or item you want to attach to the record.

3. Save and close the contact record.

Creating Electronic Business Cards

When you enter information in a contact record, the first 10 lines of information appear in the business card in the upper-right corner of the contact record window. If the contact record includes an image, the image appears on the left side. You can change the types of information that appear; rearrange the information fields; format the text and background; and add, change, or remove images such as a logo or photograph.

Creating a business card for yourself provides you with an attractive way of presenting your contact information to people you correspond with in email. You can send your business card to someone else by attaching the card to an email message. The recipient can then save the contact information in his or her own address book.

You can also use your business card as your email message signature. Then Outlook not only embeds the business card at the bottom of your messages but also attaches it to the message.

> **See Also**   For information about automatic email signatures, see section 3.4, "Manage Automatic Message Content."

➤ To modify the information that appears in a business card

1. In the contact record window, on the **Contact** tab, in the **Options** group, click the **Business Card** button.

2. In the **Edit Business Card** dialog box, below the **Fields** box, click **Add**, point to the type of field you want, and then click the specific field.

> **Tip** Use custom user fields to add text that is not part of the contact record to the business card.

3. With the new field selected in the **Fields** list, click the **Move Field Up** button or **Move Field Down** button to position the field where you want it to appear on the business card.

4. In the **Edit** area, enter the field's value in the box and format it the way you want. If necessary, select a label location from the list, and then enter the field's label.

5. In the **Fields** box, click any field you want to remove, and then click **Remove**.

6. Click **OK** to save the modified business card.

➤ To format the appearance of a business card

1. Open the **Edit Business Card** dialog box.

2. To change the background color, in the **Card Design** area, click the **Background** button. Then in the **Color** dialog box, click a color you like, and click **OK**.

3. To add or change the picture attached to the card, to the right of **Image** in the **Card Design** area, click **Change**. Then browse to the folder containing the image, click the image, and click **OK**.

4. In the **Image Area** box, enter or select the image area size.

5. In the **Image Align** list, click a type of alignment.

6. Click **OK** to save the business card.

➤ To embed an electronic business card in a message

1. In the message window, on the **Insert** tab, in the **Include** group, click the **Business Card** button, and then click **Other Business Cards**.

> **Tip** Business cards that you've previously sent appear in the Business Card list. You can insert a card in a message by selecting it from the list.

2. In the **Insert Business Card** dialog box, select the card or cards you want to embed, and then click **OK**.

➤ **To attach an electronic business card to a message**

1. In the message window, on the **Message** tab, in the **Include** group, click the **Attach Item** button, point to **Business Card**, and then click **Other Business Cards**.

2. In the **Insert Business Card** dialog box, select the card or cards you want to attach, and then click **OK**.

Practice Tasks

The practice file for these tasks is located in the Outlook\Objective4 practice file folder.

- Create a contact record for John Evans, the assembly plant manager of Wingtip Toys, which is located at 111 Magnolia Lane, Flower Mound, TX 98053. John's email address is *john@wingtiptoys.com*, and the company website's URL is *www.wingtiptoys.com*.

- Using the quickest method, create a contact record for Heidi Steen, a sales associate for Wingtip Toys, whose email address is *heidi@wingtiptoys.com*.

- Edit the John Evans contact record so that it is filed as *John Evans* instead of *Evans, John*. Then note that John's nickname is Jack, his spouse's name is Jill, and his birthday is July 31.

- If you haven't already done so, create a contact record for yourself. Include your name, company, job title, business and mobile phone numbers, fax number, one or more email addresses, and one or more postal addresses.

- From your contact record, create a business card that includes only your name, company name, business phone number, and business email address. Then add the slogan *We'll take it from here* to the bottom of the card.

- Format the information on the business card, so that your name appears under and is smaller than your company name. Make the slogan italic.

- Add the OTSI-Logo graphic to the upper-left corner of your business card, allowing it to occupy 20 percent of the card. Then change the background color to beige.

- Forward your contact record to a friend as an Outlook contact. Enter *MOS Contact Information* as the message subject, and embed your business card as a signature.

4.2 Create and Manipulate Contact Groups

If you frequently send messages to a specific group of people, such as employees in a department, clients in a particular region, or players on a sports team, you can create a contact group containing the email addresses of all the people in the group. Then when you send a message or meeting request to the contact group, each member of the group receives it.

You can add people to a contact group by selecting them from an address book or by manually entering their email addresses.

> ➤ **To create a contact group from existing contact records**

1. In the Contacts module, click the **New Contact Group** button in the **New** group on the **Home** tab.

   Or

   In any Outlook module, click the **New Items** button in the **New** group on the **Home** tab, and then, in the **More Items** list, click **Contact Group**.

2. In the **Name** box, enter a name for the contact group.

3. On the **Contact Group** tab, in the **Members** group, click the **Add Members** button, and then click **From Address Book**.

4. In the **Select Members** dialog box, in the **Address Book** list, click the address book from which you want to add one or more contacts.

5. In the **Name** list, double-click the name of each contact you want to add.

6. In the **Select Members** dialog box, click **OK**.

7. On the **Contact Group** tab, in the **Actions** group, click the **Save & Close** button.

➤ **To add people to a contact group without using contact records**

1. In the **Contacts** pane, double-click the contact group to open it in a contact group window.

2. On the **Contact Group** tab, in the **Members** group, click the **Add Members** button, and then click **New E-mail Contact**.

3. In the **Add New Member** dialog box, enter the **Display name** and **E-mail address**.

4. If you want Outlook to also create a contact record for this person, select the **Add to Contacts** check box.

5. In the **Add New Member** dialog box, click **OK**.

6. Save and close the contact group.

➤ **To update a contact group with new contact information**

1. Open the contact group window.

2. On the **Contact Group** tab, in the **Members** group, click the **Update Now** button.

3. Save and close the contact group.

➤ **To remove contacts from a contact group**

1. Open the contact group window.

2. In the contact group member list, click the contact you want to remove.

> **Tip** You can select multiple contacts for simultaneous removal by holding down the Ctrl key and clicking each contact.

3. On the **Contact Group** tab, in the **Members** group, click the **Remove Member** button.

4. Save and close the contact group.

➤ **To record notes about a contact group**

1. In the contact group window, in the **Show** group, click the **Notes** button.

2. On the **Notes** page, enter notes in the form of text, images, illustrations, tables, and so on.

3. Save the contact group record.

Practice Tasks

There are no practice files for these tasks.

- Create a new contact group named *MOS Clients*, and select the *John Evans* contact record you created earlier in this chapter as a member. Then add *Heidi Steen* to the contact group, and save and close the contact group.

- Add the following people to the *MOS Clients* contact group and to your contact list:

  Holly Dickson holly@consolidatedmessenger.com

  Max Stevens max@consolidatedmessenger.com

  Linda Mitchell linda@lucernepublishing.com

  Jill Shrader jill@lucernepublishing.com

- Open the contact record for *Jill Shrader*, and change her email address to *jill@wingtiptoys.com*. Then update the *MOS Clients* contact group to reflect Jill Shrader's new email address.

- Send a message with the subject *MOS Group Test* to the *MOS Clients* contact group. (You will receive non-deliverable message alerts in response.)

Objective Review

Before finishing this chapter, ensure that you have mastered the following skills:

4.1 Create and Manipulate Contacts

4.2 Create and Manipulate Contact Groups

5 Managing Calendar Objects

The skills tested in this section of the Microsoft Office Specialist exam for Microsoft Outlook 2010 relate to creating and managing appointments, events, and meetings, and displaying information in the Calendar pane. Specifically, the following objectives are associated with this set of skills:

5.1 Create and Manipulate Appointments and Events

5.2 Create and Manipulate Meeting Requests

5.3 Manipulate the Calendar Pane

Outlook 2010 provides full calendar and scheduling functionality to help you manage business and personal appointments, meetings, and events. Knowing how to use the calendar effectively can help you stay organized, on task, and on time.

This chapter guides you in studying ways of creating and customizing Outlook calendar items, scheduling meetings and managing meeting requests, customizing your Calendar settings to fit the way you work, and displaying different views of one or more calendars.

> **Practice Files** Before you can complete the practice tasks in this chapter, you need to copy the book's practice files to your computer. The practice files you'll use to complete the tasks in this chapter are in the Outlook\Objective5 practice file folder. A complete list of practice files is provided in "Using the Book's Companion Content" at the beginning of this book.

5.1 Create and Manipulate Appointments and Events

Scheduling Appointments

Appointments are blocks of time you schedule for only yourself (as opposed to meetings, to which you invite other Outlook users). An appointment has a specific start time and a specific end time (as opposed to an event, which occurs for one or more full 24-hour periods).

You can enter an appointment directly in the Calendar pane, in which case the time is shown on your calendar as Busy and the appointment reminder is set to 15 minutes. If you want to change those default settings, or if you want to schedule an appointment to start or end at a time that does not fit the default half-hour increments shown in the Calendar pane, you can enter the appointment in an appointment window.

Show your availability

Reminder time

Time scheduled for an appointment can be shown as Free, Tentative, Busy, or Out Of Office. You can change the reminder time or turn it off completely. You can also include information such as driving directions or website links in the content pane, and attach related files so that they are easily available to you at the time of the appointment.

> **Tip** If you synchronize your Outlook installation with a mobile device such as a Windows Phone, an iPhone, or a BlackBerry, you can also receive reminders on your device.

You can also create an appointment based on an email message or task simply by dragging it to the Calendar button in the Navigation Pane. When you release the mouse button, an appointment window opens with the message or task subject as the appointment subject and the message or task details in the appointment window's content pane. The start and end times are set to the next half-hour increment following the current time. You can then make any necessary adjustments before saving the appointment.

> **Tip** When you create an appointment based on an email message, the appointment window might open behind the Outlook program window. Click the Outlook button on the Windows taskbar and then click Untitled - Appointment to display the new appointment window.

> **Tip** You can convert an appointment to a meeting by opening the appointment window, clicking the Scheduling Assistant button in the Show group on the Appointment tab, and then adding one or more attendees. For more information, see section 5.2, "Create and Manipulate Meeting Requests."

➤ **To create an appointment with default settings**

1. In the **Calendar** pane, click the desired time slot, or drag through consecutive time slots.

2. Enter the information you want to appear as the appointment subject, and then press Enter.

➤ **To create an appointment with custom settings**

1. In the Calendar module, on the **Home** tab, in the **New** group, click the **New Appointment** button.

2. In the appointment window, enter the information you want to appear on the calendar in the **Subject** and **Location** boxes.

3. Click the appointment start date in the left **Start time** list and, if the appointment extends across multiple days, click the appointment end date in the left **End time** list.

4. Click or enter the appointment start time in the right **Start time** list and the appointment end time in the right **End time** list.

5. On the **Appointment** tab, in the **Options** group, click your availability during the specified appointment time—**Free**, **Tentative**, **Busy**, or **Out of Office**—in the **Show As** list.

6. In the **Options** group, in the **Reminder** list, click the length of time prior to the appointment (or **None**) when you would like Outlook to display an appointment reminder.

> **Tip** You can specify the sound to play for reminders by clicking Sound at the bottom of the Reminder list and then browsing to the sound file you want to use. You can remove the sound effect from reminders by clicking Sound and then clearing the Play This Sound check box.

7. Add notes about the appointment in the content pane.

> **Tip** To attach a file to an appointment or event, click the **Attach File** button in the Include group on the Insert tab, and then browse to and double-click the file.

8. On the **Appointment** tab, in the **Actions** group, click the **Save & Close** button.

➤ **To change the time of an existing appointment**

→ In the **Calendar** pane, drag the appointment to a different date or to a different time slot.

→ In the **Calendar** pane, in Day view, Work Week view, or Week view, drag the top or bottom border of the appointment up or down to change the start or end time.

→ In the **Calendar** pane, click the appointment one time to select it, press Ctrl+X, click the time slot to which you want to move the appointment, and then press Ctrl+V.

→ In the appointment window, adjust the **Start date**, **End date**, **Start time**, and **End time** settings. Then on the **Appointment** tab, in the **Actions** group, click the **Save & Close** button.

➤ **To create an appointment from an email message**

1. In the Mail module, drag the message from the **Mail** pane to the **Calendar** button at the bottom of the **Navigation Pane**.

2. In the appointment window that opens, edit the appointment details as necessary.

3. On the **Appointment** tab, in the **Actions** group, click the **Save & Close** button.

Scheduling Events

Events are day-long blocks of time that you schedule on your calendar. In all other respects, events are identical to appointments. In Day, Work Week, or Week view, events are shown in the space below the header, above the schedule for the day. In Month view, events are shown above appointments and meetings.

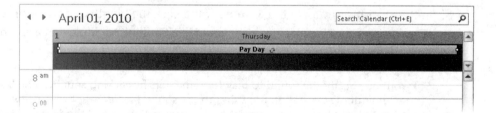

You can enter an event directly in the Calendar pane, in which case the time is shown on your calendar as Free and the event reminder is set to 15 minutes. You can change those settings by opening the event window.

You can create an event from an email message or task by first creating an appointment and then converting it to an event.

> ➤ **To create an event with default settings**

1. In the Calendar module, display the date on which you want to schedule the event in Day view, Work Week view, or Week view.

2. At the top of the **Calendar** pane, click (don't double-click) the space between the header and the first time slot.

> **Tip** appears in the space when you point to the correct space.

3. Enter the event subject, and then press Enter.

Or

1. Display the Calendar module in Month view.

2. Click an empty area of the cell below the header of the date on which you want to schedule the event.

> **Tip** The cell color changes to indicate that the date is selected, but no text indicator appears.

3. Enter the event subject, and then press Enter.

> ➤ **To create an event with custom settings**

1. In the Calendar module, display the date on which you want to schedule the event.

2. In Day view, Work Week view, or Week view, double-click the space between the header and the first time slot.

Or

In Month view, double-click the cell below the date header.

> **Tip** You can also open a new event window by clicking All Day Event on the New Items menu without first clicking the space above the time slots.

3. In the **Untitled - Event** window that opens, fill in the **Subject** and **Location** boxes and set the **Show As** and **Reminder** options.

4. On the **Event** tab, in the **Actions** group, click the **Save & Close** button.

> **Strategy** Practice creating appointments, meetings, and events from scratch and from email messages; then practice changing a calendar item from one type to another, changing its details, and attaching files to it.

Setting Recurrence and Privacy Options

If an appointment, event, or meeting will happen more than once at specific intervals, such as every Tuesday or every month, you can set it up as a recurring appointment, event, or meeting series. Outlook then creates multiple instances of the appointment in your calendar at the time interval you specify. Calendar items in a recurring series are linked; if you need to make changes, you can choose to update a specific occurrence or all occurrences.

Recurrence indicators

Recurrence details

You can mark any item in your calendar as Private. Then when other people look at your calendar, they can see that you are free, busy, or out of the office, but they can't see why.

Recurring appointment

Availability   Location   Private appointment

➤ **To mark a Calendar item as private**

→ In the item window, on the **Appointment**, **Event**, or **Meeting** tab, in the **Tags** group, click the **Private** button.

➤ **To create a recurring Calendar item**

1. In the item window, on the **Appointment**, **Event**, or **Meeting** tab, in the **Options** group, click the **Recurrence** button.

2. In the **Recurrence pattern** area of the **Appointment Recurrence** dialog box, click a frequency option.

3. In the adjacent area, which changes according to the frequency option you select, adjust the settings to reflect the desired recurrence.

4. In the **Range of recurrence** area, select the appropriate end date for the series of appointments or events.

5. Click **OK**.

➤ **To cancel the recurrence of a Calendar item**

1. In the Calendar pane, click (don't double-click) the item.

2. On the Calendar Tools **Appointment Series**, **Event Series**, or **Meeting Series** contextual tab, in the **Options** group, click the **Recurrence** button.

3. In the **Appointment Recurrence** dialog box, click the **Remove Recurrence** button.

Strategy Practice creating private appointments on your calendar; then ask a coworker to verify that he or she can't see the appointment details in Outlook.

➤ **To edit one or all occurrences of a recurring Calendar item**

1. In the **Calendar** pane, double-click the recurring item.

2. In the **Open Recurring Item** dialog box, click **Open this occurrence** to edit only the item you clicked, or click **Open the series** to edit all occurrences in the series. Then click **OK**.

Working with Appointments and Events

To share information about an appointment or event, without specifically creating a meeting and inviting people to the meeting as attendees, you can forward the appointment or event information as an email attachment or you can distribute a printout of the appointment or event information.

➤ **To forward an appointment or event**

1. In the appointment or event window, on the **Appointment** or **Event** tab, in the **Actions** group, do one of the following:

   ○ Click the **Forward** button to create an email message that has the appointment or event attached as an Outlook item.

   ○ Click the **Forward** arrow and then click **Forward as iCalendar** to create an email message that has the appointment or event attached as an iCalendar file.

> **Tip** You can forward an appointment or event as an iCalendar attachment to people who use email programs other than Outlook.

2. Address and send the email message.

➤ **To print appointment or event details**

1. Open the appointment or event window.

2. On the **Print** page of the Backstage view, specify the print options you want, and then click the **Print** button.

Practice Tasks

The practice file for these tasks is located in the Outlook\Objective5 practice file folder.

- Display tomorrow's date in the Calendar pane. Create a half-hour appointment from 11:30 A.M. to 12:00 P.M., with the subject *MOS Lunch with Jane*. Accept all other default settings.

- Without opening the appointment window, change the start time of the *MOS Lunch with Jane* appointment to 10:30 A.M and the end time to 11:30 A.M.

- Specify the location of the *MOS Lunch with Jane* appointment as *Fourth Coffee*, and set a reminder to appear at 9:30 A.M. Set the appointment options so that other Outlook users see that you will be out of the office from 10:30 A.M. to 11:30 A.M. but can't see any appointment details.

- Create a recurring one-hour appointment on the first Monday of the month at 6:00 P.M. with the subject *MOS Book Club*. Set the series to end after six occurrences.

- Create a two-day event on Tuesday and Wednesday two weeks from now in Portland, Oregon, with the subject *MOS Annual Meeting and Retreat*. Attach the *Agenda* document to the event.

- Forward the *MOS Annual Meeting and Retreat* event information to yourself as an email message attachment.

5.2 Create and Manipulate Meeting Requests

Creating Meeting Requests

You can send a meeting invitation (referred to as a *meeting request*) to any person who has an email account (even to people who don't use Outlook). You can let people who don't have to attend the meeting know that it is taking place by marking their attendance as optional. The meeting request can include text and web links, as well as file attachments to ensure that attendees have specific information available to them.

Meeting requests include two pages: the Appointment page and the Scheduling Assistant page. You can change the date and time and invite attendees on either page. You can specify whether a specific attendee is required or optional on the Scheduling Assistant page.

Attendance options

> **See Also** For information about the Scheduling Assistant page, see "Scheduling Meetings" later in this section.

By default, meeting requests that you send include a standard set of response options that allow meeting request recipients to accept, tentatively accept, or decline the meeting request; to propose a new meeting time; to reply to the meeting organizer or to all attendees; or to forward the meeting request. You can remove the option to propose a new meeting time, or remove the response options entirely (for example, when sending a meeting request to a particularly large group of people).

You can add an attendee to a meeting at any time. If this is the only change you make to the attendee list, Outlook gives you the option of sending an update only to the new attendee.

Just as you can create recurring appointments and events, you can create recurring meetings by setting the recurrence options in the Appointment Recurrence dialog box.

➤ **To invite required attendees to a meeting**

1. In the Calendar module, display the date on which you want to schedule the meeting.

2. On the **Home** tab, in the **New** group, click the **New Meeting** button.

3. In the meeting window, enter the email addresses of the meeting attendees in the **To** box.

4. In the **Subject** box, enter the name of the meeting; and in the **Location** box, indicate where the meeting will take place.

5. Adjust the **Start time** and **End time** settings, and then click **Send**.

➤ **To invite an optional attendee to a meeting**

1. On the **Appointment** page of the meeting window, enter the email address of the optional attendee in the **To** box.

2. On the **Meeting** tab, in the **Show** group, click the **Scheduling Assistant** button.

3. In the **All Attendees** list, click the icon immediately to the left of the optional attendee's name and then, in the list, click **Optional Attendee**.

➤ **To set response options**

1. In the meeting window, on the **Meeting** tab, in the **Attendees** group, click the **Response Options** button.

2. To remove the option for attendees to propose alternative meeting times, click **Allow New Time Proposals** to clear the selection of this default setting.

3. To remove all meeting response options, click **Request Responses** to clear the selection of this default setting.

➤ **To create a recurring meeting**

1. In the meeting window, on the **Meeting** tab, in the **Options** group, click the **Recurrence** button.

2. In the **Recurrence pattern** area of the **Appointment Recurrence** dialog box, click a frequency option, and adjust settings to reflect the desired recurrence.

3. In the **Range of recurrence** area, select the appropriate end date for the series of meetings. Then click **OK**.

➤ **To add a meeting attendee**

1. In the meeting window, enter the new attendee in the **To** box.

2. To the left of the **To** box, click the **Send Update** button.

3. In the **Send Update to Attendees** dialog box, click **Send updates only to added or deleted attendees**, and then click **OK**.

Scheduling Meetings

An important factor when scheduling a meeting with many attendees is finding a time that works for everyone. The Scheduling Assistant page of a meeting request window displays the availability of people within your organization and of people outside of your organization who have published their schedules to the Internet. Colored blocks indicate the availability of each invitee: time is shown as white (Available), blue (Busy), purple (Out of Office), or gray (outside of working hours). Light-blue diagonal stripes indicate tentatively scheduled time. Gray diagonal stripes indicate that no information is available (either because Outlook can't connect to a person's calendar or because the proposed meeting is further out than the scheduling information stored on the server). The selected meeting time is light gray bordered by green (start time) and red (end time) vertical bars.

The All Attendees row at the top of the schedule indicates the collective schedule of all the invitees for the displayed time period. The calendar in the upper-right corner of the Scheduling Assistant page indicates the collective availability of the group by color:

- Days when all attendees are available are white (Good).
- Days when most attendees are available are light blue (Fair).
- Days when most attendees are not available are medium blue (Poor).
- Days that occur in the past and non-working days are gray; scheduling suggestions are not provided for those days.

Selecting a date in the calendar displays suggested meeting times for that day. The availability of required attendees is shown separately from that of optional attendees and resources.

If your organization is running Microsoft Exchange Server 2010 or Exchange Server 2007, Outlook simplifies even further the process of selecting a suitable meeting time by displaying a list of suggested meeting times on the right side of the Scheduling Assistant page. The Suggested Times list displays meeting times of any duration you specify in the Duration list and indicates for each time the number of required and optional attendees who are available.

Start time and end time bars   Collective availability

Suggested meeting times

If your organization is running Exchange Server and the Exchange Server directory includes shared resources such as conference rooms or presentation equipment, you can include these resources when scheduling a meeting.

> **See Also** For information about comparing multiple schedules in a horizontal Schedule view, see section 5.3, "Manipulate the Calendar Pane."

➤ **To schedule a meeting with a message sender**

1. In the message window or **Reading Pane**, point to the message sender's name or email address.

2. In the contact card that appears, click the **View more options for interacting with this person** button and then, in the list, click **Schedule a Meeting**.

> **See Also** For information about contact cards, see section 4.1, "Create and Manipulate Contacts."

➤ **To schedule a meeting with any person**

1. In the Calendar module, display the date on which you want to schedule the meeting.

2. On the **Home** tab, in the **New** group, click the **New Meeting** button.

3. On the **Appointment** page of the meeting window, enter the meeting attendees in the **To** box.

   Or

   On the **Scheduling Assistant** page of the meeting window, enter the meeting attendees in the **All Attendees** list.

> **Tip** Click the To button on the Appointment page or click the Address Book button in the Attendees group on the Scheduling Assistant page to display the Select Attendees And Resources dialog box from which you can select contacts from any address book.

4. On the **Appointment** page, enter the meeting dates, start time, and end time in the appropriate boxes.

   Or

   On the **Scheduling Assistant** page, enter or select a meeting time.

5. On the **Appointment** page or the **Scheduling Assistant** page, click the **Send** button.

➤ **To use Smart Scheduling to schedule a meeting**

1. On the **Scheduling Assistant** page of the meeting window, specify the required and optional attendees, as well as any necessary resources.

2. In the **Suggested times** list on the right side of the window, click a meeting time when all or most of the required attendees are available.

Responding to Meeting Requests

When someone schedules a meeting with you as an attendee, Outlook sends you a meeting request, which you receive in your Outlook Inbox. When you receive the meeting request, Outlook automatically schedules the meeting on your calendar as Tentative.

You can respond to a meeting request in one of four ways:

- **Accept** Outlook deletes the meeting request and shows the scheduled time on your calendar as the meeting organizer indicated in the meeting request.

- **Tentatively accept** Outlook deletes the meeting request and shows the time on your calendar as tentatively scheduled.

- **Decline** Outlook deletes the meeting request and removes the meeting from your calendar.

- **Propose a new time** Outlook sends your proposal to the meeting organizer for confirmation and shows the original time on your calendar as tentatively scheduled.

When a meeting attendee responds to a meeting request from you, you receive a meeting response in your Inbox. The icon and subject of the meeting response message indicate the attendee's response. In the meeting window, Outlook displays the number and type of responses from attendees in a banner below the ribbon. Either way, you always have an up-to-date report of how many people will be attending your meeting.

If you set up a meeting that includes resources, such as a conference room, the meeting request sent to that resource might be automatically approved, or the person assigned responsibility for the resources might approve the request.

➤ **To accept, tentatively accept, or decline a meeting request**

1. In the meeting request window or **Reading Pane**, click the **Accept** button, the **Tentative** button, or the **Decline** button.

2. Choose one of the following response options:

   ○ Click **Edit the Response before Sending**. In the meeting response window that opens, enter a message to the meeting organizer in the content pane, and then click the **Send** button.

   ○ Click **Send the Response Now** to send a standard meeting response without an additional message.

   ○ Click **Do Not Send a Response** to not send a meeting response. Your response will be tallied by Outlook and included in the up-to-date attendee information available to the meeting organizer in the meeting window.

➤ **To propose a new meeting time**

1. In the meeting request window or **Reading Pane**, click the **Propose New Time** button, and then do one of the following:

   ○ Click **Tentative and Propose New Time** to mark the meeting time on your calendar as tentatively scheduled.

   ○ Click **Decline and Propose New Time** to remove the meeting from your calendar.

2. In the **Propose New Time** dialog box, set the proposed meeting date, start time, and end time, and then click the **Propose Time** button.

3. In the meeting response window that opens, enter a message to the meeting organizer, and then click the **Send** button.

➤ **To track responses to a meeting request**

➜   In the meeting window, do one of the following:

○   In the information bar below the ribbon, view the tally of attendees who have accepted, tentatively accepted, or declined.

○   On the **Meeting** tab, in the **Show** group, click the **Tracking** button to see a complete list of attendees' responses.

> **Tip** To send an email message to everyone you've invited to a meeting, open the meeting window, and click the Contact Attendees button in the Attendees group on the Meeting tab. Then click New E-mail To Attendees to open a blank message composition window or Reply To All With E-mail to open a message composition window that contains the meeting details.

Rescheduling and Canceling Meetings

If it is necessary to change the date, time, or location of a meeting, you can easily do so in the meeting window. You can also cancel the meeting entirely. If the meeting you want to change is recurring, you can change an individual occurrence of the meeting or the entire meeting series. After you make changes, Outlook sends an updated meeting request to the invited attendees to keep them informed. Changes to the meeting details are clearly indicated.

If an invitee cannot attend the meeting at the scheduled time and proposes a new meeting time, as the organizer of the meeting, you can accept or decline the proposal. If you accept, Outlook updates the entry in your calendar and opens the meeting window so you can send an updated meeting request to the attendees. If the proposed time doesn't work for you, reply to or delete the proposal.

> **Tip** You can specify that attendees cannot propose new meeting times. To do this for all meetings, open the Outlook Options dialog box, click Calendar, and then clear the Allow Attendees To Propose New Times For Meetings check box. To do it for the current meeting request, click Response Options in the Attendees group on the Meeting tab, and then clear the Allow New Time Proposals check box.

> ➤ **To update a one-time meeting**

1. Double-click the meeting in the **Calendar** pane.

2. In the meeting window, make any necessary changes.

3. Click the **Send Update** button.

> ➤ **To update a recurring meeting**

1. Double-click the meeting in the **Calendar** pane.

2. In the **Open Recurring Item** dialog box, click either **Open this occurrence** or **Open the series**, and then click **OK**.

3. In the meeting window, make any necessary changes.

4. Click the **Send Update** button.

> ➤ **To cancel a meeting**

1. In the meeting window, on the **Meeting** tab, in the **Actions** group, click the **Cancel Meeting** button.

2. If the meeting is a recurring one, in the **Confirm Delete** dialog box, click either **Delete this occurrence** or **Delete the series**, and then click **OK**.

3. To inform attendees that the meeting has been canceled, click the **Send Cancellation** button.

➤ To accept a proposed meeting time change

→ In the meeting response window, in the **Respond** group, click **Accept Proposal**, and then click **Send Update**.

➤ To decline a proposed meeting time

1. In the meeting response window, in the **Respond** group, click the **Reply** button.

2. In the email message, enter text to inform the attendee that you are not accepting the proposed time, and then click **Send**.

3. Delete the **New Time Proposed** message.

Practice Tasks

There are no practice files for these tasks. Before you begin, alert two colleagues that you are going to practice scheduling meetings.

- Create a request for a half-hour meeting with a colleague, with the subject *MOS Status Meeting*, at 3:00 P.M. tomorrow. Enter *Test – please accept* as the location, and send the request to one person.

- Add a second colleague as an optional attendee to the meeting request for the *MOS Status Meeting*, and then send the meeting request only to the new attendee.

- Schedule a one-hour *MOS Budget Meeting* with two colleagues at the first available time next week. Set up this meeting to occur at the same time every month for three months.

- Reschedule the *MOS Budget Meeting* to the week after next, and then send the updated meeting request.

- Ask a colleague to send you a meeting request for a meeting with the subject *MOS Project Meeting*. When the meeting request arrives, tentatively accept the meeting and propose that the meeting be held at the same time on the following day.

- Cancel the *MOS Status Meeting* and *MOS Budget Meeting* meetings and send cancellation notices to the attendees.

5.3 Manipulate the Calendar Pane

Arranging Calendar Content

You can arrange the Calendar module to display specific time periods in the Calendar pane. The standard time periods are available from the Arrangement group on the View tab or the Arrange group on the Home tab. These time periods are:

- **Day** Displays one day at a time separated into half-hour increments.

- **Work Week** Displays only the days of your work week. The default work week is Monday through Friday from 8:00 A.M. to 5:00 P.M. Time slots that fall within the work week are white on the calendar; time slots outside of the work week are colored.

> **See Also** For information about modifying the days and hours of the work week shown in Outlook, see section 1.1, "Apply and Manipulate Outlook Program Options."

- **Week** Displays one calendar week (Sunday through Saturday) at a time.

- **Month** Displays one calendar month at a time, as well as the preceding and following weeks (for a total of six weeks, the same as the Date Navigator). When displaying Month view, you can choose one of three detail levels:

  - **Low Detail** Displays a calendar that is blank except for events.

  - **Medium Detail** Displays events and shaded, unlabeled bars to indicate ppointments and meetings.

  - **High Detail** Displays events and labeled bars to indicate appointments and meetings.

You can also display a horizontal Schedule view of one or more calendars. Schedule view is a new feature in Outlook 2010 that is designed to simplify the process of comparing short periods of time across multiple calendars.

◄ ► October 24 - 30, 2010

Search Calendar (Ctrl+E)

10 am   11 00   12 pm   1 00   2 00

Tuesday, October 26, 2010

Jean Trenary

Joan Lambert — Real estate agent tour — Core meeting; Jo — Biz meeting 866-500-‹ Joan L

Joyce Cox

Susie Carr

Marlene Lambert

Lisa Van Every

► **To change the time period displayed in the Calendar pane**

→ On the **View** tab, in the **Arrangement** group, click the **Day**, **Work Week**, **Week**, or **Month** button.

► **To change the amount of information shown in Month view**

→ On the **View** tab, in the **Arrangement** group, click the **Month** arrow, and then click **Show Low Detail**, **Show Medium Detail**, or **Show High Detail**.

► **To display a specific day, week, or month from the Calendar pane**

→ In Month view, click the week tab at the left edge of a week to display only that week.

→ In Month, Week, or Work Week view, double-click the header of an individual day to display only that day.

→ Display the previous or next time period by clicking the **Back** button or the **Forward** button next to the date or date range.

→ Display the current day by clicking the **Today** button in the **Go To** group on the **Home** tab.

➤ **To display a specific day, week, or month from the Date Navigator**

→ To display a day, click that day.

> **Tip** If you're displaying the calendar in Day, Work Week, or Week view, the day appears and is highlighted in the current view. If you're displaying the calendar in Month view, the display changes to Day view.

→ To display a week, click the margin to the left of that week. Or, if you display week numbers in the Date Navigator and Calendar, click the week number to display that week.

> **See Also** For information about displaying week numbers, see section 1.1, "Apply and Manipulate Outlook Program Options."

> **Tip** In any calendar view, selecting a week in the Date Navigator changes the display to Week view.

→ To display a month, click the **Previous** or **Next** button to scroll one month back or forward, or click the current month name and hold down the mouse button to display a range of months, point to the month you want to display, and then release the mouse button. To scroll beyond the seven-month range displayed by default, point to the top or bottom of the month list.

> **Tip** In Month view, scrolling the month displays the entire month; in Day view, it displays the same date of the selected month; and in Week or Work Week view, it displays the same week of the selected month.

➤ **To display multiple calendars in Schedule view**

1. On the **View** tab, in the **Arrangement** group, click the **Schedule View** button.

2. In the **Navigation Pane**, select the check boxes of the calendars or calendar groups you want to display.

> **See Also** For information about modifying the way Outlook displays information in Schedule view, see section 1.1, "Apply and Manipulate Outlook Program Options."

Displaying Different Views

The Calendar module offers four distinct views of content. These views are:

- **Calendar** This is the standard view in which you display your Outlook calendar. In the Day, Work Week, or Week arrangement, Calendar view displays the subject, location, and organizer (if space allows) of each appointment, meeting, or event, as well as the availability bar and any special icons, such as Private or Recurrence.

- **Preview** In the Day, Work Week, or Week arrangement, this view displays additional information, including information from the notes area of the appointment window, as space allows.

- **List** This list view displays all appointments, meetings, and events on your calendar.

- **Active** This list view displays only future appointments, meetings, and events.

When working in a list view, you can group calendar items by selecting a field from the Arrangement gallery on the View tab.

> **Tip** In this book, we assume you are working in Calendar view, and refer to the standard Calendar view arrangements as *Day view*, *Work Week view*, *Week view*, and *Schedule view*.

➤ **To display a different view of the Calendar module**

→ On the **View** tab, in the **Current View** group, click the **Change View** button, and then click **Calendar**, **Preview**, **List**, or **Active**.

Displaying Multiple Calendars

Secondary calendars are calendars that you create, import, or subscribe to, or that other people share with you. You can view secondary calendars either individually or at the same time as your primary calendar. You can view multiple calendars next to each other, or you can overlay them to display a composite view. When you view and click a date in the Date Navigator or scroll one calendar, all the currently displayed calendars show the same date or time period.

Overlaid calendars

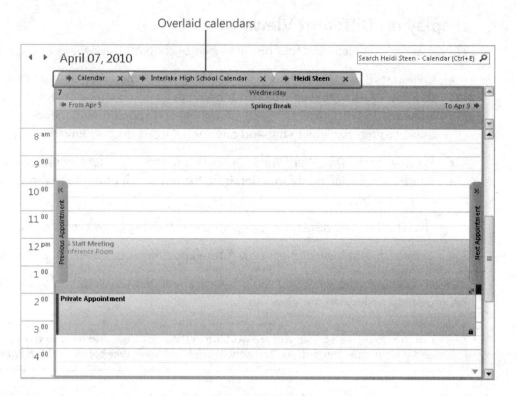

In the Calendar module, the Navigation Pane displays a list of the available calendars. You display or hide a calendar by selecting or clearing its check box.

In the Mail module, calendars are shown in the expanded folder list. You display a calendar in the Calendar module by clicking it in the folder list.

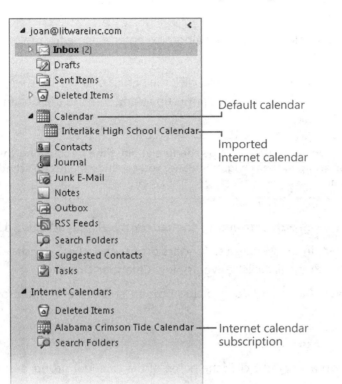

If you meet frequently with the same people, you can create a calendar group that displays the schedules of multiple people within your organization in one place. Then any time you need to schedule a meeting with that group of people, you can display the calendar group in Schedule view, visually compare schedules, and then send a meeting request for a time when everyone is available.

➤ **To create a secondary calendar**

1. In the Calendar module, on the **Folder** tab, in the **New** group, click the **New Calendar** button.

2. In the **Create New Folder** dialog box, name the calendar, select its location, and then click **OK**.

➤ **To create a calendar group by choosing group members**

1. In the Calendar module, on the **Home** tab, in the **Manage Calendars** group, click the **Calendar Groups** button and then, in the list, click **Create New Calendar Group**.

2. In the **Create New Calendar Group** dialog box, enter a name for the group and then click **OK**.

3. In the **Select Name** dialog box, double-click the names of the people whose calendars you want to include in the calendar group to add them to the **Group Members** box, and then click **OK**.

> **Tip** You can display an up-to-date group schedule at any time by selecting the check box of the calendar group in the Navigation Pane. You can hide the group schedule by clearing the check box.

➤ **To create a calendar group containing the currently displayed calendars**

1. On the **Home** tab, in the **Manage Calendars** group, click the **Calendar Groups** button and then, in the list, click **Save as New Calendar Group**.

2. In the **Create New Calendar Group** dialog box, enter a name for the group and then click **OK**.

➤ **To delete a calendar group**

1. In the **Navigation Pane**, right-click the name of the calendar group, and then click **Delete Group**.

2. In the confirmation dialog box, click **Yes**.

➤ **To display multiple calendars**

→ In the **Navigation Pane**, select the check boxes of the calendars or calendar group you want to view.

➤ **To switch between Overlay Mode and Side-By-Side Mode**

→ On the title bar tab of any secondary calendar, click the **View in Overlay Mode** button. In Overlay Mode, click either calendar tab to display that calendar on top of the other calendar.

→ On either of the overlaid calendars, click the **View in Side-By-Side Mode** button to return to the standard display.

Changing Calendar Colors

Each calendar you display in Outlook has 1 of 15 standard colors assigned to it. The calendar color is used in the Navigation Pane, in the calendar header, and when creating appointments and meetings in the Calendar pane. The calendar color helps you to visually differentiate between calendars, and is especially useful when viewing multiple calendars in Overlay Mode. By default, Outlook automatically assigns a color to each new calendar that is different from the colors of existing calendars. You can change the color of any calendar.

> ➤ **To change a calendar color**

   1. Display the calendar for which you want to change the color. If you're displaying multiple calendars, select the calendar you want to change by clicking its tab.

   2. On the **View** tab, in the **Color** group, click the **Color** button. Then in the **Color** gallery, click the color you want to assign to the calendar.

Practice Tasks

There are no practice files for these tasks. Before you begin, alert a colleague that you are going to practice sharing your calendar.

   • Display the calendar for next month. By clicking in the Calendar pane, display only the second week of the month. By clicking in the Date Navigator, display only the fifteenth day of the month.

   • Create a secondary calendar named *MOS Schedule*, and display it beside your primary calendar.

   • Change the color of the *MOS Schedule* calendar to one of your choosing.

   • Create a calendar group named *MOS Team* that includes the secondary calendar and the calendar of a colleague, and display the calendar group in Schedule view.

   • Display the *MOS Team* calendar group in Overlay Mode.

   • Delete the *MOS Team* calendar group.

   • Hide the *MOS Schedule* calendar.

Objective Review

Before finishing this chapter, ensure that you have mastered the following skills:

5.1   Create and Manipulate Appointments and Events

5.2   Create and Manipulate Meeting Requests

5.3   Manipulate the Calendar Pane

6 Working with Tasks, Notes, and Journal Entries

The skills tested in this section of the Microsoft Office Specialist exam for Microsoft Outlook 2010 relate to working with the Tasks module, the Notes module, and the Outlook Journal. Specifically, the following objectives are associated with this set of skills:

6.1 Create and Manipulate Tasks

6.2 Create and Manipulate Notes

6.3 Create and Manipulate Journal Entries

Outlook 2010 provides functionality for tracking tasks in a to-do list, storing miscellaneous items of information as notes, and recording activities as journal entries. You can view your tasks for each day at the bottom of the Calendar pane as well as in the To-Do Bar, and you can manage tasks from the To-Do Bar or from the Tasks module. In the Notes module, you can quickly jot down text notes about any subject, and in the Journal module, you can track interactions with contacts.

This chapter guides you in studying ways to create tasks, mark tasks as complete or private, assign tasks to other people, accept and decline tasks, and send status reports about assigned tasks. You will also study ways to create notes and journal entries, change the current view while working with notes, categorize notes, automatically record Outlook items and record files in the Journal, and edit journal entries.

> **Practice Files** Before you can complete the practice tasks in this chapter, you need to copy the book's practice files to your computer. The practice file you'll use to complete the tasks in this chapter is in the Outlook\Objective6 practice file folder. A complete list of practice files is provided in "Using the Book's Companion Content" at the beginning of this book.

6.1 Create and Manipulate Tasks

Creating Tasks

If you use your Outlook task list to its fullest potential, you'll frequently add tasks to it. You can create tasks in several ways:

- In the Tasks module, add a task to the task list.
- In other modules, add a task to the To-Do Bar Task List.
- Create a new task in the task window.
- Base a task on an existing Outlook item (such as a message).

Just as you can create recurring appointments, events, and meetings, you can create recurring tasks. You can set the task to occur every day, week, month, or year; or you can specify that a new task should be generated a certain amount of time after the last task is complete.

You may frequently need to take action based on information you receive in Outlook—for example, information in a message or in a meeting request. You might want to add information from another Outlook item to your task list, to ensure that you complete any necessary follow-up work. Depending on the method you use, you can either create a new task from an existing item or simply transfer the existing item to your task list by flagging it.

Regardless of how or where you create a task, all tasks are available in the Tasks module and in the To-Do Bar Task List. Only individual tasks are available in the Tasks List.

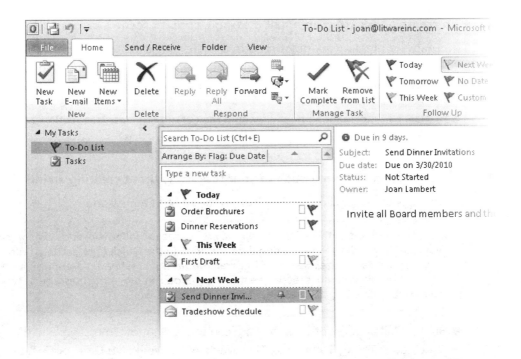

> ### To create a task in the Tasks module

→ On the **Home** tab, in the **New** group, click the **New Task** button. Enter the task details in the task window that opens, and then save and close the task.

→ When displaying the To-Do List view of the Tasks module, enter the task description in the **Type a new task** box, and then press Enter to create a task with the default settings.

→ When displaying the Tasks List view of the Tasks module, enter the task description in the **Click here to add a new Task** box, press Tab to move to subsequent fields, fill in other information, and then press Enter.

> **Tip** The fields available in the Tasks List vary based on the list view you're displaying. For information about the available views, see the "Displaying Views of Tasks" topic later in this section.

> ### To create a task in any module

→ On the **Home** tab, in the **New** group, in the **New Items** list, click **Task**. Enter the task details in the task window that opens, and then save and close the task.

→ In the To-Do Bar, enter the task description in the **Type a new task** box at the top of the To-Do Bar Task List.

➤ To create a task from an email message, contact record, or note

→ Drag the message, contact record, or note to the **Tasks** button at the bottom of the **Navigation Pane**, pause until the **Navigation Pane** changes to display the Tasks module content, and then release the mouse button.

> **See Also** For information about changing the default due date, see section 1.1, "Apply and Manipulate Outlook Program Options."

➤ To transfer an email message to your task list without creating an individual task

→ In the **Mail** pane, click the flag icon to the right of a message.

> **Tip** This method, referred to as *flagging a message for follow-up*, adds the message to your task list with the default due date specified in the Quick Click settings, and adds an information bar to the message. However, it does not create a separate task item, so to retain the task, you must retain the message—you can move the message between mail folders, but deleting the message deletes the task as well.

→ In the **Mail** pane, right-click the flag icon to the right of a message, and then specify a due date: **Today**, **Tomorrow**, **This Week**, **Next Week**, **No Date**, or **Custom** (which allows you to set specific start and end dates).

→ Drag the message to the To-Do Bar Task List and drop it under the heading for the due date you want to assign it to. (If the desired due date doesn't already have a heading in the To-Do Bar Task List, you need to drop the message under another heading and then assign the due date you want.)

> **Tip** This method also adds the message to your task list but doesn't create a separate task item.

➤ To transfer a contact record to your task list without creating an individual task

1. In the **Contacts** pane, click the contact record to select it.
2. On the **Home** tab, in the **Tags** group, click the **Follow-Up** button, and then click a due date.

Displaying Views of Tasks

Outlook 2010 makes it simple to keep your task list at your fingertips. You can view tasks in several different locations, including the following:

- In the Tasks module, you can display either the To-Do List, which is the default view of this module and includes both tasks and flagged messages, or the Tasks List, which includes only tasks. There are many options for viewing and arranging each list.

- In any module, the expanded To-Do Bar displays the To-Do Bar Task List, where tasks are grouped and sorted under due date headings. (You can also sort this list by category, start date, folder, type, or importance, or you can create a custom arrangement.) You can scroll through the list to display all your tasks or collapse the groups you don't want to view. To increase the space available for your task list, you can close the Date Navigator or show fewer or no appointments.

- In the Calendar module, the Daily Task List appears at the bottom of the Calendar pane in Day, Work Week, or Week view. When expanded, the Daily Task List displays the tasks due, including the category and task type, during the displayed time period. In Day view, the start date, due date, and reminder time also appear.

> **Tip** You can schedule a specific block of time to complete a task by dragging it from the Daily Task List to your calendar. When you mark the task complete, Outlook removes it from your calendar. If you don't see the Daily Task List in Day, Work Week, or Week view, click the Daily Task List button in the Layout group on the View tab, and then click Normal.

You can display different views of your Tasks List and, within each view, different arrangements of the tasks.

Tasks List views include:

- Active
- Assigned
- Completed
- Detailed
- Next 7 Days
- Overdue
- Prioritized
- Server Tasks
- Simple List
- Today
- To-Do List

You can select from the following standard arrangements of items within the To-Do List or a Tasks List view:

- Assignment
- Categories
- Due Date
- Folder (Available in the To-Do List only, this view separates tasks and flagged messages that are stored in different folders.)

> **See Also** For information about organizing tasks in custom folders, see the "Managing Tasks" topic later in this section.

- Importance
- Modified Date
- Start Date
- Type

Completed tasks remain in the Tasks List until you actually delete them, so they are available there if you want to view them.

> **See Also** For information about completing and deleting tasks, see the "Finalizing Tasks" topic later in this section.

➤ **To change the Tasks List view**

→ On the **Home** tab, in the **Current View** gallery, click the view you want.

→ On the **View** tab, in the **Current View** group, click the **Change View** button, and then click the view you want.

➤ **To change the arrangement of tasks in the Tasks List view or To-Do List**

→ On the **View** tab, in the **Arrangement** gallery, click the arrangement you want.

➤ **To reorder the tasks in a list view**

→ Click the column header of the field you want to sort on.

> **See Also** For information about adding and removing fields from a list view, see section 1.3, "Arrange the Content Pane."

Managing Tasks

To help you organize your tasks, you can assign them to color categories in the same way that you do any other Outlook item.

If your task list gets too big, or if you want to maintain separate task lists for different purposes, you can organize tasks into separate folders.

➤ **To create a task folder**

1. On the **Folder** tab, in the **New** group, click the **New Folder** button.

2. In the **Create New Folder** dialog box, enter the name and select the location of the folder.

3. In the **Folder Contains** list, click **Task Items**, and then click **OK**.

➤ **To move a task to another folder**

1. In the **Tasks** pane, select the task you want to move.

2. On the **Home** tab, in the **Actions** group, click the **Move** button, and then click the folder to which you want to move the task.

   Or

1. Expand the **Navigation Pane** to display the new folder.

2. Display the contents of the original folder.

3. Drag the task from the original folder to the new folder.

> **Tip** If you drag a task into a Mail, Calendar, Contact, or Note Items folder, a message, meeting, contact, or note window opens with the task's subject entered in the Subject field and details of the task in the message body or Notes pane.

➤ **To create a copy of a task in another folder**

1. In the **Tasks** pane, select the task you want to copy.

2. On the **Home** tab, in the **Actions** group, click the **Move** button, and then click **Copy to Folder**.

3. In the **Copy Items** dialog box, click the folder to which you want to copy the task, and then click **OK**.

Managing Task Details

When you create a task item, the only information you must include is the subject. As with many other types of Outlook items, you can set several options for tasks to make it easier to organize and identify tasks.

- **Start date and due date** You can display tasks on either the start date or the due date in the various Outlook task lists. The color of the task flag indicates the due date.

- **Status** You can track the status of a task to remind yourself of your progress. Specific status options include Not Started, In Progress, Completed, Waiting On Someone Else, or Deferred. You also have the option of indicating what percentage of the task is complete. Setting the percentage complete to 25%, 50%, or 75% sets the task status to In Progress. Setting it to 100% sets the task status to Complete.

- **Priority** Unless you indicate otherwise, a task is created with a Normal priority level. You can set the priority to add a visual indicator of a task's importance. Low priority displays a blue downward pointing arrow and High priority displays a red exclamation point. You can sort and filter tasks based on their priority.

- **Recurrence** You can set a task to recur on a regular basis; for example, you might create a Payroll task that recurs every month. Only the current instance of a recurring task appears in your task list. When you mark the current task as complete, Outlook creates the next instance of the task.

- **Category** Tasks use the same category list as other Outlook items. You can assign a task to a category to associate it with related items such as messages and appointments.

- **Reminder** You can set a reminder for a task in the same way you do for an appointment. The reminder appears until you dismiss it or mark the task as complete.

- **Privacy** Marking a task as private ensures that other Outlook users to whom you delegate account access can't see the task details.

None of the options are required, but they can be helpful when sorting, filtering, and prioritizing your tasks.

To track tasks to completion, you can update the Status and % Complete information in the task window.

> **Tip** You can attach files to tasks, and you can include text, tables, charts, illustrations, hyperlinks, and other content in the task window content pane.

➤ **To create a recurring task**

1. On the **Task** tab of the task window, in the **Recurrence** group, click the **Recurrence** button.

2. In the **Task Recurrence** dialog box, select the **Recurrence pattern** and **Range of recurrence** options you want, and then click **OK**.

➤ **To assign a task to a category**

→ In your To-Do List or To-Do Bar Task List, right-click the category icon to the right of the task subject in the task list, and then click the category you want.

→ Click the task in your Tasks List to select it. On the **Home** tab, in the **Tags** group, click the **Categorize** button, and then click the category you want.

→ On the **Task** tab of the task window, in the **Tags** group, click the **Categorize** button, and then click the category you want.

➤ **To assign a due date to a task**

→ In your To-Do List or To-Do Bar Task List, right-click the flag icon, and click the due date you want.

> **See Also** For information about automatically setting task reminders, see section 1.1, "Apply and Manipulate Outlook Program Options."

➤ **To mark a task as private**

→ On the **Task** tab of the task window, in the **Tags** group, click the **Private** button.

Managing Task Assignments

You can assign tasks from your Outlook task list to other people within your organization, and other people can assign tasks to you. You can't assign flagged Outlook items; only tasks.

When you assign a task, Outlook sends a task request, similar to a meeting request, to the assignee. If the assignee declines the task, you can return it to your task list or reassign it. If the assignee accepts the task, ownership of the task transfers to that person, and you can no longer update the information in the task window. You can choose whether to keep a copy of the task on your own task list or transfer it entirely to the assignee's task list. (Either way, the task remains on your own task list until it is accepted, so you won't lose track of it.) If you keep a copy of the task on your task list, you can follow the progress as the assignee updates the task status and details, and you can communicate information about the task to the owner by sending status reports. You can choose to have Outlook send you a status report on an assigned task when the assignee marks the task as complete.

If you are assigned a task, you receive an email message with the assignment in your Inbox. You can accept or decline the task assignment by clicking the corresponding button in the Reading Pane or in the task window.

Task assignment

Task response options

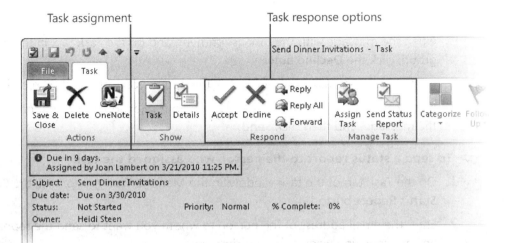

Tip Outlook indicates assigned tasks in your task list by an outstretched hand on the task icon, similar to that of a shared folder in Windows Explorer.

➤ To assign a task to someone else

1. On the **Task** tab of the task window, in the **Manage Task** group, click the **Assign Task** button.

2. In the **To** box that appears, enter the email address of the assignee.

3. If you don't want to keep the task on your task list or receive a report when the task is complete, clear the corresponding check box.

4. Click **Send**.

5. If a message notifies you that the task reminder has been turned off, click **OK**.

➤ To accept an assigned task

1. Open the message with the task assignment, and on the **Task** tab, in the **Respond** group, click the **Accept** button.

2. In the **Accepting Task** dialog box, click **Edit the response before sending** or **Send the response now**, and then click **OK**.

3. If you chose to send a message with your acceptance, enter the message, and then click **Send**.

➤ **To decline an assigned task**

1. Open the message with the task assignment, and on the **Task** tab, in the **Respond** group, click the **Decline** button.

2. In the **Declining Task** dialog box, click the option you want, and then click **OK**.

3. If you chose to send a message explaining your rejection of the assignment, type the message, and then click **Send**.

➤ **To send a status report to the person who assigned the task**

1. On the **Task** tab of the task window, in the **Manage Task** group, click the **Send Status Report** button.

2. Enter the email address of the person to whom you want to send the report, type any message you want, and then click **Send**.

Finalizing Tasks

You can remove a task from your active task list by marking it as complete, or by deleting it. You can remove a flagged item from the active task list by removing the follow-up flag.

☐ ☑	Subject	Due Date ▲	Categories	🏳 ▲
	Click here to add a new Task			
🗓 ☑	~~Order Brochures~~	~~Tue 3/23/2010~~		✓
🗓 ☑	~~Dinner Reservations~~	~~Wed 3/24/2010~~		✓
🗓 ☐	Send Dinner Invitations	Tue 3/30/2010		🏳

> **Tip** When you mark an instance of a recurring task as complete, Outlook generates a new instance of the task at whatever interval you specified when creating the task. When you delete a task or flagged message, it moves to the Deleted Items folder. When you empty that folder, it is permanently deleted, and no record of it remains on your task list.

➤ **To mark a task as complete**

→ In the task window, set **% Complete** to **100%**.

→ On the **Task** tab of the task window, in the **Manage Task** group, click the **Mark Complete** button.

➤ **To remove a follow-up flag**

→ In the To-Do List, Tasks List, To-Do Bar Task List, Mail pane, Contacts pane, or Notes pane, click the flag icon to the right of the message subject to change the flag to a check mark.

→ In the Tasks module, in the To-Do List, Tasks List, or To-Do Bar Task List, click the flagged item to select it. Then on the **Home** tab, in the **Manage Task** group, click the **Remove from List** button.

→ In a module other than the Tasks module, in the To-Do Bar Task List, click the flagged item to select it. Then on the Task Tools **Task List** contextual tab, in the **Manage Task** group, click the **Remove from List** button.

➤ **To delete a task**

→ On the **Task** tab of the task window, in the **Actions** group, click the **Delete** button.

→ In the Tasks module, in the To-Do List or Tasks List, click the flagged item to select it. Then on the **Home** tab, in the **Delete** group, click the **Delete** button.

Practice Tasks

There are no practice files for these tasks. Before you begin, alert a colleague that you will need his or her assistance to practice working with task assignments.

- From the To-Do Bar, create a task with the subject *MOS Dinner Reservations*, flag it for completion this week, and assign it to the Management category (or another category you choose).

- Open a new task window, and create a task with the subject *MOS Send Dinner Invitations*. Set a due date of next Tuesday with a reminder at 5:00 P.M., and then set the status to Waiting On Someone Else.

- Open the *MOS Dinner Reservations* task, and mark it as private and high priority. Then set it to 25 percent complete.

- Create a new task with the subject *MOS Status Report* that must be carried out on the first Monday of every month for six months.

- Assign the *MOS Dinner Reservations* task you created in the previous practice tasks to a colleague, without retaining the task on your task list.

- Ask your colleague to assign two tasks to you. When you receive the first task assignment, accept it. When you receive the second assignment, reject it with a polite message explaining why.

- Open the task you accepted in the previous practice task, mark it 50 percent complete, and set its status to In Progress. Then send a task status report to the colleague who assigned the task.

6.2 Create and Manipulate Notes

Creating Notes

In the Notes module, you can create and store text notes about any subject. If your organization uses Microsoft Exchange Server, the notes are available to you whenever you connect to your account through Outlook, through your Internet browser, or from a mobile device.

Outlook Notes support plain text, formatted text, and hyperlinks. You can't format text within a note but you can paste formatted text from a document, message, or other source into a note and retain its formatting.

> **Tip** The first line of text in the note is shown as its subject.

Displaying Views of Notes

You can view the content of the Notes module in three standard views:

- **Icon** This view depicts each note as a colored square with a turned up corner, reminiscent of a pad of sticky notes. In Icon view, you can display large icons organized in rows and columns, or small icons organized either in rows or in columns.

- **Notes List** This list view displays a small icon, the note subject, and up to three lines of note content.

- **Last 7 Days** This list view is identical to Notes List view but displays only notes that have been modified within the last seven days.

In either list view, you can choose from two standard arrangements: Categories and Created Date. As with other list views, you can sort notes by a specific field by clicking the column header for that field, and you can add or remove fields from the list view.

> **See Also** For information about adding and removing fields in a list view, see the "Displaying Views of Tasks" topic of section 6.1, "Create and Manipulate Tasks."

If none of the standard views meets your needs, you can create a custom view.

➤ **To change the Notes module view**

→ On the **Home** tab, in the **Current View** gallery, click the view you want.

→ On the **View** tab, in the **Current View** group, click the **Change View** button, and then click the view you want.

➤ **To change the arrangement in Notes List view or Last 7 Days view**

→ On the **View** tab, in the **Arrangement** gallery, click the arrangement you want.

➤ **To create a custom view of the Notes module**

1. On the **View** tab, in the **Current View** group, click the **Change View** button, and then click **Manage Views**.

2. In the **Manage All Views** dialog box, do one of the following:

    ○ To modify an existing view, click **Current view settings** or the name of one of the standard views.

    ○ To design a view from scratch, click the **New** button. In the **Create a New View** dialog box, enter a name, select the type of view you want to create, and specify the folders in which the view will be available. Then click **OK**.

3. To modify a copy of the view rather than the original, click the **Copy** button. In the **Copy View** dialog box, enter a name and specify the folders in which the view will be available. Then click **OK**.

4. Click the **Modify** button. In the **Advanced View Settings** dialog box, make the changes you want to the **Sort**, **Filter**, and other settings of the selected view. Then click **OK**.

> **See Also** For information about changing the color, size, and font of notes, see section 1.1, "Apply and Manipulate Outlook Program Options." For information about adding and removing fields from a list view, see section 1.3, "Arrange the Content Pane."

Organizing Notes

You can organize notes by assigning them to color categories. In Icon view, uncategorized notes are depicted in the default color set in the Outlook Options window; categorized notes are depicted in the most recently assigned category color. You can also assign a note to one or more contact records. Notes that are assigned to a contact record are available from the Notes folder and from the Activities page of the contact record window.

➤ **To assign one or more notes to a color category**

1. In the **Notes** pane, select the note or notes you want to assign to the same category.

2. On the **Home** tab, in the **Tags** group, click the **Categorize** button and then, in the list, click the category you want to assign.

➤ **To associate a note with one or more contact records**

1. In the upper-left corner of the note window, click the note icon and then, in the list, click **Contacts**.

2. In the **Contacts for Note** dialog box, do one of the following:

   ○ Enter the contacts to whom you want to assign the note.

   ○ Click the **Contacts** button. In the **Select Contacts** dialog box, select the contact or contacts you want, and then click **OK**.

3. In the **Contacts for Note** dialog box, click the **Close** button.

Practice Tasks

There are no practice files for these tasks.

- In the Notes module, create a note that contains your full name.

- Modify the note content so that only your first name appears as the note subject.

- If you haven't already done so, create a color category named *MOS*. Assign the note to the MOS color category.

- If you haven't already done so, create a contact record for yourself. Associate the note with your contact record.

6.3 Create and Manipulate Journal Entries

Activating the Outlook Journal

By default, the Outlook Journal is turned off and its button is not available in the Navigation Pane. You can activate the Journal and configure it to track the interactions you have with contacts so that you can easily locate messages, meetings, tasks, and files associated with specific people.

Tip It is not necessary to use the Journal if you want to track only email messages for an existing contact; these are automatically tracked on the Activities page of each contact record.

When you display the Journal, if it isn't already turned on, Outlook gives you the option to turn it on. You can display the entire Journal as you do any other module, or display only the activities and files associated with a contact from that person's contact record.

December 2010

| Thu 9 | Fri 10 | Sat 11 | Sun 12 | Mon 13 | Tue 14 | Wed 15 | Thu 16 | Fri 17 | Sat 18 |

Entry Type: E-mail Message

Entry Type: Microsoft Office Excel

C:\OTSI\OTSI Employee schedule.xlsx   C:\Users\Joan\AppData\Local\Microsoft\Windows\Temp

C:\OTSI\OTSI Employee schedule.xlsx

Entry Type: Microsoft Word

\Fictitious Names.docx   C:\Users\Joan\Documents\SharePoint Drafts\MOS_P3_PowerPoint_01.docx   C:\Users\Public\Documents\PROJECTS\M

C:\Users\Joan\Documents\SharePoint Drafts\MOS_P2_Excel_01.docx   C:\Users\Joan\Documents\SharePoint Drafts\31cab_663BS_M:

C:\Users\Public\Documents\PROJECTS\MOS2010\External_OD_882 Excel Core FINAL v2.d...   C:\Users\Joan\Documents\SharePoint Drafts

C:\Users\Public\Documents\PROJECTS\MOS2010\External_OD_882 Excel Core FINAL v2.d...   C:\Users\Joan\Documents\SharePoint Drafts

C:\Users\Public\Documents\PROJECTS\MOS2010\External_OD_882 Excel Core FINAL v2.d...   C:\Users\Joan\Documents\SharePoint Draft:

C:\Users\Public\Documents\PROJECTS\MOS2010\External_OD_888 Excel Expert FINAL v2...   C:\Users\Joan\Documents\SharePoint Draft:

C:\Users\Public\Documents\PROJECTS\MOS2010\MCAS_P4_Outlook_To-Do.doc   C:\Users\Joan\Documents\SharePoint Drafts\25bea_

C:\Users\Public\Documents\PROJECTS\MOS2010\External_OD_881_Word_Core_FINAL_v2.do...   C:\Users\Joan\Docun

➤ **To display the Journal button in the Navigation Pane**

→ In the lower-right corner of the **Navigation Pane**, click the **Configure buttons** button, click **Add or Remove Buttons**, and then click **Journal**.

➤ **To display the Journal module**

→ At the bottom of the **Navigation Pane**, click the **Journal** button.

→ Press Ctrl+8.

Automatically Recording Information

When you first turn on the Journal, you can specify the types of items and files you want to record, and the contacts for whom you want to record them. At any time thereafter, you can change the Journal settings from the Notes And Journal page of the Outlook Options dialog box.

The Journal can record the following types of Outlook items associated with a contact:

- Email messages
- Meeting requests, responses, and cancellations
- Task requests and responses

In addition, the Journal can record Microsoft Access, Excel, PowerPoint, Project, and Word files sent to or received from contacts.

➤ **To automatically record Outlook items for one or more contacts**

1. On the **Notes and Journal** page of the **Outlook Options** dialog box, click the **Journal Options** button.

2. In the **Journal Options** dialog box, do the following, and then click **OK**:

- ○ Select the check box for each type of Outlook item you want to record.
- ○ Select the check box for each type of file you want to record.
- ○ Select the check box for each contact for whom you want to record Outlook items and files.

3. In the **Outlook Options** dialog box, click **OK**.

Editing Journal Entries

Each item recorded by the Journal is saved as a journal entry with the original item attached to the entry. The journal entry includes information about the item and commands for working with it. You can assign properties to a journal entry just as you can to other Outlook items.

➤ To open a journal entry

→ In the **Journal** pane, double-click the recorded item.

➤ To edit a journal entry

→ In the journal entry window, do any of the following, and then click the **Save & Close** button:

- ○ On the **Journal Entry** tab, in the **Tags** group, click the **Categorize** or **Private** button to assign properties to the entry.

- ○ On the **Journal Entry** tab, in the **Timer** group, click the **Start Timer** button to begin recording time spent working with the journaled item, and the **Pause Timer** button to stop recording time.

> **Tip** The Duration field changes to reflect the time you record.

- ○ In the **Subject** box, change the subject to one that will more easily allow you to identify the entry.

- ○ In the **Entry type** list, click **Conversation**, **Document**, **E-mail Message**, **Fax**, **Letter**, a meeting item type, an Office document type, **Note**, **Phone call**, **Remote session**, or **Task** to move the item to a different Journal group.

- ○ In the content pane, add text, graphics, or other information that you want to save with the entry. Use the same methods as you would when adding content to a message.

Practice Tasks

The practice file for these tasks is located in the Outlook\Objective6 practice file folder. Before you start, alert a colleague that you will be testing the Journal functionality by sending a message to him or her.

- Turn on the Journal and configure it to automatically record email messages and Word documents associated with your colleague.

- Send an email message to your colleague. Attach the *ServiceProject* document, and request that the colleague respond to the message.

- After you receive the response, display the Journal and open the journal entry that contains the received message.

- Assign the journal entry to a color category, and then close the journal entry.

Objective Review

Before finishing this chapter, ensure that you have mastered the following skills:

6.1   Create and Manipulate Tasks

6.2   Create and Manipulate Notes

6.3   Create and Manipulate Journal Entries

Index

A

absolute references (Excel), 243
  to range of cells, 250
activating charts (PowerPoint), 415
Active view (Outlook), 625
adding values in worksheets, 189
add-ins (PowerPoint), 316
address block (Word), 147
address books, 591
  adding members to contact groups from, 600
  finding email addresses in, 484
  multiple, searching, 484
  printing, *See* printing contact records
  searching, default behavior, 484
  selecting contacts from, 616
  Suggested Contacts, 503
address lists. address books
addressing email messages, 484
alerts. notifications (email)
aligning (Excel), text in worksheet cells, 205, 206
aligning (PowerPoint)
  graphics, 371
  text boxes, 359
  text in slides, 347, 349, 362
  text in tables, 403
alphanumeric index (Outlook Contacts module),
  502, 503
Animation gallery, 422
Animation Painter, 424
Animation pane, 428, 430
  adding sound, 431
  changing animation order, 431
  changing effect options, 429, 431
  changing timing, 431
  viewing animation details, 428
animations, slide. slide animations
annotating slides, 468
Appointment page, for meeting requests, 611
Appointment Recurrence dialog box, 609, 613
appointments, 604
  across multiple days, 605
  and events, compared, 604
  and meetings, compared, 604

  attaching information to, 604
  availability choices, 604, 605
  canceling recurrence, 609
  categorizing, 512
  converting to meetings, 605
  creating from email messages, 606
  creating from tasks, 604
  entering in appointment window, 604
  entering in Calendar pane, 604
  forwarding, 609
  forwarding as iCalendar files, 609
  marking as Private, 608
  notes, adding to, 605
  on mobile devices, 604
  printing, 610
  recurring, 608
  reminders, 497, 605
  scheduling, 604
  searching for, 531
  selecting times for, 605
  setting options for, 496
  time, changing, 606
archiving, mailbox items, 509, 573
arguments, conditional logic (Excel), 246
artistic effects, applying to pictures (Word), 104
aspect ratio (PowerPoint)
  in graphics, maintaining, 369
  in text boxes, locking, 358
  settings, for cropping, 374
assigning items to categories (Outlook), 514
assignments, task
  accepting, 641
  declining, 642
  options, changing, 504
attaching
  electronic business cards, to email messages, 599
  items to contact records, 596
attachments, email. email attachments
attendees, meeting. meetings
  optional, availability of, 614
  optional, inviting to meetings, 613
  required, availability of, 614
  required, inviting to meetings, 612
  sending email messages to, 619

audio (PowerPoint)
   automatic play, setting, 394
   clips, in slides, 392
   editing, 395
   fading in/out, 395
   files, inserting into slides, 392, 393
   hiding during show, 394
   icons, 393
   in slides, 392, 394
   looping, 394
   recording, 393
   rewinding, 394
   settings, changing, 394
   trimming, 395
   volume, changing, 394
audio/visual equipment, scheduling, 502
AutoArchive (Outlook), 573
AutoComplete (Outlook), 493
AutoCorrect (Outlook), 487
AutoCorrect (PowerPoint), 438
   adding entries to, 439
   customizing, 314
AutoCorrect (Word), 125
   adding entries to, 126
   default settings, modifying, 126
   exceptions, 127
AutoFill (Excel), 193
   custom data series, 194
   options, 193
AutoFit (Excel), 210
Autofit (PowerPoint), 356
   behavior, setting, 358
   options, 356
AutoFormat (Outlook), 487
Automatic Replies (Outlook), 579
   and rules, compared, 579
   out-of-office, 580
   rules, specifying, 580
AutoSave (Excel), 184
AutoSave (Word), 28
AutoSum. Excel functions, SUM
availability
   in Scheduling Assistant page, 614
   options for appointments, 604
Available Windows gallery (Outlook), 555
averages, calculating, 245
axes, chart (PowerPoint), 410
   adding/removing, 412
   formatting, 418

B

background. *See also* **page backgrounds (Word);**
      slide backgrounds
   email message, changing, 587
   page, color, 95
   page, pattern, 95
   page, watermark, 95, 96
Background Removal tab (pictures), 377
Backstage view (Excel), 168
balloons (Word), 127, 129
banner, web page, 324
Bcc field (email message), 544
blank page, 83
Blocked Senders list (Outlook), 582, 584
blog posts
   creating, 34
   publishing, 35
booklets, printing contacts as, 538
bookmarks (Word), 135
borders (Excel), 207
borders (PowerPoint), 368
breaks. page breaks (Excel); page breaks (Word);
      section breaks (Word)
brightness, adjusting (PowerPoint), 377
broadcasting slide shows, 473
browsers, 278
browsing document elements, 53, 54, 57
Building Block Organizer (Word), 90
building blocks. Quick Parts (Word)
bulleted lists (PowerPoint)
   animating, 429
   bullet style, changing, 352
   changing items to/from titles, 350
   converting SmartArt graphics to, 388
   converting to/from paragraphs, 350, 352
   creating SmartArt graphics from, 385
   customizing, 350
   demoting, 352
   formatting, 350
   indenting, 352, 353
   pictures as bullets, 353
   promoting, 352
bulleted lists (Word)
   automatic formatting, turning on/off, 78
   creating, 77
   level, changing, 77
   sorting, 77
   symbol, changing, 77

Bullets gallery (PowerPoint), 353
business cards, electronic
    as email message signatures, 597
    Business Card list, 598
    creating contact records from, 595
    custom user fields, 598
    editing, 598
    formatting, 598
    images in, 596, 598
    in contact records, 596
    in email messages, 599
    in email signatures, 586
buttons
    Quick Access Toolbar (Excel), 182
    Quick Access Toolbar (PowerPoint), 312, 313
    ribbon, appearance of, xxxii
    ribbon (Excel), 178
    ribbon (PowerPoint), 316

C

Cached Exchange Mode (Outlook), 523
calculations. Excel formulas
calendar groups, 627, 628
calendar items
    appointments. *See* appointments
    attaching to email messages, 569
    canceling recurrence, 609
    charts in, creating or modifying, 554
    clip art, inserting, 551
    grouping, 625
    hyperlinks in, creating, 557
    marking as Private, 608
    modifying visual elements, 556
    pictures, inserting, 550
    recurring, 608
    reminders for, default, 497
    screen images, inserting, 555
    shapes, inserting, 551
    SmartArt graphics, creating, 552
    visual elements, inserting, 550
Calendar module
    content pane in, 526
    Daily Task List in, 635
    defining week settings, 497
    displaying list views in, 527
    Free/Busy options, customizing, 498
    holidays, adding, 497
    new meeting time proposals on, 497

    setting options for, 501
    tasks in, 635
    time zones, 501
Calendar pane
    displaying specific day, week, or month, 623
    entering appointments in, 604
    entering events in, 606
    views in, 622
Calendar view, 625
calendars
    color, changing, 500, 629
    controlling information displayed, 499
    displaying/hiding, 626
    hiding details from meeting invitees, 501
    imported, 627
    in content pane, 526
    in Mail module (Outlook), 627
    Internet subscription, 627
    limiting access to, 498
    meetings in. *See* meetings
    multiple, displaying, 624, 628
    permissions, controlling, 499
    printing. *See* printing calendars
    scheduling tasks in, 635
    secondary, 625, 627
    setting options for, 496
    view modes, switching, 628
calling contacts, 594
captions, photograph. photographs (PowerPoint)
capturing screen clippings (Outlook), 555
capturing screen clippings (Word), 103
cards, printing contacts as, 538
cascading program windows (Excel), 230
cascading program windows (PowerPoint), 308
catalogs, setting up mail merge for (Word),
        151, 155
categories (Outlook). color categories (Outlook)
category axis, 255, 410
    adding/removing, 412
    formatting, 418
CDs, packaging presentations for, 454
cell ranges (worksheet)
    adding to print areas, 169
    mathematical operations and, 189
    pasting formula results in, 189
    removing from print areas, 170
    specific, moving to, 167

cell references. *See* Excel formulas
cells, table (Word). tables (Word)
cells, worksheet
  aligning text, 206
  borders, adding/removing, 207
  Cell Styles gallery, 222
  color/pattern fill, 207
  comments, displaying/hiding, 286
  copied or cut, inserting, 191
  custom styles, creating, 223
  deleting, 190, 192
  error when inserting, 191
  fill, applying based on cell value, 298
  fill color, 207, 298
  first, moving to, 167
  formatting, 204. *See also* conditional formatting
    (Excel)
  formatting, copying, 206
  formatting text in, 205
  inserting, 189, 190, 191
  inserting comments in, 285
  merging, 216
  moving between, 166
  nonblank, moving to next or last, 167
  number formatting in, 210
  splitting merged, 216
  styles, creating, 223
  styling, 223
  text alignment, 205
  text format, default, 204
  text orientation, changing, 205, 206
  text wrapping, 205, 206
  unmerging, 216
  wrapping text in, 206
  zooming on, 233
character formatting (Excel), 204
character formatting (PowerPoint), 346
character formatting (Word), 48
character spacing (PowerPoint), 347
character spacing (Word), 48
character styles (Word), 51
chart area, 410
  selecting, 415
chart axes, 410
  adding/removing, 412
  category, 255
  data points, 255
  displaying/hiding, 262
  formatting, 418

  series, 255
  titles, adding/removing, 261
  value, 255
chart gridlines
  displaying/hiding, 262
  formatting, 418
chart legends, 410
  adding/removing/moving, 261, 413
  formatting, 418
charts (Excel)
  axes, displaying/hiding, 262
  axis, adding/removing, 261
  axis titles, adding/removing, 261
  category axis, 255
  chart sheets, moving chart to, 258
  chart type, changing, 256
  chart types, listed, 254
  data labels, displaying, 261
  data points, 255
  data range, changing, 259
  data table, displaying, 262
  editing data, 259
  formatting elements, 263
  gridlines, displaying/hiding, 262
  in Outlook items, 553
  layout, applying/changing, 257
  legend, adding/removing/moving, 261
  moving to different worksheet, 258
  plotting selected data, 256
  rows/columns, switching, 256
  series axis, 255
  size, changing, 258
  styles for, 257
  title, adding, 260
  value axis, 255
charts (Outlook)
  creating, 554
  modifying, 554
charts (PowerPoint)
  3D, formatting, 413
  activating, 415
  adding/removing elements, 412
  analysis elements, adding/removing, 413
  chart area, styling/formatting, 417, 419
  chart types, 410
  data source, switching, 408
  editing data, 408
  elements of, 410
  Format dialog box for, 417, 419

gridlines, displaying/hiding, 411, 413
inserting, 406
layout, applying/changing, 411
plot area, formatting, 417
plotting data, 408
positioning elements in, 415
rotating, 415
selecting elements, 414
size, changing, 415
styles for, 416, 418
titles, 411
WordArt styles, applying, 419
checking addresses (Outlook), 594
checking spelling. spell checking
circles, drawing, 382
cleaning up conversations (Outlook), 490
clip art. graphics
background, removing, 377
brightness, adjusting, 377
color, changing, 378
compressing, 378
contrast, adjusting, 377
cropping, 374, 375
discarding changes, 379
downloading from Internet, 551
effects, applying, 377, 378
formatting, 376
inserting (Excel), 264
inserting (Outlook), 551
inserting (Word), 113
locating, 113, 551
modifying, 377
replacing, 379
saving as a file, 114
sharpening/softening, 376, 377
storing in Clip Organizer, 114, 264, 265
tinting options, 376
transparency, changing, 378
viewing information, 551
clip art videos, 389
inserting into slides, 390
Clip Organizer. Microsoft Clip Organizer
Clipboard. Microsoft Office Clipboard
color (Excel)
assigning to worksheet tabs, 227
cell, changing, 207
conditional formatting, 298
filtering data by, 292
scale, displaying based on cell value, 299

color (Outlook)
calendar, changing, 629
notes icon, setting, 505
pictures, changing, 556
task, changing, 504
color (PowerPoint)
pictures, changing, 378
SmartArt graphics, changing, 387
color categories (Outlook), 512
appearance of, 513
assigning email messages to, 517
assigning items to, 514
assigning notes to, 645
custom, creating, 515
default, setting, 511
keyboard shortcuts, assigning, 515
multiple, assigning items to, 514
Quick Click, 513, 515
renaming, 515
color scheme. colors, theme
colors, theme (PowerPoint)
changing, 333, 335
creating, 334
colors, theme (Word), changing, 89
column references. Excel formulas
columns (Excel)
adjusting manually, 209
aligning text in, 206
deleting, 190, 192
freezing, 228
headings, hiding/displaying, 232
headings, printing, 173
hiding, 219
inserting, 189, 191
merging, 215
selecting, 162, 209
selecting data in, 163
sizing, 162
sorting by, 294
titles, printing, 217
transposing with rows, 189
unfreezing, 229
unhiding, 219
width, changing, 208, 210
wrapping text in, 206
columns (PowerPoint), 362, 363
columns (Word)
aligning text, 85
changing width, 86
formatting part of a document in, 86

columns (Word) *(continued)*
  lines between, displaying, 86
  multiple, formatting entire document, 85
  table, deleting, 74
  table, inserting, 74
  table, width, 74
comma delimited file (Excel), 279
command groups (ribbon), 179, 180
commands
  accessing from minimized ribbon, 178
  adding to Quick Access Toolbar, 312
  old, restoring to ribbon, 180
  ribbon, xxxi, 182
comments (Excel)
  appearance in worksheets, 285
  deleting, 286
  displaying/hiding, 285, 286
  editing, 286
  inserting, 285
  moving, 286
  moving among, 286
  resizing, 286
comments (PowerPoint)
  default placement of, 436
  deleting, 437
  displaying/hiding, 436, 437
  editing, 437
  inserting, 437
  moving among, 437
  printing, 459
  user name attached to, 436
comments (Word)
  appearance of, 127, 128
  deleting, 130
  displaying, 129
  editing, 129
  hiding, 129
  inserting, 128
  moving among, 129
  responding to, 130
  reviewing, 128
Common Feed List (CFL), 511
comparing presentations, 444
Compatibility Checker (PowerPoint), 449, 450
Compatibility Mode (Excel), 279
compressing media for presentations, 453
compressing pictures, 103, 378
conditional formatting (Excel)
  based on cell value, 298
  deleting for selected cells, 299

display options, 299
  modifying for selected cells, 299
  rules, creating, 299
  rules, managing, 296
  rules, types of, 296
  stopping test if rule is met, 299
conditional logic arguments (Excel), 246
conference rooms, scheduling (Outlook),
    502, 615, 618
connecting shapes (PowerPoint), 383
contact groups (Outlook), 591, 500
  adding to Safe Recipients list, 582
  creating from existing contact records, 600
  creating new contact records from, 601
  creating new contacts in, 601
  members, adding from address book, 600
  notes, recording, 601
  removing contacts, 601
  updating contact information in, 601
contact records (Outlook), 591
  addressing email messages from, 594
  alphanumeric index, 502
  alphanumeric indices, multiple, displaying, 503
  assigning flags to, 518
  assigning tasks from, 594
  associating with email messages, 517
  associating with notes, 646
  attaching items to, 596
  categorizing, 512
  changing default mailing address, 596
  changing filing order, 596
  charts in, creating/modifying, 554
  clip art, inserting, 551
  creating, 594, 595
  creating contact groups from, 600
  creating journal entries from, 594
  creating tasks from, 634
  displaying maps from, 594
  displaying websites from, 594
  electronic business cards in, 596
  filing order, 502, 503, 593
  flagging, 517, 634
  flags, listed, 517
  hyperlinks in, creating, 557. *See also* hyperlinks
  images in, 596
  in content pane, 526
  initiating actions from, 593, 594
  initiating phone calls from, 594
  meeting requests, creating from, 594
  modifying visual elements, 556

phone numbers in, 594
pictures in, 503
presence information in, 503
preventing creation of, 503
printing. *See* printing contact records
screen images, inserting, 555
searching for, 531
sending, 595
setting options for, 502
shapes, inserting, 551
SmartArt graphics, creating, 552
types of information in, 592
visual elements, inserting, 550
contacts. contact records (Outlook)
addresses, mapping, 594
assigning tasks to, 594
calling, 594
display information, specifying, 503
finding quickly, 483
in groups, updating, 601
journal entries, assigning to, 594
name structure, specifying, 503
removing from contact groups, 601
tracking email messages for, 646
website, displaying, 594
**Contacts module (Outlook). contact records
    (Outlook)**
contact pictures in, 503
content pane in, 526
displaying list views in, 527
filing order in, 502
finding contacts in, 483
Navigation Pane in, 483
presence information in, 503
setting options for, 502
content pane (Outlook), 525
Calendar module views, 526
Contacts module views, 526
Mail module views, 525
Tasks module views, 526
continuous section breaks (document), 84
contrast (picture), adjusting, 377
conventions of book, xxiv
Conversation view (Outlook), 574
conversations (Outlook)
cleaning up, 490
managing, 574
converting
table to text (Word), 75
text to table (Word), 67

copying (Excel), 188
currency amounts, in worksheets, 197
formatting, 206
formatting only, in worksheets, 197
numeric data, in worksheets, 197
text, in worksheets, 197
worksheet data, 404
worksheets, 226
copying (Outlook)
email messages, automatically. *See* rules (Outlook)
formatting, 561
tasks, 638
copying (PowerPoint)
formatting, 347
slide animations, 424
slide text, 345
copying (Word)
pictures, to new location, 104
text boxes, 116
cover page, inserting (Word), 93
cropping frame, 374, 375
cropping handles, 375
cropping pictures (Outlook), 556
cropping pictures (PowerPoint), 374
after background removal, 377
by hand, 375
to aspect ratio, 375
to fill or fit shapes, 375
cropping pointer, 375
CSV file (comma delimited) (Excel), 279
currency amounts, copying (Excel), 197
currency formatting (Excel), 213
custom slide shows
creating, 475
delivering, 476
editing, 475
Cycle diagrams (SmartArt), 384

D

Daily Task List (Outlook), 635
data (Excel). data series (Excel)
editing, setting options for, 176
filtering, 289, 291
moving, setting options for, 176
sorting, 293
data bars (Excel), 299
data entry (Excel), 164
data labels (Excel), 261

data labels (PowerPoint), 413
data markers (PowerPoint), 410, 418
data points (Excel), 255
data range, changing for charts (Excel), 259
data regions, moving in (Excel), 167
data series (Excel), 193
    AutoFill, 193, 194
    capitalization in, 196
    custom, creating/applying, 196
    date, 193
    date, advanced options, 196
    date, filling, 195
    day, advanced options, 196
    day, filling, 195
    excluding formatting when filling, 196
    growth, 193
    increasing/decreasing, 195
    linear, 193
    numeric, advanced options, 196
    numeric, filling/formatting, 195
data tables (PowerPoint), 411
    formatting, 418
data values, filtering by (Excel), 292
Date Navigator (Outlook)
    date range, changing, 524
    dates, selecting in, 524
    displaying specific day, week, or month, 624
    in To-Do Bar, 524
    secondary calendars in, 625
    week numbers in, 500
    weeks, displaying, 524
date range in Date Navigator, changing, 524
date series (Excel), 193
    advanced options, 196
    filling, 195
date/time
    in Date Navigator, changing (Outlook), 524
    in headers/footers (Word), 99
day
    displaying in Calendar pane, 623
    displaying in Date Navigator, 624
day series (Excel)
    advanced options, 196
    filling, 195
Day view (Outlook), 622
    events in, 606
    scrolling in, 624
decreasing indentation level (PowerPoint), 349
delaying delivery of email messages, 517
deleted items, retaining on exit (Outlook), 509

Deleted Items folder (Outlook)
    emptying, 573
    viewing size of, 573
deleting (Excel)
    cells, 190, 192
    rows/ columns, 190, 192
deleting (Outlook)
    calendar groups, 628
    email messages, automatically. *See* rules (Outlook)
    junk mail, automatically, 584
    Outlook items, permanently, 573
    rules (Outlook), 579
    tasks, 642, 643
deleting (PowerPoint)
    comments, from presentations, 437
    graphics with attached hyperlinks, 372
    shapes, 386
    table columns/rows, 400
    tables, 399
delimited text file (Excel), 279
delivery receipt (email), requesting, 517, 543
demoting sections, in Outline view, 14
deselecting text (Word), 2
Design contextual tab (Chart Tools), 411
Design contextual tab (SmartArt), 367
    adding shape/texts from, 385
    changing color/layout from, 387
    converting graphics from, 388
    converting graphics to independent shapes, 388
    moving shapes from, 386
    promoting/demoting from, 386
    resetting shapes from, 388
    switching direction from, 387
    ungrouping graphics from, 388
Design contextual tab (Table Tools)
    creating styles from, 403
    drawing tables from, 400
    editing chart data from, 408
    erasing table borders, 401
    Quick Styles, applying from, 403
    switching chart data source from, 408
    table columns, adding, 400
desktop alerts, customizing (Outlook), 489
Developer tab (Word), displaying, 43
diagrams. SmartArt graphics
dictionary, adding a word (Word), 123
digital signatures (PowerPoint)
    attaching, 465
    removing, 466
    viewing, 465

dismissing reminders, 529
distributing graphics (PowerPoint), 371
dividing values (Excel), 189
Document Information Panel (Excel), 183
Document Inspector (PowerPoint), 462
documents
  AutoSave, changing frequency, 28
  blank page, inserting, 83
  blog posts, creating/publishing as, 34, 35
  bookmarks, inserting, 135
  bookmarks, moving to, 135
  breaking lines, 81
  Building Block Organizer, 90
  bulleted lists, creating, 77
  bulleted lists, formatting, 77, 78
  bulleted lists, sorting, 77
  character formatting, applying, 48
  character spacing, changing, 48
  character styles, applying, 51
  clip art, locating/inserting, 113
  clip art, storing, 114
  columns in, 85, 86
  comments. *See* comments (Word)
  cover page, inserting, 93
  demoting/promoting sections, 14
  diagrams. *See* SmartArt graphics
  drawing canvas, opening, 106
  editing, restricting, 25
  expanding/collapsing sections/subdocuments, 14
  fields, inserting, 93
  font size, changing, 48
  fonts, changing, 89
  footnotes/endnotes, creating, 137, 138
  formatting, copying, 52
  formatting, replacing, 56
  formatting, restricting, 25
  formatting marks, displaying/hiding, 16
  formatting text, 49
  grammar checking, 123. *See also* grammar
    checking
  grammar errors, fixing, 122
  grammar errors, hiding, 123
  grammar errors, ignoring, 122
  headers/footers, 96, 99
  headings, displaying, 53
  headings, moving to, 53
  hidden characters, displaying/hiding, 16
  highlighting search results, 56
  highlighting text, 48
  hyperlinks, inserting, 133, 134
  hyphenation, 81
  jumping to a page/section, 10
  locating elements, 56, 57
  mail merge. *See* mail merge
  marking as final, 23
  moving around in, 3
  multiple columns, 85
  navigating, 3
  navigating pages, Full Screen Reading view, 10
  opening in multiple windows, 20, 21
  page background color, adding, 95
  page backgrounds, 94
  page border, adding, 94
  page breaks, 82, 83
  page margins, changing, 81
  page settings, 80
  page thumbnails, displaying, 6
  pages, displaying, 54
  pages, moving to, 54
  paragraph indentation, changing, 59
  paragraphs, applying a style, 51
  paragraphs, line spacing, 63
  password, 26, 27
  pictures in, applying artistic effects, 104, 105
  program windows, arranging multiple, 21
  promoting/demoting sections, 14
  protection, removing restrictions, 25
  Quick Parts, 90, 92
  Quick Styles, applying, 51
  Quick Table, inserting, 69
  removing splits, 19
  reorganizing in Outline view, 14
  restrictions, removing, 25
  rulers, displaying/hiding, 16
  saving, as PDF files, 41
  saving, as XPS files, 41
  saving, specific format, 40
  saving to SharePoint, 32
  saving to Windows Live SkyDrive, 32
  screen clipping, 103
  section breaks, 83, 85
  sending as email attachments, 30
  shapes. *See* shapes
  shared, sending link to, 30
  soft page breaks, 82
  spaces, hiding/displaying, 6
  special effects, adding to text, 48
  spell checking, 123. *See also* spell checking (Word)
  splitting, 19
  stacking shapes/text boxes, 108

documents *(continued)*
  style area pane, displaying, 51
  styles, clearing instances, 52
  styles, displaying/hiding in Draft view, 15
  styles, displaying/hiding in Outline view, 13
  Styles pane, 51
  subdocuments, opening, 14
  tab stops, 61
  tab stops, changing position, 61
  tables. *See* tables (Word)
  tables of contents, creating custom, 140, 141
  templates, attaching, 43
  text, replacing, 56
  text boxes. *See* text boxes (Word)
  text case, changing, 48
  themes, 87, 88
  versions, 28
  versions, deleting/displaying, 28, 29
  view options, Full Screen Reading view, 10
  views, switching, 6
  watermarks, adding, 94, 96
  WordArt objects. *See* WordArt objects
  zooming, 18
domains, email. email domains
Drafts folder (Outlook), 492
Draft view (Word)
  style area pane, displaying/hiding, 15
drag-and-drop editing (PowerPoint), 345, 346
drawing canvas, opening (Word), 106
drawing guides (PowerPoint), 359
drawing on slides, 468
drawing shapes (Excel), 267
drawing shapes (PowerPoint), 382
drawing tables (PowerPoint), 399
drawing tables (Word), 67
due date for tasks (Outlook), 504, 638

E

editing (Outlook)
  electronic business cards, 598
  email messages, 487
  hyperlinks, 558
  journal entries, 649
  recurring calendar items, 609
editing (PowerPoint)
  audio, 395
  comments, 437
  graphics with attached hyperlinks, 372
  photo albums, 322

  shapes, 382
  tables, 399
  text, 345
  videos, 392
editing (Word), restricting changes, 25
effects (Outlook), 567
  applying to pictures, 556
  text, changing, 560
  theme, changing, 567
effects (PowerPoint)
  animation. *See* slide animations
  applying to graphics, 368
  applying to pictures, 377, 378
  applying to text boxes, 361, 362
  applying to WordArt text, 381
  as email message signatures, 597
  attaching to email messages, 599
  Business Card list, 598
  creating contact records from, 595
  custom user fields, 598
  editing, 598
  embedding in email messages, 598
  formatting, 598
  images in, 596, 598
  in contact records, 596
  in email signatures, 586
  theme, creating, 334
email accounts
  in Junk E-Mail Options dialog box, 582
  multiple, and Quick Steps, 546
  multiple, signatures in, 585, 586
  specifying for sending messages, 544
email addresses
  adding to Safe Recipients list, 584
  adding to Safe Senders list, 584
  AutoComplete list, clearing, 493
  default, in contact records, changing, 596
  directing replies to, 517, 543
  Exchange Server network and, 484
  finding from address book, 484
  multiple, sending email messages to, 484
  semicolons in, 484
  suggestions displayed by Outlook, 484
email aliases, 484
email attachments, 569
  attaching multiple files, 569
  creating contact records from, 596
  documents, sending a link to, 30
  documents, sending as, 30
  electronic business cards as, 599

encrypting, 516
forwarding, 569
linking to shared documents, 30
multiple, saving, 575
opening, 569
Outlook items as, 569
previewing, 569
printing, 535
processing messages based on, 576
recording in Outlook Journal, 648
saving, 569, 575
workbooks as, 284

email domains
adding to Safe Recipients list, 584
adding to Safe Senders list, 582, 584
blocking, 584
top-level, blocking, 585

email messages
adding signatures, 517
addressing, 484
advanced editing features, 488
appearance, changing, 542, 587
archiving, 573
arrival notification, customizing, 489
assigning flags to, 518
associating with contact records, 517
attaching electronic business cards to, 599
attachments. *See* email attachments
AutoCorrect options, 487
AutoFormat options, 487
Automatic Replies, 579
backgrounds, changing, 587
Bcc field, displaying/hiding, 544
business graphics in, 551
categorizing, 512, 517, 576
charts in, creating/modifying, 554
clip art, inserting, 551
colors, changing, 587
commenting on, 491
conversations, cleaning up, 490
conversations, ignoring, 575
creating appointments from, 606
creating contact records from, 595
creating events from, 607
creating from contact records, 594
creating tasks from, 634
cut/paste options, customizing, 488
deleting, and flags, 634
deleting permanently, 573
delivery, delaying, 517

delivery, scheduling, 543
delivery options, changing, 542
delivery receipt, requesting, 495, 517, 543
drafts, 492
drafts, customizing save options, 492
Drafts folder, 492
editing options, setting, 487
embedding electronic business cards in, 598
encrypting, 516
expiration, setting, 517, 544
flagged, 634, 642
flagging, 517, 634
fonts, changing, 587, 588
format, setting, 487
formatting, 587
formatting in plain text, 542
formatting in Rich Text Format (RTF), 542
forwarding, 490, 491
From field, displaying/hiding, 544
graphics in, 551
header fields, 493, 544
headers, content of, 482
headers only downloaded, 482
HTML, 487
hyperlinks in, creating, 557. *See also* hyperlinks
importance, setting/removing, 516
information bar in, 581
inline responses, 491, 589
Internet headers, displaying, 517
junk. *See* junk mail
languages, blocking, 585
Math AutoCorrect options, 487
measurements in, customizing, 488
meeting requests, keeping after response, 493
modifying visual elements, 556
moving, and flags, 634
notification requests, processing, 495
options, setting/changing, 542
outgoing, flagging for follow-up, 518
out-of-office replies, creating, 580
Overtype mode in, 488
participants, shown in People Pane, 522
pictures in, 503, 550, 556
plain text, 487, 542
poll, creating, 543
presence information in, 503
printing, 535
printing list views of, 535
priority, setting/removing, 516
processing automatically. *See* rules (Outlook)

email messages *(continued)*
Properties dialog box, displaying, 517
Quick Steps and. *See* Quick Steps (Outlook)
reading without opening, 482
read receipts, requesting, 489, 495, 517, 543
read status, setting, 519
receipts, requesting, 493, 495, 543
receiving, 482
recipients, processing based on, 576
recording in Outlook Journal, 648
redundant, deleting, 574
replies, automatic. *See* Automatic Replies (Outlook)
replies, routing to different email address, 543
responses, customizing, 490
responses, including original text in, 491
Rich Text Format (RTF), 487, 542
rules. *See* rules (Outlook)
Safe Senders list, 582, 584
saving, 545, 575, 576
screen images, inserting, 555
Search Folders, 533
search results, working with, 532
searching for, 531, 532
send/receive options, accessing, 511
senders, blocking, 582, 584
senders, processing based on, 576
senders, scheduling meetings with, 616
sending, 544
sending from different accounts, 544
sending to meeting attendees, 619
sending to multiple recipients, 484
send/receive status, viewing, 528, 530
sensitivity, setting, 516
sent, saving, 492, 545
sent items, customizing save options, 492
Sent Items folder, 492
shapes, inserting, 551
SmartArt graphics in, 551
spell checking, customizing, 488
stationery, 587
styles, changing, 587
text, customizing how Outlook works with, 488
theme, default, 566, 587
to recipients not using Outlook, 542
tracking, 495, 646
unread, viewing number of, 528
viewing text of, 482
visual elements, inserting, 550
voting buttons, 517, 543

email signatures, 585
creating, 586
electronic business cards, 597
in responses, 587
inserting manually, 587
removing, 587
embedding electronic business cards in email
messages, 598
emptying
Deleted Items folder, 573
Junk E-Mail folder, 582
encrypting email messages, 516
encrypting presentations, 464
endnotes (Word)
creating, 137
deleting, 138
formatting, 138
envelopes (Word), addressing using mail merge,
149, 154
environment. working environment
erasing slide annotations, 469
erasing table borders, 401
errata, submitting, xli
error checking, options for (Excel), 176
Even Page section break (Word), 84
events (Outlook)
appearance in Calendar, 606
appointments and, compared, 604
canceling recurrence, 609
creating, 607
entering in Calendar pane, 606
entering in event window, 606
forwarding, 609
marking as Private, 608
printing, 610
recurring, 608, 609
reminders for, default, 497
selecting dates for, 607
event window (Outlook), 606, 607
Excel 97-2003
opening .xlsx files in, 278
.xls file format, 278, 279
Excel 2010. worksheets
advanced options, setting, 176
AutoFill feature, 193
charts, in Outlook items, 553
Compatibility Mode, 279
opening multiple windows, 229
Paste Special dialog box, 188

program window, 176, 230, 231
ribbon, customizing, 178
saving workbooks in other formats, 278
workbook formats, 278
working environment, managing, 165
.xlsb file format, 278
.xlsm file format, 278
.xlsx file format, 278
Excel formulas. Excel functions
average of a range, 238
calculation, changing order in, 241
cell reference range, absolute, 250
cell reference range, relative, 250
cell references, absolute, 243
cell references, relative, 242
cell references, relative to range in formula, 250
column references, absolute, 243
conditional logic arguments, 246
counting cells with values, 238
counting empty cells, 238
highest value in a range, finding, 239
lowest value in a range, finding, 239
named ranges, changing name, 249
named ranges, defining, 248, 249
named ranges, deleting, 249
nesting functions, 246
options for, 176
results, pasting, 189
sum of values in range, 237
worksheet references, different workbook, 244
worksheet references, same workbook, 243
Excel functions
AVERAGE, 238
AVERAGEIF, 245
AVERAGEIFS, 245
COUNT, 238
COUNTA, 238
COUNTIF, 245
COUNTIFS, 245
IF, 246
IFERROR, 245
MAX, 239
MIN, 239
nesting, 246
SUM, 237
SUMIF, 245
SUMIFS, 245
Excel Macro-Enabled Workbook, 278

Excel Options dialog box, 175
Advanced page, 176
Formulas page, 176
Quick Access Toolbar page, 181
Exchange Server
connecting to account, 530
connection status, viewing, 528
email addresses on, 484
MailTips, in Outlook, 494
notes in, 644
Outlook Cached Exchange mode and, 523
Outlook People Pane limitations and, 523
rules, applying to multiple accounts, 578
rules, setting up, 576
scheduling meetings and, 614
expanding ribbon, 179
expiration (email messages), setting, 517
exporting
content from Outlook, 510
RSS feeds from Outlook, 510

F

feedback, submitting, xli
Field Chooser (Outlook), 528
fields, inserting (Word), 93
fields, list view (Outlook)
adding, 528
removing, 528
file formats (Excel), 278, 279
file formats (PowerPoint), 448
files
linking graphics to, 373
worksheet hyperlinks to, creating, 200
filing order, contacts (Outlook), 502
filling data series (Excel), 193
custom, 194, 196
excluding formatting, 196
filtering data (Excel), 289, 290
applying a common criterion, 292
by data values, 292
by formatting, 292
for a specific column value, 291
removing, 291
filters (Excel)
custom, creating, 292
filter buttons, 291
filtering arrows, displaying/hiding, 292

finding/replacing text (PowerPoint), 441
flags (Outlook)
   adding reminders to, 518
   assigning, 518, 634
   custom, setting, 518
   for email recipients, 518
   for outgoing messages, 518
   reminders for, 517
   removing, 642
Folder List, accessing (Outlook), 525
folders (Outlook)
   creating, 483
   task, 637
fonts (Excel), worksheet, conditional formatting,
      298
fonts (Outlook)
   changing, 560
   color, changing, 560
   email message, changing, 587
   for specific email message types, 588
   size, changing, 560
   style, changing, 560
fonts (PowerPoint)
   replacing, in presentations, 442
   theme, changing, 334, 335
   theme, creating, 334
   theme, deleting, 335
fonts (Word)
   theme, changing, 89
   theme, deleting, 89
footers (Excel), 174
   changing, 175
   height, changing, 221
   inserting, 174
footers (PowerPoint), 338
footers (Word)
   creating/modifying, 96
   date/time, inserting, 99
   deleting, 99
   Different First Page, 98
   Different Odd & Even Pages, 98
   inserting, 98
   page numbers in, 99
   setting for sections, 84
footnotes (Word), 137, 138
Format contextual tab (audio), 394
Format contextual tab (Chart Tools), 414, 419
Format contextual tab (graphics), 369, 371
Format contextual tab (pictures), 375, 377, 378, 379
Format contextual tab (shapes), 382, 383
Format contextual tab (SmartArt), 367, 387, 388

Format contextual tab (video), 391
Format contextual tab (WordArt), 381, 382
Format Painter (Excel), 206
Format Painter (Outlook), 561
Format Painter (PowerPoint), 347, 350
Format Painter (Word), 52
formatting (Excel). conditional formatting (Excel)
   cells, 204, 298
   chart elements, 263
   copying, 206
   copying only formatting, 197
   currency, 213
   filtering by, 292
   number. See number formatting (Excel)
   shapes, 268, 383
   text in shapes, 268
formatting (Outlook)
   applying from Paste Options button, 564
   copying, 561
   creating new styles from, 563
   electronic business cards, 598
   email messages, 487, 542, 587
   local, applying, 560
   notes, 644
formatting (PowerPoint)
   3D charts, 413
   adjusting text layout, 362
   audio icons, 394
   charts, 417, 419
   graphics, 366, 369
   gridlines, 418
   shapes, 358, 360, 361, 362
   tables, 402
   text, 346
   videos, 391
formatting (Word)
   bulleted lists, automatic (Word document), 77
   copying, 52
   footnotes/endnotes, 138
   locating, 56
   marks, displaying/hiding, 16
   page numbers in headers/footers, 99
   restricting changes, 25
   restrictions, removing, 25
   shapes, 107
   text, 49
   text boxes, 116, 117
   text in shapes, 107
   WordArt objects, 109
Formula Bar, hiding/unhiding (Excel), 232

formulas. *See* Excel formulas
forwarding email messages, automatically.
      rules (Outlook)
framing slides, 459
freezing columns/rows (Excel), 228
From field (email message), displaying/hiding, 544
Full Screen Reading view (Word), 10
Full Screen view (Excel), 231
functions. Excel functions

G

Go To (Word)
    bookmarks, 135
    document elements, 57
Go To Special (Excel), 166, 167
grammar checking
    AutoCorrect options, 125
    email messages, 488
    entire document, 123
    options, setting, 124
graphics
    aligning, 371
    applying borders to, 368
    applying effects to, 368
    applying SmartArt picture layouts to, 370
    applying styles to, 367
    bringing forward in stack, 370
    distributing, 371
    dragging, 369
    flipping vs. rotating, 368
    formatting in Outlook items, 561
    grouping, 371
    hyperlinks attached to, 372
    in junk mail, 581
    in slides, animating. *See* slide animations
    linked, creating ScreenTip for, 373
    linking, 373
    manipulating, 366
    moving, 369
    proportional sizing, 369
    regrouping, 371
    rotating, 368, 369
    saving slides as, 450, 451
    scale, changing, 369
    selecting in a stack, 370
    sending backward in stack, 370
    sizing, 369
    SmartArt. *See* SmartArt graphics
    stacking order, 370
    ungrouping, 371

greeting line, inserting, 148
gridlines
    chart, displaying/hiding (Excel), 262, 411, 413, 418
    displaying (Word), 16
    displaying in tables (Word), 71
    displaying/hiding (Excel), 232
    displaying/hiding (PowerPoint), 368, 369
    formatting (PowerPoint), 418
    printing (Excel), 173
    sizing grid, 359
grouping
    calendar items (Outlook), 625
    graphics (PowerPoint), 371
    shapes (Word), 108
    tasks (Outlook), 635, 636, 637
    worksheets, 227
groups, ribbon
    displaying all commands in, xxxii
    displaying hidden, xxxii
growth data series (Excel), 193

H

handout master, customizing, 461
Handout Master view (PowerPoint), 302
handouts, changing orientation (PowerPoint), 325
handouts, creating/printing in Word, 459, 460
header row, specifying in table (Word), 71
headers (Word)
    creating, 96
    date/time, inserting, 99
    deleting, 99
    Different First Page, 98
    Different Odd & Even Pages, 98
    inserting, 98
    modifying, 96
    page number, 99
    setting for sections, 84
headers (Excel), 174
    changing, 175
    height, changing, 221
    inserting, 174
headings (Word), 53
hidden cells, finding (Excel), 219
hidden characters, displaying/hiding (Word), 16
hidden columns, sorting on (Excel), 294
hidden panes, displaying (PowerPoint), 310
hidden slides, displaying, 332, 341
hidden worksheets, displaying, 227

hiding
calendar details from meeting invitees, 501
columns/rows (Excel), 219
comment (PowerPoint), 436, 437
Excel program window elements, 231
Formula Bar (Excel), 232
gridlines (Excel), 232
nonprinting characters (Word), 83
note modification date (Outlook), 505
panes (PowerPoint), 310
ribbon tabs, 179
slides, 332
worksheets, 226
Hierarchy diagrams (SmartArt), 384
subordinate points in, 386
highlighter tool (PowerPoint), 468, 469
highlighting (Word)
search results, 56
text, 48
holidays, adding to calendar, 497
.html file format (Excel), 278
hyperlinks. linking
changing target of, 558
creating pre-addressed email messages, 134, 558
default behavior, 557
editing, 558
formatting, 333
in Excel. *See* worksheet hyperlinks
in junk mail, treatment of, 581
inserting/modifying, 133, 134
removing, 559
testing, 373
to bookmarks, 558
to files, 557
to headings, 133
to webpages, 133, 558
to Word documents, 557
**Hypertext Markup Language (HTML), email
messages in, 487**
hyphenation (Word), 80, 81

images. See *also* **graphics; pictures**
in contact records, 596
in electronic business cards, 596, 598
Import And Export wizard (Outlook), 510
importance (email message), 516
importing content into Outlook, 510
Inbox
cleaning up, 574
Conversation view, 574
managing conversations in, 574
new messages in, 482
searching specific folders, 532
increasing indent level (PowerPoint), 349
indentation, changing (Word), 59
**inline responses (email messages), adding
identifiers, 491, 589**
inserting (Excel)
cells, 189, 190, 191
clip art, 264
comments in cells, 285
copied or cut cells, 191
rows/columns, 189, 191
inserting (Word)
bookmarks, 135
cells in tables, 74
footnotes/endnotes, 137
headers/footers, 98
hyperlinks, 133
page numbers, 99
pictures, 103
screen clipping, 103
tables, 66
text boxes, 115, 116
inserting hyperlinks (Outlook), 557
**instant messages, replying to email messages
with, 594**
Instant Search (Outlook), 531, 532
Internet fax, sending workbooks as (Excel), 283
Internet headers, displaying (Outlook), 517
inviting attendees to meetings, 612

I

iCalendar files, attaching to email messages, 609
Icon view (Outlook), 644
icons (Excel)
displaying based on cell value, 299
ignoring conversations (Outlook), 575
illustrations. clip art; pictures

J

journal entries
assigning properties to, 649
assigning to contacts, 594
categorizing, 512
editing, 649
opening, 649
recording automatically, 505
searching for, 531

Journal module (Outlook). *See also* Outlook
    Journal; journal entries
  displaying, 647
  Navigation Pane in, 483
  setting options for, 505, 648
Junk E-Mail folder, 581, 582
junk mail, 581
  adding addresses to Safe Recipients list, 584
  adding domains to Safe Senders list, 582, 584
  adding groups to Safe Recipients list, 582
  allowing messages from safe senders, 582, 584
  allowing responses to sent mail, 584
  appearance of, 581
  blocking, 584, 585
  deleting automatically, 584
  graphics in, 581
  hyperlinks in, 581
  information bar in, 581
  marking as Not Junk, 582
  options, setting, 582
  phishing messages, appearance of, 581
  processing, 582
  protection level, setting, 584
justifying slide text, 349

K

keyboard shortcuts
  assigning to color categories (Outlook), 515
  navigation (Word), 3
keywords (Excel), 183
keys, directional
  navigating documents, with, 3
  navigating worksheets with, 166

L

labels
  creating using mail merge, 150
  creating using Mail Merge wizard, 154
landscape, aspect ratios for cropping, 374
language
  blocking email based on, 585
  changing (PowerPoint), 315
  setting options for (Outlook), 506
Last 7 Days view (Outlook), 644
  changing arrangement in, 645
Layout contextual tab (Chart Tools), 412, 413, 415
Layout contextual tab (Table Tools), 400, 401, 403

layout of diagrams, changing, 111
legends. chart legends
levels, displaying in Outline view (Word), 13
line charts, elements, adding/removing, 413
line spacing, changing (Word), 63
linear data series (Excel), 193
lines, breaking automatically (Word), 81
linked graphics, creating ScreenTips for, 373
linking. hyperlinks
  graphics to different presentations or files
      (PowerPoint), 373
  graphics to different slides (PowerPoint), 373
  graphics to email message form (PowerPoint), 373
  graphics to webpages (PowerPoint), 373
  text boxes (Word), 116
  to workbooks, 284
  worksheet cells, 188
List diagrams (SmartArt), 384
List view (Outlook), 625
list views (Outlook), 527
  adding fields, 528
  Calendar module, displaying, 527
  Contacts module, displaying, 527
  Mail module, displaying, 527
  modifying, 527
  Notes module, displaying, 527
  removing fields, 528
  resetting to default, 528
  saving, 528
  sorting content, 527
  Tasks module, displaying, 527
lists. bulleted lists
local template, attaching to documents (Word), 43
Location Information dialog box (Outlook), 594
locking aspect ratio of graphics (PowerPoint), 369

M

magnification. zooming
mail merge
  address block, inserting, 147
  catalog/directory, 151
  envelopes, addressing, 149, 150
  errors, checking for, 156
  greeting line, inserting, 148
  into document, 159
  into email message, 159, 160
  labels, creating, 150
  Mail Merge wizard, for catalog/directory, 155
  Mail Merge wizard, for email messages, 153

mail merge *(continued)*
  Mail Merge wizard, for envelopes, 154
  Mail Merge wizard, for labels, 154
  Mail Merge wizard, for letters, 152
  main document, multiple merge fields, 147
  main document, preparing, 146
  main document, single merge field, 147
  manual process, 148
  previewing results, 158
  printing using Mail Merge wizard, 160
  recipients, creating list, 145
  recipients, excluding, 159
  recipients from contacts, 146
  recipients from file, 145
  setting up for email messages, 149
  setting up for letters, 148
  validating, 156
Mail module (Outlook)
  content pane in, 525
  displaying list views in, 527
  flagging email messages in, 634
  Navigation Pane in, 525
  setting options for, 486, 488- 490, 492, 494,
    495, 496
mailbox (Outlook)
  archiving items, 573
  Deleted Items folder, 573
  locating large items, 572
  locating old items, 572
  searching, 531
  size, managing/viewing, 572
Mailbox Cleanup tools (Outlook), 572
mailing lists, adding to Safe Recipients list
    (Outlook), 582
MailTips (Exchange Server), preferences, setting in
    Outlook, 494
mapping contact addresses, 594
margins
  of documents, 81
  of slide text, 362, 363
  of table cells (PowerPoint), 403
  of worksheets, 221
marking documents as final, 23, 24
marking email messages as read/unread, 519
marking presentations as final, 465
masters, viewing (PowerPoint), 302, 306
Math AutoCorrect options (Outlook), 487
mathematical operations (Excel), 189
Matrix diagrams (SmartArt), 384
meeting requests, 611
  accepting, 618
  Appointment page, 611
  attaching information to, 611

  creating from contact records, 594
  declining, 618
  keeping, after response, 493
  optional attendees, 611
  processing, 495
  proposing a new time, 497, 618
  recording in Outlook Journal, 648
  responding to, 617
  response options, 612, 613, 617
  responses, tracking, 619
  Scheduling Assistant page, 611
  tentatively accepting, 618
meeting window (Outlook)
  canceling meetings in, 619
  changing meetings in, 619
  responses in, 618
meetings
  accepting proposed time change, 621
  adding attendees to, 613
  and appointments, compared, 604
  attendees, inviting, 612, 613
  canceling, 620
  canceling recurrence, 609
  converting appointments to, 605
  declining proposed time change, 621
  hiding calendar details from invitees, 501
  marking as Private, 608
  preventing new time proposals, 498, 620
  recurring, creating, 608, 613
  recurring, editing, 609
  recurring, updating, 620
  resources, scheduling automatically, 502
  response options, setting, 620
  scheduling, 616. *See also* Scheduling Assistant
  scheduling, and Exchange Server, 614
  Scheduling Assistant options, changing, 501
  scheduling conference rooms, 615, 618
  scheduling presentation equipment, 615, 618
  scheduling with a message sender, 616
  sending email messages to attendees, 619
  setting options for, 496
  Smart Scheduling, 616
  time proposal options, changing, 498
  updating, 613, 620
members of contact groups, adding from address
    book, 600
memos, printing contacts as, 539
merge fields (Word)
  inserting address block, 147
  inserting greeting line, 148
  inserting multiple, 147
  inserting single, 147

merged worksheet cells, splitting, 216
merging documents. mail merge
merging table cells (PowerPoint), 401
merging worksheet cells, 215, 216
Microsoft Certification ID, xxi
Microsoft Certified Professional website, xxi
Microsoft Clip Organizer, 114, 265
Microsoft Exchange Server. Exchange Server
Microsoft Office 2010. Office 2010
Microsoft Office Clipboard, 114
  saving formatting to (Outlook), 561
Microsoft Office Communicator. Office
  Communicator
Microsoft Office Open XML Formats. .xml file
  format
Microsoft Office Specialist Expert (MOS Expert), xix
Microsoft Office Specialist (MOS), xix
Microsoft Office Specialist program, xx
Microsoft Outlook 2010. Outlook 2010
Microsoft PowerPoint 2010. PowerPoint 2010
Microsoft PowerPoint Viewer, 454
Microsoft SharePoint Server. SharePoint Server
Microsoft Word 2010. Word 2010
minimizing ribbon, 178
mobile devices, appointment reminders on, 604
modules (Outlook), switching between, 525, 526
monochrome presentations, 458
month, displaying (Outlook), 623, 624
Month view (Outlook)
  changing detail level, 623
  events in, 606
  scrolling in, 624
  week numbers in, 500
motion path slide animations, 422, 426
  adjusting, 427
  rotating, 427
  schematics of, 426
moving
  charts to chart sheet (Excel), 258
  charts to different worksheet (Excel), 258
  email messages, automatically. See rules (Outlook)
  graphics (PowerPoint), 369
  pictures (Word), 104
  shapes (PowerPoint), 386
  slide text, 345
  tasks (Outlook), 637
  text boxes (PowerPoint), 357, 358
  worksheets, 226
multiple columns (Word). columns (Word)
multiplying values in worksheets, 189

N

name structure of contacts, specifying, 503
named ranges (Excel)
  changing name, 249
  defining, 248
  deleting, 249
  redefining, 249
  specific, moving to, 167
  worksheet hyperlinks to, creating, 200
narrating presentations, 471
narrations, attaching to slides, 393
national holidays, adding to calendar, 497
navigating
  among comments in presentations, 437
  in documents, in Full Screen Reading view, 10
  in documents, with directional keys, 3
  in documents, with scroll bars, 3
  in presentations, 303
  in worksheets, 166
Navigation Pane (Outlook)
  buttons, changing order, 508, 521
  buttons, changing space for, 521
  buttons, displaying/hiding, 507, 521
  changing font in, 508
  closing, 520
  customizing, 520
  displaying, 520
  expanding, 521, 525
  in Outlook modules, 482, 483
  minimized, information on, 525
  minimizing, 521
  multiple calendars in, 626
  switching between modules from, 525
  width, changing, 521
Navigation Pane (Word)
  browsing, 53, 54, 57
  locating formatting, 56
  locating special characters, 56
  locating styles, 56
  locating text, 55
  page thumbnails, displaying, 6
New Slide gallery (PowerPoint), 326
Next Page section break (Word), 84
nonbreaking spaces (Word), 81
nonprinting characters, displaying/hiding
  (Word), 83
Normal view (Excel), 231

Normal view (PowerPoint), 302, 310
adjusting pane size, 310
hiding panes, 310
Notes pane, 310
Overview pane, 310
panes in. *See* panes (PowerPoint)
presentation sections in, 340
rearranging slides in, 331
setting transitions in, 432
Slide pane, 310
switching to, 306
notes (Outlook)
adding to appointments, 605
assigning to categories, 645
associating with contact records, 646
attaching to email messages, 569
categorizing, 512, 645
creating tasks from, 634
default font, setting, 505
Exchange Server and, 644
filtering, 644
formatting, 644
Icon view, 505, 644
Last 7 Days view, 644
modification date, hiding, 505
Notes List view, 644
organizing, 645
recording for contact groups, 601
searching for, 531
setting options for, 505
sorting, 644
viewing, 644
notes (PowerPoint). speaker notes (PowerPoint)
Notes List view (Outlook), 644
changing arrangement in, 645
notes master, customizing (PowerPoint), 461
Notes Master view (PowerPoint), 302
Notes module (Outlook)
displaying list views in, 527
Navigation Pane in, 483
setting options for, 505, 648
view, changing, 644
Notes Page view (PowerPoint), 302
displaying, 461
Notes pane (PowerPoint), 310
notifications (email)
customizing, 489
processing requests, 495

number formatting (Excel)
automatic, 210
changing, 210
custom, 211, 212
default, applying, 213
refining, 213
numbered lists (PowerPoint)
converting to/from paragraphs, 353
customizing, 351
demoting items, 352
indenting, 352, 353
number style, changing, 353
Numbering gallery (PowerPoint), 353
numbers, appearance in Excel, 163
numeric data, copying (Excel), 197
numeric data series (Excel)
advanced options, 196
filling, 195
filling/formatting, 195

O

objective domain, in MOS exams, xx
objects (Word)
clip art, locating/inserting, 113
WordArt, creating from text, 109
WordArt, formatting, 109
WordArt, inserting, 109
Odd Page section break (Word), 84
Office 2010
getting help, xli
new image modification functionality, 556
theme, default, 587
Office Communicator
and Outlook To-Do Bar, 524
using with contact records, 594
Office.com
clip art, 551
sounds, 392
online edition of book, downloading, xxxviii
OpenDocument presentations, 450, 452
optional attendees, inviting to meetings, 613
organizing tasks (Outlook), 637
orientation. page orientation (Excel); worksheet cell orientation
orphans/widows, avoiding (Word), 83
Outline tab, editing lists on (PowerPoint), 352

Outline view (Word)
levels, displaying, 13
reorganizing documents with, 14
sections, expanding/collapsing, 14
sections, promoting/demoting, 14
style area pane, displaying/hiding, 13
styles, displaying/hiding in, 13
subdocuments, expanding/collapsing, 14
subdocuments, opening, 14
outlines (PowerPoint)
creating presentations based on, 330
expanding/collapsing, 330
inserting slides from, into presentations, 330
orientation, changing, 325
Rich Text Format, 330
saving presentations as, 450, 452
Word, in PowerPoint presentations, 330
Outlook 2010
address book, 591
archiving items automatically, 509
connecting to social networks from, 523
Conversation view (new feature), 574
creating folders, 483
Date Navigator, 624
email download settings, 482
Excel charts in, 553
exporting/importing, 510
formatting text in, 560
hyperlinks in, 557
Inbox. *See* Inbox (Outlook)
items, printing, 535
Journal. *See* Outlook Journal
junk mail in. *See* junk mail
mailbox size, managing, 572
modules, switching between, 525, 526
program window, customizing, 519, 520
Quick Print, 535
Quick Steps, 545
rules, 576
Schedule view (new feature), 622
ScreenTips in, 488
settings, changing, 486
SmartArt graphics in, 551
startup/exit behavior, changing, 509
styles, 562
text in, formatting, 560
themes, 566
views. *See* views (Outlook)
working environment, managing, 485, 519

**Outlook Journal. Journal module (Outlook);
    journal entries**
accessing, 525
activating, 646
button, displaying, 647
display options, 647
recording information in, 647
settings, changing, 647
Timer, recording with, 649
Outlook Options dialog box, 486
Advanced page, 507, 509, 510, 511
Calendar page, 496, 497, 499, 500, 501
Contacts page, 502
Language page, 506
Mail page, 486, 488, 489, 490, 492, 494, 495, 496
Notes And Journal page, 505, 648
Tasks page, 504
out-of-office replies (Outlook), 580
overhead projector, sizing slides for, 324
Overlay Mode (Outlook), 628
Overtype mode, in email messages, 488
Overview pane (PowerPoint), 310
closing, 310
entering text in, 344
rearranging slides in, 330
sizing, 310

P

packaging presentations for CDs, 454
page backgrounds (Word), 94
color, adding, 95
pattern, adding, 95
watermarks, adding, 95, 96
page borders (Word), 94
Page Break Preview view (Excel), 231
page breaks (Excel), 170
adjusting, 172
deleting, 172
inserting, 172
manual, deleting all, 172
previewing, 172, 231
page breaks (Word), 82
avoiding widows/orphans, 83
deleting, 83
forcing, 83
inserting, 82
keeping paragraphs together, 83

Page Layout view (Excel), 231
page margins (Word), 81
page numbers (Word), 99
page orientation (Excel), 221
pages, browsing (Word), 54
panes (PowerPoint), 310
panes, freezing (Excel), 228
paragraphs (Outlook), formatting, 561
paragraphs (Word)
  indentation, changing, 59
  keeping lines together, 83
  keeping together, 83
  line spacing, changing, 63
  page breaks, inserting before, 83
  selecting, 2
  spacing of, changing, 64
  styles, applying, 51
passwords (PowerPoint)
  deleting, 464
  opening presentations with, 463
  setting, 455, 463, 464
passwords (Word)
  deleting, 27
  modifying documents with, 27
  opening documents with, 26
  setting, 26
Paste gallery, previewing in (Excel), 189
Paste Special (Excel), 188
pasting (Excel), 188, 189
  formula results, 189
pattern, adding to page background (Word), 95
pausing presentation recording, 479
PDF file format
  saving documents in, 41
  saving presentations in, 450, 452
  saving workbooks in, 279, 281
pen tool (PowerPoint), 468, 469
People Pane (Outlook)
  and Exchange Server accounts, 523
  collapsed view, 522
  contact information in, 522
  contracting, 523
  expanded view, 522, 523
  finding items in, 522
  switching between views, 523
  Toggle button, missing, 523
percentage complete (Outlook), 638
Personal, marking email messages as, 515
phishing. junk mail
phone directory, printing contacts as, 539

phone numbers, entering in contact records, 594
photo albums (PowerPoint), 320
  adding captions, 322
  adding photographs, 322
  black-and-white photographs in, 322
  creating, 320, 321, 322
  editing, 320, 323
  layout of photographs in, 322
  photograph frames in, 322
  templates, creating other presentations with, 320
  templates, replacing photographs, 321
  themes in, 322
photographs (PowerPoint). pictures; images
  adding to photo albums, 322
  background, removing, 377
  black-and-white, in photo albums, 322
  brightness, adjusting, 377
  captions, adding in photo albums, 322
  color, changing, 378
  compressing, 378
  contrast, adjusting, 377
  cropping, 374, 375
  discarding changes, 379
  effects, applying, 377, 378
  formatting, 376
  frames, in photo albums, 322
  layout in photo albums, 322
  modifying, 377
  rearranging in photo albums, 322
  replacing, 379
  replacing in photo album templates, 321
  sharpening/softening, 376, 377
  tinting options, 376
  transparency, changing, 378
Picture diagrams (SmartArt), 384
picture presentations, 450, 451
Picture Tools contextual tab, 556
picture watermark, adding as a background
    (Word), 96
pictures. photographs; graphics; images
  applying artistic effects to, 104, 272, 556
  as bullets (PowerPoint), 353
  as document watermark, 96
  as slide backgrounds, 336, 338
  background, removing, 377, 556
  brightness, adjusting, 377
  clip art, saving as a file, 114
  color in, 378, 556
  compressing, 103, 378

contact, in email messages, 503
contrast, adjusting, 377
copying to new location, 104, 272
cropping, 374, 375, 556
discarding changes, 379
effects, applying, 378
effects, options, 377
formatting, 376
in email responses, modifying, 556
inserting (Excel), 271
inserting (Outlook), 550
inserting (Word), 103
inserting in header/footer (Excel), 272
inserting multiple (Outlook), 550
modifying, 377
moving, 104, 272
replacing, 273, 379
sharpening/softening, 376, 377, 556
size/shape, changing, 104, 272
styles, applying, 105, 272
three-dimensional effects, applying, 556
tinting, 376
transparency, 378
plain text, email messages in, 487, 542
Playback contextual tab (audio), 394, 395
Playback contextual tab (video), 391, 392
plot area, 410
plotting charts. charts (Excel)
poll, email, creating, 543
Portable Document Format (PDF). PDF file format
portrait aspect ratios for cropping, 374
pound sign (#) in Excel, 163
PowerPoint 2010
customizing, 314
Professional Plus, and slide libraries, 327
program options, accessing, 318
themes, 333
views. *See* views (PowerPoint)
PowerPoint Options dialog box
Add-ins page, 317
Advanced page, 316
General page, 314
Language page, 315
Proofing page, 314
Quick Access Toolbar page, 311
Save page, 314
Trust Center page, 317
PowerPoint presentations. presentations
PowerPoint Show, 450, 451

PowerPoint Viewer, 454
.ppt file format, 449
.pptx file format, 450, 451
presence information, in email messages, 503
presentation equipment, scheduling with Outlook,
    615, 618
presentation sections, 339
adding, 340
appearance of, 340
applying themes to, 341
hiding slides in, 341
naming, 341
rearranging, 341
removing, 341
presentations
adding audio. *See* audio (PowerPoint)
adding slides, 326, 327
adding slides from outlines, 330
adding video. *See* videos
animating. *See* slide animations
annotations in, 344, 469
audio narration, adding, 479
autorun file, creating, 454
broadcasting, 473
cascading, 309
changing slide layout, 327
checking compatibility, 449, 450
colors, changing, 89, 333, 335
combining versions of, 444
commenting in, 436
comparing versions of, 444
compressing media, 453
creating based on Word outline, 330
creating from photo album template, 320
creating Quick Access Toolbar for, 312
customizing, 474
deleting slides, 331
delivering, 472
digital signatures in, 465
displaying on multiple monitors, 472
displaying specific slide, 303
dragging slides between, 331
effects, creating, 334
encrypting, 464
Excel worksheets, inserting, 404
file formats, 448
finding/replacing text, 441
fonts, changing, 89, 334, 335
fonts, finding/replacing, 442
handouts, 302, 325, 461

presentations *(continued)*
  hyperlinks. *See* hyperlinks
  linking graphics, 373
  linking worksheets, 405
  marking as final, 465
  masters, viewing, 302, 306
  moving around in, 303
  multiple, viewing, 308
  narrations, enabling, 471
  navigating in, 476
  opening, in Slide Show view, 450, 451
  packaging for CDs, 454
  panes. *See* panes (PowerPoint)
  password-protecting, 455, 463, 464
  pausing recording of, 479
  pen color, changing, 469
  personal information, removing, 462
  photo albums, 320
  previewing, 457, 458, 459
  printing, settings for, 458, 459
  printing as transparencies, 457
  protecting information in, 462
  rearranging slides, 330
  recording, 478
  reducing size, 453
  rehearsing, 477
  reusing slides, 327
  reviewing, 444
  revisions, accepting/rejecting, 444
  Rich Text Format outlines in, 330
  save options, customizing, 314
  saving, as earlier version, 450
  saving, as OpenDocuments, 450, 452
  saving as outlines, 450, 452
  saving, as PDF or XPS, 450, 452
  saving, as picture presentations, 450, 451
  saving, as videos, 455
  saving, in different file formats, 450
  saving, to removable media, 454
  scrolling in, 303
  setting up for delivery, 471
  slide timings, setting up, 471
  source citations in, 344
  speaker notes. *See* speaker notes (PowerPoint)
  switching among, 308, 309
  tables, creating, 398
  themes, 88, 334
  transitions, 432
  variations for different audiences, 474
  viewing, 309, 310
  views, switching, 302
  Word outlines in, 330
  worksheets, embedding, 405
  zooming, 307
Presenter view (PowerPoint), 472
Preview view (Outlook), 625
previewing
  presentations, 457, 458, 459
  slide animations, 423
print areas (Excel)
  adding ranges to, 169
  clearing, 170
  defining, 169
  ignoring, 170
  removing ranges from, 170
printers, specifying, 458
printing
  address books. *See* printing contact records
  calendars. *See* printing calendars
  comments, in presentations, 459
  contact records. *See* printing contact records
  email attachments, 535
  email message list views, 535
  email messages, 535
  handouts, 459
  hidden slides, 458
  Outlook items, 535
  presentations, settings for, 458, 459
  row/column titles (Excel), 217
  slides, 458
  transparencies, 457
  workbooks, 168
  worksheets, 168, 172, 231
printing calendars, 536, 537
  excluding private appointments, 537
  previewing, 537
  styles, listed, 536
printing contact records, 538, 539
priority (email message), setting/removing, 516
priority (task), 638
privacy, marking
  appointments, 608
  calendar items, 608
  email messages, 515
  events, 608
  meetings, 608
  tasks, 639
Process diagrams (SmartArt), 384

program windows (Excel)
arranging multiple, 230
cascading, 230
hiding elements, 231
tiling, 230
unhiding elements, 231
program windows (Outlook), 519
customizing, 520
program windows (Word)
arranging multiple, 21
resizing, xxxii
stacking, 21
Styles pane, displaying, 51
promoting sections in Outline view (Word), 14
properties (Excel)
adding to display, 184
editing, 183
removing from display, 184
server, viewing, 183
viewing, 183, 184
properties (Outlook email message), 517
publishing (Excel). saving
publishing (Word). blog posts
Pyramid diagrams (SmartArt), 384

Q

Quick Access Toolbar (Excel), 181
adding buttons, 182
moving, 182
Quick Access Toolbar (PowerPoint), 311
adding buttons, 311, 312
restoring default buttons, 313
Quick Click setting (Outlook), 511
Quick Parts (Word), 90
cover pages, 93
dynamic document properties, 92
fields, 93
inserting, 92
repositioning, 92
resizing, 92
saving, 117
Quick Print (Outlook), 535
Quick Steps (Outlook), 545
actions, adding/changing, 547, 548
changing, 545
creating, 546
custom, creating, 548

default actions, resetting to, 548
deleting, 548
gallery, 545
managing, 547
multiple accounts and, 546
names, changing, 547
performing, 547
properties, changing, 547
properties, viewing, 547
resetting, 548
setting up, 546
shortcut keys in, 546, 547
tooltip message, changing, 547
Quick Styles. WordArt text
applying to tables (PowerPoint), 403
applying to text (Word), 51
Quick Styles gallery (Outlook), 562
creating style sets, 565
including/excluding styles, 564
Quick Tables (Word), 69

R

read receipt (email)
requesting, 517, 543
responding to automatically, 495
read status (Outlook)
determination, customizing, 489
setting, 519
Reading Pane (Outlook), 521
closing, 523
customizing, 489
displaying, 523
in Mail module, 525
People Pane in. *See* People Pane (Outlook)
Reading View (PowerPoint), 302, 306
receipts (email)
delivery, requesting, 495, 543
read, requesting, 543
read, responding to automatically, 495
receiving email messages, 482
recipients, mail merge
creating list, 145
excluding, 159
selecting, 145, 146
recording audio, 393
recording presentations, 478

recurrence
  in appointments, 608
  in calendar items, 608
  in events, 608
  in meetings, 608
  in tasks, 638
  pattern, setting, 609
recurring
  appointments, canceling recurrence, 609
  appointments, creating, 608
  appointments, editing, 609
  calendar items, canceling recurrence, 609
  calendar items, creating, 608
  calendar items, editing, 609
  events, canceling recurrence, 609
  events, creating, 608
  events, editing, 609
  meetings, canceling recurrence, 609
  meetings, creating, 608, 613
  meetings, editing, 609
  meetings, updating, 620
  tasks, completing, vs. deleting, 642
  tasks, creating, 639
redirecting email messages. rules (Outlook)
references. Excel formulas
regrouping graphics, 371
rehearsing presentations, 477
Relationship diagrams (SmartArt), 384
relative cell references (Excel)
  to cell contents, 243
  to range in formula, 250
reminders (Outlook). flags (Outlook)
  adding to flagged items, 518
  default, modifying, 498
  dismissing, 529
  overdue, displaying on status bar, 529
  preventing, 498, 510
  receiving on mobile devices, 604
  rescheduling, 529
  sound, setting, 510
  task, assigning, 639
  task, setting automatically, 504
reorganizing in Outline view (Word), 14
replacing formatting (Word), 56
replacing text (PowerPoint), 441
replacing text (Word), 56
replying to email messages
  automatically. See rules (Outlook)
  with instant messages, 594

required attendees, inviting to meetings, 612
rescheduling reminders, 529
resizing ribbon, xxxii
resources, scheduling automatically (Outlook), 502
reusing slides, 327
reviewers, displaying comments by (Word), 129
Reviewing Pane (Word)
  comments, appearance in, 128
  resizing, 129
reviewing presentations, 444
revisions, accepting/rejecting (PowerPoint), 444
ribbon, xxxi
  buttons, appearance of, xxxii
  commands on, xxxi
  customizing (Excel), 178
  customizing (PowerPoint), 316
  expanding, 179
  groups, displaying all commands in, xxxii
  groups, displaying hidden, xxxii
  minimized, selecting commands, 178
  minimizing, 178
  Office 2010 vs. older versions, 180
  resetting to default, 180
  resizing, xxxii
  restoring old features, 180
  tabs. See ribbon tabs
ribbon tabs
  command groups, creating custom, 179
  custom, creating, 180
  Developer tab, displaying, 43
  groups, adding/removing commands, 179, 180
  groups, moving, 180
  hiding, 179
  moving, 180
  removing command groups, 179
  resetting to default, 180
Rich Text Format (RTF)
  compatibility with email programs, 487
  email messages, 487, 542
  outlines, in presentations (PowerPoint), 330
rotating (PowerPoint)
  charts, 415
  graphics, 369
rows (Excel)
  adjusting manually, 209
  and columns, freezing, 229
  deleting, 190, 192
  freezing, 228
  headers, selecting, 209

headings, hiding/displaying, 232
headings, printing, 173
height, and text wrapping, 206
height, changing, 204, 208, 209, 210
hiding, 219
inserting, 189, 191
merging, 215
moving in, 167
references, 243
selecting, 162, 209
selecting data in, 163
sizing, 162
sorting by, 294
titles, printing, 217
transposing with columns, 189
unfreezing, 229
unhiding, 219
rows, table (Word)
deleting, 74
height, changing, 74
inserting, 74
RSS feeds (Outlook)
importing/exporting, 510
making available to other programs, 511
marking as unread, 511
rulers (PowerPoint)
changing list indent with, 353
displaying, 353
rulers, displaying/hiding (Word), 16
rules (Outlook), 576
actions, selecting, 578
applying, 578
Automatic Replies, 579
client, 576
conditions, selecting, 577
creating, 577, 578
criteria, 576
deleting, 579
dialing, 594
editing, 578
exceptions, selecting, 578
Exchange Server, 576
out-of-office replies, creating, 580
running on existing messages, 579
server, 576
rules, conditional formatting (Excel), 296
creating, 299
defining, 297

S

Safe Recipients list (Outlook), 582, 584
Safe Senders list (Outlook), 582, 584
saving
clip art as a file, 114
delimited text files (Excel), 279
email attachments, 575
email messages as files, 575, 576
presentations, as earlier version, 450
presentations, as outlines, 450, 452
presentations, as videos, 455
presentations, file options for, 450, 452
slides, as graphics, 450, 451
text box as building block (Word), 117
Word documents, AutoSave, changing frequency, 28
Word documents, options for, 41
Word documents, to SharePoint site, 32
Word documents, to Windows Live SkyDrive folder, 32
workbooks, as templates, 279
workbooks, AutoSave, changing frequency, 184
workbooks, file options for, 281
workbooks, locations, 280
workbooks, to SharePoint site, 282
workbooks, to Windows Live SkyDrive folder, 282
scale of graphics, changing, 369
scaling worksheets, 221
Schedule View (Outlook), 622
display options, modifying, 500
displaying multiple calendars, 624
scheduling
appointments, 605
events, 606
meetings. *See* meetings
Smart Scheduling, 616
Scheduling Assistant, 614
availability in, 614
color coding in, 614
for meeting requests, 611
options, changing, 501
scope of search, changing (Outlook), 532
Screen Clipping tool, 555
screen clippings. screen images
screen images
capturing, 103, 270, 555
inserting, 103, 270

screen shots. screen images
ScreenTips
   comments, displaying in (Word), 129
   creating for linked graphics (PowerPoint), 373
   language, changing (Outlook), 506
scroll bars (Word), 3
scrolling
   in documents, 3
   in presentations, 303
Search Folders (Outlook), 533
   accessing, 533
   creating, 534
   customizing, 534
searching (Outlook). Instant Search (Outlook);
      Search Folders (Outlook)
   multiple address books, 484
section bars (PowerPoint). presentation sections
section breaks (Word), 83
   deleting, 85
   headers/footers, specifying, 84
   inserting, 84
   page settings, 84
   types, 84
sections, presentation. presentation sections
security (PowerPoint), 317
security, junk mail. junk mail
selecting (Excel), 163
   data, 163
   individual columns/rows, 162
   worksheet content, 162
selecting (PowerPoint)
   chart elements, 414
   table elements, 400
   worksheet data, 409
selecting (Word)
   selection area, 2
   text, 2
semicolons in email messages, 484
sending workbooks as Internet faxes, 283
send/receive status of email, viewing, 530
sensitivity of email messages, setting, 516
Sent Items folder (Outlook), 492
sentence, selecting (Word), 2
series, data. data series (Excel)
series axis, 255
shading, adding to SmartArt graphics, 386
shape of WordArt text, changing, 381

shapes
   adding text to, 107, 268, 383
   adding to SmartArt graphics, 385
   changing, 107, 268, 382
   connecting, 383
   converting SmartArt graphics to, 388
   copying, 381
   cropping graphics to fill or fit, 375
   customizing, 107, 268
   deleting, 386
   drawing, 106, 267, 382
   editing, 382
   formatting, 107, 268
   grouping, 108, 269
   handles, 383
   inserting into Outlook items, 551
   moving, 386
   positioning, 382
   promoting/demoting in slides, 386
   rotation, maintaining, 383
   setting styles for, 381
   size, maintaining, 383
   sizing, 382
   SmartArt, changing, 387, 388
   SmartArt, changing color, 387
   stacking multiple, 108, 268
   text, adding, 268
   text, formatting, 107
   ungrouping, 108, 269
Shapes gallery (Outlook), 551
Shapes gallery (PowerPoint), 354
SharePoint
   saving documents to, 32
   saving workbooks to, 282
SharePoint Server, slide libraries, 327
sharpening pictures, 376, 377
shortcut keys, in Quick Steps (Outlook), 546, 547
shortcuts, accessing (Outlook), 525
Side-By-Side Mode (Outlook), 628
signatures, email, 585
   adding, 517
   creating, 586
   electronic business cards as, 597
   electronic business cards in, 586
   in responses, 587
   inserting manually, 587
   removing, 587
Single File Web Page (Excel). .html file format
      (Excel)

sizing
   chart elements, 415
   charts, 415
   columns, in worksheets, 162
   graphics, 369
   pictures, 104
   PowerPoint panes, 310
   rows in worksheets, 162
   shapes, 382
   slides, 324, 325
   table elements, 401
   text boxes, 356, 357, 358
   worksheets in PowerPoint presentations, 405
sizing handles (graphics), 369
SkyDrive. Windows Live SkyDrive
slide animations, 421
   adjusting, 425, 428
   advanced, 423
   Animation gallery, 422
   Animation Painter, 424
   Animation pane, 428
   built-in, adding, 423
   copying, 424
   custom, applying, 424
   duration, changing, 426
   effect options, changing, 426
   emphasis, 422
   entrances/exits, 422
   motion paths, 422, 426, 427
   multiple, applying, 424
   multiple, viewing details, 428
   order, changing, 423, 426, 431
   previewing, 423
   removing, 423
   repeating, 431
   schematics for, 426
   sound, adding, 431
   start, delaying, 426
   start action, specifying, 426
   start triggers, 426
   text, by word or letter, 431
   text, changing after animation, 431
   text, changing direction, 431
   text, grouping paragraphs, 431
   timing, 426, 431
   viewing details, 428
slide backgrounds, 336
   custom, applying to all slides, 338
   filling, 337, 338, 360, 362

   gallery, 336
   pictures, adjusting, 338
   predefined, applying to all slides, 337
slide layouts, 326, 327
slide libraries
   in SharePoint Server, 327
   storing slides in, 329
Slide Master view (PowerPoint), 302, 342
   changing slide size/orientation in, 325
   closing, 343
   switching to, 343
   working in, 343
slide masters, 342
   changing formatting, 343
   default components, 342
   exam coverage, 342
Slide pane (PowerPoint), 310
   entering text in, 344
   fitting slides in, 308
slide projectors, sizing 35mm slides for, 324
Slide Show view (PowerPoint), 302, 306
slide shows
   broadcasting, 473
   controlling from separate monitor, 472
   customizing, 475
   Presenter view, 472
   sizing slides for, 324
Slide Sorter view (PowerPoint), 302
   presentation sections in, 340
   rearranging slides in, 330
   setting transitions in, 432
   switching to, 306
slide text
   alignment, 347, 349, 362
   animating, 431
   case, changing, 347, 348
   character spacing, changing, 347, 348
   color, changing, 346, 348
   columns, setting, 363
   converting to lists, 350, 352, 353
   copying/pasting, 345
   creating new item, 344
   deleting, 345
   demoting, 344
   direction, changing, 347, 349
   direction, setting, 362, 363
   editing, 345, 346
   effects, changing, 347, 348

slide text *(continued)*
  embedded, animating, 429
  entering, 344
  font, changing, 346, 347
  formatting, 346
  formatting, clearing, 347, 350
  formatting, copying, 347, 350
  justifying, 349
  layout, adjusting, 362
  line/paragraph spacing, 347, 349
  margins, setting, 362, 363
  moving/copying, 345, 346
  pasting, 346
  promoting, 344
  redoing a change, 346
  replacing, 345
  selected, appearance of, 304
  selecting, 303, 304
  sizing, 346, 347, 348
  stacking, 362
  style, changing, 347, 348
  text effect, changing, 347
  undoing changes, 345, 346
  WordArt. *See* WordArt text
  wrapping, 362, 363
slide timings
  applying, 477
  default, in videos, 455
  setting up, 471
slide transitions, 421
  adding, 433
  adding sound to, 433
  applying to all slides, 434, 477
  automating, 434
  refining, 433
  removing, 434
  speed, changing, 433
slides
  accepting all changes on, 445
  adding to presentations, 326, 327, 328, 329
  animations. *See* slide animations
  annotating, 468
  attaching sounds/narration to, 393
  audio in, 392. *See also* audio
  bullet points, animating, 429
  changing layout, 327
  cutting/pasting, 331
  date/time in, 338
  deleting, 331, 332

design, changing. *See* slide masters
displaying specific, 303
dragging between presentations, 331
drawing on, 468
duplicating, 327
entering text, 344
erasing annotations, 469
fitting to window, 308
footers, adding, 338, 339
framing, when printing, 459
graphics in. *See* graphics
hidden, displaying, 332, 341
hidden, printing, 458
hiding, 332
hiding bullet points in, 330
hiding under section bar, 341
hiding/displaying objects on, 304
highlighter tool, 468
hyperlinks in, 372
inserting audio, 393
inserting from outlines, 330
inserting SmartArt graphics into, 385
inserting videos into, 390
linking graphics to, 373
masters. *See* slide masters
navigating, 476
orientation, changing, 325
pen tool, 468, 469
playing audio in, 394
playing videos in, 391
printing, 458
promoting/demoting shapes in, 386
rearranging, 330, 331
reused, formatting, 329
reusing, 327, 328, 329
saving as graphics, 450, 451
selecting text/objects, 304
sizing, 324, 325
slide numbers in, 338
storing in slide library, 329
thumbnails, dragging, 330
thumbnails, sizing, 330
transitions. *See* slide transitions
undoing deletion, 331
videos in, 389. *See also* videos
zooming, 307
SmartArt graphics, 384
  adding shapes to, 385
  adding text to, 111, 266, 385, 552

applying styles to, 111, 266, 367
Basic, importance of, 384
changing layout, 111
color, changing, 387
color scheme, changing, 111, 266
converting to bulleted lists, 388
converting to independent shapes, 388
creating, 385, 552
customizing, 386
Cycle type, 384
deleting a shape, 111, 266
diagram, inserting, 266
diagram layout, changing, 111
direction, switching, 387
elements, inserting, 553
elements, modifying, 553
elements, removing, 553
formatting text in, 386
hidden text in, 386
Hierarchy type, 384
in Outlook items, 551
inserting into documents, 110
inserting into slides, 385
layout, changing, 266, 387
List type, 384
Matrix type, 384
picture layout, applying to graphics, 370, 553
Picture type, 384
populating, 552
Process type, 384
promoting/demoting in, 386
Pyramid type, 384
Relationship type, 384
shading, 386
shapes, changing, 387
shapes, deleting from diagram, 111
shapes, resetting, 388
shapes, sizing, 387
styles, applying, 111
text, adding, 111
Text pane, displaying or hiding, 553
three-dimensional effects, 386
types, listed, 384
Smart Scheduling, 616
snapping objects to grid (PowerPoint), 369
Snooze option, for reminders (Outlook), 529
social networks, connecting to from Outlook, 523
softening pictures, 377
soft page breaks (Word), 82

sorting data (Excel), 293
by column/row, 294
on hidden columns, 294
on multiple columns, 294
on one column, 294
removing sort level, 295
sorting table content (Word), 71
sorting tasks (Outlook), 635, 636, 637
sounds. audio (PowerPoint)
adding to animations, 431
adding to slide transitions, 433
as email message notifications, 489
attaching to slides, 393
downloading from Office.com, 392
for appointment reminders, 605
Outlook reminders, setting, 510
spaces, hiding/displaying (Word), 6
sparklines (Excel), 273
changing type, 275
creating, 274
deleting, 275
style, applying, 275
speaker notes (PowerPoint)
adding, 302, 460
displaying, 306
orientation, changing, 325
special characters, locating (Word), 56
special effects, adding to text (Word), 48
spell checking (Outlook), 488
spell checking (PowerPoint), 440. AutoCorrect (PowerPoint)
appearance of, 440
as you type, 440
customizing, 314
entire presentation, 440
spell checking (Word)
appearance of, 120
AutoCorrect exceptions, 127
AutoCorrect options, 125, 126, 127
automatic corrections, reversing, 126
dictionary, adding a word, 123
entire document, 123
error indicators, ignoring, 122
errors, fixing, 122
errors, hiding, 123
errors, visual indicators, 120
options, setting, 124
settings, customizing, 124
split bar (Word), 18, 19

split bars (Excel), 228, 229
splitter bars (PowerPoint), 310
splitting document windows, 19
splitting table cells (PowerPoint), 401
splitting worksheet windows, 229
square aspect ratio for cropping, 374
squares, drawing, 382
stacking order, changing
  graphics, 370
  shapes, 108, 268
  text boxes, 108
stacking program windows (Word), 21
start date (tasks), 638
startup folder (Outlook), 509
stationery, email message, 587
status, read (Outlook). read status (Outlook)
status bar (Outlook), 528
  customizing, 529
  displaying overdue reminders, 529
status reports for tasks, sending, 642
step values for data series (Excel), 193
style area pane (Word), 13, 15, 51
style sets (Outlook), 565
styles, 366, 562
  applying to cells, 223
  applying to chart shapes, 257
  applying to charts, 257, 416, 418
  applying to email text, 563, 587
  applying to graphics, 367
  applying to paragraphs, 51
  applying to pictures, 105, 272
  applying to SmartArt graphics, 266
  applying to sparklines, 275
  applying to tables, 68, 403
  applying to WordArt, 380
  clearing, 52
  creating, 223, 563
  displaying/hiding, 13, 15
  galleries, 366
  including/excluding from Quick Styles gallery, 564
  locating, 56
  modifying, 563
  previewing, 51, 563
  saving to templates, 563
Styles pane, 50, 562
  displaying, 51, 563
  displaying visual preview of styles, 51
styling, WordArt text, 380
subdocuments (Word), 14

subordinate points (PowerPoint), 386
subtracting values in worksheets, 189
Suggested Contacts address book, 503
sum of values, in a range (Excel), 237
switching direction (SmartArt), 387
switching time zones (Outlook), 501
synchronous scrolling (Word), 21
synonyms, finding (PowerPoint), 444

T

tab delimited file (Excel), 279
tab stops
  changing position, 61
  clearing all, 61
  deleting, 61
  setting, 61
table of contents (Word)
  creating, 140, 141
  updating, 141
table properties (Word), 73
tables (Excel). worksheets
  cell width, 163
  columns. See columns (Excel)
  data entry, completing, 164
  entering text in, 163
  inserting, 404
  rows. See rows (Excel)
  selecting data, 163
  sizing columns/rows, 162
  sorting, 294
tables (Outlook)
  formatting, 561
  printing contacts as, 539
tables (PowerPoint)
  aligning text in, 403
  cell margins, setting, 403
  columns, adding, 400
  columns, deleting, 400
  creating, 398
  distributing column/rows evenly, 402
  drawing, 399
  editing, 399
  erasing borders, 401
  formatting, 402
  formatting selected cells, 403
  inserting, 398
  merging cells, 401

navigating in, 398
populating, 398
Quick Styles, applying, 403
resizing elements in, 401
rows, adding, 400
rows, deleting, 400
selecting elements of, 400
splitting cells in, 401
structure, changing, 399
styles, applying, 403
text direction, setting, 403
tables (Word)
built-in style, applying, 68
cells, deleting, 74
cells, inserting, 74
cells, merging/splitting, 75
column width, changing, 74
columns, deleting, 74
columns, inserting, 74
converting table to text, 75
converting text to table, 67
deleting, 74
drawing, 67
gridlines, displaying, 71
header row, specifying, 71
inserting, 66
properties, displaying, 73
Quick Table, inserting, 69
row height, changing, 74
rows, deleting, 74
rows, inserting, 74
size of, changing, 73
sorting content, 71
tabs. tab stops
tabs, worksheet. worksheet tabs
tags (Excel), 183
task requests, recording in Outlook Journal, 648
Tasks button. creating tasks from, 634
Tasks List (Outlook), 526, 635
changing sort order, 637
changing view, 637
completed tasks in, 636
creating tasks from, 633
fields in, 633
views of, listed, 635
Tasks module (Outlook)
content pane in, 526
creating tasks in, 633
displaying list views in, 527

Navigation Pane in, 483
setting options for, 504
Tasks List in, 635
To-Do List in, 635
viewing tasks in, 635
tasks (Outlook)
assigned, appearance of, 641
assigned, changing options, 504
assigning, 640, 641
assigning due dates, 639
assigning flags to, 518
assigning to contacts, 594
assignments, accepting/declining, 641, 642
attaching items to, 639
attaching to email messages, 569
categorizing, 512, 639. *See also* color categories
 (Outlook)
changing view, 637
charts in, creating/modifying, 554
checklist view, 526
clip art, inserting, 551
color, changing, 504
completed, 636
copying, 638
creating, 632, 633, 634
creating appointments from, 604
creating events from, 607
default due date, changing, 504
deleting, 643
dismissing reminders, 529
finalizing, 642
flagging, 517
folders, creating, 637
grouping, 635, 636, 637
hyperlinks in, creating, 557. *See also* hyperlinks
in Calendar module, 635
in content pane, 526
marking as complete, 642
moving, 637
organizing, 637
percentage complete, 638
pictures, inserting, 550
priority, 638
privacy, assigning, 639
recurring, creating, 632, 639
reminders for, 639
reordering, 637
scheduling in calendar, 635
screen images, inserting, 555

tasks (Outlook) *(continued)*
  searching for, 531
  setting automatically, 504
  setting options for, 504
  shapes, inserting, 551
  sorting, 635, 636, 637
  start date/due date, 638
  status, 638
  status reports, sending, 504, 642
  task list, updating, 504
  text in. *See* text
  tracking, 639
  viewing, 635
  visual elements, inserting, 550
telephoning contacts, 594
templates (Excel), saving workbooks as, 279
templates (Outlook)
  basing rules on, 576
  saving styles to, 563
templates (PowerPoint)
  creating photo albums with, 320, 321
  photo album, creating other presentations
    with, 320
  replacing photographs in, 321
templates (Word)
  local, attaching, 43
  web, attaching, 43
testing hyperlinks (PowerPoint), 373
text
  adding to diagrams, 111
  adding to shapes, 107, 383
  adding to SmartArt graphics, 385, 552
  alignment, changing, 560
  alignment in tables, 403
  applying local formatting, 560
  applying styles, 563
  as document watermark, 95
  case, changing, 48
  character formatting, applying, 48
  character spacing, changing, 48, 560
  character styles, changing, 560
  color, changing, 560
  columns, aligning text, 85
  converting to table, 67
  copying, 197
  copying formatting, 561
  creating styles, 563
  deselecting, 2
  effects, changing, 560
  finding/replacing, in presentations, 441
  font, changing, 560
  font size, changing, 48
  font style, changing, 560
  formatting, 49, 560
  formatting in shapes, 107, 268
  formatting in SmartArt graphics, 386
  highlighting, 48
  highlighting search results, 56
  in SmartArt graphics, hidden, 386
  in worksheet cells, formatting, 204
  indentation, changing, 560
  locating (document), 55
  modifying styles, 563
  on slides. *See* slide text
  paragraph formatting, changing, 561
  paragraph styles, changing, 560
  previewing styles, 563
  Quick Styles, applying, 51
  replacing, 56
  selecting, 2. *See also* selecting (Word)
  size, changing, 560
  special effects, adding, 48
  tables, converting from, 75
  text boxes, inserting text into, 116
  WordArt. *See* WordArt text
  worksheet cell, orientation, changing, 205, 206
  worksheet cell, wrapping, 205, 206
text boxes (PowerPoint). text placeholders
    (PowerPoint)
  aligning, 359
  applying styles to, 360, 362
  aspect ratio, locking, 358
  Autofit, 356, 358
  columns in, 363
  displaying Format Shape dialog box, 358
  distributing, 359
  editing text in, 344
  effects, 361, 362
  fills (background), 360, 362
  fixed height, 344, 345
  fixed width, 344, 345
  formatting, 360, 363
  gridlines/drawing guides, 359
  horizontal alignment, 359
  margins in, 363
  moving, 344, 357, 358
  outlines, 361, 362
  overlapping, fixing, 359

selecting, 344
shape, changing, 355
shape, default, 354
sizing, 356, 357, 358
stacking order, 359
text alignment in, 362
text direction in, 363
text layout in, 362
text wrapping in, 363
vertical alignment, 359
text boxes (Word)
  copying, 116
  direction of text, changing, 116
  formatting, 116, 117
  inserting, 115, 116
  inserting text in, 116
  linking, 116
  saving as building block, 117
  stacking order, changing, 108
text case, changing, 48
text direction, in tables, setting, 403
text files (Excel), 279
text font, changing, 48
text placeholders (PowerPoint), 344
  Autofit and, 357
  fitting text into, 357
  formatting, 354
  selecting text in, 303
text watermark, adding, 95
Themes gallery (Outlook), 567
Themes gallery (PowerPoint), 333, 334
themes (Outlook), 566, 587
  applying, 567
  colors, 567
  creating, 567
  default, resetting, 588
  effects, 567
  fonts, 567
  modifying, 567
  Office, described, 587
  previewing, 567
  saving, 567
themes (PowerPoint), 333
  applying, 334, 341
  changing, 334
  colors, 333, 334, 335
  deleting, 335
  effects, 334

fonts, 334, 335
in photo albums, 322
saving, 334
themes (Word)
  applying, 88
  changing, 88
  colors, 89
  deleting, 89
  fonts, 89
  saving, 89
Thesaurus (PowerPoint), 442
three-dimensional (3D)
  charts, formatting, 413
  effects, adding to SmartArt graphics, 386
  picture effects, applying, 556
tick-mark labels, 411
tiling program windows (Excel), 230
tiling program windows (Word), 21
time, inserting in headers/footers, 99
time zones, 500
  changing, 501
  multiple, displaying, 501
  switching between, 501
Timer, recording journal entries with (Outlook), 649
tinting pictures, 376
To-Do Bar (Outlook), 524
  and Office Communicator, 524
  changing content, 508
  closing, 524
  creating tasks from, 633
  Date Navigator in, 524
  displaying, 524
  expanding/minimizing, 524
  width, changing, 521
To-Do Bar Task List (Outlook), 635
To-Do List (Outlook tasks), 526, 635
  changing sort order, 637
  creating tasks from, 633
  sorting tasks in, 636
tracking email messages, 495
tracking meeting request responses, 619
transitions, slide. slide transitions
Transitions gallery (PowerPoint), 433
transparencies, printing (PowerPoint), 457
transparency of pictures, changing, 378
transposing rows/columns (Excel), 189
trendlines, chart, adding/removing, 413
tri-fold, printing calendar as, 537
triggers, slide animation, 426

U

unfreezing columns/rows (Excel), 229
ungrouping graphics, 371
unhiding
  columns/rows (Excel), 219
  Formula Bar (Excel), 232
  worksheets, 227
unified messaging system, Outlook contact
      options and, 594
updating linked worksheets, 405
user interface. working environment

V

value axis, 255, 410
  adding/removing, 412
  formatting, 418
values (Excel)
  adding/subtracting/multiplying/dividing, 189
  in formulas, pasting, 189
versions (Excel), 184
  replacing current with previous, 184
  saved, displaying, 184
  temporary (unsaved), deleting, 185
  temporary (unsaved), displaying, 184
versions (Word), 28
  replacing current with previous, 29
  saved, displaying, 28
  temporary (unsaved), deleting, 29
  temporary (unsaved), displaying, 29
vertical ruler, displaying/hiding (Word), 16
videos
  automatic play, setting, 391
  clip art, inserting into slides, 389, 390
  configuring, 456
  digital files, inserting into slides, 389, 390
  editing, 392
  fading in/out, 392
  formatting, 391
  full-screen play, setting, 391
  hiding while not playing, 391
  inserting, 389, 3990
  inserting from websites, 389, 390
  looping, 391
  previewing, 456
  rewinding, 391

saving presentations as, 455
settings, changing, 391
trimming, 392
volume, changing, 391
view options, changing (Word), 10
View Shortcuts toolbar (PowerPoint), 306
View toolbar (Excel), 231
viewing
  different parts of same presentation, 309
  multiple presentations, 308
views (Excel), 228
  freezing columns/rows, 228, 229
  Full Screen, 231
  multiple workbook windows, 230
  Normal, 231
  Page Break Preview, 231
  Page Layout, 231
  splitting, 229
  View toolbar, 231
  zooming, 232
views (Outlook)
  Active, 625
  Calendar, 625
  Conversation, 574
  custom, defining, 483
  Day, 622
  Day, events in, 606
  for tasks, 635
  List, 625
  Month, 622
  Month, events in, 606
  Notes module, changing, 644
  Overlay Mode (calendars), 628
  Preview, 625
  Schedule, 622
  Side-By-Side Mode (calendars), 628
  switching, 483
  task, changing, 637
  time periods in, 622
  Week, 622
  Week, events in, 606
  Work Week, 622
  Work Week, events in, 606
views (PowerPoint), 302
  Handout Master, 302
  Normal, 302, 306, 310, 331
  Notes Master, 302
  Notes Page, 302

Reading View, 302, 306
Slide Master, 302, 325, 342
Slide Show, 302, 306
Slide Sorter, 302, 330
views (Word)
multiple document windows, 21
splitting, 19
switching, 6
voting buttons, email, 543
adding to messages, 517
labels, changing, 543
voting requests, email, processing, 495

W

watermarks
adding, 95
picture, adding, 96
web beacons. graphics, in junk mail
attaching to documents, 43
webpages. .html file format (Excel)
banner, sizing slides for, 324
hyperlinks to, creating, 558
linking graphics to, 373
worksheet hyperlinks to, creating, 199
websites
displaying from contact records, 594
videos from, inserting in slides, 389, 390
videos from, unable to copy, 390
week numbers (Outlook), 496, 499, 624
displaying, 500
Week view (Outlook), 622
events in, 606
scrolling in, 624
weeks. work week (Outlook)
displaying in Calendar pane, 623
displaying in Outlook Date Navigator, 624
widows/orphans, avoiding (Word), 83
windows
cascading (Excel), 230
cascading (PowerPoint), 308
side by side (PowerPoint), 308
side by side (Word), 20
stacking (Word), 20
Windows Live SkyDrive, 31, 281
folder, creating (Excel), 282
folder, creating (Word), 32
saving documents to, 32
saving workbooks to, 282

Word 2010
AutoCorrect, 125
documents, hyperlinks to, 557
grammar checking, 120
opening multiple windows, 20
outlines, in PowerPoint presentations, 330
program windows, arranging multiple, 21
Quick Parts, 90
spell checking, 120
Word Options dialog box, 121, 124
WordArt objects
creating from text, 109
inserting, 109
WordArt text, 380. Quick Styles
adding effects to, 381
changing shape of, 381
creating, 380
formatting, 109
formatting in charts, 419
handles, 381
styling, 380, 381
transforming, 381
words, selecting (Word), 2
work week (Outlook), 496, 497
Work Week view (Outlook), 622
events in, 606
scrolling in, 624
workbook properties, 183
adding to display, 184
editing, 183
removing from display, 184
server, viewing, 183
viewing, 183, 184
workbooks
adding Quick Access Toolbar buttons, 182
AutoSave, changing frequency, 184
copying worksheets between, 226
inserting worksheets into, 162
moving worksheets in, 226
new, creating worksheet hyperlinks to, 200
opening in multiple windows, 229
opening second instance in separate window, 230
printing worksheets in, 168, 169
program windows, arranging multiple, 230
save locations, 280
saving, options for, 278, 281
saving as template, 279
saving for web browsers, 278
saving to a SharePoint site, 282

workbooks *(continued)*
  saving to Windows Live SkyDrive, 282
  sending as email attachments, 284
  sending as Internet faxes, 283
  sending links to, 284
  versions, displaying/deleting temporary (unsaved),
    184, 185
  versions, displaying saved, 184
  versions, replacing current with previous, 184
  worksheets in, default number, 165
workday limitations (Outlook), 497
working environment
  Excel, managing, 165, 305
  Outlook, managing, 485, 519
  PowerPoint, changing language of, 506
worksheet cell orientation, 205, 206
worksheet hyperlinks, 198
  appearance of, 199
  creating email messages with, 201
  editing, 201
  removing, 201
  selecting for formatting, 199
  targets, changing, 201
  to files, creating, 200
  to named ranges, creating, 200
  to new workbooks, creating, 200
  to webpages, creating, 199
  to worksheets, creating, 200
worksheet tabs, 227
worksheets. tables (Excel), workbooks
  aligning cell text in, 206
  AutoFill feature, 193
  average of a range, 238
  cell borders, adding, 207
  cell borders, removing, 207
  cell fill color, changing, 207
  cell reference range, absolute, 250
  cell reference range, relative, 250
  cell references, 242
  cell references, absolute, 243
  cell references, in different workbook, 244
  cell references, relative, 243
  Cell Styles gallery, 222
  cell text wrapping in, and row height, 205, 206
  cells, formatting, 204, 205, 206
  cells, merging/splitting, 215, 216
  cells, moving among, 166, 167

chart axes, displaying/hiding, 262
chart legend, adding/removing/moving, 261
chart types, 254
charts, adding/removing titles, 260, 261
charts, applying styles, 257
charts, changing data range, 259
charts, changing layout, 257
charts, changing size, 258
charts, changing type, 256
charts, data labels, 261
charts, displaying data table, 262
charts, editing data, 259
charts, formatting elements, 263
charts, gridlines, 262
charts, moving, 258
charts, plotting selected data, 256
charts, switching rows/columns, 256
clip art, inserting, 264
colors, changing theme, 89
column references, absolute, 243
column/row headings, hiding/displaying, 232
column/row headings, printing, 173
columns in. *See* columns (Excel)
comments, deleting, 286
comments, editing, 286
comments, inserting, 285
comments, moving among, 286
comments, resizing/moving, 286
comments, temporarily displaying, 285
conditional logic arguments, 246
copied or cut cells, inserting, 191
copying, 226
copying cell formatting, 206
copying currency amounts, 197
copying data from, 404
copying formatting only, 197
copying numeric data, 197
copying text, 197
counting cells with values, 238
counting empty cells, 238
customizing, 232
custom styles, creating, 223
data regions, moving in, 167
data series in. *See* data series (Excel)
deleting, 162
deleting cells, 190, 192
deleting rows/columns, 190, 192

diagrams, adding text to shapes, 266
diagrams, changing layout, 266
diagrams, deleting a shape, 266
diagrams, inserting, 266
displaying, 231
embedding in presentations, 405
error when inserting cells, 191
filling data series in, 193
filtering data, 290
fitting on page, 221
fonts, changing, 89
footers, changing height, 221
Format Painter in, 206
formulas, order of calculation, 241
freezing rows/columns in, 228
full screen mode, 231
gridlines in, 232
gridlines, printing, 173
grouping, 169, 227
headers, changing height, 221
headers/footers in, 174
hidden, displaying, 227
hidden cells, finding, 219
hiding, 226
hyperlinks to, creating, 200
inserting cells, 189, 190, 191
inserting in PowerPoint presentations, 404
inserting new, 162
inserting rows/columns, 189, 191
insertions, formatting, 191
linked, updating, 405
linking cells in, 188
linking to, from PowerPoint, 405
margins, changing, 221
mathematical operations in, 189
maximizing work area, 231
moving, 226
moving around in, 166, 167
named ranges, changing name, 249
named ranges, defining, 248, 249
named ranges, deleting, 249
navigating, 166
number formatting in, 210
number in workbook, default, 165
page breaks, adjusting, 172
page breaks, deleting, 172
page breaks in, 170

page breaks, inserting, 172
page breaks, previewing, 172
page orientation, changing, 221
pasting data in, 188
pasting formula results in, 189
pictures, applying artistic effects, 272
pictures, changing size/shape, 272
pictures, copying to new location, 272
pictures, inserting, 271, 272
pictures, moving, 272
pictures, replacing, 273
plotting charts, 254
print areas in. *See* print areas (Excel)
printing, 168, 169
properties, searching by, 167
references, different workbook, 244
references, same workbook, 243
removing splits, 229
renaming, 162, 227
rows in. *See* rows (Excel)
rows, moving in, 167
scaling, 221
screens, moving between, 166
selecting data in, 162, 409
shapes, adding text, 268
shapes, changing, 268
shapes, customizing, 268
shapes, drawing, 267
shapes, formatting, 268
sizing, in PowerPoint, 405
sizing columns/rows, 162
SmartArt diagrams, inserting, 266
SmartArt graphics, applying a style, 266
SmartArt graphics, changing layout, 266
sorting data, 293, 294
sparklines in, 273, 274, 275
splitting, 229
styling, 223
text alignment in cells, 205
text orientation in, 205, 206
themes, applying, 88
themes, changing, 88
themes, saving, 89
transposing rows/columns, 189
wrapping cell text, 206
zooming, 232
zoom level, changing, 233

X

.xls file format (Excel), 278, 279
.xlsb file format (Excel), 278
.xlsm file format (Excel), 278
.xlsx file format (Excel), benefits of, 278
.xml file format, 279
   saving workbooks in, 278
XML Paper Specification (XPS). .xps file format
.xps file format
   saving documents in, 41
   saving presentations in, 450, 452
   saving workbooks in, 281

Y

year, defining first week of (Outlook), 497

Z

Zoom controls (Outlook), 528
zoom level (Excel), 233
zoom level (PowerPoint), 307
Zoom toolbar (Excel), 232
zooming
   documents, 18
   presentations, 307
   on selected worksheet cells, 233
   worksheets, 232

About the Authors

Joan Lambert

Joan has worked in the training and certification industry for 14 years. As President of Online Training Solutions, Inc. (OTSI), Joan is responsible for guiding the translation of technical information and requirements into useful, relevant, and measurable training and certification tools.

Joan is a Microsoft Office Master (MOM), a Microsoft Certified Application Specialist (MCAS) Instructor, a Microsoft Certified Technology Specialist (MCTS), a Microsoft Certified Trainer (MCT), and the author of more than two dozen books about Windows and Office (for Windows and Mac).

Joyce Cox

Joyce has 30 years' experience in the development of training materials about technical subjects for nontechnical audiences, and is the author of dozens of books about Office and Windows technologies. She is the Vice President of OTSI.

As President of and principal author for Online Press, she developed the Quick Course series of computer training books for beginning and intermediate adult learners. She was also the first managing editor of Microsoft Press, an editor for Sybex, and an editor for the University of California.

The Team

This book would not exist without the support of these hard-working members of the OTSI publishing team:

- Jan Bednarczuk
- Susie Carr
- Patty Gardner
- Kathy Krause
- Marlene Lambert
- Jaime Odell
- Jean Trenary
- Elisabeth Van Every

We are especially thankful to the support staff at home who make it possible for our team members to devote their time and attention to these projects.

Rosemary Caperton provided invaluable support on behalf of Microsoft Learning.

Online Training Solutions, Inc. (OTSI)

OTSI specializes in the design, creation, and production of Office and Windows training products for information workers and home computer users. For more information about OTSI, visit:

www.otsi.com